Cognitively Informed Intelligent Interfaces:

Systems Design and Development

Eshaa M. Alkhalifa
University of Bahrain, Bahrain

Khulood Gaid
Royal University for Women, Bahrain

Managing Director:	Lindsay Johnston
Senior Editorial Director:	Heather A. Probst
Book Production Manager:	Sean Woznicki
Development Manager:	Joel Gamon
Development Editor:	Hannah Abelbeck
Acquisitions Editor:	Erika Gallagher
Typesetter:	Lisandro Gonzalez
Cover Design:	Nick Newcomer

Published in the United States of America by
Information Science Reference (an imprint of IGI Global)
701 E. Chocolate Avenue
Hershey PA 17033
Tel: 717-533-8845
Fax: 717-533-8661
E-mail: cust@igi-global.com
Web site: http://www.igi-global.com

Library of Congress Cataloging-in-Publication Data

Cognitively informed intelligent interfaces: systems design and development / Eshaa M. Alkhalifa and Khulood Gaid, editors.
    p. cm.
  Includes bibliographical references and index.
  Summary: "This book analyzes well-grounded findings and recent insights on human perception and cognitive abilities and how these findings can and should impact the development and design of applications through the use of intelligent interfaces"-- Provided by publisher.
  ISBN 978-1-4666-1628-8 (hardcover) -- ISBN 978-1-4666-1629-5 (ebook) -- ISBN 978-1-4666-1630-1 (print & perpetual access) 1. User interfaces (Computer systems) 2. Artificial intelligence. 3. Cognition. I. Alkhalifa, Eshaa M., 1966- II. Gaid, Khulood, 1989-
 QA76.9.U83C58 2012
 005.4'37--dc23
                                   2012000166

British Cataloguing in Publication Data
A Cataloguing in Publication record for this book is available from the British Library.

All work contributed to this book is new, previously-unpublished material. The views expressed in this book are those of the authors, but not necessarily of the publisher.

Table of Contents

Section 1
Phones and Browsers

Section 2
Visual Representations of Images and Graphics

Section 3
Monitoring Human Workflow, Collaborating with Intelligent Systems, and Recognizing Human Traits exhibited by Computers

Section 4
Interface Design, User Profile Design, and System Evaluation Models

Section 5
Education and Interactive Picture Book

Detailed Table of Contents

Section 1
Phones and Browsers

Phones have entered into almost every single house on the planet and Browsers are quickly trying to catch up. Modern lifestyles are becoming fast with a need to optimize use of these gadgets that support our cognitive memories, display, and organize information in a way that we find more meaningful. The four chapters in this section present realistic approaches to achieve these goals.

Chapter 1

> *Qing Wang, Sun Yat-Sen University, China*
> *Huiyou Chang, Sun Yat-Sen University, China*
> *Huiyang Liu, Sun Yat-Sen University, China*

This chapter clarifies two common patterns of multitasking on the Web, namely Multiple Tasks (MT) and Multiple Session Tasks (MST). Multi-Tasks (MT) is defined as executing a set of tasks simultaneously where the execution often depends on bundles of Web pages. Multi-Session Task (MST), on the other hand, is defined as executing a single task spanning multiple Web sessions. To support both of these, the task concept needs to be introduced into a browser. An online pilot survey has revealed which attributes of the task concept are most significant to Web users, and as a result, a simple prototype, the Multitasking Bar (MB), has been proposed based on these findings. The MB copes with the multitasking needs of both MT and MST in the browser by providing functions for task related Web page management and task schedule management. A two-session controlled experiment has been conducted to evaluate the MB and to compare user performance and experience when multitasking on the Web with and without support for MT and MST. Results show that support for both MST and MT significantly improves user task performance efficiency and greatly enhances the user experience when multitasking on the Web.

Chapter 2

> *Bruno Merlin, UFPA, Brazil*
> *Mathieu Raynal, Université Paul Sabatier, France*

Predictive models, based on cognitive and motor laws (modeling some aspect of human behaviors), were supposed to provide an efficient tool to compare quickly soft keyboards performances, but these models are confronted with some limitations. Moreover, they failed to predict efficiently the performances during the first usage that got an important impact on soft keyboard acceptability. To improve these models, the authors integrated into them the character search strategies oriented by the user's background. They illustrate their purpose by modeling three keyboards and comparing the results with experimental ones. The models integrating the user's background predicted results close to the experimental ones. However, those models must be adapted to the function of the keyboard and the targeted population. The applicability of the models as a rapid comparison tool for soft keyboards must be questioned.

Chapter 3

Siu-Tsen Shen, National Formosa University, Taiwan
Stephen D. Prior, Middlesex University, UK

With roughly a third of the world's population now having access to the internet, the area of web efficiency and its optimal use is of growing importance to all online users. We are approaching a tipping point where the majority of people will have spent more time online than offline. With this in mind, the function of revisitation, where a user wants to return to a website that they have visited in the recent past, becomes more important. Current static, textual-list approaches developed within the latest versions of mainstream web browsers such as Internet Explorer, Firefox, and Chrome leave much to be desired. This chapter suggests a new approach via the use of organic, visual, and contextual cues to support users in this vital task area.

Chapter 4

Takashi Nagamatsu, Kobe University, Japan
Michiya Yamamoto, Kwansei Gakuin University, Japan
Hiroshi Sato, Kwansei Gakuin University, Japan

Today, touch-screen-based handheld mobile devices are widely used; however, they are awkward to use with one hand. The authors propose MobiGaze, which is a user interface that uses one's gaze to operate a handheld mobile device. By using MobiGaze, one can target the entire display area easily, even when the device is quite large. Moreover, MobiGaze can use both gaze and touch interactions. The combination of gaze and touch becomes a novel interaction paradigm. A gaze-and-touch interface effectively avoids the Midas-touch problem. The authors adopted a gaze-tracking method that uses a stereo camera to develop MobiGaze, because the user's line of sight is detected in 3D. This allows the user to move the handheld mobile device freely. They constructed a prototype MobiGaze system, which consists of two cameras with IR-LEDs, a Windows-based notebook PC, and iPod touches. The authors evaluated the accuracy in a laboratory experiment and developed several applications for MobiGaze.

Section 2
Visual Representations of Images and Graphics

The following chapters present applications that show the importance of visual representations and image analysis. Medicine, for example, is a field where mistakes cannot be tolerated; therefore, attracting the doctor's attention to the troubled area is essential. Another application could be to attract a surfer's attention in an online market or attracting student attention while learning online. In essence, understanding how humans represent space/time is an essential concept that influences all these applications.

Boris W. van Schooten, University of Twente, The Netherlands

Betsy M. A. G. van Dijk, University of Twente, The Netherlands

Avan Suinesiaputra, University of Auckland, New Zealand

Anton Nijholt, University of Twente, The Netherlands

Johan H. C. Reiber, Leiden University Medical Center, The Netherlands

Visual search is a task that is performed in various application domains. The authors examine it in the domain of radiological analysis of 3D vascular images. They compare several major visualisations used in this domain, and study the possible benefits of automatic warning systems that highlight the sections that may contain visual targets and hence require the user's attention. With help of a literature study, the authors present some theory about what result can be expected given the accuracy of a particular visual cue. They present the results of two experiments, in which they find that the Curved Planar Reformation visualisation, which presents a cross-section based on knowledge about the position of the blood vessel, is significantly more efficient than regular 3D visualisations, and that automatic warning systems that produce false alarms could work if they do not miss targets.

Jeremiah D. Still, Missouri Western State University, USA

Christopher M. Masciocchi, Frostburg State University, USA

In this chapter, the authors highlight the influence of visual saliency, or local contrast, on users' searches of interfaces, particularly web pages. Designers have traditionally focused on the importance of goals and expectations (top-down processes) for the navigation of interfaces (Diaper & Stanton, 2004), with little consideration for the influence of saliency (bottom-up processes). The Handbook of Human-Computer Interaction (Sears & Jacko, 2008), for example, does not discuss the influence of bottom-up processing, potentially neglecting an important aspect of interface-based searches. The authors review studies that demonstrate how a user's attention is rapidly drawn to visually salient locations in a variety of tasks and scenes, including web pages. They then describe an inexpensive, rapid technique that designers can use to identify visually salient locations in web pages, and discuss its advantages over similar methods.

Minyoung Song, University of Michigan, USA

Teaching and learning the vast range of the sizes that are too small to see (called imperceptible sizes) has been a challenging topic, and a need for a novel form of representation that may provide learners with an alternative way of perceiving and conceptualizing imperceptible sizes emerged. From this, the author introduces a multimodal representation called Temporal-Aural-Visual Representation (TAVR). Unlike commonly used conventional representations (e.g., visual representation), TAVR employs a temporal modality as the main vehicle for conveying imperceptible sizes. In this chapter, the author elaborates on the design process and the details of TAVR. Informed by cognitive psychology research, the mental model and the challenges for learners in understanding imperceptible sizes were identified to form the design requirements of TAVR. Following the design and implementation, the evaluation of TAVR aimed to assess the changes in the participating students' mental model of the range of imperceptible sizes, which showed TAVR's positive impact on student learning.

The specification of layout behavior for visual language editors is a challenging task. To support the user in an interactive environment, it is not sufficient to apply the same layout behavior in every situation. Instead, the user wants to select and alter the layout behavior at runtime. The authors present a user study in which students created several visual language editors, mainly focusing on the layout engine. With the help of this user study, they demonstrate that different editors require similar layout behavior. They also show evidence that the combination of graph drawing algorithms and other layout algorithms is reasonable. The authors also describe a framework that enables the creation of a layout engine, which satisfies the user demands identified in a user study. The approach is capable of defining layout behavior for various visual languages like graphs, class diagrams, mindmaps, business process models, or even GUI forms. The framework enables the combination of different layout approaches and provides the possibility to reuse already defined layout behavior.

Chapter 9

This chapter describes a geometric approach to human cognition centering on the concept of mental configuration space. As a case study of the approach, this work details a study that derives performance models for an important class of motor behavior—pointing in the two dimensional space. The five derived models and three existing models in the literature are compared using an experimental study. It is found that the models developed on the basis of mental configuration space fit the empirical data better than other models. It is argued that the mental configuration space concept points to a potentially fruitful direction of research. Finally, the chapter discusses the implications of such an approach for user interface research and development.

Section 3
Monitoring Human Workflow, Collaborating with Intelligent Systems, and Recognizing Human Traits exhibited by Computers

Section 3 starts by monitoring humans using a workflow system for conflicts of opinion and biases that may jeopardize work efficiency. The second chapter in this section lays out a plan for collaboration between humans and computer systems to produce pseudo code and from there working programs. The third, analyzes characteristics that one can describe in humans like having a sense of humor, extremely serious, calculating, and taking these as a basis for giving software agents human-like traits. Perhaps someday one would complain that their computer is too sensitive for the type of work in which they are involved.

Chapter 10

The chapter presents a question-answer approach to the programming of Human-Computer Interactions (HCI) during collaborative development of software intensive systems. Efficiency of the general work can be essentially increased if the human part of the work is informed by precedents and executed with a special kind of pseudo-program by "intellectual processors." The role of any processor of such type is fulfilled by a designer. The suggested approach was investigated and evolved until an instrumental system providing the pseudo-code programming of intellectual processors combined with computer processors. Interactions between processors are based on question-answer reasoning. Pseudo-code programs and their corresponding instrumental means can be combined easily with traditional HCI.

Chapter 11

François Bouchet, McGill University, Canada
Jean-Paul Sansonnet, LIMSI-CNRS, France

Conversational agents are a promising interface between humans and computers, but to be acceptable as the virtual humans they pretend to be, they need to be given one of the key elements used to define human beings: a personality. As existing personality taxonomies have been defined only for description, the authors present in this chapter a methodology dedicated to the definition of a computationally-oriented taxonomy, in order to use it to implement personality traits in conversational agents. First, a significant set of personality-traits adjectives is registered from thesaurus sources. Then, the lexical semantics related to personality-traits is extracted while using the WordNet database, and it is given a formal representation in terms of so-called Behavioral Schemes. Finally, the authors propose a framework for the implementation of those schemes as influence operators controlling the decision process and the plan/ action scheduling of a rational agent.

Chapter 12

Marcello Sarini, University of Milano-Bicocca, Italy

The chapter describes the Activity Circle, a social visualization mechanism based on the concept of Social Proxy, a minimalist graphical representation that portrays socially salient aspects of users' interactions. The Activity Circle allows users to socialize how they perceive the accomplishment of work activities that are regulated by a workflow technology. The social information visualized by the Activity Circle should primarily allow people to share the distributed viscosity perception about the workflow technology used; perceived distributed viscosity concerns the perception of the extra amount of work required by this technology to fulfill the users' organization goals, where "distributed" indicates that different groups of users perceive the impact of workflow technology differently. Making this information explicit may help groups of users reconcile the conflicts about disparities introduced by workflow technology. This information could also be used by management to design more equitable workflow technology.

Section 4
Interface Design, User Profile Design, and System Evaluation Models

In order for computer systems to become wise partners in work, it is essential to benefit from all available tools in interface design. It is also essential to minimize errors in user profiles to avoid misunderstanding the user of a computer system. Additionally, it may be time to review previous assumptions of how many people are necessary to evaluate newly developed systems with the current advances in technology and complexity.

Chapter 13

Sybille Caffiau, University Joseph Fourier – Grenoble, France
Patrick Girard, University of Poitiers, France

In user interface design, model-driven approaches usually involve generative solutions, producing interface by successive transformations of a set of initial models. These approaches have obvious limitations, especially for advanced user interfaces. Moreover, top-down design approaches (as generative approaches are) are not appropriate for interactive application development in which users need to be included in the whole design process. Based on strong associations between task models and dialogue models, the authors propose a global process, which facilitates the design of interactive applications conforming to their models, including a rule-checking step. This process permits either to start from a task model or a user-defined prototype. In any case, it allows an iterative development, including iterative user modifications, in line with user-centered design standards.

Chapter 14

Daniel Scherer, State University of Paraiba, Brazil & Federal University of Campina Grande, Brazil
Ademar V. Netto, Federal University of Campina Grande, Brazil
Yuska P. C. Aguiar, Federal University of Campina Grande, Brazil
Maria de Fátima Q. Vieira, Federal University of Campina Grande, Brazil & University of Strathclyde, UK

In order to prevent human error, it is essential to understand the nature of the user's behaviour. This chapter proposes a combined approach to increase knowledge of user behaviour by instantiating a programmable user model with data gathered from a user profile. Together, the user profile and user model represent, respectively, the static and dynamic characteristics of user behaviour. Typically, user models have been employed by system designers to explore the user decision-making process and its implications, since user profiles do not account for the dynamic aspects of a user interaction. In this chapter, the user profile and model are employed to study human errors—supporting an investigation of the relationship between user errors and user characteristics. The chapter reviews the literature on user profiles and models and presents the proposed user profile and model. It concludes by discussing the application of the proposed approach in the context of electrical systems' operation.

Chapter 15

Simone Borsci, Brunel University, UK
Stefano Federici, University of Perugia, Italy
Maria Laura Mele, Sapienza University of Rome, Italy
Domenico Polimeno, University of Perugia, Italy
Alessandro Londei, Sapienza University of Rome, Italy

The chapter focuses on the Bootstrap statistical technique for assigning measures of accuracy to sample estimates, here adopted for the first time to obtain an effective and efficient interaction evaluation. After introducing and discussing the classic debate on p value (i.e., the discovery detection rate) about estimation problems, the authors present the most used model for the estimation of the number of participants needed for an evaluation test, namely the Return On Investment model (ROI). Since the ROI model endorses a monodimensional and economical perspective in which an evaluation process, composed of only an expert technique, is sufficient to identify all the interaction problems—without distinguishing real problems (i.e., identified both experts and users) and false problems (i.e., identified only by experts)—they propose the new Bootstrap Discovery Behaviour (BDB) estimation model. Findings highlight the BDB as a functional technique favouring practitioners to optimize the number of participants needed for an interaction evaluation. Finally, three experiments show the application of the BDB model to create experimental sample sizes to test user experience of people with and without disabilities.

Chapter 16

Chris Harrison, Carnegie Mellon University, Pittsburgh, USA
Zhiquan Yeo, Carnegie Mellon University, Pittsburgh, USA
Brian Amento, AT&T Labs, USA
Scott E. Hudson, Carnegie Mellon University, Pittsburgh, USA

Human perception of time is fluid, and can be manipulated in purposeful and productive ways. In this chapter, the authors describe and evaluate how progress bar pacing behaviors and graphical design can alter users' perceptions of an operation's duration. Although progress bars are relatively simple, they provide an ideal playground in which to experiment with perceptual effects in user interface design. As a baseline in the experiments, the authors use generic, solid-color progress bars with linear pacing behaviors, prevalent in many user interfaces. In a series of direct comparison tests, they are able to rank how different progress bar designs compare to one another. Using these results, it is possible to craft perceptually-optimized progress bars that appear faster, even though their actual duration remains unchanged. Throughout, the authors include design suggestions that can contribute to an overall more responsive, pleasant, and human-centric computing experience.

Section 5
Education and Interactive Picture Book

Although the Internet serves as a means to offer education everywhere, in many cases it merely displays online books that replace paper books. The next chapter introduces a dynamic changing course that adapts to an instructor changing their mind during the course, while maintaining basic intelligent features and a student profile describing that student's level of concept mastery. The chapter that follows it makes the books in Harry Potter a reality. It presents a paper book that displays interactive changing words and pages that allow a child to change the storyline of the story being read.

Chapter 17

Khulood Gaid, Royal University for Women, Bahrain
Eshaa Mohamed Alkhalifa, University of Bahrain, Bahrain

Adaptive Educational Systems are able to alter an online course as per the needs of each student. Existing technologies require significant time and effort to design and build such courses. This chapter offers a solution allowing instructors to build a practical adaptive system as they upload their lessons and tests to the online site. The system asks the instructor to associate multiple choice answers that are incorrect with error pattern names and to associate the error patterns with lessons students need to review. The result is that the adaptable system is dynamically built as the course progresses. A student views a student profile screen that is adapted to that student's level of knowledge and displays that student's misconceptions. On the other hand, an instructor can use a reports view of the system to extract common error co-occurrences and infer information about the difficulties faced by students in that course.

Chapter 18

Hiroki Yamada, The University of Tokyo, Japan
Michitaka Hirose, The University of Tokyo, Japan

In this chapter, the authors introduce SequenceBook system, an interactive picture book that consists of a paper book with very thin IC (Integrated Circuit) tags embedded in each page and an RFID (Radio Frequency IDentification) antenna. This system uses a traditional paper book as an interface and realizes natural interface that keeps the affordance of traditional book and thus smoothly prompts users to experience its contents by just flipping pages in the same way as they read an ordinary book. Another important feature of the system is that users can change its storylines as they like. The system is designed like a bookbinder so that users can easily shuffle pages and make several patterns of stories.

Foreword

KNOWLEDGE IS THE KEY

Presenting information in a visual way is increasing since the advent of the tablet PC, which altered the meaning of mobility. The end user has become very demanding: they would like to configure their webpage, they ask to customize the way their preferred e-newspaper is represented, to be updated by the latest technology, to subscribe to some e-magazines, etc. All these features are available today by using configurable databases interacting with the visual page, namely the front-page. Some end-users would like to use this technology without any restrictions. The only restriction which makes any difference is the behavior of the user, and the user's knowledge of the different steps. Cognitive learning process integrated in the different aspects of web design can help the user.

Cognitively Informed Interfaces arrive into the world at a time when cognitive science is gradually attracting an increasing amount of attention to its findings and projects. For example, Siri, which is an application on the new iPhone 4S, is in fact an implementation of an artificial intelligence voice recognition software that uses production rules in the form of {**If**…, **then**…, **else**…} to perform the role of a cognitive assistant to users of the iPhone 4S. Siri is a cognitively informed Interface.

This book represents a set of solutions to a variety of problems, which use the graphical interface as a medium of visualization. It goes from healthcare-based problems, to learning method problems, ending in some new approaches on future methods, which could be promising for the next market need.

All chapters show the ability of implementing interactive systems, which can adapt with the behavior of each user, to increase the productivity in the business area, to promote the quality of analysis in the domain of educational process, or as a tool used in the healthcare sector. Nowadays, most of the Information Technology tools are based on a cloud area available to users regardless of place and time of delivery. This can be configured by the user or automatically by studying the behavior of the end user. The choice depends on the application and the type of user; this, in turn, determines the importance of the cognitively informed interface.

In education, an idea is presented to make a difference in the next generation of eLearning resources and eBooks. It is the change from a classical eResource (static), to a dynamic eResource, which gives a margin of flexibility to the words by representing their meanings, whether by sound or by animation. It is the first step to create a global repository of resources, which offers an adaptable resource to each learning model. More details of the idea can be found in Chapter 18.

Nowadays, the Learning Management Systems (LMS) that track student activities need a personal tutoring interaction, which necessitates additional staff. To reduce this effort, and to have a dynamic generation of student activity, it's a must to have an adaptive tutoring system integrated to the LMS which can be the agent to track and analyze student activities in the dedicated course.

Despite the importance of education as a highly considered area of application, healthcare is indeed a strong competitive domain with the same level of importance, where human interaction is not sufficient to make some serious and crucial decisions. An idea was presented to improve the observation of the black hole in a vascular system by identifying the suspicious areas, in comparison to other images taken from the same patient by implementing Curved Planar Reformation visualization; this can result in a significant efficiency improvement, compared to older methods.

Another domain where healthcare is concerned is when gazing is added to the communication protocol of the mobile phone, thus enabling the disabled to deal with mobile phones by giving orders or interacting with the mobile either by touch screen or by gazing. It is a very promising application for the full interactivity between humans and mobile phones. It can be equally applied to Tablet PCs and deployed to schools to help students be guided to their educational interests.

All the ideas presented in this book, creative and enjoyable as they are when gone through in detail, end up in the very same vision of improving our lifestyle and leading us to a better future, especially in the education and health systems. It will be a great loss not to see most of the presented ideas implemented in future generations of mobile learning devices, such as the Tablet PC, and integrated into our Identity Card, where our own healthcare personal info is stored, and when our future reading would involve a dynamic eBook.

Ahmed Dabbagh
Ankabut Project, UAE

Ahmed Dabbagh *is Manager of Technology and Services Development at the UAE Advanced Network for Research and Education "Ankabut." His main work is to enhance collaboration between the different Higher Education Institutions over UAE by using the state-of-the-art technology to connect and communicate and to create a common sense in research and education, like eLearning, eLibrary, and Grid Computing. Dr. Dabbagh is leading the UAE initiatives in Grid-Cloud Computing and the Certification Authority. Prior to joining Ankabut, Dr. Dabbagh was the Director of the Academic e-Services Department at Ajman University of Science and Technology, UAE. Dr. Dabbagh was working in France and Germany for several years in the domain of micro-controllers and a wide range of micro-processors architectures ranging from 16 bits up to 64 bit with the very known Semiconductors industry like STMicroelectronics, Siemens, Motorola. He is the inventor of several patents in this important field. Dr. Dabbagh gained a Master of Science "D.E.A." in Images and Signal Processing from the University of Rennes in 1991 and a PhD in Telecommunications from the University of Rennes, France, in 1995.*

Preface

WINDOWS TO THE WORLD!

A human being can only experience the world through the mind's eye. Human senses perceive the inputs received from the environment, and the mind interprets them to produce understanding. Limitations in the cognitive system directly impacts what we understand. An example that is established exists in visual tricks. Limitations in the visual system cause interpretations of what is seen to be manipulated.

However, this book does not describe old knowledge. Instead, it covers new emerging concepts. To understand for example, how our conceptualization of time limits how we analyze a question, ponder this question.

"I do not believe what you believe and you do not believe what I believe,

I will not believe what you will believe and you will not believe what I will believe in the future.

Did we at any time in the past share the same belief?"

Now, if the reader tries to forget that question and think only of the following one:

"I did not believe what you believed and you did not believe what I believed in the past,

I do not believe what you believe and you do not believe what I believe in the now.

Can we at anytime in the future share the same belief?"

The two questions are logically equivalent, with the first question setting the scene for the present and future time slots as having a disagreement while leaving the past without any input about it while the second places disagreement in the past and present time slots while leaving the future without input. Human inability to change the past caused those tested to mostly answer NO to the first question and YES to the second. It is not a logical choice as the possibility should be technically possible for both questions.

These limitations that guide the way we analyze the world can be studied and utilized to increase the efficiency and effectiveness of interfaces. This book focuses on interfaces that are designed for computer based systems, for smart phones, or for intelligent paper books. Screen set up, attention paid to different color arrangements, and general interface design issues are discussed here. One critical example is to detect suspicious areas in images of patients in order to attract doctor attention to those areas. Human perception is limited and confused if the images have uniform shade or color. Consequently, software is designed to detect suspicious areas and to highlight them with a bold color to ensure that doctors attend to those areas. The doctors can then dismiss the area or submit it to further testing. Here, suggested systems assist limits in perception to reduce human error in medicine.

Another emerging direction is to make devices more human like. An agent can be designed to exhibit human characteristics to resemble a specific teacher that the designer once knew, or to resemble a very creative salesman. Visitors of these sites can remember that agent and describe him as being shy, honest, and funny, for example. Adding the human traits would make a site more distinguishable from the others.

This book is of interest to a vast spectrum of readers that range from managers who wish to see where interface technology is heading, to average people who are just curious about the inventions that are just around the corner. The information contained may be crucial to managers of companies involved in interface design or applications that interact with customers. The reason is that the chapters of this book exhibit advances in various areas that bid attention.

Chapter 1 is entitled "**Multitasking Bar: Prototype and Evaluation of Introducing the Task Concept into a Browser**" and written by Eric Wang, Huiyon Chang, and Huiyang Liu. People multitask in two ways whenever using a web browser. They can either open multiple tabs to perform a single task. For example, if one is searching for a hotel to stay in when visiting a foreign country, it is quite typical to browse different hotel pages on several tabs all open simultaneously. On the other hand, it is also possible that the same person wishes to perform a task during more than one online session. One day, one browses a few hotel sites then one leaves the task at that point. The next day after speaking to a friend, one comes back to browse a different hotel in the same site. This chapter introduces a Multitasking Bar that can be added to browsers with the ability of classifying historical data of task performance. The goal is to offer more support to people who surf the Internet whether it is professional or for leisurely activities.

Chapter 2 is entitled "**Soft Keyboard Evaluations: Integrating User's Background in Predictive Models**" and written by Bruno Merlin and Mathieu Raynal. The authors examine soft keyboard predictive evaluation models. Soft keyboards are currently used in touch screen phones and Ipads. Increasing input speed of these keyboards has become a very important issue. Existing keyboards as in Qwerty are based upon very old typewriter technology which have nothing in common with touch screen mobile phones. The authors indicate that predictive models of evaluation of best and worst possible performance do not conform to empirical data. Additionally, new keyboard designs are possible in the new mediums that now exist.

Chapter 3 is entitled "**A Fresh Look at Graphical Web Browser Revisitation Using an Organic Bookmark Management System**" and written by Siu-Tsen Shen, Stephen D. Prior, and Kuen-Meau Chen. This chapter presents a graphical medium to represent information displayed in the history folder of web browsers. The graphical representation resembles a pot with a growing plant that relates different sites visited in the history folder. The goal is to relate webpage to each other to make it easier to find previously visited web paged. Since existing searches in the History folder is more like searching for a needle in a haystack unless the visit of the site was extremely recent, this is an avenue that bids researcher attention of how to make that representation more meaningful to users of the browsers.

Chapter 4 is entitled "**MobiGaze: Gaze Interface for Mobile Devices**" and written by Takashi Nagamatsu, Michia Yamamoto, and Hiroshi Sato. This chapter describes a user interface that uses human's gaze to operate a handheld mobile device. It is difficult to use a touch screen device with one hand so a touch plus gaze tracking interface was designed. This interface uses the surface revolution around the optical axis of the eye as a basis. One implementation that the authors may consider in the future is to utilize this interface to serve the physically impaired people to enable them to increase their level of interaction with the world and increase their quality of life.

Chapter 5 is entitled **"Evaluating Visualisations and Automatic Warning Cues for Visual Search in Vascular Images"** and written by Boris Van Shooten, Betsy Van Dijk, Avan Suinesiaputra, Anton Nijholt, and Johan H. C. Reiber. This chapter evaluates visualization approaches that assist in visual search in vascular images. A patient wishes that his or her doctor can immediately and correctly diagnose the existence of a condition or the lack of it. They compare four visualization techniques then discuss the professional opinions of users of these systems which indicate a preference to "paranoid" highlighting of areas of suspicion. In other words, the authors recommend that physician support systems should leave the decision in cases of confusion to the doctor in change rather than try to build systems that may cause misdiagnosis. They also note that if the system does not highlight an area, then the doctor is not likely to examine that area at all even though it may have a small tumor. Consequently, visual interfaces should take this tendency to ignore areas that are not highlighted into account especially in the field of medicine where human life may be at risk.

Chapter 6 is entitled **"Considering the Influence of Visual Saliency during Interface Searches"** and written by Jeremiah D. Still and Christopher M. Masciocchi. The authors examine the areas on the screen visitors of the web pages attend to. Saliency represents how unique an object is on the screen when compared to its surroundings. The authors compare the bottom-up approach to the top-down approach. The bottom-up approach investigates how parts of the screen attract attention in the presence of distracters. The top-down approach is goal driven when a person visually searches the screen looking for an object. The authors highlight the role of bottom-up mental processes that can be easily extended to web pages. Web page designers can use this knowledge to attract the attention of web page visitors to specific areas on the screen. The authors also examine the existence of a correlation between saliency and eye fixations using an eye tracker.

Chapter 7 is entitled **"Design and Evaluation of a Multimodal Representation for Conveying the Vast Range of Imperceptible Smallness"** and written by Minyoung Song. When teaching students about objects that are too small to see, these objects are frequently enlarged and displayed. The author of this chapter argues that students fail to grasp the distinct classes of sizes these objects fall into. Some of these very small objects may be much larger than others. The chapter describes an education tool that uses time in addition to enlarging the object image. Objects are also placed next to a reference object with a given visible size like 1 millimeter. The larger the small object is, the longer the animation takes to place it on the screen when compared to a smaller object that is placed more quickly on the screen. The author justifies this approach to be based upon cognitive science research that found that the mental representation of space and time are interwoven. The educational tool is tested with 7th grade students with positive results.

Chapter 8 is entitled **"Interactive Diagram Layout"** and written by Sonja Maier and Mark Minas. Layouts in general are relevant to any work that involves drawing a structure as in the structure of a text, or representing how different concepts relate to each other. The authors of this chapter assigns different groups of students the task of developing layout editors. They found a similarity between the layout editors that different groups of students created. The chapter also discusses a proposed pattern based layout approach that allows the definition of a combination of different layout algorithms rather than to display each algorithm alone. This approach produces good results according to the authors when integrated with existing visual language editors.

Chapter 9 is entitled **"Optimization in Mental Configuration Space: The Case of Pointing Behavior"** and written by Huahai Yang. This chapter investigates how humans mentally represent points in two dimensional space. It starts by reviewing a number of existing behavior models. Configuration space is defined as a space with one axis per variable. Finding points represented in two dimensions will require a representation on two axes (x,y). If there are three dimensions, then the representation will be in the form (x,y,z) and this would point to one point that is described in three dimensions. The authors gave students a pointing task on the screen and found that their behavior was best explained by the configuration space model. Other models failed to compete with this predictive ability of the configuration space model. This may be indicative of how humans conceptualize and reason about physical configuration in real life.

Chapter 10 is entitled "**Question-Answer Approach to Human-Computer Interaction in Collaborative Designing**" and written by Petr Sosnin. A software intensive system is software in one or more locations that continually adapt to the environment by interacting continually with it. This chapter presents a question/answer approach as a communication medium between humans and the system, and also between computer processors. Question/answer pseudo code programs are explained to be a useful means of interaction that adapt to problems' needs and can be automatically and easily translated to an executable that is run on a compiler. One outcome of such a theory may be a system that generates software codes upon interacting with a human through the question/answer communication medium provided.

Chapter 11 is entitled "**Intelligent Agents with Personality: From Adjectives to Behavioral Schemes**" and written by François Bouchet and Jean-Paul Sansonnet. The authors describe an extensive effort made to offer a tool to scholars who wish to give intelligent agents a personality. They used two references for their work and found a good match between them. Their first source of information included psychological research that classified human personality traits. Their second source of information came from a complete list of adjectives that describe people in the English Language. Perhaps the assumption made here is that the word would not exist unless there is a personality trait it can describe. Their contribution is a taxonomy available on the Internet that describes all personality traits and can be used to give intelligent agents a personality.

Chapter 12 is entitled "**The Activity Circle: A Social Proxy Interface to Display the Perceived Distributed Viscosity about Workflow Technology**" and written by Marcello Sarini. Workflow technologies are designed to allow collaboration between employees and to streamline their output to perform the organization's objectives. Simultaneously social software focuses on conversation and interaction between users. The goal of this chapter is to visually display perceived viscosity to help employees realize more about themselves, the roles they assume, and others in the organization. Management may also use this information to identify conflicts and issues that may impede work in the organization.

Chapter 13 is entitled "**A Global Process for Model-Driven Approaches in User Interface Design**" and written by Sybille Caffiau and Patrick Girard. The authors of this chapter present a process for user interface design that can start from a task based model or from a user defined simple prototype. A task model is based upon specifying the tasks an interface has to perform and generating the design from that point. A hierarchical design on the other hand, starts by defining the main tasks performed and based upon them, the subtasks are designed and so on. User defined prototypes are designed as small working systems that are shown to clients following which they are either replaced or expanded into the full working system. The chapter shows how iterative modifications using rule additions while checking these rules. The generative approach generally is associated with errors that are avoided by the authors in this approach because new rules are added without affecting the process.

Chapter 14 is entitled "**Programming a User Model with Data Gathered From a User Profile**" and written by Danial Schere, Ademar V. Netto, Yuska P. C. Aguiar, and M. F. Q. Vieira. Interfaces in general need to learn about those who use them in order to reduce the cognitive load on users. This chapter proposes a combined approach of building a user profile and a programmable user model. The relationship between the two is explored to examine the erroneous assumptions that are sometimes made in user characteristics and correct them. Future directions of work may incorporate biometrical data in the user model.

Chapter 15 is entitled "**The Bootstrap Discovery Behaviour Model: Why Five Users are not Enough to Test User Experience**" and written by Simone Borsci, Stefano Federici, Maria Laura Mele, Domenico Polimeno, and Alessandro Londei. This chapter examines how to estimate the number of users necessary to test user experience. The authors examine the Return On Investment model that helps predict the number of users necessary to evaluate a system. They argue that this mode is not suitable if testing has to be performed by more than one category or users. They proposed that the bootstrap model makes a more accurate estimation of the number of users needed to test any system. They find that in their case, 5 is not enough for testing.

Chapter 16 is entitled "**Designing 'Faster' Progress Bars: Manipulating Perceived Duration**" **and** written by Chris Harrison, Zhiquan Yeo, Brian Amento, and Scott E. Hudson. Progress bars are an integral part of the installation process. The main goal of their presence is for the system to inform the person performing the installation that the process is in progress. However, not all progress bars were created equal. Some get stuck at one location for a long while before starting to advance again. This may happen if the folder being copied is larger than the others. Many complaints are sent by impatient customers who stopped the installation because they assume the installation was stuck and could not proceed to completion. This chapter is cognitively informed about customers so it uses knowledge about human perception to retain human confidence in the installation process and gives the impression that it is also a fast installation.

Chapter 17 is entitled "**Dynamic Generation of Adaptive Tutoring**" and written by Khulood Gaid and Eshaa M. Alkhalifa. Adaptive Educational Systems are able to alter the online course as per the needs of each student. Such a powerful system has a large overhead in the time and effort required to design and build such courses. This chapter offers a practical adaptive system that is automatically built as instructors upload their tests to the online site. In short, the system asks the instructor to associate multiple choice questions that are incorrect with error pattern names and to associate the error patterns with lessons they need to review. The result is that the adaptable system is dynamically built as the course progresses. An instructor can use reports to extract common error co-occurrences and infer information about misconceptions at the end of the course.

Chapter 18 is entitled "**Interactive Picture Book with Story-Changeable System by Shuffling Pages**" and written by Hiroki Yamada and Michitaka Hirose. The authors of this chapter hope to add digital content to paper books. The idea is not as farfetched as it may seem. They use very thin Integrated Circuit (IC) tags and a Radio Frequency Identification Antenna (RFID). Users can flip through the pages of this book that allows them to change the story line in one of many possible patterns. A particular feature that may be of interest in this work is that this makes it possible to add some action to "kototama" words. The authors indicate that in Japan words are believed to have their own spirits and special force since early times so they call them spiritual words. Words come to life in this chapter as their meanings turn into actions, whether by sound or animation. "Kototama words are projected around the pages of the book as if they were 'floating' outside the world of the book" (excerpt from the chapter). Since in many cases fictional movies predict the future path of science, it may not be purely magic that allows words to float on a page, if science catches up with human imagination. This chapter is a definite 'must read'.

To sum up, this book presents work that may enter our lives in the not so distant future as devices or upgrades to existing tools. It is merely a stage, in the explosive reaction of cognitively informed systems.

Eshaa Mohamed Alkhalifa
University of Bahrain, Bahrain

Acknowledgment

I would like to thank the God that graced and protected my steps towards who I am. It is not a career position, nor is it a set of accomplishments. It is instead a sense of inner satisfaction and a tranquil pride of who I have become.

I would like to also thank my husband, and soul-mate, Sh Nawaf bin Ebrahim Alkhalifa. Thank you for continually reminding me of the capacity of my brain cells, and for continually challenging them with ideas, dreams, and plans.

I would also like to thank my two teenage sons, Ebrahim and Mohamed. They are a perfect example of everything a mother wants in her sons.

I would also like to thank all the scholars who contributed to this book for their patience with the constant nagging to meet deadline. Without YOU, there would be no great edited book like this one.

I can only thank some people with warm tears and gentle smiles but words cannot express me. To the greatest mother and father any one could have, I hope I will make you always proud. To my financial and mental supporters: Khalid and Abdullah, I hope I will be able to pay you back!

To my little brother and sisters: Mansoor, Amera, AlAnood, and Arwa, you are the joy of my life. To my beloved friends: Asila, Batool, and Zeina, you supported me in ways you yourselves do not realize, and I hope I will always do the same. To the person who strengthened me to rise up to the challenge: Mr. Parsa Zoqaqi, you are one blessing I thank God for.

To the person who believed in me and implanted hope, patience, and persistence in my soul: Dr. Eshaa Al Khalifa, thank you for guidance, time, efforts, and patience. To the person who was the reason I wanted to challenge myself, thank you. And to all who cooperated with us to make this project a success, thank you! May Allah bless this work and may praise be to Allah.

Eshaa Mohamed Alkhalifa
Royal University for Women, Bahrain

Khulood Gaid
Royal University for Women, Bahrain

Section 1
Phones and Browsers

Chapter 1
Multitasking Bar:
Prototype and Evaluation of Introducing the Task Concept into a Browser

Qing Wang
Sun Yat-Sen University, China

Huiyou Chang
Sun Yat-Sen University, China

Huiyang Liu
Sun Yat-Sen University, China

ABSTRACT

This chapter clarifies two common patterns of multitasking on the Web, namely Multiple Tasks (MT) and Multiple Session Task (MST). Multi-Tasks (MT) is defined as executing a set of tasks simultaneously where the execution often depends on bundles of Web pages. Multi-Session Task (MST), on the other hand, is defined as executing a single task spanning multiple Web sessions. To support both of these, the task concept needs to be introduced into a browser. An online pilot survey has revealed which attributes of the task concept are most significant to Web users, and as a result, a simple prototype, the Multitasking Bar (MB), has been proposed based on these findings. The MB copes with the multitasking needs of both MT and MST in the browser by providing functions for task related Web page management and task schedule management. A two-session controlled experiment has been conducted to evaluate the MB and to compare user performance and experience when multitasking on the Web with and without support for MT and MST. Results show that support for both MST and MT significantly improves user task performance efficiency and greatly enhances the user experience when multitasking on the Web.

INTRODUCTION

Currently with the ubiquity of the Internet, we are doing more and more of our jobs online (UCLA, 2003; USC, 2009; GVU, 1998), with the most important workplace for these jobs be-

DOI: 10.4018/978-1-4666-1628-8.ch001

ing the browser. On the other hand, humans are naturally multitasking beings, often either doing several tasks simultaneously and alternatively, or executing a single task through several working sessions. For instance, there are several reports in the literature that a great many managerial tasks can be characterized by their brevity, variety, and fragmentation (González & Mark, 2004; Mintzberg, 1970, 1980). This leads to simultaneously executed activities, interruptions and resumption of tasks both on and off the Web (Mayer, 2007, p. 173-278). Meanwhile, a diary study of knowledge workers has identified an average of 50 task shifts per person during a typical working week (Czerwinski, Horvitz, & Wilhite, 2004, p. 175-182), and a log study has identified an average of 3.74 e-mail or IM-driven task shifts per hour, taking between 8 and 10 minutes on average for the person to return to the interrupted task (Iqbal & Horvitz, 2007, p. 677-686).

Cognitive psychologists have studied many aspects of multitasking or task switching, providing several definitions of multitasking (Carlson & Sohn, 2000; Miyata & Norman, 1986, p. 265-284). Just et al. (2001) and Rubinstein et al. (2001) stated that multitasking is the ability of humans to handle simultaneously the demands of multiple tasks through task switching, and that it allows people to cope with ever increasing complex environments by handling multiple tasks through task switching (Burgess, 2000, p. 465-472; Lee & Taatgen, 2002, p. 572-577). We follow these definitions in this chapter and concentrate especially on tasks that depend on Web resources, typically Web pages. When users multitask while working on the Web, they switch among several tasks running simultaneously, often suspending and then resuming their task(s). In doing so, they tend to follow one of two common patterns, which we define as Multi-Tasks (MT) and Multi-Session-Task (MST). In this chapter, Multi-Tasks (MT) is defined as the pattern of executing a set of tasks simultaneously, where the execution often depends on bundles of Web pages. MST on the other hand, is the pattern of executing a single task spanning multiple Web sessions (as in MacKay's [2008] definition). For example, whilst shopping on an e-commerce web site, and doing other task(s) on the Web at the same time, i.e., planning the itinerary of a vacation, constitutes MT. Furthermore, the shopping task is classed as an MST if it spans more than one Web session; in other words, if at

some point the browser is closed and the shopping task temporarily suspended, and then later resumed in a new instance of the browser.

These patterns of MT and MST in Web use are very common, and have frequently been reported in the literature. Spink et al. (2002) found that multitasking information seeking and searching is common human behavior as many IR system users conduct information seeking and searching on related or unrelated topics. The study by Sellen et al. (2002) of knowledge workers' Web use reported that 40% of the "information gathering" activities they observed were not completed in a single sitting, often due to external interruptions. MacKay and Watters (2008) found that users with tabbed browsing typically worked on several tasks during a single web session. Morris et al. (2008) presented evidence that users often conduct multi-session tasks, such as Web investigations, and they also found that "such tasks are not adequately supported by current tools."

In summary, there is significant evidence that both MT and MST are typical patterns of Web use, and should be well supported by browsers. This means that there should be some effective functions within the browser to help users manage tasks whilst multitasking on the Web, including functions for managing bunches of Web pages for corresponding tasks both simultaneously and across Web sessions, and functions for managing a task's status and schedule. For example, in the aforementioned shopping example, while shopping online a user may browse several related web pages simultaneously. Some pages may be commodity pages from the actual e-commerce site, while others may be web pages from other sites about these commodities, such as user comments, background information, and reviews. In this situation, all these web pages comprise a bundle of resources forming the context for the user's shopping task. Consequently, this resource bundle should be able to be saved, found, and restored as a whole whenever needed. Furthermore, when work is done on more than one task, the browser should provide better support than it does at present. It should intuitively make sense of and present the user with tasks to help switch quickly and easily between them. It also should manage the status of the tasks, to remind the user when these tasks must be completed, and what their current status is. In short, what is needed is support for (multi) task resource (Web pages) management and (multi) task schedule management in a browser.

Unfortunately, contemporary browsers do not provide these kinds of functions, at least, not very well. In almost all widely-used browsers, there is neither the concept nor awareness of a task or task session, making it difficult to detect or explicitly define a task, manage its status, and hence save or resume work on it accordingly (Morris, Morris, & Venolia, 2008). To resolve this issue, users have resorted to various workarounds, such as opening several browser windows or tabs simultaneously for different tasks (Kellar, Watters, & Shepherd, 2007, p. 999-1018), bookmarking all related Web pages for a task as a group, and even writing the URLs of the relevant Web pages for a task on paper (Cockburn & Mckenzie, 2001, p. 903-922; Jhaveri & Räihä, 2005) to enable continuing the task between sessions. Besides these workarounds, the most effective approaches hitherto lie in various research prototypes and browser extensions and plugins (for details, see the RELATED WORK section).

We believe that if we explicitly introduce the task concept into a browser and allow the browser to manage the task status and related Web pages for both MT and MST, it will promote user performance efficiency and enhance user experiences when multitasking on the Web. Our study attempts to answer two research questions:

How will the introduction of the task concept into a browser impact a user's multitasking performance efficiency on the Web?

How will this introduction impact a user's experience while multitasking on the Web?

In the rest of this chapter, we first review related works on multitasking in a browser. We then introduce the pilot survey used to investigate how users expect to cope with multitasking in a browser. Next, we describe the design and implementation details of our prototype, the Multitasking Bar (MB). Thereafter, we report on the user study conducted to test the impact of introducing the task concept into a browser by comparing user performance efficiency and experience when multitasking on the Web with and without support for MT or MST in the browser. Next, we analyze data collected from our user study to ascertain research results and implications. Finally, we conclude by discussing the contributions of this chapter and suggesting possible future work.

BACKGROUND

Various studies have been conducted to investigate the multitasking features and patterns in current browsers. Jhaveri and Räihä (2005) argued that the weakness of a browser's support for MST is inherited from the weakness of revisitation support in a browser. Keelar et al. (2007) provided a taxonomy of Web tasks and argued that task oriented revisiting functionality should be provided in a user's Web interactions. Moreover, MacKay and Watters (2008) revealed the importance of better task session resumption support in a browser through a field study that investigated users' interactions with the Web on MST. They also identified three main features needed by browser tools to support MST. However, all these studies typically focused on MST and hardly considered MT.

Previous studies also proposed approaches to enhance MST in a browser. Jhaveri and Räihä (2005) proposed Session Highlights to support MST in web-based research tasks, in which a research task is visualized as a workspace and each related Web page is represented as a thumbnail. Spink et al. (2006) proposed an approach for interactive information retrieval contextually within a multitasking framework. Morris et al. (2008) built a search-centric task management tool named SearchBar as a plugin for Internet Explorer. By using search queries as a fundamental organizational metaphor, the SearchBar groups a user's browsing history into topic-centric tasks, and provides a quick task context resumption function. MacKay and Watters (2009) developed 3 prototypes to enhance a browser's support for MST. These prototypes can store and resume a bundle of web pages as a task context across Web sessions, and can switch between saved tasks by selecting the task in a dropdown list.

However, all these approaches concentrated solely on MST, and ignored MT. They investigated how to save and resume a task across Web sessions, and not how to present multiple tasks running simultaneously in a browser in such a way as to make sense to the user. Moreover, with the exception of MacKay and Watters' study, the other studies did not even incorporate the task concept, which means that in these approaches users are not able to explicitly define and track a task on its necessary attributes, such as end date (deadline), status, etc. Furthermore, in these approaches tasks differ in that they are specific to different application domains in the different approaches. Each of these studies, except for MacKay and Watters,' can only support multitasking for a particular kind of Web tasks, and not for generic Web tasks. In addition, except for MacKay and Watters' approach, none of them considered task schedule management.

Besides these publications, there are also many plug-ins, extensions and even built-in functions for browsers that can be used to support MST and MT partially. Save Session (https://addons. mozilla.org/en-US/firefox/addon/4199) and Session Manager (https://addons.mozilla.org/en-US/ firefox/addon/2324) for Firefox and TabSaver for Internet Explorer (http://tabsaver.codeplex. com/) can save a current Web session and restore it at the next startup of the browser. In fact, in Firefox 2.0+, Internet Explorer 7.0+, Safari 0.9+, and Opera 4.0+, this is a built-in feature of the browser. However, although this feature can sup-

port MST in two adjacent sessions (instances) of the browser, it cannot support either defining task related Web pages explicitly or resuming a task to a state before several browser running sessions. Another function that can be used to support MT is tab grouping, which is provided by some Firefox extensions such as Multi Row Bookmarks Toolbar (https://addons.mozilla.org/en-US/firefox/ addon/6937), Group/Sort Tabs (https://addons. mozilla.org/en-US/firefox/addon/5627), Tab Kit (https://addons.mozilla.org/en-US/firefox/ addon/5447), and TabGroups Manager (https:// addons.mozilla.org/en-US/firefox/addon/10254), etc. Nevertheless, none of these have the explicit task concept built in. Therefore, once again, they cannot resume tasks across more than one Web session and do not support task schedule management. Moreover, we have not found any literature on the impact of these extensions on the user's performance or experience when multitasking on the Web, and most of the time the improvement in user efficiency and enhancement of user experience are just taken for granted.

In summary, previous studies and tools seldom introduce the concept of a task into a browser directly and explicitly, and provide little in the way of task schedule management. Furthermore, the impact of incorporating the task concept in a browser has not been studied thoroughly. To extend these studies we have implemented a simple prototype, the Multitasking Bar (MB), which explicitly incorporates the task concept in a browser and supports both MT and MST.

PILOT SURVEY

Before introducing the task concept into a browser for multitasking, we need to answer the question of what attributes the task concept should have in a multitasking-enabled browser or, in other words, what attributes of a task are most significant to users multitasking on the Web? Unfortunately, although some previous studies explored multitasking features of Web tasks, they typically concentrated on task types, task resumption times or task dwelling times, and browser functions to support multitasking (Czerwinski, Horvitz, & Wilhite, 2004; Kellar, Watters, & Shepherd, 2007; MacKay & Watters, 2008). They did not answer the questions we have posed here.

For this reason, we conducted an online survey at SurveyGizmo (http://www.surveygizmo.com/) about multitasking on the Web between April 10 and May 10, 2009. We received 582 valid responses with 82% of the respondents being male. Age of the respondents ranged from 18 – 57 years old (median=28). The respondents had varied occupations, including teachers, software developers, librarians, salespersons, assistants and secretaries, marketing specialists, managers, and students. All respondents identified themselves as either average (31%) or expert (69%) web users; none were novice users. Our survey asked 32 questions about a variety of Web use habits, including their usage of the browser, and their experience with multitasking (having experience of MT or not, having experience of MST or not), etc.

It should be noted that the data presented in this section are self-reported, and thus we have used these results as design guidelines only, since we cannot verify their absolute accuracy.

In the survey, respondents reported having experience of MT (92%) and MST (94%), and when multitasking on the Web, on average they often had 2 – 8 tasks (μ=3.46, σ= 1.56) ongoing simultaneously. The most important question in the survey is Question 19, which relates to the significance of 6 attributes[1] of the task concept which we considered to be candidates for incorporation in a browser in our research prototype. The results are shown in Figure 1. Of the 582 respondents, 560 (96%, having either MT or MST experience) answered the question[2], and more than half of these identified Name (93%), End Date (71%), Status (53%), and Active Time (51%) as significant.

We also recruited 48 participants who are Firefox users familiar with tabs for our subsequent user study (the limit of this sample population is discussed in DISCUSSION).

SYSTEM DESIGN AND IMPLEMENTATION

We designed a simple prototype, the Multitasking Bar (MB), to evaluate the impact of introducing the task concept into a browser. It was implemented using the open source Firefox extensions Tab

Figure 1. Distribution on significance of task attributes

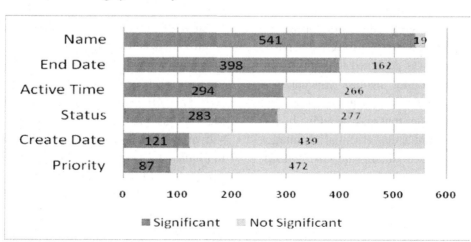

Figure 2. Screenshots of the MB: 1) multitasking bar, 2) context menu of task tab, 3) context menu of multitasking bar, 4) status icon, 5) tabs of web pages of current task, 6) tooltip of task tab

Kit (https://addons.mozilla.org/en-US/firefox/addon/5447), TabGroups Manager (https://addons.mozilla.org/en-US/firefox/addon/10254), and Tlogger (http://dubroy.com/tlogger/). Three screenshots of the MB are shown in Figure 2.

The MB supports both MT and MST. It groups Web pages for a task into a bundle and presents a task as a tab in the Multitasking Bar (1 in Figure 2). It manages the status of tasks, and can store, resume, rollback, and close related Web pages as a whole. It also collects user interactions with the browser for our user study, and can be configured with different function sets for different users[3].

Since the MB was designed to evaluate the impact of incorporating the task concept in a browser, we made it as simple as possible. That is, we excluded values that may be added by additional functions rather than essential advantages brought about by introducing the task concept into a browser.

Task Concept

The task concept in the MB only has four attributes, namely name, status, end date, and active time, which were significant to most of the respondents in our PILOT SURVEY. It is worth mentioning here that none of these attributes, except name, have generally been incorporated in a browser in previous studies; MacKay and Watters (2008, 2009) used end date, but without status and active time.

In the MB, the name of a task is either defined by the user or automatically generated by the MB by using the title of the first Web page (excluding the search engine web pages) opened in the task. The MB represents a task as a Task Tab in the Multitasking Bar, and its name and status are shown as label and status icons, respectively (1 in Figure 2). Users can also optionally define the end date of a task, from which the accumulated active time of the task will automatically be calculated by the MB and shown in the tooltip of the tab for the task (6 in Figure 2). Furthermore, according to its end date, at any time a task may be in one of the four states, namely IN PROCESS, APPROACHING END DATE, DELAYED, and CLOSED. If a task is approaching its deadline it will be shown with an APPROACHING END DATE status with the yellow icon on its tab, and if it has already missed its end date it will be shown with a DELAYED status using the red icon.

Tasks have states, especially a MST. At different times, the related Web pages for a task may be different. This feature has often been neglected by previous studies all of which assumed the user only wanted to resume a task to the state at its last running, but in fact, users occasionally need to roll a task back to a state other than that at the last running. The MB supports this feature; a user can roll back a task to any previous state stored, by selecting it from a drop down list in the context menu of the task tab (see 2 in Figure 2).

Tasks have structure. A large task often consists of a few smaller tasks, and sometimes the relationships between these child tasks can be complex. There may be certain business rules in these relationships, or these child tasks may even comprise complicated business processes or workflows. This complexity is beyond the scope of this study and we merely leave the management of the task structure to the user.

Sometimes tasks may be reused, especially the routine tasks recognized by Kellar et al. (2007). Although the MB has no dedicated function to reuse a task and does not even distinguish tasks running once from tasks running many times, it implicitly supports this feature. This means that a user can 'reuse' a task by rolling it back to a preferred stored state.

Grouping Strategy

There are several strategies for grouping Web pages to a related task in previous studies (Jhaveri & Räihä, 2005; MacKay & Watters, 2009; Morris, Morris, & Venolia, 2008). To make this as simple as possible, the MB follows and extends the strategy of Mackay and Watters (2009), that

is first grouping any newly opened Web page into the current active task unless the user explicitly defines it as a new task, and then permitting the user to move any Web page to another task or even to drop it to the special "Non-Task" task. Here the "Non-Task" task is a dummy task in the MB, which represents any casual Web surfing without a specific goal. Hence, it collects Web pages that do not belong to any real task. It is always shown at the end of the Multitasking Bar as a task tab with a grey background (on the far right of 1 in Figure 2).

User Scenario

A typical scenario for using the MB follows. In the beginning, a user starts a task by optionally giving it a name and end date. Any newly opened Web page is then collected unless the user moves it to another task or drops it to the "Non-Task." Users can store the state of a task at any time. When the browser is about to close, the MB automatically stores the states of all tasks active in the browser. Hence, afterwards the user can resume from a stored state. Users can also easily switch between tasks running simultaneously in the browser, and can suspend, resume, or close any of them as desired. The MB also highlights the status, end date, and accumulated active time of the tasks, making the user aware of her task schedule painlessly.

Data Collection

The MB can collect user interactions with the browser and itself, including any opening, closing, leaving, or returning to a Web page, and creating, renaming, storing, and resuming a task, as well as moving and dropping a Web page from a task. The MB also takes and stores screenshots when any new task is defined or any new tab is opened. This data can be used to calculate the time a user has spent on a particular task, and to compare the different usage patterns of users.

Configuration

After installation, the MB can be configured with or without MT and/or MST support. When the MT functions are disabled, the plus button on the Multitasking Bar disappears and there is only one real task available in the browser. When both MT and MST are disabled, the Multitasking Bar disappears and the MB acts only as a user browser interaction data collector.

USER STUDY

Our study goal is to evaluate the impact of incorporating the task concept in a browser on a user's performance efficiency and experience when multitasking on the Web. We conducted a two-session experiment on July 6 and July 13, 2009. Our experimental method was inspired by the method of Morris et al. (2008), and we extended it to cope with our study goal. In the experiment, we simulated a manager – secretary working scenario, in which participants acted as secretaries and were instructed by their managers, us the experimenters, to complete several tasks. They were required to do several tasks spanning the two sessions and their interactions with the browser and other useful data were collected for analysis.

Demographics

We recruited 48 participants (15 female). They ranged in age from 19 to 43 years (median = 24.5), and had a variety of occupations, including 25 students majoring in computer science, 3 students majoring in economics, 6 students majoring in psychology, 2 student majoring in management, 3 teachers, a librarian, 4 insurance salespersons, and 4 marketing specialists. Participants were given vouchers for food or beverages from the cafeteria as a gratuity.

Methodology

We used a between subjects design for our user study, with 16 participants each in one of 3 different groups. Participants in Group 1 (G1) were controlled like ordinary Web users without explicit multitasking support, while participants in Group 2 (G2), similar to users of previous approaches discussed in RELATED WORK, had MST support provided by the MB. Finally, participants in Group 3 (G3) had full support for MT and MST provided by the MB. We conducted the experiment in two separate sessions at our lab. Sessions lasted 110 minutes each including an additional questionnaire, and were scheduled one week apart.

We created the same Web working environment for each participant in both sessions, including a computer with a 19' screen with the following software installed: Windows XP Professional, Firefox with MB, Microsoft Instant Messenger (MIM), and Windows Office 2003. We instructed the participants that they could use any available tools to assist them in their tasks, including pen and paper (provided).

On June 29, a week before the beginning of the first session, we held a 20-minute training session of the MB for the participants in G2 and G3 according to their different configurations (with or without MT support) and asked them to practice using the MB during the following week. They reported their tasks created in MB in their practices, G2 (μ=4.47, σ=.79), G3 (μ=4.02, σ=.47).

First Session

In the first session, all participants were required to complete 5 tasks[4], and the manager (experimenter) launched these tasks one by one at 10 minute intervals by sending MIM group messages and delivering the required documents to all participants. All these tasks had been completed by the researchers in a pilot study to estimate the time needed for each task. The results showed that about 142 minutes were required to complete all tasks, which means that the participants were not likely to finish all of these tasks in a single experiment session. It is worth emphasizing here that although we asked participants to resume and complete these tasks in the second session, we did not inform them of this until the start of the second session.

For each task, we asked the participants each to submit a Microsoft Word document containing the results of their work. They did this based on a semi-complete Word file issued by the experimenter at the beginning of the task, and were asked to fill in all blanks in the file, i.e., street name of a particular place, date of a specific event, etc., and to complete several unfinished paragraphs.

Task 1 was the same as task 1 in Morris et al.'s (2008) methods. The manager requested that the assistants complete the itinerary for his upcoming business trip to Prague no later than July 14 (none of the participants had ever visited Prague). He told participants his itinerary requirements, such as the dates of travel, his desire to visit three famous historic sites and see three theatre productions, etc. and asked the participants to finalize his itinerary no later than the following week.

Task 2 was an easy job, and the same as task 2 in Morris et al.'s (2008) methods. Participants were required to find a restaurant for the manager in Chicago where he could take a client for lunch. They were asked to finish this task immediately in no more than 10 minutes, and were asked to fill in the blanks of restaurant name, address, telephone, 5 recommended cuisines, reasons for recommendations, etc. When the time was up, the experimenter instructed all unfinished participants to stop working on the task.

In task 3, we required participants to finish a semi-complete report on a 2008 summary of the environmental industry in the United States (none of the participants were engaged in the environmental industry at the time). Participants were required to fill in the blanks of the Industry Gross Product, leading equipment manufacturers of advanced waste disposal, smog mitigation and

water purification, etc., and to finish two paragraphs about technology and investment trends, with each paragraph having at least 500 words.

Task 4 was another long-term task whose deadline was July 11. Participants were asked to complete a semi-complete speech script for the manager's speech at an environmental forum. The report contained 20 blanks, such as the name of the chairman of the forum, city of the event, etc., and two uncompleted paragraphs about environmentalism and ecologicalism, both requiring more than 500 words.

Task 5 was also easy. Participants were required to write a recommendation for a digital camera the manager wished to purchase that met certain resolution and zoom requirements.

At the end of the session, the experimenter instructed all participants to stop working, and then asked them to complete an online questionnaire soliciting demographic information, information about their browsing habits, and multitasking strategies employed by them, and feedback on the MB tool (G2 and G3). Specifically, they were required to state how many minutes they had spent on each task, and for the unfinished tasks how many minutes they would need to complete them.

After each participant left, the experimenter saved all states by storing the Firefox's profile of the participant and any documents created in the session in a zip file, and collecting paper notes left on the desk in a file folder marked with the participant's name.

Second Session

When the participants returned for the second session, one week later on July 13[5], the setup was the same as in the first week, and Firefox had retained any settings they had accrued during the first session (bookmarks, history, MB entries, etc.), plus 280 history visitation records and 4 bookmarks intentionally added to each participant's profile[6] to populate it as if it had been used by the participant during the week. All their paper notes were on the desk as they had left them. However, we replaced the in-process result documents for their tasks with the unprocessed blank template files originally issued by the experimenter.

We informed the participants that they would continue in their role as secretary to the manager and that the computer was in the exact state they had left it the previous week, except that a computer virus had destroyed their work result files. Then we instructed all participants to report on the progress on their tasks giving task name, end date, status, time they had spent, and time still needed to complete the task. Each of them was asked to submit a report within 10 minutes. It is worth mentioning here that we did not tell them how many tasks there were or what they were; instead, we told them that if they could not remember, they could ask the experimenter for help, but not the other participants. Ten minutes later, we gave participants the correct information about their tasks' status according to the records from the first session and instructed them to carry on with the tasks. At the end of the second session, the experimenter distributed another questionnaire similar to session 1, and specifically with respect to the question on how much time participants had spent on each task, including both completed and uncompleted tasks.

Data Gathered

Data gathered during the study included notes and observations from four experimenters who observed each session, questionnaires completed after each session, the participants' task result documents from each of the two sessions, the transcripts of the instant messages, any other digital or paper notes made by participants, and the participants' Firefox profiles at the end of each session including history, bookmarks, and user browser interaction data collected by the MB.

RESULTS

During the two sessions[7], the MB clearly impacted users' multitasking on the Web. The MB was used by participants in G2 (times of using MB functions, $\mu=23.99$, $\sigma=4.14$) (11% in all browsing actions) and G3 ($\mu=16.07$, $\sigma=4.64$) (10%).

Throughout the experiment, they used the MB to create tasks G2 ($\mu=5.48$, $\sigma=.59$), G3 ($\mu=5.02$, $\sigma=.46$), and then to hibernate and resume these G2 ($\mu=6.47$, $\sigma=2.77$), G3 ($\mu=4.15$, $\sigma=0.40$). Analyses of the MB log data also show that the introduction of the task concept by the MB changed the participants' browsing behavior (Table 1). MB users in G2 ($\mu=37.20$, $\sigma=11.14$) and G3 ($\mu=30.59$, $\sigma=14.44$) opened fewer web pages than those without it, G1 ($\mu=48.73$, $\sigma=19.13$), ($p21<.04$, $p31<.01$), and they performed fewer navigation actions. The MB also changed participants' revisitation strategies. Participants with the MB used fewer history tools provided by the browser than those without it (Table 1). However, all groups had few bookmarks because they were not aware that their tasks would be continued in the second session (number of bookmarks for G1, G2, and G3 are 2, 0, and 1, respectively). Moreover, the MB changed the way participants used tabs. From Table 1 we can see that MB users used fewer tabs than the others.

Multitasking Performance Efficiency

The MB improved participants' multitasking performance. Except for one user in G2 who failed to finish task 4, all other MB users (97%) accomplished all their tasks in the experiment. Yet, among the participants not using the MB, 3 users (18%) had 4 tasks unfinished at the end of session 2. There are differences between the groups' mean times for accomplishing all five tasks in our experiment. Firstly, MB users accomplished the tasks in less time than the others; participants of G2 ($\mu=156.81$, $\sigma=16.80$) and G3 ($\mu=144.94$, $\sigma=12.69$) used less time than those

Table 1. Group statistics of interactions with browser (when p-value of t-test is less than .05, the null hypothesis is rejected)

	G1		G2		G3		G1:G2	G1:G3	G2:G3
	μ	σ	μ	σ	μ	σ			
Window and Tab Interactions							t-Test		
Window Actions	9.87	2.78	9.9	2.51	8.23	2.31	0.98	0.07	0.06
Tab Actions	88.61	20.85	74.54	15.64	60.82	17.73	0.03	0.01	0.03
Task Tab (MB)Actions	n/a	n/a	n/a	n/a	23.99	4.64	n/a	n/a	0.01
Revisitation									
History List	7.41	1.86	0.36	1.03	0.24	0.1	0.01	0.01	0.03
Task Resume	n/a	n/a	n/a	n/a	6.47	0.4	n/a	n/a	0.02
Followed Links	40.53	7.52	31.73	7.16	32.08	5.98	0.01	0.01	0.88
Navigation									
Search Engine	36.96	8.23	24.14	5.7	20.7	7.48	0.01	0.01	0.15
Look in page (find)	6.07	3.34	5.94	2.18	5.14	2.47	0.90	0.36	0.33
Copy/Paste Actions	43.68	4.24	30.28	3.57	31.27	5.25	0.01	0.01	0.54

of G1 (μ=172.44, σ=22.71), (p21<.04, p31<.01) to accomplish the tasks[8]. Secondly, participants with both MT and MST (G3) support worked more efficiently than participants with only MST support (G2) (p<.04). Moreover, the decrease in mean task time consumed brought about by MT is 11.87 minutes, which is close to the decrease of 15.63 minutes brought about by MST.

Meanwhile, MB users performed fewer other browsing actions. Table 1 shows that participants in G2 and G3 used search engines significantly fewer times and copied and pasted fewer times than those in G1. This fact plus the fact mentioned previously that MB users accessed fewer web pages indicate that the MB helped its users find the required Web resources quickly and accurately. Equally important, the MB was also helpful in "Keeping found things found" (Jones, Bruce, & Dumais, 2001), since the participants in G2 and G3 also performed fewer revisitation actions (Table 1).

We also found that to accomplish the tasks in the experiment, participants in G2 (μ=15.17, σ=1.92) and G3 (μ=12.76, σ=2.18) switched fewer times between tasks than those in G1 (μ=17.86, σ=2.39),

(p21<.01, p31<.01, p23<.01). Once again, participants with MT support in G3 performed better.

Moreover, we found that MB users in G2 (μ=66%, σ=8%) and G3 (μ=69%, σ<6%) revisited most of the web pages they had used in the first session, whereas only 43% (σ=9%) of the web pages visited in the first session were revisited by participants in G1 (p21<.02, p31<.01).

Finally, the MB improved the user's performance on resuming tasks across Web sessions. In session 2 of our experiment, all participants in G2 and G3 successfully resumed all their tasks left unfinished in session 1, but only 4 participants (25%) in G1 could achieve this without experimenter's help. Other participants in G1 failed to resume their tasks for various reasons. 6 of them (38%) could not remember how many tasks there were in the experiment, while 4 (25%) forgot at least one of their unfinished tasks. It is astonishing to note that 2 in G1 (13%) even forget that they had finished Task 2 in the first session and tried to do it again in session 2.

Table 2. Experimental group's median Likert-scale ratings of MB tools in two sessions (questions for all groups, ² session 2 only)

Question	G1	G2	G3	G1: G2	G1:G3	G2:G3
Easy to work on multiple tasks simultaneously.	2	2.5	4	z=2.11, p<.04	z=4.82, p<.01	z=4.41, p<.01
Easy to remember tasks unfinished in session 1.²	1.5	4	4.5	z=4.82, p<.01	z=4.78, p<.01	z=2.75, p<.01
Easy to re-find information used in session 1. ²	2	4	4.5	z=4.78, p<.01	z=4.82, p<.01	z=2.58, p<.01
Easy to remember the end date and progress of each of unfinished tasks. ²	1	4	4	z=4.82, p<.01	z=4.81, p<.01	z=.53, p>.05

User Experience

Participants reported favorably about their experience using the MB; they felt that it was easy to multitask on the Web with the MB's help. Table 3 shows the participants' Likert-scale rating for the usability of the MB and their user experience when multitasking on the Web after both the first and second sessions (see Table 2 for questions).

Table 3. Experimental groups median Likert-scale ratings of MB tools in two sessions.* (¹ session 1, ² session 2)

Question	G2		G3	
MB is useful, and I want to install it in my browser.	z=1.80, p>.07			
	4.5		5	
Easy to learn how to use MB.	5		5	
Easy to remember usage of MB.	z=1.70, p>.08			
	4.5		4.5	
MB was confusing to me.	1		1	
MB helped me work on multiple tasks simultaneously.	z=4.56, p<.01			
	2.5		4.5	
Easy to create a task.	z=.44, p>.7			
	4		4	
Difficult to remember how to create a new task.	z=.43, p>.6			
	3.5		3.5	
MB took up too much space in browser.	z=.15, p>.8			
	3.5	3.5		
Multiple task tab feature helpful.	N/A		4.5	
Hibernate/Resume helpful.	5		5	
Automatic naming task helpful.	5		5	
MB helped me remember what I did last week.2	5		5	
MB was useful for my tasks. 1	3	z=4.67, p<.01	3.5	z=4.67, p<.01
MB was useful for my tasks.2	5		5	
Schedule management helpful.1	3	z=4.06, p<.01	3	z=4.48, p<.01
Schedule management helpful.2	4		4.5	

* When there was no significant difference between data from sessions 1 and 2, we used the two data sets as one sample and between groups U-test results were presented, otherwise we additionally presented Wilcoxon Test results between sessions.

A participant in G3 said in her questionnaire that the MB released her from the cognitive burden of remembering the status and resources of tasks both within and across Web sessions and made working on multiple tasks pleasant and efficient. An interesting observation is that, although participants using the MB rated it as only moderately useful during the first session, when they were able to use the MB to resume their tasks, the usability rating increased greatly for the second session. Likewise, MB users with MT support agreed significantly more with the statement that the MB is helpful when working on multiple tasks simultaneously.

The usability rating for schedule management of the MB increased dramatically after session 2. A conversation between a participant in G2 and an experimenter during session 2 explains this change. She said, "*I admit that I downgraded the schedule management feature of MB in Session 1. You know, although technically saying the end date and active time is critical when having several tasks, nobody really realizes it and bothers themselves to track these data until these data are required.*"

The MB helped participants track the time consumed on each task. When we asked participants to report their task status at the beginning of session 2, almost all participants in G2 (*14, 88%*) and G3 (*15, 94%*) accurately reported the name, current status (completed or not), and end date required by manager, but none of participants in G1 could do this. Moreover, when estimating the total time needed for all tasks, MB users in G2 ($\mu=17.42, \sigma=4.91$) and G3 ($\mu=18.20, \sigma=5.55$) deviated significantly less than the other group, G1 ($\mu=23.15, \sigma=7.79$), ($p_{21}<.02, p_{31}<.04, p_{23}>.06$) and thus they could make more accurate plans than the others.

Unlike what Morris et al. (2008) found in a user study on the SearchBar, we found that participants agreed moderately with the statement that the MB took too much space in the browser. The reason for this difference might be due to the fact that the SearchBar was shown in a left pane of the browser which consumes horizontal screen real estate, while the MB was shown in a toolbar of the browser which consumes more precious vertical screen real estate.

DISCUSSION

The results presented in the previous section confirm that the participants found the MB is easy to use. It introduces the task concept into a browser thereby improving a user's experience with multitasking. Users thought that the MB was easy to learn and to use, and they also thought that it decreased their cognitive burden and improved their performance when multitasking on the Web. Data collected in the experiment support this view. MB users opened fewer Web pages, performed fewer navigation actions, and made little use of traditional history tools, yet re-found required Web pages more easily. At the same time, they used less time to accomplish tasks, and were better aware of and had better control over their tasks. Moreover, they were able to switch between tasks and resume interrupted or suspended tasks more quickly. In addition, they could remember the deadline and current status of their tasks and were aware of the time consumed on these tasks with little effort.

We also observed that the user performance improvement brought by MT is as much as by MST. Users with MT support always showed better performance and experience in almost all kinds of data we collected, especially when multiple tasks were running simultaneously. It might be a little surprising that in our experiment the overall improvement in task time consumed brought about by MT is close to that brought about by MST. We could not compare MB against other prototypes in previous studies owing to their unavailability, but according to our comparison, users with support for both MT and MST showed significantly better performance and experience in tasking switching, tab using, navigating, and revisiting than users with support for only MST.

One of the main unexplored questions here is that of users' browsing pattern shifts when introducing the task concept into a browser. As observed in this experiment, the introduction greatly impacted users' usage of browsers. It is obvious that users will gradually cope with this impact and alter their browsing behavior in many aspects, such as their refinding and revisitation strategy, searching strategy, and even collaborative strategy. These pattern shifts are more likely to occur in long-term, real-world use than in the lab. Therefore, a long-term study is required to ascertain how users will eventually adapt to the task concept in browsers through exploring and trying out the new features, and finally integrating them with their own browser habits.

We also acknowledge the limitations of this study. Firstly, we used a selected sample population consisting mainly of university students with specific characteristics (using Firefox, having multitasking experience on the Web). This means that we cannot expect that our results will generalize to a more general population. Instead, the results of this study have provided insight into how the introduction of the task concept into browsers impacts skilled Firefox users' performance and experience when multitasking on the Web. Although it is very likely that these results also apply to skilled users of other browsers, further studies are needed. Secondly, although we decided to introduce the task concept into a browser with 4 attributes based on our survey results, there are possibly other attributes that can bring great benefit to users, the importance of which users cannot appreciate before actually experiencing them. We intend pursuing a study in this direction to compare different impact factors for all attributes of a task. Finally, although we have tried our best to simulate an ordinary multitasking scenario in our experiment, the "Hawthorne Effect" (Reiss, 1979) may still exist, and a long-term study is needed to verify our results.

FUTURE RESEARCH DIRECTIONS

Future work includes extending this study to ascertain the impact of introducing tasks into browsers for users who do not use tabs, which was neglected in this work, and a broader deployment of the MB to explore its impact over longer periods of time and within a larger user population. Future development of the MB will focus on a better visualization method, a more sophisticated task grouping algorithm, and tighter and more seamless integration with history and bookmark utilities of the browser.

CONCLUSION

We have clarified two common patterns in multitasking on the Web, namely Multiple Tasks and Multiple Session Task. We found that unlike MST, MT has often been ignored in previous studies and implementations. Nevertheless, we found that supporting MT in a browser is as effective as supporting MST for improving a user's performance and experience when multitasking on the Web.

We have presented results from a pilot survey of users' expectations of tasks in browsers and their task-related browsing habits. These show that the four attributes of a task, namely name, status, end date, and active time, are most significant to users when coping with tasks in a browser.

We have presented the Multitasking Bar, a novel tool to help users multitask on the Web. With its help, users can define task(s) and manage related Web pages, and also switch between, suspend and resume task(s) as required. It also helps users in schedule management and releases their cognitive burden by informing them of deadlines and time consumed on task(s) when needed.

We have presented a user study on the impact of introducing the task concept into a browser on users' performance and experience when multitasking on the Web. This evaluation is based on the MB. We found that with the MB's help, the performance and experience of users improved dramatically. The results provide answers to the two research questions posed in the introduction. Introducing the task concept into a browser definitely improves a user's performance and experience when multitasking on the Web. Therefore, it is worthwhile considering when designing and implementing browsers and tools.

REFERENCES

Burgess, P. W. (2000). Real-world multitasking from a cognitive neuroscience perspective. *Control of Cognitive Processes: Attention and Performance, 18*, 465–472.

Carlson, R. A., & Sohn, M. H. (2000). Cognitive control of multistep routines: Information processing and conscious intentions. *Control of Cognitive Processes: Attention and Performance, 18*, 443.

Cockburn, A., & Mckenzie, B. (2001). What do web users do? An empirical analysis of web use. *International Journal of Human-Computer Studies, 54*, 903–922. doi:10.1006/ijhc.2001.0459

Czerwinski, M., Horvitz, E., & Wilhite, S. (2004). A diary study of task switching and interruptions. In *Proceedings of the SIGCHI Conference on Human Factors in Computing Systems*, (pp. 175-182). ACM Press.

González, V. M., & Mark, G. (2004). Constant, constant, multi-tasking craziness: Managing multiple working spheres. In *Proceedings of the SIGCHI Conference on Human Factors in Computing Systems*, (pp. 113-120). ACM Press.

GVU. (1998). *10th WWW user survey*. Retrieved from http://www.cc.gatech.edu/gvu/user_surveys/survey-1998-10/.

Iqbal, S. T., & Horvitz, E. (2007). Disruption and recovery of computing tasks: Field study, analysis, and directions. In *Proceedings of the SIGCHI Conference on Human Factors in Computing Systems*, (pp. 677-686). ACM Press.

Jhaveri, N., & Räihä, K. (2005). The advantages of a cross-session web workspace. In *Proceedings of CHI 2005 Extended Abstracts on Human Factors in Computing Systems*, (pp. 1949-1952). ACM Press.

Jones, W., Bruce, H., & Dumais, S. (2001). Keeping found things found on the web. In *Proceedings of the Tenth International Conference on Information and Knowledge Management*, (pp. 119-126). ACM Press.

Just, M. A., Carpenter, P. A., Keller, T. A., & Emery, L. Z. (2008). Interdependence of non-overlapping cortical systems in dual cognitive task. *NeuroImage, 14*, 417–426. doi:10.1006/nimg.2001.0826

Kellar, M., Watters, C., & Shepherd, M. (2007). A field study characterizing Web-based information-seeking tasks. *Journal of the American Society for Information Science and Technology, 58*(7), 999–1018. doi:10.1002/asi.20590

Lee, F. J., & Taatgen, N. A. (2002). Multitasking as skill acquisition. In *Proceedings of the Twenty-Fourth Annual Conference of the Cognitive Science Society*, (pp. 572-577). Cognitive Science Society.

MacKay, B., & Watters, C. (2008a). Understanding and supporting multi-session web tasks. *Proceedings of the American Society for Information Science and Technology, 45*(1), 1–13. doi:10.1002/meet.2008.1450450266

MacKay, B., & Watters, C. (2008b). Exploring multi-session web tasks. *Proceeding of the Twenty-Sixth Annual SIGCHI Conference on Human Factors in Computing Systems*, (pp. 1187-1196). ACM Press.

MacKay, B., & Watters, C. (2009). Building support for multi-session tasks. In *Proceedings of the 27th International Conference Extended Abstracts on Human Factors in Computing Systems*, (pp. 4273-4278). ACM Press.

Mayer, M. (2007). Web history tools and revisitation support: A survey of existing approaches and directions. *Foundations and Trends in Human-Computer Interaction*, 2(3), 173–278. doi:10.1561/1100000011

Mintzberg, H. (1970). Structured observation as a method to study managerial work. *Journal of Management Studies*, 7(1), 87–104. doi:10.1111/j.1467-6486.1970.tb00484.x

Mintzberg, H. (1980). *The nature of managerial work*. Englewood Cliffs, NJ: Prentice-Hall.

Miyata, Y., & Norman, D.A. (1986). Psychological issues in support of multiple activities. In *User Centered SYSTEM design* (pp. 265–284). Boca Raton, FL: CRC Press.

Morris, D., Morris, M. R., & Venolia, G. (2008). SearchBar: A search-centric web history for task resumption and information re-finding. In *Proceeding of the Twenty-Sixth Annual SIGCHI Conference on Human Factors in Computing Systems*, (pp. 1207-1216). ACM Press.

Reiss, F. (1979). *The hawthorne effect in a pilot program*. Unpublished.

Rubinstein, J. S., Meyer, D. E., & Evans, J. E. (2001). Executive control of cognitive processes in task switching. *Journal of Experimental Psychology. Human Perception and Performance*, 27(4), 763–797. doi:10.1037/0096-1523.27.4.763

Sellen, A. J., Murphy, R., & Shaw, K. L. (2002). How knowledge workers use the web. In *Proceedings of the SIGCHI Conference on Human Factors in Computing Systems: Changing our World, Changing Ourselves*, (pp. 227-234). ACM Press.

Spink, A., Jansen, B. J., Wolfram, D., & Saracevic, T. (2002). From e-sex to e-commerce: Web search changes. *Computer*, 35(3), 107–109. doi:10.1109/2.989940

Spink, A., Park, M., Jansen, B. J., & Pedersen, J. (2006). Multitasking during Web search sessions. *Information Processing & Management*, 42(1), 264–275. doi:10.1016/j.ipm.2004.10.004

UCLA. (2011). *The UCLA Internet report: Surveying the digital future*. Retrieved from http://www.digitalcenter.org/pdf/InternetReportYearThree.pdf.

USC. (2009). *Center for the digital future: 2008 digital future report*. Retrieved from http://www.digitalcenter.org/pages/current_report.asp?intGlobalId=19.

ADDITIONAL READING

André, P., Teevan, J., & Dumais, S. T. (2009). From x-rays to silly putty via Uranus: Serendipity and its role in web search. In *Proceedings of the 27th International Conference on Human Factors in Computing Systems*. ACM Press.

Aula, A., & Käki, M. (2003). *Understanding expert search strategies for designing user-friendly search interfaces*. Retrieved from http://www.iadis.net/dl/final_uploads/200302C098.pdf.

Bell, M., Reeves, S., Brown, B., Sherwood, S., MacMillan, D., Ferguson, J., & Chalmers, M. (2009). EyeSpy: Supporting navigation through play. In *Proceedings of the 27th International Conference on Human Factors in Computing Systems*. ACM Press.

Bergman, O., Tucker, S., Beyth-Marom, R., & Cutrell, E. (2009). It's not that important: Demoting personal information of low subjective importance using Gray Area. In *Proceedings of the 27th International Conference on Human Factors in Computing Systems.* ACM Press.

Broder, A. (2002). A taxonomy of web search. *ACM SIGIR Forum, 36*(2).

Brush, A. J. B., Meyers, B. R., Scott, J., & Venolia, G. (2009). Exploring awareness needs and information display preferences between coworkers. In *Proceedings of the 27th International Conference on Human Factors in Computing Systems.* ACM Press.

Chan, B., Wu, L., Talbot, J., Cammarano, M., & Hanrahan, P. (2008). Vispedia: Interactive visual exploration of Wikipedia data via search-based integration. *IEEE Transactions on Visualization and Computer Graphics, 14*(6), 1213–1220. doi:10.1109/TVCG.2008.178

Chen, J., Geyer, W., Dugan, C., Muller, M., & Guy, I. (2009). Make new friends, but keep the old: Recommending people on social networking sites. In *Proceedings of the 27th International Conference on Human Factors in Computing Systems.* ACM Press.

Choo, C. W., Brian, D., & Don, T. (1999). Information seeking on the web--An integrated model of browsing and searching. *Proceedings of the ASIS Annual Meeting, 36*, 3-16.

Cutrell, E., Dumais, S. T., & Teevan, J. (2006). Searching to eliminate personal information management. *Communications of the ACM, 49*(1), 58–64. doi:10.1145/1107458.1107492

Dubroy, P. (2011). *My talk at Mozilla.* Retrieved from http://dubroy.com/blog/my-talk-at-mozilla/.

Dubroy, P. (2011). *Field study of tab.* Retrieved from http://dubroy.com/blog/category/research/.

Dubroy, P. (2011). *Tlogger: Captures click-stream web browsing logs.* Retrieved from http://dubroy.com/tlogger/.

Fong, D. (2009). *Enhancing multitasking to enhance our minds.* Retrieved from http://faster-proxy.com/browse.php?u=Oi8vZGFuaWVsbG Vmb25nLmNvbS8yMDA4LzA4LzI0L2VuaGF uY2luZy1tdWx0aXRhc2tpbmctdG8tZW5oYW 5jZS1vdXItbWluZHMv&b=5.

Gerber, E. (2009). Using improvisation to enhance the effectiveness of brainstorming. In *Proceedings of the 27th International Conference on Human Factors in Computing Systems.* ACM Press.

Gonzales, A. L., Finley, T., & Duncan, S. P. (2009). (Perceived) interactivity: Does interactivity increase enjoyment and creative identity in artistic spaces? In *Proceedings of the 27th International Conference on Human Factors in Computing Systems.* ACM Press.

Hacker, S., & Ahn, L. V. (2009). Matchin: Eliciting user preferences with an online game. In *Proceedings of the 27th International Conference on Human Factors in Computing Systems.* ACM Press.

Hansen, D. L., & Golbeck, J. (2009). Mixing it up: Recommending collections of items. In *Proceedings of the 27th International Conference on Human Factors in Computing Systems.* ACM Press.

Harry, D., Green, J., & Donath, J. (2009). Backchan.nl: Integrating backchannels in physical space. In *Proceedings of the 27th International Conference on Human Factors in Computing Systems.* ACM Press.

Hong, L., & Chi, E. H. (2009). Annotate once, appear anywhere: Collective foraging for snippets of interest using paragraph fingerprinting. In *Proceedings of the 27th International Conference on Human Factors in Computing Systems.* ACM Press.

Jakobsen, M. R., & Hornbæk, K. (2009). Fisheyes in the field: Using method triangulation to study the adoption and use of a source code visualization. In *Proceedings of the 27th International Conference on Human Factors in Computing Systems*. ACM Press.

Jones, W. (2004). Finders, keepers? The present and future perfect in support of personal information management. *First Monday, 9*(3), 2005–2006.

Ko, A. J., & Myers, B. A. (2009). Finding causes of program output with the Java Whyline. In *Proceedings of the 27th International Conference on Human Factors in Computing Systems*. ACM Press.

Law, E. L., Roto, V., Hassenzahl, M., Vermeeren, A., & Kort, J. (2009). Understanding, scoping and defining user experience: A survey approach. In *Proceedings of the 27th International Conference on Human Factors in Computing Systems*. ACM Press.

Lichtschlag, L., Karrer, T., & Borchers, J. (2009). Fly: A tool to author planar presentations. In *Proceedings of the 27th International Conference on Human Factors in Computing Systems*. ACM Press.

MacKay, B., Kellar, M., & Watters, C. (2005). An evaluation of landmarks for re-finding information on the web. In *Proceeding CHI 2005 Extended Abstracts on Human Factors in Computing Systems*. ACM Press.

Mathur, P., & Karahalios, K. (2009). Using bookmark visualizations for self-reflection and navigation. In *Proceedings of the 27th International Conference Extended Abstracts on Human Factors in Computing Systems*. ACM Press.

MSDN. (2006). *Relevant to you? The nature of browsing is changing - report from WWW 2006.* Retrieved from http://blogs.msdn.com/andyed/archive/2006/06/21/641450.aspx.

Obendorf, H., Weinreich, H., Herder, E., & Mayer, M. (2007). Web page revisitation revisited: Implications of a long-term click-stream study of browser usage. In *Proceedings of the SIGCHI Conference on Human Factors in Computing Systems*. ACM Press.

Oleksik, G., Wilson, M. L., Tashman, C., Rodrigues, E. M., Kazai, G., & Smyth, G. … Jones, R. (2009). Lightweight tagging expands information and activity management practices. In *Proceedings of the 27th International Conference on Human Factors in Computing Systems*. ACM Press.

Reichling, T., & Wulf, V. (2009). Expert recommender systems in practice: Evaluating semi-automatic profile generation. In *Proceedings of the 27th International Conference on Human Factors in Computing Systems*. ACM Press.

Rosner, D., & Bean, J. (2009). Learning from IKEA hacking: I'm not one to decoupage a tabletop and call it a day. In *Proceedings of the 27th International Conference on Human Factors in Computing Systems*. ACM Press.

Science Blogs. (2008). Casual Fridays: Who's tab-happy -- And who's not. *Cognitive Daily*. Retrieved from http://scienceblogs.com/cognitive-daily/2008/12/casual_fridays_whos_tabhappy_a.php.

Shami, N. S., Ehrlich, K., Gay, G., & Hancock, J. T. (2009). Making sense of strangers' expertise from signals in digital artifacts. In *Proceedings of the 27th International Conference on Human Factors in Computing Systems*. ACM Press.

Suhm, B., & Peterson, P. (2009). Call browser: A system to improve the caller experience by analyzing live calls end-to-end. In *Proceedings of the 27th International Conference on Human Factors in Computing Systems*. ACM Press.

Beauvisage, T. (2009). Computer usage in daily life. In *Proceedings of the 27th International Conference on Human Factors in Computing Systems*. ACM Press.

Toomim, M., Drucker, S. M., Dontcheva, M., Rahimi, A., Thomson, B., & Landay, J. A. (2009). Attaching UI enhancements to websites with end users. In *Proceedings of the 27th International Conference on Human Factors in Computing Systems*. ACM Press.

William, J., & Ross, B. H. (2007). Personal information management. In *Handbook of Applied Cognition* (pp. 471–495). New York, NY: John Wiley & Sons.

Won, S. S., Jin, J., & Hong, J. I. (2009). Contextual web history: Using visual and contextual cues to improve web browser history. In *Proceedings of the 27th International Conference on Human Factors in Computing Systems*. ACM Press. Paul, S. A., & Morris, M. R. (2009). CoSense: Enhancing sensemaking for collaborative web search. In *Proceedings of the 27th International Conference on Human Factors in Computing Systems*. ACM Press. Auer, S., Bizer, C., Kobilarov, G., Lehmann, J., Cyganiak, R., & Ives, Z. (2008). DBpedia: A nucleus for a web of open data. In *Proceedings of the Semantic Web,* (pp. 722-735). ACM.

Zimmerman, J. (2009). Designing for the self: making products that help people become the person they desire to be. In *Proceedings of the 27th International Conference on Human Factors in Computing Systems*. ACM Press.

Zimmerman, J., Forlizzi, J., & Martens, J. (2009). User experience over time: an initial framework. In *Proceedings of the 27th International Conference on Human Factors in Computing Systems*. ACM Press.

KEY TERMS AND DEFINITIONS

Browser: Here is a computer application which is responsible for fetching, parsing, rendering and displaying Web pages, and it also has other functions for the Web surfing, such as navigation aids and favorites management.

Tasks: Are a series of things to be done for a particular goal.

Multitasking: Is defined as the ability of a person to perform more than one task at the same time.

Revisitation: Here refers to a common user behavior pattern that people revisit Web pages.

Multi-Tasks (MT): Is defined as executing a set of tasks simultaneously where the execution often depends on bundles of Web pages.

Multi-Session-Task (MST): Is defined as executing a single task spanning multiple Web sessions.

ENDNOTES

[1] Here we selected the 6 attributes from task attributes which appear in almost all well-known task management tools, such as Microsoft Project (http://office.microsoft.com/en-us/project/default.aspx), Microsoft Outlook (http://office.microsoft.com/en-us/outlook/default.aspx), iGTD (http://bargiel.ho me.pl/iGTD/), Todolist (http://todoist.com/), etc. Other attributes such as remind method, remind time, assign to, report to, etc. were discarded based on the results of a pilot survey of this pilot survey in which

most of the 20 respondents marked these attributes as irrelevant to multitasking on the Web.

[2] This question was not posed to respondents who identified themselves as Web users without multitasking experience.

[3] We used 3 different MB configurations for 3 groups in our user study; see USER STUDY for the details.

[4] According to our pilot study, participants had 3.46 tasks on average and a maximum of 5.21 tasks. Therefore we designed 5 tasks for our experiment, 2 of which (tasks 2, 5) were simple and could be done quickly.

[5] Two participants (one in G1, and another in G3) deviated from this one-week gap between sessions, returning after 8 and 10 days, respectively.

[6] According to our survey, participants view 38 Web pages per day on average, and create a bookmark every two days.

[7] We use a t-Test for normally distributed data, and a Mann-Whitney U Test and Wilcoxon Test for non-normally distributed data in between groups in same session analysis and in same group between sessions analysis respectively. Likert scale responses are on a scale of 1 to 5, where 1 = strongly disagree and 5 = strongly agree.

[8] According to the average time spent by experimenters in the pilot study on every section (blanks, paragraphs to be completed) of each result document, we estimated a proportionate completion time for the unfinished tasks of participants based on the result document they submitted at the end of the experiment and the time they spent on it.

Chapter 2
Soft Keyboard Evaluations:
Integrating User's Background in Predictive Models

Bruno Merlin
UFPA, Brazil

Mathieu Raynal
Université Paul Sabatier, France

ABSTRACT

Predictive models, based on cognitive and motor laws (modeling some aspect of human behaviors), were supposed to provide an efficient tool to compare quickly soft keyboards performances, but these models are confronted with some limits. Moreover, they failed to predict efficiently the performances during the first usage that got an important impact on soft keyboard acceptability. To improve these models, the authors integrated into them the character search strategies oriented by the user's background. They illustrate their purpose by modeling three keyboards and comparing the results with experimental ones. The models integrating the user's background predicted results close to the experimental ones. However, those models must be adapted to the function of the keyboard and the targeted population. The applicability of the models as a rapid comparison tool for soft keyboards must be questioned.

INTRODUCTION

With the expansion of mobile phones with touch screens, increasing the input speed with soft keyboards became an important challenge. Several authors demonstrated that the classical soft keyboards, such as mini-QWERTY (Goldberg & Richardson, 1993; Raynal & Vigouroux, 2005; Merlin & Raynal, 2009) or phone keyboards (Foulds, et al., 1987; Lesher & Moulton, 2000; Levine, et al., 1987) are non-optimal solutions to input text with mobile devices or as assistive technologies. However, in spite of several alternatives elaborated to improve the soft keyboard performances, these classical input solutions remain the most popular ways to input text with a pointing device (finger, stylus, mouse, etc.) until now.

DOI: 10.4018/978-1-4666-1628-8.ch002

Toward this difference between the evaluated performances and the usage reality, we implicitly observe that the variables studied to compare soft keyboard performances are not able to reflect the motivation for these users' preferences. A brief state of art illustrates that, in general, the variables used to compare the different input systems refer to the expert performances: text input speed in word per minute (wpm) or character per second (cps) and error rate obtained after a long period of usage. However, some other researches (Isokoski, 2004; Raynal & Vigouroux, 2005) point out that, out of experimental contexts, a user may not accept a regression of his performances during the first usages. Therefore, a new artifact should provide beginner performances better or at least close to the performances obtained with the classical soft keyboards. More other, some characteristics (such as a high cognitive cost required to use the keyboard), may prejudiced a solution acceptation. However, these criteria are ignored in the global comparative reviews (MacKenzie & Zhang, 1999) of soft keyboards.

Long term usage is the only way enabling a user to reach expert performance. Out of an experimental context, it means that a tool must get a good acceptability at short term to enable a usage during a long term. Thus, the beginner performances should be one of the main comparison criteria.

In order to ease this comparison, Soukoreff and MacKenzie (1995) proposed a model establishing predictive performances for both expert and novice users: the upper and lower-bound. This model is based on behavior models such as Fitts' law (Fitts, 1954) and Hick-Hyman's law (Hick, 1952; Hyman, 1953). However, they concluded that the model is bad for novice performances. Das (Das & Stuerzlinger, 2008) improved this model, but identified that the notion of beginner is very relative because the user "learn[s] some features of a technique very quickly," prejudicing the reliability of the results. Therefore, an improved

model to compare the beginner performances should be very valuable.

Out of the problem identified by MacKenzie and Das, we think that the user's background may influence users' performances in the first usages of a new soft keyboard. The background of the targeted population is frequently used (Isokoski, 2004) to justify design choices for soft keyboards. Therefore, it would be reliable to integrate it in a model predicting beginner performances.

In this chapter, we relate the practical and theoretical problems encountered in the application of the predictive models. Then, we propose to improve the model predicting the novice performances. We integrated the features representing user cultural experience toward the keyboards into this model.

To illustrate our study, we selected three soft keyboards as examples and compared the performances calculated by the initial predictive models, by our predictive models and performances measured experimentally.

Then we discuss the constraints to apply the model, and moreover the global limits of predictive model in HMI so as to keyboard evaluation. At last, we present our future axes of research to improve soft keyboard evaluation and comparison.

BACKGROUND: PREDICTING HMI PERFORMANCES AND TEXT INPUT SPEED WITH SOFT KEYBOARDS

In HMI, several cognitive models (such as KLM model [Card, et al., 1980] and GOMS [Card, et al., 1983]) and cognitive laws (such as Fitts's [Fitts, 1954] and Hick-Hyman's law [Hick, 1952; Hyman, 1953]) enable quick comparisons of different tasks and interaction patterns by predicting the time required to perform the interaction / the task. However, these models do not take into account complex cognitive processes or design criteria. Their results remain reliable for repetitive and simple tasks. They do not enable to compare a whole interface.

Because the text input task consists in a succession of pointing, this task has frequently been used to study these predictive models. At last, predictive models were specifically adapted to study the text input and compare soft keyboards performances. Among them, the Soukoreff and MacKenzie model (Soukoreff & MacKenzie, 1995) aims at comparing the soft keyboards by defining a performance range between a novice (lower-bound) and an expert user (upper-bound).

However, out of practical limits due to the new keyboard improvement strategies (proposing dynamic optimization), Sears (Sears, et al., 2001), Pavlovych (Pavlovych & Stuerzlinger, 2004), Das (Das & Stuerzlinger, 2008), and Guiard (Guiard, 2009) identified several theoretical bias in the calculus of the both limits.

Based on these observations, Das (Das & Stuerzlinger, 2008) proposes a new model modeling the performances evolution from a novice to an expert user, but as we will highlight, in spite of interesting consideration, the model is not robust enough.

In this section, we briefly present the laws and models used to evaluate HMI and explain the initial model established to compare soft keyboards: the Soukoreff and MacKenzie (1995) model. Then we relate several problems and limits encountered in the model usages: practical limits toward new soft

keyboard paradigms and theoretical bias in the upper bound calculus; and theoretical bias in the lower bound calculus. Then we introduce works attempting to correct these problems by proposing a new calculus for the both bounds and by modeling the evolution of performances during the learning period between beginner to expert. However, we demonstrate that the new calculus does not match when applied on different soft keyboards. We conclude this section by explaining the needs to better understand the novice behavior toward a soft keyboard to improve the lower-bound calculus.

Fitts' Law

The Robert S. Woodworth researches in experimental psychology (Woodworth, 1899) showed for the first time an incompatibility between velocity and high precision of movements. These works, associated to the Shannon's Theory of Information (Shannon, 1948), motivated the Fitts' researches. Fitts quantified the difficulty of pointing tasks. In analogy with the theory of information, Fitts models the pointing task as a message transmission in a perceptuo-motor system. The pointing task precision (the task difficulty) hinders the message transmission.

Based on 3 experimentations repeating pointing tasks (cf. Figure 1), Fitts deduces the following relationship:

Figure 1. Fitts' experimentation

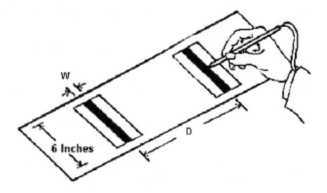

$$T = a + b * \log_2(\frac{2 * D}{W})$$

where:

- T is the time to perform the task in seconds
- D represents the movement amplitude
- W represents the target width
- a and b are coefficient (calculated by linear regression) depending on the kinesthetic properties of the pointing device and on the psychomotor capacity of the targeted population.

Later, Fitts and Peterson (Fitts, 1964), demonstrated that the law is valid for discrete pointing task. Then Card et al. (Card, 1978) demonstrated that the law works in a virtualized context where the pointing is indirect (pointing through a mouse for instance). At last, MacKenzie (1992), confirmed by the Douglas results (Douglas, 1997), adapted the law for a usage in 2 dimensions. In HMI, the law is used on this last form:

$$T = a + b * ID = a + b * \log_2(\frac{D}{W} + 1)$$

Hick-Hyman's law (Hick [Hick, 1952] and Hyman [Hyman, 1953]) independently established a model inspired by the Shannon Theory of Information. They both modeled a search task of an item among a list of N equally probable ordered items by the following relationship:

$$TR = b * \log_2(N)$$

where:

- TR is the search time in seconds,
- N is the number of items,
- b, obtained by linear regression, depends on the targeted population (is the literature,

b is generally fixed at 4.9 when the user is a beginner in the task performing and at 7 when the user is expert).

We can observe that when no choice is required (N=0), the formula presents a mathematical anomaly. To correct this anomaly, Card, Moran et Newell (Card 83) add 1 to the number of items (justified by the decision time to act or not).

GOMS and KLM Models

The GOMS (Card, 1983; Gray, 1993; John, 1996) and KLM (Card, 1980) models aim at dividing the tasks in several elementary subtasks. The subtasks can be cognitive activities (for instance, thinking about the process required to perform the task, waiting for a feedback, response time to a stimulus, etc.) or actions (cursor motion, mouse button click, keystroke, etc.). The time required for each subtasks is evaluated empirically (cf. Table 1). The sum of every subtask time determines the whole task execution time. The medium pointing time can also be substituted by a calculus more precise made through the Fitts' law (Dunlop, 2000).

As we can observe, the times (mainly the cognitive times) do not depend on the task and interface designs. Therefore, the models ignore ergonomics criteria that could enable to improve or prejudice the task execution. Moreover, the models cannot provide predefined time for complex cognitive processes. Thus, the models can only be reliable for simple repetitive tasks.

Upper-Bound and Lower-Bound

Soukoureff and MacKenzie proposed a model to predict the Minimum Time (MT) to input characters (Soukoreff & MacKenzie, 1995). This model predicts expert's performances by adding the movement times—calculated according to Fitts' law (Fitts, 1954)—between each digraph[1] of the 26 Latin characters plus the space character. The

Table 1. Empirical evaluation of subtasks (Card, 1980)

Press a key or button	
Best typist	0.08 seconds
Good typist	0.12 seconds
Average skilled typist	0.20 seconds
Typing random letters	0.50 seconds
Worst typist	1.20 seconds
Point with a mouse (excluding click)	1.10 seconds
Move hands to keyboard from mouse (or vice-versa)	0.40 seconds
Mental preparation	1.35 seconds

performance for every digraph is weighed by the frequencies (Pij) of the digraph in the language.

Thus, the average time in seconds for typing a character was:

$$\overline{MT} = \sum_{i=1}^{27} \sum_{j} P_{ij} T_{ij}$$

With $T_{ij} = a + b \log_2(\frac{D_{ij}}{W} + 1)$ and

$$\sum_{i=1}^{27} \sum_{j} P_{ij} = 1$$

D_{ij} is the distance between the center of the keys associated to the character i and j. W represents the size of the key, a and b are parameters depending on the device and the population. They will be discussed in the section "character selection model" according to the keyboard design.

Considering an average of 5 characters per word (Gentner, 1983), we obtained the maximum number of words typed per minute, the upper-bound (WPM$_{max}$), by the formula:

$$WPM_{Max} = \frac{60}{\left(5 \times MT\right)}$$

The Minimum Time (MT) models the text input as a mechanical succession of pointing. Time to look for the key is reduced to 0. Consequently, the minimum time is supposed to represent the expert's performances.

Soukoreff and MacKenzie model the input time for beginner by adding the Hick-Hyman (Hick, 1952; Hyman, 1953) scan time between the keyboard characters to the expert input time. According to this model, we used ST the scanning time for 26 Latin characters and the space:

$$ST = 0.2 \times \log_2\left(27\right) = 0.951 \sec$$

We obtained the minimum number of words typed per minute, the lower-bound, by:

$$WPM_{Min} = \frac{60}{\left(5 \times \left(MT + ST\right)\right)}$$

Practical Limits for the Upper-Bound

This model is interesting to compare some mechanical properties of keyboards, whereas it presents several limits to predict the input time.

At first, if we can easily use a physical keyboard blindly, using a standard mini-QWERTY soft keyboard needs a visual retro-control even for an expert. Therefore, we can severely discuss the choice turning to 0 the cognitive costs in the Soukoreff and MacKenzie model. Moreover, the strategy consisting in evaluating the expert performances by eliminating the cognitive costs with keyboards dynamically modified in interaction with prediction systems cannot be representative of real users' performances.

As illustration, a presentation video of TouchPal[2] explains that an expert user can reach 72wpm with this keyboard. This input speed is exceptionally high if we consider that the maximal performances with a QWERTY soft keyboard on touch screen with a stylus are 28wpm (Zhai, et al., 2002). However, TouchPal gets a completion list that enable to input several characters, the end of words, by a simple click. Although this, the speed of 72wpm provokes an interesting question.

The video illustrates this performance: the user makes an intensive usage of the completion list with a perfect anticipation of the list content. In the "true live," the use of completion list is not so efficient (Badr & Raynal, 2010). In this case, the user is not only expert of the keyboard usage, but he is expert of the sentences typed during the demonstration too. Thus, with the input sentence, the user is able to anticipate every word that appears in the completion list and its position. Consequently, the user is able to reach this speed only for the predefined sentences used during the demonstration, but, in order to reach this speed whatever the sentence, he should be able to learn an optimum use of the completion list for every word of the dictionary. Consequently, 72wpm does not represent the performances for an expert user, but the performances for a "perfect" user.

Therefore, in practical terms, the notion of expert user maybe questioned to evaluate the performances of standard keyboards, but its representativeness clearly disappears if we compare keyboards with dynamic assistances or alternative interactions.

Moreover, Guiard (2009) then Yang (Yang & Xu, 2010), demonstrated several bias in the design of experimentation based on Fitts' law. They mainly concluded that the scale for the Fitts' task impacts the task difficulty and then the calculus for the index of difficulty of the task should be reconsidered.

Theoretical Limits for the Upper- and Lower-Bound: Research or Selection Time?

The lower-bound calculus also presents some problems.

Sears (Sears, et al., 2001) first questioned the use of the Hick-Hyman's law to measure the search time. Indeed, the Hick-Hyman's law is supposed to represent the decision time to select a target between N ordered targets through a dichotomous scan process, a binary search (for instance: selecting a menu item in an alphabetical ordered menu).

A novice user is supposed not to know the keyboard layout. Consequently, Sears observes that the task consisting in searching a character among an unknown character layout does not fit with the prerequisite of the Hick-Hyman's law. The user does not have condition to perform a binarian search into an unknown character distribution. Therefore, the time to perform the task should be linear[3] and proportional to the character number.

Confirming the observation of Sears, Pavlovych (Pavlovych & Stuerzlinger, 2004) proposed an experiment aiming at measuring the search time. He determined a medium search time of 680ms to find a character among 27 characters randomly dispatched.

Based on the Sears and Pavlovych observations, Das (Das & Stuerzlinger, 2008) explains that, if the Hyck-Hyman's law does not fit with the novice model, it fits with the expert model. According to Das, even for expert users, because of a need to select the key to point, the cognitive aspect of the task should not be ignored like it is done in the Soukoreff and Mackenzie model. Thus, the Hick-Hyman's law should model the selection time for a character by an expert. He consequently proposed a model, explained in the following section, supposed to model the evolution of performances between a novice user and an expert user.

Modeling the Performances during the Learning Period

At first, Pavlovych (Pavlovych & Stuerzlinger, 2004) observes that the time required by a novice user to copy a text is not completely dedicated to move the pointer and to look for a character. Therefore, to compare efficiently the performances between theoretical and experimental results with novice, we should take into account other cognitive costs. Consequently, he decomposed the copy task involved in experimental evaluations as following:

- Time to search a character
- Time to point the key

and:

- Time to think about the character that must be input
- Time to select the number of pressure required to input the character (when the keyboard key are ambiguous ones)
- Time to read the sentence to copy
- Time to verify the character input

Pavlovych measured the time for every task and extends both the model of Soukoreff and MacKenzie (adapted for two-thumb interaction [Silfverberg, et al., 2000]) and the KLM (Card, et al., 1983) model (adapted by Dunlop [Dunlop & Crossan, 1999] to model the input performances on phone keyboards) in order to take into account the complete task of text copy and to model the performances for a novice user.

Das (Das & Stuerzlinger, 2008) distinguishes two different tasks involved in the character localization. When the user is a novice, the localization of a character is a linear searching task (such as measured by Pavlovych [Pavlovych & Stuerzlinger, 2004]). When the user is an expert, the localization of a character is a selection task modeled by the Hick-Hyman's law. Based on this observation, he suggests that during transition from novice to expert, the Localization Task (LT) is in part a Searching Task (FT) and in part a Selection Task (ST). In parallel, the others Cognitive Costs (CC) involved in the copying process decrease

linearly in function of the expertise level. He proposes a unified model where:

$$LT = \left(1\text{-}\alpha\right)\text{FT} + \alpha ST$$

with α the expertise level of the user, $\alpha \in [0;1]$

Considering MT the medium pointing time calculated in the upper-bound model, the input time is defined by the following formula:

$$T = (1\text{-}\alpha)(\text{FT} + \text{CC}) + \alpha\text{ST} + \text{MT}$$

Theoretical Limits for the Model

In his unified model, Das uses the search time measured by Pavlovych (680ms). Because the model is designed for cellular phones, he considers the selection time between 8 keys (instead of 27 for a mini-QWERTY keyboard), and because the user is expert he uses a coefficient of 1/7 for the Hyck-Hyman law (bandwidth of 7 in the information theory of Shannon [1948]). Consequently, the selection time is:

$$SeT = \frac{1}{7} \times \log_2\left(8\right) = 0.429\,\text{sec}$$

Now, instead of applying the model on an ambiguous cellular keyboard, we apply it on a simple mini-QWERTY soft keyboard. Sears (Sears, et al., 2001) showed that the searching time on an ambiguous keyboard is lightly higher than the searching time with a soft keyboard containing one character per key. Consequently, the searching time for novice users with our mini-QWERTY should be down to 680ms.

In parallel, in this context, because the keyboard contains 27 distinct targets, there is no rational motivation to use 8 instead of 27 items in the

Hyck-Hyman's law. Therefore, the selection time SeT for expert users should be:

$$SeT = \frac{1}{7} \times \log_2\left(27\right) = 0.680 \, \text{sec}$$

Thus, applying the model to a mini-QWERTY, the selection time (time an expert requires to locate a character) becomes higher than the search time! (time a novice requires to locate a character). Moreover, considering only the selection time of 680ms, ignoring the movement time needed to point the key, the input speed should be limited to 17.65wpm[4] with a mini-QWERTY keyboard (whatever the key distribution and whatever the apparatus). Several experiments (Raynal & Vigouroux, 2005; Zhai, et al., 2000) illustrate performances much higher with these kinds of soft keyboards.

Consequently, the use of the Hyck-Hyman law to model the selection time should be reconsidered.

How to Better Predict Novice Performances?

As we previously explained, the performances during the first usages are an important challenge to ensure new keyboard acceptability. Thus, a reliable model illustrating these performances could be an efficient way to compare rapidly the keyboards. The initial intention of the lower-bound is illustrating the user performances in the least favorable context: the user ignores the keyboard layout and has no heuristic to locate the characters. However, if we want to compare the initial performances between different soft keyboards differing by their layout (for instance QWERTY, GAG [Raynal & Vigouroux, 2005], Metropolis [Zhai, et al., 2000], etc.), the predictive models failed to establish results matching with the experimental results. Two explanations justify it: at first, the user is able to integrate some

features of the keyboard very quickly (Pavlovych & Stuerzlinger, 2004) and does not remain novice a long time; but, above all, the user may have a former experience or heuristics guiding him during the first usages.

Thus, to obtain representative predictive results, the lower-bound models should take into account the cultural experience of the user and other heuristic clues that may orient him in the characters research.

EXPERIMENTING THE LOWER-BOUND LIMITS

In order to illustrate the limits for the lower-bound, we modeled three different keyboards and compared them toward the classical lower-bounds models. As hypothesized, the results obtained by the predictive models are just the opposite of the results intuitively expected.

Keyboard Design

We compared the theoretical and experimental performances for three soft keyboards: MessagEase (Nesbat, 2003), DashKey, and a standard soft keyboard (called Alpha) with characters ordered by alphabetic order (cf. Figure 2).

MessagEase (Nesbat, 2003) mixes the characteristics of an ambiguous keyboard and gesture recognition. As an ambiguous keyboard, every key contains a group of characters. The user selects the character groups by pointing. The selection of a character within the group is discriminated by a simple click for the main central character, or a flick in the direction of the character for the other characters[5]. A click is considered as a flick if the distance between the pressed and released position is up to a threshold.

The MessagEase layout during this evaluation is optimized for the language of the users who did the experimentation (French). It contains 9 keys

Figure 2. MessagEase (left), DashKey (center), and Alpha (right) layouts

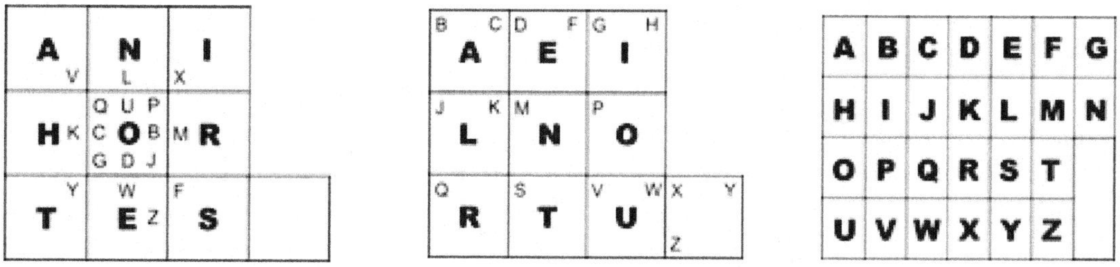

with alphabetic characters and an additional key for the space character. Each of the 9 keys displays one of the nine more frequent characters in French in the center of the key. The other characters are positioned in respect of the MessagEase original layout. The central character gets a higher size and is accessible by a simple click. The other characters are displayed in a lower size and accessible by the flick interaction.

DashKey implements the same interaction concepts (click for the key central character input and flick in direction of the character for the other character input). It differs only by the character layout. DashKey aims at reducing the character search time for beginners by giving a simple heuristic: the alphabetic order. The keys are grouping 2 or 3 characters respecting the alphabetical order. The more frequent character (in French) into each character group is displayed in the center of the key.

The Alpha keyboard gets as possible the same design characteristics of the other keyboards: same look and feel (fonts and colors), same interaction feedbacks, and same dimensions for the whole keyboard, but, the size of keys and the number of them are different. The 27 keys are unambiguous.

They cover the same surface as the 10 keys of the other keyboards. The selection of every character is performed by a simple click.

Character Selection Model

The main character selection for the DashKey/ MessagEase keys and the character selection in the Alpha keys are modeled by the Fitts' law as a simple pointing task. The size of the key is Wj = key height = key width.

Different coefficients for a and b are frequently used to model this task (Soukoreff & MacKenzie, 1995; MacKenzie & Soukoreff, 2002). We compared the keyboards according to the two mainly used set of parameters (cf. Table 2).

We used the Isokoski's model (Isokoski, 2004) to model the secondary character selection with DashKey and MessagEase. In the evaluation of a virtual keyboard augmented by a marking menu, Isokoski modeled the following task: a selection of the first character by simple pointing; then, in a continuous movement, a selection of another character by marking menu. The time for the interaction is given by the Fitts' law for the pointing task and a constant penalty time for the action

Table 2. Coefficients used for the modeling

	Simple pressure		Flick selection	
	a	b	a	b
MacKenzie	0	0.204	Pe	0.204
Isokoski/Zhai	0.083	0.127	0.083 + Pe	0.127

in the marking menu. The constant penalty (Pe = 0.16s) used by Isokoski is extracted from McQueen (McQueen, et al., 1995) experiment on a 12-slice pie menu[6].

We compared the secondary character selection to this model: key pointing for selection of a key (a group of characters) and a flick selection between 1 and 8 items for the selection of the character within the key.

Modeling Results

We compared the three keyboards according to these selection models with different values for the coefficients a and b in the Fitts' law: the coefficients established by Zhai et al. (2002) (used by Isokoski) and the coefficient of Soukoreff and MacKenzie (1995). A constant Pe = 0.16 is used for the flick selection.

According to the Soukoureff and MacKenzie's model, whatever the coefficient used, MessagEase should provide performances lightly better than the performances provided by DashKey for an expert user (cf. Table 3). The results are not surprising because:

- The sum of the frequencies for the characters accessible by a simple click is 70.5% with MessagEase against 68% with DashKey; so the time penalty required to input the secondary characters weights the input 32% of the times with DashKey against 29.5% with MessagEase.
- The central key of MessagEase contains 9 characters what tends to reduce the distance covered by the pointing device (reducing the ratio D/W in the Fitts's law).

The Alpha keyboard remains theoretically the least efficient of the three soft keyboards.

To evaluate the lower-bound, the input time increases equally for every keyboard (adding the Hyck-Hyman selection time for Soukoreff and MacKenzie or a linear search time for Das). Consequently, the order of the theoretical performances for a beginner remains unchanged (cf. Table 3).

However, the alphabetic order is a natural heuristic to orient the character search. In addition, performing simple clicks should be cognitively easier and more spontaneously than an interaction alternating simple clicks and flicks. Therefore, we intuitively imagine that the results may be inverted for the lower-bound in an experimental context.

In order to validate this hypothesis, we performed an experimentation. This experimentation aimed at comparing the novice effective performances with the three keyboards.

Experiment Design

The experiment was conduct on an HTC Touch HD with touch-screen running on windows mobile 6.1. The three soft keyboards (Dashkey, MessageEase, and Alphabetical keyboard) were developed with C++. Users used a stylus to interact with the soft keyboard. We recruited 18 participants volunteered for the experiment (11 men and 7 women, all right-handed). They ranged in age from 24 to 36 and are all computer specialists.

Table 3. Lower-bound and upper-bound results for the three keyboards with the two coefficient sets

	Mackenzie		Isokoski	
	low	up	low	up
Dashkey	9.4	37.9	9.6	40.4
MessagEase	9.6	39.7	9.7	42.5
Alpha	8.85	29.7	9.3	35.3

Figure 3. Experimental display (right) and error feedback (left)

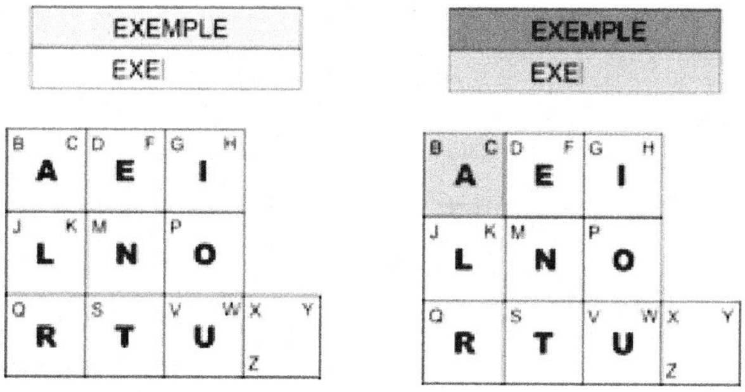

Each subject had to perform word copy with the three input devices: Alpha, DashKey, and MessagEase. Before each session, the keyboard characteristics were described (interaction technique and layout characteristic). The 18 subjects had been divided in six groups in order to balance the order of the 3 conditions. For each condition the subjects had to copy out 42 words which were the same for the three conditions but displayed in a random order. Words were chosen to respect the frequency of letters and digraphs in French (user's natural language).

The source word was presented in a strip, and the user input appears in a strip below.

The text entry errors were not displayed on the result line but provide a visual and audio feedback (cf. Figure 3). The strip did not move when the subject enters an erroneous character. Therefore, at the end of the input, the text was error free. After each word, participants must type on the space character to switch the word.

The users began by a training session in order to understand only the MessagEase and DashKey interaction technique. They performed ten character inputs with a reduced keyboard containing just two keys with a layout different of DashKey and MessagEase layout (cf. Figure 4). This different layout targets to avoid layout learning during this interaction training session.

The experimentation concluded by a brief questioner requesting the user's opinion toward: the interaction technique; the preferential layouts;

the perspective to use these different keyboards out of an experimental context.

Results

The ANOVA shows that the order in which was realized the exercises had no impact on the results.

The experimentation confirmed the results expected. The users were most efficient with the Alpha keyboard, then with DashKey and less efficient with MessagEase (cf. Table 4).

The users classified the MessagEase/DashKey interaction technique as recreating but more complex and requiring more concentration. Consequently, it generates a higher number of errors than Alpha. They also mentioned that, in spite of the recreating technique, they probably would not

Figure 4. Training layout

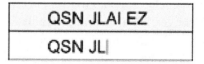

Table 4. Comparison model versus experimental results

	MacKenzie	**Isokoski / Zhai**	**Experimental results**
MessagEase	9.6	9.7	9.13
DashKey	9.4	9.6	11.1
Alpha	8.85	9.3	11.6

use DashKey or MessagEase out of an experimental context.

They preferred the DashKey layout to MessagEase layout unanimously.

Experimentation Conclusion

The experiment highlighted that the novice models proposed by Soukoreff or Das do not fit with the user's reality. The users are not novice. They are beginners in the usage of a keyboard whereas they are able to exploit former experiences to improve their performances in front of a new keyboard.

Consequently, we proposed a beginner model taking into account how the user may use his knowledge.

TAKING INTO ACCOUNT THE USER KNOWLEDGE

In Soukoreff and MacKenzie (1995), the lower bound use a constant time (ST = a * log2 [number of characters]) given by the Hick-Hyman law (Hick, 1952; Hyman, 1953) to estimate the time penalty for the character search. Pavlovych (Pavlovych & Stuerzlinger, 2004) measures a value of 680ms used in the Das model. However, in their model Das and Soukoreff estimate that a user is in front of n equally probable items. So the two models presuppose that the user do not have any heuristic to optimize its search for a character.

However, in several circumstances, the user can use knowledge to orient the character search in front of a new keyboard. For example, if a user must input an "F" on an alphabetical keyboard, he will not scan every character of the layout. Guided by the alphabetical heuristic, he will spontaneously target a restricted zone of the keyboard and look for the "F" among the characters contained in this zone. Consequently, we cannot consider, for every keyboard, that the N characters contained in the keyboard are N equally probable alternatives.

Thus, to make the lower-bound more accurate, we must be able to model these search strategies.

For the rest of the article we will reuse the character search time (Search time among 27 characters equally probable) of 680ms to evaluate our model. Because the search is linear, we will consider this search time as proportional to the character number. Thus, if the user must look for a character into a set of X character, we will consider a search time ST:

$$ST = \frac{680 \times X}{27}$$

Knowledge Model for MessagEase

Due to the design of the keyboard, our hypothesis is that the perception of the character frequency in the language is a natural guideline to orient the character search.

Perception of Character Frequency

In order to improve the model for MessagEase, we performed a preliminary experimentation aimed at measuring the perception by users of the character occurrence frequency in the language.

Figure 5. Results of the preliminary experimentation

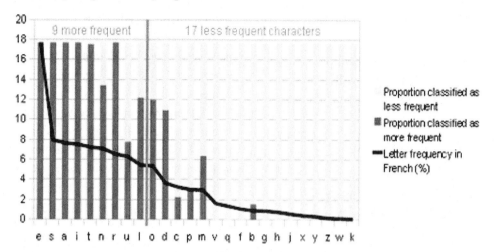

The experimentation involved 20 participant volunteers range in age from 22 and 46 (4 women and 13 men). They were all computer graduates.

The experimentation consists in a session of about 10 minutes. During the session, 260 characters (10 times each of the 26 Latin alphabet characters) were successively displayed in a random order. The users had to classify the character between two groups: the character makes part of the 9 more frequent characters in the language; the character makes part of the 17 less frequent characters. The users selected the group to classify the character by a button pressure. The errors were not displayed.

The results (cf. Figure 5) showed that the users had no significant doubt in classifying 6 among the 7 more frequent characters and 11 among the 12 less frequent characters in their correct group. However, the perception of frequency for the other characters was not so precise. Thus, 9 characters where frequently classified in the wrong group.

Impact of User Cultural Experience on the Search Time

We supposed that the space character is instantaneously identified and memorized because of its specific position and aspect (cf. Figure 1), and the high frequency of the character input. The user will look for a character considered as frequent among the 9 other characters displayed in the center of the keys and look for a low frequent character among the 17 displayed in the border of the keys. The central character is much bigger than the secondary characters. This property makes the two character groups graphically clearly distinct. Consequently, we consider that, when the user will search a character in a character group, the characters contained in the other character group will not interfere in the search.

However, like demonstrated during the preliminary experiment, we cannot consider the perception frequency as perfect. If the user will spontaneously classify characters such as "E, S, A, I, T, R" among the more frequent characters and "W, Z, Y, X, J, H, …" among the less frequent ones, the user will frequently search other characters such as "N, U, L, O, D, C, P, M, B" in the wrong character group at first and then look for into the good character group in a second time.

Consequently, we recalculated the lower bound considering three different search times:

The search time for the 6 more frequent characters classified without ambiguity. The user will search the character among the 9 main characters instead of 27 characters:

$$ST\left(E\;/\;T\;/\;A\;/\;O\;/\;I\;/\;S\right) = \frac{680 \times 9}{27}$$

The search time for the 11 unambiguous low frequent characters. The user will search the character among the 17 secondary characters:

$$ST\left(K/W/Z/Y/X/J/H/G/F/Q/V\right) = \frac{680 \times 17}{27}$$

The search time for the 9 characters with medium frequency of occurrence. We consider E (φ) the percentage of classification error for the character "φ" evaluated during the preliminary experimentation. The user will have to search the character in the correct group, but get a probability of E (φ) to search these characters in the wrong group first:

$$ST\left(N/U/L\right) = \frac{680 \times \left(9 + E(N\;/\;U\;/\;L) \times 17\right)}{27}$$

and:

$$ST\left(O/D/C/P/M/B\right) = \frac{680 \times \left(17 + E(O/D/C/P/M/B) \times 9\right)}{27}$$

Knowledge Model for DashKey and Alpha

Our hypothesis is that the alphabetic order is a natural heuristic that may guide the character searches with DashKey and Alpha soft keyboards.

Perception of Alphabetic Order

In a preliminary experimentation, we measured the user's imprecision in the perception of the alphabetic order. The experimentation consisted in determining a zone in which a user will look for a character in a set of 26 characters ordered by alphabetic order.

The experimentation involved 20 participant volunteers range in age from 22 and 43 (6 women and 14 men). They were all graduated in computation.

The experimentation consists in a session of about 10 minutes. During the session, 260 characters (10 times each of the 26 Latin alphabet characters) were successively displayed in a random order. The user had to select a key corresponding to the displayed character in a keyboard with the Alpha layout, but the characters were not displayed on the keys. The users had to perform as quickly and spontaneously as possible.

The selections occurring in a time up to 2.5 were ignored to prevent the user from counting the keys. The errors were not shown to the user. Instead, we measured the distance between the click and the key to be input.

The average of oriented distances between the selected key and the key containing the good character delimited an incertitude zone for the character (cf. Figure 6). With a visual retro-control, the user will look for a character among the key into this zone.

The characters at the beginning and the end of the alphabet are logically more easily located (distance between 0 and 2 keys for the characters A, B, C, D, X, Y, Z). The middle of the alphabet seems to be another reference point easing the localization of character (distance between 2 and 2.5 for the characters M, N, O). More the character is far from these referenced points, more the distance increases.

Impact of User Cultural Experience on the Search Time

Consequently, for Alpha and DashKey, considering Z (φ) the size of the incertitude zone and ST (φ) the search time for the character φ:

Figure 6. Size of the incertitude zone

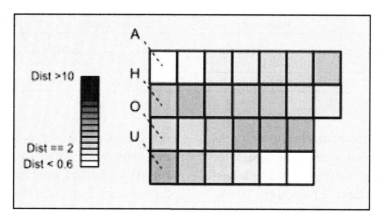

$$ST\left(\phi\right) = 680 * \frac{Z\left(\phi\right)}{27}$$

Cognitive Impact for the Flick Interaction and the Copy Task

With MessagEase and DashKey, the beginner must equally choose between two interaction techniques: the simple pressure or the flick. Consequently, we add a "choose time" in the input model. The "choose time" (CT) is modeled by the Shannon's law:

$$CT = \frac{1}{4,9} \times \log_2\left(2\right)$$

With Alpha, the user gets a unique interaction alternative. Consequently:

$$CT = \frac{1}{4,9} \times \log_2\left(1\right) = 0$$

As shown Pavlovych (Pavlovych & Stuerzlinger, 2004), the lower-bound models only the input task. Therefore, in order to compare the model with experimental result, we must add the time needed to perform the whole copying task:

time for reading the word to copy (RT), time for preparing and performing the input (T+ST+CT), and time (VT) for verifying the input.

In our experiment, we measure the time between the first and the last character input of each word. Therefore, the reading time is out of the measured sequence and we do not have to take into account this reading time (RT = 0). We used VT = 0.14s, measured by Pavlovych.

The copying task is consequently divided in 4 subtasks: the search time STj (from now dependant of the character j), the time to select the interaction CT, the input time Tij and the time to verify the input VT. The time to perform the task is MT with:

$$\overline{MT} = \sum_{i=1}^{27}\sum_{j=1} P_{ij} T_{ij}^{'} \text{ and}$$
$$T_{ij}^{'} = T_{ij} + ST_j + CT + VT$$

Beginner Model vs. Experimental Results

The new values for our beginner model (cf. Table 5) are more representative of the expected results. For a beginner, Alpha should be the keyboard the more efficient, DashKey the second, and MessagEase the least.

Table 5. Comparison model versus experimental results

	MacKenzie	**Isokoski / Zhai**	**Experimental results**
MessagEase	8.66	8.77	9.13
DashKey	10.15	10.39	11.1
Alpha	11.30	12.04	11.6

The experimental results are close to the results found with our models. However, the models for DashKey and MessagEase seem to be a little pessimistic. We suppose that the fix costs (CT + Pe) may be a little over estimated. The value of Pe, extracted from McQueen experimentation (McQueen, et al., 1995), should be reevaluated for this specific selection task.

SYNTHESIS

We observed that the results provided by the theoretical comparison of keyboards (through the calculus of the lower-bound) did not correspond to our intuitive expectations. Consequently, we improved the models by integrating search strategies oriented by the user's background. It leads us to measure experimentally the user's perception of some characteristics of the language: frequency of the letter, and position of the letters in the alphabet. Moreover, we observed that some other features of the keyboards (such as cognitive complexity of interaction) must be integrated into the model. The new model gave results more reliable toward the experimental ones.

DISCUSSION: APPLICABILITY OF PREDICTIVE MODELS FOR PERFORMANCE EVALUATIONS

The limits observed for predictive models calculating expert performances reduced their applicability contexts. The models enabled to determine keyboard layouts efficiency toward mechanical properties but they were not able to take into account other features of the keyboards such as dynamic changes due to prediction systems or alternative interaction techniques.

Moreover, by ignoring all the cognitive costs, the values calculated in the Soukoreff and Mackenzie model (Soukoreff & Mackenzie, 1995) do not fit adequately with the subtasks required for a user to perform a real input task. Thus, the model can be used to compare mechanical properties of soft keyboards but it cannot be used to predict user's performances efficiently. The model proposed by Das (Das & Stuerzlinger, 2008) tried to improve this previous model by integrating the cognitive costs for an expert, but we observed that the calculus for the cognitive costs does not fit with the reality.

Therefore, the existing models can be useful to compare the expert performances for a little subset of existing keyboards and they do not reach the new strategies proposed to improve text input (mainly dynamic helps based on prediction systems).

Tackling the question of performance prediction for novice, we observed that the models were not able to deal with the natural heuristic guiding the novice user in the character searches. This observation leads us to reconsider the way to think the models. They should not model the interface but the interaction: how a user interacts with a soft keyboard. They should depend both on the user and the soft keyboard. Then, we modeled this interaction by taking into account how a user should react in front of the specific features of a soft keyboard.

As predicted, these models provide results more reliable in comparison with experimental ones. However, because the models are relative to the user's knowledge and to the soft keyboard, they must be adapted both in function of the targeted population and in function of the soft keyboard. Some characteristic such as language, age, culture, or social category may impact the results for the same soft keyboard.

Therefore, even if the models can be improved to be more representative of the real user's performances, because of the soft keyboard diversity, modeling is not a simple generic tool to predict the performances, but, above all, the model design for the soft keyboards and the population is oriented by an observation of the soft keyboard features and the population characteristics. Every model must be validated through an experimental evaluation.

Thus, we conclude that the predictive models are losing their predictive capabilities and are not an efficient way to compare quickly the soft keyboards. They may are adapted to study some human behavior in front of an HMI but the cognitive models are not robust enough to predict user's performances with soft keyboards accurately.

FUTURE WORKS

Even with the improvement we suggested, predictive models failed to provide a quick tool to compare soft keyboards. However, our works highlighted that an attentive observation could provide interesting comparison results (this observation guided the design of our models). Consequently, purchasing the goal to obtain a robust and rapid comparison tool for soft keyboard, our future works will lead us to organize and standardize this observation as a heuristic evaluation (Nielsen & Molich, 1990; Nielsen & Phillips, 1993) comparing the soft keyboard efficiency toward criteria such as: the targeted population (age, culture, and eventual motor impairment, etc.), the usage frequency of the soft keyboard, the nature of the input texts (formal or informal SMS, emails, documents, etc.), the context of use (mobile or not, usage in double task, etc.).

Through this heuristic evaluation, we do not expect numerical results whereas we expect to be able to highlight the more adapted artifacts responding to different real condition of text input through a soft keyboard.

REFERENCES

Badr, G., & Raynal, M. (2009). Optimized interaction with word prediction list: A use case with a motor impairment. In *Proceedings of the European Conference for the Advancement of Assistive Technology in Europ (AAATE 2009)*. IOS Press.

Card, S. K., Thomas, T. P., & Newall, A. (1980). The keystroke-level model for user performance time with interactive systems. *Communications of the ACM, 23*(7), 396–410. doi:10.1145/358886.358895

Card, S. K., Thomas, T. P., & Newall, A. (1983). *The psychology of human-computer interaction.* London, UK: Lawrence Erlbaum Associates.

Das, A., & Stuerzlinger, W. (2008). Modeling learning effects in mobile texting. In *Proceedings of the 7th International Conference on MUM 2008.* ACM Press.

Douglas, S. A., & Mithal, A. K. (1997). *The ergonomics of computer pointing devices.* Berlin, Germany: Springer-Verlag.

Dunlop, M. D., & Crossan, A. (1999). *Dictionary based text entry method for mobile phones*. Paper presented at the Second Workshop on Human-Computer Interaction with Mobile Devices. Edinburgh, UK.

Fitts, P. M. (1954). The information capacity of the human motor system in controlling the amplitude of movement. *Journal of Experimental Psychology, 47*, 381–391. doi:10.1037/h0055392

Fitts, P. M., & Peterson, J. R. (1964). Information capacity of discrete motor responses. *Journal of Experimental Psychology, 67*(2), 103–112. doi:10.1037/h0045689

Foulds, R. A., Soede, M., & Van Balkom, H. (1987). Statistical disambiguation of multi-character keys applied to reduce motor requirements for augmentative and alternative communication. *Augmentative and Alternative Communication, 3*, 192–195. doi:10.1080/07434618712331274509

Gentner, D. R., Grudin, J. T., Larochelle, S., Norman, D. A., & Rumelhart, D. E. (1983). A glossary of terms including classification of typing errors. In Cooper, W. E. (Ed.), *Cognitive Aspects of Skilled Typewriting* (pp. 39–43). New York, NY: Springer-Verlag. doi:10.1007/978-1-4612-5470-6_2

Goldberg, D., & Richardson, C. (1993). Touch-typing with a stylus. In *Proceedings of the INTERCHI 1993 Conference on Human Factors in Computing Systems*, (pp. 168-176). ACM Press.

Gray, W. D., John, B. E., & Atwood, M. E. (1993). Project ernestine: A validation of GOMS for prediction and explanation of real-world task performance. *Human-Computer Interaction, 8*(3), 237–309. doi:10.1207/s15327051hci0803_3

Guiard, Y. (2009). The problem of consistency in the design of Fitts' law experiments: Consider either target distance and width or movement form and scale. In *Proceedings of the 27th International Conference on Human Factors in Computing Systems (CHI 2009)*, (pp. 1809-1818). ACM Press.

Hick, W. E. (1952). On the rate of gain of information. *The Quarterly Journal of Experimental Psychology, 4*(1), 11–26. doi:10.1080/17470215208416600

Hyman, R. (1953). Stimulus information as a determinant of reaction time. *Journal of Experimental Psychology, 45*, 188–196. doi:10.1037/h0056940

Isokoski, P. (2004). Performance of menu-augmented soft keyboards. In *Proceedings of the SIGCHI Conference on Human Factors in Computing Systems (CHI 2004)*, (pp. 423-430). ACM Press.

John, E. B., & Kieras, E. D. (1996). Using GOMS for user interface design and evaluation: Which technique? *ACM Transactions on Computer-Human Interaction, 3*(4), 287–319. doi:10.1145/235833.236050

Lesher, G. W., & Moulton, B. J. (2000). A method for optimizing single-finger keyboards. In *Proceedings of Rehabilitation Engineering Society of North America - RESNA Annual Conference*, (pp. 91-93). RESNA.

Levine, S. H., Goodenought-Trepagnier, C., Getschow, C. O., & Minneman, S. L. (1987). Multi-character key text entry using computer disambiguation. In *Proceedings of the 10th Annual Conference of Rehabilitation Engineering*, (pp. 177-179). Washington, DC: RESNA.

MacKenzie, I. S., & Soukoreff, R. W. (2002). Text entry for mobile computing: Models and methods, theory and practice. *Human-Computer Interaction, 17*(2), 147–198. doi:10.1207/S15327051HCI172&3_2

MacKenzie, I. S., & Zhang, S. X. (1999). The design and evaluation of a high-performance soft keyboard. In *Proceedings of CHI 1999*, (pp. 25-31). ACM.

McQueen, C., MacKenzie, I. S., & Zhang, S. X. (1995). An extended study of numeric entry on pen-based computers. In *Proceedings of Graphics Interface, 1995*, 215–222.

Merlin, B., & Raynal, M. (2009). *SpreadKey: Increasing software keyboard key by recycling needless ones*. Paper presented at AAATE 2009. Florence, Italia.

Nesbat, S. B. (2003). A system for fast, full-text entry for small electronic devices. In *Proceedings of the Fifth International Conference on Multimodal Interfaces, ICMI 2003*. ACM Press.

Nielsen, J., & Molich, R. (1990). Heuristic evaluation of user interfaces. In *Proceedings of the SIGCHI Conference on Human Factors in Computing Systems: Empowering People (CHI 1990)*, (pp. 249-256). ACM Press.

Nielsen, J., & Phillips, V. L. (1993). Estimating the relative usability of two interfaces: Heuristic, formal, and empirical methods compared. In *Proceedings of the INTERACT 1993 and CHI 1993 Conference on Human Factors in Computing Systems (CHI 1993)*, (pp. 214-221). ACM Press.

Pavlovych, A., & Stuerzlinger, W. (2004). Model for non-expert text entry speed on 12-button phone keypads, In *Proceedings of the SIGCHI Conference on Human Factors in Computing Systems*, (pp. 351-358). ACM Press.

Raynal, M., & Vigouroux, N. (2005). Genetic algorithm to generate optimized soft keyboard. In *Proceedings of CHI 2005 Extended Abstracts on Human Factors in Computing Systems (CHI 2005)*, (pp. 1729-1732). ACM Press.

Sears, A., Jacko, J. A., Chu, J., & Moro, F. (2001). The role of visual search in the design of effective soft keyboards. *Behaviour & Information Technology*, *20*(3), 159–166. doi:10.1080/01449290110049790

Shannon, C. (1948). A mathematical theory of communication. *Bell System Technical Journal, 27*, 379–423 & 623–656.

Silfverberg, M., MacKenzie, I. S., & Korhonen, P. (2000). Predicting text entry speed on mobile phones. In *Proceedings of the SIGCHI Conference on Human Factors in Computing Systems (CHI 2000)*, (pp. 9-16). ACM Press.

Soukoreff, R. W., & MacKenzie, I. S. (1995). Theoretical upper and lower bounds on typing speeds using a stylus and soft keyboard. *Behaviour & Information Technology, 14*, 370–379. doi:10.1080/01449299508914656

Woodworth, R. S. (1899). The accuracy of voluntary movement. *Psychological Review, 3*(2), 1–4.

Yang, H., & Xu, X. (2010). Bias towards regular configuration in 2D pointing. In *Proceedings of the 28th International Conference on Human Factors in Computing Systems (CHI 2010)*, (pp. 1391-1400). ACM Press.

Zhai, S., Hunter, M., & Smith, B. A. (2000). The metropolis keyboard - An exploration of quantitative techniques for virtual keyboard design. In *Proceedings of the 13th Annual ACM Symposium on User Interface Software and Technology*, (pp. 119-128). San Diego, CA: ACM Press.

Zhai, S., Sue, A., & Accot, J. (2002). Movement model, hits distribution and learning in virtual keyboarding. *CHI Letters, 4*(1), 17–24.

ENDNOTES

[1] Combination of two character using on of the 26 Latin characters or the space: aa ab ac… ba bb bc …

[2] http://www.cootek.com/

[3] The time is logarithmic in the Hick-Hyman dichotomous task

[4] $S = 60 / (5 * ST) = 17.65$ wpm

[5] The flick is performed in the continuity of the character group selection. Thus, character group selection and the character selection are a unique interaction: a simple pointing for the main character, and a flick for secondary characters.

[6] McQueen did not notice a significant effect of the flick direction. We neglected this aspect in this model.

Chapter 3

A Fresh Look at Graphical Web Browser Revisitation using an Organic Bookmark Management System

Siu-Tsen Shen
National Formosa University, Taiwan

Stephen D. Prior
Middlesex University, UK

ABSTRACT

With roughly a third of the world's population now having access to the internet, the area of web efficiency and its optimal use is of growing importance to all online users. We are approaching a tipping point where the majority of people will have spent more time online than offline. With this in mind, the function of revisitation, where a user wants to return to a website that they have visited in the recent past, becomes more important. Current static, textual-list approaches developed within the latest versions of mainstream web browsers such as Internet Explorer, Firefox, and Chrome leave much to be desired. This chapter suggests a new approach via the use of organic, visual, and contextual cues to support users in this vital task area.

INTRODUCTION

Cisco Visual Networking Index (VNI) Forecast has projected that there will be nearly 3 billion internet users by 2015, that is to say that there will be more than 40% of the world's population who have access to the benefits and drawbacks of the World Wide Web (Cisco, 2011). With so many people online, internet traffic and data flows are becoming as congested and overloaded as our roads. Computer users report that they find it difficult and sometimes impossible to manage their online lives in an efficient manner, and they experience increasing frustration when finding and re-finding important information. The design and utility of web browsers are therefore becoming

DOI: 10.4018/978-1-4666-1628-8.ch003

more and more important. What will happen when 80% of the world's population is online?

Current browsers offer standardized functions such as Bookmarks (Favorites) and History to assist people with data retrieval i.e. revisitation. The management of Bookmarks (Favorites) requires a great deal of effort in terms of personal organization if it is to work efficiently. A long list of History records could actually end up preventing the finding of information. Many internet users would rather carry out a new search in revisiting their desired web pages than find them from within their bookmark and history collections, which for an experienced user might amount to several hundred websites per week. A number of recent studies have shown that between 46-81% of users web pages had been revisited (Tauscher, 1997; Cockburn & McKenzie, 2001; Weinreich, et al., 2006). Further, Weinreich, Obendorf, Herder, and Meyer (2008) found that the history feature was used in only 0.2% of all revisitation events (Weinreich, et al., 2008), even though its purpose was meant to aid re-finding. Recent ad hoc modifications to the popular IE browser, i.e. the right-clickable back button that shows a list of recently visited websites and the larger sized back button in IE 9 all help with revisitation; however, they do not tackle the main cognitive issue of information presentational overload.

RELATED WORK

Generally speaking, web browsers provide short term revisitation with the functions of Back and Forward, and long term revisitation with the functions of Bookmarks (Favorites) and History. Several research studies have indicated that the Back button is more often used, compared to the Forward button. The Back button made up of 35.7% of actions by Catledge and Pitkow (1995), 31.7% of actions by Tauscher and Greenberg (1997), and 14.3% of actions by Weinreich et al. (2006). The Forward button only made up

1.5% of actions from the research by Catledge and Pitkow (1995), 0.8% of actions by Tauscher and Greenberg (1997), and 0.6% of actions by Weinreich et al. (2006). Latest research has shown that the use of the Back and Forward buttons has been in decline over the last decade. The reason for this is that they have their natural limitations to support revisitation, because of their temporal mechanism, which only allows a certain amount of the recent visited pages.

For long-term revisitation, the function of Bookmarks offers the management system for the users to store their desired links. It heavily relies on personal efforts to categorize and organize. It is a common experience that users have to spend a lot of time on retrieval, and might not be able to succeed in finding the webpage from their big collection of Bookmarks. When getting frustrated, most users would rather launch a search engine in order to re-find the lost information. Current bookmark management systems depend on either directory or keyword mechanisms for labeling bookmarks. The retrieval of information could become very difficult, if they have not been well organized.

The History function is supposed to allow users to easily track their previously visited web pages. For example, Internet Explorer 9 has combined Bookmarks with RSS feed, whereby the user could sort history lists up to 999 days by site name, most visited sites, order visited today, date and search. However, the textual list of history has its drawbacks; it is often the case that users face the same experience as Bookmarks in that the required websites could not be recovered within the history list. Several recent studies conducted by the authors have concluded that a high proportion of users do not know how to use these features, or even that they exist.

There have been many suggestions in reinforcing the above-mentioned features. Milic-Frayling, Jones, Rodden, Smyth, Blackwell, and Sommerer (2004) proposed SmartBack that allows the user to jump directly to key pages based on their navigation trials to supplement the standard Back function. Kaasten and Greenberg (2001) attempted to merge Back, Bookmarks and History into one function. Nagel and Sander (2005) presented HyperHistory to solve the web browser's History function drawbacks and enhance bookmark organization to support revisitation. Further, Tabard, Mackay, Roussel, and Letondal (2007) developed PageLinker for biologists so that they could create and present links on specific pages or set of pages on bookmarks without prior planning. There have been other commercial and open source products available such as BrowseBack where the user can search the web history through keywords and view thumbnails of web pages, and MindRetrieve which is a search engine that indexes web pages, these can then be viewed offline and are ranked by relevance (BrowseBack, 2009; MindRetrieve, 2009).

Symbaloo (www.symbaloo.com) is a new free way to organize your online life. It brings the users Bookmarks (Favorites) directly onto the main screen allowing the user to configure and use its so called 'webmix' of tiled thumbnails (10 x 6 matrix) of stored WebPages. The centre feature panel (4 x 2 matrix) is set aside for a Google Search screen. In a similar way to delicious users are able to share their bookmarks with each other via the online portal.

None of these attempts have been intuitive or engaging enough to encourage regular and sustained use from the general public. To some extent, this has been as a direct result of the limited power of the previous generation of computer systems. As time progresses we see the technological fix providing increased power at reduce cost to the user. Maybe the time is right for the introduction of a new, more intuitive and engaging interface for re-finding information.

ALTERNATIVE METAPHORS AND DESIGNS

There have been several researchers who proposed to use other metaphors to support web browser revisitation. Brown and Shillner (1995) came up with an experimental web browser, DeckScape, based on a "deck" metaphor. A deck includes a collection of web pages and multiple decks could overlap each other. Users can move and copy pages between decks, and decks can provide a flexible way to organize web pages through hotlists and history lists. Card, Robertson, and York (1996) suggested WebBook based on a "book" metaphor which allowed the user to collect HTML pages and save them as a book. WebBook presented an interesting 3D visualization by viewing the contents of a book, flipping of pages to the desired page, and storing pages on a bookcase. WebView integrates revisitation capabilities into a single display, including zoomable thumbnail images (Mander, et al., 1992) and a customizable scheme for displaying pages either by temporal properties or by 'hub-and-spoke' structural relationships (Cockburn, et al., 1999).

Further, the implementation of the "dog ear-ring" metaphor appeared in some research. Kaasten and Greenberg (2001) used dog-ears to mark pages on a list in order to replace Bookmarks. HyperHistory was employed by the metaphor of dog-earing as a way to mark the level of the importance of the pages (Nagel and Sander, 2005). Rose, Mander, Oren, Ponceleon, Salomon, and Wang (1993) employed a "pile" metaphor to assist the filing systems and data management. Agarawala and Balakrishnan (2006) applied the "pile" metaphor in organizing objects and a physics simulation afforded a casual, potentially more realistic interaction. Their pen-centric interface named Drag'n'Cross allowed the user to drag documents, cross leaf widget, and scrub to specify an insertion point.

It is true that current bookmarking functions within most browsers allow users to establish mas-

Figure 1. Original 2D i-pot schema

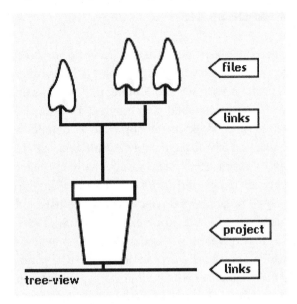

sive collections of their bookmark pages; however, they still require user effort in re-organizing their bookmarks in an unnatural way. In light of this, the authors developed a new system, which they called the 'Information Plant Organic Technique' (i-Pot) which simulated the process of seeding and growing plants with the aim to facilitate information retrieval and organize data in a more natural (organic) way (see Figure 1).

The Origins of i-Pot

As mentioned above, several previous research teams have tried to employ metaphors to aid recall and cognizance, such as the two dimensional dog-erring and three dimensional pile metaphors, without a great deal of success. The idea of developing an organic bookmark management system was inspired by Frank Lloyd Wright who wrote that:

"So here I stand before you preaching organic architecture: declaring organic architecture to be the modern ideal and the teaching so much needed if we are to see the whole of life, and to now serve the whole of life, holding no 'traditions'

essential to the great TRADITION. Nor cherishing any preconceived form fixing upon us either past, present or future, but—instead—exalting the simple laws of common sense—or of super-sense if you prefer—determining form by way of the nature of materials..." (Wright, 1971).

Furthermore, Pearson (2001) listed the rules for organic architecture and design, as well known as the Gaia Charter:

"Let the design be inspired by nature, unfold like organism, from the seed within; exist in the 'continuous present' and 'begin again and again'... grow out of the site... and be unique" (Pearson, 2001).

The concept of the 'Information Plant Organic Technique' (i-Pot) encapsulates these thoughts. The i-Pot concept is highly associated with the garden metaphor that was proposed by Shen, Prior, and Woolley (2006, 2009). It is evident that there are some similarities between a garden and i-Pot, in that both would require personal maintenance, organization, management, and devotion. Moreover, digital formats have their own organic cycles, such as the elements that seed, grow, reproduce, die off and recycle (Bentley, 2004). Therefore, the i-Pot prototype is based on the concept of the garden metaphor in order to develop and support web browser revisitation.

So, to recap, i-Pot is based upon the garden metaphor, which we believe to be an intuitive method, which cuts across cultural boundaries and allows a natural (organic) context to storage, retrieval and re-finding of information. The engaging, colourful, and three-dimensional nature of the interface also provides a user friendly and visually stimulating environment where information is presented in an easy to find and locate manner. The system is fully customizable and is easily adaptable to the needs of the user.

Table 1. Analysis of study participants

Feature	Male	Female
Age (Mean)	23.45 (sd=4.82)	24.10 (sd=5.53)
University Degree	85%	75%
> 10 yrs Computer Experience	60%	60%
> 8 hr/day internet usage	55%	60%
> 10 hr/day internet usage	20%	20%
Internet Explorer	65%	70%
Firefox	30%	20%
Chrome	20%	10%
KKMan (Local Browser)	5%	0%

PRELIMINARY USER STUDY

In order to gain a qualitative understanding of how people use bookmark management techniques and how user behavior varies with regards to revisitation, an empirical study was conducted at the National Formosa University in Taiwan during the spring of 2011. This user study combined questionnaires with recognition tasks (selected participants only). We recruited 40 participants (20 males, 20 females) from the online social network at campus. Participants were compensated with 800 New Taiwanese Dollars (approx. 25 USD) for their time when the study was completed (see Table 1).

Apart from the general browsing pattern of the participants, we also wanted to confirm their knowledge and experience with the default browser functions: History and Bookmark (Favorites). Despite the fact that all the participants were aware of the History function, it was found that 40% of the males and 65% of the females did not frequently use it. This indicated that it was either perceived as unhelpful or difficult to use. Most of the participants were aware that the History function could display the previously visited websites in the past few weeks. However, 25% of the males and 45% of the females did not realize that they could change the default History function. For example, the users were allowed to

trace History to 999 days as a maximum in IE 9. Making use of a keyword to search within the personal History record was still not well known by 25% of the males and 50% of the females. In terms of the Bookmark (Favorites) function, most of the participants were found to use it regularly, and yet 20% of the males and 5% of the females found it complex to use to organize their data. The study found that 10% of the males did not know how to manage their Bookmark (Favorites).

It was found that 40% of the males and 35% of the females regularly experienced problems when revisiting a web page, in that they could not remember its stored location. In order to solve this problem, most of the participants preferred to re-launch a search engine such as Google. When the participants History logs were reviewed over the previous 21 days, it was found that these ranged between 69 and 300 websites. In terms of the numbers of the participants' Bookmark (Favorites) folders, a mean of 16 folders was found for the males, and 14 folders for the females. When we take all the above data into consideration, this showed that there is still room to improve the History and Bookmark (Favorites) features to enhance information retrieval and management tasks.

Recognition Tasks

Recognition tasks were used to test the participants' ability to recognize attributes of the primitive 'look and feel' of the i-Pot prototype within the context of the garden metaphor. We therefore selected two males (one was classified as an advanced user, and another was an intermediate user), and one female who was a novice user, based on the first part of the questionnaire that they had submitted. This prototype was run using a Flash based platform, and was provided to the chosen participants to experience and test without time limits. They were asked to figure out how to bookmark a website including the use of the 'add' and 'delete' functions, how to organize Bookmark (Favorites) such as creating a new folder and moving the tags, and how to view the History records. Based on the Likert scale, they agreed that i-Pot was easy to recognize and to understand its overall visual design. With regards to the simplified Bookmark (Favorites) function, all three participants found i-Pot was easy to manage. For the History function, the two males involved agreed that History was easy to view, whilst the female disagreed. They suggested further improvements to the i-Pot functions and the desire to incorporate more features. For a complete review of the preliminary user study refer to (Shen, Prior, & Chen, 2011).

ITERATIVE DESIGN OF THE I-POT PROTOTYPE

Following on from the preliminary user study above (Shen, Prior, & Chen, 2011), the authors continued focusing on supporting the process of revisitation with its relevant tasks. The research team aimed to create an organic simulation that offers similar Bookmark (Favorites) function that allows the users to add and organize a new link, and a History function that allows the users to review their browsing records. The earlier itera-

tions of i-POT were built from scratch, through multi-sketching structures, and then developed into two kinds of interactive prototypes i.e. 2D (Flash-based) and 3D (Q3D-based). The implementation of these would be built on Firefox extensions, because of its great availability on crossing different OS platforms such as Mac, Linux, and Windows. Furthermore, the installation of a Firefox extension is simple and easy, in that the users only need to click the link of the extension they want to install.

In our 2D design prototype of i-Pot, the main window could be viewed (first person perspective) with a maximum of ten pots in a horizontal spiral order (see Figure 2).

The reason for this was because users generally kept around ten folders in their Bookmark (Favorites) based on our preliminary study. Each pot could be labeled by customized color and with different categories. The user could add their own bookmark by clicking the green plus symbol, and delete their own bookmark by clicking the right key of the mouse. The more bookmarks the pot contained, the bigger the plant itself grew. Once the user selected his specific pot to view, they would be led to another set of sub-pots. For example, when the user opened the 'Sports Pot,' they would find another set of pots, which specify different kinds of sports such as volleyball, football and basketball. By moving the mouse over the leaves, the user would find that there were smart boxes popping out to show information such as titles, dates, thumbnail and URLs (see Figure 3).

The user could also view their history records by clicking the pink-reddish History icon. There were two main features within the History function (see Figure 4).

The first one was the horizontal timeline that indicates the date when the user had browsed. From left to right, it shows the newest to the oldest date record. The second one was the rainbow tree, which corresponds to the timeline. When selecting a date on the timeline, the user could

Figure 2. 2D flash-based i-pot prototype

Figure 3. Example sports category sub-level

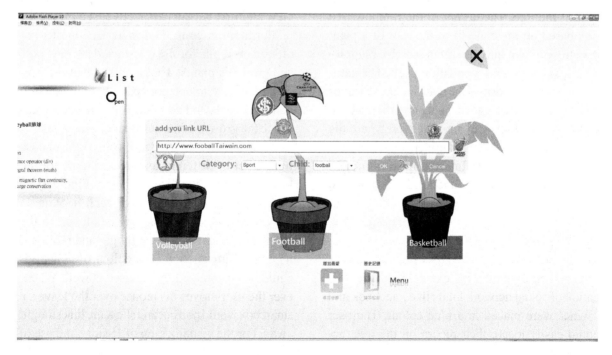

Figure 4. History rainbow tree with timeline scrollbar

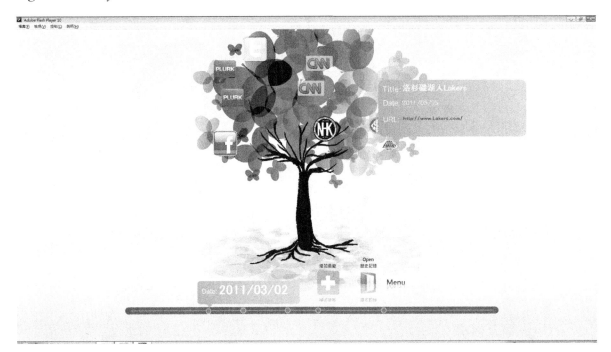

identify the highlighted information on a certain spot of the tree. The design of the rainbow tree was based on the concept of the root of a plant that grows down into the soil in search of supplements, as the central foundation itself. The natural growth mechanism of the plant including leaves and branches is irregular and unpredictable, in that they could grow in any direction where the appropriate environment of mineral nutrients and water meet their needs. Interestingly, this notion was similar to the History function that is supposed to record the users' daily activities and is unlikely to foresee their next actions. Furthermore, the advantage of the use of color to assist the history record was to give the user freedom to customize their own tree. For example, the identification of social network logos like Facebook and Twitter were placed in a blue colour. The user could easily locate their record on the tree, according to the history timeline they made.

In contrast to our 2D version of i-Pot, the advantage of using 3D space allows the user to view their garden in multiple angles such as aerial view and first person perspective (see Figure 5).

Furthermore, our 3D design version of i-Pot offered no limits for the user to add his new pots and grow his plants. That is to say that the user could feel free to categorize his bookmarks into numerous pots and add new links that could enhance the growth of the new leaves in any desired pot. On the right panel, the user could choose from a set of different textured patterns for the look of their personalized pots (see Figure 6).

For better identification of each bookmark, the concept of dewdrops was employed to the edge of each leaf cusp to highlight and represent its unique information. The colour of dewdrops could be customized by the user as well. Whenever the user moves his mouse over the leaves, a smart box would pop out and show the link straight away. For the visualization of History, the use of distinctive corporate identity color design from each website such as red for CNN and BBC was to help the user to recall and relocate records within the tree map. If the selected website did

Figure 5. 3D i-pot garden perspective view

Figure 6. User customization panel

Figure 7. Interactive view showing hot links to selected web pages

not have a distinct corporate identity symbol or logo, i-Pot would offer a thumbnail scan/preview from this website and show its main headline or keyword on the history tree for better recognition (see Figure 7).

FUTURE RESEARCH DIRECTIONS

In the opening paragraphs of this chapter, we alluded to the growth in data flows over the internet. To put this into perspective, it might be helpful to recap on what exactly this will mean for the future. In the context of data flow, it has been stated that Google now processes 24 Petabytes of data every day, this can only increase with time (MOD, 2011). In her recent presentation at the PARC Forum entitled 'The Physics of Data' Google Vice President Marissa Mayer stated that:

"...there were about 5 Exabytes of data online in 2002, which has now risen to 281 Exabytes in 2009. That's a growth rate of 56 times over seven years. This has partly been the result of people uploading more data. The average person uploaded 15 times more data in 2009 than they did just three years ago" (Mayer, 2009).

The problem of revisitation of web information is the same 'search and retrieval' problem as the wider World Wide Web, and as such, the solution to this problem will be the same solution as to the world's solution. At the heart of these solutions is the area of real-time data visualization, sometimes referred to as Visual Analytics, this is the science of presenting information in the most optimum visual way.

The future design of web browser programs will have to cope with greater amounts of data in real time and with greater visual contextualization. The world is indeed becoming a much bigger and a much smaller place (through technology) at the same time!

There exist several trends in online browsing which have developed over the last few years. The most important of these being the shift from individual fixed computers to mobile devices and the requisite need for online information portals, such as the cloud computing model, to support such activities.

Several 'Social Citation and Bookmarking' portals now exist to provide for these new services such as Connotea, Diigo, Faves, Graasp, Symbaloo and Webdocs; one of the first and most popular being the delicious (http://www.delicious.com/) website (Delicious, 2011), currently owned by Yahoo. Delicious, is a 'Social Bookmarking' service, which enables the user to save all their bookmarks online, share them and see what other people are bookmarking. The website also provides search and tagging tools to help the user to keep track of their entire bookmark collection.

Although this might appear to be the perfect solution, it does raise the subject of privacy, data protection, and abuse by spammers. The recent loss of 24.6 million user accounts by SONY has done nothing to assuage people's doubts over placing their personal information online. Recent trends in terms of web browser design are sometimes self-evident, but always insightful, some of these are listed in Table 2.

Table 2. Recent trends in web browser design

Current Feature		Future Feature
Static	➜	Dynamic
2D	➜	3D
B&W	➜	Colour
Unilateral	➜	Multi-Modal
User Tagging	➜	Autonomous Tagging
Data	➜	Data and Context

The implementation of the i-Pot concept has attempted to adhere to these trends in its design, rationale, and data visualization techniques. Like many of its predecessors over the last 20 years, the acid test will be the uptake and use of this system by the general public. Clearly, there is still much work to be done to refine, develop, and validate this concept into a functional and practical system. In this respect a series of further evaluation steps are currently ongoing to test and validate the user interface with a larger number of users. This work will be undertaken over the next 18 months and will lead to further publications and a live user evaluation online website. The researchers believe that an important first step has been achieved which shows improvements over the current range of web browsers in terms of an engaging, three dimensional environment which supports revisitation and visual cues to re-finding data. All future systems must move with the times and follow how people work now and into the future in terms of multi-modal, multi-tasking, across platform, time, and space (Wang & Chang, 2010).

CONCLUSION

Given everything that has been said previously, the central problem still remains, how to help the vast majority of people who either do not use Bookmarks (Favorites) or do not know how to organize them correctly, and also how to help users with the correct operation and use of the History function.

The current generation of web browsers clearly works, and in most cases, users are able to function just well enough to get by. However, all users from the novice to the most experienced have had the frustration of trying to find a website that they know they have visited before. Trying to find that 'needle in the haystack,' many users resort to the tried and tested Google Search engine to repeat the earlier search. This is both wasteful and inefficient and does not guarantee success. Clearly, all current web browsers can and are being incrementally improved over time, however, the authors believe that only a radical departure from the norm will provide the step change in performance required if we are to keep pace with the ever increasing rate of data overload.

Implementation of the 2D and 3D versions of i-Pot challenges preconceptions of web browser functionality in terms of outmoded textual list-based conceptualizations. Combining an organic metaphor with a 3D designer-led, intuitive, and colorful graphical medium, we believe will lead to a new level of user experience, which will promote intuitive operation and use.

Further work on the design of the i-Pot concept will involve testing and validation with multiple user populations and further refinements to the real-time user environment. The authors hope that this platform will inspire a radical shift in design thinking in this most important area of human computer interaction.

REFERENCES

Agarawala, A., & Balakrishnan, R. (2006). Keepin' it real: Pushing the desktop metaphor with physics, piles and the pen. In *Proceedings of CHI 2006: Interacting with Large Surfaces*. Montreal, Canada: ACM.

Bentley, P. J. (2004). *Software seeds: The garden where perfect software grows*. Paper presented at New Scientist. London, UK.

Brown, M., & Shillner, R. (1995). DeckScape: An experimental web browser. In *Proceedings of the 3rd International World Wide Web Conference*. Darmstadt, Germany: IEEE.

BrowseBack. (2009). *Visual web history you can search*. Retrieved from http://www.smileonmy-mac.com/browseback/.

Card, S., Robertson, G., & York, W. (1996). The WebBook and the Web forager: An information workspace for the world-wide web. In *Proceedings of the ACM CHI 1996 Conference on Human Factors in Computing Systems*. Vancouver, Canada: ACM.

Catledge, L., & Pitkow, J. (1995). Characterizing browsing strategies in the world-wide web. In *Proceedings of the 3rd International World Wide Web Conference*. Darmstadt, Germany: IEEE.

Cisco. (2011). *Global internet traffic projected to quadruple by 2015*. Retrieved June 29, 2011, from http://newsroom.cisco.com/press-release-content?type=webcontent&articleId=324003.

Cockburn, A., Greenberg, S., McKenzie, B., Smith, M., & Kassten, S. (1999). WebView: A graphical aid for revisiting web pages. In *Proceedings of the 1999 Computer Human Interaction Specialist Interest Group of the Ergonomics Society of Australia (OzCHI+99)*. Wagga Wagga, Australia: OzCHI.

Cockburn, A., & McKenzie, B. (2001). What do web users do? An empirical analysis of web use. *International Journal of Human-Computer Studies, 54*(6), 903–922. doi:10.1006/ijhc.2001.0459

Delicious. (2011). *Delicious.com*. Retrieved June 29, 2011, from www.delicious.com.

Kaasten, S., & Greenberg, S. (2001). Integrating back, history, and bookmarks in web browser. In *Proceedings of CHI 2001 extended Abstracts on Human Factors in Computing Systems*. Seattle, WA: ACM Press.

Mander, R., Salomon, G., & Wong, Y. Y. (1992). A pile metaphor for supporting casual organization of information. In *Proceedings of CHI 1992*. ACM Press.

Mayer, M. (2009). *Innovation at Google: The physics of data*. Palo Alto, CA: Palo Alto Research Center.

Milic-Frayling, N., Jones, R., Rodden, K., Smyth, G., Blackwell, A., & Sommerer, R. (2004). SmartBack: Supporting users in back navigation. In *Proceedings of WWW 2004*. New York, NY: ACM Press.

MindRetrieve. (2009). *Search your personal web*. Retrieved from http://www.mindretrieve.net/.

MOD. (2011). *The UK approach to unmanned aircraft systems*. London, UK: Ministry of Defense.

Nagel, T., & Sander, R. (2005). HyperHistory. In *Proceedings of HT 2005*. Salzburg, Austria: ACM Press.

Pearson, D. (2001). *New organic architecture: The breaking wave*. London, UK: Gaia.

Rose, D. E., Mander, R., Oren, T., Ponceleon, D., Salomon, G., & Wong, Y. Y. (1993). Content awareness in a file system interface: Implementing the pile metaphor for organizing information. In *Proceedings of SIGIR 1993*. Pittsburgh, PA: ACM Press.

Shen, S.-T., Prior, S. D., & Chen, K.-M. (2009). Comparing the perspicacity, appropriateness, and preference of web browser icons. *Digital Creativity*, *20*(1), 59–78. doi:10.1080/14626260902868012

Shen, S.-T., Prior, S. D., & Chen, K.-M. (2009). Testing of a novel web browser interface for the Chinese market. *Lecture Notes in Computer Science*, *5623*, 413–418. doi:10.1007/978-3-642-02767-3_46

Shen, S.-T., Prior, S. D., & Chen, K.-M. (2011). Revisiting revisitation in computer interaction: Organic bookmark management. *Design Principles and Practices: An International Journal*, *5*(4), 327–344.

Shen, S.-T., Prior, S. D., & Woolley, M. (2006). Towards culture-centred design. *Journal of Interacting with Computers*, *18*(4), 820–852. doi:10.1016/j.intcom.2005.11.014

Tabard, A., Mackay, W., Roussel, N., & Letondal, C. (2007). PageLinker: Integrating contextual bookmarks within a browser. In *Proceedings of CHI 2007*. San Jose, CA: ACM Press.

Tauscher, L., & Greenberg, S. (1997). How people revisit web pages: Empirical findings and implications for the design of history systems. *International Journal of Human-Computer Studies*, *47*(1), 97–138. doi:10.1006/ijhc.1997.0125

Wang, Q., & Chang, H. (2010). Multitasking bar: Prototype and evaluation of introducing the task concept into a browser. In *Proceedings of CHI 2010*. Atlanta, GA: ACM Press.

Weinreich, H., Obendorf, H., Herder, E., & Mayer, M. (2006). Off the beaten tracks: Exploring three aspects of web navigation. In *Proceedings of WWW 2006*. Edinburgh, UK: ACM Press.

Weinreich, H., Obendorf, H., Herder, E., & Mayer, M. (2008). Not quite the average: An empirical study of web use. *ACM Transactions on the Web*, *2*(1), 5.1-5.31.

Wright, F. L. (1971). *The natural house*. London, UK: Pitman.

ADDITIONAL READING

Adar, E., Teevan, J., & Dumais, S. T. (2008). Large scale analysis of web revisitation patterns. In *Proceedings of CHI 2008: Web Visits in the Long*. Florence, Italy: ACM Press.

Amershi, S., & Morris, M. R. (2008). CoSearch: A system for co-located collaborative web search. In *Proceedings of CHI 2008 Collaboration and Cooperation*. Florence, Italy: ACM Press.

Blanc-Brude, T., & Scapin, D. L. (2007). What do people recall about their documents? Implications for desktop search tools. In *Proceedings of Intelligent User Interfaces 2007*. Honolulu, HI: ACM Press.

Bruce, H., Jones, R., & Dumais, S. T. (2004). Keeping and re-finding information on the Web: What do people do and what do they need. In *Proceedings of ASIST 2004*. ASIST.

Cockburn, A., & Greenberg, S. (2000). Issues of page representation and organisation in web browser's revisitation tools. *Australian Journal of Information Systems*, 7, 120–127.

Cockburn, A., Greenberg, S., Jones, S., McKenzie, B., & Moyle, M. (2003). Improving web page revisitation: Analysis, design, and evaluation. *Information Technology and Society*, 3(1), 159–183.

Cockburn, A., McKenzie, B., & Jason-Smith, M. (2002). Pushing back: Evaluating a new behaviour for the back and forward buttons in web browsers. *International Journal of Human-Computer Studies*, 57(5), 397–414. doi:10.1006/ijhc.2002.1025

Dumais, S. T., Cutrell, E., Cadiz, J. J., Jancke, G., Sarin, R., & Robbins, D. C. (2003). Stuff I've seen: A system for personal information retrieval and re-use. In *Proceedings of SIGIR 2003*. Toronto, Canada: ACM Press.

Dziadosz, S., & Chandrasekar, R. (2002). Do thumbnail previews help users make better relevance decisions about web search results? In *Proceedings of SIGIR 2002*. Tampere, Finland: ACM Press.

Jones, R., Bruce, H., & Dumais, S. T. (2003). How do people get back to information on the web? How can they do it better? In *Proceedings of the Ninth IFIP TC13 International Conference on Human-Computer Interaction*. Zürich, Switzerland: IFIP.

Jones, W., Bruce, H., & Dumais, S. T. (2001). Keeping found things found on the web. In *Proceedings of The Tenth International Conference on Information and Knowledge Management (CIKM 2001)*. Atlanta, GA: ACM Press.

Jones, W., Dumais, S. T., & Bruce, H. (2002). Once found, what then? A study of "keeping" behaviors in the personal use of web information. In *Proceedings of the American Society for Information Science and Technology (ASIST 2002)*. Philadelphia, PA: ASIST.

Kaasten, S., & Greenberg, S. (2000). Designing an integrated bookmark / history system for web browsing. In *Proceedings of the Western Computer Graphics Symposium 2000*. Panorama Mountain Village, Canada: Western Computer Graphics.

Karlson, A. K., Robertson, G., Robbins, D. C., Czerwinski, M., & Smith, G. (2006). FaThumb: A facet-based interface for mobile search. In *Proceedings of CHI 2006: Search & Navigation: Mobile & Audio*. Montreal, Canada: ACM Press.

Kawase, R., Papadakis, G., Herder, E., & Nejdl, W. (2011). Beyond the usual suspects: Context-aware revisitation support. In *Proceedings of the 22nd ACM Conference on Hypertext and Hypermedia*. Eindhoven, The Netherlands: ACM Press.

Kulkarni, C., Raju, S., & Udupa, S. (2010). Memento: Unifying content and context to aid webpage re-visitation. In *Proceedings of the 23rd ACM UIST Symposium on User Interface Software and Technology*. New York, NY: ACM Press.

Kumar, C., Norris, J. B., & Sun, Y. (2009). Location and time do matter: A long tail study of website requests. *Decision Support Systems*, 47, 500–507. doi:10.1016/j.dss.2009.04.015

Langville, A. N., & Meyer, C. D. (2006). *Google's PageRank and beyond: The science of search engine rankings*. Princeton, NJ: Princeton University Press.

LeeTiernan. S., Farnham, S., & Cheng, L. (2003). Two methods for auto-organizing personal web history. In *Proceedings of CHI 2003: Extended Abstracts on Human Factors in Computing Systems*. Ft. Lauderdale, FL: ACM Press.

Morris, D., Morris, M. R., & Venolia, G. (2008). SearchBar: A search-centric web history for task resumption and information re-finding. In *Proceedings of the 2008 Conference on Human Factors in Computing Systems, CHI 2008*. Florence, Italy: ACM Press.

Obendorf, H., Weinreich, H., Herder, E., & Mayer, M. (2007). Web page revisitation revisited: Implications of a long-term click-stream study of browser usage. In *Proceedings of CHI 2007*. San Jose, CA: ACM Press.

Ruddle, R. A. (2009). How do people find information on a familiar website? In *Proceedings of the 23rd BCS Conference on Human-Computer Interaction (HCI 2009)*. Cambridge, UK: British Computer Society.

Teevan, J., Cutrell, E., Fisher, D., Drucker, S. M., Ramos, G., Andre, P., & Hu, C. (2009). Visual snippets: Summarizing web pages for search and revisitation. In *Proceedings of CHI 2009*. Boston, MA: ACM Press.

Zhang, L., Chen, L., Jing, F., Deng, K., & Ma, W.-Y. (2006). EnjoyPhoto - A vertical image search engine for enjoying high-quality photos. In *Proceedings of MM 2006*. Santa Barbara, CA: MM.

KEY TERMS AND DEFINITIONS

Revisitation: To visit a web page again, that you have previously visited.

Bookmark: A locally stored Uniform Resource Identifier (URI); also called Favorites or an internet shortcut.

History: The History function is a tracker for recent browsing history to allow quick and easy re-navigation or documentation of sites visited.

GUI: A Graphical User Interface is a type of user interface to allow users to interact with electronic devices with images rather than text commands.

Web Browser: This is a software application for retrieving, presenting and traversing information resources on the WWW.

Metaphor: This is a literary figure of speech that uses an image, story or tangible thing to represent a less tangible thing or some intangible quality or idea.

Color: Is the visual perceptual property corresponding in humans to the categories called red, blue, green or others.

Chapter 4
MobiGaze:
Gaze Interface for Mobile Devices

Takashi Nagamatsu
Kobe University, Japan

Michiya Yamamoto
Kwansei Gakuin University, Japan

Hiroshi Sato
Kwansei Gakuin University, Japan

ABSTRACT

Today, touch-screen-based handheld mobile devices are widely used; however, they are awkward to use with one hand. We propose MobiGaze, which is a user interface that uses one's gaze to operate a handheld mobile device. By using MobiGaze, one can target the entire display area easily, even when the device is quite large. Moreover, MobiGaze can use both gaze and touch interactions. The combination of gaze and touch becomes a novel interaction paradigm. A gaze-and-touch interface effectively avoids the Midas-touch problem. The authors adopted a gaze-tracking method that uses a stereo camera to develop MobiGaze, because the user's line of sight is detected in 3D. This allows the user to move the handheld mobile device freely. They constructed a prototype MobiGaze system, which consists of two cameras with IR-LEDs, a Windows-based notebook PC, and iPod touches. The authors evaluated the accuracy in a laboratory experiment and developed several applications for MobiGaze.

INTRODUCTION

Today, handheld mobile devices that have a touch screen are used widely; users can interact with these devices intuitively.

When using a mobile device, the user holds the device in one hand and touches the screen using the other hand. However, when the user is holding something or has one hand occupied with something else, the device is difficult to control with the single available hand. In this common circumstance, most users touch the screen using their thumb, as shown in Figure 1. It is difficult, however, to touch the entire area of the display with one's thumb; when one touches the top area of the screen, the device becomes unstable

DOI: 10.4018/978-1-4666-1628-8.ch004

Figure 1. Difficulty of usage of mobile touch screen device with one hand

Area that is difficult to touch

Area that thumb reaches easily

Thumb occludes the screen

and there is a possibility that the user will drop the device. Moreover, as the displays on devices become increasingly larger (e.g., iPad), one-hand control becomes even more difficult. In addition, the thumb blocks a large portion of the display; consequently, the user cannot look at the display area under the thumb and has difficulty touching the display accurately (fat finger problem).

To solve these problems, we propose the use of a gaze-tracking technique in mobile devices. Gaze tracking can be used as a means of pointing in a mobile device, and it does not require the use of both hands and eliminates the problem of blocking of the screen. If a mobile device features a gaze-tracking function for pointing, the user could just gaze at the object and touch it with his/her thumb anywhere on the screen to activate the selected object. Moreover, pointing with one's gaze is quicker than using a track ball or pointing stick, and the technique can be easily learned.

There are several types of gaze tracking technologies such as search coil, Electro-Oculogram (EOG), infrared corneal limbus tracker, and camera-based system. The search coil is a coil embedded in a scleral contact lens. The EOG uses electrodes that are placed on the skin around an eye. The infrared corneal limbus tracker uses infrared LEDs and photodiodes mounted on a kind of glasses. The camera-based system uses a video camera and can be divided into two categories: head-mounted and remote. Because a head-mounted gaze tracker (EOG, infrared corneal limbus tracker, and head-mounted type camera-based system) is not suitable for everyday life, we concentrate on developing a remote-type camera-based gaze tracker for a mobile device.

There are a number of technical problems associated with the introduction of gaze-tracking technology to a mobile device. Because a mobile device is small, the measurements made by a gaze-tracking system require a high degree of accuracy to indicate objects on a small screen. Moreover, the user moves the hand that holds the mobile device. Because the camera is attached to the mobile device, this hand movement causes quick changes in the direction that the camera is pointing. A successful gaze-tracking method must allow free hand movement while still providing the requisite accuracy.

In this chapter, we present a user interface that uses one's gaze (gaze interface) for a mobile device (MobiGaze). We describe a gaze-tracking method that we adopted and the implementation of our current prototypes. MobiGaze controls a mobile device not only by gaze but also by a combination of gaze and touch, which is a new interaction technique. We describe the benefits of gaze-and-touch interaction. Using gaze-and-touch interaction, we developed some applications for this new interaction device.

RELATED WORKS

Several studies have sought to detect the Point Of Gaze (POG) on the display of mobile devices.

Lukander constructed a system that makes it possible to measure the POG on the screen surface of a handheld mobile device (Lukander, 2006). Lukander's system used a commercial head-mounted eye tracker and a magnetic positional tracker.

Drewes et al. investigated how gaze interaction can be used to control applications on handheld devices (Drewes, Luca, & Schmidt, 2007). They used a commercial tabletop eye tracker in combination with a mobile phone attached to a screen.

Tobii provided an eye-tracking testing solution for a mobile device (Tobii, 2011). However, this is a tabletop-type solution, so it is useful only in a laboratory.

Miluzzo et al. presented EyePhone, which tracks the user's eye movement across the phone's display by using the camera mounted on the front of the phone and by employing a machine learning algorithm (Miluzzo, Wang, & Campbell, 2010). Although Miluzzo et al. proposed eye-tracking technology that uses the front camera of a mobile phone, the system is limited to distinguishing nine areas of the display.

Bulling et al. investigated mobile eye-based human-computer interaction (Bulling, 2010). In their paper, they indicated that efforts to implement eye tracking on a mobile device are just beginning.

Thus far, there has been no gaze-tracking system that delivers high resolution, is handheld, and has no need for headgear.

GAZE-AND-TOUCH INTERACTION ON MOBILE DEVICE

As shown in Figure 2, when a user holds a mobile device with one hand, the area that he/she can easily touch is only the small gray area near the thumb.

Gaze tracking enables us to point anywhere on the screen easily. Gaze tracking can be used with other means of interaction. We propose a novel interaction technique, which employs gaze-and-touch interaction.

Gaze-and-touch interaction has many possibilities. Although the user can typically touch the entire area of the touch screen on a mobile phone with one's thumb, they cannot touch the entire area of the display when they are using a larger device, such as an iPad. By using MobiGaze, the user moves the cursor with their eye and selects an object by touching somewhere on the screen.

Figure 2. Gaze-and-touch interface allows new interaction

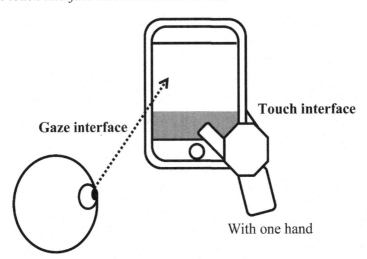

Looked at from another perspective, gaze interfaces encounter a common problem known as the Midas-touch problem; i.e., "everywhere you look, another command is activated; you cannot look anywhere without issuing a command" (Jacob, 1991). A gaze-and-touch interface easily avoids the notorious Midas-touch problem by using a combination of both gaze and touch.

The user's action is not limited to a simple touch; they can also perform a swiping action, etc. Therefore, various interactions will be considered.

In this way, the quick and easy interaction of the gaze interface and the familiar touch interface are effectively combined.

ESTIMATION OF POINT OF GAZE

A method that successfully realizes gaze tracking on a mobile device must allow free movement of the hand. Furthermore, because the display size of a mobile device is very small, the gaze estimation method for a mobile device needs high accuracy.

Gaze-tracking methods that use a stereo camera (Guestrin & Eizenman, 2006; Nagamatsu, Iwamoto, Kamahara, Tanaka, & Yamamoto, 2010; Nagamatsu, Kamahara, & Tanaka, 2008; Shih & Liu, 2004; Villanueva & Cabeza, 2008) are accurate and allow head-free movement. These methods can estimate the optical axis of the eye in 3D with high accuracy by one-point calibration.

To estimate a gaze accurately and allow the user to move the mobile device held in his/her hand, we adopted Nagamatsu's method (Nagamatsu, et al., 2010). This method allows one to measure the position of the center of the cornea and the vector along the line of sight relative to the two cameras that are employed. Nagamatsu's method models the eye, including the boundary region of the cornea, so the estimation accuracy is higher than a method that uses a spherical model of the cornea (Guestrin & Eizenman, 2006; Nagamatsu, et al., 2008; Shih & Liu, 2004; Villanueva & Cabeza, 2008) when the user gazes at areas far

apart from the cameras. Moreover, the method uses an integrated camera with light sources, so the arrangement of cameras is more flexible than other stereo camera methods (Guestrin & Eizenman, 2006; Nagamatsu, et al., 2008; Shih & Liu, 2004; Villanueva & Cabeza, 2008), as described in Yamamoto, Nagamatsu, and Watanabe (2010). The probability that the user's hand interferes with the cameras and light sources is low.

Next, we briefly explain the method using a corneal model of the surface of revolution about the optical axis that is described in Nagamatsu et al. (2010). Figure 3 shows a cross section of the eyeball. The geometric center line of the eye is called the optical axis. $\mathbf{A}$ is the center of the corneal curvature. $\mathbf{L}_j$ and $\mathbf{C}_j$ denote the position of the light source j and the nodal point of camera j, respectively; $\mathbf{C}_j$ is assumed to be the same as $\mathbf{L}_j$. The value of $\mathbf{C}_j (= \mathbf{L}_j)$ is determined by calibrating the camera beforehand.

A ray originating from the center of the pupil, $\mathbf{B}$, gets refracted at point $\mathbf{B}''_j$; passes through the nodal point of camera j, $\mathbf{C}_j$; and intersects the camera image plane at point $\mathbf{B}'_j$.

A ray from $\mathbf{L}_j$ is reflected at point $\mathbf{P}_j$ on the corneal surface, back along its incident path. It passes through $\mathbf{C}_j$ and intersects the camera image plane at point $\mathbf{P}'_j$. If the cornea is perfectly spherical, the line connecting $\mathbf{L}_j$ and $\mathbf{P}_j$ would pass through $\mathbf{A}$, and $\mathbf{A}$ can be determined using the two cameras. However, the position of $\mathbf{A}$ cannot be estimated accurately when light is reflected from an aspherical surface of the eye.

Because we use the model of a surface of revolution about the optical axis of the eye, the ray from $\mathbf{L}_j$ is reflected from the surface of the eye back in the plane that includes the optical axis of the eye. Therefore, $\mathbf{A}$, $\mathbf{B}$, $\mathbf{B}'_j$, $\mathbf{B}''_j$, $\mathbf{C}_j$, $\mathbf{L}_j$, $\mathbf{P}_j$, $\mathbf{P}'_j$, and the optical axis of the eye are coplanar. The normal vector of the plane is

$$\left(\mathbf{C}_j - \mathbf{B}'_j\right) \times \left(\mathbf{P}'_j - \mathbf{C}_j\right),$$

Figure 3. Cross section of eyeball showing center of corneal curvature, along with center of pupil, position of light source, and nodal point of camera

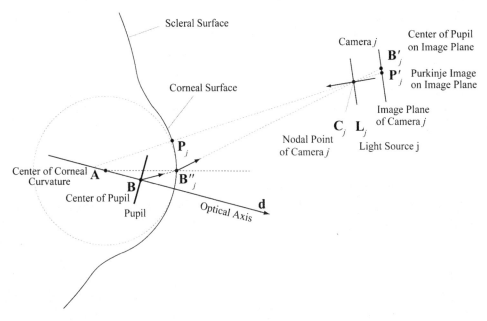

and the plane is expressed as:

$$\left\{\left(\mathbf{C}_j - \mathbf{B}'_j\right) \times \left(\mathbf{P}'_j - \mathbf{C}_j\right)\right\} \cdot \left(\mathbf{X} - \mathbf{C}_j\right) = 0,$$

where $\mathbf{X}$ (= $(x, y, z)^T$) is a point on the plane. We obtain two planes when we use two cameras (j = 0, 1). The optical axis of the eye can be determined from the intersection of the two planes, which must not be coplanar.

The line of sight connecting the fovea and the POG is called the visual axis of the eye. The user calibration that determines the offset between the optical and visual axes is performed using the one-point calibration method described in Nagamatsu et al. (2008).

HARDWARE IMPLEMENTATION

Because current mobile devices do not have two cameras or the power to process the eye image, we constructed a prototype system using a Windows-based notebook PC for image processing. Figure 4 shows the system configuration at this time. We developed two kinds of prototype systems: a single screen type and dual screen type. Most tabletop gaze-tracking systems are usually put under the display. Because they have cameras and Infrared LEDs (IR-LEDs) under their displays, the hand may hide the camera or LED when a person touches the display. Therefore, it is suitable to use a mobile device that the user touches where the cameras and IR-LEDs are located on the upper side of the display.

Single Screen Type

As shown in Figure 4a, the single screen system consists of two synchronized monochrome IEEE-1394 digital cameras (Firefly MV, Point Grey Research Inc.), a mobile device (iPod touch, Apple Inc.), and a Windows-based notebook PC (Windows XP, Intel Core 2 Duo T7500 2.2GHz). The two cameras and the mobile device are connected to the notebook PC via IEEE 1394 and a wireless

Figure 4. System configuration and prototype of the system

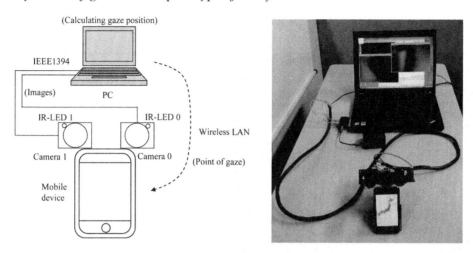

(a) Single screen type prototype

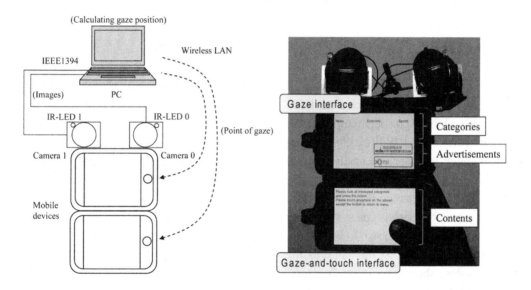

(b) Dual screen type prototype

LAN, respectively. Each camera is equipped with a 1/3″ CMOS image sensor with a resolution of 752 × 480 pixels. A 25-mm lens and an IR filter are attached to each camera. One IR-LED is attached to each camera near the camera's nodal point. These cameras are positioned on the top of the mobile device. The software on the PC was developed using OpenCV 1.0 (Intel). The frame rate for estimating the POG was approximately 10 fps.

Figure 5 depicts the system in operation. The PC captures the eye images via stereo camera, which are processed to detect the centers of the pupil and Purkinje images.

Figure 5. Prototype single screen system

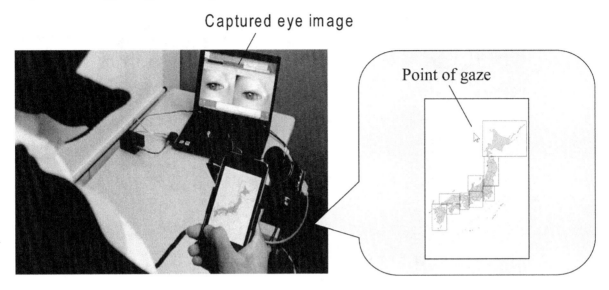

Captured eye image

Point of gaze

Dual Screen Type

Some mobile devices such as the Nintendo DS have a dual display. When using such a dual display device, it is no longer possible to operate the mobile device with one hand. With a gaze-tracking technique, however, the user can easily interact with a dual screen. The same goes for a single large display device such as the iPad.

We have constructed a prototype system for a dual screen device, which is shown in Figure 4b. The system structure is almost the same as the single screen system shown in Figure 4a. Here, when a user swipes the lower screen, the display images in the upper screen and lower screen move in synchronization. In this way, even if the display of a mobile device becomes much larger and the area that the thumb can touch remains small, the user can handle the entire area of the two screens.

Different functions can be assigned to the two screens. For example, the upper screen provides a gaze interaction, and the lower screen provides a gaze-and-touch interaction.

The current prototype system was constructed so that it can be used in a "mobile" scenario by having a notebook PC in a bag, as show in Figure 6.

EVALUATION

We evaluated the accuracy of the prototype system in a laboratory with 3 adult participants (3 men) who did not wear glasses or contact lenses. The ages of the participants range from 21 to 22.

The proposed gaze estimation method mathematically allows the user to move; however, the current implementation cannot capture the user's eyes in a large area. Therefore, to measure the performance of the gaze estimation method while

Figure 6. The current prototype system is "mobile"

Figure 7. Experimental setup and the result for 3 participants

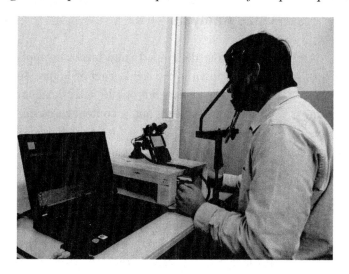

(a) Experimental setup

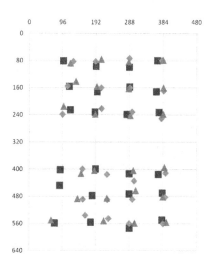

(b) Results

avoiding the errors caused by head movement, the head was supported by a chin rest to prevent it from being out of the focus/field of view of the cameras in this experiment.

Figure 7a shows the experimental setup. The eyes were approximately 300 mm from the displays. The participants were asked to fixate on 24 points that appeared sequentially on the displays. The procedure of the experiment was as follows:

1. The experimenter displayed one fiducial point using the keyboard.
2. The experimenter asked the participant to fixate on the fiducial point.
3. The experimenter checked the image processing result using the 14.1″ display on the notebook PC. If there was a problem with the image processing, the experimenter adjusted the thresholds of binarization.
4. The experimenter pressed the keyboard to start recording the POG. The data recording continued until 10 data points were obtained. If the experimenter found that the participant blinked or looked somewhere else, the experimenter repeated recording of the data.
5. The experimenter displayed another fiducial point using the keyboard.
6. The experiment was finished when data for 24 fiducial points were recorded.

Figure 7b shows the experimental results of the 3 participants. The cross points of the grids represent the fiducial points that were intentionally gazed at by the participants. The view angles between grid points are approximately 3.81° horizontally and 3.43° vertically. The triangle-, square-, and diamond-shaped points indicate the average POGs of the participants. The results of the upper screen were good; however, the lower screen was not so good, because the participant's eyelash or eyelid interfered with detection of the position of the center of the pupil and the first Purkinje image in the image processing.

APPLICATION EXAMPLE

Map Browser

We developed a map browser as an example application for MobiGaze. Figures 8A-C show a situation where the user uses a map browser. In Figure 8A, the display shows a map that indicates the islands of Japan. When a user gazes at a region (Figure 8A) and touches the screen, a detailed map is displayed (Figure 8B). Ultimately, the user can obtain a close-up map (Figure 8C). Figures 8A-E show detailed display images of the map browser. This map browser also works on a dual screen device.

Novel Browsing Application with Gaze Analysis

We have also developed a new browsing application, as shown in the right panel of Figure 4b. It provides on-screen buttons to select categories on the upper screen, and a contents area on the lower screen.

First, a user gazes at a category and then taps anywhere on the lower screen. One of the categories is selected and its content is displayed on the lower screen. The user can proceed to read by employing a swiping gesture.

Banner ads are also found on the upper screen. By analyzing the user's gaze, the banner ads can be displayed near the user's gaze, chasing it slowly, but the banner ads avoid being placed over the on-screen button. Because the banner adds movement is slow, the user can look at the banner and select by gaze and touch. Furthermore, the banner ads that

Figure 8. Map browser and its display images

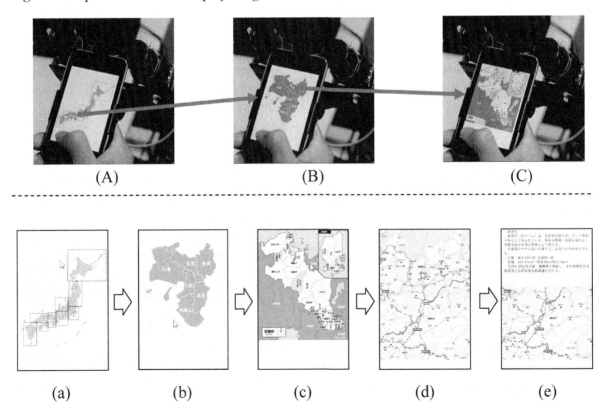

(A)　　　　　　　　(B)　　　　　　　　(C)

(a)　　　　　(b)　　　　　(c)　　　　　(d)　　　　　(e)

the user seems to be interested in can be selected on the basis of the history acquired. This can be achieved by just looking at banners, rather than by intentionally selecting the intended banners.

DISCUSSION

Because mobile devices are small, the usability of MobiGaze depends on its accuracy of measurement. Generally, the accuracy of a gaze tracker is 0.5–1.0°, because "a user generally need not position his eye more accurately than the width of the fovea (about one degree) to see an object sharply" (Jacob, 1991). This represents the limitation of the accuracy of gaze measurement. However, if the user can move the mobile device closer to his/her face, the accuracy of measurement in the view angle remains the same, but the accuracy of measurement in the screen coordinate system, in pixels, improves. Therefore, although the current implementation allows the user only limited movement, MobiGaze can realize a high and effective resolution in the future.

Because it is expected that in the near future, mobile devices will have sufficient power and will be equipped with stereo cameras, gaze tracking will be able to be integrated directly into mobile devices.

As with an ordinary gaze-tracking system, not everyone finds the current implementation of MobiGaze easy to use, and some people cannot use it. However, individuals can choose whether or not to adopt this technology because mobile devices are for personal use.

In another application, if an E-book reader is equipped with gaze-tracking technology, the history of an individual's reading can be recorded and the data can be used to estimate important parts for the reader and to abstract the contents.

Therefore, MobiGaze will expand the potentiality of mobile devices. Our future work in the development of MobiGaze will not only focus on improving the performance of its gaze measurement, but also on seeking possible applications to various fields.

CONCLUSION

In this chapter, we have proposed MobiGaze, which is a gaze interface for handheld mobile devices. With the use of stereo cameras, a user's line of sight is detected in 3D, which enables the user to interact with a mobile device by means of his/her gaze. We have constructed a prototype system of MobiGaze, which consists of two cameras with IR-LEDs, a Windows-based notebook PC, and iPod touches. We have also developed several applications for MobiGaze that take advantage of its gaze-and-touch interface. We believe that gaze-tracking technology will be widely used in mobile devices in the near future.

ACKNOWLEDGMENT

This work was partially supported by KAKENHI (23300047).

REFERENCES

Bulling, A. (2010). Toward mobile eye-based human-computer interaction. *IEEE Pervasive Computing / IEEE Computer Society and IEEE Communications Society, 9*, 8–12. doi:10.1109/MPRV.2010.86

Drewes, H., Luca, A. D., & Schmidt, A. (2007). Eye-gaze interaction for mobile phones. In *Proceedings of the 4th International Conference on Mobile Technology, Applications, and Systems*, (pp. 364-371). IEEE.

Guestrin, E. D., & Eizenman, M. (2006). General theory of remote gaze estimation using the pupil center and corneal reflections. *IEEE Transactions on Bio-Medical Engineering*, *53*(6), 1124–1133. doi:10.1109/TBME.2005.863952

Intel. (2011). *Open source computer vision library*. Retrieved from http://www.intel.com/technology/computing/opencv/index.htm.

Jacob, R. J. K. (1991). The use of eye movements in human-computer interaction techniques: What you look at is what you get. *ACM Transactions on Information Systems*, *9*(2), 152–169. doi:10.1145/123078.128728

Lukander, K. (2006). A system for tracking gaze on handheld devices. *Behavior Research Methods*, *38*(4), 660–666. doi:10.3758/BF03193899

Miluzzo, E., Wang, T., & Campbell, A. T. (2010). EyePhone: Activating mobile phones with your eyes. In *Proceedings of the 2nd ACM SIGCOMM Workshop on Networking, Systems, and Applications on Mobile Handhelds*, (pp. 15-20). ACM Press.

Nagamatsu, T., Iwamoto, Y., Kamahara, J., Tanaka, N., & Yamamoto, M. (2010). Gaze estimation method based on an aspherical model of the cornea: Surface of revolution about the optical axis of the eye. In *Proceedings of the 2010 Symposium on Eye Tracking Research & Applications*, (pp. 255-258). IEEE.

Nagamatsu, T., Kamahara, J., & Tanaka, N. (2008). 3D gaze tracking with easy calibration using stereo cameras for robot and human communication. In *Proceedings of the 17th International Symposium on Robot and Human Interactive Communication (IEEE RO-MAN 2008)*, (pp. 59-64). IEEE Press.

Shih, S.-W., & Liu, J. (2004). A novel approach to 3-D gaze tracking using stereo cameras. *IEEE Transactions on Systems, Man, and Cybernetics. Part B*, *34*(1), 234–245.

Tobii. (2011). *Tobii mobile device stand*. Retrieved from http://www.tobii.com/en/analysis-and-research/global/products/hardware-accessories/tobii-mobile-device-stand/.

Villanueva, A., & Cabeza, R. (2008). A novel gaze estimation system with one calibration point. *IEEE Transactions on Systems, Man, and Cybernetics. Part B*, *38*(4), 1123–1138.

KEY TERMS AND DEFINITIONS

Cornea: The transparent outer surface of the eye.

Gaze interface: A user interface that uses one's gaze to operate a machine or computer.

Gaze tracking/eye tracking: Procedure to estimate where the user gazes.

iPod touch: A portable information device produced by Apple Inc.

iPad: A tablet computer produced by Apple Inc.

Midas-touch problem: A common problem with gaze interfaces, where the user cannot look anywhere without issuing a command when the user controls a computer with their gaze. It results from the fact that the gaze alone cannot be used to separate activation from pointing.

POG: The point of gaze, which is the point that the user gazes at.

Purkinje image: Reflections of objects from the structure of the eye. In particular, the first Purkinje image indicates the reflection of objects from the outer surface of the cornea.

Section 2
Visual Representations of Images and Graphics

Chapter 5

Evaluating Visualisations and Automatic Warning Cues for Visual Search in Vascular Images

Boris W. van Schooten
University of Twente, The Netherlands

Betsy M. A. G. van Dijk
University of Twente, The Netherlands

Avan Suinesiaputra
University of Auckland, New Zealand

Anton Nijholt
University of Twente, The Netherlands

Johan H. C. Reiber
Leiden University Medical Center, The Netherlands

ABSTRACT

Visual search is a task that is performed in various application domains. The authors examine it in the domain of radiological analysis of 3D vascular images. They compare several major visualisations used in this domain, and study the possible benefits of automatic warning systems that highlight the sections that may contain visual targets and hence require the user's attention. With help of a literature study, the authors present some theory about what result can be expected given the accuracy of a particular visual cue. They present the results of two experiments, in which they find that the Curved Planar Reformation visualisation, which presents a cross-section based on knowledge about the position of the blood vessel, is significantly more efficient than regular 3D visualisations, and that automatic warning systems that produce false alarms could work if they do not miss targets.

DOI: 10.4018/978-1-4666-1628-8.ch005

INTRODUCTION

The main goal of this chapter is to study visual search tasks in the medical (vascular radiology) domain from a cognitive perspective. In the medical domain, cognitive studies are generally rare. Cognitive aspects of clinical processes are generally not the main focus, and most studies are clinical studies, only studying general clinical outcome of a process as a whole. We also found that knowledge from other domains and generic experiments does not transfer well because of difference in assumptions between the different domains of study. We study the visualisations by introducing the concept of target detection cues. These are visual cues that represent visual targets with a certain probability. This concept is used to examine both regular visualisations (where target detection cues are implicit in the nature of the visualisation) and warning cues generated by automatic target detection systems (where the cues are explicitly added). This enables us to compare research on target detection cues in different domains, and identify some important experimental variables.

One important aspect of target detection cues is their accuracy. Erroneous cues may be either false positives (a cue is visible but there is no target) and false negatives (no cue is visible when there is a target). We find that the error rate and the type of error is important for the effectiveness of a visualisation. Besides a study of the literature, we discuss two of our experiments, which we conducted for visual search tasks in the 3D vascular radiology domain. We conclude with some recommendations for vascular radiology visualisation and visual search tasks in general.

The visualisations in our domain are based on 3D imaging data. 3D images are significantly more complex to navigate than 2D images. In our domain, we were able to simplify navigation by restricting it to movement along a blood vessel. This is a choice that proved to work well in previous research. Other, more minor, choices in 3D navigation are also examined. We also conclude with some recommendations for 3D navigation.

BACKGROUND

In the following sections, we examine visual search in the area of medical imaging, more specifically, 3D vascular imaging. Vascular disease diagnosis can be done effectively by means of 3D imaging techniques such as Magnetic Resonance Angiography (MRA) and Computed Tomography Angiography (CTA). The most common vascular diseases that these imaging techniques help diagnose are stenoses (abnormal narrowings in blood vessels) and aneurysms (abnormal widening or ballooning of blood vessels). We focus on Contrast Enhanced MRA as this is the area of our current research (Suinesiaputra, et al., 2009). CE-MRA involves injection of a contrast agent in the blood stream, making the relevant blood vessels show up as high-density areas on the MRA scan. The output of CE-MRA is a 3D density field (typically around 128x128x128 pixels), with higher densities representing blood flow.

With help of 3D imaging techniques, the thickness of the inside of the vessel (the vessel lumen) can be determined precisely, and assessed quantitatively. This is a very attractive tool in diagnosis. Determination of the vessel lumen is called segmentation. It results in a 3D (usually tubular) surface representing the vessel lumen circumference. Since manual segmentation is time-consuming, automatic segmentation is proposed (Boskamp, et al., 2004; Suinesiaputra, et al., 2009). Automatic segmentation typically first constructs a pathline, which is a line that goes through the lumen of the vessel to be segmented (Boskamp, et al., 2004). From the pathline, a triangle mesh is constructed indicating the lumen. The pathline is also useful as a basis for "intelligent" visualisations.

In automatic segmentation, occasional errors are currently inevitable. Therefore, clinicians have to detect (and correct) errors in the automatic segmentations by means of visual search. This visual search task is the task that we examine in this chapter.

A number of visualisations have been developed specifically for visualising 3D vascular image data (see van Schooten, et al., 2009 for an overview). However, there exists little in the way of either clinical or cognitive studies that compare these visualisations. We examine three visualisations: Direct Volume Rendering (DVR) (Mueller, et al., 2005), isosurface rendering (Preim & Oeltze, 2007), and Curved Planar Reformation (CPR) (Kanitsar, 2004). DVR and isosurface are more generally used in medical visualisation, while CPR is an "intelligent" visualisation specific to vascular imaging, which makes use of the pathline to create a curved cross-section following the vessel. Later we discuss the visualisations.

Additionally, we wish to examine the potential for automatic warning cues. This involves visually highlighting areas, which have a higher probability of containing a target, and warrant closer attention by the searcher. We will call this target highlighting or suspicious area highlighting. The areas to highlight are determined by a separate algorithm, or, in our domain, can be based on uncertainty information from the segmentation algorithm itself. For example in model-based segmentation, low conformance to the model indicates low-credibility areas (Levy, et al., 2007). The errors made by a target highlighting system can be classified as either false positives (false alarm: a highlight is displayed but no target is located there) or false negatives (missed targets). Especially the absence of false negatives is often seen as a prerequisite for their medical applicability. Some of the underlying cognitive theory is explained later. The proportion of correctly identified positives is called sensitivity, while the proportion of correctly identified negatives is called specificity. In many cases, an algorithm parameter α can trade off sensitivity for specificity. In the areas of colonoscopy and mammography, some target highlighting systems manage to reach near 100% sensitivity (i.e. no false negatives) while minimising false positives to an acceptable level (i.e. not needing to mark a substantial part of the image) (Hong, et al., 2006; López-Aligué, et al., 2004). Others only manage 85%-90% sensitivity (Wang, et al., 2007) or less.

Cognitive Studies

We can bring together regular visualisations and visual highlighting systems by considering that both produce *error detection cues*, distinct visual cues that show that there is a potential error in the segmentation. A task of the searcher is to find these cues and determine if they correspond to targets. For visual highlighting systems, cues are *explicit*, that is, they are shown by explicitly defined signs. For regular visualisations, cues are *implicit*, showing them through particular visual configurations, which are an indirect result of the visualisation used. All error detection cues have a particular level of sensitivity and specificity.

The presence of errors in warning systems in general (for both visual search tasks and other tasks) are known to cause problems for users, such as over- or under-reliance. While various studies have been made, experimental variables vary widely among different application areas: the presence or absence of a moving scene or navigation, the prevalence of false positives or negatives, whether the search is self-terminating or not (that is, whether the search ends when the target is found), task difficulty (examined in Maltz & Shinar, 2003), target rarity (Fleck & Mitroff, 2007), the level of information about the system given to the users, and of course the task itself, which varies widely in nature. While some of these variables have been examined, most have not, and we can expect different applications to have quite different outcomes. These are too many variables to examine all at once, and the research coverage remains as yet spotty. Examining different application areas is still a very meaningful exercise.

For our domain, search is non-self-terminating, and the users normally have a high degree of knowledge about the system they are using. Additionally, navigation is required to examine all data properly, which may include translation, rotation, and zooming in 3D. In fact, it is normal practice to examine a blood vessel serially along the length of the vessel.

Assuming a simple cognitive processing model, the absence of false negatives can be expected to yield the best performance because it reduces the search space to only those parts highlighted by the highlighting system. Since we expect search to be serial, this will increase search speed. There are some caveats, though. In some studies, users were not found to conform to similar models. Also, users may make more errors due to visual confusion due to the highlights. It is also interesting to see if a performance improvement can be achieved with less than 100% sensitivity.

Studies of generic self-terminating target finding tasks with target highlighting found that imperfect highlighting often increased rather than decreased overall user response time, due to increase in response time for the cases where the wrong target was highlighted (Fisher & Tan, 1989; Tamborello & Byrne, 2007). This increase is found to be suboptimal w.r.t. a naive cognitive processing model. For some non-self-terminating tasks, users were also found to spend more time double-checking the data in case of false positives, resulting in increased overall response times in the presence of warnings (Dixon, et al., 2007). Overall, user performance is found to be suboptimal, even when users have a good estimate of the system's reliability (Ezer, et al., 2008; Rice, 2009).

Another theory considers focused attention (attention localised to a particular visual area) versus integrative attention (attention necessary to combine different visual elements in different locations). Wickens and Andre (1990) found that distinction of visual elements by highlighting helps focused attention but hinders integrative attention. A similar detrimental effect is called *attention tun-*

neling, which means the highlights distract the user from seeing other elements in the scene. Yeh and Wickens (2001) found that, even if highlighting of one target served to predict with 100% accuracy a target in the vicinity rather than the highlighted target itself, performance worsened.

Studies on the reliance (or trust) of users on (visual and non-visual) automatic warnings as related to the failure rate of the warning system has been studied fairly extensively. One common finding is that false positives are more damaging to trust and hence performance than false negatives (Maltz & Shinar, 2003). Maltz and Shinar (2003) also finds that target cueing works best if the targets are otherwise very difficult to detect.

None of these studies were conducted in the medical domain. One of the rare medical studies in this area, done by Freer and Ulissey (2001), seems to contradict some of these findings. It indicates a positive effect on clinical outcome in a mammogram-reading study with as much as 97.4% false positives. This involves using mammograms (2D X-ray images of the breast) to screen for early signs of breast cancer. Freer et al. use a double-reading scheme, taken from medical practice, but used by none of the other studies. This scheme involves first examining each mammogram as a plain image, and then examining it with the visual highlights shown. This reduces any possible effect of attention tunneling. Additionally Freer et al.'s task is more difficult than most of the other experiments (experts miss 50% or more of targets). This is a good example of a study in one domain that has a different outcome due to differences in (implicitly assumed) experimental variables.

Visualisations

In this section, we will discuss the visualisations used and the theory we used to analyse them. It is our experience that segmentation errors are usually close to visually apparent local density decreases in the MRA. This indicates the most common types of segmentation error: crossing

Figure 1. Density deviation around error areas in real life data. Top: segmentation error in bifurcation. Top left: a bifurcating vessel with separate segmentations for each bifurcation. Top right: cross-sections of the bifurcating vessel, showing that the blue (right side) segmentation follows partially down the wrong vessel. Bottom left: the pathline bypasses a stenotic area in the right bifurcation. Bottom right: segmentation error in tortuous area. The pathline skips part of the vessel's curvature.

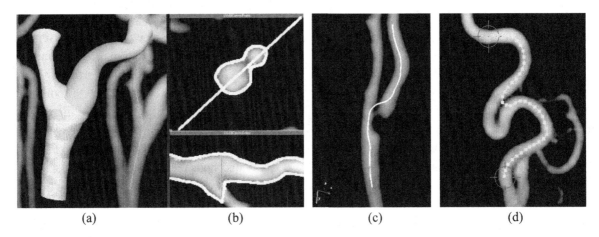

(a)　　　　　(b)　　　　　(c)　　　　　(d)

through vessel boundaries (in cases of high tortuosity or stenosis), and thickness determination problems near bifurcations (a bifurcation is a branching point in a blood vessel). See Figure 1 for examples. If we assume there is always a local density decrease, we can more easily assess the different visualisations. We will call this the *density deviation assumption*. If we do not make this assumption, our assessment depends on the particular segmentation algorithm.

We shall now focus on the three visualisations that we shall evaluate. The visualizations are chosen from a set of "promising" visualisations which were categorised and qualitatively assessed in previous work (van Schooten, et al., 2009) (See Figure 2).

- DVR (Direct Volume Rendering) is a commonly used visualisation (Mueller, et al., 2005). It involves rendering the volume as a semi-transparent 3D object, representing the densities as greyscale values. We visualise the segmentation in DVR by means of a wireframe mesh. DVR will show almost all segmentation errors if inspected closely enough, but only when the model is rotated suitably. Sensitivity and specificity are thus 100%.

- Isosurface (Preim & Oeltze, 2007) renders the data as a solid object, which is relatively easy to interpret visually, enabling clear occlusion cues and shading. It involves converting the greyscale volume to a plain mesh by choosing a density level threshold, which determines what, is "inside" and "outside." This means that information is lost in this visualisation. It has strong error detection cues for the ideal case of a properly chosen density threshold and raw data with relatively uniform density. Then, the segmentation goes outside of the surface boundary where an error occurs. This can be explicitly visualised using occlusion cues, though some camera rotation may be required to see them. This capability has 100% specificity under the density deviation assumption, but less than 100% sensitivity because areas where the segmentation is thinner than required are not marked.

Figure 2. The visualisations used in the experiments. The pictures visualise software phantoms with two types of artificial segmentation errors: veering errors (segmentation veers from vessel) and thickness errors (segmentation and vessel thickness do not match). Top left: DVR with veering error in the center. Top right: DVR with suspicious area highlighting in red; highlighted veering error at top left, highlighted thickness error at bottom right. Bottom left: isosurface with veering error in the middle; the segmentation is marked in blue where it sticks out. Bottom right: CPR with thickness errors at the left and right.

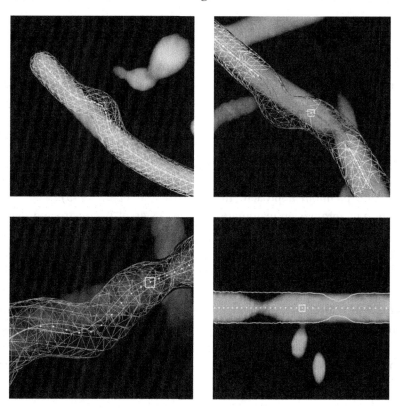

- CPR (Curved Planar Reformation) (Kanitsar, 2004) is a curved cross-section, following a vessel's pathline. This results in useful cross-sectional information along the entire vessel, capable of removing distracting parts of the volume data (Achenbach, et al., 1998). Because our vessels curve in all directions, we use the straightened variant of CPR, where the cross-section is topologically distorted so that the path line becomes a straight line. The intersection of the segmentation with the curved plane is represented as a line. This enables the user to see immediately where the segmentation crosses a lower-density area, in most cases without any rotation. The visual cue is simply the line not following the densest parts of the vessel.

We summarise the visualisations in Table 1. We also included explicit target highlighting in this table for comparison.

EMPIRICAL ANALYSIS

In this section, we summarise and discuss the results of two previously published experiments in the area of vascular visualisation. The first one concerns an evaluation of the three proposed

Table 1. The three visualisations compared to suspicious area highlighting

Name	Type	Sensitivity	Specificity	Requires rotation?	Cue difficulty
DVR	implicit	100%	100%	yes	difficult
CPR	implicit	100%	100%	rarely	difficult
Isosurface	implicit	< 100%	Up to 100%	yes	easy
Target Highl.	implicit	depends	depends	no	easy

visualisations plus a target highlighting system (van Schooten, et al., 2010a). The second one compares target highlighting systems with different α settings (van Schooten, et al., 2010b). In both experiments, our task consists of checking the correctness of automatic segmentations of vessels in MRA scans.

We used a software phantom approach. In medical terminology, a phantom is an inanimate object designed to evaluate imaging devices or techniques. A software phantom is an algorithm that likewise generates a mock imaging result. Our software phantom generates mock MRA data, along with segmentations with artificially generated segmentation errors. This way it is easy to generate dozens of cases with a clear distinction between correct and erroneous, an unambiguous ground truth, and similar difficulty levels. While

software phantoms are as of yet only used in the medical field on an ad-hoc basis, we recommend their use for both visualisation and automatic segmentation studies. We also used similar software phantoms in other work (van Schooten, et al., 2009; van Schooten, et al., 2011), and a similar approach can be found in other research as well (Rolland, et al., 1995).

A vessel is constructed using a sum of sine waves. Three distracter vessels were added in each phantom. Thickness of the vessel was varied in a stylized manner with thinner and thicker areas. When looking at a cross-section, density in the center of the vessel was highest, gradually lowering towards the boundaries of the vessel, and zero outside of the vessel. No noise or other distracters were added, neither were bifurcations present. See Figure 3. Though we have not

Figure 3. Left: real life data (MRA of carotid arteries, the arteries that supply the head and neck with oxygenated blood). Right: typical software phantom.

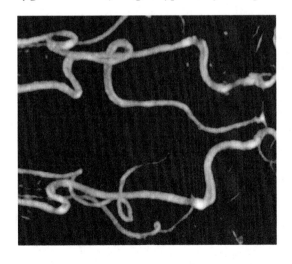
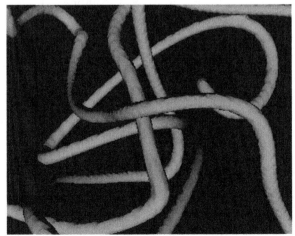

made a thorough quantitative comparison of our phantoms with the real MRA data we use in our segmentation domain, the phantom vessels have similar thickness and curvature as those found in our real data.

Errors are simply defined as a deviation between the segmentation and the densest parts of the volume. Only three error types exist: a veering away of the path line and segmentation from the vessel, the segmentation being thinner than the vessel, and the segmentation being thicker. These are explained to the user as part of an interactive tutorial (See Figure 2).

We generated 6-8 segmentation errors per model, with approximately equal numbers of veering and thickness errors. The number of errors was varied to ensure the search was not self-terminating.

Controls

Control is with the mouse only, and each button is designed to map to a single function as much as possible. We have two essentially different navigation methods, namely CPR (essentially 2D, plus rotation around the vessel axis), and the 3D visualisations.

Controls are an important issue in 3D visualisation, because of the large number of degrees of freedom (Russo Dos Santos, et al., 2000). However, because the path line is almost always in the vicinity of the target vessel, we can navigate by moving along the path line. In another study (van Schooten, et al., 2011), where we compared pathline-based navigation with free 3D navigation, we found that this is a quite effective navigation technique.

In 3D, the camera is always centered around a point on the path line. The user can navigate along the path line by either using the mouse wheel or by clicking on a path line point with the Middle Mouse Button (MMB). The camera is also rotated so that the relative angle of the vessel w.r.t. the viewer remains the same.

In 3D, the model is rotated by moving the mouse while the Right Mouse Button (RMB) is held. A standard "two-axis valuator" method is used (Bade, et al., 2005). A fourth button below the left button (the left side-button or LSMB) was used to rotate around the view axis, by moving the mouse horizontally with the button pressed. In CPR, there is only one rotational degree of freedom. Both the RMB + moving vertical and the LSMB + moving horizontal could be used to rotate around the vessel axis.

The selection of errors is designed to take as little effort as possible; the user's task concentrates only on finding the errors. When the user clicks with the left button (LMB) on a part of the path-line that contains an error, the error is selected. Selections are highlighted in green.

First Experiment: Comparison of the Main Visualisations

Setup. In the first experiment, we wanted users to be able to zoom at will. The camera starts in the middle of the vessel and is zoomed out to provide an overview. We chose to do this so users do not get disoriented. We did ask users to proceed systematically, that is, from end to end. Zooming was performed by moving the mouse vertically with the LSMB pressed.

Besides the three visualisations, we added a fourth condition which is DVR with suspicious area highlighting added. Both false positives and negatives were generated: between 1 and 3 of each in each trial, yielding an average of 25% false positives and negatives.

We used a within-subjects design for the four conditions, which we name:

1. DVR (Direct Volume Rendering)
2. DVRSUS (DVR with suspicious areas highlighted in red)
3. ISOSURF (Isosurface with non-occluded segmentation shown in blue)
4. CPR (Curved Planar Reformation)

The path line was visualised in yellow, the segmentation either as an orange mesh (in 3D) or as an orange line intersecting the CPR plane (in CPR). Each condition was repeated four times. Trials took about 25-80 seconds. All users received the same set of software phantoms in the same order, but with different, randomly ordered and counterbalanced, conditions. The users had to complete 4 trials per condition, totaling 16 trials. This was achieved by cycling through the conditions 4 times, each time in a different order, effectively counterbalancing for learning effects within a single session. Total time for the entire session was about 30-40 minutes. At the end of a trial, time taken and number of errors made was recorded, and shown to the user, before the next trial began. The experiment was concluded with a subjective survey, including questions about the overall quality of the visualisation, and which visualisation elements they prefer (CPR versus 3D; whether to show occlusion cues; whether to show suspicious areas). More details can be found in (van Schooten, et al., 2010a).

Because we used somewhat stylised models, medical laypersons could easily do the task. We recruited 12 participants from the Human Media Interaction department of our CS faculty, invited through personal invitation. The users' ages ranged from 25 to 51 years, with an average of 32, and 2 users above 40. Four users were female.

Results. Overall, there were no real problems with interaction, and the task was successfully performed by all users. Users quickly learned to identify errors with help of the tutorial. Some users kept making mistakes in the controls during the main trial (pressing the wrong buttons), but none of these mistakes were costly in terms of ruining the task performance. Most mistakes could be corrected in a fraction of a second. The error rate (number of errors missed and falsely identified errors) was near zero for almost all users. Users found the graphical render quality good, with all users finding the animation smooth enough, and only 3 users finding some details somewhat hard to see.

We expect time performance data to be multiplicative rather than additive, so to analyse time performance, we transformed the data using the log transform. We used a second transformation to increase sensitivity. It is based on the fact that the sequence of trials was the same for all users. We divided the time for each trial by the overall average of that trial over all users (note that all conditions occurred equally often). This has the effect of normalising for variations in trial difficulty.

We then performed a repeated-measures ANOVA with a Sidak post-hoc analysis. ($F(3,33)=16.384, p<0.0005$). We found that CPR was by far the fastest ($p=0.008$). This seems to be attributable to the fact that users could see all errors without needing to rotate. However, differences between the other visualisations were not significant. The averages were also very close to each other (see Table 2).

Because of the difficulty of the task, we may expect learning effects to occur during the experiment. If we look at the progress over time, it seems that the conditions go through different learning curves. DVRSUS and ISOSURF seem slower at first, then become equally fast as DVR.

We analysed the learning effect by grouping the trials into four phases. Recall that one session consists of four cycles, each cycling through all four conditions. We analysed each cycle separately,

Table 2. The averages

Condition	CPR	DVR	DVRSUS	ISOSURF
Mean trial time (sec)	43.28	60.44	68.00	64.96

as well as cycle 1 and 2 together (the first eight trials) and cycle 3 and 4 together (the last eight trials). Different learning effects are apparent, especially in cycle 1. For each cycle, we used again a repeated-measures ANOVA with Sidak post-hoc analysis, considering all conditions except CPR. We found that DVR was faster than DVRSUS in the first eight trials ($p = 0.015$), and also that DVR was faster than both DVRSUS and ISOSURF in the first four trials ($p <= 0.036$). No other significant differences were found.

While these results are tentative, we can conclude that DVRSUS and ISOSURF have a steeper learning curve, possibly caused by users learning to process the cues, or ignore them. This is consistent with our qualitative observations, which indicate that users spent a noticeable amount of time double-checking the suspicious areas, which gradually became less. One user even remarked: you quickly learn to ignore the suspicious areas.

Mistakes (user errors) were made in 17% of the trials, most of which were single mistakes. If we consider the number of mistakes per clickable vessel region, only 3.4% of the user selections were erroneous, almost all of which were omitted regions. We analysed mistakes by means of a χ^2 table (Table 3), assuming that trials and selection of selectable regions are independent events.

A χ^2 goodness of fit test over trials with and without mistakes reveals χ^2 ($3,N =192$) = 13.3, $p = 0.0041$, a χ^2 test over total segmentation errors and total number of user mistakes reveals a lower value, χ^2 ($3,N = 1344$) = 9.094, $p = 0.028$, but still significant. Apparently, users made more mistakes in CPR and possibly less in ISOSURF.

Contrary to theory, we did not find that users made more mistakes in the explicit-cues conditions DVRSUS and ISOSURF.

We will now consider subjective preferences. Users' preferences for the different conditions were not always consistent with their performance. Users were strongly divided about CPR, either preferring or dispreferring it strongly, with an average slightly below neutral, even though CPR scores significantly faster on average. We used the non-parametric Kendall's τ to check if there was a correlation between preference and time performance. We found a significant positive correlation, both absolute ($p = 0.046$) and relative ($p = 0.004$).

As concerns occlusion cues and suspicious area highlighting, most users preferred having them, and no one strongly preferred their absence. We again correlated them with time performance using Kendall's τ, but found no significant correlations.

In order to find out how the controls were used, we analysed the interaction data, in particular the time spent rotating and zooming. Users spent only an average of 0.51 sec. per trial on zooming, and 0.24 sec. on rotating around the view axis. In contrast, they spent around 11.5 sec. (18.3% of the time) on rotating around the other two axes using the RMB. Zoom behaviour differed between users. Most (8 of 12) users would navigate to one end, and then zoom in quite far to see details clearly, then proceed to the other end without zooming out. Therefore, a majority of users proceeded systematically with a fixed zoom level. Only four users liked to zoom in and out in particular cases to see context better. We conclude that the RMB

Table 3. The analysis

Condition	# trials	# segment. errors	# mistakes	# trials w/ mistakes
CPR	48	336	19	16
DVR	48	336	12	7
DVRSUS	48	336	10	7
ISOSURF	48	336	5	3

rotation controls are by far the most important, and that a fixed zoom level would probably suffice for this task.

Discussion. CPR was clearly the fastest, but also has higher error rate. Users were strongly divided over their preference for CPR, reflecting their relative individual time performance differences. We do not have an explanation for the higher error rate. CPR showed all errors in our models without rotation, so it is not caused by the users rotating too little to discover all errors. Possibly the high interaction speed also made users double-check less often. It would be interesting to find out why error rate was higher in a future experiment.

Contrary to some previous studies (e.g. Maltz & Shinar, 2003), we found that suspicious area highlighting (as in ISOSURF and DVRSUS) did not lead to increased error rate as compared to DVR. After learning effects leveled out, we found that DVRSUS and ISOSURF performed about equally well as DVR. Most users did prefer both DVRSUS and ISOSURF over DVR. While this is not a positive result, the presence of suspicious area highlighting was not detrimental either.

Possibly, the probability of false positives and negatives in DVRSUS (averaging 25% each) was

too high for this feature to be useful. Also, in part because of the learning effects, our experiment should be made more sensitive by increasing the number of trials. Therefore, it is still possible that some users would benefit from suspicious areas. Therefore, we ran a second experiment to find out.

Second Experiment: Comparison of Different Highlighting Conditions

Setup. In the second experiment, we use DVR to visualise the volume data. Again, the warning system highlights parts of the path line and mesh in red to indicate possible errors. Based on the outcome of the first experiment, we simplified the controls in the following way: the zoom level is fixed; the camera is zoomed in close to the vessel, so details can be seen clearly. Also, the initial position is at one end of the vessel and not in the middle. We compare user performance (time taken and error rate) for the following four conditions (See Figure 4):

1. *NONE* - no suspicious areas (baseline)
2. *PAR* (paranoid suspicious areas) yields only false positives - the user only has to search within the suspicious areas

Figure 4. Illustration of the visual stimuli as presented to the users. Left: with thickness error in the center and marked as potential error. Right: with veering error in the center but not marked.

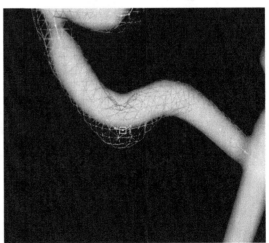

3. *CON* (conservative suspicious areas) yields only false negatives - the user can simply click the suspicious areas but has to search the rest for missed errors
4. *PER* (perfect detection) - while not realistic, this indicates an upper limit to performance of suspicious areas. It is basically an interaction task rather than an interpretation task.

We chose conditions to have 6-8 errors with 1-2 false positives or negatives. We used a within-subjects design. All users received the same set of software phantoms in the same order, but with different, randomly ordered and counterbalanced, conditions. The users had to complete 6 trials per condition, totaling 24 trials. Total duration of the main experiment was 10-20 minutes. A short subjective survey was conducted at the end, asking whether the users actually used the suspicious areas, and which type they preferred.

For the second experiment, we recruited 8 of the 12 subjects of the first experiment. Age ranged between 25 and 51; 7 were male and 1 female. Training for this experiment consisted of a 4-minute interactive tutorial, explaining the differences between the four conditions. Users were told in each condition whether to expect false positives or negatives, but not how many of these they could expect. More details can be found in van Schooten et al. (2010b).

Results. We shall begin with time performance. We expect time performance effects to be multiplicative rather than additive, so we transformed the data using the log transform. We used a second transformation to increase statistical sensitivity. It is based on the fact that the sequence of software phantoms used for the trials was the same for all

users. We divided the time for each trial by the overall average of that trial over all users (note that all conditions occurred equally often for each trial in the sequence). This has the effect of normalising for variations in trial difficulty.

Although PER is meant as a baseline condition, we first used repeated-measures ANOVA with Sidak posthoc analysis over all conditions including PER. The ANOVA yields $F(3,21) = 214.1$, $p < 0.0005$. PER is, as we might expect, very significantly different from the others: $p<0.0005$. It is almost twice as fast as the NONE condition, which shows that there may be quite a lot to gain from suspicious areas. We disregard it from here on.

We performed a second repeated-measures ANOVA on the remaining three conditions, which yields $F(2,14)=5.172, p=0.021$. A Sidak post-hoc analysis reveals that PAR is significantly faster than NONE ($p = 0.038$). The other comparisons (NONE-CON, CON-PAR) are not significant ($p >= 0.391$). This shows that PAR does provide benefit. Mean performance over all users is given in Table 4.

We analysed error rate by means of a χ^2 table, assuming that trials are independent events. User errors (mistakes) were rare events, with a total of 17 mistakes, which makes them more difficult to analyse. Number of mistakes made in NONE and CON were almost equal, while number of mistakes made in PAR was slightly lower. None of these differences were significant. We tentatively conclude that CON and PAR do not seem to result in significantly more mistakes as compared to NONE.

The sample is a bit small for serious statistical analysis of the subjective results, but we found that all users used the suspicious areas, and almost

Table 4. Mean performance of all users

condition	NONE	CON	PAR	PER
mean trial time (sec):	36.8	35.0	34.0	19.7

all preferred having both PAR and CON over NONE. We can at least conclude that users did not find the suspicious area markings annoying. There was little difference in preference between PAR and CON, although PAR was preferred more often than CON. However, a larger sample would be required to test if there is a significant difference here.

Discussion. We found that users perform significantly faster with paranoid highlighting than with no highlighting, and they make insignificantly less errors. There were no other significant differences. Users also prefer suspicious areas over no suspicious areas, and appear to prefer paranoid over conservative highlighting.

This contradicts most previous findings, which generally indicate that especially paranoid highlighting is often detrimental for both speed and error rate. While false positive rate was fairly low (about 20%), other experiments demonstrated a detrimental effect for similar rates (Dixon, et al., 2007; Yeh & Wickens, 2001). Somehow, it appears our results more closely follow a rationally based cognitive model: for the false positives case users will have to search only the marked areas, and hence, search space is much reduced, in contrast to the false negatives case, where it is less reduced. Our contradictory result cannot be explained by high difficulty or low target prevalence (the task was easy, as is illustrated by the low error rate). A possible explanation is the system reliability information given to the users. However, previous studies also showed a detrimental effect under similar reliability levels, when the users did have an accurate estimate of system reliability (Ezer, et al., 2008; Rice, 2009). The difference in outcome may alternatively be explained by a difference in task domain or visual stimuli.

CONCLUSION

We conducted two experiments, which compared task performance and subjective preference for visual search tasks involving finding segmentation errors in segmented MRA data. In the first experiment, we compared four visualisations, namely Direct Volume Rendering (DVR), Curved Planar Reformation (CPR), and Isosurface (ISOSURF), and DVR with Suspicious areas highlighted (DVR-SUS). In the second experiment, we examined different versions of suspicious area highlighting, namely the following four conditions: no warning highlights, only false positives (paranoid), only false negatives (conservative), and perfect highlighting. We compared user time and error performance as well as subjective preference.

Of the main visualisations, CPR was clearly the fastest, but also has higher error rate. Users were strongly divided over their preference for CPR, reflecting their relative individual time performance differences. We do not have an explanation for the higher error rate. It would be interesting to find out why error rate was higher in a future experiment. This result may have repercussions for search tasks in the 3D vascular domain, and also for domains which deal with similar structures, such as colon imaging.

As regards explicit suspicious area highlighting, we found that, contrary to some previous studies (e.g. Maltz & Shinar, 2003), suspicious area highlighting (as in ISOSURF and DVRSUS) did not lead to increased error rate as compared to DVR. Most users preferred both DVRSUS and ISOSURF over DVR. However, no significant time performance improvement is seen for either DVRSUS or ISOSURF over DVR either. In the second experiment, we found that users perform significantly faster with Paranoid highlighting (PAR) than with no highlighting (NONE), and they make insignificantly less errors. Users also prefer paranoid over Conservative (CON) highlighting.

We believe this result has wider applicability than just the medical domain. Our results follow a rationally based cognitive model: for the false positives case users will have to search only the marked areas, and hence, search space is much reduced, in contrast to the false negatives case, where it is less reduced. This contradicts previous findings (Dixon, et al., 2007; Yeh & Wickens, 2001), even for studies where most experimental variables are similar (i.e. Ezer, et al., 2008; Rice, 2009). The difference in outcome may be explained by a difference in task domain or visual stimuli, but also by a difference in general approach resulting from different paradigms found in the different domains. We argue that further experiments will be necessary to cover this research area more thoroughly.

Future Research Directions

In our study, we found both major differences in assumptions between different experiments, and apparently contradictory experimental outcomes. One major issue is the level of information given to users about the failure probabilities of target detection systems. Arguably, not giving information about this leaves the users to infer it, which leads to a learning effect (that is, users finding out what the failure probabilities are) which is likely undesirable. Another is the assumption that targeted highlighting systems always lead to distractors, which can be cleverly circumvented by the aforementioned double-reading scheme (Freer & Ulissey, 2001). Taking a fresh look at the different assumptions made may lead to new major perspectives and new ideas for experiments.

In our experiments, we have evidence that users follow a rationally-based cognitive processing model, while this is not so in some other studies, which found worse time and error performance for "paranoid" target detection for relatively easy visual targets. In fact, the outcomes seem contradictory enough to be worth exploring further.

While we found that CPR yielded the best time performance of the basic visualisations, we still have to explain why error rates are higher. Is this because users interacted so quickly that they started missing targets more frequently, or is this some issue with the visualisation itself? This is-

sue requires future studies to determine if CPR is really superior to regular 3D visualisations.

ACKNOWLEDGMENT

This work was carried out under the NWO (Netherlands Organization for Scientific research) Multivis project (N 643.100.602), which is part of the NWO VIEW program.

REFERENCES

Achenbach, S., Moshage, W., Ropers, D., & Bachmann, K. (1998). Curved multiplanar reconstructions for the evaluation of contrast-enhanced electron-beam CT of the coronary arteries. *American Journal of Roentgenology*. Retrieved from http://www.ajronline.org/content/170/4/895.full.pdf.

Bade, R., Ritter, F., & Preim, B. (2005). Usability comparison of mouse-based interaction techniques for predictable 3D rotation. In *Proceedings of the 5th International Symposium on Smart Graphics: SG 2005*, (pp. 138–150). Springer.

Boskamp, T., Rinck, D., Link, F., Kümmerlen, B., Stamm, G., & Mildenberger, P. (2004). New vessel analysis tool for morphometric quantification and visualization of vessels in CT and MR imaging data sets. *Radiographics, 24*(1), 287–297. doi:10.1148/rg.241035073

Dixon, S. R., Wickens, C. D., & McCarley, J. S. (2007). On the independence of compliance and reliance: Are automation false alarms worse than misses? *Human Factors, 49*(4), 564–572. doi:10.1518/001872007X215656

Ezer, N., Fisk, A. D., & Rogers, W. A. (2008). Age-related differences in reliance behavior attributable to costs within a human-decision aid system export. *Human Factors, 50*(6), 853–863. doi:10.1518/001872008X375018

Fisher, D. L., & Tan, K. C. (1989). Visual displays: The highlighting paradox. *Human Factors, 31*(1), 17–30.

Fleck, M. S., & Mitroff, S. R. (2007). Rare targets are rarely missed in correctable search. *Psychological Science, 18*(11), 943–947. doi:10.1111/j.1467-9280.2007.02006.x

Freer, T. W., & Ulissey, J. M. (2001). Screening mammography with computer-aided detection: Prospective study of 12,860 patients in a community breast center. *Radiology, 220,* 781–786. doi:10.1148/radiol.2203001282

Hong, W., Qiu, F., & Kaufman, A. (2006). A pipeline for computer aided polyp detection. *IEEE Transactions on Visualization and Computer Graphics, 12*(5), 861–868. doi:10.1109/TVCG.2006.112

Kanitsar, A. (2004). *Curved planar reformation for vessel visualization.* PhD Thesis. Vienna, Austria: Vienna University of Technology.

Levy, J. H., Broadhurst, R. R., Ray, S., Chaney, E. L., & Pizer, S. M. (2007). Signaling local non-credibility in an automatic segmentation pipeline. In *Proceedings of the International Society for Optical Engineering Meetings on Medical Imaging,* (vol 6512). IEEE.

López-Aligué, F. J., Acevedo-Sotoca, I., García-Manso, A., García-Orellana, C. J., & Gallardo-Caballero, R. (2004). Microcalcifications detection in digital mammograms. In *Proceedings of the IEEE Engineering in Medicine and Biology Society.* IEEE Press.

Maltz, M., & Shinar, D. (2003). New alternative methods of analyzing human behavior in cued target acquisition. *Human Factors, 45*(2), 281–295. doi:10.1518/hfes.45.2.281.27239

Mueller, D. C., Maeder, A. J., & O'Shea, P. J. (2005). Enhancing direct volume visualisation using perceptual properties. In *Proceedings of SPIE* (*Vol. 5744,* pp. 446–454). SPIE. doi:10.1117/12.594003

Preim, B., & Oeltze, S. (2007). *Visualization in medicine and life sciences. In 3D Visualization of Vasculature: An Overview* (pp. 39–60). Berlin, Germany: Springer Verlag.

Rice, S. (2009). Examining single and multiple-process theories of trust in automation. *The Journal of General Psychology, 136*(3), 303–319. doi:10.3200/GENP.136.3.303-322

Rolland, J. P., Muller, K. E., & Helvig, C. S. (1995). Visual search in medical images: A new methodology to quantify saliency. In *Proceedings of SPIE* (*Vol. 2436,* pp. 40–48). SPIE. doi:10.1117/12.206851

Russo Dos Santos, C., Gros, P., Abel, P., Loisel, D., Trichaud, N., & Paris, J. P. (2000). Metaphor-aware 3D navigation. In *Proceedings IEEE Symposium on Information Visualization,* (p. 155). IEEE Press.

Suinesiaputra, A., de Koning, P. J., Zudilova-Seinstra, E. V., Reiber, J. H. C., & van der Geest, R. J. (2009). *A 3D MRA segmentation method based on tubular NURBS model.* Paper presented at the International Society for Magnetic Resonance in Medicine 2009. Honolulu, HI.

Tamborello, F. P., & Byrne, M. D. (2007). Adaptive but non-optimal visual search behavior with highlighted displays. *Cognitive Systems Research, 8*(3), 182–191. doi:10.1016/j.cogsys.2007.05.003

van Schooten, B., van Dijk, E. M. A. G., Suinesiaputra, A., & Reiber, J. H. C. (2010a). Effectiveness of visualisations for detection of errors in segmentation of blood vessels. In *Proceedings of IVAPP 2010.* IVAPP.

van Schooten, B. W., van Dijk, B. M., Nijholt, A., & Reiber, J. H. (2010b). Evaluating automatic warning cues for visual search in vascular images. In *Proceeding of the 14th International Conference on Intelligent User Interfaces*, (pp. 393–396). New York, NY: ACM Press.

van Schooten, B. W., van Dijk, E. M., Suinesiaputra, A., & Reiber, J. H. (2011). Interactive navigation of segmented mr angiograms using simultaneous curved planar and volume visualizations. *International Journal of Computer Assisted Radiology and Surgery*, *6*(1), 591–599. doi:10.1007/s11548-010-0534-4

van Schooten, B. W., van Dijk, E. M. A. G., Zudilova-Seinstra, E. V., de Koning, P. J. H., & Reiber, J. H. C. (2009). Evaluating visualisation and navigation techniques for interpretation of MRA data. In *Proceedings of GRAPP, 2009*, 405–408.

Wang, Y., Gao, X., & Li, J. (2007). A feature analysis approach to mass detection in mammography based on RF-SVM. In *Proceedings of ICIP, 2007*, 9–12.

Wickens, C. D., & Andre, A. D. (1990). Proximity compatibility and information display: Effects of color, space, and objectness on information integration. *Human Factors*, *32*(1), 61–77.

Yeh, M., & Wickens, C. D. (2001). Display signaling in augmented reality: Effects of cue reliability and image realism on attention allocation and trust calibration. *Human Factors*, *43*(3), 355–365. doi:10.1518/001872001775898269

KEY TERMS AND DEFINITIONS

Target Detection Cue: Visual cue which helps detect a target in a visual search task.

Attention Tunneling: Cognitive phenomenon where subjects pay reduced attention to other (related or unrelated) stimuli when a particularly salient stimulus is presented.

Segmentation: The determination of the contour of a particular object in an image.

Magnetic Resonance Angiograpy: A medical imaging technique that results in a 3D density field that represents blood flow levels a vascular structure.

Direct Volume Rendering: Visualisation technique that visualises a 3D density field as a semi-transparent 3D object.

Isosurface: A surface mesh that represents a particular density in a 3D density field.

Curved Planar Reformation: Visualisation technique that shows a curved cross-section following the curvature of a blood vessel.

Software Phantom: An algorithm that generates output that is similar to the output of a particular imaging device.

Chapter 6

Considering the Influence of Visual Saliency during Interface Searches

Jeremiah D. Still
Missouri Western State University, USA

Christopher M. Masciocchi
Frostburg State University, USA

ABSTRACT

In this chapter, the authors highlight the influence of visual saliency, or local contrast, on users' searches of interfaces, particularly web pages. Designers have traditionally focused on the importance of goals and expectations (top-down processes) for the navigation of interfaces (Diaper & Stanton, 2004), with little consideration for the influence of saliency (bottom-up processes). The Handbook of Human-Computer Interaction (Sears & Jacko, 2008), for example, does not discuss the influence of bottom-up processing, potentially neglecting an important aspect of interface-based searches. The authors review studies that demonstrate how a user's attention is rapidly drawn to visually salient locations in a variety of tasks and scenes, including web pages. They then describe an inexpensive, rapid technique that designers can use to identify visually salient locations in web pages, and discuss its advantages over similar methods.

INTRODUCTION

Why is it that some interfaces guide us to the information we are searching for while others do not? In this chapter, we argue that visual saliency, a measure of an item's visual uniqueness compared to its surroundings, plays a critical role in guiding our attention through an interface in cooperation

with traditionally considered influences, such as goals. Visual saliency is inherent in natural and artificial scenes and interfaces, and cues the viewer to certain spatial regions over others. These cues may affect search difficulty. For instance, when a target is collocated with a salient region, searching can be accomplished in less time and with less effort and frustration for the user. The first objective of this chapter is to illustrate how visual saliency can be used to reduce user search times

DOI: 10.4018/978-1-4666-1628-8.ch006

and aid task completion by implicitly guiding users to important information within an interface.

For an object to be visually salient, it must be visually unique relative to its surroundings (for a review see Healey, Booth, & Enns, 1996; Wolfe & Horowitz, 2004). For example, bolded and irregularity spaced text (s a l i e n t) amongst regularly-spaced, non-bolded text "pulls" the viewer's attention making it more likely to be noticed. This aspect of salience is understood by the design community as illustrated by the use of bold, underlining, italics, color, and images to highlight important information. Making an item salient or identifying salient regions within an interface is unproblematic when the interface is primarily uniform. However, the same task is difficult in non-uniform interfaces, such as in web pages that are composed of pictures, logos, texts and varying spatial layouts. Thus, designers are often required to make a "best guess" about what is salient. The second objective of this chapter is to demonstrate that a saliency model, from the cognitive science literature, can help with the difficult but important task of determining which regions in a display are visually salient, and consequently the best locations for displaying critical information. In doing so, we will discuss research examining the processing of low-level cues that guide observers' searches, as well as a computational model (Itti, Koch, & Niebur, 1998) that accurately predicts where users will look based purely on measures of visual saliency.

The saliency processes, which guide attention, can be demonstrated in relatively simple experimental displays. Further, these processes operate in essentially the same way regardless of one's task: whether looking for a bird in the forest or a movie on a web page. Most of the research discussed in this chapter uses basic displays – natural scenes, experimental displays, web pages—and basic tasks—participants completing visual searches, or making responses to a target displayed among non-target (i.e., distractor) items.

BACKGROUND

Cognitive Processing, Visual Saliency, Attention, and Eye Tracking

Visual salience is a type of stimulus property that influences whether or not items are attended to and enter awareness. Two basic processes govern human attention: bottom-up and top-down. Several different descriptions of these processes appear within the literature, thus they are worth clearly defining. A bottom-up process is one that is driven by stimulus properties, like saliency. It occurs early in the processing stream, is rapid, and largely independent of knowledge (Wolfe, Butcher, Lee, & Hyle, 2003). Saliency is thought to influence bottom-up processing by biasing it toward the selection of areas that are locally unique. When an area of a display is uniform, salient items appear to pop-out. Under these conditions it does not matter how many non-target items are in the search display; the salient object is rapidly found (see Figure 1).

Many studies have shown that salient items affect attention. For example, in a study by Theeuwes (1992), a target object with a unique shape (i.e., circle) was presented amongst uniform distractors with a different shape (i.e., diamond). On some trials, one of the distractors was presented in a unique, salient color. Theeuwes found that participants were slower to make a response to the target when a salient distractor was present. This finding suggests that the salient distractor captured attention despite the fact that it was irrelevant to the task, as the unique-colored item was never the target. Furthermore, Pashler (1988) found that search performance was reduced even when the location of uniquely colored distractors were known ahead of time. In a follow-up study, Theeuwes (1994) found a similar effect when a distractor appeared abruptly (onset) and the target was a uniquely colored item. Thus, attention was captured by a salient abrupt onset even though the target never had an abrupt onset. Finally, Kim

Figure 1. These search arrays demonstrate how a circle is salient among stars and how increasing the number of surrounding stars does not increase the difficultly of detecting the circle

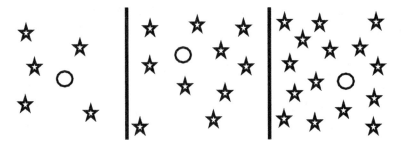

and Cave (1999) demonstrated that participants were faster to respond to probes appearing at locations of salient distractors than non-salient distractors, suggesting that salient distractors attract attention. Additionally, in some conditions participants responded just as quickly to probes appearing at locations of salient distractors as to probes appearing at target locations, suggesting that salient distractors may attract as much attention *as a target*.

In contrast to bottom-up processes, a top-down process is one that is goal driven. It occurs later in the processing stream, is more effortful and is knowledge dependent. When attention is primarily guided by top-down processes the speed of completion is typically dependent on the number of non-target items and their similarity with the target (Wolfe, Horowitz, Kenner, Hyle, & Vasan, 2004). It is common for visual searches to be heavily influenced by top-down processes. For example, when searching for a remote control in a living room one might first look on the coffee table. When searching for the power button on the remote one might look to the upper-right or upper-left corner of the interface. Each of those tasks has a clearly defined target, and visual search is heavily guided by long-term memory based conventions (Still & Dark, 2010).

However, it is artificial to refer to bottom-up or top-down processing independent of each other. These processes work together to accomplish attentional selection. Given the abundance of visual information in our environments and

the limitations of our visual system, attention must be selective (Johnston & Dark, 1986). The conceptualization of attentional selection depends on what metaphor or model of attention is being used (Fernandez-Duque & Johnson, 2002). We prefer Desimone and Duncan's (1995) neurologically-based biased-competition model. The model describes attention as being guided by an interaction between bottom-up and top-down processes (c.f. Wolfe, 2007). In the model, an interaction between visual saliency and user goal (e.g., defining features of the target) determine the amount of neural activity devoted to an item, which then affects the likelihood that the item will be selectively attended and enter awareness.

Although attention to an item can be inferred from user self-report (e.g., if an item is reported it must have been attended) and search times, it can also be inferred by tracking eye movements. Under normal viewing conditions, people make approximately four eye movements per second with stationary periods, fixations, in between. It has been suggested that eye-movement programming has a direct and natural relationship with visual attention. Studies suggest attention is often directed to whichever item is currently or next-to-be fixated (Hoffman & Subramaniam, 1995; Kowler, Anderson, Dosher, & Baser, 1995). Furthermore, only information that falls directly on the fovea during a fixation is encoded with high resolution. Thus, it is critical that users fixate on relevant visual information or that content may not reach awareness.

Attention and Web Pages

Both top-down and bottom-up processes are involved in attentional guidance, but depending on available search time, it can be difficult to see their unique contributions. There is ample evidence that top-down processes influence the guidance of attention within web pages. Eye-tracking research has shown that changing the task during a search changes users' fixation patterns (Cutrell & Guan, 2007). Additionally, given enough time, user expectations can elicit a consistent F-shaped, or reading, pattern of fixations (e.g., left-right, top-bottom) across web pages (Rayner, 1998). However, top-down and bottom-up effects interact, making the bottom-up influences particularly difficult to examine (McCarthy, Sasse, & Riegelsberger, 2003). Some might argue that if top-down processes override bottom-up processes, then there is no practical reason to understand and exploit bottom-up process. This is an incorrect assumption. When search times are short, bottom-up processes drive attentional selection even if the user has a goal in mind. When searching for information users might spend 4 to 9 seconds per web page, skimming approximately 18 words (Chen, Anderson, & Sohn, 2001; Nielsen, 2008). Consequently, it is critical to understand bottom-up processing, as these effects influence attention more rapidly than top-down processes.

Some designers have effectively used bottom-up processes to override top-down control in web page interfaces. According to Albert (2002), users learn where banner ads are commonly located (i.e., top of a page) and look less often at those locations. This top-down strategy, avoiding distracting ads, is referred to as banner blindness. To overcome banner blindness designers capture users' attention using salient transient signals within the ad, such as presenting an animation, which shakes or flashes (Burke & Hornoff, 2001). However, using such strong transients creates a double-edged sword: they draw users' attention,

but they can be disruptive if they are incongruent with the ongoing task (Rensink, 2002). Given that web pages are complex—supporting several tasks—using a transient signal to demand attention from all users, independent of task, is likely to be distracting and frustrating. Other researchers have also highlighted the negative effects of blind task interruptions (Iqbal & Bailey, 2008). Our recommendation is not that attentional control be taken from the user (as with transient signaling), rather that attention be implicitly guided to potential objects of interest.

Saliency Model: Predicting Bottom-Up Processing

To better understand the influences of saliency on attention, Itti, Koch, and Niebur (1998) developed a model to compute an image's visual saliency without any semantic input (i.e., meaning of objects or structure in a scene). Their model is based on the assumption that eye-movement programming is driven by a serial search based on *local* image contrast. These searches are guided by low-level primitives (i.e., color, light intensity, orientation) that are extracted from a scene. The saliency model was developed under the pretense that these feature primitives rapidly influence overt attention (i.e., eye movements). Thus, the underlying assumption is that visual saliency guides the fovea to unique areas within a scene that might provide the most efficient processing of information (Itti & Koch, 2000). Evidence supporting a role for salience in attention can be found in the results of a visual search task using line segments of varying orientation. Morgalia (1989) found that observers were slower to respond to the orientation of a line segment when adjacent line segments had a similar orientation (see Figure 2).

The computational model (Itti, Koch, & Niebur, 1998) produces "saliency maps" of digital pictures (see Figure 3). To create a saliency map, the model receives input from pixels within a

Figure 2. This figure demonstrates varying local image contrast and its affect on target detection ease. Within this display there are four 90⁰ vertical lines. The vertical line on the left side is easy to detect as it has a high amount of local contrast. However, the three identical vertical lines on the right side of the display are difficult to detect due their low local contrast.

picture. Then, it extracts three feature channels—color, intensity, orientation—at eight different spatial scales. These channels are normalized and differences of center-surround are calculated for each. The separate channels are additively combined to form a single saliency map. An image's saliency map provides predictions of where attention should be deployed, beginning at the location of highest saliency and then linearly selecting regions with less activation. Two other popular theories explain attentional selection in a similar manner: Guided Search (Wolfe, 2007) and Feature Integration Theory (Treisman & Gelade, 1980).

For detailed explanations of the saliency model refer to Itti, Koch, and Niebur (1998), Itti and Koch (2000), and Parkhurst, Law, and Niebur (2002). The saliency model is available for download from <SalinecyToolbox.net> as a collection of Matlab functions and scripts (Walther & Koch, 2006).

Many studies have used this saliency model to explore the relationship between saliency and attention in complex scenes. For example, visually salient items have been shown to attract eye

Figure 3. Two examples of web page screenshots and their corresponding saliency maps. Brighter areas indicate regions of higher saliency.

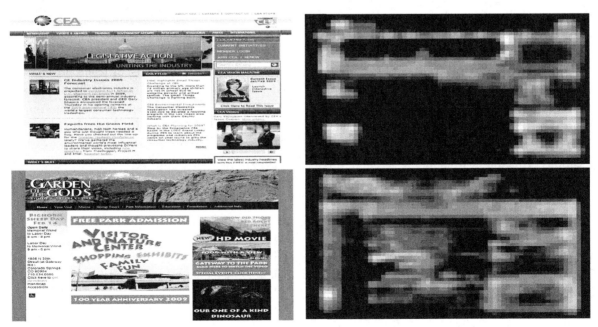

movements. Using the saliency model to identify salient regions of natural scenes (e.g., landscapes, buildings, home interiors) and artificial scenes (e.g., complex fractals), Parkhurst et al. (2002) and Masciocchi, Mihalas, Parkhurst, and Niebur (2009) found that fixations were drawn to salient locations more so than expected by chance. The effect of saliency was highest for initial fixations than later fixations, presumably because bottom-up processes influence attention more rapidly than top-down processes.

A saliency model has even been found to outperform participants in detecting a unique object within a cluttered background. To show this Itti and Koch (2000) used 44 photographs each containing a military vehicle within a rural background. They had participants search for the vehicle in each scene, and compared their performance to the saliency model's predictions. Itti and Koch found that the saliency model required fewer shifts of attention to find the vehicle than the humans; in other words the model detected the target faster than participants. This study provides some insight into the importance of bottom-up processing for detecting unique objects within complex scenes. Further, it illustrates that top-down processes may actually slow users if they are not applicable. Not only may salient distractors harm search performance, but so do incorrect search strategies.

CONTROVERSIES, PROBLEMS, AND ISSUES

Which are More Influential: Bottom-Up or Top-Down Processes?

The precise nature of the interaction between bottom-up and top-down processes is a point of controversy in the cognitive science literature. Specifically, do salient non-target items capture attention when they do not share properties with the target? If salient distractors do capture attention, it would suggest that bottom-up processes can inde-

pendently drive attention. If not, it would suggest that some top-down processes can override the influence of salient yet irrelevant features. Recall that Theeuwes (1992) showed that the presence of a uniquely colored item slowed response time to a target, indicating that attention is automatically captured by the most salient item within a display regardless of top-down processing. Bacon and Egeth (1994) disagreed proposing instead that a top-down strategy, "feature search mode," could be used to prevent attention from being captured by irrelevant salient stimuli *provided* the target's features are known ahead of time. However, Theeuwes (2004) more recently found that by increasing the number of distractors the salient objects are uncontrollably distracting; dismissing the feature search mode theory. It appears that decreasing the target and distractor similarity within the display increased the effectiveness of bottom-up processing. Overall, this controversy is far from settled.

Alternative Methods for Predicting the Deployment of Attention in Interfaces

The result of bottom-up and top-down processing is the deployment of attention. However, web page designers are left with the challenge of predicting where users are attending when viewing a web page. If important information on the website is not located in an area that users naturally attend to, they might abandon their searches early, finding them tedious and frustrating. Thus, it is advantageous for web designers to predict where users will attend, and collocate attended regions and important information.

Given the relationship between attention and eye fixations, it is no surprise that eye movements are often tracked to monitor the deployment of attention. Eye tracking systems allow designers to test whether or not their web pages actually guide users' fixations to important locations. Typically, eye movements reveal a combination of bottom-up and top-down processing, which in some cases is advantageous. However, eye tracking systems have a number of recognized costs; they are expensive, not easily accessible, time consuming to employ, and gradually lose calibration (Arroyo, Selker, & Wei, 2006; Chen, Anderson, & Sohn, 2001; Johansen & Hansen, 2006; Tarasewich, Pomplun, Fillion, & Broberg, 2005).

An alternative method for predicting the deployment of attention is the *squint test* (Cooper, Reimann, & Cronin, 2007; Mullet & Sano, 1995; Sears & Jacko, 2009). To perform a squint test, designers simply squint their eyes to make the text unreadable while preserving the overall layout of the design. The purpose of the test is to ensure important elements of a web page are discernible even under blurred conditions. It is thought that these discernible elements will be easily found by users. Several usability tools (e.g., Enhanced Restricted Focus Viewer: Tarasewich, Pomplun, Fillion, & Broberg, 2005; Stompernet Scrutinizer Foveal Gaze Simulator) emulate the squint test by blurring the display while keeping a small portion surrounding the mouse cursor in focus. Cursor position is recorded as users explore the page, and those data are used to determine where users' attention was allocated.

We are currently exploring another method of tracking user's attention in a web page: having users select the five most interesting locations in web page screenshots. The *interest point method* was developed based on Masciocchi et al.'s (2009) finding that locations in a scene rated by users as being interesting were more likely to be fixated than less interesting locations. This method has an advantage over the squint test in that it is less artificial. However, it still requires participants to formulate predictions, which may not be an option for some studies.

SOLUTIONS AND RECOMMENDATIONS

Understand the Importance of Bottom-Up Processes

The first objective of this chapter was to clarify and highlight the role that bottom-up processes have on visual search. While most of the supporting evidence presented comes from studies using artificial scenes, a few studies have demonstrated that these influences generalize to web pages. Our hope is that designers will use this understanding of bottom-up processes to enhance their designs, for example, by collocating important information and salient regions to aid users' search through their interfaces.

Using a Saliency Model to Predict Bottom-Up Attentional Processes

The second objective of this chapter was to introduce a computational model that identifies visually salient regions thereby making predictions about where in a scene participants will attend. As Norman (1993) highlighted, computers are best used to compensate for our weaknesses and one of our weaknesses is predicting where users will fixate in complex displays. For example, Johansen and Hansen (2006) found that users could only remember 70% of viewed web elements, while web designers were only able to predict 46% of the elements fixated. Their study highlights the limitation of both users' explicit report and expert predictions in anticipating fixated web elements. Although our visual attention systems may be hardwired for automatic saliency detection, we simply do not have the working memory resources (Baddeley, 1992; Vogel, Woodman, & Luck, 2001) required for the conscious calculations. We propose the use of the computational saliency model developed by Itti, Koch, and Niebur (1998) to overcome our difficulty in identifying salient regions in complex interfaces.

To test the effectiveness of the saliency model for predicting attentional deployment in web page viewing, Still and Masciocchi (2010) compared saliency model predictions to eye tracking data collected from eight participants. Participants viewed 50 web page screenshots while their eye movements were monitored using an eye tracker. They were instructed to, "Look around the image like you normally would if you were surfing the internet." Participants' eye fixations were recorded for 5 seconds. The saliency model was also run on those 50 screenshots to create a saliency map for each screenshot. Each pixel in the saliency map had a value between 0 (depicted as black) and 100 (depicted as white) to reflect its relative level of saliency in that image (see Figure 3).

To examine whether there was a correlation between saliency and eye fixations, we first determined the x, y coordinates for each participant's first 10 fixations for each screenshot. Next, we referred to the screenshot's saliency map to find the saliency value for each of those fixated locations. We then compared those results to a random shuffled distribution by taking the fixation locations for a given saliency map (e.g., web page #1), and finding the saliency values at the same x, y coordinates for each other screenshot's saliency map (e.g., web page #2-50). The shuffled distribution removes irrelevant factors (easily determined by designers) associated with spatial conventions, such as placing the navigational bar on the top or left side of a web page, and is more conservative than assuming that locations are fixated at random. The results showed that the mean values of the saliency maps at participants' actual fixation locations were larger than the mean values from the shuffled distribution. Thus, participants were likely to fixate on regions higher in visual saliency than expected by the random shuffle distribution, suggesting that their attention was guided by the location of salient information in the web pages.

We also examined whether or not the influence of saliency changed across fixations. Recall that previous studies suggest that saliency has a larger effect on early versus later fixations (e.g., Parkhurst, et al., 2002). A similar effect was found in our study. Specifically, saliency values for the first fixation were higher than the saliency values for the other nine fixations. However, the influence of saliency was not restricted to the first fixation as all 10 fixations fell on regions of higher salience than expected by chance. Given that users often spend a short time searching web pages and that the influence of saliency persists beyond the first fixation, it is clear that saliency is an important component of web page search. Previous research had shown a modest correlation between saliency and eye fixations in natural scenes (Parkhurst, et al., 2002). We extended this research by demonstrating that even in web pages, which contain more semantic information, fixations are correlated with saliency.

According to Wickens and McCarley (2008), a "computational model guided solely by bottom-up salience calculations can do a reasonable job of simulating human search behavior (Itti & Koch, 2000), but models incorporating a top-down component perform better (Navalpakkam & Itti, 2005)" (p. 71). One of the primary drawbacks to models with a top-down component is that, to be truly effective, they would require calibration for each user. Top-down processes are necessarily tied to personal experiences, and therefore semantics, schemas, expectations, and goals would vary across users. Many models utilizing top-down processes rely on a nebulous "average" user whose "experiences" are gathered via norming studies. For these reasons we recommend a saliency model specifically because it identifies bottom-up processes that are constant across users.

Some might wonder, why not use the squint test instead of a saliency model? The answer for us is simple: The squint test blurs the interface removing critically important contrast information. Processing of information outside foveal vision is fundamental for programming upcoming fixation locations (He & Kowler, 1989). This information is distorted by squinting. In addition, the squint test removes high frequency contrast with local spatial averaging. This is problematic if, as suggested in the saliency model, local contrast is an important contributor to saliency and the guidance of attention. Therefore, we suspect that squinting actually changes how users process the interface, making squint data an invalid information source for predicting attention deployment.

Although we have advocated for the consideration of visual saliency during interface design, there is one situation in which this consideration is essentially irrelevant. To take full advantage of visual saliency, the interface can only contain a few salient regions. If all interface elements are equally salient, bottom-up influences are nullified and the model is useless. In this situation, users would be equally guided to all areas—in short, guided nowhere. In this instance, top-down processes would completely control the search. However, such a case is rare, and it is more common that an irrelevant salient element pulls attention away from critical areas.

Our data suggests that saliency maps alone can provide reasonable predictions of attention, as measured by fixations. In addition, saliency maps can be generated quickly, and require no additional equipment or participants. Even with these positive attributes, one may be hesitant to abandon eye tracking altogether. Our recommendation is to choose the method of tracking user's attention that is most appropriate for your project given your constraints and needs. It is often the case that developing effective interfaces requires many levels of analysis. For example, during the early formative testing process it would be appropriate to begin with the saliency model to ensure that important regions are also visually salient. Then, during the later prototype development stage one can use eye tracking to verify that participants are actually looking at critical elements in the design.

FUTURE RESEARCH DIRECTIONS

In this chapter, we have started to translate basic visual search research into knowledge usable by the design community. However, more research is needed to test the viability of the presented concept of saliency in design contexts other than web pages as many questions remain unanswered. For instance, could a saliency model be used to ensure that critical items, such as warning signs, in work environments are indeed salient? Although it seems obvious that an orange or red warning sign should be salient, this is not guaranteed: an orange sign posted in front of orange painted machinery will not be visually salient. What about other visual characteristics contributing to the sign's salience like orientation or light intensity? While it may be easy to explicitly consider local contrast when large differences exist between components this is not the case when differences between components are subtle or when several factors interact. Future work should explore the applicability of the saliency model in these types of richer, design settings.

Also, an emerging trend within the development of saliency models is to include top-down information. It has been shown that doing so increases the predictive ability of the models (Navalpakkam & Itti, 2005). It has also been shown that top-down processing can have an earlier effect on processing than once believed possible. This rapid top-down influence has been coined "pop-out priming" (Kristjansson & Wang, 2002; Maljkovic & Nakayama, 1994). However, it remains unclear how this top-down information could be included in a saliency model and remain cost effective for designers. We speculate that models simulating top-down processes in web pages might begin by incorporating general schematic information—content that is generally similar across web pages—like positioning and format of navigational bars.

CONCLUSION

Designers studying interface use have traditionally concentrated on top-down processes. They focus on improving the reflective communication channel between the user and their interface. While it is important that we continue to consider this explicit level of communication, it is only half of the story. The user's cognitive system interprets interfaces using *both* bottom-up and top-down processes. The present research uniquely focuses on understanding bottom-up processes that occur during interface interactions, especially those influencing visual searches within web pages. We have proposed that one way to explore the implicit guidance of attention is by using a computational saliency model from the cognitive science literature. This approach makes explicit the properties that implicitly guide attention, particularly visual saliency, in interfaces.

REFERENCES

Albert, W. (2002). Do web users actually look at ads? A case study of banner ads and eye-tracking technology. In *Proceedings of Usability Professional Association Conference*. Orlando, FL: Usability Professional Association.

Arroyo, E., Selker, T., & Wei, W. (2006). Usability tool for analysis of web designs using mouse tracks. In *Proceedings of the Computer-Human Interaction Extended Abstracts on Human Factors in Computing Systems*, (pp. 484-489). ACM Press.

Bacon, W. F., & Egeth, H. E. (1994). Overriding stimulus-driven attentional capture. *Perception & Psychophysics*, *55*, 485–496. doi:10.3758/BF03205306

Baddeley, A. D. (1992). Working memory. *Science*, *255*, 556–559. doi:10.1126/science.1736359

Burke, M., & Hornoff, A. J. (2001). *The effects of animated banner advertisements on a visual search task. Computer and Information Science Report*. Nantes, France: University of Nantes.

Chen, M., Anderson, J. R., & Sohn, M. (2001). What can a mouse cursor tell us more? Correlation of eye/mouse movements on web browsing. In *Proceedings of the Computer-Human Interactions Extended Abstracts on Human Factors in Computing Systems*, (pp. 281-282). ACM Press.

Cooper, A., Reimann, R., & Cronin, D. (2007). *About face 3: The essentials of interaction design*. Indianapolis, IN: Wiley.

Cutrell, E., & Guan, Z. (2007). What are you looking for? An eye-tracking study of information usage in web search. In *Proceedings of the SIGCHI Conference on Human Factors in Computing Systems,* (pp. 407-416). ACM Press.

Desimone, R., & Duncan, J. (1995). Neural mechanisms of selective visual attention. *Annual Review of Neuroscience*, *18*, 193–222. doi:10.1146/annurev.ne.18.030195.001205

Diaper, D., & Stanton, N. A. (Eds.). (2004). *The handbook of task analysis for human-computer interaction*. Mahwah, NJ: Lawrence Erlbaum Associates.

Egeth, H. E., & Yantis, S. (1997). Visual attention: Control representation and time course. *Annual Review of Psychology*, *48*, 269–297. doi:10.1146/annurev.psych.48.1.269

Fernandez-Duque, D., & Johnson, M. L. (2002). Cause and effect theories of attention: The role of conceptual metaphors. *Review of General Psychology*, *6*(2), 153–165. doi:10.1037/1089-2680.6.2.153

He, P., & Kowler, E. (1989). The role of location of probability in the programming of saccades: Implications for "COG" tendencies. *Vision Research*, *29*, 1165–1181. doi:10.1016/0042-6989(89)90063-1

Healey, C. G., Booth, K. S., & Enns, J. T. (1996). High-speed visual estimation using preattentive processing. *ACM Transactions on Human Computer Interaction*, *3*(2), 107–135. doi:10.1145/230562.230563

Hoffman, J. E., & Subramaniam, B. (1995). The role of visual attention in saccadic eye movements. *Perception & Psychophysics*, *57*, 787–795. doi:10.3758/BF03206794

Iqbal, S. T., & Bailey, B. P. (2008). Effects of intelligent notification management on users and their tasks. In *Proceedings of the SIGCHI Conference on Human Factors in Computing Systems*, (pp. 93-102). ACM Press.

Itti, L., & Koch, C. (2000). A saliency-based search mechanism for overt and covert shifts of visual attention. *Vision Research*, *40*(10-12), 1489–1506. doi:10.1016/S0042-6989(99)00163-7

Itti, L., Koch, C., & Niebur, E. (1998). A model of saliency-based fast visual attention for rapid scene analysis. *IEEE Transactions on Pattern Analysis and Machine Intelligence*, *20*(11), 1254–1259. doi:10.1109/34.730558

Johansen, S. A., & Hansen, J. P. (2006). Do we need eye trackers to tell where people look? In *Proceedings of Computer-Human Interaction Extended Abstracts on Human Factors in Computing Systems* (pp. 923–928). ACM Press. doi:10.1145/1125451.1125630

Johnston, W. A., & Dark, V. J. (1986). Selective attention. *Annual Review of Psychology*, *37*, 43–75. doi:10.1146/annurev.ps.37.020186.000355

Kim, M. S., & Cave, K. R. (1999). Grouping effects on spatial attention in visual search. *The Journal of General Psychology*, *126*, 326–352. doi:10.1080/00221309909595370

Kowler, E., Anderson, E., Dosher, B., & Blaser, E. (1995). The role of attention in the programming of saccades. *Vision Research*, *35*, 1897–1916. doi:10.1016/0042-6989(94)00279-U

Kristjansson, A., Wang, D., & Nakayama, K. (2002). The role of priming in conjunctive visual search. *Cognition*, *85*, 37–52. doi:10.1016/S0010-0277(02)00074-4

Maljkovic, V., & Nakayama, K. (1994). Priming of pop-out: Role of features. *Memory & Cognition*, *22*(6), 657–672. doi:10.3758/BF03209251

Masciocchi, C. M., Mihalas, S., Parkhurst, D., & Niebur, E. (2009). Everyone knows what is interesting: Salient locations which should be fixated. *Journal of Vision (Charlottesville, Va.)*, *9*(25), 1–22.

McCarthy, J. D., Sasse, M. A., & Riegelsberger, J. (2003). Can I have the menu please? An eyetracking study of design conventions. In *Proceedings of Human-Computer Interaction* (pp. 401–414). ACM Press.

Moraglia, G. (1989). Display organization and the detection of horizontal lines segments. *Perception & Psychophysics*, *45*(3), 265–272. doi:10.3758/BF03210706

Mullet, K. E., & Sano, D. (1995). *Designing visual interfaces: Communication oriented techniques*. Mountain View, CA: SunSoft Press.

Navalpakkam, V., & Itti, L. (2005). Modeling the influence of task on attention. *Vision Research*, *45*, 205–231. doi:10.1016/j.visres.2004.07.042

Nielsen, J. (2008). *How little do users read?* Retrieved May 12, 2009 from http://www.useit.com/alertbox/percent-text-read.html.

Norman, D. A. (1993). *Things that make us smart: Defending human attributes in the age of the machine*. Cambridge, MA: Perseus Books.

Parkhurst, D., Law, K., & Niebur, E. (2002). Modeling the role of salience in the allocation of overt visual attention. *Vision Research*, *42*, 107–123. doi:10.1016/S0042-6989(01)00250-4

Pashler, H. (1988). Cross-dimensional interaction and texture segregation. *Perception & Psychophysics*, *43*, 307–318. doi:10.3758/BF03208800

Rayner, K. (1998). Eye movements in reading and information processing: 20 years of research. *Psychological Bulletin*, *124*(3), 372–422. doi:10.1037/0033-2909.124.3.372

Rensink, R. A. (2002). Internal vs. external information in visual perception. In *Proceedings of the 2nd International Symposium on Smart Graphics*, (pp. 63-70). IEEE.

Sears, A., & Jacko, J. A. (Eds.). (2009). *Human-computer interaction: Design issues, solutions, and applications*. Boca Raton, FL: CRC Press.

Still, J. D., & Dark, V. J. (2010). Examining working memory load and congruency effects on affordances and conventions. *International Journal of Human-Computer Studies*, *68*(9), 561–571. doi:10.1016/j.ijhcs.2010.03.003

Still, J. D., & Masciocchi, C. M. (2010). A saliency model predicts fixations in web interfaces. In *Proceedings of the 5th International Workshop on Model-Driven Development of Advanced User Interfaces*. Atlanta, GA: ACM Press.

Stompernet. (2011). *Scrutinizer foveal gaze simulator*. Retrieved from http://about.stompernet.com/scrutinizer.

Tarasewich, P., Pomplun, M., Fillion, S., & Broberg, D. (2005). The enhanced restricted focus viewer. *International Journal of Human-Computer Interaction*, *19*(1), 35–54. doi:10.1207/s15327590ijhc1901_4

Theeuwes, J. (1992). Perceptual selectivity for color and form. *Perception & Psychophysics*, *51*, 599–606. doi:10.3758/BF03211656

Theeuwes, J. (1994). Stimulus-driven capture and attentional set: Selective search for color and visual abrupt onsets. *Journal of Experimental Psychology. Human Perception and Performance*, *20*, 799–806. doi:10.1037/0096-1523.20.4.799

Theeuwes, J. (2004). Top-down search strategies cannot override attentional capture. *Psychonomic Bulletin & Review*, *11*(1), 65–70. doi:10.3758/BF03206462

Treisman, A. M., & Gelade, G. (1980). A feature-integration theory of attention. *Cognitive Psychology*, *12*, 97–136. doi:10.1016/0010-0285(80)90005-5

Vogel, E. K., Woodman, G. F., & Luck, S. J. (2001). Storage of features, conjunctions, and objects in visual working memory. *Journal of Experimental Psychology. Human Perception and Performance*, *27*, 92–114. doi:10.1037/0096-1523.27.1.92

Walther, D., & Koch, C. (2006). Modeling attention to salient proto-objects. *Neural Networks*, *19*, 1395–1407. doi:10.1016/j.neunet.2006.10.001

Wickens, C. D., & McCarley, J. S. (2008). *Applied attention theory*. Boca Raton, FL: CRC Press.

Wolfe, J. M. (2007). Guided search 4.0: Current progress with a model of visual search. In W. Gray (Ed.), *Integrated Models of Cognitive Systems*, (pp. 99-119). New York, NY: Oxford.

Wolfe, J. M., Butcher, S. J., Lee, C., & Hyle, M. (2003). Changing your mind: On the contributions of top-down and bottom-up guidance in visual search for feature singletons. *Journal of Experimental Psychology. Human Perception and Performance*, *29*, 483–502. doi:10.1037/0096-1523.29.2.483

Wolfe, J. M., & Horowitz, T. S. (2004). What attributes guide the deployment of visual attention and how do they do it? *Nature Reviews. Neuroscience*, *5*, 1–7. doi:10.1038/nrn1411

Wolfe, J. M., Horowitz, T. S., Kenner, N., Hyle, M., & Vasan, N. (2004). How fast can you change your mind? The speed of top-down guidance in visual search. *Vision Research, 44,* 1411–1426. doi:10.1016/j.visres.2003.11.024

ADDITIONAL READING

Eckstein, M. P., Thomas, J. P., Palmer, J., & Shimozaki, S. S. (2000). Further predictions of signal detection theory on visual search accuracy: Conjunctions, disjunctions, and triple conjunctions. *Perception & Psychophysics, 62*(3), 425–451. doi:10.3758/BF03212096

Fecteau, J. H., & Munoz, D. P. (2006). Salience, relevance, and firing: A priority map for target selection. *Trends in Cognitive Sciences, 10*(8), 382–390. doi:10.1016/j.tics.2006.06.011

Folk, C. L., Remington, R. W., & Johnston, J. C. (1992). Involuntary covert orienting is contingent on attentional control settings. *Journal of Experimental Psychology. Human Perception and Performance, 18,* 1030–1044. doi:10.1037/0096-1523.18.4.1030

Henderson, J. M., & Hollingworth, A. (1999). High-level scene perception. *Annual Review of Psychology, 50,* 243–271. doi:10.1146/annurev.psych.50.1.243

Koch, C., & Ullman, S. (1985). Shifts in selective visual attention: Towards the underlying neural circuitry. *Human Neurobiology, 4,* 219–227.

Ludwig, J. H., & Gilchrist, I. D. (2002). Stimulus-driven and goal-driven control over visual selection. *Journal of Experimental Psychology. Human Perception and Performance, 28*(4), 902–912. doi:10.1037/0096-1523.28.4.902

Most, S. B., & Astur, R. S. (2007). Feature based attentional set as a cause for traffic accidents. *Visual Cognition, 15*(2), 125–132. doi:10.1080/13506280600959316

Peters, R. J., Iyer, A., Itti, L., & Koch, C. (2005). Components of bottom-up gaze allocation in natural images. *Vision Research, 45,* 2397–2416. doi:10.1016/j.visres.2005.03.019

Reynolds, J. H., & Desimone, R. (2003). Interacting roles of attention and visual salience in V4. *Neuron, 37,* 853–863. doi:10.1016/S0896-6273(03)00097-7

Theeuwes, J., Kramer, A. F., Hahn, S., & Irwin, D. E. (1998). Our eyes do not always go where we want them to go: Capture of the eyes by new objects. *Psychological Science, 9*(5), 379–385. doi:10.1111/1467-9280.00071

Treisman, A. M. (1982). Perceptual grouping and attention in visual search for features and for objects. *Journal of Experimental Psychology. Human Perception and Performance, 8,* 194–214. doi:10.1037/0096-1523.8.2.194

Wolfe, J. M. (1994). Guided search 2.0: A revised model of visual search. *Psychonomic Bulletin & Review, 1,* 202–238. doi:10.3758/BF03200774

Yantis, S., & Egeth, H. E. (1999). On the distinction between visual salience and stimulus-driven attentional capture. *Journal of Experimental Psychology. Human Perception and Performance, 25,* 661–676. doi:10.1037/0096-1523.25.3.661

Zoest, W., Donk, M., & Theeuwes, J. (2004). The role of stimulus-driven and goal driven control in saccadic visual selection. *Journal of Experimental Psychology. Human Perception and Performance, 30*(4), 746–759. doi:10.1037/0096-1523.30.4.749

KEY TERMS AND DEFINITIONS

Attention: The process where individuals become aware of certain items, but not others

Bottom-up Processes: Properties of items in a display that influence whether they are attended and enter awareness (e.g., visual saliency)

Top-down Processes: Characteristics of the user that influence whether items are attended and enter awareness (e.g., goals, intentions)

Visual Saliency: A measure of an item's visual uniqueness compared to its surroundings

Visual Search: A task where observers make responses to a target displayed among non-target/distractor items

Chapter 7
Design and Evaluation of a Multimodal Representation for Conveying the Vast Range of Imperceptible Smallness

Minyoung Song
University of Michigan, USA

ABSTRACT

Teaching and learning the vast range of the sizes that are too small to see (called imperceptible sizes) has been a challenging topic, and a need for a novel form of representation that may provide learners with an alternative way of perceiving and conceptualizing imperceptible sizes emerged. From this, the author introduces a multimodal representation called Temporal-Aural-Visual Representation (TAVR). Unlike commonly used conventional representations (e.g., visual representation), TAVR employs a temporal modality as the main vehicle for conveying imperceptible sizes. In this chapter, the author elaborates on the design process and the details of TAVR. Informed by cognitive psychology research, the mental model and the challenges for learners in understanding imperceptible sizes were identified to form the design requirements of TAVR. Following the design and implementation, the evaluation of TAVR aimed to assess the changes in the participating students' mental model of the range of imperceptible sizes, which showed TAVR's positive impact on student learning.

INTRODUCTION

Teaching and learning the sizes of the objects that are too small to see[1] (called imperceptible objects) has been a challenging issue in science education. Although there exists a vast range of imperceptible sizes, Research by Tretter, Jones, Andre, Negishi, and Minogue (2006a) shows that middle school students tend to think that the sizes of imperceptible objects (e.g., cells, bacteria, viruses, DNA, molecules, and atoms) are similar with each other, even with the size of a small macroscopic object such as a grain of sand or a dust particle. For example, middle school

DOI: 10.4018/978-1-4666-1628-8.ch007

students classified the imperceptible objects into one "small" group when they are asked to classify a number of objects (including macroscopic) by similar size, while experts divided the objects into at least three different groups; sub-nano, nano, and microscopic objects (Tretter, et al., 2006a). These misconceptions arise mainly because of the nature of human perception; we cannot see imperceptible objects with naked eyes. While people instantly form a visual mental image, which plays a critical role in size perception, of a perceptibly big object when they directly see it, they are unable to generate a visual mental image of something that is too small to see.

Hence, due to this nature that learners cannot have direct and holistic visual experience with imperceptible objects, they have to depend on representations to perceive and conceptualize the sizes of the objects. Representations involve symbols, rules, constraints, and relations embedded in figures such as spatial relations of written digits, visual and spatial layouts of diagrams, even thematic colors of certain items, etc. Such representations may allow a learner to understand concepts which are absent in space and time and to access knowledge and skills that would be beyond his or her cognitive capability. These roles of representations are particularly more important when students learn about imperceptible worlds because what learners perceive and conceptualize is mediated only by the representations they use. No one has ever directly seen what a Hydrogen atom looks like, but representations enable learners to visualize it.

A number of learning technologies have been developed to support learners to understand the vast range of imperceptible sizes. Commonly used learning technologies normally present learners with the representations that are presented in Figure 1. The examples in Figure 1 are created to convey the size of a Hydrogen atom in six different ways. These are commonly used representations among expert scientists and also in science textbooks. The first example is an absolute size of a Hydrogen atom. Experts use measurement units such as micrometer[2] or nanometer[3] to discuss the absolute sizes of imperceptible objects (e.g., "the diameter a Hydrogen atom is about 0.1 nanometer."), or one may use relative size (the second example) such as "the diameter of a DNA helix is about 10,000,000,000 times smaller than one millimeter." The logarithmic scale (third example) particularly aims to convey the range of different sizes. Visual representations (fourth example) perhaps are the most commonly used representations for learners in learning technologies and textbooks. The macroscopic graphics of imperceptible objects are usually aligned in line for size comparison. Interactive visual representations (example not included in Figure 1) present learners with the macroscopic depictions of visual representations such as video (e.g., Powers of Ten) or interactive graphic images (e.g., Scale Ladder). For example, the visual representations of imperceptible objects are enlarged to a visible scale through automatic zooming-in animation or via an interactive action such as click-to-zoom, frequently coupled with relative sizes that require students to mentally visualize the sizes of the objects through proportional reasoning.

These representations require one to be able to mentally visualize something that is one billion times smaller than one meter, which is beyond human's cognitive capability according to the studies on proportional reasoning (Tourniaire & Pulos, 1985). Hence, these notions of size are meaningless to learners. Also, because learners tend to focus on the surface features of representations rather than trying to interpret the underlying meanings and theories (Kozma, Chin, Russell, & Marx, 2000), students are highly likely to misinterpret the representation and in consequence to construct misconceptions. A logarithmic scale also provides representational features that a learner may have difficulty with interpreting. It makes the difference between certain sizes look smaller than it actually is. As in the example in Figure 1, the difference between the thickness of

Figure 1. Commonly used expressions of an imperceptible size. The examples in the box are created for the size of a hydrogen atom.

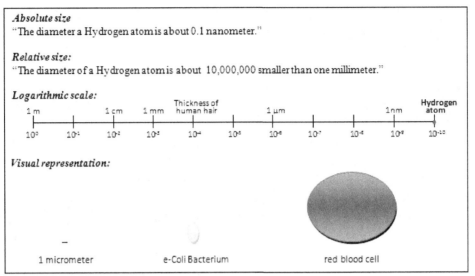

human hair and a Hydrogen atom is 6 bars, and the difference between a Hydrogen atom and 1 micrometer is 4 bars. However, the actual difference is by one million (Hydrogen atom and hair) and ten thousand (Hydrogen atom and 1 micrometer), which means that the relative difference between two objects may appear smaller to learners than it actually is.

Especially, the visual representations, which are the most commonly used representation in multimedia learning technologies, are misconception-laden. The exposures to these macroscopic visual representations of imperceptible objects are likely to inadvertently lead students to construct inaccurate mental models of the sizes of imperceptible objects.. In Tretter et al.'s (2006b) study, their participants answered, "when I picture [microscopic objects] I see the drawing [in textbooks]." In an interview that the author of this chapter conducted, it was noticed that some 7th grade students even thought that bacteria and viruses (called "germs" in their term) are as big as dust or a particle of fine-grained salt, but they are only invisible because they are transparent. These misconceptions seem to be developed under

the influence of the big-enough-to-see images of imperceptible objects, which is the exact opposite of the definition of imperceptibleness. They are designed and used in an assumption that the perception and cognition of the imperceptible size may somehow happen in the same way we do the sizes of perceptible objects, while the way people conceptualize a perceptible phenomenon and an imperceptible phenomenon is different because the modality of the mental image cannot be the same; one can build a concrete visual mental image from a perceptible experience while he cannot from an imperceptible experience. Macroscopic graphics are very effective for illustrating the shape, features, movement, or physical relationship between certain objects, as in the way they are frequently and effectively used to illustrate many scientific concepts. However, the macroscopic visual representations of imperceptible sizes are telling learners the contradictory to "too small to see."

Not all representations are useful for novices or learners. Different representations that have same abstract structure can make problem solving easier or more difficult (Norman, 1993; Rapp & Kurby, 2008; Scaife & Rogers, 1996; Zhang,

1997). Overly simplified representations that are designed for expert scientists would be meaningless to learners. On the contrary, a representation that requires a learner to focus on many components would overwhelm their cognitive capacity. In this regard, a novel form of representation that represents "too small to see" as "too small to see" is needed. A representation that does not require learners to depend on visual representations may help them achieve better comprehension of the vast range of imperceptible smallness. Representations co-determine the very nature of the human cognitive task, and interaction with representation may enhance and transform human cognition. This role of representation has been discussed by many scholars. Salomon, Perkins, and Globerson (1991) argued that higher order thinking skills are either activated during an activity with an intellectual tool or are explicitly modeled by it, through the "intellectual partnership" between a learner and a tool. Hutchins (1995) discussed that cognitive processes may be distributed in the sense that the operation of the cognitive system involves coordination between internal and external information structure. Pea (1993) used the term "distributed intelligence" to explain the cognitive activities that are socially constructed via the interaction between people and tools and the reciprocal development between human minds and the tools. The representational effect theory (Zhang & Norman, 1994), also implies that different external representations can have different impact on the cognitive tasks that learners have to deal with even if the represented information is the same. It is also known that a new type of representation that directs learners to explore the concepts in a different way may help them realize and revise their misconceptions by revealing the inconsistencies between their mental model and the new representation (Ainsworth, 1999; Chi, 2005).

To achieve this goal, an alternative representation, called Temporal-Aural-Visual Representation (TAVR) is designed to alter the way learners perceive and conceptualize the vast range of the imperceptible smallness. The representation takes temporal sense as a main modality for representing the imperceptible scale. The 'time' here refers to the duration of a sequential accumulation that happens in a limited space (i.e., placing strands of hair across the head of a pin at a certain velocity). It sequentially places an imperceptible object across the head of a pin (1 millimeter in diameter). This sequential accumulation of an imperceptible object is continued until the objects are fully lined up across the pinhead. Hence, the duration of the sequential action inferentially implies the sizes of the placed objects. The temporal representation is incorporated with visual and aural modalities, which are adopted to augment learners' temporal experience, together in a Temporal-Aural-Visual Representation (TAVR).

TAVR was designed following these steps:

1. The cognitive psychology literature on how people perceive and conceptualize sizes was reviewed to understand what it means to know the size of something and what compose the mental model of size.

2. The cognitive challenges to learners in understanding imperceptible sizes were examined as well as the reason why traditional representations (e.g., the macroscopic depictions) of imperceptible sizes are not as effective as they do for perceptible sizes. This work also was helpful for figuring out what does not.

3. The list of the necessary features of the representation was configured. The literature on the principles of representation design was taken into account in the design process to address learners' cognitive capability and pre-existing knowledge for better sense-making of the representation.

In the following, the discussion on each step of the design of TAVR is elaborated in detail. It will also show how this research was benefited from the research in cognitive psychology.

FIGURING OUT HOW TO REPRESENT "TOO SMALL TO SEE"

Different representations that have the same abstract structure can make problem solving easier or more difficult (Norman, 1993; Rapp & Kurby, 2008; Scaife & Rogers, 1996; Zhang, 1997). Deciding how to design a representation for learners can be informed much by the literature in cognitive psychology. Particularly, the three representation design principles that were discussed by Norman (1993) provides us with insights for representation design processes. According to Norman, a representation must meet the following three criteria.

First, a representation should capture the essential elements of represented phenomena, deliberately leaving out the rest to enhance a learner's cognitive ability because learners are likely to focus only on the surface features of the representations (as also discussed by Chi, Feltovich, & Glaser, 1981). This allows learners to concentrate on the important aspects of the representation and the target knowledge without getting distracted by the irrelevant or unimportant components. If the representation misleads learners away from the key aspects of the referent, it will direct them to ignore critical aspects of the event or perhaps form incorrect conclusions.

Second, a representation must be appropriate for the person's cognitive capacity. Working memory is the storage in which people maintain attentional focus for things that they are currently thinking about, whether those thoughts are driven by information from the environment or concepts we have retrieved from prior knowledge. Working memory has limits in its capacity and hence cannot process much information at the same time. Representations should address this nature of memory to help students deal with unfamiliar problem solving situations (Rapp & Kurby, 2008).

Consistently, cognitive load theory (Sweller, 1988) also argues that a learning material must direct a learner to use his/her most of the cognitive resource (working memory capacity in particular) on processing the key features of the target knowledge by reducing the cognitive burden that may be generated by irrelevant components in the material because the format of instructional materials has a direct effect on learner's cognitive performance. Hence, to make effective learning out of an instructional material, extraneous cognitive load that is caused by inappropriate designs must be eliminated.

Third, the properties of the representation must match the properties of what is being represented. Learning with a representation is most effective when the properties of the representation match the properties of what is being represented (Norman, 1993). To support learners to revise their mental models, it is critical to map the components of learning experience with the components of goal knowledge, or they are likely to construct even more idiosyncratic mental models of the knowledge. For example, children (age 6 to 7) find it very difficult to believe that the earth is a sphere because the information they collect from their daily physical experience that is tied to years of confirmation contradicts with the statement (Vosniadou & Brewer, 1992). Even after they were told that the earth is spherical, many of them maintained misconceptions, but in different forms, such as flattened sphere, hollow sphere, dual earth, disc earth, and etc.

These three principles of representation design imply that one must attempt to design a representation first by appreciating how humans perceive and conceptualize the target phenomena to effectively represent it without making learners to get distracted by unimportant or irrelevant features that do not coincide with the way people think about the target phenomena. Secondly, a designer ought to figure out the cognitive challenges that learners face, so that he/she can find alternative solution that may transform the ways learners perceive and conceptualize the target information respecting learners' cognitive limits. Lastly, a designer shall comprise the necessary features of the new representation. In this process, carefully examining why some of the preexisting representations have not been successful and what aspects of them contributed to the development of learners' misconceptions may also be helpful for identifying the required features of the new representation. In the below, the details of the design processes of TAVR are discussed.

Step 1: Reviewing Literature on How People Perceive and Conceptualize Size

To first understand how people conceptualize sizes, literature review of the cognitive psychology research on size perception and cognition was conducted. A cognitive model of how people compare different sizes, suggested by Kosslyn (1980, p. 363; 1994, p. 341), gives an implications for what compose the knowledge of size—the mental model of size. According to the model, the following information about size is stored in our long-term memory when we see an object or think about the size of an object, and they are recalled when we conduct a mental size comparison:

- *Conceptual size category tags:* These are labels for separable and distinct scale category (e.g., large, small). In a mental comparison task, people think of the size category tags as being relatively discrete.
- *Visual mental image[4]:* Visual mental image is "the mental invention or recreation of an experience that resembles the experience of actually perceiving an object or an event, either in conjunction with, or in the absence of, direct sensory stimulation."

Figure 2 illustrates the parallel process of mental size comparison of two different objects that involves conceptual size category tags and visual mental images of the objects. When a size comparison task is given, people simultaneously access and use both category tags and visual mental image in a parallel process (Route A and B in Figure 2). For example, when one attempts to compare the sizes of two objects with significantly different sizes (e.g., rat and cow) to decide which one is bigger, he/she simultaneously compares: (1) the category tags of rat and cow, and (2) the visual mental image of a rat and cow to develop an answer. In this case, the category tags of the animals' sizes differ with each other (e.g., rat is 'small' and cow is 'big'), therefore, the category

Figure 2. Mental size comparison process by Kosslyn (1980). Originally excerpted from Kosslyn, Murphy, Bemesderfer, and Feinstein's (1977) study and recreated for better readability. Route A and B are processed in parallel.

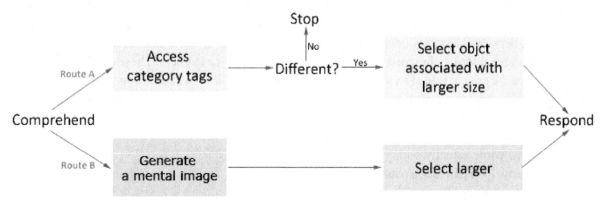

tags comparison process proceeds to the end of the Route A with the conclusion that a cow is bigger than a rat.

On the contrary, when one attempts to compare the sizes of two objects with the same category tags (e.g., both rat and chick are 'small'), the process of Route A stops at the interim step where the category tags are compared. Then only Route B that compares the visual mental image of the objects is processed to conclude which one of the objects is bigger. Therefore, a person depends on the visual mental images of the objects when they share the same scale category. The importance of category tags was also discussed in Tretter et al.'s (2006a) study. They used the term "unitizing" to describe how people use the distinctive size categories to conceptualize sizes. In their study, the experts whom they interviewed redefined inconvenient units when it was helpful for them to do so (e.g., converting the description of the size range from 1/10000 meter to a millimeter). They said that rewriting the size ranges in terms of these other units helped them better conceptualize the sizes than leaving everything in terms of a meter. Based on this observation, the authors discussed that supporting learners to become proficient at unitizing (categorization) may increase their ability to conceptualize the range of imperceptible sizes.

The process in route B implies that: (1) the visual mental image of the corresponding objects is retrieved from one's long-term memory whenever one tries to compare the sizes of different objects, and (2) the visual mental image of an object is a critical resource for conceptualizing its size and the difference between the sizes. Consistently, the findings from recent studies in spatial cognition also emphasize the critical role of a visual mental image in spatial cognition; people recall and evaluate visual mental image in memory in the same way that they would evaluate the representations that are evoked while actually seeing the object (Sims & Hegarty, 1997). In fact, a neuro-imaging study shows that the same parts of the brain were activated when people think of an image of an object as if they were seeing the actual object (Roland & Gulyas, 1994).

To summarize, Kosslyn's model indicates that conceptual category tags of sizes are important in constructing the mental models of sizes. Conceptual size category tags enable one to accurately differentiate between distinctively different sizes, and they also facilitate the learning of the size of a novel object by allowing the assignment of a scale category to the object.

Step 2: Defining the Challenges in Understanding Imperceptible Size

When representations stand between the target knowledge and learners, they act as an intermediary, requiring the learners to be proficient in both interpreting the representations and understanding the concept. At all times, there is a possibility that learners do not always benefit from all representations because they may impose constraints and challenges to learners. For example, overly simplified representations that are designed for scientists are likely to be interpreted incorrectly or meaninglessly by learners whose background knowledge is very poor and whose cognitive capabilities are limited. On the contrary, a representation that requires a learner to focus on many components would overwhelm their cognitive capacity. Existing literature on the way humans create visual mental image and conceptual categories implies that generating the visual mental image and conceptual size categories of imperceptible objects in the similar way we do for perceptible sizes is highly likely to be impossible for learners. These studies on human size perception and cognition give implications for why some representations have failed and what features may work.

Absence of Visual Mental Image

Among the information that learners construct through multimodal senses (e.g., tactile, olfactory, visual, aural), direct and holistic visual experience plays an especially critical role in spatial cognition (Kosslyn, Behrmann, & Jeannerod, 1995). Learning outcome, especially in science education, increase as a function of how easily one can develop a visual mental image of the to-be-studied information (Jenkins, 2010; Rapp & Kurby, 2008). The most accurate visual mental image of an object is created through a direct experience with the object (Jenkins, 2010), however, the direct and holistic visual experience is unavailable for imperceptible sizes, and it is the main reason why the challenges in understanding the imperceptible sizes occur. For instance, in Tretter et al.'s (2006a) study all participants exhibited the most accurate knowledge for the sizes of objects that are available for direct and holistic visual experience, while their performance tended to be relatively less accurate for imperceptible objects.

The absence of an accurate visual mental image becomes another form of challenge for learners because they have to depend on the representations to perceive and conceptualize the sizes of imperceptible objects. When a learner looks at a representation, he retrieves the elements of his mental model of the represented information and compares the representation and the mental model to decode which components of the representation stands for which aspects of the represented. Because learners' pre-existing mental models influence the way they make sense of representations (Buckley, 2000; Rapp & Kurby, 2008; Zhang & Norman, 1994), without an appropriate mental model, learners may not be able to benefit from a representation and even develop a misconception. The mental model of the size of an object heavily depends on the visual mental image and it is unlikely for learners to have the visual mental images of imperceptible objects because humans cannot see them. Therefore, this problem will make it even more difficult for learners to interpret the representations of imperceptible sizes.

Absence of Conceptual Size Categories

The role of conceptual size category tags becomes more critical in constructing a mental model of imperceptible sizes because it is almost impossible for a learner to develop the second component of the mental model of size - visual mental image. Lakoff (1987) and Chi and Roscoe (2002) argued that categorization is the main way that people make sense of experience. Kosslyn et al.'s (1977) model of mental size comparison also implies that conceptual size categories of sizes are likely to be particularly important in conceptualizing the sizes of imperceptible objects because it is impossible for humans to develop accurate visual mental image of such objects. However, it is known that learners lack conceptual size categories of the unseen sizes in quantity and quality (Tretter, et al., 2006a, 2006b), and therefore making advanced understanding of imperceptible sizes is difficult for them. For example, in Tretter et al.'s (2006a) study, middle school students categorized everything smaller than a human into one "Small" category that cannot be divided any further. Only a few students grouped the sizes smaller than a human into "small" and "too small to see." In contrast, experts formed more categories for the sizes smaller than a person, creating one category for small but visible objects (Small) and two separate groups (Many atoms and Atomic) for imperceptible objects that are too small to see, incorporating with the measurement units such as millimeter, micrometer, and nanometer. This lack of conceptual size categories amplifies the challenges for students in refining their mental model of the range of imperceptible sizes not only because the conceptual size category is a critical component of the mental model of a size (Kosslyn, 1994; Kosslyn, et al., 1977) but also because misconceptions are more difficult to fix when students lack an alternative category to shift concepts into (Chi & Roscoe, 2002).

The challenge of the absence of conceptual size categories is also derived from the ultimate problem of not being able to have a direct and holistic visual experience with imperceptible objects. Researchers discuss that the development of conceptual categories is highly experience-oriented. Rosch and Mervis (1975) and Lakoff (1987) argued that cognitive categories and concepts are typically generated through human interaction with the world. However, this interaction is direct and straightforward only at perceptible scales. Further, Rosch's category learning theory (1988) helps us understand why it is difficult for learners to develop the conceptual size categories for imperceptible sizes. The theory discusses that category learning is equivalent to learning the category prototype. That is, each category is represented by corresponding prototypes. A conceptual category is developed by first constructing a category prototype, and the exemplars of the category are created by randomly altering the prototype. When an unfamiliar stimulus is encountered, it is assigned to a category with the most similar prototype. For imperceptible sizes it is unlikely that students have formed the prototypes of each imperceptible size categories (e.g., atom for sub-nanoscopic, virus for nanoscopic, and bacterium for microscopic scale) because it has been very difficult for learners to make sense of 'how small' such objects are even before trying to make the connections between the objects and corresponding conceptual scale categories.

The limits in mental proportional reasoning capacity also contribute to the problem of the absence of conceptual size categories. A strong foundation in proportional reasoning ability is considered to be a prerequisite for developing unitizing skills because the process of converting units involves proportional reasoning (Tretter, et al., 2006a). For example, one has to know that one millionth of a meter equals one micrometer and must be able to convert the numbers through mathematical calculation. However, many students simply tend to think of something big as "large" without any mathematical computations, and it is difficult for them to make sense of large numbers through both mathematical calculations and analog representations because visualizing through mental proportional reasoning that involve large numbers is out of their cognitive capacity (Tourniaire & Pulos, 1985).

In conclusion, an alternative form of mental image that may help learners better conceptualize imperceptible sizes, not via visual representation, is deemed to be required. A mental image can be formed in different modalities (Kosslyn, 2005). Also, supporting learners to develop the conceptual size category tags is another critical goal to be achieved to help students construct a more refined mental model of imperceptible sizes.

Step 3: Addressing the Principles of Representation Design to Create a Representation that makes Sense to Learners

The previous steps covered how people think about sizes and what kinds of cognitive limits they have. It is thought that a representation can support learners better conceptualize the vast range of imperceptible sizes by meeting the following features. To represent "too small to see" as "too small to see, a representation for imperceptible sizes should:

1. Provide learners with non-visual mental image of imperceptible size.
2. Provide learners with conceptual size categories of imperceptible sizes.

Now, a representation designer has to ponder how to implement and integrate the required features to compose a representation, which demands a careful concern for learners and attentions to the fine details of the representation. How can a representation designer implement the two properties that are listed in the above into a representation? Cognitive mapping theory (Downs & Stea, 1973) provides an insight on how to approach this task. A learner has a mental model (called a "cognitive map" in this theory) of how to interpret the representation, and the representation also yields a conceptual model of how it can be interpreted. When the two models coincide, then there is a close "mapping" which is "the mental structuring process leading to the creation of a cognitive map." Addressing this theory, it becomes clear that sizes that are "too small to see" have to be represented as "too small to see," and this confirms that the main modality that conveys the imperceptibleness must be non-visual. In this regard, cognitive mapping theory also reinforces the explanation on why macroscopic visual representations have not been successful in helping learners better conceptualize imperceptible sizes: the macroscopic depictions of imperceptible objects perceptually contradict with what the representations are claiming to represent—the sizes that are too small to see. Therefore, to conceptualize sizes that are "too small to see," a learner may benefit from having an experience in non-visual modality.

Constructivist learning theory gives an inspiration for a solution to how to represent "too small to see." It discuss that learning is most effective when a learner can construct new knowledge upon their preexisting knowledge (Piaget, Gruber, & Vonèche, 1977; Wood, Bruner, & Ross, 1976). This implies that, without a comprehensible connection between a representation and what is represented, the representation can become ambiguous and misleading. Therefore, embedding a perceptible and familiar object as a reference size in the representation may help learners reconstruct their mental models based on what they already know. In this study, the head of a pin is chosen to be a reference object. Its diameter is one millimeter; it is small enough to be felt like a very small perceptible object. To convey the sizes of imperceptible objects by incorporating it with

a reference object, an approach of "conceptual metaphor" (diSessa, 2004) was made. A conceptual metaphor facilitates the abstraction of an unfamiliar knowledge by the mapping between the target domain (the conceptual domain from which we draw metaphorical expressions) and the source domain (the conceptual domain that learners try to understand). Considering this mechanism of conceptual metaphor and the necessity of conveying imperceptible sizes via non-visual modality, it was decided to use the concept of time to represent the imperceptibleness (the details are discussed in the next section).

To create an effective conceptual metaphor for scale categories, one can refer to the category learning theory by Rosch (1988) which discusses that category learning is equivalent to learning the category prototype. Each category is represented as prototype and developed by first constructing a category prototype and the exemplars of the category are created by randomly altering the prototype. When an unfamiliar stimulus is encountered, it is assigned to a category with the most similar prototype. According to Rosch (1988), there are two basic cognitive principles involved in the process of prototype category learning. The first is to achieve maximum differentiation between the prototypes of categories, allowing a learner to distinguish it clearly from all other categories. The second is to avoid cognitive overload, which would result from over-differentiating and a consequent loss in flexibility in grouping exemplars, which share important characteristics. In the representation that is designed for this study, the difference between the sizes of imperceptible objects can be recognized by the easily distinguishable units of time.

In the next section, the details of TAVR that is designed in respect to the requirements in the above is introduced, followed by the description of how its preliminary evaluation with middle school students was designed and conducted.

Figure 3. An illustration of how the accumulation is carried out in TAVR. The first imperceptible object is placed on the pinhead and one click is played (a). Then the second object is placed on the pinhead next to the first one, and one click is played (b). The process continues until the object spans the pinhead (c).

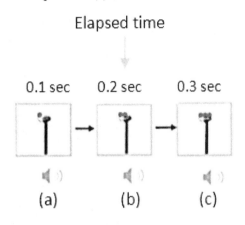

TEMPORAL-AURAL-VISUAL REPRESENTATION (TAVR)

In Temporal-Aural-Visual Representation (TAVR), the size of an imperceptible object is represented by the duration of sequential accumulation, and visual and aural representations are added to augment learners' temporal experience with imperceptible sizes. A number of an imperceptible object is placed consecutively across the head of a pin per 0.1 second until the accumulated line fully spans the diameter of the pinhead. When one object is placed, an audio clip that sounds like a single click of a mouse button is played once. The accumulation at imperceptible scale is represented only via sound, and visual representation is added once after the length of

Figure 4. A screen capture of the TAVR of Hydrogen atom. The images were captured at three different phases: (a) before a learner presses the Play button, (b) the progress of the accumulation during about 11 hours (notice the short red line that indicates the current progress of the accumulation), (c) the accumulation is completed. It is notified by the bright cyan-colored square around the icon and the label on the button (says Replay). Students can fast forward the accumulation by clicking >>FF button below the Play button.

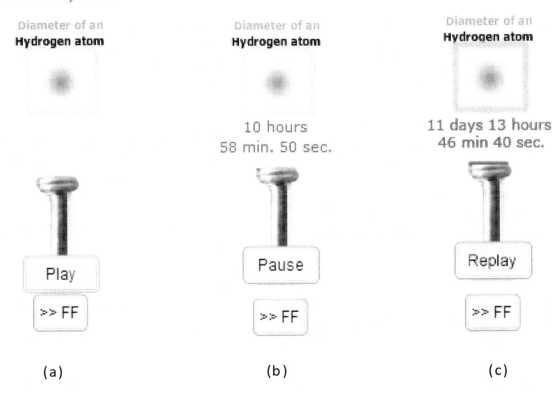

the accumulation enters macroscopic scale. The elapsed time (clock) is shown. See Figure 3 for an illustration of how the accumulation is carried out in TAVR and Figure 4 for a screen capture of how an actual TAVR works.

In TAVR there exists an inverse relationship between the duration of accumulation and the size of an imperceptible object. The smaller the object, the more objects are required to span the head of a pin. Therefore, the duration of the accumulation of the selected objects becomes longer as the sizes of the objects gets smaller.

The Rationale behind the use of Temporal Modality

The temporal component of the representation is the time it takes for the object to span across the pinhead. It is expected to play the main role in helping a learner conceptualize the relative small-ness of imperceptible objects. By observing the difference in the duration of accumulation, learn-ers are expected to conceptualize out that: (1) the sizes of imperceptible objects are very small, and (2) there exist drastic differences between their sizes. Temporal modality was chosen based on many literature that discuss that the concept of time and the concept of spatial information are interwoven in people's mental representation (Droit-Volet, 2001; Friedman, 1979; Jarman, 1979; McCormack & Hoerl, 2008; Tretter, et al., 2006a; Vallesi, Binns, & Shallice, 2008). This suggests that our mental models of things we can never see or touch may be built, in part, out of the representations of physical experiences in perception and action that happen over a certain period of time. Tretter et al. (2006b) also argue that a multimodal tool that provides a learner with sequential experience of the size of imperceptible objects over a certain period of time may be helpful for students to understand imperceptible sizes. Students have the sense of time (in terms of duration) that is acquainted through their daily lives. Many meaningful events are attached to certain periods of time.

In fact, the concept of time and the concept of spatial information are interwoven in people's mental representation (Casasanto & Boroditsky, 2008; Droit-Volet, 2001; Friedman, 1979; Gentner, Imai, & Boroditsky, 2002; Jarman, 1979; Mc-Cormack & Hoerl, 2008; Tretter, et al., 2006a; Vallesi, et al., 2008). There exist many examples in our daily lives that use the duration of an event to communicate about abstract spatial information. As shown in Table 1, people often talk about time using spatial language. The metaphorical relation-ship between space and time observed in language also exists in our more basic representations of distance and duration (Casasanto & Boroditsky, 2008). The land size measuring unit "acre" has its historic origin in the amount of land that a man behind an ox could plow in a day (Wikipedia). Astronomers have been using the unit "light years" to describe the planetary distances. Tretter et al. (2006a) noticed that people conceptualized sizes too big to see by inferring from the sequential actions (e.g., walking, running, or driving) on the distance over a certain period of time. The

Table 1. Space-time correspondences in language, excerpted from Gentner et al. (2002)

Space	Time
At the corner	At noon
From here to there	From two o'clock to four o'clock
Through the tunnel	Through the night
He stood before the house	It happened before evening
He was running ahead of me	He arrived ahead of me

students participating in their study compared the time it took to drive across a town and the time it took to drive across the state of North Carolina to reason which size is bigger than the other and also how distinctively different they are. Based on this observation Tretter et al. discussed that perceptions of time and perceptions of size are interwoven in people's mental models of sizes.

As the examples illustrate, the metaphorical relationship between space and time observed in language exists in our more basic mental representations of space and time. Our mental representations of things we can never see or touch may be built, in part, out of representations of physical experiences in perception and action that happen over a certain period of time (Casasanto & Boroditsky, 2008).

Furthermore, the units of time (e.g., second, minute, hour, day, week, month, and year) may provide a set of pre-set conceptual categories to learners. A conceptual metaphor (which here is created through the mapping between the units of time and the distance) may facilitate the abstraction of an unfamiliar knowledge (diSessa, 2004)—the imperceptible sizes. As discussed in the previous section, a conceptual metaphor is created by analogically extending the conceptual structure from richer, experience-based domains (the units of time in this study) to structure learners' understanding of relatively more abstract domains (the imperceptible sizes) (Boroditsky, 1997; Boroditsky & Ramscar, 2002; Lakoff & Johnson, 1980). In TAVR, the units of time (e.g., second, minute, hour, and day) can be a convenient method for conveying different imperceptible scales. It may be easier for learner to understand the vast range of imperceptible sizes. Calculating the difference between 6 micrometer and 0.1 nanometer is likely to be beyond learners' cognitive capacity, but the difference between 14 seconds and 12 days (in TAVR time) may be less challenging to them.

The virtual sequential experience with macroscopic sizes that was briefly suggested, though not designed, in Tretter et al.'s (2006a) study

was a non-inverse relationship that the duration is relative to the distance that involved a imperceptible object traveling across a macroscopic object. However, imperceptible objects cannot be used as the size reference to make a non-inverse relationship, as using the size of a human as a reference to measure the size of a football field, because learners do not know the size of an atom (and any other imperceptible objects), for instance. Learning happens when a learner can construct new knowledge based on their pre-existing knowledge (Piaget, et al., 1977) and hence the learning would not be meaningful when it involves subjects that learners are not familiar with. Therefore, to help learners make connections with the sizes they already know, the head of a pin is used as a reference size. One millimeter is one of the standard measurement units such as centimeter or micrometer that learners can connect with certain sizes in the future.

In summary, referring back to Kosslyn's model of mental size comparison, the difference between the durations of accumulation may help learners understand the difference between the sizes of imperceptible objects (addresses the Route B in Figure 2), while the units of time for the duration of sound of each imperceptible object (e.g., seconds, hours, and days) may help learners conceptualize the vast range of imperceptible smallness (addresses the Route A in Figure 2).

Aural and Visual Representation

Aural and visual representations in TAVR are adopted as vehicles to convey the action of accumulation. When it comes to the matter of representing how small an imperceptible object is, the representation for an object that is "too small to see" should not be visual (or visible) because it can misguide learners to overestimate the sizes of imperceptible objects. In TAVR, there exists only sound feedback to represent the accumulation of imperceptible scales. Visual representation is added only after the sequential accumulation enters

Figure 5. The sizes and the duration of accumulation for the imperceptible objects used in this study

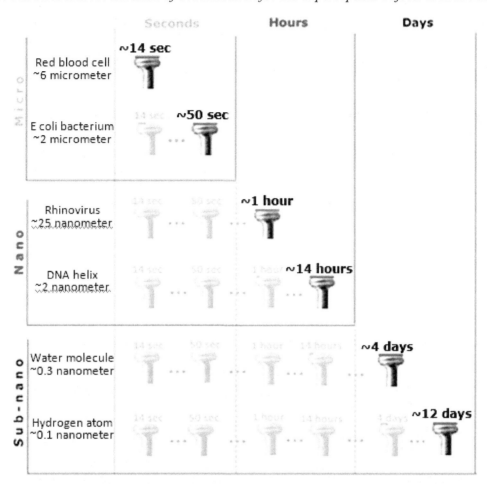

macroscopic scale. Therefore, when an object is macroscopic, learners can see the object being placed on a pinhead and hear the click simultaneously as soon as they begin playing TAVR. When the object is imperceptible, students have to wait for an enough number of objects to be accumulated, as illustrated in Figure 5. During this time they can only hear the sound of objects being placed one after another without being able to see them being placed.

Among different types of non-visual modalities (e.g., tactile) that may be useful for representing the accumulation in imperceptible scale, sound was chosen to represent the imperceptible size based on the way our working memory processes two different channels of modality (Paivio,

1986)—information is processed through two separate, but parallel, channels, visual and auditory. According to this theory, effective learning happens when the information in two channels match and interact closely. Through this process, a learner integrates the mental representations from two channels. In TAVR, the accumulation of an object is represented via sound. When the accumulation is in imperceptible scale, there exists sound only. When the accumulation enters macroscopic scale, a learner can see the visual representation (red line) growing as the accumulation continues. Through the accumulation in TAVR, learners have to simultaneously attend to both visual and aural representations to observe the sequential accumulation, and the theory of dual coding theory suggests a learner is highly likely to be capable of paying attention to both aural and visual stimuli.

Application: Wow, It Is Small! (WIIS)

Wow, It Is Small! (WIIS), a Flash-based application was designed to provide a set of learning activities where students can interact with TAVRs for selected imperceptible objects. WIIS is composed of a set of TAVRs for different imperceptible object (see Figure 5 for selected objects) and an interface to support learners' sense-making, following the scaffolding work in Quintana et al. (2004) (see Figure 6 for the screen captures

for each learning phase). Students can directly manipulate the TAVRs in drag-and-drop fashion to order the represented objects by size while interacting with TAVRs. In WIIS, the largest units of the accumulation time of the selected sample imperceptible objects match with the scale category they belong to as illustrated in Figure 5. For example, it takes several seconds for microscopic objects, hours for nanoscale objects, and days for sub-nanoscale objects.

Figure 6. Three phases of learning activity in WIIS: Students order the objects from the smallest to biggest depending on their preexisting knowledge.

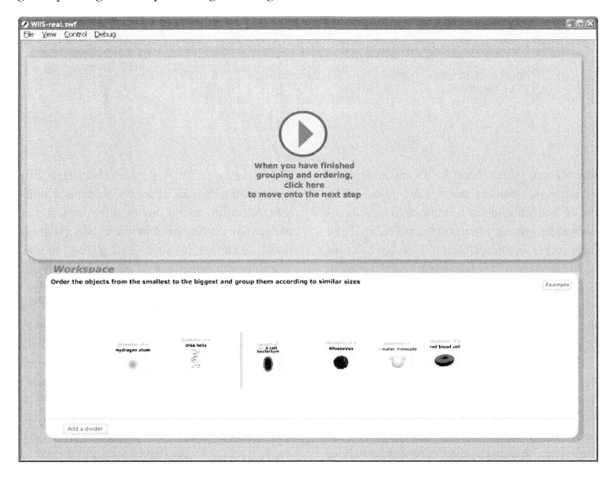

EVALUATING TAVR

The TAVR evaluation (Song & Quintana, 2009) introduced in this section was conducted to explore whether middle school students could interpret what TAVR represents and how their mental models change of the range of imperceptible sizes after the learning activity with TAVRs in WIIS. The research questions were framed into two themes: (1) examining whether students could appropriately interpret TAVRs (research question 1 in the following), and (2) investigating how their mental model of the range of imperceptible smallness changes over the learning activity with TAVRs (research question 2). The following list is the specific research questions and sub-questions:

1. *Do students understand what TAVR represents?* Since TAVR is a novel form of representation that learners are not familiar with, I thought it important to first investigate whether learners can correctly interpret what TAVR represents and how it works. With this purpose in mind, three sub-questions that address the specific aspects of TAVR were developed.
   a. Do students understand that one click corresponds to one object placed on the pinhead?
   b. Do students understand that there exists only sound until the accumulation of imperceptible object becomes macroscopic?
   c. Do students understand that the smaller the object the longer the duration of sound?

2. *Does TAVR help learners more accurately conceptualize the sizes of imperceptible objects? How do learners use the temporal aspect of TAVR to conceptualize the sizes of the imperceptible objects?* If the duration of the accumulation of an imperceptible object in TAVR was meaningful to the students in more accurately conceptualizing the imperceptible sizes, they would exhibit the evidence in performing the tasks. For example, representations of the sizes of imperceptible objects they created before and after the learning activity with TAVRs would reflect the difference they observed.

Methods

Participants

Forty-five middle school students from local public and private schools located in mid-west region of the United States participated in the study. The participants were composed of a focus interview group and two in-class learning activity groups. A focus group was formed with eleven 7th grade students who volunteered for individual interview. Every student was given a PC laptop computer, with WIIS installed, computer mouse, and personal headphone (see Table 2).

Data Collection and Analysis

Before interviewing, the researcher checked if the students were equipped with the basic idea of what the selected imperceptible objects are (e.g., the names of the objects and that they are too small to see with human eyes). Then their knowledge

Table 2. Demographics of the participants in prior study

Gender		Grade		Total
M	**F**	**7th**	**8th**	
23	22	30	15	45

about the sizes of the objects (card-sorting task) was examined. The card sorting task was composed of three sub-tasks:

1. *Ordering:* students order the imperceptible objects by size—from the smallest to the biggest.
2. *Grouping:* Then they classify the objects by similar size and divide them into several groups. The number of groups could vary from 1 to 6.

To investigate whether the students could understand what TAVR represents, the researcher asked them a set of questions after they explored the sample TAVRs. The questionnaire for research question 1 was developed to investigate whether the students could understand the basic mechanism of TAVR: (1) that one click represents one object placed on a pinhead, (2) that there exists only sound until the accumulation becomes macroscopic, and (3) the inverse relationship between the time it takes for an object to span the pinhead and the size of the object.

To observe how the students' mental model of the range of imperceptible sizes changes over time (research question 2), students were asked to order the objects from the smallest to the biggest before they began exploring the sizes of the objects in WIIS (as in Phase 1 in Figure 5). After they interacted with the TAVRs for each imperceptible object (as Phase 3 in Figure 5 shows), they were told to revise their initial ordering based on the experience with TAVRs. Further, to investigate how the students used the temporal component of TAVR to refine their mental model of the imperceptible sizes, the researcher asked them to predict the accumulation time for each imperceptible object.

After the learning activity, the students were told to reflect upon the difference between their prediction and the actual result. Students represented their reflections by editing the drawings of the objects and marking on a seven-point bipolar

Likert scale that ranged between "extremely smaller than I thought," "similar with what I thought," and "extremely bigger than I thought" (see Figure 9). After students finished reflecting in the scale, a researcher asked them to explain the logic behind their selection of the scales. In this way, the researcher attempted to investigate how the learners revised their mental model of the range of imperceptible sizes using the accumulation time in TAVR. If the unit of time was meaningful for them in conceptualizing the sizes of imperceptible objects, the participants would reflect that experience in the scale. For example, if a participant's prediction on the duration of sound for an atom was one hour, then she would find out that her prediction was way off than the actual result (~12 days). If she made a meaningful relationship between the unit of time and the represented size, she would mark on one of 'smaller than I thought' bars in the scale. To analyze the participants' response in Likert scale, the consistency between the participants' reflection on bipolar Likert scale and the difference between their prediction and the result of TAVRs was assessed.

The students were provided with a TAVR that accumulates strands of hair for grasping at least the vague sense of accumulation time for imperceptible objects, using the accumulation time for hair as the maximum accumulation time that may be possible for the imperceptible objects. The thickness of hair is almost the smallest size that human can see with the naked eye (about 100 micrometer), and it takes one second to simulate the accumulation on the head of a pin in TAVR. Since the students knew that the sizes of imperceptible objects are smaller than the thickness of hair, at least they could predict that the accumulation of imperceptible objects in TAVR should take shorter than 1 second. The students' interaction with WIIS that was showing on the computer screen and their verbal responses were recorded by using a screen recording software called Camtasia Studio.

The coding schemes were developed to quantify the collected data based on Chi's (1997) discussions that quantifying the subjective or qualitative verbal utterance is useful to objectively assess learners' knowledge. The rubrics were developed following the guideline suggested by Stix (1996):

- Decide whether the rubric addressed the most important aspects of student performance.
- Decide whether or not the rubric addresses the instructional outcome(s) to be measured.
- Decide whether the rubric includes anything extraneous. If so, change the rubric or use a different one.
- Do not pay too much attention to the rubric's stated grade level. It may be usable at other grades with little or no modification.
- See if a rubric from a different subject area can be adapted to fit your needs.
- Make sure the rubric is clear.
- Try the rubric out on some actual samples of student work.

- See if you and your colleagues can usually arrive at consensus about what scores to assign a piece of student work (Stix, 1996).

Stix also provided a framework of rubrics (see Table 3), which was used as the framework for the coding scheme for data analysis in this research. Table 4 is an example of the coding rubric that is used to analyze the participants' performance of card sorting task.

Results and Discussions

In the preparation interview that assessed the participants' pre-existing knowledge, it was noticed that all of the students had a basic idea of what the objects were and that the objects were too small to see with human eyes. The ordering and grouping tasks by all students were incorrect.

Research Question 1

In students' answers to the questions that aimed to probe their understanding of the mechanism of

Table 3. Framework of coding scheme used in this study

	Novice	Apprentice	Veteran
Content	Incorrect or few facts, hardly any detail (0 pt.)	Some facts are accurate, some detail (1 pt.)	Substantial amount of facts, good amount of detail (2 pts.)
Logic	Vague and unclear (0 pt.)	Some focus, but not organized enough (1 pt.)	Well organized and clearly presented (2 pts.)

Table 4. Coding scheme for a task given to the participants, modified from Stix's (1996) framework in Table 3

	Novice	Apprentice	Veteran
Content	1 group (0 pt.)	Ordered 1-3 objects incorrectly and formed 2 groups or more than 4 groups (1 pts.)	Correct order of the objects and classification of 3 groups with correct membership (2 pts.)
Logic	Illogical justification or random guess (0 pt.)	Can provide a logical justification but not consistent across all objects (1 pt.)	Can provide a logical justification (2 pts.)

Table 5. Types of the participants' grouping task

Object	Size	duration	Scale groups	What the participants did (in posttest)				
				Group category 1 (N = 3)	Group category 2 (N =3)	Group category 3 (N =2)	Group category 4 (N =1)	Group category 5 (N = 2)
Hydrogen atom	~0.1 nm	~12 days	(days) Sub-nano	Group 1	Group 1	Group 1	Group 1	Group 1
water molecule	~0.3 nm	~4 days			Group 2	Group 2		Group 2
DNA helix	~2 nm	~14 hours	(hours) Nano	Group 2	Group 3	Group 3	Group 2	Group 3
Rhinovirus	~25 nm	~1 hours			Group 4		Group 3	Group 4
E Coli bacterium	~2 μm	~ 50 sec	(seconds) Micro	Group 3	Group 5	Group 4	Group 4	Group 5
red blood cell	~6 μm	~ 14 sec						Group 6

TAVRs, 91% of the participants showed that they had correctly comprehended what TAVRs represent. In detail, 41 out of 45 students accurately stated that: (1) one click corresponds to one object placed on the head of a pin, (2) it takes a longer time for an imperceptible object to become macroscopic and visible and complete the accumulation, and (3) drastic differences exist between the duration of simulations for imperceptible objects with different sizes. This implies that such simulation, and the inverse relationship between the time (that it takes for an object to span the pinhead) and the size of the object, may not be a difficult concept for middle school students to understand.

Research Question 2

The data showed that TAVR was useful for the students in refining their mental models of imperceptible sizes. All participants correctly sorted the objects by size using the temporal information given in the TAVRs because they all understood the inverse relationship between the accumulation time and size. Most of the participants exhibited enhanced differences in their conception of the sizes of imperceptible objects after the exploration. 86% of them created a more number of groups in posttest then in pretest, which implies that their mental model of the range of imperceptible sizes has been expanded. In the focus group interview, it was found that some students classified the

objects into three groups by referring to the biggest unit of time (e.g., by several days, hours, and seconds), while some other students classified the objects in more numbers because they thought the differences between the accumulation time for some imperceptible object were large enough to be separated in different scale groups (see Table 5). It appears that this difference occurred mainly because of the difference in the participants' conception of time. Here, the strategies that the students of each case used are introduced.

Group Category 1 (N=3)

These students classified the objects into three groups only based on the biggest unit of the time of the duration of sound (e.g., by several days, hours, and seconds). They commented that they simply focused on the biggest units of the duration of sound and grouped objects with same biggest units of time into one group.

Group Category 2 (N=3)

These participants stated that the differences between atom, molecule, DNA, and virus are large enough to put them in separate groups, but the difference within a range of several seconds occurred between a bacterium and red blood cell is insignificant. They stated that the difference of several seconds between a bacterium and red blood cell is short enough to put them in one group, but the differences in several hours or days are too large compared to the difference of several seconds. It seemed that they used 'several seconds' as a standard of evaluating whether different objects have similar sizes or not.

Group Category 3 (N=2)

These students stated that the difference between atom and molecule (several days) was large enough to put them in separate groups but the differences within a range of several seconds or hours are not very significant. One student commented, *"...some seconds (bacterium and red blood cell) are very short, and ... these [DNA and virus] can happen within one day, I mean much less than a day. But this [molecule] needs several days, so it's much longer than those. And for the atom it takes almost two weeks. These are just way longer than the others like DNA, and they are also very different with each other."* These students referred to the units of time in their justification, although the way conceptualized and used the units of time was different with what I expected them to do.

Group Category 4 (N=1)

This student made three groups at first, but soon changed it to four groups. He commented that he first grouped the objects according to the biggest unit of time but he soon thought that the difference between DNA and virus was too large compared to the difference between bacterium and red blood cell or the difference between atom and molecule.

Group Category 5 (N=2)

These students thought that the differences in the accumulation time for each imperceptible object were significantly different with each other and the differences between each object and red blood cell seemed large enough to be *"by themselves."*

The ratio of the revisions that the students made to their own drawings of the objects tended to be consistent with the amount of the difference between their prediction and the result, although it was not mathematically accurate. For example, when their prediction was shorter than the actual result only by a few seconds, they made relatively smaller changes to their drawings than to the drawings of the objects of which their predictions were off by more than several hours.

The students' reflections in the seven point bipolar Likert scale are summarized in Figure 7. 82% (37 out of 45 students) of the students stated that all of the given imperceptible objects turned out to be smaller than they thought. 18% (8 students) answered that the size of red blood cells was similar to their initial beliefs and the rest of the objects were smaller than they had thought. Figure 10 shows that the smaller the size of the objects, the more dramatic reactions students tend to make after interacting with TAVRs, and this may imply that TAVR is particularly effective for conveying sizes that are extremely small.

During the focus group interviews, it was noticed that: (1) all students actively referred to the difference between their prediction and the actual result to respond to the Likert scale question, (2) the responses in the scale were consistent with the difference between the prediction and result they noticed, and (3) their responses in the scale were consistent with the scale of the difference between the prediction and result. For example, a student who predicted that it would take less than one hour for an atom to span the pinhead (it takes about 12 days) answered that the size of an atom was "extremely smaller than I thought" in the scale. The same student responded that the size of a red blood cell was similar to what he thought because his prediction was 10 seconds, which was only 4 seconds short of the actual duration (it takes about 14 seconds for a red blood cell). This consistency in the justification was noticed in all participants' responses.

Figure 7. Three phases of learning activity in WIIS: Students play sample TAVRs and solve quizzes to check their understanding of what TAVR simulates.

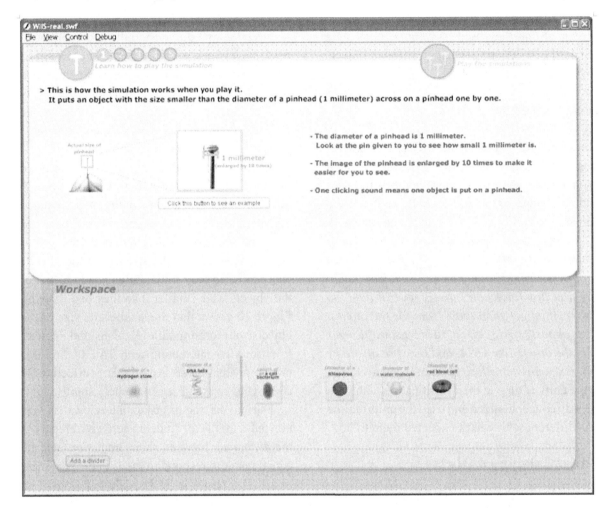

In summary, students accurately ordered the given imperceptible objects by size based on their experience with TAVRs and exhibited positive change in their conception of relative smallness of the imperceptible sizes through the representations they created. Taken together, these results imply that: (1) 7th grade students could understand that TAVR represents the size of an imperceptible object by the inverse relationship between the duration of sound and the size, and (2) TAVR was useful for the students to construct more useful mental images of the range of imperceptible sizes. Further, it is clear that time is a meaningful concept for learners and that they can analogically achieve better comprehension of abstract spatial knowledge using it. Relating these findings with Kosslyn's model of size comparison (Figure 2), TAVR was useful in supporting the students conceptualize the relative smallness of imperceptible objects (which concerns Route B in Figure 2) and was also effective for providing a support for the development of conceptual size category tags (Route A in Figure 2).

Figure 8. Three phases of learning activity in WIIS: Students explore the sizes of imperceptible objects by interacting with TAVRs created for the objects. Students can revise their initial object ordering from Phase 1.

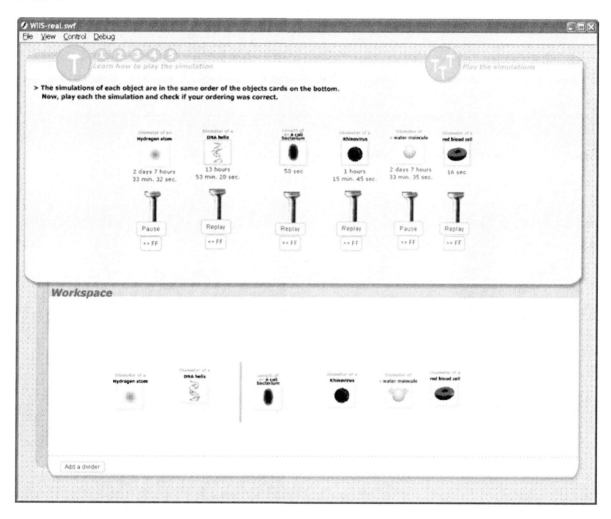

CONCLUSION

This chapter presented the design process of multimodal representation that incorporates a temporal modality for supporting learners to explore the vast range of imperceptible sizes. It was designed by carefully reviewing what cognitive psychology research informs as to how humans perceive and conceptualize size as well as the properties of a representation for learning. The research on the human mental model of sizes enabled the researcher to the design of TAVR and to develop assessment tasks for learners. The tasks for students were designed to detect the changes in the mental models of the range of imperceptible sizes. Overall, it was clear that time is a meaningful concept for middle school students that they can analogically build further understanding of an abstract concept upon by providing learners with a new channel of non-visual mental image creation. The temporal representations of imperceptible sizes helped learners construct more refined mental models of the range of imperceptible sizes. It may be easier for learners to communicate imperceptible

Figure 9. An example of Likert-like bipolar scale used to probe the student's conceptual change of size of imperceptible objects

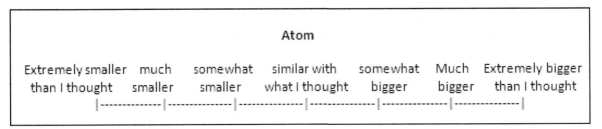

Figure 10. The students' reflections in the seven point bipolar Likert scale

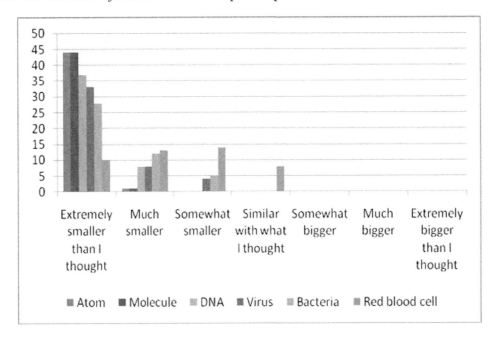

sizes in terms of TAVR time (e.g., "The size of a Hydrogen atom is about 12 days.") rather than absolute sizes (e.g., "The size of a Hydrogen atom is 0.1 nanometer.") or relative sizes (e.g., "The size of a Hydrogen atom is about ten million times smaller than 1 millimeter.").

A greater number of interfaces are becoming multimodal. Unlike visual representations, temporal representation has not been explored much even in conjunction with other modalities for conveying an abstract concept in the field of learning technologies. The research introduced in this chapter shows that interacting with a novel

form of technology can alter the ways people think about an abstract concept and consequently improves the comprehension of abstract information that humans cannot perceive. This study may inform the community of interface researchers and designers about whether and how the temporal modality can be used to expand the potentials of learning technologies.

The author of this article would like to emphasize that, although visual representation and other conventional representations of imperceptible sizes are difficult for learners to comprehend, it does not mean that learning about imperceptible sizes must exclude such representations. In addition to supporting students to construct a more refined mental model of the range of imperceptible sizes, TAVR may also be useful for them to make better sense of preexisting representations which are commonly used by scientists and contemporary science literature and media. Learning with multiple representations can offer unique benefits when people learn new ideas (Ainsworth, 1999; Kozma & Russell, 2005; Mayer & Sims, 1994). According to Ainsworth (1999), learners can benefit from using multiple representations in two ways. First, multiple representations may complement each other with regard to their content, their computational efficiency and with regard to learner characteristics and preferences. Second, multiple representations may constraint the interpretation of another representation. The combination of different representations enables learners to deal with the material from different perspectives and with different strategies. Working with two different representational formats engenders two different ways of insight to the same target knowledge and may have synergetic effects on the construction of coherent knowledge structures. In this regard, providing learners with a more number of representations that convey imperceptible sizes may help them to construct an even better mental model of the range of imperceptible sizes.

However, these benefits may not always be easily achieved. Interpreting and integrating the multiple representations will be additional challenges to the learners. It is known that learners tend to have difficulty not only in interpreting representation, but also in making connections between different representations (Kozma, et al., 2000). Therefore, one must carefully approach to providing learners with multiple representations. Students' preexisting misconceptions and the potential misconceptions that may be generated by the representations must be thoroughly investigated first.

REFERENCES

Ainsworth, S. (1999). The functions of multiple representations. *Computers & Education, 33*(2-3), 131–152. doi:10.1016/S0360-1315(99)00029-9

Boroditsky, L. (1997). *Evidence for metaphoric representation: Perspective in space and time.* Paper presented at the 19th Annual Conference of the Cognitive-Science-Society. Palo Alto, CA.

Boroditsky, L., & Ramscar, M. (2002). The roles of body and mind in abstract thought. *Psychological Science, 13*(2), 185–189. doi:10.1111/1467-9280.00434

Buckley, B. C. (2000). Interactive multimedia and model-based learning in biology. *International Journal of Science Education, 22*(9), 895–935. doi:10.1080/095006900416848

Casasanto, D., & Boroditsky, L. (2008). Time in the mind: Using space to think about time. *Journal of Cognition, 3*(4).

Chi, M. T. H. (1997). Quantifying qualitative analyses of verbal data: A practical guide. *Journal of the Learning Sciences, 6*(3), 271–315. doi:10.1207/s15327809jls0603_1

Chi, M. T. H. (2005). Commonsense conceptions of emergent processes: Why some misconceptions are robust. *Journal of the Learning Sciences, 14*(2), 161–199. doi:10.1207/s15327809jls1402_1

Chi, M. T. H., Feltovich, P. J., & Glaser, R. (1981). Categorization and representation of physics problems by experts and novices. *Cognitive Science, 5*(2), 121–152. doi:10.1207/s15516709cog0502_2

Chi, M. T. H., & Roscoe, R. D. (2002). The processes and challenges of conceptual change. In Mason, M. L. A. L. (Ed.), *Reconsidering Conceptual Change: Issues in Theory and Practice* (pp. 3–27). Dordrecht, The Netherlands: Springer Netherlands. doi:10.1007/0-306-47637-1_1 diSessa, A. A. (2004). Metarepresentation: Native competence and targets for instruction. *Cognition and Instruction*, *22*(3), 293–331. doi:10.1207/s1532690xci2203_2

Downs, R. M., & Stea, D. (1973). Cognitive maps and spatial behavior: Process and products. In Downs, R. M., & Stea, D. (Eds.), *Image & Environment: Cognitive Mapping and Spatial Behavior* (pp. 8–26). New Brunswick, NJ: Aldine Transaction. doi:10.1002/9780470979587.ch41

Droit-Volet, S. (2001). Temporal bisection in children. *Journal of Experimental Child Psychology*, *80*(2), 142–159. doi:10.1006/jecp.2001.2631

Friedman, W. (1979). *The development of relational understandings of temporal and spatial terms*. Retrieved from http://www.eric.ed.gov/PDFS/ED178176.pdf.

Gentner, D., Imai, M., & Boroditsky, L. (2002). As time goes by: Evidence for two systems in processing space-time metaphors. *Language and Cognitive Processes*, *17*(5), 537–565. doi:10.1080/01690960143000317

Jarman, R. F. (1979). Matching of auditory–visual and temporal–spatial information by seven- and nine-year-old children. *Child Development*, *50*(2), 575–577. doi:10.2307/1129438

Jenkins, M. H. (2010). *The effects of using mental imagery as a comprehension strategy for middle school students reading science expository texts*. Retrieved from http://search.ebscohost.com/login.aspx?direct=true&db=psyh&AN=2010-99051-321&site=ehost-live.

Kosslyn, S. M. (1980). *Image and mind*. Cambridge, MA: Harvard University Press.

Kosslyn, S. M. (1994). *Image and brain: The resolution of the imagery debate*. Cambridge, MA: MIT Press.

Kosslyn, S. M. (2005). Reflective thinking and mental imagery: A perspective on the development of posttraumatic stress disorder. *Development and Psychopathology*, *17*(3), 851–863. doi:10.1017/S0954579405050406

Kosslyn, S. M., Behrmann, M., & Jeannerod, M. (1995). The cognitive neuroscience of mental imagery. *Neuropsychologia*, *33*(11), 1335–1344. doi:10.1016/0028-3932(95)00067-D

Kosslyn, S. M., Murphy, G. L., Bemesderfer, M. E., & Feinstein, K. J. (1977). Category and continuum in mental comparisons. *Journal of Experimental Psychology*, *106*(4), 341–375.

Kozma, R., Chin, E., Russell, J., & Marx, N. (2000). The roles of representations and tools in the chemistry laboratory and their implications for chemistry learning. *Journal of the Learning Sciences*, *9*(2), 105–143. doi:10.1207/s15327809jls0902_1

Kozma, R., & Russell, J. (2005). Multimedia learning of chemistry. In Mayer, R. E. (Ed.), *The Cambridge Handbook of Multimedia Learning* (pp. 409–428). Cambridge, UK: Cambridge University Press.

Lakoff, G. (1987). *Women, fire, and dangerous things: What categories reveal about the mind*. Chicago, IL: University of Chicago Press.

Lakoff, G., & Johnson, M. (1980). *Metaphors we live by*. Chicago, IL: University of Chicago Press.

Mayer, R. E., & Sims, V. K. (1994). For whom is a picture worth a thousand words? Extensions of a dual-coding theory of multimedia learning. *Journal of Educational Psychology*, *86*(3), 389–401. doi:10.1037/0022-0663.86.3.389

McCormack, T., & Hoerl, C. (2008). Temporal decentering and the development of temporal concepts. *Language Learning*, *58*(1), 89–113. doi:10.1111/j.1467-9922.2008.00464.x

Norman, D. A. (1993). *Things that make us smart: Defending human attributes in the age of the machine*. Reading, MA: Addison-Wesley Pub. Co.

Paivio, A. (1986). *Mental representations: A dual coding approach*. Oxford, UK: Oxford University Press.

Piaget, J., Gruber, H. E., & Vonèche, J. (1977). *The essential Piaget*. New York, NY: Basic Books.

Quintana, C., Reiser, B. J., Davis, E. A., Krajcik, J., Fretz, E., & Duncan, R. G. (2004). A scaffolding design framework for software to support science inquiry. *Journal of the Learning Sciences, 13*(3), 337–386. doi:10.1207/s15327809jls1303_4

Rapp, D. N., & Kurby, C. A. (2008). The 'ins' and 'outs' of learning: Internal representations and external visualizations. In Gilbert, M. R. A. M. N. J. K. (Ed.), *Visualization: Theory and Practice in Science Education (Vol. 3*, pp. 29–52). Dordrecht, The Netherlands: Springer Netherlands. doi:10.1007/978-1-4020-5267-5_2

Roland, P., & Gulyas, B. (1994). Visual imagery and visual representation. *Trends in Neurosciences, 17*(7), 281–287. doi:10.1016/0166-2236(94)90057-4

Rosch, E. (1988). Principles of categorization. In Collins, A. M., & Smith, E. E. (Eds.), *Readings in Cognitive Science: A Perspective from Psychology and Artificial Intelligence* (pp. 312–322). San Mateo, CA: Morgan Kaufmann.

Rosch, E., & Mervis, C. B. (1975). Family resemblances: Studies in the internal structure of categories. *Cognitive Psychology, 7*(4), 573–605. doi:10.1016/0010-0285(75)90024-9

Scaife, M., & Rogers, Y. (1996). External cognition: How do graphical representations work? *International Journal of Human-Computer Studies, 45*(2), 185–213. doi:10.1006/ijhc.1996.0048

Sims, V. K., & Hegarty, M. (1997). Mental animation in the visuospatial sketchpad: Evidence from dual-task studies. *Memory & Cognition, 25*(3), 321–332. doi:10.3758/BF03211288

Song, M., & Quintana, C. (2009). WIIS: Multimodal simulation for exploring the world beyond visual sense. In *Proceedings of the 27th International Conference Extended Abstracts on Human Factors in Computing Systems*. Boston, MA: ACM Press.

Stix, A. (1996). *Creating rubrics through negotiable contracting and assessment*. Retrieved from http://www.interactiveclassroom.com/pdf/Creating_Rubrics_Through_Negotiable_Contracting_and_Assessment.pdf.

Sweller, J. (1988). Cognitive load during problem solving: Effects on learning. *Cognitive Science: A Multidisciplinary Journal, 12*(2), 257-285.

Tourniaire, F., & Pulos, S. (1985). Proportional reasoning: A review of the literature. *Educational Studies in Mathematics, 16*(2), 181–204. doi:10.1007/BF02400937

Tretter, T. R., Jones, M. G., Andre, T., Negishi, A., & Minogue, J. (2006a). Conceptual boundaries and distances: Students' and experts' concepts of the scale of scientific phenomena. *Journal of Research in Science Teaching, 43*(3), 282–319. doi:10.1002/tea.20123

Tretter, T. R., Jones, M. G., & Minogue, J. (2006b). Accuracy of scale conceptions in science: Mental maneuverings across many orders of spatial magnitude. *Journal of Research in Science Teaching, 43*(10), 1061–1085. doi:10.1002/tea.20155

Vallesi, A., Binns, M. A., & Shallice, T. (2008). An effect of spatial-temporal association of response codes: Understanding the cognitive representations of time. *Cognition, 107*(2), 501–527. doi:10.1016/j.cognition.2007.10.011

Vosniadou, S., & Brewer, W. F. (1992). Mental models of the earth: A study of conceptual change in childhood. *Cognitive Psychology, 24*(4), 535–585. doi:10.1016/0010-0285(92)90018-W

Wikipedia. (2011). *Historical origin of acre*. Retrieved from http://en.wikipedia.org/wiki/Acre#Historical_origin.

Wood, D., Bruner, J. S., & Ross, G. (1976). Role of tutoring in problem-solving. *Journal of Child Psychology and Psychiatry, and Allied Disciplines, 17*(2), 89–100. doi:10.1111/j.1469-7610.1976.tb00381.x

Zhang, J. (1997). The nature of external representations in problem solving. *Cognitive Science, 21*(2), 179–217. doi:10.1207/s15516709cog2102_3

Zhang, J., & Norman, D. (1994). The representation of relational information. In *Proceedings of the Sixtheenth Annual Conference of the Cognitive Science Society*, (pp. 952-957). Cognitive Science Society.

KEY TERMS AND DEFINITIONS

Educational Representation: An educational representation is a representation that is exclusively designed to support a group of learners to understand a specific concept.

Imperceptible Objects: Imperceptible objects are the objects that are too small to see with human eyes. Humans usually cannot see an object that is smaller than one hundred micrometer.

Learning Technology: A learning technology is a technology tool that is designed to support learning in various domains.

Mental Image: Mental images are a specific type of internal representation that are produced during the first phases of perception, but are created from stored representations in memory (not from sensory input). Mental images occur in each sensory system, and hence, they can exist in the form of many different modalities such as kinesthetic, spatial (which includes size), auditory, and tactile in addition to visual.

Mental Model: A mental model is an internal structure of knowledge of an external reality. A mental model plays a critical role in cognition (and even perception, sometimes), reasoning, decision-making, and problem-solving strategies. The mental model of a phenomenon in a person's mind is constructed through the interaction with external reality. A mental model usually is not the same with the structure of the external reality. A mental model is also called as internal representation, mental representation, or knowledge representation.

Modality: A modality refers to the type of sensation such as visual, tactile, olfactory, aural, temporal, kinesthetic, etc.

Multimodal Representation: Multimodal representation is a representation that incorporates two or more modalities to deliver the target knowledge.

Perception: Perception is the process of attaining awareness or understanding of the environment by organizing and interpreting sensory information.

Reference: Pomerantz, James R. (2003): "Perception: Overview." In: Lynn Nadel (Ed.), Encyclopedia of Cognitive Science, Vol. 3, London: Nature Publishing Group, pp. 527–537.

ENDNOTES

[1]   The limit of human vision lies at about 100 micrometer (μm).

[2]   1 micrometer is one millionth of one meter (one thousandth of one centimeter)

[3]   1 nanometer is one thousandth of one micrometer

[4]   Mental images are a specific type of internal representation that are produced during the first phases of perception, but are created from stored representations in memory (not from sensory input) (Kosslyn, 2005). Mental images occur in each sensory system, and hence, they can exist in the form of many different modalities such as kinesthetic, spatial (which includes size), auditory, and tactile in addition to visual. Mental image becomes a component of a mental model.

Chapter 8
Interactive Diagram Layout

Sonja Maier
Universität der Bundeswehr München, Germany

Mark Minas
Universität der Bundeswehr München, Germany

ABSTRACT

The specification of layout behavior for visual language editors is a challenging task. To support the user in an interactive environment, it is not sufficient to apply the same layout behavior in every situation. Instead, the user wants to select and alter the layout behavior at runtime.

The authors present a user study in which students created several visual language editors, mainly focusing on the layout engine. With the help of this user study, they demonstrate that different editors require similar layout behavior. They also show evidence that the combination of graph drawing algorithms and other layout algorithms is reasonable.

The authors also describe a framework that enables the creation of a layout engine, which satisfies the user demands identified in a user study. The approach is capable of defining layout behavior for various visual languages like graphs, class diagrams, mindmaps, business process models, or even GUI forms. The framework enables the combination of different layout approaches and provides the possibility to reuse already defined layout behavior.

INTRODUCTION

Layout is present in diverse areas, e.g., in text documents, webpages, or GUI forms. In this chapter, we focus on visual language editors (also called diagram editors), although our layout approach could be applied in many different domains. In Figure 1, a simple graph editor is shown, which will serve as the running example in this chapter.

In visual language editors, a layout engine is responsible for layout computation. This engine usually runs continuously and improves the layout in response to user interaction in real-time. Layout improvement includes all sorts of changes concerning the position or shape of diagram components. For instance, in case rectangle E is

DOI: 10.4018/978-1-4666-1628-8.ch008

Figure 1. Graph editor

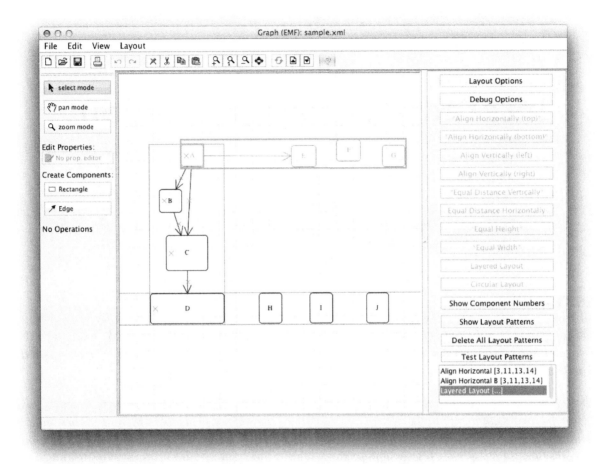

moved (cf. Figure 1), the start point of the incoming edge is updated accordingly. In visual language editors, however, it is not reasonable to completely automate layout improvement. Instead, the editor users want to influence the layout at runtime. E.g., in Figure 1, the editor user has "defined" that nodes *D, H, I,* and *J* are aligned horizontally, indicated by the two gray horizontal lines.

Two facts are highly relevant concerning layout in visual language editors: Users do not want to just visualize diagrams, but rather want to interact with them. They do not handle diagrams with more than 100 components, but usually diagrams with less than 100 components. Based on these facts, we can conclude that users favor predictable layouts

that preserve the users' mental map (Purchase, et al., 2007), instead of high quality layout derived from a standard layout algorithm, which aims at fulfilling some sort of graph aesthetics.

In general, we distinguish graph-like from non-graph-like visual languages. Many visual languages, however, fit into both categories. For instance, some parts of class diagrams show a graph-like structure, e.g., classes together with associations and generalizations. Other parts of class diagrams (c.f. Figure 4) show a non-graph-like structure, e.g., lists of attributes or the nesting of packages and classes.

In the context of visual language editors, the layout engine is usually implemented using one of the following approaches: hand-coded, graph drawing algorithms, constraint-based layout algorithms, or rule-based layout algorithms. Each of these approaches has its strengths, hence, existing rightfully. Graph drawing algorithms are usually written by hand and are specifically tailored to graph-like structures. Constraint-based layout algorithms are defined via declarative constraints, using a constraint solver to compute the layout. They are usually used for non-graphlike structures, and are helpful in case "global" layout computations are required. Rule-based layout algorithms (Maier & Minas, 2009) are a variation of constraint-based layout algorithms, which do not require evoking a constraint solver. They are usually used for non-graph-like structures, and are the best chosen if (only) "local" layout computations are needed.

We have developed a layout approach that is fitted to visual language editors. This approach enables the usage and even the combination of different layout algorithms, such as the ones described above. Hence, the approach benefits from the strengths of the different layout algorithms. Further goals are the specification of layout on an abstract level, and the possibility of reusing already defined layout behavior.

The rest of this chapter consists of three parts: In the first part, a user study is presented examining the desired properties of a layout engine for visual language editors. The second part gives an overview of layout patterns, which are the underlying concept of our layout approach. The third part discusses some challenges concerning the integration of the layout approach into a visual language editor.

BACKGROUND

Some comparable tools, like the editor generators AToM³ (de Lara & Vangheluwe, 2002) or Tiger (Ehrig, et al., 2005), offer only rudimentary layout support. Some tools provide the possibility of using a graph drawing algorithm, such as layered layout (di Battista, et al., 1998), while others provide the possibility of using constraints for layout specification. All these tools have in common that only a small subset of desired layout behavior can be realized by the mechanisms provided. To overcome this issue, most tools additionally allow writing the layout engine by hand, which, in practice, is excessively used. Our approach aims at reducing the necessity of writing the layout engine by hand. This is achieved by providing different approaches for layout specification, and by enabling the combination of these approaches.

Some hand-coded graph editors exist that are somewhat related to our approach. The "godfather" of tools that deal with dynamic diagram drawing is Sketchpad (Sutherland, 1988). Like many "modern" tools, Sketchpad is based on constraints. Interestingly, besides solving the constraints via a relaxation method, it also provides an additional mechanism called "one pass method" to layout the diagram in only one run, to overcome performance problems. Most of the more recent tools use one-way or multi-way constraints (Sanella, 1993). Two examples are GLIDE (Ryall, et al., 1997) and Dunnart (Dwyer, et al., 2009), which deal with interactive graph drawing. Both tools are based on declarative constraints and provide some user-controlled layout behavior, for instance, a mechanism to align nodes. All those tools have in common that a constraint solver needs to be invoked for layout computation, hence performance is an issue. In our approach, we do not define every layout behavior via a constraint-based layout algorithm. We only make use of a constraint-based layout algorithm in the rare cases such a layout algorithm is necessary. This way, it avoids performance issues.

Our approach is based on the concept of layout patterns, which are similar to design patterns (Gamma, et al., 1995), as they are known in the area of software engineering. Schmidt and Kastens (2003) coined the term pattern in the context of layout. Their layout approach is syntax-directed, and so is ours. However, they use tree grammars for specifying diagram syntax, whereas we use meta-models.

Rules are the underlying concept of our rule-based layout algorithm. Rules are widely used in the context of visual language editors, e.g., in the approach described in Guerra and de Lara (2007) interaction dynamics are defined via rules. In this work, the definition of interaction is based on one language-independent meta-model for all diagram languages. In contrast, we introduce several language-independent meta-models, one for each layout pattern, to enable reuse.

Branke (2001) discusses special aspects that should be considered when dealing with dynamic graph drawing, which focuses on graph layout. In this context, predictable results that preserve the mental map (Purchase, et al., 2007; Purchase & Samra, 2008) are favored, instead of high quality layout derived from a standard layout algorithm. Purchase et al. (2007) state that dynamic graph layout algorithms have only recently been developed. They anticipate that maintaining the users' "mental map" between time slices assists with the comprehension of the evolving graph. Purchase and Samra (2008) further claim that "extreme" changes should be favored in comparison to small changes made by the layout engine. As most diagram languages show a graph-like structure, these aspects also apply in our context and are considered in our approach.

It is widely accepted that an editor user should have the possibility to alter the layout of a diagram at runtime. Some approaches were introduced already trying to tackle this challenge, but could not be established. In our opinion, the reason for that is that the usage of these approaches is rather unintuitive and quite complicated. For instance, in some tools, the user has to define constraints textually in order to influence the layout. One quite easy layout feature, which does not have these drawbacks, is hypersnapping (Masui, 2001). This feature became widely accepted, and should serve as an archetype.

MAIN FOCUS OF THE CHAPTER

Issues, Controversies, Problems

Automatic graph layout dominates the research in the area of layout. As a consequence, graph aesthetics are usually the main measure for the quality of the layout, hence for the quality of the layout algorithm. This is a good measure in the context of graph visualization, but not in the context of graph editors or visual language editors. Here, usability is more important; hence, other criteria should be used, such as predictability and mental map preservation.

There is a lack of standardization and formalization concerning the layout functionality of visual language editors. As a consequence, each editor developer, who makes his own design decisions, is usually unable to cope with the layout engine, and finally neglects this part of the editor.

Solutions and Recommendations

It is a common fact that layout is a challenging task. Nevertheless, developers tend to reinvent the wheel, meaning that the layout engine is built form scratch for every tool. To avoid this needless effort, we think that a framework is needed, which enables the reuse of certain layout modules.

As our experience shows, developers tend use only one layout approach and utilize it for the specification of every layout behavior imaginable. We argue that each layout approach has its own strengths, and therefore a combination of different approaches is more reasonable than the usage of only one of them.

Most tools either solely provide automatic layout, which may not be influenced by the user, or only provide a quite restricted form of user-controlled layout. We are convinced that tools should provide the possibility to allow the user to strongly influence the layout at runtime.

The user study, which is described in detail in the next section, supports our claims:

- It is reasonable to reuse and combine layout modules in different layout engines.
- Instead of applying just a single layout approach, it makes sense that different layout approaches are combined.
- Users do not want diagrams to "look nice," they mainly require the layout engine to make the interaction with the diagram easier.

Based on the created framework, we can draw the following conclusions:

- It is feasible to develop a framework that creates layout engines that combine different layout approaches.
- The layout engines created may be used in an interactive environment.

USER STUDY

We have performed a user study in order to examine the desired properties of a layout engine for visual language editors. We had the following expectations, which turned out to be true:

- Different visual language editors require similar layout modules.
- The combination of graph drawing algorithms and other layout algorithms is reasonable.

Setup

The setup of the user study was as follows: We asked seven groups of students, consisting of two or three students each, to use DiaMeta (Minas, 2006), an editor generation framework. First, each group had to create a visual language editor to get familiar with the system. Afterwards, each group had to define a layout algorithm for this visual language. First, they were asked to implement a "standard" layout algorithm, meaning a layout algorithm that was designed for graph visualiza-

tion, following the descriptions of di Battista et al. (1998). Afterwards, they had to adapt the algorithm to the special requirements of their visual language editor.

The visual languages were chosen with respect to two criteria: We wanted visual languages that comprise graph-like as well as non-graph-like parts and we tried to cover a wide range of visual languages. The graph drawing algorithms were chosen by examining the visual languages and selecting the ones that fit well.

The following "pairs" were chosen:

- Mindmaps, tree layout
- Business process models, layered layout
- Class diagrams, edge routing
- Reducer rules (a visual language for editor specification), force-directed layout
- Orgcharts, incremental connector routing
- Entity relationship diagrams, polyline drawings
- Circuit diagrams, interactive orthogonal drawings

Results

To show some of the students' design decisions, three representative examples are described in the following: tree drawing applied to mindmaps, layered drawing applied to business process models, and edge routing applied to class diagrams. For each layout algorithm, we list the layout behavior that was defined via graph drawing algorithms and the layout behavior that was defined outside the graph drawing algorithms.

Mindmaps: A tree drawing algorithm was applied to the obvious tree structure of a mindmap (Figure 2). The students implemented a circular and a layered layout strategy.

- *Layout behavior defined via graph drawing algorithms:* Nodes should stay near the position where the user has placed them.

Figure 2. Mindmaps: circular and layered layout strategy

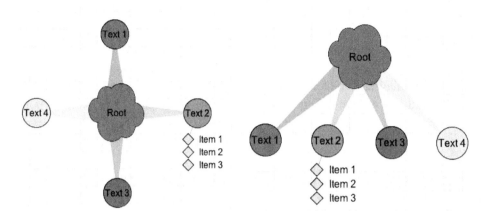

Besides, the different node shapes (e.g. a cloud) and sizes need to be considered.

*   *Layout behavior defined outside graph drawing algorithms:* Lists (diamonds followed by text) are required to remain attached to their owner nodes, and the order of list entries should be preserved. Links between different branches need to stay attached and must be routed without crossing other nodes.

Business Process Models: A layered drawing algorithm was applied to business process models (Figure 3). Here, flow objects serve as nodes and connecting objects as edges. To alter the drawing, the students have provided many options, e.g., horizontal or vertical alignment of components.

*   *Layout behavior defined via graph drawing algorithms:* Changing the diagram should not result in flow objects being moved to a (completely) different layer.

*   *Layout behavior defined outside graph drawing algorithms:* A special edge router is used to cope with nodes of different sizes. Swimlanes allow for node nesting, which has to be preserved. The layout engine should further maintain the vertical or horizontal order of these lanes.

Class Diagrams: For class diagrams, the students have implemented two edge routers, which may be combined. Edge routers are a somewhat different category of drawing algorithms as node positions are fixed. For class diagrams, the edge

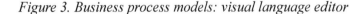

Figure 3. Business process models: visual language editor

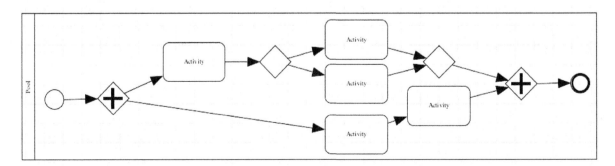

Figure 4. Class diagrams: the same class diagram before and after moving the class person

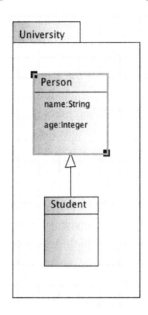 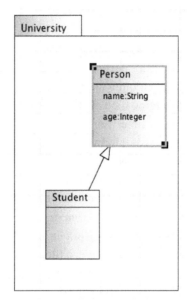

routers are applied to associations and generalizations.

- *Layout behavior defined outside graph drawing algorithms:* Nodes should not overlap. Besides, attributes need to be aligned and the nesting of packages and classes needs to be preserved.

The first implemented edge router is an *edge follower* that makes sure that edges follow a component and start exactly at the contour of this component.

- *Layout behavior defined via graph drawing algorithms:* For class diagrams, edges need to follow classes, which are visualized as rectangles, or packages, whose shape is a bit more complex.

The second implemented edge router is an *edge positioner*, whose purpose is to route edges, e.g., to introduce bend points. The algorithm especially avoids that edges cross nodes.

- *Layout behavior defined via graph drawing algorithms:* Again, the shape of nodes is important. For simplification, the bounding box of nodes is used as the basis of the computation. Other important requirements are that edge crossings are avoided and that two edges do not start or end at the same point.

Discussion

As expected, different groups defined similar layout modules. We can conclude that it is reasonable to reuse and combine layout modules in different layout engines.

We further examined that some layout behavior was built into the graph drawing algorithms themselves, while other layout behavior was defined outside of the graph drawing algorithms. Most students defined the preservation of the size of nodes, the containment of nodes and the order of nodes (lists) outside the graph drawing algorithms. This functionality could be easily defined via constraint-based layout algorithms or rule-based layout algorithms. Hence, the combination of graph drawing algorithms and other layout algorithms is reasonable.

One finding was a bit surprising: The students rather preferred to be in control of the layout engine instead of achieving a "perfect" layout. Without being asked, they put quite an effort on the adaption of the layout engine such as allowing influencing the layout at runtime. For instance, several options, such as the distance between nodes were provided for most of the graph drawing algorithms. In addition, the algorithms were adjusted to allow for options such as the preservation of the horizontal and/or vertical ordering of nodes. Most groups also modified the framework in a sense that layout algorithms were no longer called automatically after user changes. Instead, the algorithm is explicitly called by clicking a button. Here, a tendency was apparent: Graph drawing algorithms that perform major structural changes, such as the layered layout or the circular layout, are explicitly triggered by the user. Graph drawing algorithms that only perform minor structural changes, such as the edge follower or the edge positioner, are called automatically.

PATTERN-BASED LAYOUT APPROACH

We have developed a pattern-based layout approach[1] that is tailored to the requirements identified in the last section, and hence to an interactive environment. In this section, we give an overview of the approach with the help of the graph editor shown in Figure 1. The editor was created by the help of the editor generation framework DiaMeta. In such frameworks, an editor is generated from an abstract specification, whereas the layout engine is usually hand-coded. To change this, we introduced layout patterns, which enable the specification of layout on an abstract level and which allow to generate the layout engine from this specification.

Graph Editor

The core of the specification of an editor, which was created with DiaMeta, is a meta-model called *language-specific meta-model*, which is created with the Eclipse Modeling Framework (Steinberg, et al., 2009). This meta-model comprises two parts: The abstract syntax meta-model, representing the language's abstract syntax, and the concrete syntax meta-model, representing the language's concrete syntax. The language-specific meta-model that corresponds to the graph editor is visualized in Figure 5. It consists of the two classes *Arrow* and *Rectangle*, which, together with the association *attach,* form the concrete syntax meta-model. The class *Node* together with the associations *from* and *to* form the abstract syntax meta-model. The association *modelObject* connects both meta-models.

Several layout patterns have been integrated into the graph editor:

- **Non-Overlap:** Removes overlapping of nodes by performing force-directed layout.
- **Edge Follower:** Makes sure that edges stay attached to nodes.
- **Alignment (Horizontal and Vertical):** Aligns certain nodes vertically or horizontally, respectively.
- **Equal Distance (Horizontal and Vertical):** Makes sure that certain nodes have an equal distance to each other.
- **Equal Size (Width and Height):** Makes sure that certain nodes have the same height or width, respectively.
- **Layered Layout:** Creates a layered layout for certain nodes and edges.
- **Circular Layout:** Creates a circular layout for certain nodes and edges.

When the editor user changes the layout manually, e.g., moves a node, the layout engine is called and the diagram layout is automatically adjusted. In our example, the user may move node *A* right

Figure 5. Language-specific meta-model (left) and pattern-specific meta-models (right)

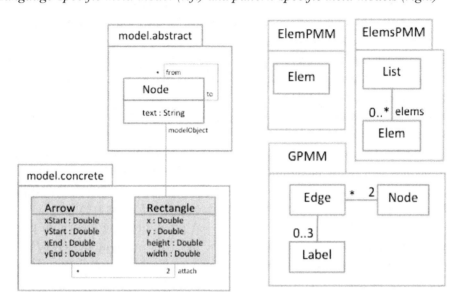

(Figure 1). During this movement, the nodes *C*, *D*, and *E* are also moved to the right by the layout engine. In addition, the connected edges are updated accordingly. Each of these changes is performed by a different layout pattern, hence, by a different layout algorithm. Generally speaking, several layout algorithms may be applied to a diagram simultaneously, even to diagram parts that overlap.

Layout Patterns

Our approach is based on the concept of layout patterns, which was introduced in Maier and Minas (2009). With the help of layout patterns, automatic and user-controlled layout behavior is made possible.

Each layout pattern encapsulates certain layout behavior. Different layout algorithms can be included as certain patterns, e.g., graph drawing algorithms, such as the Sugiyama algorithm, and constraint-based layout algorithms, which compute the layout by the help of a constraint solver. Our own version of rule-based layout algorithms

may be also used, which is specifically tailored to the interactive nature of visual language editors.

Each layout pattern is based on a language-independent, but *pattern-specific meta-model*. Algorithms are defined on top of these pattern-specific meta-models. In order to apply a layout pattern to a certain visual language, i.e., in order to instantiate the pattern, the pattern-specific meta-model must be mapped to the language-specific meta-model. This way, reuse of layout behavior is enabled, and the complexity of the layout specification is usually decreased, due to the customized meta-model.

In order to allow for pattern-based reuse, graph drawing algorithms have to be based on a pattern-specific meta-model, the *GPMM* (Graph Pattern Meta-Model). This meta model is shown in Figure 5: A graph consists of several edges, nodes, and labels. An edge has up to three labels and connects exactly two nodes.

The constraint-based layout algorithms as well as the rule-based layout algorithms are based on different meta-models, e.g., on the meta-model *ElemPMM* or *ElemsPMM*, which are also shown in Figure 5. The meta-model *ElemPMM* consists of a single class *Elem*, which stands for the component(s) the layout algorithm is applied to. The meta-model *ElemsPMM* consist of the classes *List* and *Elem* and the association *elems*. It describes an ordered list of diagram components the layout algorithm is applied to.

The pattern-specific meta-model of a layout pattern is an abstraction of the situation in the language-specific meta-model, meaning that concrete classes in the pattern-specific meta-model correspond to classes in the language-specific meta-model. However, the pattern-specific meta-model usually does not exactly match the part of the language-specific meta-model where the layout pattern shall be applied. Instead, some variation can be found. Hence, the correspondence between language-specific meta-model and pattern-specific meta-model must be defined for each pattern. The mapping between the instances of different meta-models can be seen in Figure 6. Here, the language-specific model is an instance of the language-specific meta-model. Instances of the meta-models shown in Figure 5 are *GPM*, *ElemsPM*, and *ElemPM*. The dashed edges indicate the transformations between different models. Every ellipse connected with a rectangle forms a pattern instance, e.g., Alignment together with *ElemsPM*, or Edge Follower together with *GPM*.

For instance, the alignment pattern is based on the *ElemsPMM*. To use the pattern, a correspondence between the language-specific model and the *ElemsPM* needs to be established. For the alignment pattern, a correspondence between the class *Rectangle* and the class *Elem* is created. In addition, in case the components should be aligned horizontally, a correspondence between the attribute *x* and the association *elems* is created. In case the components should be aligned vertically, a correspondence between the attribute *y* and the association *elems* is created.

A graph drawing algorithm gets an instance *GPM* of the meta-model *GPMM*, a list of options and a history as input. The algorithm is either hand-coded or provided by a graph drawing library, such as yFiles (Wiese, et al., 2002) or JUNG (Madadhain, et al., 2005). The graph drawing algorithms edge follower, non-overlap, circular layout and layered layout, which are integrated in the graph editor, all operate on the same *GPMM*. Graph drawing algorithms are usually quite complex, and performance is crucial in an interactive environment. Hence, it is reasonable to implement them, not to define them on an abstract level. Graph drawing algorithms are usually used for the graph-based portions of the diagram language.

Figure 6. Correlation of diagram, language-specific model, pattern-specific models, and patterns

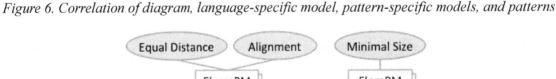
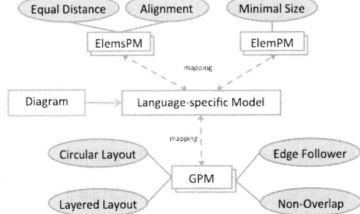

A constraint-based layout algorithm gets an instance of the corresponding pattern meta-model, a list of options, and a history as input. The layout is defined via a set of declarative constraints, and a constraint solver is used to compute the layout. In our example, the constraint-based layout algorithm equal distance is included. Constraint-based layout algorithms are usually used in case "global" layout modifications are required.

A rule-based layout algorithm also gets an instance of the corresponding pattern meta-model, a list of options, and a history as input. A rule-base layout algorithm is some sort of constraint-based layout algorithm: The layout is also defined via a set of declarative constraints. Instead of using a constraint solver to compute the layout, some layout rules are provided. In our example, the rule-based layout algorithms alignment and minimal size are included. In contrast to standard constraint-based layout algorithms, a more predictable layout behavior may be defined via rule-based layout algorithms. In case the layout needs to be updated, and the layout engine is called, roughly speaking, several layout rules are applied to the diagram and predictably update the values of certain attributes. Rule-based layout algorithms are usually used in case more "local" layout modifications are required.

Pattern Combination

While computing the layout, a certain set of pattern instances comes into play. Our approach comprises an algorithm that enables an automatic pattern combination, which was described in detail in Maier and Minas (2010). The idea is: Changes made by the user are propagated through the diagram, trying to find a layout satisfying all pattern instances. Starting with the attribute(s) changed, all pattern instances are checked that involve these attributes. Each "violated" pattern instance changes one or more attribute value(s) in order to "repair" the layout. Afterwards, all

pattern instances are checked that involve these attributes. This procedure is continued until all pattern instances are satisfied, or until the algorithm signals a failure. A failure is signaled when no "valid" layout exists. As the user is allowed to add pattern instances, it might be the case that two or more pattern instances contradict each other, and hence, it is not possible to compute a "valid" layout.

Discussion

In our setting, the layout needs to be computed, and the diagram needs to be updated accordingly, after each modification of the diagram performed by the user. Hence, one critical aspect of layout computation is performance. Performance tests showed that the approach fits into an interactive environment, meaning that the user is not "disturbed" by layout computation, e.g., in the diagram shown in Figure 1 the layout computation after any user modification requires less than 15 milliseconds on standard hardware. For larger diagrams, performance is not an issue also. One reason for the good performance is that the pattern combination algorithm is a local propagation algorithm, which means that in most cases only a small part of the diagram needs to be analyzed. Furthermore, the editor user usually changes a small part of the diagram, e.g. the position of node D, and only a small part of the diagram needs to be updated, e.g. the position of the nodes H, I, and J. Of course, choice of layout patterns is crucial concerning performance. As it can be imagined, rule-based layout algorithms exhibit the best performance, followed by graph drawing algorithms and constraint-based layout algorithms bring up the rear.

Another issue is the usability of visual language editors that include a pattern-based layout engine. Usability does not fade into existence, meaning that the visual language editors had to be adapted. Some details will be discussed in the next section.

EDITOR INTEGRATION OF THE LAYOUT ENGINE

Using the pattern based layout approach described in the last section, we specified several layout patterns, and integrated them into various visual language editors, e.g., they were integrated into the graph editor presented earlier, into a class diagram editor, into a GUI forms editor that allows to create GUIs, or into a VEX (Citrin, et al., 1995) editor that allows to draw lambda expressions visually.

The creation of the layout modules as well as their inclusion in different visual language editors turned out to be (more or less) straightforward. But we noticed that simply including the different layout patterns was not sufficient. The editor users could not utilize the whole functionality of the layout approach and the usability of the editors was unsatisfactory. To overcome these "problems," several features were added. Namely automatic and user-controlled layout, pattern visualization, layout suggestions, and syntax preservation, will be described in the following.

Automatic and User-Controlled Layout

First of all, we extended the user interface to enable automatic and user-controlled application of layout patterns.

Automatic instantiation means that the layout engine automatically adds pattern instances as soon as their corresponding meta-model parts are instantiated in the diagram. The editor user "only" has the possibility to completely turn such patterns on or off. In the graph editor, the non-overlap pattern and the edge-follower pattern are such patterns.

An alternative to automatic instantiation is *user-controlled instantiation*. By selecting one or more components, the user may define a part of a diagram to which a certain pattern shall be applied. An instance of this pattern is then added, triggered by the user. This pattern instance is now applied until the editor user explicitly removes it again. In the graph editor, the user has the possibility to create instances of the patterns equal distance, alignment, equal size, layered layout and circular layout. All patterns that were added by the user are shown in a list at the bottom-right of the editor.

In the example shown in Figure 1, the user added three pattern instances: A layered layout algorithm rearranges the nodes *A*, *B*, *C,* and *D* and the corresponding edges. The nodes *D*, *H*, *I*, and *J* are aligned horizontally at the top *and* at the bottom. When the user modifies the diagram, two alignment pattern instances and one layered layout pattern instance preserve the layout that was "defined" by the user. In addition, several non-overlap pattern instances move the nodes to assure that they do not overlap, and several edge follower pattern instances update the start and end point of the edges to keep them correctly connected to the nodes.

Internally, the difference between automatic and user-controlled pattern instantiation is only marginal: In both cases, one or more instances of the corresponding pattern-specific meta-model are created. Pattern-specific models are created on the basis of a certain model. In case of automatic instantiation, the whole language-specific model is taken as the basis, whereas in case of user-controlled instantiation, only a certain part of the language-specific model is used.

Pattern Visualization

After users applied several layout patterns, while editing a diagram, they had some troubles "understanding" the layout dependencies between components. To cope with this problem, we added a special feature, which visualizes pattern instances in the diagram. In the example shown, the horizontal alignment pattern instances are visualized via gray lines, and the layered layout pattern is visualized via a colored box. It is possible to instantiate the same layout pattern several times in one diagram. To distinguish different pattern instances, they are highlighted in different colors.

If the user selects one of the pattern instances in the list at the bottom-right of the editor, the involved components are highlighted via a gray cross in the middle of each component. In the editor shown in Figure 1, the user has selected the layered layout pattern instance, and the nodes *A, B, C, D,* and the four edges are highlighted.

Layout Suggestions

To further support the user, the editor is able to suggest layout patterns that can be applied. After selecting one or more components, the user may click the button *Test Layout Patterns*. As a consequence, the buttons on the right side of the editor are highlighted in a certain color. Black indicates that the corresponding pattern cannot be applied to the component(s) selected, while blue indicates that the corresponding pattern can be applied. Stars are added to the label of the button, if the application of the pattern results in minor changes of the diagram. No stars are added, if it results in major changes.

In Figure 1, layout suggestions for the rectangles *A, E, F,* and *G* were computed. For instance, stars are added to the button *Align Horizontal (top)*, as only minor diagram changes would be necessary after applying the pattern, whereas no stars are added to the button *Align Vertical (left)*, as major diagram changes would be necessary.

Layout suggestions are computed by "trying out" each layout pattern. Therefore, a pattern instance is added, and the pattern is applicable if the layout engine is able to compute a "valid" layout. Based on the attribute changes performed by the layout engine, it is decided whether a star is added or not.

Syntax Preservation

The layout engine may be included in any visual language editor. For editors that support freehand editing, the *syntax preservation* feature proved useful. "Freehand" means that components may be freely positioned on the screen, and that the syntax of the diagram is computed on the basis of components´ locations. As a consequence, the layout engine may cause syntax changes. This usually results in an unexpected behavior of the editor, and hence should be avoided.

In the graph editor, a syntax change may occur in case the layout engine moves one node on top of another node. (The example assumes that the non-overlap pattern is turned off.) If an edge is connected to one of these nodes before moving the node, the diagram does not answer the question to which node this edge is connected to after moving the node.

Syntax preservation is achieved by an examination of the diagram, or more specifically, by comparing the internal graph representation before and after a layout adaption. In case the layout engine changes this graph, the user changes that led to this violation are undone.

FUTURE RESEARCH DIRECTIONS

A platform was built that allows for the specification of layout behavior, tailored for an interactive environment. This platform provides a playground for further investigations. For instance, during the development of the layout approach and its integration into several editors, some interesting questions arose, e.g., Which layout patterns should be defined? Which ones should be included in a certain visual language editor? How should they be visualized?

It is possible to apply our approach in other areas where layout is required. Even "modern" input devices, such as large screens or mobile devices, could benefit from the approach. With the help of our approach, some useful functionality could be rapidly defined, like grids and guides, as described in Frisch et al. (2011).

CONCLUSION

In this chapter, we have examined the layout requirements of visual language editors by presenting a user study. We have demonstrated that the combination of different layout algorithms is reasonable by outlining three visual language editors that have been created by students. Besides, the reuse of certain layout behavior was motivated.

We also gave an overview of our pattern-based layout approach. The approach enables the combination of different layout algorithms and is capable of defining layout behavior for diverse visual languages.

We gave some details about the integration of the layout engine into an editor and focused on some useful features, namely user-controlled layout, pattern visualization, layout suggestions and syntax preservation. There are several other features imaginable that could also be included, e.g. automatic layout support after diagram import.

As a proof of concept, we successfully integrated our approach into various visual language editors. In practice, the approach produces good results, and the overall performance is convincing.

REFERENCES

Branke, J. (2001). Dynamic graph drawing. In *Drawing Graphs: Methods and Models*. Berlin, Germany: Springer. doi:10.1007/3-540-44969-8_9

Citrin, W., Hall, R., & Zorn, B. (1995). Programming with visual expressions. In *Proceedings of the 11th International IEEE Symposium on Visual Languages*. IEEE Press.

de Lara, J., & Vangheluwe, H. (2002). AToM3: A tool for multi-formalism and meta-modeling. In *Proceedings of the 5th International Conference on Fundamental Approaches to Software Engineering*. IEEE.

di Battista, G., Eades, P., Tamassia, R., & Tollis, I. G. (1998). *Graph drawing: Algorithms for the visualization of graphs*. Upper Saddle River, NJ: Prentice Hall.

Dwyer, T., Marriott, K., & Wybrow, M. (2009). Dunnart: A constraint-based network diagram authoring tool. In *Proceedings of Graph Drawing: 16th International Symposium*. Springer.

Ehrig, K., Ermel, C., Haensgen, S., & Taentzer, G. (2005). Generation of visual editors as eclipse plug-ins. In *Proceedings of the 20th IEEE/ACM International Conference on Automated Software Engineering*. IEEE Press.

Frisch, M., Kleinau, S., Langner, R., & Dachselt, R. (2011). Grids & guides: Multi-touch layout and alignment tools. In *Proceedings of the 2011 Annual Conference on Human Factors in Computing Systems*. ACM Press.

Gamma, E., Helm, R., Johnson, R., & Vlissides, J. (1995). *Design patterns*. Boston, MA: Addison-Wesley.

Guerra, E., & de Lara, J. (2007). Event-driven grammars: Relating abstract and concrete levels of visual languages. In *Software and Systems Modeling, 6*(3), 317-347.

Madadhain, J., Fisher, D., Smyth, P., White, S., & Boey, Y. B. (2005). Analysis and visualization of network data using JUNG. *Journal of Statistical Software*. Retrieved from http://jung.sourceforge.net/doc/JUNG_journal.pdf.

Maier, S., & Minas, M. (2009). Pattern-based layout specifications for visual language editors. In *Proceedings of the 1st International Workshop on Visual Formalisms for Patterns*. ECEASST.

Maier, S., & Minas, M. (2010). Combination of different layout approaches. In *Proceedings of the 2nd International Workshop on Visual Formalisms for Patterns*. ECEASST.

Masui, T. (2001). HyperSnapping. In *Proceedings of the IEEE 2001 Symposia on Human Centric Computing Languages and Environments*. IEEE Press.

Minas, M. (2006). Generating meta-model-based freehand editors. In *Proceedings of the 3rd International Workshop on Graph Based Tools*. ECEASST.

Purchase, H. C., Hoggan, E., & Goerg, C. (2007). How important is the "mental map"? An empirical investigation of a dynamic graph layout algorithm. In Kaufmann and Wagner (Eds.), *Graph Drawing: 14th International Symposium*. Springer.

Purchase, H. C., & Samra, A. (2008). Extremes are better: Investigating mental map preservation in dynamic graphs. In *Proceedings of the 5th International Conference on Diagrammatic Representation and Inference*. Springer.

Ryall, K., Marks, J., & Shieber, S. (1997). An interactive constraint-based system for drawing graphs. In *Proceedings of the 10th ACM Symposium on User Interface Software and Technology*. ACM Press.

Sannella, M. (1993). Multi-way versus one-way constraints in user interfaces: Experience with the DeltaBlue algorithm. *Software, Practice & Experience, 23*(5). doi:10.1002/spe.4380230507

Schmidt, C., & Kastens, U. (2003). Implementation of visual languages using pattern-based specications. *Software, Practice & Experience, 33*(15). doi:10.1002/spe.560

Steinberg, D., Budinsky, F., Paternostro, M., & Merks, E. (2009). *EMF: Eclipse modeling framework*. Boston, MA: Addison-Wesley.

Sutherland, I. E. (1988). *Sketchpad: A man-machine graphical communication system. In 25 Years of DAC Papers on Twenty-Five Years of Electronic Design Automation*. ACM Press.

Wiese, R., Eiglsperger, M., & Kaufmann, M. (2002). yFiles: Visualization and automatic layout of graphs. In Kaufmann and Wagner (Eds.), Graph Drawing: 9th International Symposium. Springer. ENDNOTE [1] Further details about the pattern-based layout approach can be found here: http://www.unibw.de/inf2/DiaGen/Layout.

Chapter 9

Optimization in Mental Configuration Space:
The Case of Pointing Behavior

Huahai Yang
IBM Research – Almaden, USA

ABSTRACT

This chapter describes a geometric approach to human cognition centering on the concept of mental configuration space. As a case study of the approach, this work details a study that derives performance models for an important class of motor behavior—pointing in the two dimensional space. The five derived models and three existing models in the literature are compared using an experimental study. It is found that the models developed on the basis of mental configuration space fit the empirical data better than other models. It is argued that the mental configuration space concept points to a potentially fruitful direction of research. Finally, the chapter discusses the implications of such an approach for user interface research and development.

INTRODUCTION

Gärdenfors (2004) proposes a geometric mode of mental representation complementary to the more prominent approaches of the symbolic (Newell, 1990) and the connectionist (Rumelhart & McClelland, 1986) mode of representations in cognitive science. He suggests that the representation of vector spaces is more satisfactory than symbolic and connectionist representations for modeling concept formation, semantics and

reasoning. For representing sensory stimuli such as spectral composition of light, intensity of sound, velocity of self-rotation and so on, Gallistel (1990) indicates that vector space representation is organism's natural means of internalizing the environment. Though promising, this geometric line of investigation has not grown outside the realm of cognitive science to influence user interface research and design. This chapter attempts to bring readers' attention to this line of inquiry, and uses a case study to illustrate the potential viability of the geometric approach.

DOI: 10.4018/978-1-4666-1628-8.ch009

The case study centers on extending Fitts' law (Fitts, 1954) to give a more detailed account of user performance in a variety of situations. As one of the best well known contributions of psychology to the field of user interface research (Card, et al., 1983), Fitts' law is generally used as a tool for evaluating user interfaces or devices (Soukoreff & MacKenzie, 2004), and has helped launching some important input devices, including the ubiquitous mouse (Card, et al., 1978). Despite its usefulness, a lack of consensus in its fundamental nature limits its applicability and hinders the development of similarly predictive laws. This work attempts to alleviate this kind of conceptual deficiency by extending the law from the perspective of mental configuration space.

In the following sections, several lines of research on mental configuration space are first briefly reviewed. The possible optimization principles in mental configuration are then proposed. Turning to the case study, 1D and 2D pointing tasks are described. The chapter proceeds to derive five models of 2D pointing performance based on progressively richer assumptions on the shape and distribution of 2D pointing mental configuration space. The derived models are tested with an experiment. Three previous models in the literature are also tested with the experimental data. Results suggest that models based the optimization principles in mental configuration space fit well with the empirical data. The chapter concludes with discussions on the implications of the work.

BACKGROUND

Concept of Mental Configuration Space

The concept of configuration space refers to a way of treating the state of an entire system as a single point in a higher dimensional vector space. It has a long history in physics and mathematics, and has known to be a fruitful method of dealing with complex problems in many fields (e.g. Latombe, 1991). *Configuration space* is an abstract space of all possible combinations of quantities (parameters) that characterize the state of a system. Every configuration or state can be thought of as a point in the space of all possible configurations. The number of dimensions or Degrees Of Freedom (DOF), of the space equals to the number of parameters specifying the configuration. These parameters can be seen as coordinates of a point in the space. Let us start with a toy example of a "system": a pendulum, the kind seen on some old mechanic clock. The state of the system can be uniquely determined by the angle between the line going through the rod of the pendulum and the line of gravity. The configuration space of the system is a one-dimensional space; in fact, a circle, as the value of an angle goes from 0 to 360 then back to 0. If the pendulum's arm consists of two rods hinged together instead, the configuration space becomes two-dimensional. Assuming the hinge is completely flexible, one angle specifies the upper rod's position, **a**, and another angle fixes the lower rod's position, **b**. The shape of the configuration space is a torus (see Figure 1): each state of the pendulum system, **p**, has a one-to-one correspondence with each point of the torus; the two angles, each changing from 0 to 360, are the coordinates of a point on the torus.

One benefit of the configuration space viewpoint is that it often forces researchers to think carefully about all the relevant parameters of a system. Perhaps more importantly, the configuration space viewpoint allows researchers to move the attention away from the superficial distinction in the ways of parameterization (coordinates systems), and instead focus on the more consequential overall structure of the space. For example, consider a three dimensional space of a ball. A position of a point of the space can be expressed in term of spherical coordinates of latitude, longitude and altitude, or be equally formulated in Cartesian coordinates of x, y, and z. They are equivalent because one set of param-

Figure 1. A pendulum of two rods and its configuration space of a torus

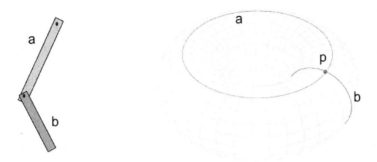

eters can be converted into another without loss of information. For this conversion to be possible, both side of the conversion must have the same number of DOFs. What determine the behaviors of the system are the shape of the space and the distribution of points therein, not the coordinates system chosen to describe them. It might be more convenient or simpler to describe a system behavior in one coordinate system than in another, but changing the coordinate system does not alter system behavior.

One of the central ideas of the geometric approach to cognition is to represent mental states as points in vector spaces. In Gärdenfors (2004), the vector spaces are labeled "conceptual space" for the topic of that work is conceptual formation and reasoning, whereas in Shepard (1987), the name "psychological space" is used to emphasize its general applicability for a wide range of psychological phenomena. In this chapter, *mental configuration space* refers essentially to a configuration space where all dimensions are psychological in nature. This choice of the term retains the broad coverage of psychological phenomena, at the same time, makes apparent the idea's connection with a broader community of sciences that employees the concept of configuration space. The underlying assumptions of the view can be laid out in the following: For a given cognitive task involving multiple task parameters, it is assumed that there are corresponding mental representations of the parameters, and thus forming a mental

configuration space. Adopting a configuration space approach to understand cognitive systems could entail two different levels of commitment. A weak view would regard the concept just as a way of thinking about the problems cognitive systems try to solve. A strong view would assume psychological processes operate in configuration space: psychological space is a configuration space. Many work in the geometric direction of cognition seem to fall into the later camp (e.g. Shepard, 1987; Gärdenfors, 2004), and some even go so far as to suggest mental configuration space is literally represented in nervous system anatomically as spaces (e.g. Gallistel, 1990).

An often cited example of a mental configuration space is the space of human color perception, with its three psychophysically measured qualities: hue, saturation, and brightness (Shepard, 1987; Gärdenfors, 2004). Any color percept is then entirely determined by its position in the three dimensional space of the qualities. The shape of the three dimensional color space can be depicted as the familiar color spindle (Sivik & Taft, 1994). It should be emphasized that the shape of mental configuration space often does not match that of the corresponding space of physical attributes (Clark, 1993). For example, the geometrical structure of wavelength is linear whereas the corresponding mental dimension of hue is a circular shape. Therefore, the shape of the mental configuration space is not determined by the direct mappings between physical attributes and mental attributes, but by the ways in which mental representations relate to one another (Shepard & Chipman, 1970). In other words, mental configuration space follows its own rules of operations. Clearly, the principles governing the operations in mental configuration space influence the performance of cognitive tasks. It is conceivable that the governing principles can be expressed as some kind of optimizations.

Optimization in Mental Configuration Space

One straightforward optimization principle in configuration space is the tendency for the system to seek the shortest distance from one state to another. Such a geometrical principle of optimization has been demonstrated in Shepard's experiments on mental rotations (Carlton & Shepard, 1990; Shepard & Farrell, 1985). For example, it is found that the imagined motions follow curved paths in the physical space that are actually straight paths in the configuration space. Although his explanation for such a geometrical optimization, as some kind of evolutionary internalization of physical world, may not be convincing (Kubovy & Epstein, 2001), or even necessary as geometry itself can be considered mental (Borovik, 2009), the observation that some mental operations are guided by simple optimization principles in configuration space is still compelling.

Cognitive systems routinely work with complex tasks that involve a large number of parameters, so the mental configuration space must cope with the high dimensionality of physical input. Since mental configuration space is normally found to be of "modest dimensionality" (Gallistel, 1990), it is reasonable to hypothesize that cognitive systems employ some kind of strategies to reduce the number of dimensions but still maintain a somewhat degraded yet acceptable performance, in the spirit of bounded rationality (Simon, 1957). Such strategies, if exist, would certainly utilize the structure of the configuration space. In perceptual organization research, Feldman (1997a, 1997b) proposes a regularity based lattice structure for perceptual configuration space. Object representations that are more regular, as defined by meeting more symmetric constraints, are placed lower in the lattice, and are the preferred interpretations compared with other models that also apply but are higher on the lattice. For example, isosceles triangles and squares are found to be "better" shapes than the generic ones in both goodness rating and shape production tasks (Feldman, 2000). These shapes are considered regular because they satisfy an extra symmetric constraint of having sides of equal length. To completely specify the shape of a square, only one parameter is needed: the length of its sides, whereas a generic rectangle needs two: the height and width. Similarly, one parameter can fully quantify the shape of an isosceles triangle: the size of its top angle, but one additional parameter is required to describe the shape of a generic triangle: the ratio of its two sides' lengths.

The preference for regular models is consistent with the principle of simplicity (Chater & Vitanyi, 2003): less regular models require more free parameters to specify, whereas more regular models need fewer free parameters to specify, due to the increased number of symmetric constraints that they must satisfy. Regular models therefore require less storage space in the cognitive system, thus explaining the preference. Looking from another perspective, less regular representations can be seen as reproducible from regular ones through some transformations (Leyton, 1982). In this sense, a regular representation can serve as a prototype for a class of representations (Rosch, 1975). The class membership of representations could be governed by the principle of convexity (Gärdenfors, 2004): if x and y are elements of a class, and if z is between x and y, then z is also likely to belong to the same class. Gärdenfors argued that cognitive systems naturally prefer the partitioning of mental configuration space into convex regions.

From the brief literature review above, the preferences for the shortest path, regular configurations and convex regions in configuration space seem to be reasonable principles for understanding certain perceptual and conceptual phenomenon. The question remains as whether such preferences exist in other domains of cognition. In particular, would it offer any explanatory power for the pointing behavior that is important for user interface research? This tantalizing question is investigated in the following case study.

CASE STUDY: POINTING IN 2D SPACE

Models of 1D and 2D Pointing

$$T = a + b \log_2 \left(\frac{D}{W} + 1 \right) \qquad (1)$$

As shown in Equation (1), the commonly accepted form of Fitts' law models pointing behavior in one dimension (1D). It predicts movement time *T*, the time duration between starting a movement at some distance *D* away from a target and stopping the movement somewhere within the target. The target is quantified by its width *W* along the movement direction. See Figure 2. In Fitts' law and all of its extensions mentioned in this chapter, *a* refers to the intercept and *b* is the slope of the

Figure 2. Schematic illustration of the 1D pointing task

linear regression. The interpretation of the two is beyond the scope of this chapter (but see Zhai, 2004), as the focus of the work is to extend the formula to situations beyond 1D and to include more parameters than *D* and *W*.

1D pointing is an idealization of real world pointing task in that the dimension of the target perpendicular to the movement direction is ignored. In addition, the movement direction does not vary. In 2D pointing, all these limitations are removed. To model 2D pointing, both the width and the height of target need to be accounted for, and all the possible movement directions need to be considered (See Figure 3). Since 2D pointing is such a pervasive task that every graphic interface user routinely performs, up to thousands of times per day, researchers in HCI have formulated various quantitative models to predict the movement time (Accot & Zhai, 2003; Appert, et al., 2008; Grossman & Balakrishnan, 2005; MacKenzie & Buxton, 1992; Murata, 1999), and have reached some impressive results in term of fitting the models to their experimental data, often obtaining R^2 well above 0.9. In spite of such modeling successes, however, 2D pointing has

Figure 3. Three different parameterizations for 2D pointing task. The shaded rectangle is the target of a pointing movement, and the ball represents the starting position of the movement.

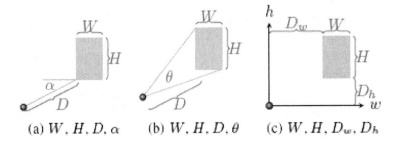

(a) W, H, D, α (b) W, H, D, θ (c) W, H, D_w, D_h

yet to achieve a conceptually satisfactory resolution, since the models were not derived from the first principles but were proposed according to intuitions.

Models in Grossman and Balakrishnan (2005) and Murata (1999) utilize the experimentally measured distribution of movement stopping points in space to predict the measured movement time, essentially fitting one type of experimental results to another. Such a modeling approach is not in the scope of this study. The remaining models in the literature are briefly reviewed here. MacKenzie and Buxton (1992) propose several models of 2D pointing. The best model confirmed by their data is this formula:

$$T = a + b \log_2 \left(\frac{D}{\min(W, H)} + 1 \right) \qquad (2)$$

This model reflects the intuition that the smaller of height **H** or width **W** should dominant overall performance. Accot and Zhai (2003) build on such understanding, but also note the importance of the **W** vs. **H** ratio. They formalize these ideas into a set of desirable mathematical properties, and arrived at a set of models based on various measures of distance between **D / W** and **D / H**. They finally settle on an Euclidean distance model:

$$T = a + b \log_2 \left(\sqrt{(\frac{D}{W})^2 + \eta(\frac{D}{H})^2} + 1 \right) \qquad (3)$$

where η depends on data. For their own data, $\eta = 0.13$; for data in [18], $\eta = 0.32$. Since the authors conclude that the value of η should be in the range of (1/7, 1/3), the median value of 0.24 is used in the model comparison here. Appert et al. (2008) proposes a model to more explicitly account for the effect of movement directions:

$$T = a + b \log_2 \left(\frac{D}{W} + \frac{D}{H} + 0.6 \cos(\alpha) \frac{D}{\min(W, H)} + 1 \right) \qquad (4)$$

where α is the absolute value of the angle between movement direction (assuming straight movement) and the vertical line. It is noted here that the later two models include constants (η and 0.6, respectively) that are difficult to explain.

Deriving 2D Pointing Models

This work attempts to derive the models from theoretical principles rather than merely following intuitions. To do that, the original argument for proposing the concept of task difficulty in Fitts (1954) is revisited:

The rational basis for this estimate of task difficulty is the maximum relative uncertainty that can be tolerated for a correct movement in a series having a specified average amplitude. Thus the minimum organization required of a particular movement is defined by the specification of one from among k possible categories of amplitude within which the movement is to terminate.

Formalizing the idea into modern information theoretical terms (Cover & Thomas, 1991), the Index of Difficulty (**ID**) of a pointing task can be defined as the logarithm of the reciprocal of the probability of terminating the movement within the target:

$$ID = \log_2 \frac{1}{P(\text{Terminating Within Target})} \qquad (5)$$

This formulation of **ID** is general. In principle, the movement time prediction for any pointing task can be calculated with this definition of **ID**. The key is to estimate the probability. In 1D idealization of the pointing task, all the possible movement terminating positions are on a single line, and thus Equation (5) can be instantiated into the classic Fitts' law formula:

$$ID = \log_2 \frac{D + W}{W} \tag{6}$$

where D is the distance from the starting position of movement to the beginning of the target line segment, W is the length of the target line segment. $D+W$ determines the total number of possible movement terminating positions, and W determines the number of possible terminating positions inside the target. It should be stressed that this entire discussion is within the realm of mental configuration space. The parameters above are mental representation of physical parameters of the task conditions. The ratio $W / (D +W)$ is the probability of terminating within the target.

Unlike a classic Fitts' experiment, a 2D pointing experiment does not ignore the height H of the target, but treats it as an independent variable. So the number of needed parameters is expanded to three: the distance from starting position to the target D, the width of the target W, and H. However, three is not enough: to fully specify a generic 2D pointing task, an additional angle parameter, as shown in Figure 3a, or alternatively as in Figure 3b, is necessary. Another way to parameterize the task is to use the parameter set $\{W, H, D_w, D_h\}$, as shown in Figure 3c. All three ways of parameterization require four parameters, and they are equivalent since each parameterization can be calculated from another via simple trigonometry. In other words, these different parameterizations characterize the same four dimensional configuration space. However, the shape of the space and the distribution of points therein, which both are unknown, might be easier to discover in one parameterization than in another. Adopting different parameterizations and equipping each with a different set of assumptions on

how the parameters are related (probabilistically dependent or independent), five different models can be developed.

Width-Height Independence Model

If 2D pointing is conceptualized as two independent 1D pointing actions combined, one horizontal and one vertical, and further assuming that both actions follow 1D Fitts' law, the following formula can be written to model movement time T:

$$T = a + b \log_2 (\frac{D_w}{W} + 1) + c \log_2(\frac{D_h}{H} + 1) \tag{7}$$

This model assumes total independence between D_w / W and D_H / H, therefore the total movement time is the sum of the two independent movement times: one moves horizontally, another vertically. Obviously, the independence condition is not well justified. This model is included as the baseline for comparison.

Angle-Fitts Additivity Model

Switching to another parameterization of the configuration space, with distance D and angle θ as shown in Figure 3b, better justification for their independence can be found. As illustrated in Figure 4a, a user may first pick a direction line connecting the start position with one point within the target, and then do a 1D Fitts task along the selected line. If these two actions are independent, the overall time is the sum of their time.

$$T = a - b \log_2 (\theta \int_0^\theta \frac{L_i(t)}{L(t)} dt) - c \log_2 \theta \tag{8}$$

The time spent selecting a direction line can be calculated according to the same ID principle of Equation (5): the larger of the probability of locating a legal direction line (a direction line is legal

Figure 4. Three different parameterizations for 2D pointing task. The shaded rectangle is the target of a pointing movement, and the ball represents the starting position of the movement.

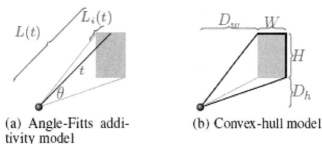

(a) Angle-Fitts additivity model   (b) Convex-hull model

if it goes across the target) among all the possible direction lines, the smaller is the **ID** of selecting such a line; from Figure 4a, it is easy to see that the probability of finding a legal direction line is proportional to the size of the angle θ; therefore the logarithm of $1/\theta$ is proportional to the line selection time, resulting in the last term of Equation (8). The above argument has essentially sketched a derivation of the law of crossing (Accot & Zhai, 1997), but the remaining details are beyond the scope of this chapter.

Once a legal direction line is selected, the time spent following the line to hit the target is governed by 1D Fitts' law. To calculate the average movement time of all the legal direction lines, it is necessary to first calculate their sum, which is the integral of the **ID** formula of 1D Fitts task in Equation (6) over a single variable t that varies in the interval **[0, θ]**. Basically, the variable t indicates which direction line is chosen, and thus determines its total length **$L(t)$**. $L_i(t)$ is the length of chosen line inside the target, and $L_i(t) / L(t)$ is then the probability of terminating within target when line t is selected. When the target is rectangular, **$L(t)$** and $L_i(t)$ can be calculated via trigonometry and the integral has closed form solution. Dividing the value of the integral by the size of angle θ, the average movement time is obtained, as shown in the second term of Equation (8).

Convex Hull Model

In order to calculate the probability of hitting the target, it is necessary to find a reasonable set of all the possible terminating positions, i.e. to classify the space into the set of possible termination positions vs. the impossible ones. According to the optimization principle of preferring convex regions in mental configuration space (Gärdenfors, 2004), the set of possible terminating positions can be reasonably assumed to be all the points within the convex hull enclosing the starting point and the target area, as outlined by thick lines in Figure 4(b). The probability of terminating within target is then obtained by dividing the area of the target by the area of the convex hull, resulting in this formula:

$$T = a + b \log_2 \left(\frac{HD_w + WD_h}{2WH} + 1 \right) \qquad (9)$$

Regular Configuration Model

As discussed earlier, regular configurations are defined as configurations that require fewer free parameters to specify than the generic ones. In other words, a regular configuration satisfies more symmetric constraints. In the following discussion, the scale of configuration is ignored, as it has been shown to be largely independent from pointing task performance (Guiard, 2009). Without considering scale, three parameters are needed to specify a 2D pointing configuration, and they should all be ratios of lengths instead of absolute lengths due to the removal of scale. Suppose that W, H, D_w and D_h are originally chosen as the set of parameters. To normalize scale, every parameter is divided by D_w, and the set is reduced to three parameters: W/D_w, H/D_w, and D_h/D_w. To define a regular configuration, at least one more parameter needs to be taken out of the set. Target shape W/H is a hard constraint prescribed by the task; so is the minimal movement distance D, which depends on D_w and D_h. There is no freedom in these once a configuration is shown. The only free parameter that can be taken away is the movement angle, as users can approach the target in any angle as along as the target is hit. Given these considerations, the only reasonable choice to define a regular configuration for 2D pointing is to add a symmetric constraint of $W/H = D_h/D_w$, as illustrated in Figure 5.

Figure 5. A regular configuration. The movement starting position is indicated by the ball, and the shaded arc represents all the starting positions with the same shortest distance **D** *to the target.*

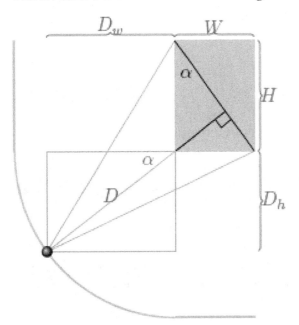

The regular configuration model can be obtained by applying the convex hull model of Equation (9) to the regular configuration defined above:

$$T = a + b \log_2\left(\frac{HD_w + WD_h}{2WH} + 1 \right) \qquad (10)$$

$$= a + b \log_2\left(\frac{HD\cos\alpha + WD\sin\alpha}{2WH} + 1 \right) \qquad (11)$$

$$= a + b \log_2\left(\frac{D\sqrt{W^2 + H^2}}{2WH} + 1 \right) \qquad (12)$$

$$= a + b \log_2\left(\frac{1}{2}\sqrt{(\frac{D}{H})^2 + (\frac{D}{W})^2} + 1 \right) \qquad (13)$$

Augmented Regular Configuration Model

The regular configuration model essentially ignores the effect of movement direction on performance, but such effect does exist (Grossman & Balakrishnan, 2005). To model it, the third term of the angle-Fitts additivity model of Equation (8) is added to the regular configuration model of Equation (13). The rationale for adding the two terms together is that the choice of movement direction is independent from the movement-terminating decision - the same argument used in the angle-Fitts additivity model.

Experimental Comparison of Models

A typical 2D pointing task was used to collect data for comparing the models. Participants performed the task with a mouse, moving the cursor between two identical rectangles used as the targets. Participants were asked to click on

Figure 6. Summary of model fit

Model	a		b		c		R^2
	Est.	SE	Est.	SE	Est.	SE	
Width-height independence (Eq. 7)	360.2	8.1	66.1	2.7	68.7	2.7	.753
Angle-Fitts additivity (Eq. 8)	207.8	10.5	107.2	4.9	85.7	9.5	.855
Convex-hull (Eq. 9)	314.2	6.0	143.9	2.7	-	-	.883
Regular configuration (Eq. 13)	191.7	5.8	135.4	1.8	-	-	.937
Augmented regular configuration	157.8	5.6	174.0	3.5	41.8	3.4	.955
MacKenzie and Buxton 1992 (Eq. 2)	227.0	6.0	133.0	2.0	-	-	.924
Accot and Zhai 2003 (Eq. 3)	233.3	5.9	136.5	2.0	-	-	.923
Appert et al. 2008 (Eq. 4)	133.8	7.7	125.6	1.9	-	-	.916

one target, then the other, and alternate back and forth between the two targets as quickly and as accurately as possible. The time durations between clicking two targets were recorded as movement time T. If a point outside the targets is clicked, the trial is counted as an error and its movement time is discarded.

As prescribed by the configuration space of 2D pointing, four independent variables were systematically varied: the width W and the height H of the targets had four levels: 30, 50, 80 and 120 pixels; the horizontal distance D_w and the vertical distance D_h between the two targets also had four levels: 0, 80, 240, 400 pixels. The final 384 conditions used in the experiment were the results of combining the levels of the four independent variables, permutating them to account for the alternating movements in both directions, and removing some illegal combinations, e.g. D_w and D_h can not both be 0 pixel.

The experiment was conducted using a repeated within-subject design. Each participant did all the 384 conditions, which appeared in dynamically generated random orders different for each participant. Each condition contains eleven trials, and the average of last ten trials' T is used in data analysis. Fifteen paid university students participated in the experiment. More details of the experiment set up can be found in Yang and Xu (2010).

Linear least square regression methods were performed to test the fits of the five models proposed above and the three previous models.

The fits of the eight models are all statistically significant with $p<.001$. Results are summarized in Figure 6. The first column contains the names of the models; the last column is the percentage of variance explained by the models, R^2. The columns in between are the estimates of model coefficients a, b, and c (if applicable), and their standard errors.

The relative poor fit of width-height independence model is not surprising because the model is equivalent to modeling a task where users first move horizontally, then vertically towards the target, or vice versa, but nobody moves in such a city-block way. Angle-Fitts additivity model, though conceptually attractive, does not seem to be an accurate model. It is likely that movements are not strictly straight lines but curved paths, so the second term of Equation (8) does not work very well. It is slightly surprising that the naive convex hull model works better than the aforementioned ones. A model based purely on the ground of the space of all possible terminating positions (a configuration space approach), the assumption of which may be grossly simplistic (the convexity preference), can still fare quite well in predicting the performance. This result indicates the value of adopting a configuration space way of thinking.

All three previous models tested perform not as well as the regular configuration model. Among them, MacKenzie and Buxton (1992) model, though the most simple, did surprisingly well. The other two models perform not as well as they were for their original data set. The significant difference in form between the regular configuration model and the Accot and Zhai (2003) model is that the later contains an extra η constant, which actually hurts the performance of the model. It is likely that the constant introduced is an artifact of over-fitting due to the limited set of conditions tested in their experiment.

The augmented regular configuration model fits the data the best. However, its advantage over the regular configuration model is not substantial, especially on account of the one more free coefficient it requires. The superiority of regular configuration model is obvious, in light of its simplicity: it has only two free regression coefficients instead of three. It does not introduce any extra constant either. To give an intuitive feel of the model fit, Figure 6 shows a scatter plot of the data fitting to the regular configuration model. Each data point in the plot represents the average performance of one experimental condition. Data points belonging to different movement directions

Figure 7. Fit of regular configuration model. Vertical bar marks indicate vertical movements, horizontal bar marks are horizontal movements, triangle and circle marks are the two diagonal movements.

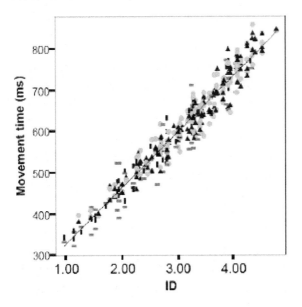

are represented with different marks. Considering how different these conditions are, the remarkable fit of the regular configuration model strongly supports the viability of the configuration space approach.

FUTURE RESEARCH DIRECTIONS

Research Methodology

For user interface research, one of the main points of this chapter may be a methodological one. First, unlike Fitts (1954), modeling work in HCI often does not attempt to propose theoretical justifications. Models are often proposed on the basis of intuitions or as the outcomes of mathematical exercises of satisfying known trends in data. This chapter demonstrates an approach to modeling that is based on formal derivation from first principles within a theoretical framework, and the results seem to be encouraging. More future research using this approach could potentially lead to better models in HCI.

Secondly, previous modeling work in HCI normally considers only a few factors at a time. Thus, the experiments used to test these models often investigate only limit cases concerning these factors, and hold other factors constant. This type of limited experimentation with a small number of factors is certainly the standard scientific practice of uncovering causal relationships between factors and effects. However, experimentation with a small number of factors alone is insufficient for obtaining a global understanding of the phenomenon. At some point, regression with a large number of testing conditions is necessary in order to achieve such an understanding.

One side effect of limited experimentation is that the resulting models often contain arbitrary constants that may happen to apply for the subset of investigated cases: the risk of overestimating model fit is high. Although it is undesirable to exhaustively test all the possible conditions, testing models in as many meaningfully varied conditions as possible can reduce such risk. The mental configuration space viewpoint introduced in this chapter offers some methodological guidance on selecting a suitable set of conditions to test. Instead of varying only a few factors in model checking, including all DOFs of the configuration space of a task is recommended. Including less than the number of DOFs of configuration space would likely lead to model over-fitting. Including more than the number of DOFs would be wasteful of resources since some of the factors would be redundant, and can be derived from the defining set of DOFs.

Another benefit of including all DOFs is the ability to see the relative contribution of individual factors. Properly designed experiments are often capable of finding statistically significant effects of individual factors if they do exist, no matter how small the effects might be. However, to see the factors' contribution to the overall performance requires studies that include all the relevant factors. For example, the 2D pointing results here show that the movement angle parameter does affect performance, but its contribution is relatively small when all parameters are tested. For HCI, this issue of choosing the proper set of factors to study is more important due to the practical nature of the discipline. It is nice to study causal relationships among a few factors as a scientific endeavor; it would be insufficient for practical purpose, since all the factors are present in the real world.

Finally, mental configuration space viewpoint urges researchers to move away from the debate of which way of parameterizations is more "correct" than others. If two set of parameters have the same number of DOFs and are characterizing the same configuration space, then they are equivalent. In this view, to understand a behavior is to understand the structure of the configuration space. The coordinate system researchers choose to impose on the space does make the job of finding a structure easier or harder, depending on the kind of structure they are looking for. It is desirable to

maintain a conceptual flexibility on parameterizations, and to choose the set of parameters that is the easiest to test for the structures the researchers are hypothesizing about.

Principle of Maximum Regularity

A common thread in the literature of motor behavior seems to be the quest to find some forms of optimization as the governing principle. In addition to the information theoretical argument of Fitts (1954), neural noise reduction (Meyer, et al., 1998) and movement smoothness (Flash & Hogan, 1985) have been proposed as the criteria of optimization. It is not the aim of this chapter to dispute these criteria, but to offer another: the preference to maximum regularity in mental configuration space. Facing the high dimensionality of stimuli, cognitive systems are likely to impose some structure on the mental configuration space in order to reduce the number of dimensions. This reduction can be done by favoring more regular configurations and treat them as the representatives of the more generic ones. In the case of the 2D pointing experiment described above, the regular configurations were nonexistent in actuality since they were not shown as part of the experimental conditions. However, the participants responded as if they were shown. Such response patterns seem to suggest the regular configurations serve as prototype of generic ones and are the preferred representation in the mental configuration space. This optimization principle saw support in the domains of perceptual organization (Feldman, 2000) and concept categorization (Rosch, 1975). The results here seem to extend its applicability to the realm of motor behavior. Obviously, more studies are needed to confirm the conclusion and to support or counter such generalization.

The preference to maximum regularity in mental configuration space has the potential to simplify research and evaluation of user interfaces. For example, in the case of 2D pointing, the number of conditions needs to be tested in order to estimate the average movement time of a design can be greatly reduces: since the regular configuration dominants the performance, and is capable of explaining the majority of performance variance, it may be sufficient to test the regular configurations only in order to obtain a good enough estimate, at least for certain engineering purposes such as selecting the best design among several alternatives. Generalizing the idea, if the dominating regular configurations for other cognitive tasks can be defined, a standard test suite of regular configurations might be developed and used by practitioners.

The mental configuration space framework seems to work well for visual oriented cognitive tasks, such as perception (Feldman, 1997), mental rotation (Shepard & Farrell, 1985), and Fitts' tasks. It is unclear whether other modalities of cognition, for example the audio or haptic tasks, are sufficiently similar for it to be applicable. It is therefore the intention of this chapter to encourage researchers to purse the geometric mode of cognitive representation further, and to apply the mental configuration space framework to analyze all domains of cognitive tasks.

In both Feldman (2000) and the present study, the strategy for reducing the number of parameters to produce regular configuration has been to set the values or ratios of several parameters to be equal to each other. However, the concrete choice of which parameters to be set as equals is currently made on the basis of geometric intuition. For example, the present study's choice of $W / H = D_h / D_w$ reflects a mirror symmetry, with the closest corner of the target as the point of reflection. Another choice, $W / H = D_w / D_h$, would not produce the same level of regularity, even though it reduces the number of parameters equally as well. Therefore, the principle of maximum regularity is not just concerned with reducing the minimum number of parameters required to describe a configuration, but also with increasing the amount of symmetry embodied in the configuration. To quantify such

notions of regularity, detailed investigation of symmetry, for example, along the line of group theory, seems to be necessary.

CONCLUSION

This chapter briefly reviews the geometric approach to human cognition based on the concept of mental configuration space. It is suggested that some optimization principles in mental configuration space have good explanatory power on cognitive behaviors, particularly, there exists a preference for regular configurations, and the classification in mental configuration favors convex regions. As a case study, several models of 2D pointing are derived based on these ideas of mental configuration space. These derived models are tested with empirical data, and are found to be well performed compared with the existing models in the literature. This chapter also critically evaluates some practices of user interface research, and advocates a research methodology based on the ideas of mental configuration space. Future research directions are suggested for this promising approach.

REFERENCES

Accot, J., & Zhai, S. (1997). Beyond Fitts' law: Models for trajectory-based HCI tasks. In *Proceedings of ACM CHI Conference on Human Factors in Computing Systems*, (pp. 295–302). ACM Press.

Accot, J., & Zhai, S. (2003). Refining Fitts' law models for bivariate pointing. In *Proceedings of ACM CHI Conference on Human Factors in Computing Systems*, (pp. 193–200). ACM Press.

Appert, C., Chapuis, O., & Beaudouin-Lafon, M. (2008). Evaluation of pointing performance on screen edges. In *Proceedings of Advanced Visual Interfaces*. ACM. doi:10.1145/1385569.1385590

Borovik, A. V. (2009). *Mathematics under the microscope*. Washington, DC: American Mathematical Society.

Card, S. K., English, W. K., & Burr, B. J. (1978). Evaluation of mouse, rate-controlled isometric joystick, step keys, and text keys for text selection on a CRT. *Ergonomics, 21*, 601–613. doi:10.1080/00140137808931762

Card, S. K., Moran, T. P., & Newell, A. (1983). *The psychology of human-computer interaction*. Boca Raton, FL: CRC Press.

Carlton, E., & Shepard, R. N. (1990). Psychologically simple motions as geodesic paths: Asymmetric objects. *Journal of Mathematical Psychology, 34*, 127–188. doi:10.1016/0022-2496(90)90001-P

Chater, N., & Vitanyi, P. (2003). Simplicity: A unifying principle in cognitive science? *Trends in Cognitive Sciences, 7*, 19–22. doi:10.1016/S1364-6613(02)00005-0

Clark, A. (1993). *Sensory qualities*. Oxford, UK: Clarendon Press.

Cover, T. M., & Thomas, J. A. (1991). *Elements of information theory*. New York, NY: John Wiley & Sons. doi:10.1002/0471200611

Feldman, J. (1997a). Regularity-based perceptual grouping. *Computational Intelligence, 13*(4), 582–623. doi:10.1111/0824-7935.00052

Feldman, J. (1997b). The structure of perceptual categories. *Journal of Mathematical Psychology, 41*, 145–170. doi:10.1006/jmps.1997.1154

Feldman, J. (2000). Bias toward regular form in mental shape spaces. *Journal of Experimental Psychology. Human Perception and Performance, 26*, 152–165. doi:10.1037/0096-1523.26.1.152

Fitts, P. M. (1954). The information capacity of the human motor system in controlling amplitude of movement. *Journal of Experimental Psychology, 47*, 381–39. doi:10.1037/h0055392

Flash, T., & Hogan, N. (1985). The coordination of arm movements: An experimentally confirmed mathematical model. *The Journal of Neuroscience, 5*, 1688–1703.

Gallistel, C. R. (1990). *The organization of learning*. Cambridge, MA: MIT Press.

Gärdenfors, P. (2004). *Conceptual space: The geometry of thought*. Cambridge, MA: MIT Press.

Grossman, T., & Balakrishnan, R. (2005). A probabilistic approach to modeling two-dimensional pointing. *ACM Transactions on Computer-Human Interaction, 12*(3), 435–459. doi:10.1145/1096737.1096741

Guiard, Y. (2009). The problem of consistency in the design of Fitts' law experiments: Consider either target distance and width or movement form and scale. In *Proceedings of ACM CHI Conference on Human Factors in Computing Systems*. ACM Press.

Hoffmann, E., & Sheikh, I. (1994). Effect of target shape on movement time in a Fitts task. *Ergonomics, 37*, 1533–1548. doi:10.1080/00140139408963719

Kubovy, M., & Epstein, W. (2001). Internalization: A metaphor we can live without. *The Behavioral and Brain Sciences, 24*(4), 618–625.

Latombe, J. C. (1991). *Robot motion planning*. Boston, MA: Kluwer.

Leyton, M. (1982). *Symmetry, causality, mind*. Cambridge, MA: MIT Press.

MacKenzie, I. S., & Buxton, W. A. S. (1992). Extending Fitts' law to two-dimensional tasks. In *Proceedings of ACM CHI Conference on Human Factors in Computing Systems*, (pp. 219–226). ACM Press.

Meyer, D. E., Abrams, R. A., Kornblum, S., Wright, C. E., & Keith, S. J. (1998). Optimality in human motor performance: Ideal control of rapid aimed movements. *Psychological Review*, *95*, 340–370. doi:10.1037/0033-295X.95.3.340

Murata, A. (1999). Extending effective target width in Fitts' law to a two-dimensional pointing task. *International Journal of Human-Computer Interaction*, *11*(2), 137–152. doi:10.1207/S153275901102_4

Newell, A. (1990). *Unified theories of cognition*. Cambridge, MA: Harvard University Press.

Rosch, E. (1975). Cognitive reference points. *Cognitive Psychology*, *7*, 532–547. doi:10.1016/0010-0285(75)90021-3

Rumelhart, D. E., & McClelland, J. L. (1986). *Parallel distributed processing* (*Vol. 1-2*). Cambridge, MA: MIT Press.

Shepard, R. N. (1987). Toward a universal law of generalization for psychological science. *Science*, *237*, 1317–1323. doi:10.1126/science.3629243

Shepard, R. N., & Chipman, S. (1970). Second-order isomorphism of internal representations: Shapes of states. *Cognitive Psychology*, *1*, 1–17. doi:10.1016/0010-0285(70)90002-2

Shepard, R. N., & Farrell, J. E. (1985). Representation of the orientations of shapes. *Acta Psychologica*, *59*, 104–121. doi:10.1016/0001-6918(85)90044-7

Simon, H. (1957). A behavioral model of rational choice. In *Models of Man, Social and Rational: Mathematical Essays on Rational Human Behavior in a Social Setting*. New York, NY: Wiley.

Sivik, L., & Taft, C. (1994). Color naming: A mapping in the NCS of common color terms. *Scandinavian Journal of Psychology*, *35*, 144–164. doi:10.1111/j.1467-9450.1994.tb00939.x

Soukoreff, R. W., & MacKenzie, I. S. (2004). Towards a standard for pointing device evaluation: Perspectives on 27 years of Fitts' law research in HCI. *International Journal of Human-Computer Studies*, *61*, 751–789. doi:10.1016/j.ijhcs.2004.09.001

Yang, H., & Xu, X. (2010). Bias towards regular configuration in 2D pointing. In *Proceedings of ACM CHI Conference on Human Factors in Computing Systems*, (pp. 1391-1400). ACM Press.

Zhai, S. (2004). Characterizing computer input with Fitts' law parameters: The information and non-information aspects of pointing. *International Journal of Human-Computer Studies*, *61*, 791–809. doi:10.1016/j.ijhcs.2004.09.006

ADDITIONAL READING

Crossman, E. R. F. W., & Goodeve, P. J. (1983). Feedback control of hand-movement and Fitts' law. *Quarterly Journal of Experimental Psychology*, *35A*, 251–278.

Dorst, L., Fontijne, D., & Mann, S. (2007). *Geometric algebra for computer science*. New York, NY: Morgan Kaufmann.

Hestenes, D. (1999). *New foundations for classical mechanics*. Berlin, Germany: Springer.

Jagacinski, R., Repperger, D., Moran, M., Ward, S., & Glass, B. (1980). Fitts law and the microstructure of rapid discrete movements. *Journal of Experimental Psychology. Human Perception and Performance*, *6*, 309–320. doi:10.1037/0096-1523.6.2.309

Kanerva, P. (1988). *Sparse distributed memory*. Cambridge, MA: MIT Press.

Keele, S. (1968). Movement control in skilled motor performance. *Psychological Bulletin*, *70*, 387–403. doi:10.1037/h0026739

Kerr, B., & Langolf, G. (1977). Speed of aiming movements. *The Quarterly Journal of Experimental Psychology, 29,* 475–481. doi:10.1080/14640747708400623

Langolf, G., Chaffin, D., & Foulke, J. (1976). An investigation of Fitts law using a wide range of movement amplitudes. *Journal of Motor Behavior, 8,* 113–128.

Latash, M. L., & Turvey, M. T. (Eds.). (1996). *Dexterity and its development.* Mahwah, NJ: Lawrence Erlbaum.

Mcdonald, A. (2011). *Linear and geometric algebra.* New York, NY: CreateSpace.

McGuffin, M., & Balakrishnan, R. (2005). Fitts law and expanding targets: Experimental studies and designs for user interfaces. *ACM Transactions on Computer-Human Interaction, 12*(4), 388–422. doi:10.1145/1121112.1121115

Porteous, I. R. (2009). *Clifford algebras and the classical groups.* Cambridge, UK: Cambridge University Press.

Prablanc, C., Echallier, J., Komilis, E., & Jeannerod, M. (1979). Optimal response of eye and hand motor systems in pointing at a visual target. *Biological Cybernetics, 35,* 113–124. doi:10.1007/BF00337436

Rosenbaum, D. A., Meulenbroek, R. G., & Vaughan, J. (2004). What is the point of motor planning? *International Journal of Sport and Exercise Psychology, 2*(4), 439–469. doi:10.108 0/1612197X.2004.9671754

Schmidt, R., Zelaznik, H., Hawkins, B., Frank, J., & Quinn, J. (1979). Motor-output variability: A theory for the accuracy of rapid motor acts. *Psychological Review, 86,* 415–451. doi:10.1037/0033-295X.86.5.415

Shepard, R. N. (1962). The analysis of proximities: Multidimensional scaling with an unknown distance function: I and II. *Psychometrika, 27*(2). doi:10.1007/BF02289630

Shepard, R. N. (1982). Geometrical approximations to the structure of musical pitch. *Psychological Review, 89,* 305–333. doi:10.1037/0033-295X.89.4.305

Shepard, R. N., & Cooper, L. A. (1982). *Mental images and their transformations.* Cambridge, MA: MIT Press.

Shepard, R. N., Kilpatrick, D. W., & Cunningham, J. P. (1975). The internal representation of numbers. *Cognitive Psychology, 7,* 82–138. doi:10.1016/0010-0285(75)90006-7

Suppes, P., Krantz, D. H., Luce, R. D., & Tversky, A. (1989). Foundations of measurement: *Vol. II. Geometrical, threshold, and probabilistic representations.* New York, NY: Academic Press.

Wallace, S., & Newell, K. (1983). Visual control of discrete aiming movements. *Quarterly Journal of Experimental Psychology, 35A,* 311–321.

Widdows, D. (2004). *Geometry and meaning.* Palo Alto, CA: Stanford University Press.

Section 3

Monitoring Human Workflow, Collaborating with Intelligent Systems, and Recognizing Human Traits exhibited by Computers

Chapter 10

Question–Answer Approach to Human–Computer Interaction in Collaborative Designing

Petr Sosnin
Ulyanovsk State Technical University, Russia

ABSTRACT

The chapter presents a question-answer approach to the programming of Human-Computer Interactions (HCI) during collaborative development of software intensive systems. Efficiency of the general work can be essentially increased if the human part of the work is informed by precedents and executed with a special kind of pseudo-program by "intellectual processors." The role of any processor of such type is fulfilled by a designer. The suggested approach was investigated and evolved until an instrumental system providing the pseudo-code programming of intellectual processors combined with computer processors. Interactions between processors are based on question-answer reasoning. Pseudo-code programs and their corresponding instrumental means can be combined easily with traditional HCI.

INTRODUCTION

One of problematic kinds of a human-computer activity is a collective creating of Software Intensive Systems (SISs) in any of which the software plays an essential role in the system functionality, cost, development risk, and development time (Software, 2006). A very low degree of success (about 35%) in the activity of such type indicates that the problem of failures is connected with an absence of very important means accessible to both developers and users of the SIS.

From the general point of view, the unsuccessfulness of the SIS development is being discovered via users interactions with the SIS that essentially differ from reactions expected by users. Similar events indicate that corresponding units of the programmed behavior have not been tested by developers or were being understood incorrectly. Usually any definite unit of the behavior has not been tested when this unit was not qualified by developer as an essential case.

DOI: 10.4018/978-1-4666-1628-8.ch010

Therefore, the developers of SISs need the effective means for adequate defining of the essential behavior units, their modeling for achieving the necessary understanding and also for testing the units in appropriate conditions of designing and using. First of all, the essential units are to be distinguished and such actions can be fulfilled experimentally by interacting with the developing system in real time of designing. Let us notice that interactions used in experiments with the chosen behavior unit can play for this unit the integrative and others helpful roles.

On a deep belief of the author, the named behavioral units are to be distinguished, defined, modeled, understood, coded, and tested as precedents. *"Precedents are actions or decisions that have already happened in the past and which can be referred to and justified as an example that can be followed when the similar situation arises"* (Precedent, 2011, p. 1).

The precedent form of a human activity was "created" by nature in an evolution of a phenomenon named "conditioned reflex." It is possible to consider, that any precedent appears as a result of the corresponding "experiment" executed by a person or a group of people. Creating of the precedent and its reusing in appropriate conditions which should be preliminary tested are based on human interactions with an environment of the precedent existence. Such interactions are impossible without the usage of the natural language and the activity of consciousness. Any human has a rich experience of such interactions and this experience should be inherited for the creation of means which support the human-computer interaction in the collaborative designing.

All that was told above can be used for formulating the following assertion: *the degree of success in collaborative designing can be significantly increased due to the use of new more effective means of HCI which are oriented on behavioral units of the precedent type.* Below this assertion is analyzed and evolved until the system of instrumental means, which provide the implementation of question-answer approach (QA-approach) to HCI.

The approach is aimed at increasing the intellectuality of HCI. We can mark the following features of such approach:

- Using the models of precedents for the presentation of appropriate kinds of activity units of developers and users;
- Using the question-answer reasoning (QA-reasoning) and their models in HCI for the rational connection of human and computer actions in their collaborative activity for hierarchical representing the tasks and also for their modeling, analyzing and programming;
- Using the QA-reasoning for pseudo-programming of the human "processor" (intellectual processor or briefly I-processor), which is executing the human actions, similarly the program works being executed by the computer processor (K-processor);
- Combining the offered means of interactions with traditional means of HCI;
- Using the knowledge base for keeping a number of metrics of usability (in the form of precedents) for the access to them for their embedding into the designing process.

BACKGROUND OF QA-APPROACH

Question-Answer Reasoning

The choice of the QA-approach to HCI is explained that consciousness has a dialog nature the existence and process of which are being opened via the usage of the natural language. Dialog processes in consciousness support an intellectual formation of any precedent model as a certain sample of an activity. Moreover the dialog is a rational form for working with the reaction part of this model and with the conditional choice of the appropriate precedent. Such working depends on the used model in the essential measure.

Basic features of the QA-approach are bound with the logical model of the precedent, which has the following structure:

```
Name of precedent P_i:
  while [logical formulae (LF) for
  motives  M = {M_k}]
    as [LF for aims  C = {C_l}]
      if [LF for precondition U' =
      {U'_n}],
        then [plan of reaction
        (program) r_q],
      end so [LF for post conditions
      U" = {U"_m}]
  --------------------------
  there are alternatives {P_j(r_p)}.
```

This model is a human-oriented scheme the human interaction with which activates the internal logical process on the level of the second signal system in human brains. As told above such logical processes have a dialog nature and for inheriting the naturalness on the computer side the interaction processes outside brains should keep the dialog form also.

When such logical model is accessible to the human the choice of the corresponding precedent starts from testing the conditioned part of this model. The experience of expert systems indicates that the best way for testing is a question-answering process the implementation of which will include discovering and registering of LF-elements in the analyzing situation.

When the logical model is being created its structure and content should be prepared for the use in the described process of choice. The essence of the preparation process is being defined by the extraction of LF-elements from the description of the investigating situation and their logical binding in the formulae the best way for which is question-answering process.

One can consider any precedent appearing after the decision of the appropriate task and the estimation of its value. It is known the use of question-answering means is a typical way for cognitive analysis (Crystal, 2004) of any task and for the creation of its conceptual decision. The last is especially important for tasks, which are being solved at the conceptual stage of the collaborative designing of complex systems when precedents are being created and interactively used by the group of designers.

Therefore, the chosen logical scheme of the precedent and described understanding of its use have been put to the base of the QA-approach. Details of this approach are being defined by the following specifications:

1. The model $M(P_i)$ of any precedent P_i is created as a solution of the definite task Z_i.
2. The solution of the task Z_i is built as a composition $M(P_i) = \cup P^X_i$ of the specialized precedent models $\{P^X_i\}$ one of which is the logical model $(P^L i)$.
3. The conceptual essence of the precedent P_i and task Z_i is defined by the text model (P^T_i) in the form of the statement of this task.
4. Any model P^X_i is created as a solution of the corresponding subtask Z^X_i (subordinated to the task Z_i) representing the definite useful view to the precedent.
5. The solution process of any task or subtask is being accompanied by QA-reasoning which is being fulfilled and registered as a protocol (QA-protocol) of the task decision.
6. The QA-protocol of QA-reasoning fulfills the role of the specialized model P^{QA}_i as for the task Z_i so for the precedent P_i.
7. The QA-protocol of the corresponding subtask uses as the QA-model of this subtask.
8. Any model $M(P_i)$ is implemented and existed in an program form the structure of which composes the object-oriented implementations of specialized models $\{P^X_i\}$.

9. Any QA-protocol can be interpreted or built originally as a text of the pseudo-program written in the natural language in its algorithmic usage. Pseudo-programs of such type (named QA-programs) are suggested by the author for the realization of HCI in collaborative designing.

10. QA-programs are destined for their collaborative execution by I-processors and K-processors and such execution is being supported by the specialized means of HCI developed by the author.

By other words and shortly the QA-approach to HCI in collaborative designing is based on QA-modeling and QA-programming of the common work with necessary precedents developed for service, instrumental and technological aims and also for creating the SIS. Such means of QA-approach will be named below as QA-means.

Related Works

For the QA-approach the nearest alternative is a scenario-oriented approach to HCI the essence of which is connected with the use of a scenario as the activity model. More formally, *"A scenario is a description that contains actors, background information about them, and assumptions about their environment, their goals, or objectives, and sequences of actions and events. It may include obstacles, contingencies, and outcomes. In some applications scenarios may omit, one of the elements or express it simply and implicitly"* (Go, 2004, p. 45).

Scenarios are expressed in various media and forms. For example, scenarios can be textual narratives, storyboards, video mockups or scripted prototypes. In the simplest understanding the scenario is a story about the human work, human collaboration, or human activities which one person tries to tell to another. The representative catalogue of scenario-based methods and methodologies is presented in the paper (Muller, 1999).

There are essential differences as in definitions of precedents and scenarios so in their understanding and especially in their usage in the development and exploitation of any SIS. In the implementation of the QA-approach the precedents models will be embedded to the developed SIS for supporting their rational usage by users (understanding, controlling, adjusting and so on). A set of precedents models {M(Pi)} which are created and applied by developers in the development stage will be opened to users in created forms of precedents including QA-models and QA-programs embedded to them. If it will be necessary some precedents models can be changed (reprogrammed) by users if such actions will be allowed to them. In these cases the users will interact as programmers with computer components of the SIS and one can count that the users will apply means of programming (in forms of pseudo-programming, QA-programming) in human-computer interactions with the SIS. In the realization of the scenario-oriented approach, the scenarios are used basically at the development stage of the SIS for answering the specific design questions (for example, for usage-guided testing of systems). After finding and/or building answers on necessary questions, the scenarios are being transformed for their partial including to the SIS as their interfaces for HCI and guides for users.

The other group of works related to QA-approach is connected with Question-Answering as a type of "an information retrieval in which a direct answer is expected in response to a submitted query, rather than a set of references that may contain the answers" (Question, 2011).

There were many different QA-methods and QA-systems, which have been suggested, investigated, and developed in the practice of the informational retrieval and extraction (Hirschman, 2001). Possible ways in the evolution of this subject area were marked in the Roadmap Research (Burger, 2001) which is now possible. This research has defined the system of concepts, classifications, and basic tasks of this subject area.

Applying concepts of the Roadmap Research we can assert that QA-means which are necessary for working with precedents samples should provide the use of "interactive QA" and "advanced reasoning for QA" (Question, 2011). In interactive QA "the questioner might want not only to reformulate the question, but (s)he might want to have a dialogue with the system." The advanced reasoning is used by questioner who "expects answers which are outside the scope of written texts or structured databases" (Question, 2011). From this point of view the useful informational sources for the creation of precedents samples is mental reasoning in dialog forms.

Finally, we mark the works which are connected with traditional means of HCI and especially with interface metrics described in standards (first of all usability metrics from standard ISO/MEC 9126) and also in libraries of corporations, for example, the list of metrics of Microsoft Corporation (User, 2011). Such metrics of interfaces are the units of the experience, which are materialized in the realization of QA-approach in the reuse forms supporting the creation of precedents of designing. In the QA-approach the named interfaces metrics are combined with QA-means. It is necessary to note that the group of interface metrics are united and included to the separate section of the library of technological precedents models.

IMPLEMENTATION OF QA-APPROACH

Preliminary Preconditions

In accordance with the previous content, the interests of the chapter are restricted by rational HCI means, which can help to increase the degree of success of the collaborative activity of a group of designers working in technologies providing the developments of SISs. The best example of such technologies is the Rational Unified Process (RUP) created by IBM corporation (Kroll, 2003).

The RUP can be used as a collection of requirements opened the specificity of designers interactions with computer components of the toolkit supported this technology. The specificity includes the following features:

- Collective activity of designers which fulfill different actions by playing corresponding roles (architect, system analyst, programmer, and many others) in frames of definite scenarios;
- Normative modeling of such activity in the form of workflows the typical units of which are tasks with guides for their repeated decisions;
- Usage by designers several hundred of typical tasks (for example, in RUP about 500 units only for conceptual designing) the enormous quantity of examples of which should be decided collaboratively in the coordination;
- Necessity to generate by designers the new ideas and to solve creatively new tasks (not only typical tasks) which evolve their personal and collective experience.

The list of specific features, which could be inherited from RUP, can be continued but the named of them are sufficient for explaining and implementing the new kind of HCI suggested by the author. First of all one can agree that conceptual and professional actions of designers connected with their work with enormous quantity of typical and creative tasks, should be automated.

Many approaches and instrumental means for the automation of such work are existed and used. For example in RUP the automation is being supported by the usage of the networking access to the Experience Factory, the units of which (templates, guides, and the others) are being applied in decisions of current tasks. Except for that, the specialized toolkit is accessible on any workplace of designers group. But all of these means do not contain means of programming for the tasks being solved by designers at the conceptual stage of designing.

Intellectual Processor

As told above one of the directions of the positive changes in the development of the SIS can be connected with the creation and usage of means for programming the designer interactions with instrumental means in the conceptual designing. By the other words, the degree of automation in the conceptual designing will be positively increased if any designer will play the role of the "processor" which executes the programs managing his(her) activity in the appropriate instrumental medium. Above such role of the designer was named "intellectual processor."

The idea of the designer model as I-processor is inherited by the author from publications (Card, 1983; Kieras, 1997) where described the model human processor (MH-processor) as an engineering model of the human performance in solving the different tasks in real time.

The especially known application of the MH-processor is Executive Process-Interactive Control (EPIC) described in detail. Means of EPIC support the programming of the human interaction with the computerized system in the specialized command language named Keystrok Level Model (KLM). A set of basic KLM actions includes the following operators: **K**—key press and release (keyboard), **P**—point the mouse to an object on screen, **B**—button press or release (mouse), **H**—hand from keyboard to mouse or vice versa and others commands. MH-processor is defined (Kieras, 1997) as a system of specialized processors which solve the common task collaboratively. One of these processors is a cognitive processor providing mental reasoning the type and content of which are not specified.

It is necessary to underline that I-processor is similar to MH-processor and includes the cognitive processor also, but the existence and work of this component of I-processor are revealed through reasoning of the question-answer type. This feature is one of the main differences between MH-processor and I-processor. Another important difference is a set of basic commands, which includes typical commands of the pseudo-code algorithmic language. There are two ways for managing the designer activity the one of which is based on QA-reasoning which is registering by designers and coming back to support the work of I-processors. The second way is aimed at the creation of pseudo-code programs being executed by I-processors.

Moreover, interactions of I-processor with K-processor should be implemented with the usage of a model of QA-reasoning as in its free form so in pseudo-code program form. QA-reasoning in all versions of their usage should support the interaction of designers with own experience and with its computer models.

Executing of this role is supported by the toolkit named WIQA (Working In Questions and Answers) which provides the collaborative execution of workflows by the group of I-processors and corresponding computer processors (K-processors) in the client-server medium (Sosnin, 2009).

Ensuring of the named coordination implements by means of WIQA aimed at modeling and using of QA-reasoning in conceptual decisions of tasks in the development of the SIS. The other useful interpretation of WIQA is a QA-processor, which provides the collaborative work of I-processors, and corresponding K-processors.

Combining of processors is schematically presented in Figure 2 which is inherited and adapted from Figure 1 of the ACM SIGCHI Curriculum for Human-Computer Interaction (Hewett, 2002).

In scheme the question is understood by the author as the natural phenomenon which appears (in human brains) at the definite situation when the human interacts with the own experience. In this case, the "question" is a symbolic (sign) model of the appropriate question. Used understanding helps to explain the necessity of fitting the "question" in QA-processes. Implicit questions

Figure 1. Combining of processors

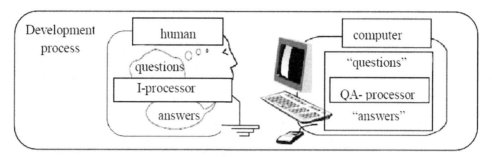

Figure 2. General structure

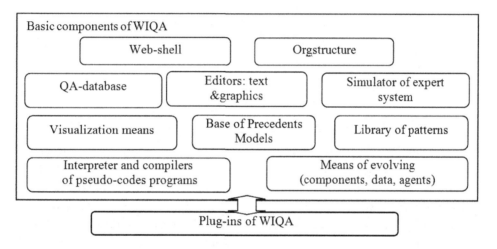

and answers exist in the reality while "questions" and "answers" present them as sign models. Let us note the task is a type of questions.

Toolkit WIQA

The system WIQA has been developed previously as the QA-processor for the conceptual designing of the SIS by the method of conceptual solving the project tasks (Sosnin, 2009). This method is based on the stepwise refining and QA-reasoning, which are being evolved in the frame of incremental designing.

Processor WIQA has been implemented in several versions. Elaborations of two last versions were based on architectural views of QA-model and the usage of the repository, MVC,

client-server, and interpreter architectural styles. Moreover in created versions have been used object-oriented, component-oriented, and service-oriented architectural paradigms.

One of the last versions named as NetWIQA has been programmed on Delphi 6.0 and the second version (named as WIQA.Net) has been created on C# at the platform of Microsoft.Net 3.5. The structure of WIQA, its functional possibilities, and positive effects are described in the publication (Sosnin, 2009). The features of WIQA are reflected by its general components structure presented in Figure 2.

The basic component of WIQA is the QA-database, which supports the real time working of designers with tasks of designing for the current project. All tasks are combined in the tasks tree

Figure 3. Accessible units of the QA-protocol

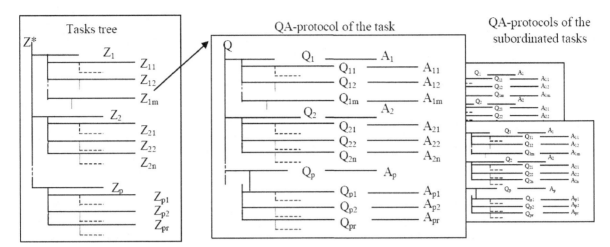

supported the visual access of designers to its units each of which is interpreted as the definite precedent used in designing or will be executed by the user of the SIS. The conceptual solution of any task Zi is being built with the help of QA-reasoning, which is being registered in the QA-protocol fulfilled the role of the QA-model of the corresponding task. Units of the QA-protocol which are accessible for designers on the monitor screen are presented in Figure 3.

In more details any unit of the Z-, Q-, or A-type is an interactive object the properties of which are being opened when any special plug-ins are used. Thus interactive tasks tree and a set of corresponding interactive QA-models of tasks present the "intermediate" between developers and the current state of the designed SIS existed in the computer environment.

This intermediate link opens opportunities for the realization of new forms HCI which are additional for forms of interactions put into the practice now. New forms are oriented to precedents and have the question-answer type. QA-means for the implementation of such forms consist of declarative and imperative parts.

The declarative part is based on data models named QA-data which present the tasks tree, QA-models, Z-, Q-, A-objects and all useful

transformations of these units supported in WIQA. QA-data is their interpretation from the informational point of view.

The specificity of QA-data is defined by typical forms of Z-, Q-, and A-objects each of which includes the numerous diversity of attributes (for example, index-name, type of object, creator, time of creation, and many others) and the hierarchical combining of such objects. The central place among attributes occupies the attribute "textual description" presenting the content of the corresponding object ("task," "question," or "answer" of the definite type).

The imperative part consists of a set of commands (QA-commands) with QA-data, their useful sequences and more complicated behavioral units from QA-commands which are specified as a kind of QA-programs. For this reason, WIQA is constructed as the specialized QA-processor. This processor supports the work of I-processor with one side of the QA-intermediate and provides the work of K-processor on the other intermediate side. The kernel of the last version of WIQA is programmed in C# and its potential is oriented on the work with precedents by the use of specialized framework.

Typical Model of Precedent

First of all the framework for precedent model was defined as the composition of the specialized models presented in Figure 6.

Additionally to models P^T and P^L described above the developer can build for any precedent its question-answer model P^{QA}, the diagrammatic model P^G, the QA-program as the source text of pseudo-code P^{SC} and the executable code P^E. These models reflect the state of the precedent in its life cycle.

So the content of any precedent model combines a number of its normative models of such types as P^T, P^L, P^{QA}, P^G, P^{SC} and P^E each of which can be understood as the specialized view to the corresponding precedent. Such combination is registered as a whole in the precedents base of WIQA. Any precedent view is accessible for any designer in any time of the precedent reuse.

HUMAN-COMPUTER INTERACTION IN FORMS OF QA-MODELING

Question-answer models, as well as any other models, are created "for extraction of answers to the questions enclosed in the model." Moreover, the model is a very important form of the representation of questions, answers on which are generated during interaction with the model. Let us remind that in WIQA we understand questions as a natural-artificial phenomenon, which initiate, orientate, and control the definite speech activity of developers and users of the created SIS. The attribute "natural" indicates that the cause of the speech activity is the development of the SIS. The attribute "artificial" reflects that any "question" is being expressed in the language of the SIS project.

The essence of QA-modeling is interactions of designers with artifacts included to the QA-model in their current state. For such interaction, the developer can use the special set of QA-commands, their sequences and a set of WIQA plug-ins.

The main subset of positive effects of QA-modeling includes:

- Controlling and testing the reasoning of the developer with the help of "integrated reasoning" and "integrated understanding" included into the QA-models;
- Correcting the understanding of designer with the help of comparing it with "integrated understanding";
- Combining the models of the collective experience with individual experience for increasing the intellectual potential of the designer on the definite working place;
- Including the individual experience of the developer in accordance with the request on the other working places in the corporate network.

Any developer can get any programmed positive effect with the help of QA-modeling as "answer" on question actually or potentially included in the QA-model (Figure 4).

As shown, in this scheme any component of the QA-model is the source of answers accessible for the developer as results of interactions with the QA-model. At the same time, the potential of the QA-model is not limited by the questions planned at defining and creating the QA-model. Another source of useful effects of QA-modeling is an additional combinatorial "visual pressure" of questions and answers, which is caused by influence on brain processes in their contacts with components of the QA-model. There is no difference based on who has created the QA-model.

There are different forms for building answers with the help of QA-modeling, not only linguistic forms. In any case, the specificity of QA-modeling is defined by the inclusion of additional interacting with "question-answer objects" into dynamics of the integrated consciousness and understanding (into natural intellectual activity of designers).

Figure 4. QA-model of task

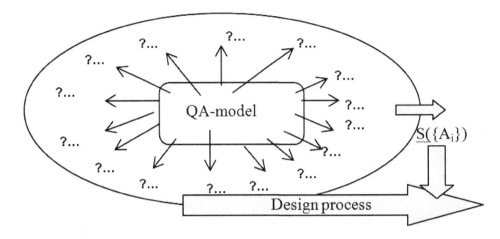

HUMAN-COMPUTER INTERACTION IN FORMS OF QA-PROGRAMMING

Means for Writing the Pseudo-Code Texts

Most essential feature of the QA-approach is the possibility of programming (preliminary or in the real time) of human-computer interactions because in accordance with definition of HCI "includes the user interface and the underlying processes which produce the interactions" (Human, 2011). Moreover, this approach assumes that necessary means of HCI are being embedded to the definite model of the precedent. For supporting such possibility, the means of QA-modeling have been evolved till their usage for pseudo-programming oriented on precedents and the execution of pseudo-programs by I-processors and K-processors collaboratively. Below we shall describe specificities of accessible (for developers) means of pseudo-programming, which was named by the author as QA-programming.

The first step of such evolving of WIQA was connected with the choice of the pseudo-code language (LP) and the "material" on which the QA-program should be written. The built and used language LP as other languages of such type is similar to the natural language in its algorithmic usage. The natural language includes universal means for the creation of QA-programs executed by I-processors. Most part of existed means of pseudo-programming is not fitted for K-processors. The language LP helps to build QA-programs, which are being executed by the I-processor and K-processor collaboratively or separately.

Any QA-program is being written on the "material" for registering of QA-reasoning. There are two additional ways for the adaptation of QA-reasoning to programming. The first way is to provide the expression of the basic constructions of programming with the help of elements of QA-reasoning. The second way is to fill such constructions by the adequate content extracted from QA-reasoning. However, both ways of the adaptation are bound with the presentation of QA-reasoning from the data point of view.

The language LP as any language for writing the programs includes means for data declarations and means for coding the programs operators. In WIQA, any line of any QA-program is being written on the "surface" of the corresponding QA-object. In this case, the used QA-object can be interpreted as a "material for writing" which has useful properties.

This "material" consists of visualized forms for writing the symbols string originally intended for registering the texts in fields "textual description" of corresponding Z-, Q- and A-objects. The initial applicability and features of such type of strings are being inherited by data and operators of QA-programs. It is possible to assume that data and operator are written on "punch-cards" the features of which (attributes of corresponding QA-objects) can be accessible for their processing together with textual descriptions if it will be necessary.

Interpretation of the QA-Data

The next step of the evolving was connected with broadening the interpretation of QA-data. Originally, the QA-data had been suggested and developed for the real-time work with such interactive objects as "tasks," "questions," and "answers" which were kept in the QA-database and used by designers in the corporate network. It is necessary to remind that "task" is a type of a question and "decision of the task" is an answer to such question.

On the logical level, the QA-data can be interpreted as the specialized hierarchical model of data emulated by means of the relational model of data. Two hierarchical trees of data the units of which are connected as questions and answers is one of specificities of QA-data. The general version of QA-data includes the dynamic tasks tree the units of which are united with a system of QA-models for corresponding tasks.

Let us remind that any unit of such model is the interactive object the unique name and symbolic expression of which are visually accessible to designers in the tasks tree or in the corresponding QA-protocol. Other characteristics (for example such basic attributes as name of creator, time attributes, indicator of changes, attribute of inheritances) are being discovered and used in different planned actions with the data unit.

One direction of broadening the interpretation of QA-data is defining the abstract type of data

with named attributes and features including the accessible set of commands. Such interpretation allow to developers to use the abstract QA-type for the emulation of the types of data, which are needed for pseudo-programming.

The emulation is based on the use of Q-objects and corresponding A-objects for the following the presentation of any normative types:

- "question" → " name of the variable for the simple type of data" and "answer" → "its value";
- "definite composition of questions" → " typical data" (for example array, record, set, array of records or table, stack, queue, and others types of composite data) and "corresponding composition of answers" → "its value."

There are sufficient reasons for the interpretation of variable (names of variables) as questions and their values as corresponding answers. So the QA-data can be used for emulating the data of many known types. For solving the emulation tasks in WIQA there is a special mechanism for assigning the necessary characteristics to the definite unit of QA-data. It is the mechanism of Additional Attributes (AA) which gives the possibility to expand the set of basic attributes for any Z-, Q-, or A-object keeping in the QA-database.

The mechanism of AA implements the function of the object-relational mapping of QA-data to programs objects with planned characteristics. One version of such objects is classes in C#. The other version is fitted for pseudo-code programming. The scheme which is used in WIQA for the object-relational mapping is presented in Figure 5.

The usage of the AA is supported by the specialized plug-ins embedded in WIQA. This plug-ins helps the designer to declare the necessary attribute or a group of attributes for definite QA-units. At any time, the designer can view declared attributes for the chosen unit. Other actions with

Figure 5. Object-relational mapping

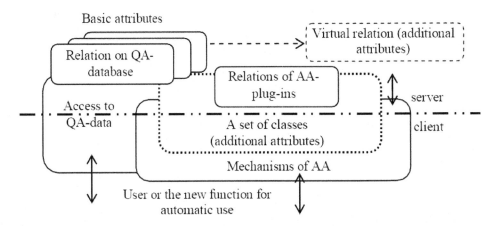

Figure 6. Keeping the array with elements of integer type

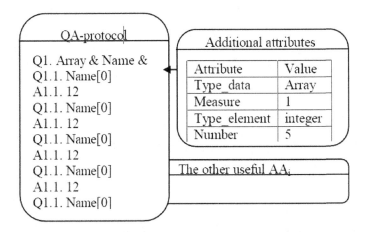

the AA must be programmed in C# or in the pseudo-code language supported by WIQA.

Broadening of the abstract type of QA-data by means of additional attributes helps to emulate any traditional data types such as scalars, arrays, records lists and the others. Moreover, means of additional attributes open the possibilities for assigning to simulated data their semantic features. An example of keeping the array with elements of integer type is presented in Figure 6 where a set of additional attributes are used for translating the array declaration to computer codes.

Attributes, which are assigned for the array, are visually accessible for the designer at any time and can be used not only for translating. The designer

can add useful attributes to the set of array attributes for example for describing its semantic features, which will be checked in creating and executing the QA-program. Any designer can create any necessary type of data as for C#-programming so for pseudo-code programming.

Emulation of Pseudo-Code Operators

The second type of pseudo-code strings is intended for writing the commands (operators). As it was for QA-data we can define for operators the next interpretations:

- "question" is " a symbolic presentation of an operator";
- "answer" indicates by the special marker about "the fact that the operator was fulfilled."

In other words, the symbol string of the "question" can be used for writing (in this place) the operator in the pseudo-code form. The fact or the result of the operator execution will be marked or registered in the symbol string of the corresponding "answer."

The next step in the emulation of operators is connected with taking into account types of operators. For simulating the basic pseudo-program operators the next constructions were chosen:

- **Appoint**: "question" → "name of variable" and "answer" → "appoint the value";
- **Goto:** "question" → "condition" and "answer" → "go to the definite operator of the QA-program";
- **If:** "question" → "condition" **Then** "answer" → **"Execute** the definite operator";
- **Command**: "question" → " the command of the QA-processor" and "answer" → "execute the command";
- **Function**: "question" → "definition of function" and "answer" → "compute the value";
- **Procedure**: "question" → "definition of procedure" and "answer" → "execute the procedure."
- **End**: "question" → "end of program" and "answer" → "finish the work with the QA-program."

In named operators, the following definitions of functions and procedures are used:

- Any function is defined as the expression of the P-language;
- Any procedure is a typical sequence of actions which are accessible in the QA-

processor for the execution by the designer playing the role of I-processor.

As for QA-data there are sufficient reasons for the interpretation of the operator (or function or procedure) description as "question" as its execution (or result of the execution) as "answer."

The set of basic operators includes traditional pseudo-code operators but each of which inherits the feature of the appropriate QA-units also. Hence, the basic attributes of the QA-unit and necessary additional attributes can be taken into account in processing the operator and not only in its translation. In order to underline the specificity of the operator emulation they will be indicated as QA-operators.

In pseudo-programming languages, a set of basic operator is being expanded usually. In described case the expansion includes cycle-operators such as "**for**," "**while-do**," and "**do-until**." Emulations of QA-data and QA-operators are implemented in WIQA and provide the creation of pseudo-code programs for different tasks (Sosnin, 2011).

Specimens of QA-Programs

First, it is necessary to underline the main difference of QA-programs for I-processor from traditional programs for K-processors and from programs for the EPIC-system the typical commands of which have been presented above. This difference can be shown on the example of the following QA-program providing the reset of Outlook Express in Box 1.

In this example, the strings of the "A"-type are excluded (for shortening the text). Moreover, the index name of any operator indicates the subtype of questions marked by the symbol "O" (operator). The answer for such type will be marked by the symbol "E" (executed). For the QA-data the symbols "N" and "V" will be indicated the name of variables and their values.

The example demonstrates that the work should be fulfilled by the human who uses com-

Box 1.

```
O1. Quit all programs.
O2. Start On the menu Run, click.
O3. Open In the box regedit, type, and then OK the click.
O4. Move to and select the following key:
HKEY_CURRENT_USER/Software/Microsoft/Office/9.0/Outlook
O5. In the Name list, FirstRunDialog select.
O6. If you want to enable only the Welcome to Microsoft Outlook greeting, on
the Edit menu Modify, click the type True in the Value Data box, and then OK
the click.
O7. If you also want to re-create all sample welcome items, move to and select
the following key:
HKEY_CURRENT_USER/Software/Microsoft/Office/9.0/Outlook/Setup
O8. In the Name list, select and delete the following keys: CreateWelcome
First-Run
O9. In the Confirm Value Delete dialog box click Yes, for each entry.
O.10. On the Registry menu, click Exit.
O11. End.
```

puter assistants. The human must understand the content of each operator and to implement actions embedded to it.

In principle, this program of actions can be written with using of the EPIC-commands, but all names of the chosen items and semantics of actions will be lost. There is a possibility to exclude the human from the execution of program if human actions will be simulated by program codes for the computer but it is not so simply and such version of program will be estimated as a very strange.

The other important difference is the orientation of QA-programs to the creation and use of precedents models. Such orientation suggests the programming of the condition part and reaction part of any precedent separately. The condition part should help to solve the task of the precedent choice from the base of precedents. Such work has a service type and it depends on the state of the base, which changes during the development of the SIS. Therefore, the program of any precedent choice should be easily changeable by the designer who is not the professional programmer usually. QA-programming helps to solve this problem.

The typical scheme of QA-programs for the conditioned parts has the following view:

```
QA-PROGRAM_1 (condition for the ac-
cess to the precedent):
N1. Variable V_1 / Comment_1?
V1. Value of V_1.
N2. Variable V_2 / Comment_2?
V2. Value of V_2.
....................................................
NM. Variable V_M / Comment_M?
VM. Value of V_M.
N0. F = Logical expression (V_1, V_2,
..., V_M)?
V0. Value of Expression.
End.
```

It is necessary to notice that the designer can build or to modify or to fulfill (step by step) the definite example of this program in the real time work with the corresponding precedent which, it may be, the designer creates. In presented typical scheme the logical expression of the choice is programmed as the program function (QA-function).

The reaction part of the precedent has very often the technique type the possibility of QA-programming of which was demonstrated above. If it is not so the designer can create the reaction part in the prototype form as the QA-program. The next typical scheme reflects the work with techniques programmed as QA-procedures:

```
QA-PROGRAM_2 (technique for the typi-
cal task):
O1.K_i, K_j, …, PL_k ?
E1. *
O2.  K_m, QA-P_n,  …, K_q?
E2.*
……………………………
ON. K_s, Pl_t,  …, QA-P_v?
EN. #
End.
```

The program text includes the symbolic names K_x and Pl-y for the Command and Plug-ins of WIQA and QA-P_z for the QA-Program written by means of WIQA. It is necessary to notice that all names of the types K_x, Pl-y, and QA-P_z are indicated positions on the monitor screen for initiating the actions by touch of the designer. In such "points" of human-computer interactions the suggested means of HCI are being combined with traditional means of HCI. In the second typical scheme the symbols "*" and "#" (as "yes" and "no") indicate the facts of the execution for operators. Let us note that in the typical case any string includes only one operator.

Creating and Processing of QA-Programs

Means for QA-programming have been developed and embedded to WIQA as its evolution. The creation and use of QA-programs are being fulfilled in the operational medium presented in Figure 7.

Creating of the definite QA-program is beginning from the choice of the point in the tasks tree and the declaration of the new task for this pro-gram. The index name of the new task (1) will be used as the initial address for computing the index names for any line of the source code of the QA-program which is written in the area (2) of the text editor. The indexed copy of the source code is registered in the editor memory and is being visualized in the area (3). After saving the current state of the source code its indexed copy transfers (4) to the QA-database (5). In any time any QA-program from the database can be loaded to the editor.

Any QA-program in any state can be loaded (6) to the interpreter for the execution. Any executed operator of the QA-program is visualized in the special area (7) of the interpreter, and at any time, the designer can declare the new synonym for the chosen keyword (8).

The reality of the designer activity is a parallel work with many tasks at the same time. Therefore, the special system of interruptions is included into WIQA. It gives the possibility to interrupt any executed task or the QA-program (if it is necessary) for working with other tasks or QA-programs. The interruption system supports the return to any interrupted task or the QA-program to its point of the interruption.

Uniting of QA-Programs in a Single Whole

In general, the precedent can be combined from sub-precedents or its reaction part can be combined from several QA-programs. For such cases, the designers should have the necessary means for the uniting of QA-programs in a single whole. The toolkit WIQA suggests two ways for such work:

- One way is a creation of the "block and line" schemes (in the special graphic editor embedded to WIQA) the names of the blocks of which help to transfer between schemes or to call the QA-programs;

Figure 7. Operational medium

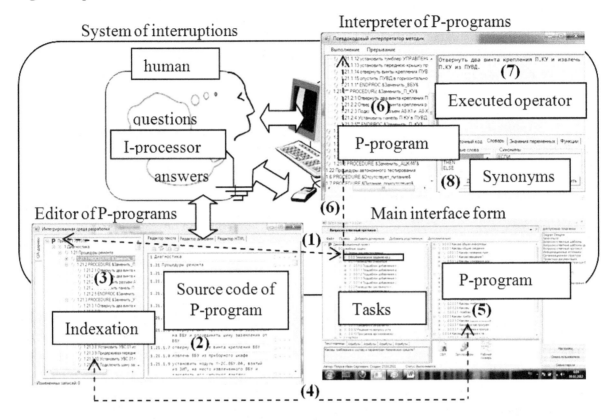

- The second way is a creation of QA-programs for interfaces which unite the necessary components.

Both ways can be used for the creation of prototypes of project decisions. Moreover, similar prototypes can be interpreted as precedents in their prototype forms. Built prototypes as simulation models open the possibility for the experimental testing of the project decisions in the conceptual designing. The second way is a more feasible in the prototyping. Moreover, this way prompts to transform the QA-programs of the interfaces to the executed codes of the designed SIS. The possibility of the transformation is being determined by the limited number of typical interface schemes.

For supporting the described possibility, the specialized means have been developed for providing the second way of the prototyping. In their realization the model-driven approach (Nguyen,

2011) has been applied. The first step of the prototyping begins from the creation of the "block and line" scheme named the "interface diagram." The interface diagrams are similar to the Use-Case diagrams of the Unified Modeling Language (UML) but their semantics is richer because this type of diagrams represents information as for interfaces so for their activity context.

The following steps are aimed at the translation of the previous model of the prototype description to the next model, which is richer. So step by step, the executed code of the prototype will be formed. The sequence of the model-driven reformation is presented in Figure 8.

The abstract model of the user interface is a result of the reformation of the initial QA-text which is aimed at the more detailed specification of tasks, actions and elements of actions. Additional units of information ($\Delta 1$) are being included to the

Figure 8. Model-driven transformation in the interface prototyping

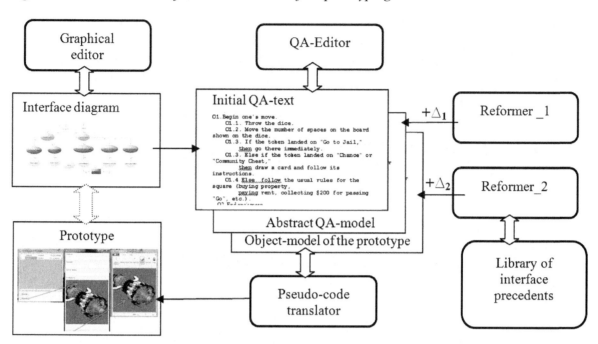

QA-text by the designer who should know about the created prototype what is necessary.

The object model of the created prototype is necessary for the definition of visualized interface forms - controls, elements of management, with their behavior, references to external modules and the other typical forms of interfaces. During this step of the reformation, the reformer_2 provides the choice of the necessary interface precedents from the special library (section in the base of precedents) and included them (Δ2) to the object model. The step includes two sub-steps on the first of which the QA-description of the object model is being saved. The second sub-step provides the translation of this description to the XML-code with using the object relational mapping. After that, the XML-code of the built QA-program is being translated to the executed code of the developed prototype (opening the possibility for experimenting).

Aspect-Oriented Designing of Interface Prototypes

The presented means of HCI open the effective possibilities for aspect-oriented designing the traditional versions of HCI. For all usability metrics, which are defined in the standard ISO/MEK–9126, corresponding precedents were created. All of them are united in the library of the typical tasks. Any task of this library is programmed with the usage of QA-means so that the corresponding usability metrics is accessible to designers as the definite interface precedent. The created library consists of 73 typical tasks any of which can be used for generating the necessary quantity of copies adjusted to the places of their materializations in the implemented system.

When in current solving of the project task, the designer discovers the next "point of human-computer interaction" then the appropriate metrics task is being included to the tasks tree of the designed SIS. Such task has two subtasks one of which is a pseudo-program of the precedent condition. The second subtask is a pseudo-code technique providing the inclusion of the chosen metrics into the solution of the project task. In order to simplify the use of the aspect-oriented technique the special plug-ins for the interface prototyping which was described above.

FUTURE RESEARCH DIRECTIONS

Nowadays, the main attention in evolving of the suggested means is focused on the agents-oriented solutions. A number of such solutions are found, tested, and embedded to WIQA in the form of program agents. Nearest plans are include investigations aimed at the use of intellectual agents in modeling of precedents.

CONCLUSION

Told above contains sufficient arguments to assert that the real time pseudo-programming of HCI by the user leads to many positive effects in the usage of SISs and their development. QA-programming is the rational way for such work, which can be implemented with the help of WIQA means. QA-programming of HCI can be implemented at the project level (as the creation of the tasks tree) and at the pseudo-code level (as writing QA-programs for I-processors and computer processors).

QA-programs are useful means of HCI, which are additional for traditional means of HCI. Such means of HCI are adjusted for the access to the human experience in the precedents forms, which were used in creating the library of the usability metrics implemented as the set of tasks with embedded interfaces precedents.

QA-programs are the kind of pseudo-programs. Any line of the source code of such pseudo-program inherits the property of the appropriate QA-unit, which is used as the "material" for writing this string. At any time, the programmer can expand the set of attributes for any line of

the definite QA-program if it helps to solve the corresponding task. The programmer has the possibility to use the line attributes of the source code in the operators of the created pseudo-program.

QA-programs also manage accustomed (habitual) semi-automatic actions when QA-programs show to the designer the sequence of actions which designer must execute by "touching" with the help of the marker the special signs or definite area on the monitor screen. Moreover, QA-programs can be translated to the form, which can be executed by the computer processors.

REFERENCES

Card, S. K., Thomas, T. P., & Newell, A. (1983). *The psychology of human-computer interaction*. London, UK: Lawrence Erlbaum Associates.

Crystal, A., & Ellington, B. (2004). Task analysis and human-computer interaction: approaches, techniques, and levels of analysis. In *Proceedings of the Tenth Americas Conference on Information Systems*, (pp. 1-9). New York, NY: Americas Conference.

Go, K., & Carroll, J. M. (2003). The blind men and the elephant: Views of scenario-based system design. *Interaction, 11*(6), 44–53. doi:10.1145/1029036.1029037

Hewett, T., Baecker, R., Card, S., Carey, T., Gasen, J., & Mantei, M. (2002). *ACM SIGCHI curricula for human-computer interaction. ACM Technical Report. New York, NY*. Verplank, W.: ACM Press.

Interaction, H.-C. (2011). *Definition*. Retrieved from http://encyclopedia2.thefreedictionary.com/human-computer+interaction.

Kieras, D., & Meyer, D. E. (1997). An overview of the EPIC architecture for cognition and performance with application to human-computer interaction. *Human-Computer Interaction, 12*, 391–438. doi:10.1207/s15327051hci1204_4

Kroll, P., & Kruchten, P. (2003). *The rational unified process made easy: A practitioners guide to the RUP*. Boston, MA: Addison-Wesley.

Microsoft. (2011). *User experience interaction guidelines*. Retrieved from http://msdn.microsoft.com/en-us/library/ aa511258.aspx.

Muller, M. J. (2011). Catalogue of scenario-based methods and methodologies: Technical Report #99-06. *IBM Watson Research Center*. Retrieved from http://domino.watson.ibm.com/cambridge/research.nsf.

Nguyen, P., & Chun, R. (2011). *Model driven development with interactive use cases and UML models*. Retrieved from http://www.pnguyen.tigris.org/SER4505.pdf.

Precedent. (2011). *Definition*. Retrieved from http://dictionary. reference.com/ browse/precedent.

Software Intensive Systems in the Future. (2006). *Final report//ITEA 2 symposium*. Retrieved from http://symposium.itea2.org/ symposium2006/main/publications/ TNO_IDATE_study_ ITEA_ SIS_ in_the_future_Final_Report.pdf.

Sosnin, P. (2009). Means of question-answer interaction for collaborative development activity. *Advances in Human-Computer Interaction*. Retrieved from http://www.hindawi.com/journals/ahci/2009/619405/.

Sosnin, P. (2011). Question-answer shell for personal expert systems. In *Expert Systems for Human, Materials and Automation* (pp. 51–74). New York, NY: InTech.

ADDITIONAL READING

Anggreeni, I., & Van der Voort, M. (2007). *Tracing the scenarios in scenario-based product design: A study to support scenario generation*. Internal Report. Retrieved from http://doc.utwente.nl/64410/.

Bass, L. (2003). *Software architecture in practice*. Boston, MA: Addison Wesley.

Bass, L., Ivers, J., Klein, M., & Merson, P. (2005). *Reasoning frameworks, software engineering institute. Technical Report*. Pittsburgh, PA: Carnegie Mellon University.

Booch, G., & Brown, A. W. (2003). Collaborative development environments. In Zelkowitz, M. (Ed.), *Advances in Computers* (p. 59). San Diego, CA: Academic Press.

Burger, J. (2001). *Issues, tasks and program structures to roadmap research in question & answering (Q&A). Technical Report*. Washington, DC: NIST.

Carroll, J. M. (2000). *Making use: Scenario-based design of human-computer interactions*. Cambridge, MA: MIT Press.

Charette, R. N. (2005). Why software falls. *IEEE Spectrum, 4*(9), 36–43.

Clements, P., Kazman, R., & Klein, M. (2002). *Evaluating software architecture*. Boston, MA: Addison-Wesley.

Clements, P., & Northrop, L. (2002). *Software product lines: Practice and patterns*. Boston, MA: Addison-Wesley.

Dijkstra, E. (1979). *Programming considered as a human activity*. New York, NY: ACM Press.

Guarino, N., Oberle, D., & Staab, S. (2009). What is an ontology? In Staab, S., & Studer, R. (Eds.), *Handbook on Ontologies* (2nd ed., pp. 1–17). Berlin, Germany: Springer. doi:10.1007/978-3-540-92673-3_0

Hirschman, L., & Gaizauskas, R. (2001). Natural language question answering: The view from here. *Natural Language Engineering, 7*, 67–87. doi:10.1017/S1351324901002807

Karray, F., Alemzadeh, M., Saleh, J. A., & Arab, M. N. (2008). Human-computer interaction: Overview on state of the art. *Smart Sensing and Intelligent Systems, 1*(1), 138–159.

Knuth, D. (2011). Computer programming as an art. *Communications of the ACM, 17*(12), 667–673. doi:10.1145/361604.361612

Kroll, P., & Kruchten, P. (2003). *The rational unified process made easy: A practitioners guide to the RUP*. Boston, MA: Addison-Wesley.

Kruchten, P., Obbink, H., & Stafford, J. (2006). The past, present, and future for software architecture. *IEEE Software, 23*(2), 22–30. doi:10.1109/MS.2006.59

Leffingwell, D., & Widrig, D. (1999). *Management software requirements: A unified approach*. Boston, MA: Addison-Wesley.

Pew, R. W. (2007). Some history of human performance models. In Gray, W. (Ed.), *Integrated Models of Cognitive Systems* (pp. 20–47). Cambridge, UK: Cambridge University Press.

Shaw, M., & Clements, P. (2006). *The golden age of software architecture: A comprehensive survey*. Technical Report CMU-ISRI-06-101. Pittsburgh, PA: Carnegie Mellon University.

Sosnin, P. (2008). Conceptual solution of the tasks in designing the software intensive systems. In *Proceedings of the 14th IEEE Mediterranean Electrotechnical Conference - MELECON 2008*, (pp. 293-298). Ajacco, France: IEEE Press.

Sosnin, P. (2010). Question-answer programming in collaborative development environment. In *Proceedings of CIS-RAM, 2010*, 273–278.

Sosnin, P. (2010). Creation and usage of project ontology in development of software intensive systems. *Polibits, 42*, 51–58.

KEY TERMS AND DEFINITIONS

Intellectual Processor: Human who fulfils the pseudo-code programs by the way which is similar to the execution of computer programs with the help of the interpreter program. (definition of the author)

Human-Computer Interaction: An interdisciplinary field focused on the interactions between human users and computer systems, including the user interface and the underlying processes which produce the interactions. http://encyclopedia2.thefreedictionary.com/human-computer+interaction

Precedent: Precedents are actions or decisions that have already happened in the past and which can be referred to and justified as an example that can be followed when the similar situation arises. Available from http://dictionary.reference.com/browse/precedent.

Pseudo-code: Pseudo-code is a compact and informal high-level description of a computer programming algorithm that uses the structural conventions of a programming language, but is intended for human reading rather than machine reading. Available from http://en.wikipedia.org/wiki/

Question-Answering: Question-Answering (QA) is a type of "an information retrieval in which a direct answer is expected in response to a submitted query, rather than a set of references that may contain the answers. Available from http://www.wordiq.com/definition/Question_answering.

Scenario: "A scenario is a description that contains actors, background information about them, and assumptions about their environment, their goals, or objectives, and sequences of actions and events. It may include obstacles, contingencies, and outcomes." (Go, 2003)

Software Intensive Systems: Systems in which "software represents a significant segment in the following points: system functionality, system cost, system development risk, development time"(Software, 2006)

Chapter 11
Intelligent Agents with Personality:
From Adjectives to Behavioral Schemes

François Bouchet
McGill University, Canada

Jean-Paul Sansonnet
LIMSI-CNRS, France

ABSTRACT

Conversational agents are a promising interface between humans and computers, but to be acceptable as the virtual humans they pretend to be, they need to be given one of the key elements used to define human beings: a personality. As existing personality taxonomies have been defined only for description, the authors present in this chapter a methodology dedicated to the definition of a computationally-oriented taxonomy, in order to use it to implement personality traits in conversational agents. First, a significant set of personality-traits adjectives is registered from thesaurus sources. Then, the lexical semantics related to personality-traits is extracted while using the WordNet database, and it is given a formal representation in terms of so-called Behavioral Schemes. Finally, the authors propose a framework for the implementation of those schemes as influence operators controlling the decision process and the plan/action scheduling of a rational agent.

DOI: 10.4018/978-1-4666-1628-8.ch011

INTRODUCTION

Context: Intelligent Agents for Assisting Human Users

Intelligent agents are autonomous software entities, which perceive their environment and acts on it to accomplish their goals. Among elements of the environment of such agents are human beings. Some categories of agents have been more and more in interaction with human users, sometimes becoming themselves the interface between the users and the system they want to use. Those are called the *conversational agents* (Maes, 1994; Cassell, Bickmore, Billinghurst, Campbell, Chang, Villiamsson, & Yan, 1999), and as many tend to be there to provide them with some kind of *assistance*, we'll therefore focus here on this subcategory of agents that are the *intelligent assistant agents* (further referred to simply as *agents*). In that kind of situation, three entities are in bilateral interaction (a human user U, an intelligent assistant agent A, and a computer system S), where the user performs some activity on/with the system, and, at times, they can solicit the agent for general advice or for direct help upon the system or the task at hand, in which case the agent might have to interact with the system directly, on behalf of the user. In such a situation (further called a UAS situation), one can see that agents need to be both able to interact with:

- A symbolic model of the application and a rational reasoning capacity about that model. In the following, we will refer to this part of an agent as the *"rational agent."* Actually, intelligent assistant agents should be able to interact with a system in the same way as autonomous agents achieve practical reasoning, in order to perform tasks in a given environment.
- The user, which requires: a) a conversational interface, which is often multimodal; b) processing, in a rational way, the input

of user's requests in order to produce as output factual replies c) expressing the answers in a way that would look and sound similar to how a human being assisting the user in the same task would.

Personality Traits for Agents: Why and How?

That last point requires taking into account what we know of the cognitive processes of human beings, in order to mimic it in a software agent. It means that it is not enough for an agent to be *technically competent* thanks to their symbolic reasoning capacities: they also need to be *psychologically relevant,* to be acceptable (in the sense of Davis, 1989), especially when they deal with people of the general public. One of the key points to ensure the consistency of an agent in the way it will provide information to the users is for it to be given what makes a human being follow the same usual patterns of behavior and emotions: *personality traits.* Having agents with personality traits is also particularly interesting in order to try to provide different kind of assistance strategies, which could be adapted to the personalities of the human users.

Those considerations led us to propose a framework dedicated to the study of the nature of the relationships between the rational and the psychological reasoning capacities: the Rational and Behavioral architecture (R&B), where "behavioral" has the particular meaning of "psychological behavior," and which can be found at http://www.limsi.fr/~jps/research/rnb/rnb.htm. R&B is a generic framework enabling the computational definition and the experimentation of various rational/psychological strategies. In recent work based on R&B (Sansonnet & Bouchet, 2010), we have proposed a model where psychological phenomena, such as personality traits, are implemented in terms of influence operators altering the rational process of an agent. Presently, the proposed model has been implemented only with few arbitrary-chosen psychological phenomena (e.g. a *lazy/gloomy/cheerful...* agent) (Bouchet & Sansonnet, 2009). This approach illustrates the principle and the feasibility of a framework like R&B, but it fails to cover significantly the main domain of the description of the psychology of a person, especially in terms of personality traits. Therefore, there is a real need for a more systematic and computationally tractable definition of the domain, covering most psychological phenomena. To do that, computer scientists can start from the literature on psychology, which provides various taxonomies of personality traits. Unfortunately, those are rarely fine-grained enough (despite the existence for some of them of second level elements called facets, like Costa and McCrae [1992]) and they are too generic to allow a straightforward computational implementation.

Concretely, we propose in this chapter to follow a methodology that can be summarized in the following four key-points:

1. We suggest refining the facets in order to propose a three-level taxonomy for describing the personality of a person (and ultimately, of an agent).
2. The third level of this extended taxonomy will be composed of so-called behavioral schemes that are intended to provide implementable instantiations of the facets, especially in terms of influences upon actions and plans of the rational agent.
3. We propose to elicit those schemes from a corpus of personality adjectives, which are in turn associated with their lexical senses and glosses in the WordNet lexical database (Fellbaum, 1998). Not only linguistics resources have long been a source for building psychological, but WordNet also offers three extra advantages: it is a computerized database, it has a standard position in natural language processing, and, above all, it provides a comprehensive set

of lexical semantics senses (called *synsets*) that will provide a solid ground for defining the schemes.

4. The scheme elicitation process is conducted in two main phases:

    Phase 1: Selection of a significant subset of personality adjectives and classification into a standard, two-level taxonomy (traits-facets)

    Phase 2: For each facet, clusterization of involved lexical senses into schemes.

In order to better understand our proposition, it appears necessary to provide readers that might not be very familiar with this field some background information about agents in general, and psychology research on personality, which we will do in a first background section. In a second section, we will develop the aforementioned methodology inn four points. Finally, we will conclude and review further works that the existence of our extended taxonomy and its implementation within an agent framework make possible.

BACKGROUND

First, we will focus on the definition of rational agents and provide an overview of the existing frameworks in this domain. Then we will introduce the major works of past decade that tried to add some personality elements to the traditional rational agents, and their motivation to do so. In a third subsection, we will then focus more particularly on the class of conversational agents (differing from rational ones by the fact they are in dialogical interaction with humans), and review attempts to bring personality elements into those. Finally, in a fourth subsection, we will review research in psychology to see, independently from the agent perspective, how researchers in that field have been treating the concept of (human) personality, which methodologies were used and to what kind of taxonomies they led.

Frameworks for Rational Agents

In our context, the term *"rational agent"* will be compliant with traditional definitions issuing from Artificial Intelligence (AI) and Multi-Agents Systems (MAS). For example, Russell and Norvig (2009) state that *"a rational agent is an AI software component that does the right thing"* while achieving commonsense reasoning, using its own current knowledge upon the state of the world (pp. 38-39). Wooldridge (2000) provides a similar definition for MAS agents by stating that *"an agent is said to be rational if it chooses to perform actions that are in its own best interests, given the beliefs it has about the world"* (p. 1). According these traditional definitions, rational agents are associated with programs capable of *practical reasoning*, i.e. building plans and choosing actions to be executed in order to achieve their goals.

One of the first attempts at modeling the cognitive reasoning process of an agent is the outstanding SOAR (State, Operator, And Result) architecture (Laird, Newell, & Rosenbloom, 1987; Anderson, Matessa, & Lebiere, 1997) which uses explicit IF-THEN rules and can synthesize plans according to several strategies (problem space search, means-ends analysis, hill-climbing, etc.). Another noticeable architecture is ACT-R (Adaptive Control of Thought-Rational) (Anderson, 1996), which operates on similar principles and

focuses on the separation between declarative and procedural representations (actually, the list of existing cognitive architectures is large: CHREST, CLARION, ICARUS, DUAL, PSI…).

Following SOAR or ACT-R architectures, the BDI (Beliefs, Desires, Intentions) approach developed by Rao and Georgeff (1995) is a theory of practical reasoning (deciding what to do next cf. Bratman, Israel, & Pollack, 1988) directed towards situated reasoning about actions and plans (Allen, Kautz, Pelavin, & Tenenberg, 1991). BDI architectures recognize the primacy of *beliefs*, *desires,* and *intentions* in rational action.

It is common for BDI platforms to use practical reasoning rules (PR-rules) of the form: < Head→ Guard: Body >, where the Head is associated to a goal, the guard to a belief (often expressed as a predicate function over the world) and the body to a procedure (an instantiated plan). The process of triggering the proper rule at a given moment is called the *deliberation cycle.*

Many operational frameworks implement the BDI model such as JAM (Huber, 1999), JACK (Howden, Rönnquist, Hodgson, & Lucas, 2001), 2APL (Dastani, 2008), etc.

These architectures have been quite successful at creating both autonomous and multi-agent systems capable of operating in computational contexts, and are therefore good candidates for the support of intelligent assistant agents.

A generic version of the deliberation cycle of a BDI architecture as given by authors such as Wooldridge (2000) or Sardina (2007) is as follows in Algorithm 1.

Algorithm 1. Agent Control Loop

```
while true do
1 Observe the world;
2 Update internal world model;            // assess the current state of affairs
3 Deliberate about what intention to achieve next;        // what to do next
4 Use means-ends reasoning to get a plan for the intention;  // how to do it
5 Execute the plan;                                       // do it
end
```

Steps 3 and 4 are specific to the BDI theory:

- Given an agent A with an initial set of possibly contradictory desires g_i, during step 3, the agent chooses within its desires a subset of so-called goals g* such that: 1) A intends to achieve goals in g* and 2) goals in g* must be non-contradictory (whereas desires g_i can be contradictory).

- Traditional rational reasoning is then performed (step 4) to synthetize all the plans, and within a plan all the sub-plans that will enable the agent to reach a goal in the set g*. Indeed, although the planner proposes a single plan expression in order to achieve the current goal, this expression often contains alternatives (equivalent sub-plans or equivalent terminal actions) and options (optional sub-plans or optional terminal actions). Hence, plans are sub-determined and the agent has to make choices between alternatives and to decide whether to execute or not options. Other kinds of decisions are required in the scheduling of the plan operators. In any case, the result of the decision process is to elicit the next atomic action to be executed.

Note that practical reasoning (deciding what to do next) is often opposed to *theoretical reasoning* (deciding what is True/False), which is directed towards the logical consistency of the knowledge base of the agent and will not be addressed here. Moreover, we also discard from our definition the Decision Theory approach, where an agent is said rational if it maximizes a function of expected utility (Russell & Norvig, 2009). For that, we rely on the argument of those authors stating that contrary to practical reasoning, *decision theory* is based on total knowledge (actually, decision theory is much addressed in current multi-agent system studies in social and economics macro-models).

Adding Personality Traits to Rational Agents

Recently, authors have attempted to integrate into rational agent architectures some psychological notions, giving two main reasons to do so: first, to propose more complete cognitive models of agents; second, to propose agents capable of sustaining more human-like interactions with people, especially ordinary people involved in conversational activities with intelligent assistant agents.

While some authors have proposed a model of emotions based on traditional SOAR architecture (Gratch & Marsella, 2004), with a significant impact upon the inner SOAR architecture, most authors have preferred to propose improvements of BDI architectures because their deliberation cycle is more flexible. In this case, they exhibit both rational reasoning modules and psychological reasoning modules (Dias & Paiva, 2005; Lim, Dias, Aylett, & Paiva, 2008). In these architectures, the psychology of the agent influences both the expression of emotions through the body modalities (the agents are embodied as graphical virtual characters for example) but also has an impact on the decision making process. For example, the eBDI model implements emotions in a BDI framework (Jiang, Vidal, & Huhns, 2007). They give a good introduction about the history of the necessity to implement emotions into rational agents: "According to Weiss (1999) there are four types of traditional agent architectures: logic based agents; reactive agents; layered architectures; BDI agents," but according to Jiang *et al.*, all these approaches have drawbacks:

- In logic-based agents, decision-making is predicated on the assumption of calculative rationality: the world will not change in any significant way while the agent is deciding what to do, but most current multi-agent systems cannot guarantee a static and deterministic environment.

- Reactive agents make decisions based on local information, so they must have sufficient information available in their local environment for them to determine an acceptable action, and it is difficult to see how such decision-making could take into account non-local information.
- Layered architectures are very general. The main problem is that while they are arguably a pragmatic solution, they lack the conceptual and semantic clarity of unlayered approaches. Another issue is that of interactions among layers.
- BDI architectures are known to reflect human practical reasoning process, and they have both widely accepted philosophical and logical roots. However, Jiang et al. claim that BDI architectures currently ignore the influence of emotions in decision-making.

Gmytrasiewicz and Lisetti (2002) worked on an interesting way to define formally, within the decision theory of a rational agent, an implementation of emotions and personality (seen there as a set of emotions available for the agents), but didn't really aim at having an exhaustive list of those based on research in psychology.

Using the well-used agent creation platform JACK (Howden, Rennquist, Hodgson, & Lucas, 2001) that implements the BDI theory, CoJACK (Norling & Ritter, 2004; Evertsz, Ritter, Busetta, & Pedrotti, 2008) is an extension layer intended to simulate physiological human constraints like a) the duration taken for cognition; b) working memory limitations (e.g. "losing a belief" if the activation is low or "forgetting the next step" of a procedure); c) fuzzy retrieval of beliefs; d) limited focus of attention; or e) the use of moderators to alter cognition. One can note that the cognitive notions handled in CoJACK are not closely related with the psychology traits of a human person, but rather to generic mental capacities. Nonetheless,

CoJACK remains an outstanding attempt at introducing cognitive notions into formal frameworks for rational agents.

Adding Personality Traits to Conversational Agents

SOAR, ACT-R, and BDI frameworks have been primarily developed to support artificial intelligent agents: in a single-agent context for SOAR or ACT-R, and in single/multi-agent context for BDI. In these systems, an agent interacts with the environment or with other artificial agents but not directly with human beings. On the contrary, conversational agents are primarily designed to support extensive multimodal conversational interacting sessions with people, often persons of the general public. This is the reason why there has been a much stronger incentive for introducing psychological notions into their architecture, which is also often based on rational agent engines.

Historically, the first works in this area were performed in the context of so-called *"believable agents,"* introduced in the mid-1990s. Several research projects and groups (the Carnegie Mellon University Oz project [Bates, 1994], the Agents group MIT [Maes, 1995], the Virtual Theater project at Stanford [Hayes-Roth, Brownston, & van Gent, 1995], etc.) have focused their efforts on the creation of computerized believable agents.

Since then, there have been various attempts at implementing psychological features into conversational cognitive architectures, either in terms of personality or emotions elements (Petta, Pelachaud, & Cowie, 2011).

The works of Rousseau and Hayes-Roth (1996) stated the principle that personality traits actually express themselves as influences on actions and plans. Another major contribution is the idea that personality traits can be associated with intensity factors so that a computational planning engine can take them into account. Rizzo, Veloso, Miceli, and Cesta (1997) prove that goals and plans can be used to represent a character's personality in an efficient way, by attributing specific behaviors to the pursuit of each goal. Personality traits are used to choose between the multiple goals of a BDI agent (*i.e.* traits influence desires), and once chosen, the goals are planned and executed. Malatesta, Caridakis, Raouzaiou, and Karpouzis (2007) use traits to create different expressions of behaviors, especially by influencing the appraisal part of the OCC theory (Ortony, Clore, & Collins, 1988; Ortony, 2003). Their work focuses on how agents evaluate results of their actions and of external events, not on the way they perform a task. Nonetheless, the idea that traits can differentiate agents' behaviors underlies this work. The PMFserv framework (Silverman, Johns, Cornwell, & O'Brien, 2006) is dedicated to the creation of culturally credible agents by using Performance Moderators Functions (PMFs). The authors claim that "*its principal feature is a model of decision-making based on emotional subjective utility constrained by stress and physiology.*" This work was partly based on Gillis & Hursh's (1999) work, introducing the notion of *behavior moderators*. Like CoJACK, they focus on a differentiation based on the physical capacities of the agents, as their aim is to simulate crowd behavior in military forces.

All these authors emphasize the fact that agents should exhibit both a rational reasoning engine and a psychological reasoning engine.

Works like those of Ball and Breese (2000) were interested in the impact of personality and emotions in the choice of vocabulary done by a conversational agent. Recently, Allbeck and Kress-Gazit (2010) have proposed a framework where complex instructions can be given by the user, especially by using natural language to control an agent. In that case, the agent is a robot (it is an autonomous agent but not strictly speaking a conversational agent) acting in a complex environment. The user's instructions constrain the execution of the agent's plan. This work is focused on dynamic actions and planning for robots. The constraints applied to the actions and plans are provided by an external source (a human user), and can sometimes impact over the action and plans (e.g. prohibiting an action, changing the actions execution order, etc.).

In the same way, works of McRorie, Sneddon, Sevin, Bevacqua, and Pelachaud (2009), based on the well-used architecture of conversational agent GRETA (Pelachaud, 2000), involve models of personality for the expression of emotions (face, gesture, etc.), and as claimed by Doce, Dias, Prada, and Paiva (2010), it is necessary to create individual agents through personality traits because "*in the era of globalization, concepts such as individualization and personalization become more and more important in virtual systems.*" They personally also use the Five Factor Model (Goldberg, 1992) as a basis for creating different personalities, by using traits that can automatically influence cognitive processes such as appraisal, planning, or coping. They also consider there is a need for an emotion model that can easily represent emotions in a systematic way.

Works on Personality Traits Classification

Although presented above as separate notions, the rational and the psychological reasoning capacities of actually work in quite an intricate manner (Ellsworth & Scherer, 2003; Frijda, 2006). Moreover, many studies mentioned above focus on low-level/transitory psychological notions such as emotions and moods, but other notions like personality traits (John, Robins, & Pervin, 2008) that are associated with high-level/long-lasting features of the personality of a human being should be integrated and could be promising for developing agents with consistent characters.

Authors in philosophy and in psychology have attempted to define the notion of personality, such as:

- An individual's characteristic pattern of thinking/feeling/acting;
- A person's general style of interacting with the world;
- Differences between people which are relatively consistent over time and place

According to Neill (2008), there have been four main historical periods, corresponding to four main paradigms: Psychoanalysis (1900's—); Behaviorism and Classifications (1950's—); Humanistic (1960's—); Social-Cognitive Transpersonal (1980's—):

1. *Psychoanalytic* by Freud is a psychodynamic perspective (there is a strong notion of personality development) which emphasizes on unconscious motivation. It is intended for therapy but it is also a theory of personality involving three main concepts: a) the *id* is mainly biological and deals with aggression and pleasure. It is unconstrained by logic or reality and does not distinguish between reality and fantasy; b) the *ego* is about rationality; and c) the *superego* is dealing with societal and moral values. It strives for the ideal and is responsible for guilt.

2. *Behaviorism and Classifications* is mainly based on personality traits. A trait is traditionally defined as: a characteristic pattern of behavior or a disposition to feel and act. In this domain, two main approaches are prevailing: a) *type-based classifications* label each person as a single type/class; b) *traits-based classifications* identify the degree to which several different personality factors occurring within an individual (notion of independent dimensions). Nowadays, the four main Personality Inventories are: EPQ (Eysenk & Eysenk, 1975); 16PF (Cattell, Eber, & Tatsuoka, 1970); MMPI (Graham, 2006), and FFM (Goldberg, 1990).

3. *Humanistic* by Maslow (1968), along with Rogers, which were discontent both with Freud's negativity and the mechanistic psychology of the behaviorists and trait-based classifications. Their approach a) emphasizes on healthy individuals and defense maneuvers (like coping) and b) defines the well-known *scale of needs*: Physiological/Safety/Belonging/Esteem/Self-actualization.

4. *Social-Cognitive* by Bandura (1986) combines social learning and cognition. They claim that human behaviors emerge from the interplay between a person and her/his environment (according to a principle of reciprocal determinism). This is an optimistic view that allows growth and change based on person centered therapy.

In the following, we will rely upon the approach based on behaviorism and classifications, because it is the most comprehensive and tractable from the computational point of view. Moreover, we will focus on trait-based classifications because there is a large consensus about their usefulness at least from the standardization point of view. When one is interested in the taxonomy of the psychological phenomena, particularly those related to personality traits, the two most successful paradigms are:

- *The Two Dimensional Model of Eysenck* (EPQ), which is mainly based on personality questionnaires, which are questionnaires (generally with yes/no questions) to assess the personality traits of a person (Eysenk & Eysenk, 1975; Eysenck, Eysenck, & Barret, 1985);
- *The Five Factor Model* (FFM), which is mainly based on lexical data. It is a convergent research from many authors in psychology, from Norman (1963) to Goldberg (1990), etc.

Following early work of Cattell's personality trait classification into 16 factors (Cattell, Eber,

& Tasuoka, 1970), which was still prominent in the 1980s, Eysenck developed in 1976 a model based on a biological approach, mainly stating that personality traits are heritable and have a foundation in the nervous system (Eysenck, 1976). In this view, they are supposed to be very stable parameters of human psychology. The three basic traits found by Eysenck were: Psychotism, Extraversion, Neuroticism (PEN), with a high and a low pole. Later, Eysenck focused on a representation of personality traits based on two axes only: Neuroticism (also denoted *emotional stability*) and Extraversion which entails four cases: phlegmatic, melancholic, choleric, and sanguine, encompassing 32 basic facets. Eysenck then proposed a set of criteria as an attempt to merge the three major systems, namely Cattell's 16 PF, Norman's Five Factor Model, and Eysenck's PEN system (Eysenck & Eysenck, 1975).

The FFM approach to the taxonomy of traits is based on natural language and more precisely lexical resources (Baumgarten, 1933), such as the glosses found in dictionaries. The *lexical hypothesis* states that most of socially relevant and salient personality characteristics have become encoded in the natural language (Allport, 1937). The lexical approach has been promoted by Goldberg who claimed that "*personality vocabulary provides an extensive, yet finite, set of attributes that people speaking a given language have found important and useful in their daily interactions*" (Goldberg, 1981). In 1990, Goldberg tried to define a small set of 475 common trait adjectives grouped into 131 sets of factors that can cover the big five domain (Goldberg, 1990). It issued in 1992 into the 50-item instrument using so-called 'transparent format' (Goldberg, 1992) that finally led to the modern version of FFM. The FFM is based on five large classes of psychological traits, often named Big Five model or OCEAN, by taking the first letter of the name of each class (the classes are listed in the first column of Table 1).

Note that while it is largely used today, the FFM model has undergone many critics since its beginning. For example, McAdams (1992) proposed an early critical appraisal of the FFM mode with six main arguments, often developed by other authors afterwards: 1) it is limited to personality *traits*; 2) it lacks actual behavior prediction power; 3) it does not address causal explanations of human behavior; 4) it does not consider any representation or knowledge about the world; 5) it does not provide a program for human personality integration and improving; 6) it relies on the notion of *short phrases* (taken either from dictionaries or questionnaires) for the description of the psychology of a person. McAdams claims that FFM describes a *generic* personality for humankind not the personality of this man (that I know of) or this woman (that I know of) by stating: "*the Five-factor model is essentially a psychology of a stranger.*"

The FFM being a very generic classification, several authors have tried to refine this taxonomy by dividing the FFM classes into so-called facets (Saucier & Ostendorf, 1999; Costa & McCrae, 1992; Soto & John, 2008). John, Naumann, and Soto (2008a) have shown that these facet lists have many similarities although their facet number varies from 16 in Saucier and Ostendorf (1999) to 30 in the so-called NEO PI-R (NEO PI-R stands for: **N**euroticism **E**xtraversion **O**penness **P**ersonality **I**nventory **R**evisited) proposition of Costa and McCrae (1992). The 30 facets of the NEO PI-R classification are listed in the second column of Table 1, together with their glosses. NEO PI-R is a long-standing model that provides a very precise facet list. For these reasons, we will rely on it for the work presented in the next sections.

BUILDING A RESOURCE FOR PERSONALITY DESCRIPTION

In this section, we will describe our contribution to the aforementioned domains by defining a computationally-oriented resource of personality for conversational agents. In a first subsection,

Table 1. Facets for enriching the FFM classes: three approaches (alignment according to John et al. judgment, based on Soto & John, 2009]). Facet names in italics correspond to a secondary possible attachment of a facet.

OCEAN Classes	Lexical facets (N=18) (Saucier & Ostendorf, 1999)	NEO PI-R facets (N=30) (Costa & McCrae, 1992)	CPI-Big five facets (N=16) (Soto & John, 2009)
Extraversion	Sociability	-	-
	Assertiveness	Gregariousness	Gregariousness
	-	Activity	-
	Activity/Adventurousness	Excitement-seeking	*(O Adventurousness)*
	-	-	Social confidence (vs Anxiety)
	-	Positive emotions	-
	Unrestraint	-	-
	(A Warmth/Affection)	Warmth	-
Agreeableness	Warmth/Affection	*(E Warmth)*	-
	Modesty/Humility	Modesty	Modesty (vs Narcissism)
	-	Trust	Trust (vs Suspicion)
	-	Tender-Mindedness	Empathy/sympathy
	Generosity	-	Altruism
	Gentleness	Compliance	-
	-	Straightforwardness	-
Conscientiousness	Orderliness	Order	Orderliness
	Industriousness	Achievement striving	-
	Reliability	Dutifulness	Industriousness
	Decisiveness	-	-
	-	Self-Discipline	Self-discipline
	(O Perceptiveness)	Competence	-
	-	Deliberation	-
Neuroticism	Insecurity	Anxiety	Anxiety
	Emotionality	-	-
	Irritability	Angry hostility	Irritability
	-	Depression	Depression
	-	-	Rumination-compulsiveness
	-	Self-consciousness	*(E Social confidence [vs Anxiety])*
	-	Vulnerability	-
	-	Impulsiveness	-
Openness	Intellect	Ideas	Intellectualism
	-	Aesthetics	Idealism
	Imagination/creativity	Fantasy	-
	-	-	Adventurousness
	-	Actions	-
	-	Feelings	-
	-	Values	-
	Perceptiveness	-	-

we shall justify our choice of a lexical approach of personality and in particular the use of Word-Net as a resource. In a second subsection, we will explain the methodology followed to classify personality adjectives within the NEO PI-R taxonomy. Then we will describe how that work allowed eliciting some concrete human behavior schemes associated to the taxonomy, based on the adjective glosses. Finally, in a fourth section, we will show how those schemes can lead to a concrete implementation within a particular agent framework as influence operators.

Lexical Semantics Senses of Personality Adjectives

Following the lexical hypothesis, we are interested in the sub set of the vocabulary that describes the personality of a person (further called personality adjectives) in order to assess the actual behaviors of people that are associated with such adjectives. Actually we are not interested in the adjectives, as words, but rather in the lexical semantic senses (in short the senses) of adjectives that describe the personality of people, in terms of their actual behaviors. Such instances of human behaviors, related to personality adjectives can be exhibited from so-called *short phrases* or *glosses*. There are three main sources for short phrases: a) Dictionary senses definitions; b) Personality questionnaires; c) Electronic lexical databases.

As an illustration of what dictionary senses definitions look like, here is the entry of the Merriam-Webster (MW) dictionary for personality adjective 'lazy' (which might not be the most important trait we would like to integrate into an agent, but provides a rich example here):

Lazy:

1a: disinclined to activity or exertion: not energetic or vigorous
1b: encouraging inactivity or indolence <a lazy summer day>
2:    moving slowly: sluggish

3:    droopy, lax <a rabbit with lazy ears>
4:    placed on its side <lazy E livestock brand>
5:    not rigorous or strict <lazy scholarship>

This entry contains five main distinct senses, the first one being divided into two sub cases. For most senses, one or several short phrases are given as instances of the corresponding sense. They are the behavioral source we are looking for in order to carry a computational implementation of the sense. Note that not all of the senses are related to personality description, e.g. droopy, lax <a rabbit with lazy ears> refers to physical proprieties of objects or people.

An alternative source to elicit the personality traits of a particular person is provided by the questions (in this context, called *items*), which are hand-built for the constitution of so-called personality questionnaires. Table 2 includes an excerpt of 10 first yes/no questions from the revised version of the original 100 items of the EPQ Model of personality of Eysenck and Eysenck (1975).

Because an item like "Are you a talkative person?" is linked with a specific personality trait (say E-Gregariousness), in an outside table, a simple transposition of the questionnaire makes it possible, for a given trait, to list the set of its associated behaviors.

Previously, we have mentioned that authors already have classified sets of adjectives in the FFM model and in the NEO PI-R model. However, when we tried to use these classifications in our works, we encountered two main problems:

- *Access to data*: Classification tables provided in the papers are too synthetic to be exploited and it is not easy to access the original resource data files.
- *Computational approach to semantics*: In order to fulfill the requirements of computational definition, we need words but also the precise lexical semantics attached to them (their precise senses). For example, the word 'kind' has three senses:

Table 2.

Occupation:		Age:	Sex:
Instructions: Please answer each question by putting a circle around the 'YES' or the 'NO' following the question. There are no right or wrong answers, and no trick questions. Work quickly and do not think too long about the exact meaning of the questions.			
1. Do you have many different hobbies?		YES	NO
2. Do you stop to think things over before doing anything?		YES	NO
3. Does your mood often go up and down?		YES	NO
4. Have you ever taken the praise for something you knew someone else had already done?		YES	NO
5. Do you take much notice of what people think?		YES	NO
6. Are you a talkative person?		YES	NO
7. Would being in debt worry you?		YES	NO
8. Do you ever feel 'just miserable' for no reason?		YES	NO
9. Do you give money to charities?		YES	NO
10. Were you ever greedy by helping yourself to more than you have share of anything?		YES	NO

… and 90 more.

/Tolerant/, /Genial/, /Openhearted/ (see Table 3) that can be classified into two distinct FFM classes and three distinct NEO PI-R facets: resp. A-compliance, E-warmth, A-tendermindedness. This example shows that the traditional word-level is insufficient. Instead we need to work at the sub level of the semantic senses attached to words.

The WordNet lexical database (Fellbaum, 1998) comes handy when one has to treat a large amount of lexical data and one has to access the lexical semantics of words. In WordNet, a word

Table 3. WordNet synsets associated with three commonly used personality adjectives. In column two, synsets with * marks are not related to personality traits.

Adjective	Not	Synset	WordNet gloss defining the synset
friendly		/Pally/	characteristic of or befitting a friend
	*	/Allied/	of or belonging to your own country's forces or those of an ally
	*	/Easy/	easy to understand or use
		/Favorable/	inclined to help or support; not antagonistic or hostile
kind		/Tolerant/	tolerant and forgiving under provocation
		/Genial/	agreeable, conducive to comfort
		/Openhearted/	having or showing a tender and considerate and helpful nature; used especially of persons and their behavior
lively		/Vital/	full of spirit
	*	/Eventful/	filled with events or activity
		/Frothy/	full of life and energy
	*	/Springy/	elastic; rebounds readily
		/Alert/	quick and energetic
		/Racy/	full of zest or vigor

is attached to several so-called *synsets* that define a unique lexical sense described by a gloss. Moreover, because the WordNet database is freely accessible, it makes it easy to build a computer-aided system for the classification process. Below, in order to compare with traditional dictionaries like MW, is the WordNet definition for personality adjective 'lazy,' which has two senses/synsets (noted here between / /):

Lazy:
1. SYNSET /Workshy/ disinclined to work and exertion = sense 1.a in MW
2. SYNSET /Slow/ moving slowly and gently = sense 2 in MW

One can see that there is some correspondence (but not bijective) between the Merriam-Webster definition and the WordNet definition for personality adjective 'lazy.'

Classification of a Set of Personality Adjectives into the FFM/NEO PI-R Taxonomy

In previous work (Bouchet & Sansonnet, 2010), we have carried out a classification of a set of personality adjectives in the FFM/NEO PI-R taxonomy. Below, we give a summary of this process carried out by two expert annotators, in three main steps:

Step 1: Personality Adjective Selection

In order to work on actually used personality adjectives, we have collected a set of personality adjectives C_{coll} from ten different Internet sources explicitly claiming to provide *"lists of adjectives describing personality traits"* (the sources are listed in Bouchet & Sansonnet, 2010). The set C_{coll} contains 1055 distinct adjectives, providing a first order approximation of the linguistic domain related to personality traits adjectives. Moreover, for each personality adjective a_i in C_{coll}, we have associated a salience rank ra_i depending on the number of lists in which a given adjective appears, which represents its usage frequency in the resources files. We have observed that ra_i values are ranging from 1 to 9. Unfortunately, some of the words appearing in set C_{coll} are not present in the WordNet database (|29|) or are present but are not listed as adjectives (|21|). However, their low salience (ra_i =1) allowed us to choose to discard them, leading to a set C_{WN} of 1005 distinct WordNet-tractable adjectives. Table 4 gives an excerpt of C_{WN}, which shows that the coverage of English language is quite large, if not exhaustive.

Step 2: Selection of the Relevant Adjective-Synset-Gloss Triplets

Each adjective a_i in the set C_{WN} has a WordNet entry, which associates with a_i a set of lexical semantics senses (i.e. its synsets). In the WordNet base, each synset is a unique identifier and defines a unique sense by means of a short phrase called a gloss. It is thus possible to obtain from the C_{WN}

Table 4. Excerpt of personality adjectives from the C_{WN} set containing 66 adjectives beginning with letter 'a' (listed not by salience rank but in alphabetic order)

abandoned, abashed, aberrant, abhorrent, abiding, abject, able, abnormal, abrasive, abrupt, absent-minded, absorbed, absurd, abusive, accepting, accomplished, acid, active, adamant, adaptable, addicted, adorable, adventurous, affective, afraid, aggressive, agonizing, agreeable, alcoholic, alert, alive, all-around, alluring, aloof, ambiguous, ambitious, amoral, amused, amusing, anal-retentive, ancient, angry, animated, annoyed, annoying, anxious, apathetic, appealing, appreciated, argumentative, arrogant, articulate, artificial, artistic, ashamed, assertive, astonishing, athletic, attentive, auspicious, automatic, awake, aware, awesome, awful, awkward.

set of adjectives, a base B_{all} of triplets of the form: < adjective, synset, gloss >. However as one can see from entries marked with a mark * in Table 2, not all triplets are related to the description of the personality of a person. In order to discard these entries, an annotating process was performed by two expert annotators (details are given in Bouchet & Sansonnet, 2010), which resulted in the selection of a base B_{sel} of 1356 relevant triplets, containing 904 distinct adjectives.

Step 3: Classification of the Triplets into the FFM/NEO PI-R Taxonomy

The NEO PI-R taxonomy proposes for each of the five FFM personality classes 6 facets, thus resulting in 30 clusters. In NEO PI-R, each facet encompasses both the concept and its antonym(s), e.g. the facet A-Modesty can stand for adjectives like '*mild*' as well as '*arrogant.*' Hence, similarly to Goldberg's works on 50 bipolar scales (Goldberg, 1992), each facet was divided into two poles: noted + for the concept and - for its antonym(s), thus resulting in 60 target clusters noted +/-NEO PI-R. The classification was performed by two expert annotators (details in Bouchet & Sansonnet, 2010), which resulted in the building of a base, further transformed into an XML resource. This resource is freely available for research and teaching purposes on the Web [http://perso.limsi.fr/jps/research/rnb/toolkit/taxo-glosses/taxo.htm]. Table 4 displays an excerpt of this XML resource listing triplets associated with FFM trait Openness.

A first attempt at classifying a subset of B_{sel} entries over the 60 established classes raised a major issue: despite the fact that the collected adjectives words were claimed by the resources to be personality-related, actually a lot of their corresponding adjective-synset-gloss triplets in WordNet are also associated with other attributes of a person, which can be divided into five main categories, called *external categories*:

- Physical descriptions, e.g. "having a sturdy and well-proportioned body" (athletic, / Muscular/);
- Mental capacities e.g. "characterized by quickness and ease in learning" (bright, / Smart/), (smart, /Bright/);
- Judgmental qualities, both physical or mental, e.g. "appealing to the emotions as well as the eye" (lovely, /Beautiful/);
- Social roles, e.g. "characterized by or indicating poverty" (poor, /Beggarly/);
- Mind states are transitory (like emotions), e.g. "in an aroused state," (excited, / Thrillful/).
- Errors are items that don't fit in any of the facets of categories.

The final distribution of gloss-oriented triplets into the categories (30 facets + external cases) is summarized by Figure 1. Although some facets like C-Dutifulness and A-Tender-mindedness appear to have gathered significantly more glosses, we can see that all NEO PI-R facets have had some associated triplets (with a minimum of two for O-Aesthetics—see Table 4, line **Facet: Aesthetics pole +**). Moreover, some negative positions have no triplets attached to them. This is due to the fact that they were introduced systematically as complement to positive poles—for example, see Table 5, line **Facet: Aesthetics pole -**.

Elicitation of Behavioral Schemes Associated with Adjectives

From the process of classification of the triplets into the FFM/NEO PI-R taxonomy, we have obtained a resource base where each facet contains two bipolar lists of triplets. The glosses contained in a given facet provide several instantiations of the psychological notion associated with the facet.

Actually, these instantiations can describe *distinct human behaviors* needing to be implemented with distinct computational heuristics. For example, considering the facet Openness-Fantasy

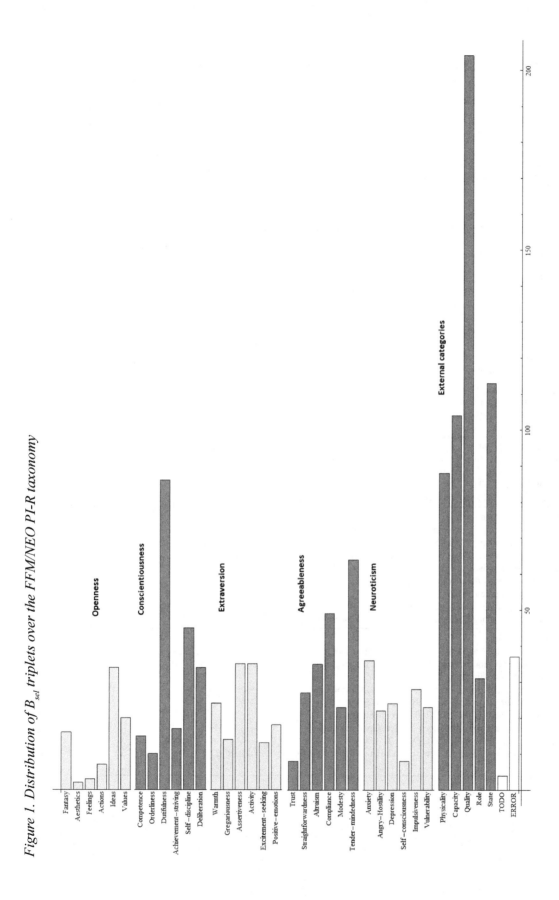

Figure 1. Distribution of B$_{sel}$ triplets over the FFM/NEO PI-R taxonomy

Table 5. Classification of B_{sel} triplets into the FFM/NEO PI-R taxonomy. An excerpt of trait **Openness** *is given for covering its facets: Fantasy, Aesthetics, Feelings, Action, Ideas, Values (facet Ideas is abridged; facet Values is no listed). Triplets are separated into two sets: pole + (the concept of the facet) and pole – (its antonym). Each line displays a triplet in the format: gloss [adjective, Synset (with '/' omitted), rank].*

FFM trait: Openness
Facet: Fantasy pole +
not sensible about practical matters; idealistic and unrealistic [romantic, WildEyed, 5]
having the ability to produce or originate [productive, Generative, 4]
concerned with sacred matters or religion or the church [religious, Spiritual, 4]
promoting construction or creation [creative, Constructive, 3]
having the ability or power to create [creative, Originative, 3]
marked by independence and creativity in thought or action [imaginative, Imaginative, 3]
concerned with or affecting the spirit or soul [spiritual, Unearthly, 3]
showing great reverence for god [godly, Worshipful, 2]
Facet: Fantasy pole -
unimaginatively conventional [conservative, ButtonDown, 3]
guided by practical experience and observation rather than theory [practical, Hardheaded, 3]
aware or expressing awareness of things as they really are [realistic, Virtual, 3]
freed from illusion [disillusioned, Disillusioned, 2]
sensible and practical [earthy, DownToEarth, 2]
denying or questioning the tenets of especially a religion [skeptical, Unbelieving, 2]
concerned with the world or worldly matters [mundane, Terrestrial, 1]
deficient in originality or creativity; lacking powers of invention [sterile, Uninspired, 1]
Facet: Aesthetics pole +
marked by refinement in taste and manners [cultured, Cultured, 5]
relating to or characteristic of art or artists [artistic, Art, 1]
Facet: Aesthetics pole -
Facet: Feelings pole +
able to feel or perceive [sensitive, Sensible, 7]
given to or marked by sentiment or sentimentality [sentimental, Tender, 2]
Facet: Feelings pole -
tired of the world [bored, WorldWeary, 3]
Facet: Action pole +
possibly accepting or permitting [capable, Open, 4]
capable of adapting (of becoming or being made suitable) to a particular situation or use [adaptable, Adaptable, 3]
willing to undertake or seeking out new and daring enterprises [adventurous, Adventurous, 3]
disposed to venture or take risks [daring, Venturous, 3]
fearless and daring [bold, Vaulting, 2]
Facet: Action pole -
excessively fastidious and easily disgusted [nice, Prissy, 6]
incapable of adapting or changing to meet circumstances [inflexible, Person, 2]
Facet: Ideas pole +
eager to investigate and learn or learn more (sometimes about others' concerns) [curious, Snoopy, 5]
having curiosity aroused; eagerly interested in learning more [curious, Interested, 5]
ahead of the times [modern, Innovative, 5]
open to arguments, ideas, or change [receptive, Pervious, 5]
ready or willing to receive favorably [receptive, Open, 5]
devoted to matters of the mind [reflective, Intellectual, 5]
ready to entertain new ideas [open-minded, Open-minded, 3]
having an open mind [hospitable, Open, 2]
of high moral or intellectual value; elevated in nature or style [idealistic, Rarified, 2]
... Etc.

Table 6. Clusterization of facet Openness-Fantasy (Ofa) into three distinct atomic bipolar schemes. For poles +/- of scheme CREATIVENESS, we give the set of its associated triplets, actually abridged here to the gloss part (text italicized)

Scheme's poles identifiers	Textual definition of the scheme + abridges 'more than average' resp. 'less than average'	Gloss count
1. IDEALISTICNESS	**O**fa = Openness-fantasy	
+ IDEALISTIC	+ inclined to like (even to believe in) imaginary ideas or situations	1
- PRACTICAL	- inclined to like (or to believe in) imaginary ideas or situations	5
2. SPIRITUALISTNESS	**O**fa	
+ SPIRITUALIST	+ interested in spirit and soul matters	6
- MATERIALIST	- interested in spirit and soul matters, even denying the tenets	2
3. CREATIVENESS	**O**fa	
+ CREATIVE	+ having power of creativity in thought or action • *Having the ability to produce or originate* • *Promoting construction or creation* • *Having the ability to create* • *[…] marked by independence and creativity in thought or action*	4
- UNIMAGINATIVE	- having power of creativity in thought or action • *Unimaginatively conventional* • *Deficient in originality or creativity; lacking powers of invention* • *Unimaginative and conformist* • *Lacking spontaneity or originality or individuality*	4

in Table 6, classified glosses are actually dealing with three distinct notions: creativity, idealness and spirituality, which are mixed in both the + or - pole of the facet.

This is the reason why we have to carry out a more precise clustering of the glosses within the facets, in terms of so-called behavioral schemes (in short *schemes*), where each scheme can reasonably be viewed as "an atomic kind of behavior." Indeed, each scheme is intended to be further associated with a specific computational implementation, for example in terms of operators influencing decisions and choices in the deliberation cycle of the BDI agents of the R&B framework.

Each scheme is a structure of the form:

```
Scheme ID
FFM/NEO PI-R category
Positive pole ID, Textual definition,
{gloss₁, .. glossₙ}
Negative pole ID, Textual definition,
{gloss₁, .. glossₙ}
```

Like facets, schemes are organized into a positive pole and a negative pole. Contrary to facet-poles that support a two-position scale (concept/antonym opposition), scheme-poles are organized onto a three-position scale: more than average (+), average (=), less than average (-). The average position implicitly is associated with the "*average behavior associated with the personality of a generic human being*" while + and - poles explicitly denote a person with a marked psychological inclination. Technically, the semantics of a scheme is only and uniquely defined by the list of its associated glosses. However, each scheme pole is provided with an informal textual definition synthetizing its glosses.

During the process of organization of the facets into behavioral schemes 766 glosses were annotated and clustered into 69 distinct schemes resulting in a total of $2 \times 69 = 138$ scheme +/- poles.

Figure 2 displays the distribution of the glosses and of the schemes in the FFM/NEO PI-R taxonomy. Globally, one observes a good

Figure 2. Distribution in FFM/NEO PI-R taxonomy of glosses (top) and schemes (bottom), where: N_{facet} = 30, N_{gloss} = 766, N_{scheme} = 69, mean number of glosses per facet = 26 and mean number of schemes by facet = 2.3

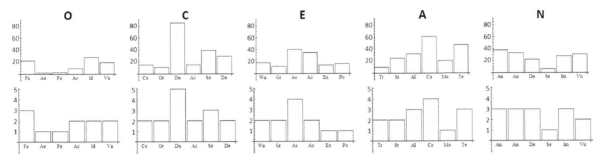

and homogeneous coverage in terms of glosses and schemes over the five OCEAN traits and over the 30 NEO PI-R facets. There is also a good and homogeneous coverage of glosses over the schemes: the distribution varies from min = 2 to max = 40, with a mean of 26 glosses by scheme.

Association of Influence Operators to the Schemes

Once the WordNet glosses of the set of personality adjectives have been reorganized into the FFM/ NEO PI-R facet taxonomy, they must be associated with an actual computational implementation. In the R&B framework, this part is taken by the so-called influence operators (further called *operators*), which are symbolic rule-based heuristics operating on/altering the rational behavior of the agent (see Bouchet & Sansonnet, 2009 for a formal definition). In this context, a final step towards the computational implementation of the schemes is required because there is often but not always a direct correspondence between a scheme and an operator. It comes from the fact that schemes are concepts elicited from the linguistic domain point of view, whereas the operators we wish to define are symbolic heuristics (or meta rules) defined from a computational point of view. This heterogeneity entails three issues:

- It can happen that a scheme requires several distinct operators to be implemented;

- Conversely, the same operator can implement distinct schemes, meaning that actually these schemes are not distinct from a computational point of view;

- Moreover, the +/- poles of the schemes can be inverted with the +/- poles of the operators (especially in the Neuroticism class).

From the set of 69 schemes, it was possible to elicit a set of 56 operators, which can be organized in a two-level taxonomy. Whereas the two-level scheme taxonomy is psychology-oriented (FFM/ NEO PI-R) the two-level operator taxonomy is computation-oriented, that is organized according to the activities of the agent. Because we consider conversational agents in UAS situation, as stated in the introduction, the first level of the classification of the operators separates:

- *Mono-agent situations*: with operators mainly related to the A ↔ S interactions. This class of operators is made of four subsets: personal knowledge; personal action; personal satisfaction; personal control of moods/affects.
- *Multi-agent situations:* with operators mainly related to the U ↔ A interactions. This class of operators is made of three subsets: knowledge exchange; multi-agent action and control of others; interactional feelings and manners.

Table 7 lists the taxonomy of the No = 56 operators and for each category the count of its operators. From this classification we could draw three main results:

CONCLUSION AND FUTURE RESEARCH DIRECTIONS

While software agents are more and more in interaction with human users, there is a real need for more human-like interactions between ordinary people and artificial agents. Hence, artificial agents should not only be mere rational entities, providing efficient services but also friendly entities, playing the mediating roles involved in presentation, assistance, teaching, game companions, coaching, etc.

A way to fulfill these requirements is to provide traditional rational agent architectures with specific features dealing with psychological notions such as personality traits and/or moods. However, this can only be achieved: 1) when a solid ground for the description of the personality of a generic person is defined, according to state of the art works in psychology; but also 2) when personality traits descriptions are computationally implementable, which entails a need for behavioral precision.

Table 7. Two-level taxonomy of the influence operators (No = 56)

1. Mono Agent	$N_{po} = 26$	2. Multi Agent	$N_{io} = 30$
Personal knowledge: Memory, fact, commonsense, learn	4	**Interaction - knowledge:** trust, frankness, curiosity, privacy, conversion	5
Personal execution of action and plans: adaptation, decision, deliberation, creativity, danger, expectation, novelty, clean, method, concern, attention, activity, work	13	**Interaction - action and control of others:** Meeting, cooperation, sacrifice, giveness, fairness, forgiveness, commitment, charisma, domination, menace, agreement, honesty, malice, conform, progress	15
Personal satisfaction: possession, success, pleasure, art	4	**Interaction - feelings and manners:** comfort, reassurance, perception, empathy, humility, tolerance, aggression, friendliness, showiness, smalltalk	10
Personal mood/affect control: moodiness, emotionality, fierceness, assurance, prone(mood)	5	-	

1. First level balance: There is a good balance between the two sets of personal operators ($N_{po} = 26$) and the interactional operators ($N_{io} = 30$). This balance is not artificial: it is the result of the distribution of the lexical semantics attached to the initial set of personality adjectives. Actually, the linguistic senses reflect the two faces of an agent: its personal face and its social face.

2. Scheme-operator alignment: The alignment between schemes and operators is quite good. Actually, most schemes (68%) are in a one to one relation with an operator and 25% of the others operators occur only in two schemes, as shown in Table 8 (where prone(mood$_i$) wraps in a single class the tendency to exhibit 7 kinds of moods).

Table 8. Alignment between schemes and operators

Type of operators counted	Frequency	% of N_o
All occurrences in schemes	82	-
With 1 occurrence (bijections)	38	67.9%
With 2 occurrences	14	25.0%
With 3 occurrences	2	5.4%
With special operator prone(mood$_i$)	7	12.5%

3. Corpus coverage: A third result is the good convergence of personality adjectives over operators: repetitive random samples of only 100 adjectives, taken from C_{WN} (*i.e. samples of* 10% of the 1005 adjectives of C_{WN}) have proved to cover about 90% of the 56 operators. Hence, we can consider that the resource base built in this work provides a good coverage of the personality trait domain in terms of schemes and operators.

We have defined and described a taxonomy of psychological behaviors through a study based 1) on standard personality traits taxonomies in psychology (FFM with NEO PI-R for the facets) and 2) on a commonly used lexical database (WordNet). Using the lexical semantic senses of an original selection of 1005 personality adjectives in that base, we have dispatched them over the 60 facets of NEO PI-R, taking into account their polarity. The glosses associated to those senses in WordNet thus provide extra and useful information about how to computationally implement a given facet. We have finally shown that although there is often a direct mapping between a psychological facet and a computational operator, there are several exceptions, which led us to define a second computationally-oriented taxonomy.

We believe that this taxonomy can become a useful resource (currently available on the Internet) for future research works focusing on the implementation of psychological behaviors in terms of the elicited operators. Once implemented, an operator would then have to be evaluated. Considering the class of multi-agent operators, for example in the context of conversational agents, it can be done by making human subjects interact with the agent. Considering the class of mono-agent operators, for example in the context of autonomous agents, it can be done by observing the agent actual actions. These experiments should confirm that people actually would notice differences in behaviors, and that those differences actually correspond to the personality traits or facets that were intended to be implemented by that operator.

From a more application-based point of view, the fact that this taxonomy has been conceived for a concrete computational application (agent-based interfaces) makes it particularly useful for agent framework designers, as opposed to taxonomies originally made exclusively to describe human personality. We have shown that they could be implemented within our own agent framework (R&B) as what we called influence operators: a similar work could be done within other existing agent frameworks, by modifying them to include such operators.

As for system designers who simply wish to add a conversational agent within their system, although choosing how their agent(s) should react in the particular context of their application still remain exclusively their decision, they can at least use this taxonomy as an exhaustive set of personality traits and associated behaviors they should consider during the agent design. Such a process would have to be done in two phases: firstly, by asking themselves what each of those influence operators would mean for them (e.g. "what would it mean for our particular agent to be trustful towards the user?"), and secondly, once this question has been answered, to decide if they want to implement it or not (e.g. "do we want our agent to behave this way or not?"), in an ad hoc way, if they don't rely on an existing agent framework.

REFERENCES

Allbeck, J. M., & Kress-Gazit, H. (2010). Constraints-based complex behavior in rich environments. In Allbeck, J., Badler, N., Bickmore, T., Pelachaud, C., & Safonova, A. (Eds.), *Intelligent Virtual Agents* (*Vol. 6356*, pp. 1–14). Berlin, Germany: Springer. doi:10.1007/978-3-642-15892-6_1

Allen, J. F., Kautz, H. A., Pelavin, R. N., & Tenenberg, J. D. (1991). *Reasoning about plans*. New York, NY: Morgan Kaufmann Publishers Inc.

Allport, G. W. (1937). *Personality: A psychological interpretation*. Oxford, UK: Holt.

Anderson, J. R. (1996). ACT: A simple theory of complex cognition. *The American Psychologist*, *51*(4), 355–365. doi:10.1037/0003-066X.51.4.355

Anderson, J. R., Matessa, M., & Lebiere, C. (1997). ACT-R: A theory of higher level cognition and its relation to visual attention. *Human-Computer Interaction, 12*(4), 439. doi:10.1207/s15327051hci1204_5

Ball, G., & Breese, J. (2000). Embodied conversational agents. In Cassell, J., Sullivan, J., Prevost, S., & Churchill, E. (Eds.), *Embodied Conversational Agents* (pp. 189–219). Cambridge, MA: MIT Press.

Bandura, A. (1986). *Social foundations of thought and action: A social cognitive theory.* Englewood Cliffs, NJ: Prentice-Hall.

Bates, J. (1994). The role of emotion in believable agents. *Communications of the ACM, 37*(7), 122–125. doi:10.1145/176789.176803

Baumgarten, F. (1933). Die charaktereigenschaften *Beiträge zue Charakter-und Persönlichkeitsforschung, 1.*

Baylor, A. L., & Kim, Y. (2004). Pedagogical agent design: The impact of agent realism, gender, ethnicity, and instructional role. In Lester, J. C., Vicari, R. M., & Paraguaçu, F. (Eds.), *Intelligent Tutoring Systems* (pp. 592–603). Maceio, Brazil: Springer. doi:10.1007/978-3-540-30139-4_56

Bouchet, F., & Sansonnet, J.-P. (2009). A framework for modeling the relationships between the rational and behavioral reactions of assisting conversational agents. In *Proceedings of the 7th European Workshop on Multi-Agent Systems (EUMAS 2009).* Agia Napa, Cyprus: EUMAS.

Bouchet, F., & Sansonnet, J.-P. (2010). Classification of wordnet personality adjectives in the NEO PI-R taxonomy. In *Proceedings of the Actes du Quatrième Workshop sur les Agents Conversationnels Animés (WACA 2010),* (pp. 83-90). Lille, France: WACA.

Bratman, M. E. (1990). What Is Intention? In Cohen, P. R., Morgan, J., & Pollack, M. E. (Eds.), *Intentions in Communication* (pp. 15–32). Cambridge, MA: The MIT Press.

Bratman, M. E., Israel, D. J., & Pollack, M. E. (1988). Plans and resource-bounded practical reasoning. *Computational Intelligence, 4*(4), 349–355. doi:10.1111/j.1467-8640.1988.tb00284.x

Cassell, J., Bickmore, T., Billinghurst, M., Campbell, L., Chang, K., Vilhjálmsson, H., & Yan, H. (1999). Embodiment in conversational interfaces: Rea. In *Proceedings of the SIGCHI Conference on Human Factors in Computer Systems,* (pp. 520-527). New York, NY: ACM Press.

Cattell, R. B., Eber, H. W., & Tatsuoka, M. M. (1970). *Handbook for the sixteen personality factor questionnaire (16 PF).* Champaign, IL: Institute for Personality and Ability Testing.

Costa, P. T., & McCrae, R. R. (1992). Normal personality assessment in clinical practice: The NEO personality inventory. *Psychological Assessment, 4*(1), 5–13. doi:10.1037/1040-3590.4.1.5

Dastani, M. (2008). 2APL: A practical agent programming language. *Autonomous Agents and Multi-Agent Systems, 16*(3), 214–248. doi:10.1007/s10458-008-9036-y

Davis, F. D. (1989). Perceived usefulness, perceived ease of use, and user acceptance of information technology. *Management Information Systems Quarterly, 13*(3), 319–340. doi:10.2307/249008

Dias, J., & Paiva, A. (2005). Feeling and reasoning: A computational model for emotional characters. In Bento, C., Cardoso, A., & Dias, G. (Eds.), *Progress in Artificial Intelligence* (*Vol. 3808,* pp. 127–140). Berlin, Germany: Springer. doi:10.1007/11595014_13

Doce, T., Dias, J., Prada, R., & Paiva, A. (2010). Creating individual agents through personality traits. In Allbeck, J., Badler, N., Bickmore, T., Pelachaud, C., & Safonova, A. (Eds.), *Intelligent Virtual Agents* (*Vol. 6356,* pp. 257–264). Berlin, Germany: Springer. doi:10.1007/978-3-642-15892-6_27

Ellsworth, P. C., & Scherer, K. R. (2003). Appraisal processes in emotion. In Davidson, R. J., Scherer, K. R., & Goldsmith, H. H. (Eds.), *Handbook of Affective Sciences* (pp. 572–595). New York, NY: Oxford University Press.

Evertsz, R., Ritter, F. E., Busetta, P., & Pedrotti, M. (2008). Realistic behaviour variation in a BDI-based cognitive architecture. In *Proceedings of SimTecT 2008*. Melbourne, Australia: SimTecT.

Eysenck, H. J. (1976). The measurement of personality. *Proceedings of the Royal Society of Medicine, 40*(2), 75–80.

Eysenck, H. J., & Eysenck, S. B. G. (1968). *Manual of the Eysenck personality questionnaire.* San Diego, CA: EdITS.

Eysenck, S. B. G., Eysenck, H. J., & Barrett, P. (1985). A revised version of the psychoticism scale. *Personality and Individual Differences, 6*(1), 21–29. doi:10.1016/0191-8869(85)90026-1

Fellbaum, C. (1998). *WordNet: An electronic lexical database.* Cambridge, MA: MIT Press.

Frijda, N. H. (2006). *The laws of emotion.* New York, NY: Psychology Press.

Gillis, P. D., & Hursh, S. R. (1999). Using behavior moderators to influence CGF command entity effectiveness and performance. In *Proceedings of the Eighth Conference on Computer Generated Forces and Behavioral Representation,* (pp. 237-251). Orlando, FL: Computer Generated Forces.

Gmytrasiewicz, P. J., & Lisetti, C. L. (2002). Emotions and personality in agent design and modeling. In Meyer, J.-J. C., & Tambe, M. (Eds.), *Intelligent Agents VIII* (*Vol. 2333,* pp. 21–31). Berlin, Germany: Springer. doi:10.1007/3-540-45448-9_3

Goldberg, L. R. (1981). Language and individual differences: The search for universal in personality lexicons. *Review of Personality and Social Psychology, 2*(1), 141–165.

Goldberg, L. R. (1990). An alternative "description of personality": The big-five factor structure. *Journal of Personality and Social Psychology, 59,* 1216–1229. doi:10.1037/0022-3514.59.6.1216

Goldberg, L. R. (1992). The development of markers for the big-five factor structure. *Psychological Assessment, 4*(1), 26–42. doi:10.1037/1040-3590.4.1.26

Graham, J. R. (2006). *MMPI-2: Assessing personality and psychopathology* (4th ed.). New York, NY: Oxford University Press.

Gratch, J., & Marsella, S. (2004). A domain-independent framework for modeling emotion. *Cognitive Systems Research, 5*(4), 269–306. doi:10.1016/j.cogsys.2004.02.002

Hayes-Roth, B., Brownston, L., & van Gent, R. (1995). Multiagent collaboration in directed improvisation. In *Proceedings of the First International Conference on Multi-Agent Systems,* (pp. 148-154). San Francisco, CA: ICMAS.

Howden, N., Rönnquist, R., Hodgson, A., & Lucas, A. (2001). JACK intelligent agents-summary of an agent infrastructure. In *Proceedings of the 5th International Conference on Autonomous Agents.* Autonomous Agents.

Huber, M. J. (1999). JAM: A BDI-theoretic mobile agent architecture. In *Proceedings of the Third Annual Conference on Autonomous Agents,* (pp. 236–243). Seattle, Washington: AGENTS.

Jiang, H., Vidal, J. M., & Huhns, M. N. (2007). EBDI: An architecture for emotional agents. In *Proceedings of the 6th International Joint Conference on Autonomous Agents and Multiagent Systems,* (pp. 11:1–11:3). Honolulu, HI: ACM Press.

John, O. P., Naumann, L. P., & Soto, C. J. (2008). Paradigm shift to the integrative big five trait taxonomy: History, measurements, and conceptual issues. In *Handbook of Personality: Theory and Research* (3rd ed.). New York, NY: The Guilford Press.

John, O. P., Robins, R. W., & Pervin, L. A. (Eds.). (2008). *Handbook of personality: Theory and research* (3rd ed.). New York, NY: The Guilford Press.

Laird, J. E., Newell, A., & Rosenbloom, P. S. (1987). SOAR: An architecture for general intelligence. *Artificial Intelligence, 33*(1), 1–64. doi:10.1016/0004-3702(87)90050-6

Lim, M. Y., Dias, J., Aylett, R., & Paiva, A. (2008). Improving adaptiveness in autonomous characters. In Prendinger, H., Lester, J., & Ishizuka, M. (Eds.), *Intelligent Virtual Agents (Vol. 5208*, pp. 348–355). Berlin, Germany: Springer. doi:10.1007/978-3-540-85483-8_35

Maes, P. (1994). Agents that reduce work and information overload. *Communications of the ACM, 37*(7), 30–40. doi:10.1145/176789.176792

Maes, P. (1995). Artificial life meets entertainment: Lifelike autonomous agents. *Communications of the ACM, 38*(11), 108–114. doi:10.1145/219717.219808

Malatesta, L., Caridakis, G., Raouzaiou, A., & Karpouzis, K. (2007). Agent personality traits in virtual environments based on appraisal theory predictions. In *Proceedings of AISB 2007: Artificial and Ambient Intelligence, Language, Speech and Gesture for Expressive Characters*. Newcastle, UK: AISB.

Maslow, A. H. (1968). *Toward a psychology of being* (2nd ed.). Princeton, NJ: Van Nostrand.

McAdams, D. P. (1992). The five-factor model in personality: A critical appraisal. *Journal of Personality, 60*(2), 329–361. doi:10.1111/j.1467-6494.1992.tb00976.x

McRorie, M., Sneddon, I., Sevin, E., Bevacqua, E., & Pelachaud, C. (2009). A model of personality and emotional traits. In Ruttkay, Z., Kipp, M., Nijholt, A., & Vilhjálmsson, H. H. (Eds.), *Intelligent Virtual Agents (Vol. 5773*, pp. 27–33). Berlin, Germany: Springer. doi:10.1007/978-3-642-04380-2_6

Neill, J. (2008). Personality reading. *Center for Applied Psychology*. Retrieved from http://wilderdom.com/JamesNeill.htm.

Norling, E., & Ritter, F. E. (2004). Towards supporting psychologically plausible variability in agent-based human modelling. In *Proceedings of the Third International Joint Conference on Autonomous Agents and Multi-Agent Systems*. AAMAS.

Norman, W. T. (1963). Toward an adequate taxonomy of personality attributes: Replicated factor structure in peer nomination personality ratings. *Journal of Abnormal and Social Psychology, 66*(6), 574–583. doi:10.1037/h0040291

Ortony, A. (2003). On making believable emotional agents believable. In Trappl, R., Petta, P., & Payr, S. (Eds.), *Emotions in Humans and Artifacts* (pp. 189–211). Cambridge, MA: MIT Press.

Ortony, A., Clore, G. L., & Collins, A. (1988). *The cognitive structure of emotions*. Cambridge, UK: Cambridge University Press. doi:10.1017/CBO9780511571299

Pelachaud, C. (2000). Some considerations about embodied agents. In *Proceedings of the Workshop on Achieving Human-Like Behavior in Interactive Animated Agents*. Barcelona, Spain: Autonomous Agents.

Petta, P., Pelachaud, C., & Cowie, R. (Eds.). (2011). *Emotion-oriented systems: The humane handbook*. Dordrecht, The Netherlands: Springer.

Rao, A. S., & Georgeff, M. P. (1995). BDI agents: From theory to practice. In *Proceedings of the 1st International Conference on Multi-Agent Systems,* (pp. 312-319). San Francisco, CA: ICMAS.

Rizzo, P., Veloso, M., Miceli, M., & Cesta, A. (1997). Personality-driven social behaviors in believable agents. In *Proceedings of the AAAI Fall Symposium on Socially Intelligent Agents,* (pp. 109-114). AAAI.

Rousseau, D., & Hayes-Roth, B. (1996). *Personality in synthetic agents. Technical Report No. KSL 96-21*. Palo Alto, CA: Stanford University.

Russell, S., & Norvig, P. (2009). *Artificial intelligence: A modern approach* (3rd ed.). New York, NY: Prentice Hall.

Sansonnet, J.-P., & Bouchet, F. (2010). Expression of behaviors in assistant agents as influences on rational execution of plans. In Allbeck, J. M., Badler, N. I., Bickmore, T. W., Pelachaud, C., & Safonova, A. (Eds.), *Intelligent Virtual Agents* (*Vol. 6356*, pp. 413–419). Philadelphia, PA: Springer. doi:10.1007/978-3-642-15892-6_45

Sardina, S. (2007). *A course on BDI architectures*. Melbourne, Australia: University of Melbourne.

Saucier, G., & Ostendorf, F. (1999). Hierarchical subcomponents of the big five personality factors: A cross-language replication. *Journal of Personality and Social Psychology*, *76*(4), 613–627. doi:10.1037/0022-3514.76.4.613

Silverman, B. G., Johns, M., Cornwell, J., & O'Brien, K. (2006). Human behavior models for agents in simulators and games: Part I: Enabling science with PMFserv. *Presence (Cambridge, Mass.)*, *15*(2), 139–162. doi:10.1162/pres.2006.15.2.139

Soto, C. J., & John, O. P. (2009). Ten facet scales for the big five inventory: Convergence with NEO PI-R facets, self-peer agreement, and discriminant validity. *Journal of Research in Personality*, *43*(1). doi:10.1016/j.jrp.2008.10.002

Weiss, G. (2000). *Multiagent systems: A modern approach to distributed artificial intelligence*. Cambridge, MA: MIT Press.

Wooldridge, M. J. (2000). *Reasoning about rational agents*. Cambridge, MA: MIT Press.

KEY TERMS AND DEFINITIONS

Intelligent Agent: An autonomous entity in interaction with its environment, from which it collects data through sensors, and upon which it acts through actuators, in order to reach a set of personal goals.

Rational Agent: Intelligent agents that rely exclusively on rational choice theory to decide its next set of actions, as opposed to an agent trying to mimic human non-rational behaviors (emotions, personality traits…).

Conversational Agent: An intelligent agent in interaction with human users, usually in a multimodal way including at least natural language (typed or speech as input, displayed on screen or vocalized as output), and possibly gesture or emotions (if the agent has an embodiment).

Gloss: short phrase used in a thesaurus (or an electronic lexical database like WordNet) to define a word (or a synset).

Personality Traits: A set of basic dispositions that influence the actions and behaviors of a person or agent, and that are stable over time (as opposed to moods or emotions).

Behavioral Scheme: The smallest unit of concrete behavior that can be inferred from a personality trait.

Influence Operator: Symbolic rule-based heuristics handled by the behavioral engine (within the R&B framework), in order to alter the rational behavior of the agent, to make it non-exclusively rational.

Chapter 12
The Activity Circle:
A Social Proxy Interface to Display the Perceived Distributed Viscosity about Workflow Technology

Marcello Sarini
University of Milano-Bicocca, Italy

ABSTRACT

The chapter describes the Activity Circle, a social visualization mechanism based on the concept of Social Proxy, a minimalist graphical representation that portrays socially salient aspects of users' interactions. The Activity Circle allows users to socialize how they perceive the accomplishment of work activities that are regulated by a workflow technology. The social information visualized by the Activity Circle should primarily allow people to share the distributed viscosity perception about the workflow technology used; perceived distributed viscosity concerns the perception of the extra amount of work required by this technology to fulfill the users' organization goals, where "distributed" indicates that different groups of users perceive the impact of workflow technology differently. Making this information explicit may help groups of users reconcile the conflicts about disparities introduced by workflow technology. This information could also be used by management to design more equitable workflow technology.

DOI: 10.4018/978-1-4666-1628-8.ch012

INTRODUCTION

Workflow technology has rarely been considered from a social perspective. In fact, literature on workflow technology has mainly focused on the technological aspects related to the design, enactment, and execution of business processes (Abbott & Sarin, 1994). Researchers emphasized how these technologies could facilitate the automatic accomplishment of work activities rather than how they could support interactions occurring among people who must accomplish related work activities. However, the CSCW research area (Schmidt & Bannon, 1992; Gerson & Star, 1986; Suchman, 1987; Brown & Duguid, 2000) has focused on "fields of work" studies, which investigate how people organize the coordination of interdependent activities; from a more technological perspective, CSCW research has considered the design of more effective collaboration technology, where effectiveness is about supporting people to accomplish interdependent activities related to common work flows.

Interdependent activities are central to CSCW because one can consider people as engaging in a cooperative work arrangement if they are mutually dependent in their work. This means that those people must cooperate to complete the work. Being mutually dependent in work means that every person relies on the work of the others to complete her work and vice versa (Schmidt & Bannon, 1992).

Recently, a trend drawing more general conclusions about workflow technology from a social perspective has emerged; specifically, Business Process Management (BPM) researchers have considered how to combine social software with BPM systems (Erol, et al., 2009). This intended to bring the richness of social relationships into technology supporting work organization. However, scholars tend to overemphasize a technological perspective without considering human interactions. These researchers often aim to build other workflow technology using social software (like Wikis) to benefit only of the functionalities promoting sociality (e.g., as proposed in Neumann & Erol, 2009).

We consider workflow technology from a social point of view because it supports people during the interactions occurring while coordinating interdependent work activities. We therefore propose to integrate standard workflow technology with the functionalities provided by social software to facilitate the acceptance of traditional workflow technology by their end users rather than to build a more advanced workflow technology.

According to Stowe Boyd (2006), *Social Software* is software built to provide support for the following: 1) conversational interactions between individuals or groups; 2) social feedback to rate others' contributions; and 3) the creation and management of social networks to handle personal relationships. Visualization techniques that help people both recognize feedback from others and manage complex social networks can provide these different forms of support. Consequently, social software is tightly related to visualization; thus, the visualization of social data (e.g., collected by the social software) for social purposes (e.g., to help managing the network of personal relationships) is called *Social Visualization* (Karahalios & Viégas, 2006).

According to this perspective, we propose to integrate usual workflow technology with a social visualization approach to facilitate actors' interactions. Using the Activity Circle, we seek to integrate social information about distributed viscosity perception when a workflow technology is used. *Distributed viscosity* is a specialization of the concept of *viscosity*, a cognitive construct first described by Green (1990) to explain how a new technology can affect a single user's interactions to complete a single task and whether this technology requires extra effort from users (i.e., the viscosity of the task is increased). Yvonne Rogers (1994) extended this concept in technology to support work within organizations, including workflow technology, to consider the extra effort required by its users to fulfill their organizational goals. Distribution arises when using technology mainly designed to support coordination and collaboration among employees; in fact, authors like Rogers (2004) and Poelmans (1999) based on their user studies, suggested that this technology can benefit some groups of users at the expense of others. Consequently, introducing a workflow technology can raise the perception of differences among groups of users, which might raise intergroup conflicts or dissatisfaction for users feeling disadvantaged by the new technology.

The main aims of the Activity Circle are the following: first, to facilitate defining a common view about workflow technology among members of the same group, which may also facilitate creating a common identity to help members handle problems; second, to make explicit the possible conflicts among different user groups and also to show whether users in different groups have a similar perception of the distributed viscosity raised by the technology; finally, to help management facilitate balancing disparities in different strategies, like rewards, or help them identify the critical points of the workflow technology to formulate more precise requests to designers for making the workflow technology more fair.

This approach is part of a broader research agenda about enhancing workflow technology with social features to improve both its flexibility and the users' acceptance. This would bring to the design of *Workflow Management Social Systems*, i.e., workflow systems emphasizing the social relations among people involved in fulfilling the organization's goal (Sarini, et al., 2010).

The chapter is organized as follows: the background section analyzes different approaches for the integration of social software with workflow technology, particularly emphasizing the recognition of different social visualization techniques used to identify an approach that better suits our requirements. The next section explains the Activity Circle in more detail: it first discusses a series of premises, presents the interfaces, and finally describes the methodology to use the Activity Circle. Future research directions about the presented proposal and a conclusion end the chapter.

BACKGROUND

The literature is full of contributions regarding workflow technology and social software. We identify contributions that enhance the fruitful integration of these two technologies, focusing on social visualization functionalities. Concerning the integration of these two technologies, the literature contains proposals to combine the functionalities of social software, including integrated revision management found in Wikis, with workflow technology. Neumann and Erol have implemented the principles underlying workflow management (including modeling processes and their executions) in a Wiki system (Neumann & Erol, 2009). The peculiarities of a Wiki also allow adding new functionalities to increase the awareness of the presence of other users, thus facilitating collaboration. Based on revision history, enriched Wiki systems can display two kinds of graphs, Activity and Personal Collaboration, that allow all members to know the relationships among users and the performed activities. Activity graphs indicate relations between users (as nodes are labeled with the corresponding user names) involved in different activities for the same artifact: two nodes are then connected if related people worked on the same artifact. The thickness of the line connecting two people depends on the number of their contributions, and each node is numbered to identify the number of activities performed by the considered user on the same workflow instance. Conversely, the Personal Collaboration graph is a personalized graph showing how a user's activities are related to others' on the same artifact. The visualizations thus provide users with information about the degree of interdependence and collaboration as well as common interests, which are indirectly suggested by the activity of the people addressing the same artifact within the same process. In a similar vein, Fuchs-Kittowski and Kohler (2005) focused on integrating wiki-based communities with process-oriented knowledge structures. However, they did not pay attention to visualizing aspects of the related social network. Instead, most other proposals focused on collaborative process descriptions. Dengler et al. (2009) suggested an extension of the Semantic Media Wiki to facilitate sharing values and reconciling different terminologies during process modeling. However, Dengler and colleagues did not focus on visualization aspects. Some approaches emphasized how social networks can be used to promote recommendations in the collaborative design of business processes (Qu, et al., 2008; Koschmider, et al., 2009). Qu et al. (2008) proposed a recommendation engine that computes the closeness among different professionals according to their traces regarding process annotation and creation. However, the authors did not provide specific visualization functionalities to exploit clusterization among similar users. In contrast, Koschminder et al. (2009) focused on visualizing the social network, which was based on the process modeling activities of the involved modelers. Two different typologies of social networks were visualized: social networks derived from either process models or from recommendations. In the former case, the network and related graph visualizations were generated by considering which users had been selected as performers of a certain activity in a process model. In the latter case, the graph related users who chose the same process fragment during the modeling phase. The proposed graph visualizations of the generated social networks can provide indirect suggestions about the similarity of people's behaviors during the modeling phase.

The above proposals still emphasize the graph-based aspect of social visualization techniques, i.e., the "shape of the social network," using nodes and arcs to represent social information about workers engaged in some relation with others. Both nodes and arcs are weighted to represent, respectively,

the strength of the involvement of a worker or the strength of the relation between two connected workers. This visualization thus provides a snapshot of a particular situation at a given time. This method makes it difficult for workers to interpret the information within a broader context, such as having indications of users' patterns of behavior in a particular situation.

An alternative to this approach to social visualization is a *Social Proxy* approach. According to Erikson (2008), a "Social proxy is a minimalist graphical representation that portrays socially salient aspects of an online interaction." This approach considers sharing visualizations of people and their activities. While graph-based visualization approaches emphasize the relationships among individuals in a more static manner, social proxy approaches do not focus on the identity of the interacting people. Instead, they dynamically identify behavioral trends and patterns during people's interactions. A social proxy visualization of a situation also represents trends in whether social norms are respected or rejected, and it can promote forms of mutual influence in users' behaviors.

The social proxy approach, making closeness/distance explicit among proxies in which either closeness or distance correlate to users' behaviors, helps interpret how other people behave in certain situations. It thus promotes the awareness of others' behaviors, which, in turn, can influence the way each person behaves in similar contexts.

To our knowledge, a social proxy approach to social visualization has been rarely integrated into workflow technology. However, we prefer this approach to the graph-based approach because it is more suited to our goals, i.e., to keep users aware of dynamic behavior patterns concerning the daily use of a workflow system during the accomplishment of the related work activities.

THE ACTIVITY CIRCLE: A PROPOSAL

Premises

Our proposal is based on the premise that workflow technology affects the commonly used practitioners' work practices. This influence happens, for instance, when management uses workflow technology as an *organizational accounting device*, i.e., as a tool for making the work activities of an organization observable-and-reportable (Dourish, 2001). In this situation, the management uses workflow technology as a tool for exerting a formal mode of control (Kirsch, 1997) on end users to guarantee the achievement of a certain standard of work. To this aim, workflow technology provides end users with a process representation, a set of formal mandatory rules with which they must comply.

The present proposal enriches another proposal in which the author (Sarini, 2010) considered a simplified situation in which only two groups were involved in the introduction of a workflow technology: the management that governed the introduction of the workflow technology and the end users who had to accept and use it. Accordingly, Sarini hypothesized that conflicts might occur between members of the two groups, especially when the rules incorporated in the process representation affected the end users' consolidated ways of accomplishing their work. We considered here workflow technology in a richer way. Workflow technology provides different functionalities to different end users according to the roles they play in the organization, and there are more than only two groups. In this way, we consider *Distributed Viscosity* as a concept that accounts for different groups (hereafter, a group is an aggregation of end users playing the same role in the organization) having different benefits from the introduction of a new workflow technology. Because the distributed viscosity can be perceived but is difficult to measure objectively,

we defined a new construct, *Perceived Distributed Viscosity (PDV)*, as a subjective measure made by each user on a 7-point Likert scale to indicate how much she considers the introduction of the workflow technology to affect the strength of the distributed viscosity. The Activity Circle aims to represent the perceived distributed viscosity as social information to workflow technology users. This subjective measure can indicate possible conflicts among different groups according to how much a group perceives that the technology benefits another group at its own expense.

The Activity Circle can promote building a *social identity* (Haslam, 2004) among different users. Achieving a common identity could help reduce conflicts. In the study by Sarini et al. (2010), a social software perspective (the use of a moderated forum) was suggested to promote the creation and perception of a common identity among end users to facilitate acceptance of the technology and to let end users more strongly express their opinions about the technology to the management. This chapter extends that previous work by considering a further specialization of a social software approach that relies on the capability of social visualization to facilitate social information sharing, which contributes to creating a social identity among different users. The focus is on a proxy-based social visualization approach, i.e., defining proxies displayed as dots in the Activity Circle that represent the different human actors' opinions about the technology.

The information displayed by a dot corresponding to the particular opinion associated to a human agent can differ according to which kind of influence the designers intend to promote with the Activity Circle. In Sarini (2010), the social proxy-based visualization mechanism was explicitly designed to report the end users' intentions of breaking the rules relating to the current activity they had to accomplish, i.e., how much the end users intended (at least in principle) to not follow the work organization imposed by the related workflow technology. In that proposal, each dot in the Activity Circle represented the related user's position on how much the rules imposed by the technology affected her working behavior.

Here, the information displayed is different: each dot in the Activity Circle represents the related user's perception about distributed viscosity concerning how the workflow technology affects her working behavior. The closer a dot is to the center of the circle, the more the user perceives an increment of distributed viscosity, and, conversely, the farther the dot is from the center of the circle, the less the user perceives an increment of distributed viscosity.

The Activity Circle thus acts as a social-proxy visualization interface that displays members' perceptions of distributed viscosity. Our social proxy visualization makes clear to all users whether the perceived increase or decrease of distributed viscosity reflects only an isolated member or an overall group. The social visualization of this information can also reinforce the perception of a common identity among different users in the same group. Moreover, the information displayed by the Activity Circle can help compare the distributed viscosity perception among different groups and make users aware if the disparity in support provided by the workflow technology is too evident. The Activity Circle also provides managers with hints about critical workflow technology aspects in managing the related business process.

The Interfaces

The proposal is mainly based on two interfaces: The *Workflow Evaluation interface* (Figure 1 presents a mock-up) and the *Activity Circle interface* (Figures 2, 3, and 4 show the mock-ups related to different presentation views). The first interface allows a workflow technology user to evaluate how much she perceives that the perceived distributed viscosity has changed due to the introduction of the workflow technology. A user can express, in that particular workflow instance and for that specific activity, the related value for the perceived

distributed viscosity: 0 if she perceives that the workflow technology did not heavily change her practices for completing related work activities; +1, or +2, or +3 to express a low, medium, or high increase, respectively, in distributed viscosity due to the introduction of the workflow technology; and -1, -2, or -3 to express low, medium, or high decreases, respectively. A positive ranking means that, for the user, the workflow technology had a negative impact on accomplishing her work; in this case, technology required extra effort to accomplish the user's related work activity. Conversely, a negative value expresses a positive effect of the technology on facilitating the accomplishment of the user's activities.

The Workflow Evaluation interface displays a process view, describing the current process representation. The process model that represents a process took inspiration from common basic constructs, usually considered when representing a business process (as in BPMN notation [White & Miers, 2008]). We considered a *Process* to contain a set of *Activities*, which can be executed sequentially or in parallel. To emphasize the social aspects of a workflow technology, we also considered constructs inspired by Ariadne (Schmidt & Simone, 1996), a flexible and malleable notation designed to smoothly describe articulation work. Articulation work is the extra work people must perform to coordinate themselves when accomplishing interdependent activities. In this way, each *Activity* is associated to a *Role* responsible for its completion, where, during process execution, a Role can be assumed by an *Actor*, i.e., by a human actor using the system to complete an *Instance* of a *Process*. Consequently, the process view in the interface (Figure 1, top-left) displays this information about a process instance. Moreover, the interface allows the Actor under consideration to express the Perceived Distributed Viscosity related to an Activity only if the Role she is playing is responsible for accomplishing that Activity; otherwise, the Activities in the process view are grayed for the Actor, and the

Figure 1. The workflow evaluation interface

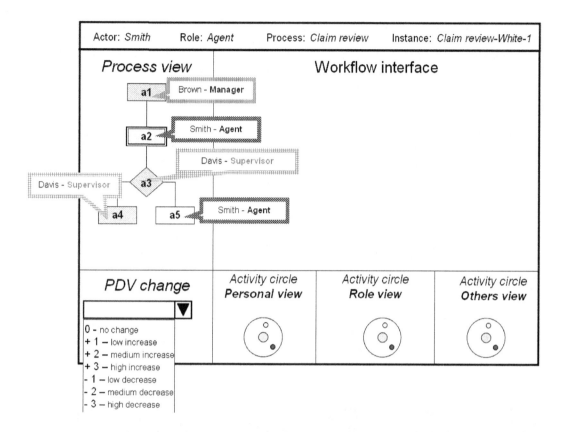

Figure 2. The activity circle interface: the personal view

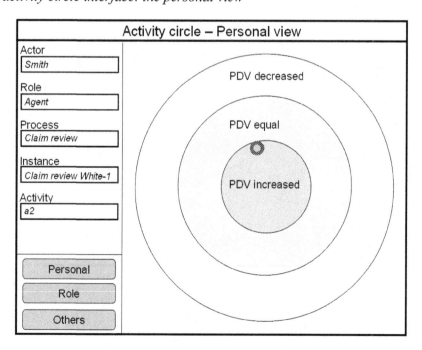

Figure 3. The activity circle interface: The role view

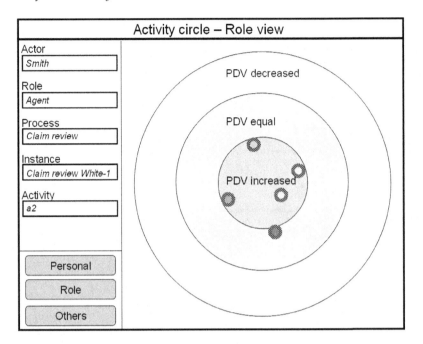

Figure 4. The activity circle interface: the others view

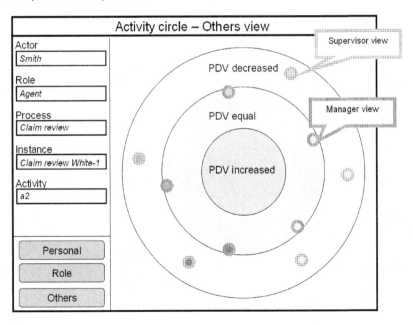

related drop down lists for describing perceived distributed viscosity change are disabled.

We intend to implement the Activity Circle without affecting the logic of the existing workflow technology. More simply, we want to provide users with the opportunity to contextually express the value related to the perceived distributed viscosity for the activity scheduled by the workflow technology. The Activity Circle interface provides the users with the generated social proxy representation accordingly. The Workflow Evaluation interface thus reflects the basic building blocks for a workflow technology and could serve as a wrapper for the interface of an existing workflow technology by adding the evaluation functionalities to it.

Three different modalities are considered for the Activity Circle interface: the *Personal, Role,* and *Others views.* For each view, the background where dots are drawn intuitively reflects the concept of viscosity of a liquid medium: the less viscous a medium, the more a mass can easily cross it, and conversely, the more viscous a medium, the less a mass (with the same initial force) can traverse it. The inner background circle hosts dots with high-perceived distributed viscosity values; in the background medium circle, dots represent users who perceived no change before and after the introduction of the workflow technology; the outer background circle hosts dots traversing a low viscosity medium, and these dots are associated to users with low distributed viscosity perceptions.

The *Personal view* reflects the Actor currently requesting the Activity Circle visualization. In this case, the interface shows the related user's dot describing how the user perceives distributed viscosity for the considered Activity. The dot's position is calculated using the same Activity for all Instances of the related Process that involved the Actor.

The second modality, the *Role view,* concerns the perceived distributed viscosity as ranked by all Actors playing the Role of the requester, accounting for the same Activity for all Instances of the

same Process. More formally, we define the PDV for a Role R_j responsible for an Activity Ac_i as a set of values related to the different Actors playing that Role in completing the Activity as follows:

$$PDV(Ac_i, R_j) = \bigcup_{k=1,..,n} PDV(IoAc_i, A_k)$$

where *PDV(IoAc$_i$, A$_k$)* specifies PDV value given by a single Actor A_k who assumed Role R_j in completing an instance of Activity Ac_i (i.e., *IoAc$_i$*)

Consequently, the number of dots displayed equals the total numbers of Actors who played that Role at the time of the request. To help each user interpret the social information displayed in the Role view, the center of each dot is displayed with a different hue of the Role's main color (a different hue for each Actor), while the border of the dot has the main Role's color to recall which Role is associated with this social information.

The third modality, the *Others view,* displays information about the perceived viscosity distribution, making a group's user aware of how other groups perceive the distributed viscosity related to an Activity she must perform. This view relates most to the distributed aspect of viscosity, in that the viscosity perceived by a group (all Actors playing the same Role) for an Activity is somehow related to the viscosity perceived by other groups about other Activities. For building the Others view, first identifying the other groups and Activities to be considered is required. To this aim, we made two assumptions. The first assumption, the *distributed* nature of viscosity, is inspired by literature related to distributed viscosity (Rogers, 2004; Poelmans, 1999) and determines how to indirectly calculate perceived distributed viscosity values. Using a workflow technology helps some groups accomplish their work, but this often happens at the expense of other groups. To build this view, we estimated the perceived distributed viscosity of a Role not responsible for completing the Activity in question by considering the PDV of that Role in an Interdependent Activity for which the Role is responsible, but that value of PDV negated in sign. This last operation considers the characteristic distributed nature of the viscosity.

The second assumption, the *locality* assumption, concerns identifying Roles in the Others view that are mutually affected by the ranking of one Role. We assumed that the propagation of distributed viscosity, and hence of the effects of a change in perceived distributed viscosity perception, was limited in space. Consequently, we decided to fix its propagation to only one step away from the Activity in question, investigating the value of perceived distributed viscosity only for the Roles responsible for the Activities occurring just before and after the considered Activity. This assumption is a sort of "locality principle" (Denning, 2005) applied to business processes to easily limit the range for searching for interdependent Activities. In this view, we consider only the Activities immediately preceding and following the reference one in the process model as interdependent.

Assuming the locality principle narrows the process context because an Activity's context is simply considered by its proximity and not by which Activities are interdependent in a process model. However, the latter definition of the Activity context requires a deeper modeling effort for both managers and end users, and we thus omit it at this stage of our proposal. More formally, we define the set of Interdependent Activities *IA* about a specific Activity Ac_i as follows:

$$IA(Ac_i) = P(Ac_i) \bigcup F(Ac_i)$$

where $P(Ac_i)$ is the set of Activities preceding Ac_i in the model and $F(Ac_i)$ is the set of Activities following Ac_i. In the future, replacing the definition of *IA(Ac_i)* with other more fine-tuned definitions according to the possibility of modeling the process in a richer and more complex way will be possible.

We define *other Roles* for an Activity Ac_i as the set encompassing all Roles responsible for an Activity which is interdependent with Ac_i in such a way:

other Roles (Ac_i) = {R_j s.t. R_j is responsible for Ac_k where Ac_k belongs to IA(Ac_i)}

After defining the *other Roles* set, the average perceived distributed viscosity value for the Activity that is interdependent with the reference Activity and for which that Role is responsible is calculated for each Role in that set. More formally, we define the value ADPV(Ac_p, R_j) as the average of PDV values as expressed by different Actors A_k playing Role R_j in completing Activity Ac_p as follows:

$$ADPV(Ac_p, R_j) = \left(\sum_{k=1,..,n} PDV(IoAc_p, A_k) \right) / n$$

This value, changed in sign, evaluates how the other Roles indicated in the set perceive the distributed viscosity for the group of the requesting Actor for the Activity the Actor has currently selected. The estimation of perceived viscosity for an Activity Ac_i with respect to *other Roles*, is the set *EPDV(Ac_i, other Roles)*:

$$EPDV(Ac_i, otherRoles) = \bigcup_{k=1,..,n} -APDV(Ac_k, R_p)$$

where each *APDV(Ac_k, R_p)* refers to the average value of PDV related to the kth Activity Ac_k under the responsibility of a Role R_p, where R_p belongs to *other Roles* and Ac_k belongs to *IA(Ac_i)*.

This is an approximation to gather the PDVs from the point of view of the Roles that are not responsible for the activity in question but for related interdependent activities; however, we consider this to be the most reasonable way to calculate PDV because this way considers users' difficulties in evaluating the perceived viscosity for an Activity they do not directly perform as well as both the locality and distributed nature of viscosity assumptions to calculate this value of perceived distributed viscosity.

The Others view displays a number of dots equal to the number of Actors playing the same Role of the requester for each Role in the set *otherRoles*, and the values encompassed by EPDV determine each dot position. Because another group provides the value of the perceived distributed viscosity used, the Other view displays the centers of the dots with their original colors, but the borders have the main color of the Role whose perceived distributed viscosity value was used.

Consider the process displayed in Figure 1 as an example of an automobile claim process. Different roles are involved in that process: Agents, who usually follow the normal process flow, Managers, who start the process, and Supervisors, who are involved when the claim requires additional verification. In Figure 1, a_1 represents the starting of the claim process, in which a Manager assigns the case to a specific Agent. The Agent must complete a preliminary analysis concerning the estimation of the claim costs (a_2); the involved Supervisor evaluates the agent's analysis (a_3) and, according to the costs, the claim is then assigned to an Agent (a_5) or a Supervisor (a_4). Let us consider the PDV about activity a_2. Figure 3 displays a situation in which five Agents, responsible for that Activity in other instances of the same process, are perceived with almost identical perceived viscosity increments; a_2, in the process defined after introducing workflow technology, required extra effort from Agents because the Managers' duties previously held part of this activity, but during process design, the management freed Managers from this work to let them concentrate more on interactions with policy holders.

Figure 4 displays the Other view, reflecting how both Supervisor and Manager Roles perceive the distributed viscosity of Activity a_2 for which they are not responsible. The viscosity is calculated for the Manager Role accounting for

the perceived viscosity of all Actors playing that Role in Activity a_1, which is interdependent with a_2. This Activity precedes a_2 in the process shown in the Process view of Figure 1. The Managers' PDV for a_2 is unchanged, which is estimated by considering that the PDV for a_1 for Managers is the same, probably because introducing the workflow technology relieved part of their work related to claim analysis, but the management requested increased client involvement. For Managers, the technology brought both a clear advantage and a disadvantage. Estimating the PDV for a_2 from the Supervisors' perspective uses PDV values from the Actors playing the Supervisor Role in Activity a_3; we considered a_3 because it is interdependent with a_2, following it in the process. Figure 4 shows that the PDV for a_2 is lower. Actors playing the Supervisor Role when completing Activity a_3 perceived an increment of viscosity. The process supported by workflow technology was designed in such a way that Supervisors became responsible for a_3, while Managers previously performed cost evaluations and identified which branch of the process the claim had to follow. Because the Supervisors had problems with claim assignments performed by Managers in many cases and because Managers who did not thoroughly consider claim documentation caused these problems, the management decided to handle this issue by entrusting this activity to Supervisors.

Comparing Figures 3 and 4 reveals that, while PDV has not changed for Managers, PDV followed a different trend for Agents and Supervisors. The perceived distributed viscosity increased in Agents for Activity a_2 and Supervisors for a_3. In this case, the Activity Circle makes users aware that there is no consensus among groups about the effects due to introducing the workflow technology. This then can raise some alerts to further investigate the way workflow technology affects the accomplishment of activities, as, in this particular case, concerns the blocks related to Activities a_2 and a_3.

Methodology

Defining a methodology to justify using the Activity Circle requires specifying two related aspects: 1) defining metrics and 2) defining a protocol to apply these metrics to discover, in this specific case, whether the Activity Circle approach is effective, i.e., if people exposed to the social influence conveyed by the Activity Circle have a better attitude towards the Workflow Technology. For the metrics, identifying what to measure, when it is relevant to measure and how to measure are all required. This approach relies on the tradition of behavioral investigation related to the acceptance and use of a technology. Literature about technology acceptance considers the definition of theoretical models based on a set of constructs that can reliably anticipate future behaviors. In particular, literature specifies, on the one hand, more general behavioral models, (e.g., the Theory of Reasoned Action [TRA] [Ajzen & Fishbein, 1980] and the Theory of Planned Behavior [TPB] [Ajzen, 1985]), which are then interpreted considering the more specific behaviors of technology acceptance and use; on the other hand, specific models, including the Technology Acceptance Model (TAM) (Davis, 1986) and its extensions, e.g., the Unified Theory of Acceptance and Use of Technology (UTAUT) (Venkatesh, et al., 2003), are designed to evaluate technology acceptance.

The Theory of Reasoned Actions specifies that the intention to perform a behavior is a predictor of a person's actual behavior, and this intention could be determined by both considering a person's attitude towards the behavior and the subjective norm associated with that behavior, where the subjective norm refers to the extent of social desirability in performing the considered behavior. TPB is an extension of the Theory of Reasoned Action that adds the Perceived Behavioral Control (PCB) construct, which involves the perception of controlling the performance of a given behavior.

In the TAM model, Davis (1986) replaced the concept of generic behaviors with the actual use of a system, and the model states that adopting a system can be predicted by considering the attitude towards system use. This attitude relates to the beliefs of both the system's perceived usefulness and the perceived ease of use. Perceived usefulness is users' perception of whether the technology will help them perform their job better. Perceived ease of use concerns the users' belief regarding the effort required to use the technology. UTUAT (Venkatesh, et al., 2003) extends TAM and unifies eight different models from user acceptance literature. We paid particular attention to the case of introducing a workflow technology in which its use is not voluntary, but mandatory. We defined a specific model, the *Workflow Technology Acceptance Model* (W-TAM), to identify how users perceive workflow technology introduction, accounting for all peculiarities of this technology: 1) its use is mandatory and not voluntary, while most technology acceptance studies refer to voluntary technology use; 2) the technology affects the usual people's work practices, and we are particularly interested in the phase related to introducing a new workflow technology in which consolidated work practices may be disrupted, as when paper-based processes are replaced by digital ones; 3) the workflow technology, as any technology, may introduce some rigidity in accomplishing work activities, and we are more interested in handling this issue by considering a more human-oriented approach than technical, where this last case seeks to design and implement more flexible workflow technology (e.g., dynamically reconfiguring work flow according to the situation [Reijers & Poelmans, 2007]). For these reasons, the W-TAM focuses on attitude and its possible antecedents, particularly on Perceived Distributed Viscosity, because scholars (e.g., Brown, et al., 2002) have identified that in mandatory settings, attitude is more important than intention. W-TAM considers other constructs associated to attitude, including resistance to change (Juntumaa, 2010), i.e., how people tend to resist to the introduction of a new technology at work (though the technology is perceived as useful) because its use requires additional effort, and habits (Wood, et al., 2002), referring here to working behaviors that an individual considers habitual and that could represent barriers to change (in this case, barriers to introducing new workflow technology). Contrasting other approaches, including the BPM success model presented in Poelmans and Reijers (2009), we focus on socio-psychological variables related to end-users instead of variables related to defining the success of Information Systems. Approaches such as the BPM success model are more suitable for evaluating a system already in use because they focus on factors associated to the system use, including the capability to provide the right information at the right time or the ability to dynamically modify the routing of documents. Instead, we are more interested in evaluating the opinions and attitudes of potential users about the possible introduction of a workflow technology, providing management with a tool to evaluate the returns of investments about introducing this kind of technology in their organization.

To define a protocol to evaluate the effectiveness of the Activity Circle, we follow the general line used to investigate the effects of social influence and conformity behaviors as described by Asch (1955). We consider work settings as "social" places where phenomena like social influence, conformisms and social identity play important roles.

In Asch's paradigm, subjects were first asked to give their opinions regarding an issue. The subjects were later asked to again state their choices, but they were also informed of the opinions held by a group of peers. The paradigm examined how many subjects changed their opinions and to what extent. The greater the changes (in both the number of subjects and extent of the change), the more the opinion of the group members influenced the subjects. Asch first investigated the influence of the majority on small groups with co-located people (Asch, 1951).

Crutchfield (Krech, et al., 1962) repeated Asch's experiments, but with an apparently insignificant difference: the subjects were not co-located. Instead, each subject was isolated in cubicles where the opinions of the others were displayed in abstractly on a screen; the subjects were thus indirectly influenced by the opinions of the others. Because this experiment again revealed the power of peer influence, our use of the Activity Circle approach is thus justified. Our approach is experienced by users in a communication technology mediating the sense of presence among people, and the effectiveness measure of our approach relies on social psychology findings regarding conformity and the influence of the majority.

In our case, subjects will be asked to express their judgment about constructs related to W-TAM in a questionnaire and will be asked to rate the PDVs for the Activities by using the Workflow Evaluation interface. The questionnaire accounts for the most common items in the studies related to technology acceptance; some items are also considered from scales related to habit measures (Verplanken & Orbell, 2003) and resistance to change (Oreg, 2003). Finally, we specifically designed some items to evaluate the nature of work within the considered organization, including items used to investigate the satisfaction of subjects about how they are currently accomplishing their work as well as items to measure the degree of coordination among workers.

Based on the data collected, we will perform a statistical analysis to evaluate which constructs are the most reliable anticipators of users' acceptance behaviors, which represent valid causal relations among constructs and which are the relations of W-TAM constructs with PDV values. In particular, in accordance with Information System research, we base this analysis on Partial Least Square (PLS) approaches (Barclay, et al., 1995), which are more suitable than other standard Structural Equation Model techniques because of their flexibility and their ability to deal with smaller sample sizes and complex models.

After analyzing the first phase of the experiment, not considering the influence of the Activity Circle, the subjects will be randomly assigned to two different groups to make the groups as homogeneous as possible: in the first group subjects will be presented with Workflow Evaluation interface and the related Activity Circle interface, while the subjects in the control group will not be shown the Activity Circle but only the Workflow Evaluation interface. The same questionnaire will be reissued and analyzed to verify whether subjects in the Activity Circle group show significantly different results than subjects in the control group. An improvement on factors related to workflow technology acceptance in the Activity Circle group will support our approach's effectiveness in facilitating Workflow Technology acceptance.

FUTURE RESEARCH DIRECTIONS

Future research will investigate theoretical and technological aspects related to using the Activity Circle. For the theoretical aspects, we must investigate the measures in which our approach could help limit conflicts among user groups and allow users to promote a positive attitude towards workflow technology. To this aim, we must implement studies in real organizations to verify the protocol for measuring the effectiveness of our approach and to gather evidence about how effective the Activity Circle is in helping different end users share and interpret the perceived distributed viscosity about workflow technology. This implies a further validation of the proposed *Workflow Technology Acceptance Model* to evaluate whether other constructs could be relevant to define metrics to measure the effectiveness of the Activity Circle. In addition to phenomena like social influence, we are also interested in studying phenomena that require more time to emerge, including social identity. In fact, people working together

over time could start to perceive themselves as part of a group and build a social identity. In this case, the group establishes a set of social norms, and people tend to conform to them to avoid the so called Black Sheep Effect (Marques & Paez, 1994), i.e., the tendency of ingroup members to treat or evaluate a deviant member of their own group more harshly than an outgroup member for a similar behavior. Moreover, an investigation in real organizations could open new scenarios for studying whether social psychology findings, such as active minority influence (Moscovici, 1976), still hold in organizational settings when people's interactions in completing work activities are mediated by a given technology.

In the technological aspects, researchers are implementing a prototype, based on the previous experience in prototyping the Activity Circle (Sarini, 2010). In this case, the prototype is implemented using Flash Action Script 3 (AS3). ActionScript (Adobe Systems) is a scripting language primarily used for website development. The language is open-source, and both an open source compiler and virtual machine are available. In the prototype, the aforementioned interfaces are being implemented with the mechanisms required to facilitate data exchange between then. AS3 was chosen to make the prototype available from the Internet with the intention of widening its possible use, especially during experimental studies.

CONCLUSION

In this chapter, we proposed the Activity Circle, a social proxy visual approach to help share perceived distributed viscosity information, i.e., how users perceive the accomplishment of work activities is affected when regulated by a workflow management technology. In this vein, the Activity Circle aims to allow users in organizations to self-monitor their behaviors and thus implement informal control modes (Kirsch, 1997), i.e., local attempts by workers to informally regulate their behavior to reach the organization's goals. These informal control modes can then be added to formal control modes exerted by workflow technology to enrich its capability to support accomplishing work activities. This approach also helps people make each other aware of their behaviors and fosters creating a common identity among people playing the same role while facilitating the reconciliation of possible conflicts, such as if users perceive that the workflow technology favor some groups at the expense of others. Our visual approach also helps an organization's management better understand the effects of introducing new technologies and facilitates introducing strategies to reduce disparities perceived by groups of users. Our approach could be especially useful in cases where introducing a workflow technology may likely disrupt consolidated work practices, as when digital processes replace paper-based ones.

REFERENCES

Abbott, K. R., & Sarin, S. K. (1994). Experiences with workflow management: Issues for the next generation. In *Proceedings of Conference on Computer Supported Cooperative Work,* (pp. 113-120). Chapel Hill, NC: ACM Press.

Ajzen, I. (1985). Action control: From cognition to behavior. In *From Intentions to Actions: A Theory of Planned Behavior* (pp. 11–39). Berlin, Germany: Springer-Verlag.

Ajzen, I., & Fishbein, M. (1980). *Understanding attitudes and predicting social behavior*. Upper Saddle River, NJ: Prentice-Hall.

Asch, S. E. (1951). Groups, leadership and men. In *Chapter Effects of Group Pressure upon the Modification and Distortion of Judgment*. Pittsburgh, PA: Carnegie Press.

Asch, S. E. (1955). Opinions and social pressure. *Scientific American, 193*, 31–35. doi:10.1038/scientificamerican1155-31

Barclay, D., Thompson, R., & Higgins, C. (1995). The panial least squares (PLS) approach to causal modeling: Personal computer adoption and use as an illustration. *Technology Studies, 22*, 285–309.

Boyd, S. (2006). Are you ready for social software? Retrieved January, 2011, from http://www.stoweboyd.com/post/2325281845/are-you-ready-for-social-software.

Brown, J. S., & Duguid, P. (2000). *The social life of information*. Boston, MA: Harvard Business School Press.

Brown, S. A., Massey, A. P., Montoya-Weiss, M. M., & Burkman, J. R. (2002). Do I really have to? User acceptance of mandated technology. *European Journal of Information Systems, 11*, 283–295. doi:10.1057/palgrave.ejis.3000438

Davis, F. (1986). *A technology acceptance model for empirically testing new end-user information systems: Theory and results*. Ph.D. Dissertation. Cambridge, MA: MIT Press.

Dengler, F., Lamparter, S., Hefke, M., & Abecker, A. (2009). Collaborative process development using semantic mediawiki. *Wissensmanagement, 145*(1), 97–107.

Denning, P. J. (2005). The locality principle. *Communications of the ACM, 48*(7), 19–24. doi:10.1145/1070838.1070856

Dourish, P. (2001). Process description as organisational accounting devices: The dual use of workflow technologies. In *Proceedings of Conference on Supporting Group Work (GROUP 2001),* (pp. 52–60.). New York, NY: ACM Press.

Erickson, T. (2008). Social systems: Designing digital systems that support social intelligence. *AI & Society, 23*(2), 147–166. doi:10.1007/s00146-007-0140-3

Erol, S., Granitzer, M., Happ, S., Jantunen, S., Jennings, B., & Johannesson, P. (2009). Combining BPM and social software: Contradiction or chance? *Journal of Software Maintenance and Evolution: Research and Practice, 22*(6-7), 449–476. doi:10.1002/smr.460

Freeman, L. (2000). Visualizing social networks. *Journal of Social Structure, 1*(1).

Fuchs-Kittowski, F., & Köhler, A. (2005). Wiki communities in the context of work processes. In *Proceedings of the 2005 International Symposium on Wikis (WikiSym 2005),* (pp. 33–39). New York, NY: ACM Press.

Gerson, E. M., & Star, S. L. (1986). Analyzing the due process in the workplace. *ACM Transactions on Office Information Systems, 4*(3), 447–465. doi:10.1145/214427.214431

Green, T. R. G. (1990). The cognitive dimension of viscosity: A sticky problem for HCI. In *Proceedings of the IFIP TC13 Third Interational Conference on Human-Computer Interaction (INTERACT 1990),* (pp. 79-86). Amsterdam, The Netherlands: North-Holland Publishing Co.

Haslam, S. A. (2004). *Psychology in organizations: The social identity approach.* Thousand Oaks, CA: SAGE Publications.

Juntumaa, M. (2010). Why consumers resist applications perceived useful? Case e-invoicing. In *Proceedings of IADIS International Conference ICT, Society and Human Beings.* IADIS.

Karahalios, K. G., & Viégas, F. B. (2006). Social visualization: Exploring text, audio, and video interaction. In *Proceedings of Extended Abstracts on Human Factors in Computing Systems (CHI 2006),* (pp. 1667–1670). New York, NY: ACM Press.

Kirsch, L. S. (1997). Portfolios of control modes and IS project management. *Information Systems Research, 8*(3), 215–239. doi:10.1287/isre.8.3.215

Koschmider, A., Song, M., & Reijers, H. A. (2009). Social software for modeling business processes. In *Lecture Notes in Business Information Processing* (*Vol. 17,* pp. 666–677). Berlin, Germany: Springer.

Krech, D., Crutchfield, R., & Ballachey, E. (1962). *Individual in society: A textbook of social psychology.* New York, NY: McGraw-Hill.

Marques, J. M., & Paez, D. (1994). The "black sheep effect": Social categorization, rejection of ingroup deviates, and perception of group variability. *European Review of Social Psychology, 5,* 3768. doi:10.1080/14792779543000011

Moscovici, S. (1976). *Social influence and social change.* London, UK: Academic Press.

Neumann, G., & Erol, S. (2009). From a social wiki to a social workflow system. In *Lecture Notes in Business Information Processing* (*Vol. 17,* pp. 698–708). Berlin, Germany: Springer. doi:10.1007/978-3-642-00328-8_70

Oreg, S. (2003). Resistance to change: Developing an individual differences measure. *The Journal of Applied Psychology, 88*(4), 680–693. doi:10.1037/0021-9010.88.4.680

Poelmans, S. (1999). Workarounds and distributed viscosity in a workflow system: A case study. *SIGGROUP Bullettin, 20*(3), 11–12.

Poelmans, S., & Reijers, H. A. (2009). Assessing workflow management systems a quantitative analysis of a workflow evaluation model. In *Proceedings International Conference on Enterprise Information Systems (ICEIS 2009).* ICEIS.

Qu, H., Sun, J., & Jamjoom, H. T. (2008). SCOOP: Automated social recommendation in enterprise process management. In *Proceedings of Services Computing (SCC 2008),* (pp. 101-108). IEEE Press.

Reijers, H. A., & Poelmans, S. (2007). Re-config-uring workflow management systems to facilitate a smooth flow of work. *International Journal of Cooperative Information Systems, 16*(2), 155–175. doi:10.1142/S0218843007001615

Rogers, Y. (1994). Exploring obstacles: Integrating CSCW in evolving organisations. In *Proceedings of Conference on Computer Supported Coopera-tive Work (CSCW 1994),* (pp. 67-77). New York, NY: ACM Press.

Sarini, M. (2010). The activity circle: Build-ing a bridge between workflow technology and social software. In *Proceedings of Advances in Human-Oriented and Personalized Mechanisms, Technologies and Services (CENTRIC)* (pp. 22–27). Nice, France: IEEE Press. doi:10.1109/CENTRIC.2010.18

Sarini, M., Durante, F., & Gabbiadini, A. (2010). Workflow management social systems: A new socio-psychological perspective on process management. In *Lecture Notes in Business In-formation Processing* (*Vol. 43*, pp. 231–242). Berlin, Germany: Springer. doi:10.1007/978-3-642-12186-9_22

Schmidt, K., & Bannon, L. J. (1992). Taking CSCW seriously: Supporting articulation work. *Computer Supported Cooperative Work, 1*(1–2), 7–40. doi:10.1007/BF00752449

Schmidt, K., & Simone, C. (1996). Coordination mechanisms: Towards a conceptual foundation of CSCW systems design. *Computer Supported Cooperative Work, 5*(2-3), 155–200. doi:10.1007/BF00133655

Suchman, L. A. (1987). *Plans and situated actions: The problem of human-machine communication.* Cambridge, UK: Cambridge University Press.

Venkatesh, V., Morris, M., Davis, G., & Davis, F. (2003). User acceptance of information tech-nology: Toward a unified view. *Management Information Systems Quarterly, 27*(3), 425–478.

Verplanken, B., & Orbell, S. (2003). Reflections on past behavior: A self-report index of habit strength. *Journal of Applied Social Psychology, 33,* 1313–1330. doi:10.1111/j.1559-1816.2003.tb01951.x

White, S. A., & Miers, D. (2008). *BPMN modeling and reference guide: Understanding and using BPMN.* New York, NY: Future Strategies Inc.

Wood, W., Quinn, J., & Kashy, D. (2002). Habits in everyday life: Thought, emotion, and action. *Jour-nal of Personality and Social Psychology, 83*(6), 1281–1297. doi:10.1037/0022-3514.83.6.1281

Section 4
Interface Design, User Profile Design, and System Evaluation Models

Chapter 13
A Global Process for Model-Driven Approaches in User Interface Design

Sybille Caffiau
University Joseph Fourier – Grenoble, France

Patrick Girard
University of Poitiers, France

ABSTRACT

In user interface design, model-driven approaches usually involve generative solutions, producing interface by successive transformations of a set of initial models. These approaches have obvious limitations, especially for advanced user interfaces. Moreover, top-down design approaches (as generative approaches are) are not appropriate for interactive application development in which users need to be included in the whole design process. Based on strong associations between task models and dialogue models, the authors propose a global process, which facilitates the design of interactive applications conforming to their models, including a rule-checking step. This process permits either to start from a task model or a user-defined prototype. In any case, it allows an iterative development, including iterative user modifications, in line with user-centered design standards.

INTRODUCTION

Since the 70's, application designers and developers have tried to define and to structure the design steps in order to improve application development. Design models were first defined (Winston, 1970).

With the popularization of the use of computerized systems (and then, the proliferation of interactive applications), they looked for integrate users in design modeling. Design models were adapted (such in the V model) and new models were created. For example, the star model (Hix, 1993) proposed a non-sequential design process centered on the evaluation step. This design model introduced

DOI: 10.4018/978-1-4666-1628-8.ch013

iteration and user feedbacks in the interactive application design process.

Design models identified design steps and links between steps, however, they did not define link semantics, and thus, they did not explain how to go to the next step from previous ones. Several works proposed model-based approaches. They developed concrete interface from abstract interface definition by combining and transforming models (Calvary, 2003).

In such model-based approaches, task models stand for the user point of view. Task model express activity as a hierarchical structure, based on the "theory of action" (Norman, 1990), which describes actions as compositions of sub-actions. The task model is often the only entry for user needs and observations. Thus, several research works (Mori, 2004; Luyten, 2003; Wolff, 2009) use a generative approach to build user interfaces—mainly skeletons to be completed—from task models. Following the analysis we made in Caffiau (2007), we can argue that this approach has several limitations.

First, generating requires adding information in order to reach interface operative stage. This information can be added to high-level models, which then loose their original goal; so doing they become hard to understand and to use, because of their multiple semantics. For example, task models use operators that schedule tasks. Associating tasks and interface components (widgets), the interface components included in the interface presentation may be deduced. Nevertheless, when tasks can be concurrently performed, there is no way to infer the position of the interface components. For instance, in a form, the order of text fields (and their associated labels) cannot be inferred from any initial model. The way generative approaches work is to affect a position to the components that depends on the place the corresponding task have in the task tree (i.e. if, in a task tree, a task *entering addressee* is placed left to a task *entering message*, in a mailer form, the text field used to edit the addressee will be placed above the text

field used to edit the message). Then, presentation information is added to task models through the addition of new semantics to this model. The other way is to insert this information during the generating process. This second approach is for example used in TERESA (Berti, 2004) by the way of heuristics, which are applied during the process. This however results in a lack of understanding of such transformations by users.

Second, all considered research issues are concerned with classical WIMP1 applications. The hierarchical structure of task models is used to build the interface navigation scheme. We demonstrated in Caffiau (2007) that introducing non menu-based interactions implies a non-automatic transformation of the application dynamic expression (named dialogue).

Last, generating is not easy to include in iterative design cycles such as HCI-adapted cycles. When changes are required, it is necessary to modify the high-level models, and to generate again a new skeleton, to be improved again by hand-made add-ons. Some results have been obtained around the definition of "round-trip engineering" (Hettel, 2008; Sendall, 2004), but have not been applied to HCI yet. More, these approaches prevent the designers to start from the prototype, which method is often used in post-WIMP design.

Our aim is to introduce a new way to use models in user interface design. Our approach proposes to link some concepts of two models (task model and dialogue model) in order to design and check the application dynamics). Leaning on meta-models of one task model (K-MAD [Lucquiaud, 2005; Baron, 2006]) and one dialogue model (HI [Depaulis, 2002; Depaulis, 2006]), we wrote equivalence rules between such models. Then, we defined a new development cycle that can be used in a user-centered iterative approach.

We present the global approach in the first section. It is based on links existing between concepts of the K-MAD task model and the HI dialogue model, which are relevant for the applica-

Figure 1. The global design process

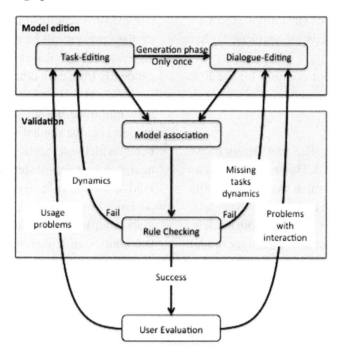

tion behavior. The second section focuses on the meta-model relationships. Models, meta-models and relations, which we identified between some of their concepts, are presented. Prior to conclude, in the third part, equivalence rules are presented. In order to present rules, we use them in an application development scenario based our global design process.

THE GLOBAL PROCESS

As stated in ISO 13407, interactive application design must be an iterative process. However, as we previously claimed, if design processes conform to this need, introducing iteration between steps (user needs collection, global design, functional design, development and evaluation), few works aim at including iteration in each phase and explain how it could be applied. In this section, we describe the model-driven global process we propose to design interactive applications. It is presented in Figure 1 and consists in including

design phases in a dynamic design process. In this work, we consider the design of only two models in the design process: the task and the dialogue models. The task model expresses the user activity and the dialogue model expresses the application dynamics (which manages user actions and system reactions in the interface). Due to their dynamic characteristics, they are implicitly linked (Bomsdorf, 1998). We propose to exploit this link (once formally defined) in our global process. Each iteration starts by model edition.

We consider three edition-starting points according to the existing models:

- *Only task model.* In user-centered design the most usual starting point is user needs collection. User needs can be expressed by several documents among which task model expressing user activity. Usually, other models are designed from it.
- *Only dialogue model.* In order to improve an existing application (adding functionalities or integrating new technology, for

example), designers may use the application dialogue model (in design report or inferred from the existing application) but not the task model.

- *Both models*. Except possibly for the first iteration, during iterative design, both models are edited.

Having both models. The first iteration can start from only one model. However, as soon as the second has been elaborated, the designer starts the design cycle from the edition of both models. Thus, the designer aims at obtaining both models. Beginning the design from only a dialogue model is less frequent than from only a task model. Moreover, designing a task model is a collective task in which people with different skills (such as users or future users, or ergonomic experts) are involved. For these two reasons, we discard the case of a design from the dialogue model only, and we consider the need to design the dialogue model from the task model.

As previously claimed in the introduction (and presented in Caffiau, 2007), generating dialogue models from task models suffers from drawbacks; the most important of them is related to the iterative nature of user-centered approaches. When changes must be made in response to new or enhanced user needs, the generating process must be run again, and all hand-made changes in the interface are lost. We argue that, if a generation phase occurs, it must be restricted to a starting point; then, the process must be able to achieve without any further generation. So, in our approach, a first skeleton for the dialogue model can be derived (e.g. generated, but only once) from the task model. Either kinds of rules, logical rules and semantic rules (see later), can be used to produce this skeleton. Then, the next step consists in adding specific dialogue elements; thus, the dialogue model can be completed.

Once both models exist, phases of joint design can start. For each iteration, the two models can be confronted for detecting inconsistencies.

Model edition. Assuming we are able to design, edit and verify each task and dialogue model, each of these phases will be called "X-editing phase" thereafter. These phases may be performed independently from each other (by using tools or not).

Validation. By editing models, the designer may introduce design inconsistencies between models (i.e: the semantics of one model is incoherent with the semantics of the second one). The next step (validation step) aims at detecting this kind of incoherence. To reach this objective, the designer must associate the two models (model association): dialogue entities might be related to task entities, and coherency rules can be automatically checked (rule checking).

After analysis, depending on the result, different solutions can be applied:

- *Fail. The two models do not match. Some tasks are missing in the dialogue model.* The dialogue model must be improved to take into account the whole task model.
- *Fail. The two models do not match. The dynamics of the two models differ.* The task model and/or the dialogue model must be modified.
- *Success. The two models match.* If the designer considers the design step as finished, the system is ready to be tested by users.

After rule checking, a failure results in redoing both Task and Dialogue Editing Phases. Notice that the designer chooses what he/she wants to validate. For example, if he wishes to validate only a part of an application, he can associate only entities that are relevant for this part.

User evaluation. A user evaluation phase may result in new requirements, which may lead us to coming back to either dialogue or task modeling, and resuming the loop. If problems are detected with usage or interaction during user evaluation, the process must also be repeated starting again from X-Editing Phases.

Edition and User Evaluation are two independent phases. They are manually performed. We propose to use models in order to assist designers during the validation step.

ASSOCIATION OF META-MODEL ENTITIES

The validation step is split into two phases (Figure 1). First, entities of the two models are associated. Second, once entities are associated, rules are automatically checked. Associations and rules were defined from studies on:

- Concepts and structure of models (Caffiau, 2009a; Caffiau 2010)
- Implicit and explicit transformations on generative approaches (Caffiau, 2007)

Two main results of these preliminary studies are (1) hierarchical structure is profitable to jointly design both models and (2) task model concepts that express dynamic implications are scheduling composed tasks (and their common characteristics) and objects. They imply restrictions for model choices. The dialogue model must be hierarchical and task model must support task and object concepts. We chose K-MAD as task model and HI as dialogue model that correspond to these needs.

Prior to present entity associations applied on K-MAD and HI models, we briefly present these models. We illustrate models, associations, and rules (presented in the next section) with the design of a *Currency converter.* In our scenario, in order to design a *Currency converter* (including the HI model), we assume that the designer owns a task model (described below and illustrated in Figure 3) and a first dialogue model (described below and illustrated in Figure 5).

The K-MAD Model

The K-MAD model was developed from literal study of other models and case studies (K-MAD was used to design several applications). The resulting task model is composed of tasks, objects, events, actors and machines.

Tasks are the main element of task models. They are performed to accomplish a specific goal. All other concepts are associated with tasks. *Objects* are handled objects used to perform tasks; they are mainly used to express task conditions and iterations. *Events* are circumstances that are not user-initiated but that influence the course of his/her activity; they trigger tasks or are triggered by tasks. When humans and/or systems perform tasks, *actors* and *machines* may be associated to task execution.

Tasks are composed of sub-tasks, with temporal operators describing a part of the dynamics of the model. Among task characteristics, some are used in order to complete the task dynamic description (such as the *optional* characteristic for example).

In addition to task characteristics, the description can be enhanced by the relationship between tasks and objects. This relation is expressed by preconditions, post-conditions, and actions that control the model dynamics more precisely.

The semantics of these different elements is defined in details and modeled. Figure 2 illustrates a sample of EXPRESS (Dehainsala, 2005) definition of the central element of the model, the task.

Application to our design scenario. Converting currency is performed by two main tasks (Figure 3a). First, the user enters the amount and second, the conversion is triggered specifying in and out currencies. Two types of objects are modeled for this activity: the conversion rate and the amount (Figure 3b). In order to perform the *Converting from $ to €* task, the *€Rate* object is used. Thus, a pre-condition (in green in Figure 3a) to the task execution is that this value does not equal zero. A similar pre-condition is expressed for the *Converting from € to $* task (with the *$Rate* object).

Figure 3. The K-MAD model of a €/$ convertor: a) task tree and b) objects

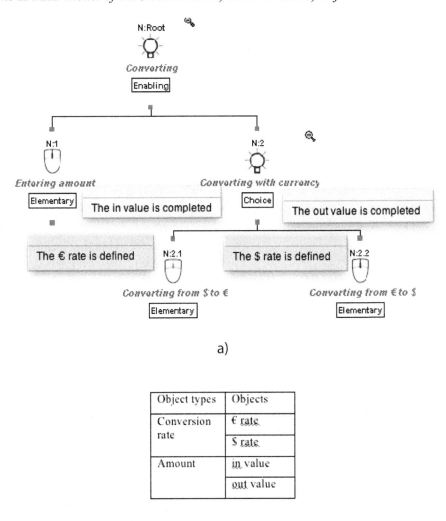

a)

Object types	Objects
Conversion rate	€ rate
	$ rate
Amount	in value
	out value

b)

In addition to the pre-conditions, two post-conditions (in yellow in Figure 3a) are expressed on the task model for the tasks *Entering amount* and *Converting with currency*. Resulting from the execution of these two tasks, the amount values are completed (the *in value* object for the *Entering amount* task and the *out value* object for the *Converting with currency* task).

Last, all tasks are performed in one machine (on which the converter runs).

The HI (Hierarchical Interactors) Model

The HI model consists in a *state machine* model where the dialogue of the application is split into independent *automata*. *Transitions* are activated by tokens that represent user inputs or automaton productions.

The hierarchical organization of the model allows automata to produce and consume *tokens*. The main advantages of this system are two-fold:

Figure 5. a) A currency converter mock-up and b) its HI model

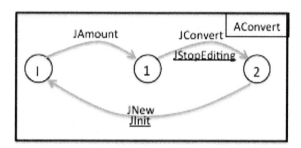

a)

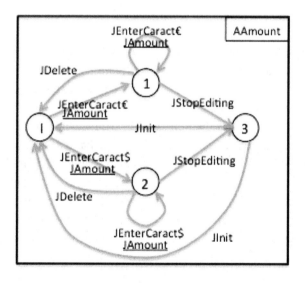

b)

- Automata are independent from each other. They can be removed or added independently, without any change to others.
- Tokens are the key element of the model. As they can refer to both user entries and

automaton productions, they break the binding between user inputs and transitions. This allows to consider the dialogue at the level of abstract level one wants.

Figure 2: EXPRESS definition of task entity (partial)

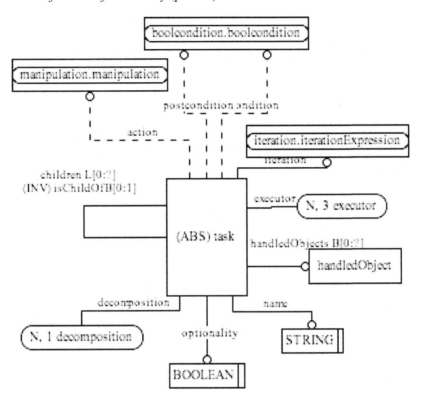

This is particularly important when post-WIMP interaction techniques are used.

Such as in advanced state machines, transitions may be guarded by expressions, which involve variables. They also can trigger actions. Figure 4 illustrates the EXPRESS HI transition meta-model.

Application to our design scenario. An interface mock-up of a currency converter and its dialogue model are illustrated in Figure 5. The HI dialogue model is composed of two automata corresponding to two abstract levels.

The less concrete automaton, *AConvert,* is a cycling automaton with three states and three transitions. From the *init* state (I), receiving the *JAmount* token changes the current state to the 1-state. Only one transition can be triggered from this state, using the *JConvert* token. The execution of this transition creates a new token (the *JSto-*

pEditing token) and puts the application on the 2-state. The last transition (triggered by a *JNew* token) brings back the *AConvert* automaton to the *init* state (*I*) and produces a *JInit* token.

The second automaton, *AAmount,* is composed of four states and nine transitions. Two transitions can be triggered from the *init* state corresponding to the entry of an amount entity either as euro (*JEnterCaract€*) or as dollar (*JEnterCaract€*). According to the entered currency, the current state becomes the 1-state or the 2-state. Following the currency choice (implicitely made when the first amount entity was entered), the whole amount is entered. If the value is deleted (*JDelete*), the current state brings back the automaton to the *init* state. When the amount edition is closed (a *JStopEditing* token is received), the current state becomes the 3-state and the only one transition that can be triggered (*JInit*) is to go back to the *init* state.

Figure 4. EXPRESS definition of transition entity

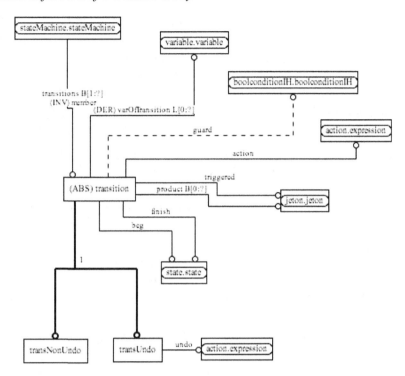

JEnterCaract€, JEnterCaract$, JDelete, JConvert, and *JNew* are tokens created by user actions on the application interface. Figure 5a shows for each widget the produced tokens. Other tokens are produced by transition executions and are underlined on Figure 5b.

Associations between K-MAD and HI Models

The general philosophy of our approach is to take advantage of the hierarchical nature of the two models in order to establish strong associations between them. Associations are manually defined by the designer and may link three kinds of relations.

Application to our design scenario. In our scenario example, the designer wants to verify the coherency between the high-level automaton (*AConvert*) and the K-MAD task model, so all associations consider only the *AConvert* automaton.

The Compound-Task/ Automaton Association

The structure of the dialogue model encourages considering each task decomposition as equivalent to a specific automaton. The structure of the automaton must then be compatible with the dynamics described through the temporal operator of the compound task. Again, the dialogue may be richer than the simple translation of the temporal operator. Another consequence of this association is the equivalence between tokens and compound tasks: each compound task may be achieved by the way of an automaton that produces a token that stands for the task achievement.

Application to our design scenario. The *Converting* composed task of the task model (presented in Figure 3a), is associated with the *AConvert* automaton of the HI model (in Figure 5b). Remind that we consider that the designer wants to validate the coherency between only this automaton and the task model.

The Task/Transition Association

The first obvious association can be made between tasks from the task model and transitions from the dialogue model. This link has been largely used in the previous research works, but for us, the link is not a bijective link: because of the need for interaction facilities in applications, there can be more transitions than user tasks.

Application to our design scenario. In the *AConvert* automaton, the *JAmount* transition is associated with the *Entering amount* task and the *JConvert* transition is associated with the *Converting with currency* task.

The Object/Variable and Expression Associations

Task model and dialogue model use expressions, which manipulate objects (for task models) and variables (for dialogue model). This link is patent, but was not described in the previous works because the used task model did not formally consider objects and expressions. As we wrote above, K-MAD expresses objects and computerized expressions that use them. Thus, we defined an association between objects and expressions of the K-MAD task model and the variables and expressions (guards and actions) of the HI dialogue model.

Application to our design scenario. The *€Rate* and *$Rate* objects are used to perform *Converting from € to $* and *Converting from $ to €* tasks. In our illustration case, these objects are not associated with variables used on HI dialogue model.

CHECKING RULES

Two kinds of rules can be established between the models (Caffiau, 2009b), based on the previously defined associations.

The first kind of rules concerns the existence of logically associated entities in both models. For example, are there one token and one automaton for each compound task? or is there one transition in the dialogue model for each task in the task model?

The second kind of rules relates to the semantics of the models. Are the semantics of the expressions we can find in each model equivalent? Is the navigation, which is allowed by the automata, consistent with the temporal decomposition of the tasks?

These rules can be exploited in two ways. They can be used in initial design to generate a skeleton of the dialogue, or they can be used in verification to state if two models are compatible. In that way, our work might be compared to Kavaldjian (2009). We illustrate the application of rules that we identified, verifying compatibility of the task and dialogue models previously presented (Figures 3 and 5) by using the associations defined before.

Logic Verification

Rules. The relations between tasks and automata are based on the hierarchical structure that organizes elements from the more abstract to the more concrete level. This hierarchical structure implies the two types of tasks that compose the K-MAD task trees:

- Compound tasks, which are compositions of more concrete tasks,
- Elementary tasks, which are not composed (they correspond to atomic tasks).

Subtasks of a compound task detail how it is performed (what tasks should be performed in order to attend its goal). An automaton represents, by a succession of transitions, a succession of user actions. The first two logical rules are defined above the similarity of the entity (task and transition) decompositions.

1. Except for the high level task, each compound task must be associated to one token,

2. All compound tasks must be associated with at least one automaton of the dialogue model.

K-MAD tasks are executed by four executant types:

- User: the task is performed by humans without computer assistance,
- System: the task is performed by systems without user intervention,
- Interactive: the task is performed jointly by users and systems,
- Abstract: the task executant is compound.

In the HI dialogue model, transitions express associations between user actions (or results of user actions) and system reactions. Then, starting points of transitions are always user actions on the system. From these observations, two logical verification rules are defined based on task executant types.

3. No task executed by the user (named user task) can be associated to a dialogue model component,
4. All tasks jointly performed by user and system (named interactive task) must be linked to at least one transition of the dialogue model.

Last, our approach aims at designing a dialogue model for the dynamic of only one system. The last logical verification rule focuses on the machines associated with tasks.

5. All tasks associated with dialogue model transitions must be performed on a common machine.

Application to our design scenario. The K-MAD task model of the *currency converter* is composed of two compound tasks. Their executant type is abstract. All other tasks are performed by interactions between the user and the system

(interactive executant). The *Converting* task is associated with the *AConvert* automaton. *Entering Amount* task is associated with the *JAmount* transition and the *JConvert* transition with the *Converting with currency* task.

1. The only one compound task associated to a dialogue model entity is the *Converting* task. It is the high level task, then this rule is not applicable to our case.
2. The *Converting with currency* task is not associated to an automaton of the dialogue model. This rule is not verified.
3. There is no task performed by the sole user. This rule is not applicable to our case.
4. Two interactive tasks are not associated with any transition (*Converting from $ to €* and *Converting from € to $*). The rule is not verified for these two tasks.
5. All tasks are performed on a common system. This rule is successful.

Sum-up: The logical verification fails: three tasks must be associated to dialogue model components (*Converting with currency, Converting from $ to €, Converting from € to $*).

Semantic Verification

Rules. Compound tasks express precisely the subtasks execution schedule by the way of four scheduling operators:

- Enabling: subtasks are performed one-by-one following their position on the subtask order,
- Choice: only one subtask is performed,
- No order: subtasks execution order is not predefined,
- Concurrent: subtasks are concurrently performed.

As stated before, automaton transitions express action successions. Based on associations between compound tasks and automata, and subtasks and transitions, we defined three semantic verification rules that verify coherency between task scheduling and transition successions.

1. When a compound task schedules its subtasks with the *enabled* scheduling operator, the transitions associated with the subtasks must follow each other. For T1 and T2, two transitions associated with two subtasks ST1 and ST2 (with ST2 as the next task after ST1). Then, the ending state of T1 is the beginning state of T2.
2. When a compound task schedules its subtasks with the *choice* scheduling operator, the transitions associated with the subtasks must begin from the same initial state.
3. When a compound task schedules its subtasks with the *no order* scheduling operator, whichever the routes followed from the common initial state, the ending state must be common.

   In addition to scheduling operators, another task characteristic expresses subtask succession information: the iteration characteristic. It indicates a (number or expression) condition that controls the task iteration. In order to take into account the task iteration on associated transitions, we defined a fourth semantic verification rule.
4. For each iterative task, the associated transition must go back to its initial state (the initial state is the same that the ending state) Tasks and transitions may be restricted by the expressed state of the world (represented by objects on task models and variables on dialogue models). In K-MAD, the task execution condition is named *precondition* and in HI, the transition execution condition is named *guard*. Both are Boolean expressions. Moreover, resulting of task and transition execution, actions are performed. Task actions are expressed by using objects and transition actions by using variables. The

last two semantic verification rules verify the use of associated objects and variables in associated expressions (preconditions/ guards and actions).

5. Variables associated with objects O_i are used in *guards* of transitions that are associated with tasks using O_i to express *preconditions*.
6. Variables associated with objects O_i are used in *actions* of transitions that are associated with tasks using O_i to express *actions*.

Application to our design scenario. In the considered task model, the *Converting* task schedules sequentially its subtasks and *Converting with currency* schedules its subtasks with the *choice* operator. *JAmount* and *JConvert* of *AConvert* are respectively associated to *Entering amount* and *Converting with currency* of the K-MAD task model. Let us check the six rules:

1. The *JAmount* ending state is the same as the *JConvert* beginning state. This rule is fulfilled.
2. *Converting from $ to €* and *Converting from € to $* tasks are not associated to any transitions. Then, this rule cannot be currently verified.
3. There is no *no order* operator used in the task model. This rule is not applicable to our case.
4. There is no iterative task in the task model. This rule is not applicable to our case.
5. No guard is expressed on the *AConvert* automaton transitions. This rule is not applicable to our case (an example will be given in the next step, below).
6. No task action is expressed on the task model. This rule is not applicable to our case.

Sum-up: According to the expressed entities and the defined associations, the semantic verification is fulfilled, for that first design step.

Completing the Scenario Design Process

In order to complete the use of our approach to design the dialogue model of a currency converter, all the defined rules have to be checked. The first iteration of the checking step (presented in the previous sections) aimed at validating coherency of the high level of the dialogue model (*AConvert*). To summarize the logical verification of this automaton, three tasks ought to be associated with dialogue model entities:

- *Converting with currency* (abstract task)
- *Converting from $ to €* (interactive task)
- *Converting from € to $* (interactive task)

The association of these tasks with dialogue model entities will increase the semantic verification adding verification of some semantic rules.

To start the second iteration, the designer must associate the second level automaton to task model entities. According to the second logical verification rule, an automaton ought to represent in the dialogue model the abstract task (*Converting with currency*). In the designed converter application (Figure 5), the second automaton (*AAmount*) expresses the amount input; it does not express the dynamics of a conversion. Therefore, the designer cannot associate the *AAmount* automaton to the *Converting with currency* task. As a conclusion, we must assume that the converter application illustrated in Figure 5 cannot map the expressed task model (illustrated in Figure 3).

Another currency converter (and its dialogue model) must be designed (Figure 6). The dialogue model of this interface is also composed of two abstract levels. The high-level automaton (*AConvert*) is the same as for the interface presented in Figure 5. Conversely, the second abstraction level is composed of two automata. *AAmount* expresses the application dynamic that corresponds to the amount entry and *ACurrency* expresses the choice of the currencies. Two of the three transitions of

this automaton have guards expressed by using two numerical variables (*$ Rate* and *€ Rate*). In addition to the previously expressed associations, the second level automata (and their components) are associated to task model entities. All associations are presented in Table 1.

Based on these associations. Logical and semantic rules can be checked.

Logical rules:

1. The *Converting with currency* task is associated to the *JConvert* token. This rule is successful.
2. *The tasks Converting and Converting with currency* are respectively associated to the *AConvert* and *ACurrency* automata. This rule is successful.
3. There is no task performed by only the user. This rule is not applicable to our case.
4. The three interactive tasks (*Entering amount, Converting from $ to €* and *Converting from € to $*) are associated to one trnsition. This rule is successful.
5. All tasks are performed on a common system. This rule is successful.

Semantic rules:

1. The *JAmount* ending state is the same as the *JConvert* beginning state. This rule is successful.
2. The *Converting from $ to €* and *Converting from € to $* tasks are associated to the transitions *JConvertTo$* and *JConvertTo€*. This rule is successful.
3. There is no *no order* operator used in the task model. This rule is not applicable to our case.
4. There is no iterative task in the task model. This rule is not applicable to our case.
5. The conversion rate K-MAD objects ($ rate and € rate) are associated to the Rate variables ($Rate and €Rate). These objects are used

Figure 6. a) A second currency converter mock-up and b) its HI model (only the second level automaton)

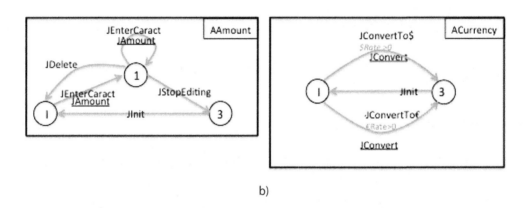

JEnterAmount
JDelete

Amount to be
converted:

$ -> €   → JConvertTo€

€ -> $ → JConvertTo$

Result:

New
Conversion

JNew

a)

b)

Table 1. Associations

Task model element	Dialogue model element
Task: Converting	Automaton: AConvert
Task: Converting with currency	Automaton: ACurrency
Task: Entering amount	Transition: JAmount
Task: Converting with currency	Transition: JConvert
Task: Converting with currency	Token: JConvert
Task: Converting from $ to €	Transition: JConvertTo€
Task: Converting from € to $	Transition: JConvertTo$
Object: € rate	Variable: €Rate
Object: $ rate	Variable: $Rate

in precondition expressions of two tasks: *Converting from $ To €* and *Converting from € To $*. The $Rate variable is used to express the guard of the *JConvertTo$* transition and the €Rate variable is used to express the guard of the *JConvertTo€* transition. These two transitions are associated to the two tasks. This rule is successful.

6. No task action is expressed on the task model. This rule is not applicable to our case.

Sum-up: All our rules are checked, and successful. At this step, the designer can either modify his/her models or start the user evaluation on a prototype.

CONCLUSION AND FUTURE WORKS

In this paper, we present a global process to use a model-driven approach in user interface design. This process uses rules that allow checking the validity of task models and dialogue models. Moreover, this process is compliant to user-centered approaches, which promote iterative design. A case study is fully described, showing how the method can be used; this example also demonstrates how the verification fails, which lead to a new design for a proposed solution.

Unlike the majority of relative works, this method is not based on the generative approach, which allows avoiding most of its known drawbacks. Instead, our process leans on rule checking, which allows improvements by adding new rules without disturbing the process.

Future works are numerous. The example we present in this paper is obviously very simple, to match with space constraints. Larger examples have to be designed, and tools should be developed in order to help users in applying the method.

Our method leans on two specific models (K-MAD and HI); hence, it should be interesting to check how it can apply with other models. Once again, the fact the method is based on explicit rules

allows to discard easily rules whose concepts are not present in the used models.

Last, evaluation should be made with designers, to prove the usability of the method.

REFERENCES

Baron, M., & Scapin, D. (2006). *K-MAD project site*. Retrieved June 28, 2011, from http://kmade.sourceforge.net/.

Berti, S., Correani, F., Mori, G., Paternò, F., & Santoro, C. (2004). TERESA: A transformation-based environment for designing and development multi-device interface. In *Proceedings of the Conference on Human Factors in Computing Systems - CHI 2004*, (pp. 793-794). Vienna, Austria: ACM Press.

Bomsdorf, B., & Szwillus, G. (1998). From task to dialogue, task-based user interface design: A CHI 98 workshop. *SIGCHI Bulletin, 30*(4).

Caffiau, S. (2009). *Approche dirigée par les modèles pour la conception et la validation des applications interactives: Une démarche basée sur la modélisation des tâches*. Unpublished doctoral dissertation. Retrieved from http://www.lisi.ensma.fr/ftp/pub/documents/thesis/2009-thesis-caffiau.pdf.

Caffiau, S., Girard, P., Guittet, L., & Scapin, D. L. (2009). Hierarchical structure: A step for jointly designing interactive software dialog and task model. In *Human-Computer Interaction: Novel Interaction Methods and Techniques* (pp. 664–673). Berlin, Germany: Springer. doi:10.1007/978-3-642-02577-8_73

Caffiau, S., Girard, P., Scapin, D., & Guittet, L. (2007). Generating interactive applications from task models: A hard challenge. In *TAsk MOdels and DIAgrams (TAMODIA)* (pp. 267–272). Berlin, Germany: Springer. doi:10.1007/978-3-540-77222-4_22

Caffiau, S., Scapin, D., Girard, P., Baron, M., & Jambon, F. (2010). Increasing the expressive power of task analysis: Systematic comparison and empirical assessment of tool-supported task models. *Interacting with Computers*, *22*(6), 569–593. doi:10.1016/j.intcom.2010.06.003

Calvary, G., Coutaz, J., Thevenin, D., Limbourg, Q., Bouillon, L., & Vanderdonckt, J. (2003). A unifying reference framework for multi-target user interfaces. *Interacting with Computers*, *15*(3), 289–308. doi:10.1016/S0953-5438(03)00010-9

Dehainsala, H., Jean, S., Dung, N. X., & Pierra, G. (2005). Ingénierie dirigée par les modèles en EXPRESS: Un exemple d'application. In *Proceedings of IDM 2005*. IDM.

Depaulis, F., Jambon, F., Girard, P., & Guittet, L. (2006). Le modèle d'architecture logicielle H4: Principes, usages, outils et retours d'expérience dans les applications de conception technique. *Revue d'Interaction Homme-Machine*, *7*(1), 93–129.

Depaulis, F., Maiano, S., & Texier, G. (2002). DTS-edit: An interactive development environment for structured dialog applications. In *Proceedings of CADUI, 2002*, 75–82.

Hettel, T., Lawley, M., & Raymond, K. (2008). Model synchronisation: Definitions for round-trip engineering. In *Theory and Practice of Model Transformations* (pp. 31–45). Zürich, Switzerland: Springer. doi:10.1007/978-3-540-69927-9_3

Hix, D., & Hartson, H. R. (1993). *Developing user interfaces: Ensuring usability through product & process*. New York, NY: John Wiley & Sons, Inc.

Kavaldjian, S., Kaindl, H., Mukasa, K. S., & Falb, J. (2009). Transformations between specifications of requirements and user interfaces. In *Proceedings of MDDAUI 2009*. Sanibel Island, FL: CEUR-WS.

Lucquiaud, V. (2005). Proposition d'un noyau et d'une structure pour les modèles de tâches orientés utilisateurs. In Proceedings of the 17th French-Speacking Conference on Human-Computer Interaction, (pp. 83-90). Toulouse, France: HCI.

Luyten, K., Clerckx, T., Coninx, K., & Vanderdonckt, J. (2003). Derivation of a dialog model from a task model by activity chain extraction. In *Proceedings of DSV-IS 2003*, (pp. 203-217). Funchal, Portugal: Springer-Verlag.

Mori, G., Paternò, F., & Santoro, C. (2004). Design and development of multidevice user interfaces through multiple logical descriptions. *IEEE Transactions on Software Engineering*, *30*(8), 507–520. doi:10.1109/TSE.2004.40

Norman, D. A. (1990). *The design of everyday things*. New York, NY: DoubleDay.

Sendall, S., & Küster, J. (2004). *Taming model round-trip engineering*. Paper presented in the OOPSLA Workshop on Best Practices for Model Driven Software Development. Vancouver, Canada.

Winston, W. R. (1970). Managing the development of large software systems. In *Proceedings of IEEE Wescon*, (pp 1-9). IEEE Press.

Wolff, A., & Forbrig, P. (2009). *Deriving user interfaces from task models*. Paper presented at MDDAUI 2009. Sanibel Island, FL.

ENDNOTE

[1]   Windows, Icons, Menus, and Pointers

Chapter 14

Programming a User Model with Data Gathered from a User Profile

Daniel Scherer
State University of Paraiba, Brazil & Federal University of Campina Grande, Brazil

Ademar V. Netto
Federal University of Campina Grande, Brazil

Yuska P. C. Aguiar
Federal University of Campina Grande, Brazil

Maria de Fátima Q. Vieira
Federal University of Campina Grande, Brazil & University of Strathclyde, UK

ABSTRACT

In order to prevent human error, it is essential to understand the nature of the user's behaviour. This chapter proposes a combined approach to increase knowledge of user behaviour by instantiating a programmable user model with data gathered from a user profile. Together, the user profile and user model represent, respectively, the static and dynamic characteristics of user behaviour. Typically, user models have been employed by system designers to explore the user decision-making process and its implications, since user profiles do not account for the dynamic aspects of a user interaction. In this chapter, the user profile and model are employed to study human errors—supporting an investigation of the relationship between user errors and user characteristics. The chapter reviews the literature on user profiles and models and presents the proposed user profile and model. It concludes by discussing the application of the proposed approach in the context of electrical systems' operation.

DOI: 10.4018/978-1-4666-1628-8.ch014

INTRODUCTION

Traditionally, software design and development are focused on system features. More recently, design methods and processes have evolved in the pursuit of user satisfaction, resulting in user centred practices. These user-centred development practices consider the user characteristics and the context of use. In spite of the general acceptance of the relevance of user characteristics for design, there are no clear specifications on how to account for these.

Some user interface conception methods, such as: ADEPT (Markopoulos, Pycock, Wilson, & Johnson, 1992), TRIDENT (Bodart, Hennebert, Leheureux, & Vanderdonckt, 1994), and MCIE (Turnell, 2004) recommend the construction of a user profile and the modelling of the task as part of the requirement gathering phase; placing user profiles at the centre of the user interface conception process.

A user profile consists of a set of user characteristics such as: age, gender, user skills and knowledge, among others, that do not take into account the dynamics of the interaction between the user and system, nor the errors that might occur during this interaction. It is important to note that a static profile may be sufficient to support the conception of a variety of systems. For systems that require a high level of reliability and low level of error incidence, knowledge of the user behaviour becomes a key requirement for the interface design. Acquiring this knowledge requires a research foundation in areas such as ergonomics and psychology, as illustrated in the following brief literature review.

In ergonomics, work analysis (Guérin, Laville, Daniellou, Duraffourg, & Kerguelen, 2001) is employed to support the building of user cognitive behaviour models, such as those proposed by Leplat and Cuny (1977), Rasmussen, Pejtersen, and Goodstein (1994), and Card, Moran, and Newell (1983). In turn, the current understanding of user behaviour supports the study of the human error (Reason, 1990).

In cognitive psychology there are various studies that focus on building user models (Leuchter, Niessen, Eyferth, & Bierwagen, 1997; Niessen & Eyferth, 2001). These studies differ in purpose from the research reported here although they do share common objectives such as observing and understanding human behaviour during task activity. Some of the studies address the human behaviour from the task effort point of view, considering the mental and physical effort, psychological stress and time constraints involved when performing a task (Weinger, et al., 2000; Wiebe, Roberts, & Behrend, 2010; DiDomenico & Nussbaum, 2008). Others try to establish the workload as perceived by the user and through its relation with parameters of the Autonomic Nervous System (ANS) (Kreibig, 2010). Yet other authors address the relationship between human behaviour and the body's physiological reactions (Huey & Wickens, 1993; Wittmann & Paulus, 2007; Baldauf, Brugard, & Wittmann, 2009). Finally, Tenenbaum and Connolly (2008) and Jung and Jung (2001) proposed models based on the NASA model Task Load Index (TLX), with similar objectives.

As previously stated, an important step in the user centred design approach consists of understanding the two-fold implications of the user-system interaction. In this investigation programmable user models, through simulations, are used to reach this goal.

According to Niessen, Leuchter, and Eyferth (1998), if the programmable user model has psychological assumptions built-in, it is possible to:

- Arrive at a more explicit and detailed description of the cognitive process during interaction than would be possible with a textual description;
- Explore a theoretical framework by reproducing anticipated effects of the user behaviour;
- Extract hypothesise from empirical work;
- Anticipate and analyze, the effect of technological changes on interaction with a

complex system and on user cognitive activities, thus giving insights into aspects that might affect cognitive performance.

In the specific context of industrial activity, due to the critical nature of the task performed, it is essential to understand the nature of user behaviour in order to prevent human error. This chapter therefore explores the relationship between an extended user profile that accounts for behavioural aspects and a programmable user model. Both of these models were conceived to represent the characteristics (static and dynamic) of operators in the electricity supply industry. This chapter describes the application of a user profile as the source of information for a programmable user model, conceived to investigate human behaviour during interaction with complex systems. The user profile and user model will be employed in human error studies, supporting the investigation of the relationship between errors and the user characteristics. The combined approach of building the user profile and mapping its data onto the programmable user model is later discussed and explored illustrating how it can contribute to an increased knowledge of user behaviour. The use of the resulting knowledge in preventing the human error is also addressed. The assumption is that this resulting knowledge, derived on the basis of cognitive sciences, will support the design of more ergonomic user interfaces, which in turn will prevent the occurrence of human errors during the operation of automated industrial systems. The proposed approach was subjected to a preliminary validation procedure, which consisted of instantiating the user profile with real data extracted from error reports originated in the electricity industry, and subsequently programming the user model with the user profile data. The user model was then run for the reported scenarios. Currently further validation is underway that consists of observing user behaviour during task performance, registering, analyzing and confronting the observations with data obtained from measuring the human

workload from the physiological, procedural and subjective points of view, as proposed in Weinger et al. (2000).

As discussed above, this chapter reflects in its structure the work's multidisciplinary approach. It therefore reviews the literature on user profiles, programmable user models and human error studies, and is organized as follows. Section 2 reviews the literature on cognitive psychology and the human error. Section 3 presents a brief literature review of user profiles and discuss the POCUs user profile. Section 4 presents a brief literature review on programmable user models and describes the Programmable User Model (MoPUs). Section 5 discusses how POCUs and MoPUs must be integrated to describe the static and dynamic user characteristics. Section 6 presents the preliminary results of the validation exercise, which has been undertaken and proposes further investigations. Section 7 concludes with the discussion of the potential impact of user behaviour knowledge on the design of human interfaces that are robust to human errors.

COGNITIVE PSYCHOLOGY AND HUMAN ERROR

The classical literature on human (Rasmussen, Pejtersen, & Goodstein, 1994; Cellier, 1990) concerns studies that aim to understand reported cases of human error. Authors such as Norman and Reason are concerned with exposing the "triggers" that lead to an error and the situations that activate those triggers, but do not relate errors to "triggers."

A study (Huey & Wickens, 1993) on team transition (i.e. the acting of an operator, or a team, in order to solve a problem caused by an event) stated that the level of difficulty posed by the task can be influenced by the following factors:

- Goals and performance evaluation criteria established for the task;

- The task structure;
- Quality, format and media in which the information is presented to the operator;
- Cognitive processing needed for the task, and;
- Characteristics of the interaction devices available to the operators.

The study also points out that there are five characteristics in common for the majority of team transition processes:

- The time:
  ○ How abruptly the demand is triggered;
  ○ The expectation (or perceived probability) of the demand (the study suggests that the level of expectation is potentially important, since it influences the speed at which the operators can respond to discrete events or system failures) and;
  ○ For how long the team must remain on standby before the demand occurs. (This has the potential to influence the quantity and quality of rest, and thus influence the performance post-demand.);
- The event structure: relates to how predictable the demand is and determines if the intended response to the demand can effectively be pre-programmed. In cognitive terms, it represents the need for update of mental maps in response to possible situations and their development;
- The environment: concerns the physical conditions to which the operator will be subject during the activity;
- The personal risk: concerns the risk assessment (personal injury or death) for the operator or for others;
- The organizational structure: this is subdivided into three components, namely (1) the team structure or chain of command,

(2) the integrity and continuity of the team structure over time, and (3) the level of team autonomy.

As it will be discussed later in this chapter, these characteristics are similar to those which must be accounted for in the domain of user interface design.

Another perspective on user characteristics is presented in Kreibig (2010), where the author draws a relationship between these and the Autonomic Nervous System (ANS), from the medical and psychological points of view. The study focused on: (1) negative emotions: anger, anxiety, disgust, embarrassment, fear, sadness; (2) positive emotions: affection, amusement, contentment, happiness, joy, anticipatory pleasure, pride, relief; and (3) emotions without clear valence connotation, such as: surprise and suspense. This relationship, although qualitative, represents evidence to support observations and behaviour analysis based on biometric measurements. The author does not provide quantitative data, since there is no consensus of opinion in the area and because it is not possible to determine specific values for different groups of individuals (Kreibig, 2010). In the literature concerning the relation between human behaviour and physiological reactions, ANS is a major reference. Therefore, the authors understand that it could equally be employed to explain the relationship between human behaviour and human error.

Rasmussen, Pejtersen, and Goodstein (1994) and Reason (1990) describe human error as a cause effect relationship between circumstances, without considering the human behaviour involved. On the other hand, Kreibig describes the relation between human behaviour and psychological and physiological reactions without accounting for the circumstances that lead into a specific behaviour. In the study here presented, error report analysis of electrical system operations shows a relationship between the context and operator behaviour, which in turn results in a decision and subsequent effect that feeds back into the context. The analysis has enabled the identification of sets of operator behaviour and contexts related to specific errors. This has formed the basis for the construction of the first programmable user model presented later.

The authors' view is that user profiles should be at the basis of the interface conception process. Nonetheless, the user profiles typically consist of a concise set of user characteristics that do not account for the dynamics of the system-user interaction. On the other hand, programmable user models have often been used to support system adaptability and automatic product testing, without considering the relation between the user behaviour and the resulting errors. Thus, in this chapter, a combined approach is proposed, in which the user profile is fed into an associated programmable user model aiming to investigate system users' characteristics and to support human error studies.

USER PROFILES

User interface conception methods vary in the degree to which they account for the user profile. Like TRIDENT (Bodart, Hennebert, Leheureux, & Vanderdonckt, 1994) and MCIE (Turnell, 2004), these methods adopt a user profile that consists essentially of objective data such as: age, gender and user experience. Alternatively, these methods categorize users through stereotypes. The knowledge of user behaviour when faced with adverse situations (such as those brought about by errors) is, therefore, usually overlooked. This section reviews user profiles.

The choice of elements that make up the user profile presented here is based on the following work:

- DePerUSI (de Queiroz, de Oliveira, & Turnell, 2005), adopted in the method MCIE (Turnell, 2004), which represents a classic user profile, containing personal information and including physical and professional aspects;

- The user profile proposed in the norm from the International Standard Organization ISO 9241 (ISO, 1998) that outlines a more complete user profile, including the personal level, the task and the user activity context. However, this general outline does not accommodate a cognitive profile (psychological/clinical profile). Rather it focuses on occupational and environmental issues;

- The International Classification of Functioning, Disability and Health (ICF) proposed by the World Health Organization (WHO) (WHO, 2001) which consists of a wide-ranging set of elements and provides a good basis for the construction of a user model. Its nature is specifically related to the medical field, however, and includes a wider list of items than is required for the purposes of this work. Nonetheless, certain relevant aspects do contribute to this research;

- The user profile proposed by Courage and Baxter (2005) that is general in nature, incorporating demographic characteristics (similarly to DePerUSI), and information on the user's values and attitudes, interests and preferences, skills, goals and beliefs. It also includes information that takes a wider view of the user and the work context such as behaviour patterns and knowledge of the interaction context.

This work adopts its information category structure from the profile proposed by Courage and Baxter (2005), i.e.:

- **Personal Profile:** Individual and personal characteristics such as name, age, and gender;

- **Clinical Profile:** Information about memory, language, and mental skills that constitute the general clinical status of the user;
- **Physical Profile:** Concerns the user's physical fitness as well as manual dexterity and balance;
- **Psychological Profile:** User behaviour characteristics directly influenced by the context;
- **Professional Profile:** Professional background comprising qualifications as well as experience in performing the professional activity;
- **Contextual Profile:** Contextual aspects that influence the user's behaviour.

Table 1 compares these profiles in terms of the number of items in each one of the categories listed above. This comparison highlights how the items are distributed in the categories and therefore the emphasis on each category given by each profile. Due to the small number of items, the categories clinical and physical were combined for the comparison.

In order to include features that would allow the analysis of the causes of human error in the proposed user profile, the scope of this study has been widened to include concepts from complementary areas such as:

- Models and taxonomies originated from human error studies, as proposed by Reason (1990), Hollnagel (1998), and Rasmussen, Pejtersen, and Goodstein (1994);
- Concepts adopted in the Human Factors Analysis and Classification System (HFACS) that have been analyzed by Shappel and Wiegmann (2000) and Paletz, Bearman, Orasanu, and Holbrook (2009) (the latter arguing the importance of the social and psychological factors in a user profile) and
- Concepts originating from Work Analysis Ergonomics (WAE) (Guérin, Laville, Daniellou, Duraffourg, & Kerguelen, 2001) and from user behaviour cognitive models as proposed by Leplat and Cuny (1977), Rasmussen, Pejtersen, and Goodstein (1994), and Card, Moran, and Newell (1983).

As stated earlier, the development of critical complex systems demands knowledge of a detailed user profile including aspects related to the human behaviour. An error when operating these systems may endanger life and/or cause material losses. It is necessary, therefore, to know those user characteristics that might influence error probability, such as physical and psychological limitations. This knowledge is essential when adapting the user interface to user requirements. From this point of view, the models and taxonomies helped to identify the context (organization, task, and equipment). On the other hand, the Human Factors Analysis and Classification System, Work

Table 1. Comparison between user profile categories

	Courage&Baxter	DePerUSI	ISO9241-11	ICF
Personal	3	2	2	6
Clinical/Physical	0	2	2	15
Psychological	3	0	3	34
Professional	12	9	10	5
Contextual	2	1	28	6
Total	20	14	45	66

Analysis Ergonomics (WAE), and user behaviour cognitive models helped to identify the variables associated with the user's physical and psychological limitations.

The *POCUs* User Profile

The proposed user profile—POCUs—is an extended set of typical user characteristics that includes features related to cognitive behaviour that are interesting for the study of human error. The user profile is structured in six sub-sets of characteristics, as proposed by Courage and Baxter (2005). These are: Personal, Clinical, Psychological, Professional, Contextual, and Physical.

The set of elements that compose POCUs was obtained as a superset of the profiles proposed by Courage & Baxter, DePerUSI, ISO 9241 Part 11 and ICF (Table 2). The resulting superset comprises 76 elements, grouped in six distinct profiles. Since gathering all this information could be an overwhelming task if performed either by the user or the designer; and since there are elements which demand a specialist's appraisal for its correct completion (product designer or a medic professional), the data gathering process is supported by a questionnaire and a checklist, as illustrated on Table 3. The 42-item questionnaire is to be answered by the user, whereas the 34-item checklist is to be answered by the professional in charge of building the user profile.

Given the extent of the data to be collected, and the degree of relevance for the intended purpose of the user profile, the information to be gathered was grouped into four levels of detail. Level "A" consists of an information set that represents the core of any user profile and the remaining three levels may be added as required to broaden the scope of the model. Each element has an associated scale or a set of parameters to facilitate profile completion. For instance, product experience level is associated to the semantic scale: none, low, medium, good, very good, and not applicable.

Table 3 (questionnaire) and Table 4 (checklist) illustrates the profile relevant to the programmable user model (MoPUs) in its current level of complexity. It comprises the categories: Personal, Professional, Contextual, and Psychological, relative to levels A and B, as instantiated for the case study. The characteristics in the questionnaire were extracted from error reports and from a real operator profile originated from the electricity industry. The characteristics in the checklist were extracted from the case study through observation of the work environment.

PROGRAMMABLE USER MODEL

Programmable user models are widely used in the area of Artificial Intelligence. The main research

Table 2. Relation between categories, elements' distribution, tools, and category origin

Categories	Elements' distribution	Tool	Category origin
Personal	8 elements	Questionnaire	DePerUSI, Courage & Baxter, ICF
Physical	9 elements		
Contextual	15 elements		ISO 9241 part 11
Professional	10 elements		DePerUSI, Courage & Baxter
	2 elements	Checklist	
Psychological	20 elements		ICF
Clinical	12 elements		

Table 3. Excerpt of POCUs questionnaire to support instantiating the MoPUs

Questionnaire			Data gathered
Personal Profile	Level A	Age	Between 35 and 65 years of age
		Gender	Male
		Quality of sleep	Unavailable information
Professional Profile	Level A	Education degree	technical background in electro technology
		Current job	operator in an electrical system substation
		Product experience level	not applicable
		System experience level	Good (over ten years of experience in the job)
		Task experience level	Good (well trained in the task)
		Job experience level	Good (always worked in the same function)
	Level B	Training level	Good (trained by the company)
		Ability with input devices	Good (trained in using the human interface –panels and computer)
		Qualifications (major)	Trained in the job and also in safety and operating norms.
		General Knowledge	Unavailable information
Contextual Profile	Level A	Working cycles	Six hours shift
		Teamwork / individual work	Teamwork
		Monitoring as pressure factor	Unavailable information
		Feedback	Unavailable information
		Equipment	Not always adequate
		Working time	Unavailable information
		Interruptions	Frequent
		Work Space Design	Adequate but with some problems

Table 4. Excerpt of POCUs checklist to support instantiating the MoPUs

Checklist			Data gathered
Psychological Profile	Level A	Motivation	Average
		Attention functions	Not always high
	Level B	Higher-level cognitive functions • judgment • cognitive flexibility • organization and planning	Unavailable information

stream follows the approach of Problem Solving Model and in particular General Problem Solver (GPS [Butterworth & Blandford, 1997]), STanford Research Institute Problem Solver (STRIPS [Fikes & Nilsson, 1971]) and the SOAR architecture (Lewis, 2001). A frequent difficulty has been how to instantiate these models, since they usually require specific knowledge of the model programming language.

There are also user models, which support adaptive interfaces. The GUIDE project (Cheverst, Mitchell, & Davies, 2002) is based on predictive models and allows for the explicit inclusion of users' interests; whereas the GECKO project (Bohnert & Zukerman, 2009) is based on non-intrusive observations to support the building of collaborative models.

A similar proposal to this work's application of a programmable user model is the one presented in Leuchter, Niessen, Eyferth, and Bierwagen (1997). There, a model of the mental processes of air traffic controllers is conceived and implemented in ACT-R. The model represents operating procedures during dynamic situations. The authors represent three information processing cycles: monitoring, anticipation and problem solving. The first two cycles are related to diagnosis (conflict detection) and the last cycle is considered the preparation stage for controller intervention (Niessen, Leuchter, & Eyferth, 1998; Niessen & Eyferth, 2001). Although similar in purpose to the research presented here, this model does not account for human error or user behaviour when confronted with error.

Model Description

The programmable user model proposed in this chapter, MoPUs *(Modelo Programável do Usuário)*—was conceived to represent user behaviour, the task, and the work environment, in the context of electrical systems operation. It was based on the descriptions contained in human error reports originated from the electricity industry in Brazil. In the current work, this model is being extended to represent information categories cited in the literature on human error. Its original aim is to support the investigation of the influence of human behaviour on the outcome of a system's operation. Although simple in terms of the represented parameters, it allows the representation of scenarios cited in the industry's human error reports through the adjustment of model parameters when simulating the chosen situations.

As presented in Netto, Aguiar, Scherer, and Vieira (2009), the programmable user model simulates the dynamic behaviour of an operator when performing tasks during situations and contexts that lead to error. The simulated situations reflect a set of data extracted from an ontology, conceived from the error report analysis. The model was built using the Colored Petri Nets (CPN) formalism (Jensen, 1992). This choice of formalism was based on its ability to represent the chosen user characteristics as well as on the tools available to support modelling and analysis. The tools used during this project were: CPN Tools (Eindhoven University of Technology, 2011), version 2.2.0 and BRITNeY (Eindhoven University of Technology, 2009).

In an attempt to minimize the complexity of the original user model, only a modest set of variables were considered to represent the operator status. The chosen variables correspond to a set of human characteristics identified in human error reports from the electricity industry, and are the most frequently mentioned in those reports. The reports describe human errors that lead to system failure at a Brazilian electricity company (Scherer & Vieira, 2008). The modelled characteristics are also represented in an ontology extracted from the human error reports. The characteristics: tiredness, stress, attention and confusion, were the causes most frequently mentioned in the human error reports.

The initial set of the user model variables comprise:

Table 5. Influential factors in the original user model parameters

		Interfering Factors					Work context			
		Phone interruption	Emergency tasks	Anxiety	Personal Problems	Extra Tiredness	Working cycle duration	Task time	Task complexity	Task status
Operator status	Attention	✓	✓	✓	✓				✓	
	Stress						✓	✓		✓
	Fatigue					✓	✓	✓		
	Confusion	✓		✓	✓					

- **Fatigue:** Which represents the level of operator tiredness;
- **Stress:** Which represents the level of operator stress;
- **Attention:** Which represents the level of operator attention;
- **Confusion:** Which represents the level of operator confusion, when performing the task;
- **Task Type:** Which represents two dimensions: the level of task complexity (simple or complex) and the task nature (rare or routine).
- **Working Cycle (shift) Duration:** Which represents the duration of a cycle for the model run. The working cycle duration, which typically is of six hours in the case study, can be extended beyond this (overtime) as a result of critical unfinished tasks or, due the absence of the operators in charge of the next shift.
- **Task Demand Time:** Which specifies when the task demand occurs in relation to the start of the shift.
- **Working Cycles:** Which specifies the number of cycles (shifts) that will be performed in the automatic simulation mode.
- **Task Status:** Which stores the task status at one point in time during the model execution (finished successfully, finished unsuccessfully and unfinished);

- **Interfering Factors:** Which represents a concatenated extra set of factors that can influence operator performance during task execution. It concerns the operator status: anxiety, personal problems, and tiredness before starting work. It also concerns other factors such as phone call interruptions and demands originating from emergency tasks.

These interfering factors influence the variables representing the operator status Attention, Stress, Fatigue and Confusion, as illustrated in Table 5.

These factors influence the operator and as a consequence influence the task final status. They belong to two groups: those that are related to the operator status before the working shift, such as the levels of anxiety and tiredness and the influence of personal problems; and factors, which appear during the working shift, such as the demand to perform emergency tasks and the occurrence of phone calls during the working shift. These variables and respective dimensions are illustrated in Table 6.

In the user model, the operator's behaviour is "simulated" during a working shift. The characteristics that define the status of the operator are updated under the influence of the variables: time, type of manoeuvre, the manoeuvre status, external factors, etc.

Table 6. Model variables and dimensions

Operator status	Task complexity	Working cycle duration	Task time	Task status	Interfering factors
Attention Stress Fatigue Confusion	Simple and routine Simple and rare Complex and routine Complex and rare	Normal (six hours shift) Overtime (extended shift)	Start-of-shift Half-way through shift End-of-shift Overtime	Unfinished Finished unsuccessfully Finished successfully	Phone interruptions Emergency tasks Anxiety Personal problem Extra tiredness

The model was built using the Coloured Petri Net formalism (Jensen, 1992), and consists of five interconnected modules. A brief description of each module is given below. Further details are found in Netto, Aguiar, Scherer, and Vieira (2009).

1. **Model Configuration:** This module allows configuration of the model's initial state (at the start of a simulation process), establishing the initial levels of the operator's status (fatigue, stress, attention and confusion); the initial task type, the task demand time, the number of working cycles, and the working cycle duration.

2. **Scenario specification:** After initialization, this module sets up the scenario to be followed by setting the task type, and causes the update of the model's log file *(log)*. The user model evolves according to a cycle (shift) duration and the number of cycles previously run;

3. **Task Status:** This module estimates an operator error rate based on the current operator status and determines the task status at the end of the working shift.

4. **Operator Status:** This module updates the operator status at the beginning of a new cycle, taking into account: the operator's previous status, the number of model cycles already run, the task status at the end of the previous cycle, the task type and the interfering factors for the current cycle.

5. **Operator Idleness:** This module registers the event "no-task-requested" in the log file, adjusts the operator status, increments the

cycle time count and checks for a new task request, leading (or not) into another idle cycle.

The user model offers two configuration modes before beginning a new simulation. The first mode allows setting up a specific scenario to run during a single model cycle. In this mode, the initial operator status is chosen (stress intensity, lack of attention, fatigue and confusion) as well as the type of task and the period during the working shift when it should be performed (beginning, middle, end or overtime). In this mode it is possible to replicate a scenario that leads to error (extracted from the error reports) and investigate the task results under the specified conditions.

In the second configuration mode, the model is set up with: an initial operator status; the type of task to be performed; the workload level for the first cycle of simulation and the total number of cycles to be run. In this mode only the initial configuration is set up and for each new cycle (that represents a working shift) new values are assigned for the type of task, with the operator workload adjusted as a consequence. This mode allows investigating the user behaviour over time, starting from a known model state.

The user model characteristics being extended are described in Section five. The set of variables is being extended to represent both the user behaviour as well as other factors that may influence the user status. The proposed extensions must improve the fidelity and level of realism of the user model.

As already stated, the model parameters and their range originated from report analysis. A weight was assigned for each model variable to be employed during simulation in order to set the degree of influence of one variable on the other model variables.

INTEGRATING THE USER PROFILE INTO A PROGRAMMABLE USER MODEL

The purpose of integrating the user profile into the programmable user model was to create a platform of human error studies based on a more realistic user model. This can be achieved though a set of model parameters originating from cognitive behaviour studies on the human error instantiated with data obtained from a corpus of reports on human error from the electricity industry.

The knowledge of user behaviour integrated into the model enabled the exploration of hypothesise about the relationship between profile characteristics such as motivation and attention (psychological profile) and the task final status in the user model. Other examples proposed for investigation are:

a. How a worried operator, already anxious and stressed would handle an emergency task and;
b. How long working hours would affect operator task performance under the influence of a combination of other influential factors.

To answer these questions it is necessary investigate the relation between ANS and user psychological reactions. In the literature review, the works of Schomer apud (Tenenbaum & Connolly, 2008) and Task Load Index (TLX) (Hart & Staveland, 1988) stand out. Schomer proposed a method to classify the user focus of attention according to the following parameters: (A) feelings and affects; (B) body monitoring, (C) command and instruction, (P) pace monitoring, (E) environmental feedback, (R) reflective activity thoughts, (S) personal problem solving, (W) work, career

and management, (I) course information, and (T) talk and conversational chatter. The parameters A, B, C, and P, are classed as associative, with the focus of attention towards the task, whereas the categories R, S, W, E, I and T are classed as dissociative, since they bare no relation to the task. This classification uses the think aloud process to extract information about the user parameters, which is appropriate for data gathering during task observation.

Schomer's classification has similar items to those adopted in the POCUs profile. For instance, the category (A) feelings and affects can be mapped into the proposed Psychological profile items (motivation, temperament, and personality characteristics) whereas category (B) body monitoring can be mapped into the Clinical Profile (perceptual functions, psychomotor functions, voice and speech functions, and consciousness characteristics). This classification poses a practical issue if it is to be used as the basis for the user profile since its application would demand the user to think aloud. Therefore, it is not adequate for building the user profile and since it was not considered appropriate, it was not included in Table 7.

Tenenbaum and Connolly (2008) explore Schomer's classification when relating physical workload with associative and dissociative attention. They concluded that there is a relationship between physical effort and attention, and that low levels of physical effort enable individuals to swap the focus of attention between external and internal sources. When the effort level rises, the attention focus narrows and internalizes; thus reducing the ability to divide attention between multiple sources of information. This view is similar to Schomer's regarding the focus of attention since according to this author when thoughts related to associative aspects arise, the user focus of attention is redirected towards the main activity and consequently the attention given to secondary activities (dissociative) is diminished; thus reducing the feeling of being overloaded.

Table 7. Evolution of the user profile and model

User Profile				User Model	
Profile Categories	Team transition characteristics	TLX characteristics	Extended POCUs characteristics	Original MoPUs	Extended MoPUs
Task	Time	Time pressure	Time management	Task time	
	How abruptly the event is triggered				Instant of time when the event is triggered (Task time)♦
	Expectation or probability of the demand to occur				Incidence level of emergency task ♦
	Time during which the team must remain on alert.		Working time	Working cycle duration	Working cycle duration♦
	Event structure	Task difficulty		Task complexity (rare, routine)	Task difficulty♦
					Rare
					Routine
		Activity type		Task complexity (complex, simple)	Task complexity♦
					Simple
					Complex
Organizational / Contextual	Organizational structure				
	Team structure		Teamwork/ Individual work		Teamwork/ Individual work♦
	Team integrity				Team integrity ♣
	Team autonomy level				Team autonomy level ♣
	Environment		Monitoring as a pressure factor		Monitoring as a pressure factor♣
			Workspace design		Workspace design ♣
			Equipment		Equipment♣
				Phone interruption	Environmental interfering factors♦/♣
Personal	Personal risk	Physical effort	Transport support		Transport support♣
			Logistic support		Logistic support♣
			Work location		Location♣
			Ease of access		Restrictions♦
		Mental/ Sensory effort	Higher-level cognitive functions		Higher-level cognitive functions♦/♣
				Operator anxiety	Operator anxiety
				Operator confusion	Operator Confusion
		Frustration level	Temperament and personality		Temperament and personality♦
		Stress level		Stress	Stress level♣
			Community, society and civic life	Operator personal problems	Community, society and civic life♣
			Major areas in life		Major areas in life ♣
		Fatigue	Quality of sleep	Tiredness	Quality of sleep♣
				Operator tiredness	

continued on following page

Table 7. Continued

User Profile				User Model	
Professional		Performance	Product experience level		Product experience level♣
			System experience level		System experience level♣
			Task experience level		Task experience level♣
			Job experience level		Job experience level♣

Data gathering tool: ♣ - Questionnaire ♦ - Checklist

The work published in Huey and Wickens (1993) follows the streamline of user interface design studies, focusing on the time of an event and the reaction demanded from the user. The factors which influence task effort confirm the findings reported in the study of human error in the set of reports from the electricity industry (Scherer, da Costa, Barbosa, & Vieira, 2010). This study was used as the basis for the user programmable model.

The proposed user characteristics, similar to most team transition situations, are clearly essential for any user model conceived to support the study of human behaviour when faced with error. Confronting the standard characteristics of team transition processes with the user model parameters (Table 7) the need for the inclusion of the following parameters in the MoPUs becomes evident.

- Time
  - Expectation or probability of a demand to occur.
- Personal risk;
- Organizational structure
  - Team structure;
  - Team integrity;
  - Team autonomy level.

Contrasting with Schomer´s classification, which is based on data collected during the task, TLX (Hart & Staveland, 1988), is a questionnaire to be answered by the user after performing the task, similarly to the POCUs questionnaire.

Table 7 presents the extended set of parameters for the user model, based on Team transition and TLX; and the extended set of parameters for POCUs. It must be pointed out that the "task time" parameter was changed from meaning "how abruptly an event is triggered" to meaning "the point in time when it is triggered."

Examining Table 7, the user profile characteristic "Personal risk," originally proposed by Huey and Wickens (1993), was sub-classified into "physical effort" and "mental/sensory effort," whereas the remaining ones were kept as proposed in TLX since they adequately represent the information on user behaviour. The user model extension adopts parameters from TLX related to physical limitations when performing a task as well as performance parameters.

The extended user model represents a superset of the information presented in Table 7, aiming to be more complete regarding the representation of the task and user characteristics.

Extended POCUs Profile and Programmable User Model (MoPUs)

The original user model has been extended with new parameters, and the original parameters have been adapted, aiming to represent user characteristics that reflect behaviour. The extended user model is incorporated in Table 7. The added parameters must be set up before model simulation using a frontend module, designed to simplify model parameterization with the values originated from the POCUs user profile.

The following parameters remained unaltered in the extended version of the user model: fatigue, stress, attention; confusion; task status; working cycle number and duration; task demand time. Whereas the following ones were adapted to reflect the model's intended scope:

- Interfering factors: the modification consisted of including the variable emergency task demand in the frontend set of variables.

- The variable task type was split into two: task frequency (rare or routine) and task complexity (simple or complex); simplifying the association of a scale of values to each of the new variables, similar to TLX.

From the study on TLX and Team transition, new parameters were added to the user model, as follows:

- From TLX, the user performance became related to: product experience level, system experience level, task experience level and job experience level. These variables were all included as frontend variables.

- Also from TLX, social life (community, society, and civic life) and major life areas are frontend variables related to stress. If the user profile indicates that the user does not have access to, or has some difficulties in accessing, a social life there is a consequent rise in stress levels. From the model point of view, if the social life or major life areas are assigned negative values, the model sets the interfering factor: operator personal problem;

- Sleep quality is a frontend variable that affects the initial value of the operator fatigue level. If the assigned value is "usu-

ally bad," the model sets the interfering factor: operator extra tiredness;

- The incidence of emergency tasks is also a variable that is set up through the frontend that incorporates in the model the "expectation of the emergency task demand" directly influencing the variables related to the "operator status."

- A group of three variables, set up through the frontend module, is related to the organizational structure available for task execution:
  ◦ Teamwork or individual work represents how the task should be performed: individually or in a team and the team composition. When the team is incomplete it impacts negatively on the operator status;
  ◦ Team integrity represents the team structure composition at the time of an event. Changes in the team structure affect interfering factors such as anxiety levels;
  ◦ Team autonomy represents the team access to critical information for decision making and the resulting task performance. The related parameters are the quality, format and media in which the information is presented. In the model, the corresponding "interfering factors" are: anxiety, confusion and stress. When running the model, if the quality of information is poor or inadequate there is a rise in confusion and stress and a fall in performance.

- Monitoring as a pressure factor: this frontend variable represents the adequacy of the time available for performing the task, as perceived by the operator. When inadequate, it impacts negatively on the user stress levels as well as on interfering factors such as anxiety.

- Workspace design: a frontend variable that represents the adequacy of the working environment to performing the task. When inadequate it impacts negatively on the operator levels of confusion and stress;
- Equipment: this frontend variable represents the adequacy of the equipment available to perform the task. When inadequate it impacts negatively on the operator fatigue and stress levels;
- Transport and logistic support: these are variables to be set up by the frontend that represent the infrastructure provided by the organization. When inadequate, the infrastructure impacts negatively on the operator fatigue level.
- Location: this frontend variable represents the ease of access to the place of work. When the access is difficult it impacts negatively on the operator's fatigue.
- Higher-level cognitive functions: this variable represents a combination of the personal traits: abstraction, organization and planning, cognitive flexibility and judgement. If this model variable (*set of user characteristics*) is set at a high level there should be a reduction in user confusion and a rise in user attention.

VALIDATING THE PROPOSED APPROACH

The user model was validated by a process that consisted in the instantiation with data from a case study before running simulations and comparing the results with data taken from a real situation reported in the case study.

The case study consisted of one report chosen from the corpus of study, describing a human error when operating an electrical substation. The error consisted of the operator performing a correct action on the wrong object, during task execution. The task itself consisted of restoring the electric system using a prescribed procedure. The error report mentions the operator's lack of attention, tiredness, and confusion, as the likely causes for the error. This particular report was chosen because it refers to three of the four factors represented in the original operator model. According to the company documents this task (system manoeuvre) was classed as complex and rare, and was an emergency task. The human error occurred towards the end of the working shift. The report mentions lack of attention due to ergonomic factors (human interface flaws), as well as to operator confusion and tiredness, due to a high workload.

The case study discussed in Netto, Aguiar, Scherer, and Vieira (2009) highlights the relationship between the model parameters and the task outcome. During simulation, as in the reported case, the task was only performed with success when the values for the variables: confusion and fatigue were at average levels; the stress level was low and attention was high; showing that the model results were compatible with the data from the human errors reports.

The original user model was conceived to investigate the impact of the user behaviour and characteristics on the task execution outcome. During its validation process it became clear that, in spite of its usefulness, it needed to be extended to shed more light on the human error study.

In the case study, the error report mentions many relevant facts that could not have been represented in the model due to its original simplicity; such as problems with the workspace at the time of the event (*obstructed angle of vision*) and equipment problems (*poor signalling on the panel*).

On the other hand, some of the new variables introduced into the extended model are not mentioned in the error report, and its potential effect on the task outcome therefore remains to be investigated. Amidst the more relevant model parameters found in the case study there are: team autonomy, product experience level, system experience level, task experience level, and job experience level. All these parameters are associated with the reported high level of operator confusion and an average level of stress. In this particular case it would be possible to investigate the following hypothesis:

a. *If the operator had had access to more precise information, the inadequate workspace would have had less impact on the operator's levels of confusion and stress, thus impacting less on the task outcome;*

b. *With a high level of experience with the system, task, job and tools (product), the operator would have been less confused and thus less influenced by the poor panel signalling.*

To validate the extended version of the model it is proposed to investigate a set of hypothesise by running the model instantiated with the same error report data and comparing the simulation outcome with the data from the error report as well as with data originating from other reports from the same corpus of study.

It is also proposed to investigate the relationships between the user behaviour modelled parameters with those mentioned in literature review on human error and compare this with data obtained from the observations of the user performing the task under similar conditions to those reported in the corpus of study. Considering the constraints of an electrical system work environment it would only be possible to perform the task on a simulated system. The following excerpts are taken from error reports, which form part of the corpus cited in Scherer, Vieira, and Neto (2010):

R.20: "...decided to go to the equipment in order to inspect it. After opening its command box directed the attention to reading the label fixed on its door. At this point stepped on false (losing the balance) and in the attempt to hold on and avoid falling, caused the equipment trip."

R25: "... the operator knows the task in detail and had the prescribed task instructions at hand...

when selecting the switch X got confused and selected switch Y instead, since both were placed on the same chassis." Assigned causes for the error: "self-confidence- simple, standard and routine task," "momentary loss of concentration due to self-confidence," "incorrect selection of switch to be manipulated."

R34: "Operator lack of concentration during task execution due to procedure disregard (task considered simple), and task execution happened during team exchange at the end of the working shift." Assigned causes for the error: "Second operator was absent, resulting in no double checking or follow up." "Lack of operator concentration... causing incomplete execution of one item in the task, aggravated by this item's characteristics, which demanded two actions to be performed in separate places of the control panel complex."

EXPECTED IMPACT ON HUMAN ERROR PREVENTION

Although the human behaviour is too complex to be represented in a parameterized model, as far as prototypes go, the user model proposed in this work can be useful as a platform to explore it under stressful work conditions. It is expected that the chosen characteristics are adequate for the study of their intricate inter-relations, and to provide some preliminary insights.

The authors expect that, through simulations, the extended user model will facilitate investigation of the dynamics of the relation between the variables considered allowing this knowledge to be applied to the design of more ergonomic user interfaces for industrial automated control environments, thereby reducing the occurrence of human errors due to human interface design flaws.

The preliminary results with the original user model suggested the need for a wider set of variables that comprise user characteristics as well as representing task and context information. This result is in line with the proposal of the MCIE

(Turnell, 2004) method for ergonomic interface conception. With an extended set of model parameters the possibilities investigating the relation between user behaviour and task outcome widens, impacting on the knowledge required to build user interfaces with higher usability. The investigations should be supported by the observation, and associated gathering, of physiological and cognitive data, adequate to evidence traits of the user's status and indicative of the user's future behaviour—particularly during stressful situations that might induce human error. This proposal for future work follows in the steps of previous work such as discussed in Kreibig (2010); although with a wider scope, since that work is restricted to relating emotions with ANS, on the basis of physiological data, at a qualitative level.

Another piece of work, a reference for the work reported here, is that of Jung and Jung (2001) which proposes ranges of values for the model parameters. These values should be obtained from user questionnaires related to specific contexts and situations. The parameters considered in that work are: physical workload, environmental factors, postural discomfort and mental workload. A proposed set of scales is associated with each user parameter, and is similar to the scales proposed for POCUs and MoPUs. There is no scale related to the mental workload due to the inherent difficulty of handling the subjectivity associated with different individuals.

For the purposes of this work, TLX with its workload parameters is the most relevant. Not only is it the basis of much other relevant work (e.g. Jung & Jung, 2001; Wiebe, Roberts, & Behrend, 2010), but it also relates directly to the POCUs and MoPUs structures, having made easier the addition of new parameters such as "time pressure," "task difficulty" and "task type." It is also pointed out that the (Huey & Wickens, 1993) set of characteristics contributed to POCUs and MoPUs with relevant information to define a team organization structure.

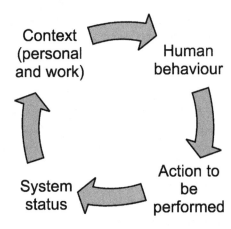

Figure 1. Dynamics of the relation between the human behaviour and the error

The user model based on the user profile widened the knowledge of user behaviour and its relation to human error. The assumption was that understanding the dynamics of the interaction could help to understand the cause of error and elaborate more effective error prevention measures.

From the literature on human error, the authors propose to represent the dynamics of the interaction in diagrammatic form as illustrated in Figure 1. This figure relates "Context," both personal and work, with human behaviour, which in turn determines the action to be performed on the system to reach the targeted system status. This then feeds back onto the operator behaviour.

Future Directions

The next step in this research will be to incorporate biometrical data into the user model. This will allow the association of mental and physical overload with related stress and their influence on the user reliability and performance. It is also intended to investigate the relationship between the previously mentioned variables and user behaviour, searching for relations that might indicate the need for improvement in working conditions that might reduce the incidence of human error.

Variables to be included in future versions of MoPUs:

- Physical Restrictions: Which represents the influence of user physical restrictions on task performance, from the view point of physiology;
- Temperament and Personality: Which represents psychological aspects of the user such as: agreeableness, confidence and impulsive behaviour, which can directly affect the operator status.

With this addition it would be possible to investigate the cross effect of the new variables on the shift duration and the resulting workload.

Final Comments

This chapter described the combined approach of building a user profile and mapping it into a programmable user model, enriching it with information relevant to studies of human error. It discussed how to employ the user model to increase knowledge of user behaviour. Finally, it discussed how to use the resulting knowledge to prevent human error during the operation of automated industrial systems, in a chosen domain. The authors hope that this knowledge, acquired on the basis of cognitive sciences, will support the design of more ergonomic user interfaces, which in turn will reduce the occurrence of human errors. The proposed approach has been subjected to preliminary validation through its application to the operation of automated systems in the electricity industry with promising results. Further validation is proposed, consisting of observing user behaviour during task performance, registering and analyzing it using methods for measuring workload from the physiological, procedural and subjective points of view, as proposed in Weinger et al. (2000).

REFERENCES

Baldauf, D., Brugard, E., & Wittmann, M. (2009). Time perception as a workload measure in simulated car driving. *Applied Ergonomics*, *40*(5), 929–935. doi:10.1016/j.apergo.2009.01.004

Bodart, F., Hennebert, A., Leheureux, J., & Vanderdonckt, J. (1994). Towards a dynamic strategy for computer-aided visual placement. In *Proceedings of 2nd ACM Workshop on Advanced Visual Interfaces AVI 1994*, (pp. 78-87). New York, NY: ACM Press.

Bohnert, F., & Zukerman, I. (2009). Non-intrusive personalisation of the museum experience. In *Proceedings of UMAP 2009*. UMAP.

Butterworth, R., & Blandford, A. (1997). *Programmable user models: The story so far*. PUMA Working Paper WP8. Retrieved from http://www.eis.mdx.ac.uk/puma/wp8.pdf.

Card, S., Moran, T., & Newell, A. (1983). *The psychology of human-computer interaction*. Wahwah, NJ: Lawrence Erlbaum Associates.

Cellier, J. M. (1990). L'erreur human dans le travail. In Leplat, J., & De Terssac, G. (Eds.), *Les Facteurs Humains de la Fiabilite dans les Systemes Complexes. France*. Marseille.

Cheverst, K., Mitchell, K., & Davies, N. (2002). The role of adaptive hypermedia in a context-aware tourist guide. *Communications of the ACM*, *45*(5). doi:10.1145/506218.506244

Courage, C., & Baxter, K. (2005). *Understanding your users: A practical guide to user requirements*. New York, NY: Morgan Kaufmann Publishers.

de Queiroz, J., de Oliveira, R., & Turnell, M. F. (2005). *WebQuest: A configurable web tool to prospect the user profile and user subjective satisfaction*. Paper presented at the 11th International Conference on Human-Computer Interaction. Las Vegas, NY.

DiDomenico, A., & Nussbaum, M. (2008). Interactive effects of physical and mental workload on subjective workload assessment. *International Journal of Industrial Ergonomics, 38*(5), 977–983. doi:10.1016/j.ergon.2008.01.012

Eindhoven University of Technology. (2009). *Suite home, experimental test-bed for new features for CPN tools.* Retrieved from http://wiki.daimi.au.dk/britney/_home.wiki.

Eindhoven University of Technology. (2011). *CPN tools homepage.* Retrieved from http://wiki.daimi.au.dk/cpntools.

Fikes, R., & Nilsson, N. (1971). STRIPS: A new approach to the application of theorem proving to problem solving. *Artificial Intelligence.* Retrieved from http://www.ai.sri.com/pubs/files/tn043r-fikes71.pdf.

Guérin, F., Laville, A., Daniellou, F., Duraffourg, J., & Kerguelen, A. (2001). *Comprendre le travail pour le transformer - La pratique de L'ergnonomie* (Ingratta, G. M., & Maffei, M., Trans.). Paris, France: Edgard Blücher Ltda.

Hart, S., & Staveland, L. (1988). Development of NASA-TLX (task load index): Results of empirical and theoretical research. In Hancock, P., & Meshkati, N. (Eds.), *Advances in Psychology: Human Mental Workload* (pp. 239–250). London, UK: Elsevier. doi:10.1016/S0166-4115(08)62386-9

Hollnagel, E. (1998). *Cognitive reliability and error analysis method (CREAM).* London, UK: Elsevier Science.

Huey, B. M., & Wickens, C. D. (1993). *Workload transition: Implications for individual and team performance.* Washington, DC: National Academy Press.

ISO. (1998). *ISO 9241 - Ergonomic requirements for office work with visual display terminals.* Geneva, Switzerland: International Organization for Standardization.

Jensen, K. (1992). *Couloured petri nets – Basic concepts, analyses methods and practical use* (*Vol. 1*). Berlin, Germany: Springer.

Jung, H., & Jung, H.-S. (2001). Establishment of overall workload assessment technique for various tasks and workplaces. *International Journal of Industrial Ergonomics, 28*(6), 341–353. doi:10.1016/S0169-8141(01)00040-3

Kreibig, S. (2010). Autonomic nervous system activity in emotion: A review. *Biological Psychology, 84*(3), 394–421. doi:10.1016/j.biopsycho.2010.03.010

Leplat, J., & Cuny, X. (1977). *Introduction à la psychologie tu travail* (Domingos, H., Trans.). Lisboa, Portugal: Fundação Calouste Gulbenkian.

Leuchter, S., Niessen, C., Eyferth, K., & Bierwagen, T. (1997). Modelling mental processes of experienced operators during control of a dynamic man maschine system. In *Proceedings of the 16th European Annual Conferece on Human Decision Making and Manual Control,* (pp. 268-276). Kassel, Germany: Universidade of Kassel.

Lewis, R. (2001). Cognitive theory, soar. In *International Encyclopedia of the Social and Behavioral Sciences.* Amsterdam, The Netherlands: Pergamon. doi:10.1016/B0-08-043076-7/01583-7

Markopoulos, P., Pycock, J., Wilson, S., & Johnson, P. (1992). ADEPT - A task based design environment. In *Proceedings of the International Conference on System Sciences,* (pp. 587-596). Hawaii, HI: IEEE Computer Society Press.

Netto, A., Aguiar, Y., Scherer, D., & Vieira, M. D. (2009). *Context analysis during task execution: An operator model.* Paper presented at the IADIS International Conference - Interfaces and Human Computer Interaction 2009. Portugal.

Niessen, C., & Eyferth, K. (2001). A model of the air traffic controller's picture. *Safety Science, 37*(2-3), 187–202. doi:10.1016/S0925-7535(00)00048-5

Niessen, C., Leuchter, S., & Eyferth, K. (1998). A psychological model of air traffic control and its implementation. In F. E. Riter, & R. M. Young (Eds.), *Second European Conference on Cognitive Modelling (ECCM-98),* (pp. 104-111). Nottingham, UK: Nottingham University Press.

Paletz, S., Bearman, C., Orasanu, J., & Holbrook, J. (2009). Socializing the human factors analysis and classification system: Incorporating social psychological phenomena into a human factors error classification system. *Human Factors, 51,* 435–445. doi:10.1177/0018720809343588

Rasmussen, J., Pejtersen, A., & Goodstein, L. (1994). *Cognitive systems engineering.* New York, NY: John Wiley & Sons, Inc.

Reason, J. (1990). *Human error.* Cambridge, UK: Cambridge University Press.

Scherer, D., da Costa, R., Barbosa, J., & Vieira, M. D. (2010). Taxonomy proposal for the description of accidents and incidents in electrical systems operation. In *Proceedings of the ACM SIGCHI Symposium on Engineering Interactive Computing Systems.* Berlin, Germany: ACM Press.

Scherer, D., & Vieira, M. (2008). Accounting for the human error when building the user profile. In *Proceedings of the Third IASTED International Conference Human-Computer Interaction,* (pp. 132-137). Insbruck, Austria: ACTA Press.

Scherer, D., Vieira, M., & Neto, J. (2010). Human error categorization: An extension to classical proposals applied to electrical systems operations. In P. Forbrig, F. Paternó, & A. Pejtersen (Eds.), *Proceedings of HCIS 2010, IFIP AICT,* (pp. 234-245). Brisbane, Australia: Springer.

Shappel, S., & Wiegmann, D. (2000). *The human factors analysis and classification system - HFACS.* Oklahoma City, OK: FAA Civil Aeromedical Institute.

Tenenbaum, G., & Connolly, C. (2008). Attention allocation under varied workload and effort perception in rowers. *Psychology of Sport and Exercise, 9*(5), 704–717. doi:10.1016/j.psychsport.2007.09.002

Turnell, M. F. (2004). Accounting for human errors in a method for the conception of user interfaces. In *Proceedings of the International Mediterranean Modelling Multi-Conference - I3M 2004,* (pp. 122-130). Genova, Italy: I3M.

Weinger, M. B., Vredenburgh, A. G., Schumann, C. M., Macario, A., Williams, K. J., & Kalsher, M. J. (2000). Quantitative description of the workload associated with airway management procedures. *Journal of Clinical Anesthesia, 12*(4), 273–282. doi:10.1016/S0952-8180(00)00152-5

WHO. (2001). *International classification of functioning, disability and health (ICF).* Retrieved from http://www.who.int/classifications/icf/en/.

Wiebe, E., Roberts, E., & Behrend, T. (2010). An examination of two mental workload measurement approaches to understanding multimedia learning. *Computers in Human Behavior, 26*(3), 474–481. doi:10.1016/j.chb.2009.12.006

Wittmann, M., & Paulus, M. (2007). Decision making, impulsivity and time perception. *Trends in Cognitive Sciences, 12*(1), 7–12. doi:10.1016/j.tics.2007.10.004

ADDITIONAL READING

Adamski, A., & Westrum, R. (2003). Requisite imagination: The fine art of anticipating what might go wrong. In Hollnagel, E. (Ed.), *Handbook of Cognitive Task Design.* Mahwah, NJ: Lawrence Erlbaum Associates.

Dekker, S. (2007). *Just culture: Balancing safety and accountability*. Farnham, UK: Ashgate Publishing Company.

Falzon, P. (2007). Enabling safety: Issues in design and continuous design. *Cognition Technology and Work, 10*(1).

Hollnagel, E., Woods, D., & Leveson, N. (2006). *Resilience engineering: Concepts and precepts*. Farnham, UK: Ashgate Publishing.

Isaac, A., Shorrock, S., & Kirwan, B. (2002). Human error in European air traffic management: The HERA project. *Reliability Engineering & System Safety, 75*(2). doi:10.1016/S0951-8320(01)00099-0

Johnson, W. B., & Rouse, W. B. (1982). Analysis and classification of human errors in troubleshooting live aircraft power plants. *IEEE Transactions on Systems, Man, and Cybernetics, 12*(3).

Naoya, H. (2001). *Intention and slips of actions*. Kyoto, Japan: Kyoto University.

Neto, J. N., Vieira, M. D., Santoni, C., & Scherer, D. (2009). Proposing strategies to prevent the human error in automated industrial environments. In *Proceedings of HCI International 2009*, (pp. 279-288). San Diego, CA: Springer-Verlag.

Norman, D. A. (1983). Design rules based on analyses of human error. *Communications of the ACM, 26*(4). doi:10.1145/2163.358092

Rasmussen, J., Pedersen, O. M., Carmino, A., Griffon, M., & Gagnolet, P. (1981). *Classification system for reporting events involving human malfunctions. RISO National Laboratory*. Denmark, The Netherlands: RISO National Laboratory.

Reason, J. (1987a). A framework for classifying errors. In Rasmussen, J., Dunkan, K., & Leplat, J. (Eds.), *New Technology and Human Error*. New York, NY: John Wiley & Sons Ltd.

Reason, J. (1987b). A preliminary classification of mistakes. In Rasmussen, J., Dunkan, K., & Leplat, J. (Eds.), *New Technology and Human Error*. New York, NY: John Wiley & Sons Ltd.

Schneiderman, B. (2004). *Designing the user interface: Strategies for effective human-computer interaction*. Boston, MA: Addison Wesley.

Shorrock, S. (2002). Error classification for safety management: Finding the right approach. In *Proceedings of a Workshop on the Investigation and Reporting of Incidents and Accidents*. Glasgow, UK: University of Glasgow.

van der Schaaf, T., & Habraken, M. (2005). *PRISMA-medical-A brief description*. Eindhoven, Germany: Technische Universiteit Eindhoven.

van Eekhout, J. M., & Rouse, W. B. (1981). Human errors in detection, diagnosis, and compensations for failures in the engine control room of a supertanker. *IEEE Transactions on Systems, Man, and Cybernetics, 11*(12), 813–816. doi:10.1109/TSMC.1981.4308621

Vidal, M., Carvalho, P., Santos, M., & Santos, I. (2009). Collective work and resilience of complex systems. *Journal of Loss Prevention in the Process Industries, 22*(4), 516–527. doi:10.1016/j.jlp.2009.04.005

Westrum, R. (2006). A typology of resilience situations. In Hollnagel, E., Woods, D., & Leveson, N. (Eds.), *Resilience Engineering: Concepts and Precepts*. Farnham, UK: Ashgate Publishing.

KEY TERMS AND DEFINITIONS

User Behaviour: Display of psychological and social characteristics that directly influence the user system interaction.

User Profile: Typically represented by a set of user characteristics such as age, gender, user skills and knowledge, among others. In this work it encompasses both the static characteristics mentioned before as well as dynamic ones related to user behaviour.

Human Error: The result of actions performed by a user that lead to unwanted or unforeseen outcomes for the system, causing human or material losses.

Programmable User Model: Conceived to support the investigation of the human behaviour during interaction with complex systems. The user profile and user model will be employed in human error studies, supporting the investigation of the relationship between the errors and the user characteristics.

POCUs: The proposed user profile – POCUs (Perfil Objetivo e Cognitivo do Usuário) is an extended set of typical user characteristics that include features related to cognitive behaviour, which are of interest for human error studies. The user profile is structured in six sub-sets of characteristics: Personal; Clinical; Psychological; Professional; Contextual and Physical Profiles; the data gathering process is supported by a questionnaire and a checklist.

MoPUs: The programmable user model (Modelo Programável do Usuário), was conceived to represent the user behaviour, the task and the work environment, in the context of industrial systems' operation, more specifically that of electrical systems operation.

Scenario: Representation of a situation that has been reported to lead into human errors. It can be extracted from the error reports and allows investigating task results under specified conditions.

Ergonomic User Interfaces: Interfaces conceived to take into account the task, the work context and the user characteristics, in order to better adapt to the user and thus contribute to prevent the human error.

Chapter 15
The Bootstrap Discovery Behaviour Model:
Why Five Users are Not Enough to Test User Experience

Simone Borsci
Brunel University, UK

Stefano Federici
University of Perugia, Italy

Maria Laura Mele
Sapienza University of Rome, Italy

Domenico Polimeno
University of Perugia, Italy

Alessandro Londei
Sapienza University of Rome, Italy

ABSTRACT

The chapter focuses on the Bootstrap statistical technique for assigning measures of accuracy to sample estimates, here adopted for the first time to obtain an effective and efficient interaction evaluation. After introducing and discussing the classic debate on p value (i.e., the discovery detection rate) about estimation problems, the authors present the most used model for the estimation of the number of participants needed for an evaluation test, namely the Return On Investment model (ROI). Since the ROI model endorses a monodimensional and economical perspective in which an evaluation process, composed of only an expert technique, is sufficient to identify all the interaction problems—without distinguishing real problems (i.e., identified both experts and users) and false problems (i.e., identified only by experts)— they propose the new Bootstrap Discovery Behaviour (BDB) estimation model. Findings highlight the BDB as a functional technique favouring practitioners to optimize the number of participants needed for an interaction evaluation. Finally, three experiments show the application of the BDB model to create experimental sample sizes to test user experience of people with and without disabilities.

DOI: 10.4018/978-1-4666-1628-8.ch015

INTRODUCTION

The ROI model, which was proposed in 1993 by Nielsen and Landauer, shows that, generally, the least number of users required for a usability test ranges from three to five. This model is an asymptotic test which allows practitioners to estimate the number of users needed through the following formula:

$$\text{Found}(i) = N[1-(1-p)^i] \qquad (1)$$

In (1), the N value corresponds to the total number of problems in the interface, the p value is defined by Nielsen and Landauer (1993) as "the probability of finding the average usability problem when running a single average subject test" (i.e., discovery detection rate), and the i value corresponds to the number of users. For instance, by applying formula (1), practitioners can estimate whether five users are sufficient for obtaining a reliable assessment and, if not, how many users (N) are needed in order to increase the percentage of usability problems. Nielsen, starting from the results obtained by many applications of the ROI model, suggests that the practitioners, in order to test different categories of users, have to divide users into multiple groups composed as follows (Nielsen, 2000):

- 5 subjects of a category if testing 1 group of users;
- 3-4 subjects from each category if testing 2 groups of users;
- 3 users from each category if testing three or more groups of users.

The value "p" (see formula 1) may be considered an index for assessing the effectiveness and efficiency of an Evaluation Method (EM). As some international studies (Lewis, 1994; Nielsen, 2000; Nielsen & Mack, 1994; Virzi, 1990, 1992; Wright & Monk, 1991) have shown, a sample size of five participants is sufficient to find ap-

proximately 80% of the usability problems in a system when the individual detection rate (p) is at least .30. The value of 30% was derived through Monte Carlo (MC) resampling of multiple evaluators, and could also be estimated using the full matrix of problems as discovered by independent evaluators (Lewis, 2001).

However, as Nielsen and Landauer (1993, p. 209) underline when discussing their model, the discoverability rate (p) for any given usability test depends on at least seven main factors:

- The properties of the system and its interface;
- The stage of the usability lifecycle;
- The type and quality of the methodology used to conduct the test;
- The specific tasks selected;
- The match between the test and the context of real world usage;
- The representativeness of the test participants;
- The skill of the evaluator.

As Borsci, Londei, and Federici (2011) claim, many studies underline that these factors have an effect on the evaluation of the interaction between system and user that the ROI model is not able to estimate (Caulton, 2001; Hertzum & Jacobsen, 2003; Lewis, 1994, 2006; Schmettow, 2008; Spool & Schroeder, 2001). In this sense, the ROI model cannot guarantee the reliability of the evaluation results obtained by the first five participants.

One of the most relevant problems that Borsci et al. (2011) underline is that the ROI model starts with a "one evaluator" condition and not at zero condition; this means that the characteristics of the system are considered only as the differences between problems found by the first evaluators. Nielsen and Mack (1994) pointed out that the first evaluator (a user or an expert) generally finds 30% of the problems, because these problems are generally the most evident. The subsequent evaluators usually find a smaller percentage of new problems, simply because the most evident ones have already been detected by the first evaluator. The number of evident problems is determined empirically and it varies because it is dependent on the evaluator's skills, which, as we have already stated, are a factor that this model does not consider.

A serious limitation of the ROI model is that it happened to be working with products for which the value of p across evaluators/users was about .3, but as J. R. Lewis (1994) showed, it is possible for the composite value of p to be much lower than .3. In order to assess the completeness of a problem-discovery usability study, the practitioner(s) running the study must have some idea of the value of p, which differs from study to study as a function of the properties of the system, the interface lifecycle stage, the methodologies selected for the evaluation, and the skill of the evaluators/users, ergo it is not necessarily .3 (30%).

FROM ECONOMIC EVALUATION TO EFFECTIVENESS AND EFFICIENCY OF THE EVALUATION METHODS

Albeit the ROI is a powerful model to obtain an economic index, it does not guarantee the efficiency and the effectiveness of the evaluation. Indeed the assumption of this model is that all problems identified in the evaluation are real problems. This assumption is true just when we consider separately all the problems found in a test.

However, when the problems identified by experts and users are matched, three different kinds of problems can be identified: false problems, which are detected only by the expert analysis; missed real problems, which are problems identified by the users during the interaction that were not detected by the experts; and real problems, which are problems identified by both the user-based and the expert-based analyses.

Our idea is that the problem with the ROI model is not only the limit in the estimation of

the p value, but we want to claim that the most important deficiency of the ROI model is the economical perspective mediated by it. In fact under this perspective, in which all the found problems are considered as real *per se*, the p value estimation problems cannot be solved.

The limits of this perspective can be summarized as follow:

1. *It is not related to a standard definition of effectiveness and efficiency*: Nielsen and Landauer created the ROI model five years before the definition of effectiveness and efficiency provided by the International Standards Organization (ISO) 9241-11 (1998). In this sense, they did not refer to the effectiveness and the efficiency as dimensions of usability (multi-dimensional perspective), but they endorsed an economical perspective (monodimensional perspective): implicitly, in the ROI model, the effectiveness is considered as the amount of problems found by a technique, while the efficiency as the amount of evaluation costs.

2. *It is focused on a quantitative point of view*: The more efficient an EM is the less it costs. The costs of an EM are mainly calculated on the number of the participants in the evaluations, because more participants require more time for the evaluation, money for the participants' fees, etc. Therefore, an EM is more efficient when it employs few participants. Moreover, an EM is considered effective when with the smallest number of participants it finds the largest number of problems (i.e., more than 80% of the probable problems in the interface). Nevertheless, as we already claimed, the model does not consider which kind of problems the EMs detected.

In order to avoid the first limit of the ROI model perspective, we try to provide a definition of evaluation technique effectiveness and efficiency that accomplishes the ISO standard.

The ISO 9241-11(1998) standard defines the effectiveness and the efficiency of a system as follows:

- *Effectiveness* is the accuracy and completeness with which users achieve specified goals;
- *Efficiency* is the amount of resources expended in relation to the accuracy and completeness with which users achieve goals.

Following this statement, and applying it to an EM technique, we wonder: how can we define the effectiveness and the efficiency of an EM? We propose these following definitions of effectiveness and efficiency by applying in the context of EMs the aforementioned content of the ISO-9241-11.

- *Effectiveness of an EM*: Considering the effectiveness as "the accuracy and completeness with which a user achieves specified goals," we define the Effectiveness of an EM as the ability to estimate which real problems are present in the evaluated system (i.e., which problems do not allow an effective interaction);
- *Efficiency of an EM*: Considering the efficiency as "the amount of resources expended in relation to the accuracy and completeness with which users achieve goals," we define the Efficiency of an EM as the amount of all the costs of the evaluation meant as the time spent by user and/or expert.

Since the aim of the evaluation process is the identification of real problems, the effectiveness of a technique should be related to the quantity of "real" problems found (and not just to the number of all problems); while the efficiency should

be linked to the cost of the evaluation—i.e., the number of participants and the time spent for the analysis.

As a second step, in order to overcome the quantitative point of view of the ROI model perspective, according to our definition of efficiency and effectiveness of an EM, we provide a new perspective on the identified problem in evaluation by distinguishing the quantity and the quality of their nature.

Nielsen and Landauer (1993) consider heuristic evaluations (i.e., expert-based analysis) to be always more powerful than any user-based evaluation: in fact, heuristic evaluation provides a large amount of problems' identification (i.e., effectiveness according to ROI) with a lower cost than the users' tests (i.e., efficiency according to ROI). Now, it is clear that, while we could endorse the idea that a high efficiency equals a low cost evaluation, we cannot endorse the idea that a high effectiveness equals a high amount of problems found, without distinguishing between real and false problems. In our opinion, an effective evaluation is that one that detects the highest number of just "real" problems.

Using a metaphor to explain the difference between the ROI model and our perspective, we can say that:

- *Following the ROI model*: A fisher (i.e., the evaluator), in order to have an effective and efficient fishing process, needs to use the largest fishing net possible (i.e., the EM); in this way, in fact, s/he would be able to obtain a low-cost process (efficiency) and a high number of fishes caught (effectiveness).
- *Following our idea*: A fisher, in order to have an effective and efficient fishing process, not only needs to use a kind of fishing net (i.e., EM) able to guarantee a low-cost process (efficiency), but s/he also needs to catch a certain kind of fishes: i) fishes that can be sold as edible and ii) fishes that can

be fished without breaking the law. Our idea is that an effective fishing net is not the largest one but the one able to catch those fishes that the fisher will not have to throw overboard. Out of our example: an effective EM must find the highest number of "real" problems, minimizing the identification of "not real" ones.

Summarizing, in this section we have divided the interaction problems into false and reals. The real ones are the problems identified during the interaction by both experts and users, while the false problems are identified only by experts. We have stressed that the ROI model does not take into consideration our previous distinction, because it endorses a monodimensional and economical perspective in which an evaluation process, composed of only an expert technique, is sufficient to identify all the interaction problems. As we discussed above, today the ROI model perspective is overcome by a multidimensional perspective (ISO 9241-11, 1998) in which the evaluation process aims at identifying problems by matching results from experts' and users' techniques (i.e., computing only the real problems). In order to extend both the ROI perspective and its mathematical model, we applied a bootstrap statistical technique for assigning measures of accuracy to sample estimates. By following this aim we create an alternative model to the ROI, based on the probabilistic behaviour in the evaluation, the Bootstrap Discovery Behaviour (BDB) model. The BDB, by considering more factors in the p value estimation and endorsing a multidimensional perspective of the evaluation, may be applied for defining the sample size of both the users and the experts needed to identify the real problems of interaction by a matching of all experienced problems.

The BDB Model

The term "bootstrapping," defined by Efron (1979), is an allusion to the expression "pulling oneself up by one's bootstraps"—in this case, using the sample data as a population from which repeated samples are drawn (Fox, 2002). The present bootstrapping approach moves from the assumption that discovering new problems should be the main goal of both users' and experts' evaluations as well as expressed in Formula (1) by Nielsen and Landauer (1993).

Given a generic problem x, the probability that a subject will find x is $p(x)$. If two subjects (experts or users) navigate the same interface, the probability that *at least* one of them will detect the problem x is:

$$p(x_1 \lor x_2) \tag{2}$$

In (2), where x_1 and x_2 represent the problem x detected by subjects 1 and 2, OR is the logic operator. According to De Morgan's law (Goodstein, 1963), (2) is equivalent to:

$$p[\neg(\neg x_1 \land \neg x_2)] \tag{3}$$

Equation (3) expresses the probability of "the degree to which it is false that none of the subjects find anything" (the logic operator for negation). So (3) can be rewritten as:

$$p(\neg x) = 1 - p(x)$$

Since the probabilities of different subjects finding a specific problem are mutually independent, Equation (3) can be written as:

$$p[\neg(\neg x_1 \land \neg x_2)] = 1 - [1-p(x_1)]*[1-p(x_2)] \tag{4}$$

Following Caulton's homogeneity assumption (2001) that all subjects have the same probability (*p*) of finding the problem *x*, then (4) can also be expressed as:

$$p(x_1 \vee x_2) = 1 - (1 - p)^2 \tag{5}$$

Of course, we can extend this case to a generic number of evaluators *L*:

$$p(x_1 \vee x_2 \vee \ldots x_L) = 1 - (1 - p)^L \tag{6}$$

Equation 6 expresses the probability that, in a sample composed of *L* evaluators, at least one of them will identify the problem *x*.

According to Nielsen and Landauer (1993), given *N* problems in an interface, the probability of any problem being detected by any evaluator can be considered constant ($p(x) = p$). Then, the mean number of problems detected by *L* evaluators is:

$$F(L) = N[1 - (1 - p)^L] \tag{7}$$

Leading to the same model presented by Nielsen (Equation 1), in (7), in order to estimate *p(x)* we adopted the bootstrap model, avoiding estimation merely based on the addition of detected problems. This kind of estimation could in fact be invalidated by the small size of the analysed samples or by the differences in the subjects' probabilities of problem detections.

As its first feature, BDB model is able to take into account the probabilistic individual differences in problem identification. The second feature of the BDB is that it considers the evaluated interfaces as an object per se. The interfaces are considered different not in terms of the number of problems found by the first evaluator (evaluation condition), but different as objects (zero condition) estimating the probabilistic number of evident problems that all the evaluators can detect by testing the interface. The third feature of the BDB model is that, in order to calculate the number of evaluators needed for the evaluation, it considers the representativeness of the sample (as regards the population of all the possible evaluation behaviours of the participants).

Our idea is that the BDB should be able to grant a more reliable estimation of the probability of identifying a problem than the ROI model, particularly when a practitioner has to carry out a User eXperience (UX) evaluation test with a mixed sample of disabled and not disabled users.

The Mixed Sample User eXperience Evaluation: BDB Model Application

The new concept of UX enlarged the role played by users within the interaction evaluation process. Indeed, as Garret underlines, the UX of the system "is about how it works on the outside, where a person comes into contact with it and has to work with it" (Garrett, 2003). At the same time, the ISO 9241-210 defines UX as "a person's perceptions and responses that result from the use or anticipated use of a product, system or service. [...] User experience is a consequence of the presentation, functionality, system performance, interactive behaviour, and assistive capabilities of an interactive system, both hardware and software. [...] It is also a consequence of the user's prior experiences, attitudes, skills, habits and personality" (2010). Following this definition, the UX concept results in an extent of the usability itself, by taking into consideration the users' experiences, attitudes, skills, and personality. According to this new framework, the analysis of the interaction of disabled users becomes a priority in order to allow practitioners to compose a mixed panel of users that guarantees the reliability of the set of data obtained during the interface evaluation process.

Although the literature on the interaction between disabled users and technology is very wide; indeed, the studies on HCI rarely take into account the UX of persons with intellectual disabilities (Luckasson, et al., 2002; Schalock & Luckasson, 2004), and, when it happens, they mostly focus on either analysing accessibility issues (Bohman

& Anderson, 2005) or describing how to improve design of the technology (Fairweather & Trewin, 2010). Moreover, these kind of studies are mostly centered on identifying the advantages of new communication technologies for persons with intellectual disabilities (Feng, Lazar, Kumin, & Ozok, 2008, 2010).

Following the distinction made by Hartson and colleagues (Hartson, Andre, & Williges, 2001), have identified two approaches endorsed in HCI evaluation studies: the first one is the summative evaluation approach by which the evaluation of the interface is conducted for assess the efficacy of the final design or to compare competing design alternatives in terms of usability; the second approach is the formative evaluation one by which the evaluation is focused on usability problems that need to be solved during the prototype design stage before a final design can be accepted for release.

We use this distinction for classify the literature on the interaction between disabled users and technology. We classify under the 'Summative Oriented' (SO) approach all the studies which aim at improving the system accessibility and analysing disabled users' skills and behaviour while performing a product. These studies (Bohman & Anderson, 2005; Fairweather & Trewin, 2010; Feng, et al., 2008, 2010) endorse an approach that considers the disabled users only as 'customers' of products, instead of users in interaction.

Conversely, we classify the studies focussed on a widening disabled users' participation to systems' creation by a User-Centred Design (UCD) perspective (Norman, 1988) under the 'Participative and Formative Oriented' (PFO) approach (Federici & Borsci, 2010; Federici, Borsci, & Mele, 2010; Federici, Borsci, & Stamerra, 2010; Federici, et al., 2005; Feng, et al., 2008, 2010; Lewis, 2005).

The main purpose of both SO and PFO approaches is to promote and diffuse the *Design for All*, according to the Stephanidis' definition: "Universal Design in information technology and telecommunications products should not be conceived as an effort to advance a single solution for everybody, but as a user-centered approach to providing products that can automatically address the possible range of human abilities, skills, requirements and preferences" (Stephanidis, 2001).

Although both the SO and PFO approaches have the aim to analyse the "match" between the technologies and the users' needs, by following the Design for All philosophy, the SO results as the most used approach by the researchers, even though it reduces the evaluation of interaction to the mere analysis of the system features.

On the other hand the PFO approach—which endorses the motto 'Nothing about us, without us' (Charlton, 1998), that we may reinterpret here as 'nothing is *for all*, without us'—aims to improve the UX of interaction by a UCD process of design and re-design which allow to extend the system's features taking into account the needs of all kind of users. While the SO approach not fully accomplishes the Design for All's goals, because it not considers the users' needs, the PFO approach aims to overcome the SO assessment process by involving disabled users ever since the first phases of both the design and the evaluation processes. In this sense, by following the PFO perspective, the only way to spread the Design for All philosophy is to develop methods and techniques that equally involve disabled and not disabled users in each step of the assessment process, starting from the recruitment of subjects until the final product evaluation. Indeed, one of the most important problems in the UX studies is not only how to test disabled users in order to analyse their interaction experience, but also how to test them by collecting data that can be compared to not-disabled users.

In the next sections after the presentation of the BDB model, we focused on the sample size of participants who must be involved into the evaluation process of a prototype during its development. Specifically, in order to identify the number needed to get the less expensive and the most efficient mixed sample of users for discovering at least the 80% of usability problems, a usability evaluation has been carried out involving users with intellectual disabilities, blind and not-disabled users. We present three experimental application of the BDB model, in order to show how large a mixed sample has to be created by a practitioner to obtain a reliable (i.e., efficient and effective) UX evaluation.

EXPERIMENTAL APPLICATION OF THE BDB MODEL

We compare the BDB and the ROI model discovery rate in a UX test conducted with three experimental groups of users—not-disabled, blind and with Down Syndrome (DS)—in order to estimate the number of users (with and without disability) needed to compose sample that can allow to discover the number of problem as lager as possible (i.e., efficacy) at the minimum costs (i.e., efficiency). Three experimental sessions are here presented, concerning the analysis of three different web interfaces. Each experiment involved a control group composed by not disabled and disabled users, with either visual or intellectual disabilities.

Methods and Tools

We compared the number of users needed in order to identify the 80% of problems by applying both the ROI model and the BDB model (for the source code of the BDB model, see Appendix 1). The analysis was carried out through the IBM® PAWS Statistics 18 software and the Matlab software.

Apparatus

For each experiment the apparatus used during the experimental setting was set up as follows: A internet connection ADSL 4 MB; an internet Explorer 8 browser; a PC AMD Athlon 64 (3,200 MHz); a Philips 190S LCD 19" monitor; a Jaws® screen reader version 12 (for both the experiment

1 and 2); a CamStudio version 20 screen recorder; two amplifiers; an audio recorder Digital Zoom h2; a Nikon L2 digital camera; a Stopwatch; and a desk bell.

Experimental Websites

In all the three experiments each user were involved in four scenario-based analyses, which have been created to allow users to recruit information with at least four actions (i.e. mouse click). The tests of the web interfaces for all the experiments were conducted between April and June 2009.

- The experiment 1 consisted on the evaluation of the Italian National Social Service website (www.serviziocivile.it) conducted by a sample of blind users and a sample of sighted users.
- The experiment 2 consisted on the evaluation of a prototype of a sonified visual search engines WhatsOnWeb (WoW)—created at the University of Perugia by Department of Electronic and Information Engineering (DIEI) (Di Giacomo, Didimo, Grilli, & Liotta, 2007; Di Giacomo, Didimo, Grilli, Liotta, & Palladino, 2008) with the collaboration of the CognitiveLab group (www.cognitivelab.it) (Mele, Federici, Borsci, & Liotta, 2010)—conducted by a sample of blind and sighted users. Differently from other common search engines, e.g. Google or Yahoo, WoW has been implemented by using sophisticated graph visualisation algorithms on semantically clustered data: in this way, the indexed information is conveyed by means of a visuospatial data representation allowing to overcome the efficiency limitations of the top-down linear output given by the most common search engines, which generally use a flat representation of the indexed dataset (Federici, Borsci, & Stamerra, 2010).

- The experiment 3 consisted on the evaluation of the website of the Public Transportation of Rome (http://www.atac.roma.it/) conducted by a sample of users with Down Syndrome and a sample of users without any intellectual disability.

Measures

- *Verbal protocols:* In each of the three experiments the Partial Concurrent Thinking Aloud (PCTA) verbal protocol has been used to analyse the interaction of disabled users. The PCTA is a new but consolidated technique (Federici, Borsci, & Mele, 2010; Federici, Borsci, Mele, & Stamerra, 2010; Borsci, Kurosu, Federici, & Mele, 2011) that respects the properties of classic verbal protocols and at the same time overcomes the structural interferences and the limits of the concurrent and retrospective protocols when used during the screen reader navigation. Furthermore, the classic Thinking Aloud (TA) (Ericsson & Simon, 1980) method was used with not-disabled subjects in all the three experiments.
- *Discovery rate measures:* We apply the BDB model with 5000 bootstrap steps. Actually, the BDB approach allows the behaviour of the whole population, the representativeness of the sample data (i.e. the problems found expressed by p value) and the different properties of the interface to be taken into account. Since it respects the assumption of the ROI and the results obtained by a Montecarlo resampling, this model opens the possibility of considering both the properties of the interface and the representativeness of data, granting to practitioners a representative evaluation of the interface.
- *The Mini Mental State Exam (MMSE):* is used for the clinical and neuropsychological evaluation (Folstein, Folstein, & McHugh, 1975) with persons with intellectual disabilities to analyse the degree of disability. The test is composed by 30 items with a scoring point from 0 to 30. The evaluation of the degree of intellectual disability follows these criteria: 1) a Scoring between 25 to 30 points indicates any disability; 2) a Scoring between 21 to 24 points indicates a mild disability degree; 3) a Scoring between 10 to 20 point indicates a moderate disability degree; iv) a scoring less than 9 point indicates an high disability degree. In experiment 3 we used the MMSE to analyse the users skills (e.g. memory, attention and, language comprehension) which are usually associated with a human-computer interaction task.

Procedure

The experiments 1 and 2 share the same experimental procedure: *1*) After 20 minutes of free navigation as training *2*) blind users started the PCTA session whereas sighted users started the TA session by following the evaluation tasks presented as scenarios. The evaluation coordinator reported all the problems identified in both the PCTA and the TA session, checking and integrating the report by means of the video recordings of the verbalizations and mouse actions made by each users.

The experiment 3 follows the same procedure adding the MMSE test before the first step.

For all the experiments all the participants are volunteers of different institutions. The not disabled participants are students of the Sapienza University of Rome, while the participants with visual disabilities are members of different institutes for blind people of Rome, and the participants with Down Syndrome are members of the Italian Association of Persons with Down Syndrome (AIPD).

Figure 1. Number of users needed for found more of the 80% of problems. For the ROI model 6 sighted users and 8 blind users are needed for create a mixed panel.

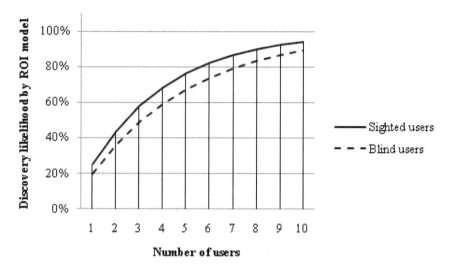

Results

Experiment 1: Blind Users' Interactions with Websites

In the experiment 1 a total of 22 interaction problems have been found: 15 problems were identified by both sighted and blind users, 4 problems were identified only by sighted users and 3 problems were identified only by blind users.

Participants:

- Control group: 6 users (3 male, 3 female, mean age = 22.7) were involved in the TA analysis of the target website.
- Experimental group: 6 blind users (3 male, 3 female, mean age = 27.3) were involved in the PCTA analysis of the target website.

Discovery rate results: According to the p value estimated by the ROI model 6 sighted users (p =.25) and 8 blind users (p =.2) are needed to find more than the 80% of problems (see Figure 1 and Table 1). While the p value, estimated by the BDB model, shows that practitioners have to add 4 more sighted users – 10 users for this category (p =.15)—and 3 mode blind users—11 users for this category (p=.14)—to obtain a reliable evaluation (see Figure 2 and Table 2).

Experiment 2: Blind Users' Interactions with Sonificated Search Engines

In the experiment 2 a total of 12 problems have been found: 8 problems were identified by both sighted and blind users and 4 problems were identified only by sighted users.

Participants:

- Control group: 4 sighted users (2 male, 2 female, mean age= 25) were involved in the TA analysis of a typical Web search session by using three typologies of graphic layout (Radial, Layered, and Spiral TreeMap) in the visual version of a search engine called WhatsOnWeb.
- Experimental group: 4 blind users (2 male, 3 female, mean age = 28) were involved in the PCTA analysis of a typical Web search session by using three typologies of layout

Table 1. Percentage of problems discovered by sighted and blind users in the experiment 1 calculated by ROI model

Number of users needed for identify more than 80% of problems in the interface	Discovery likelihood of Sighted users	Discovery likelihood of Blind users
1	25%	20%
2	44%	36%
3	58%	49%
4	68%	59%
5	76%	67%
6	**82%**	74%
7	87%	79%
8	90%	**83%**
9	92%	87%
10	94%	89%

Figure 2. Number of users needed for found more of the 80% of problems. For the BDB model 6 sighted users and 8 blind users are needed for create a mixed panel.

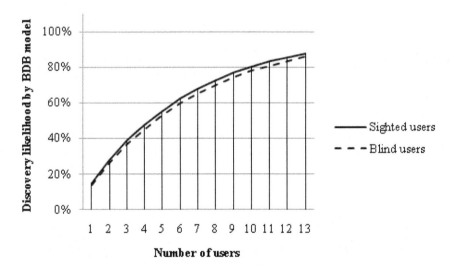

(Radial, Layered and Spiral TreeMap) by means of the PanAndPitchBlinking sonification algorithm in a sonificated version of WhatsOnWeb.

Discovery rate results: According to the p value estimated by the ROI model 3 sighted users (p =.5) and 3 blind users (p =.54) are needed to find more than the 80% of problems (see Figure 3 and Table 3). While the p value, estimated by the BDB model, from a side confirms the ROI model estimation of not-disabled users, from another side shows that practitioners have to add 1 more blind user—4 users for this category (p= .34)—to obtain a reliable evaluation (see Figure 4 and Table 4).

Table 2. Percentage of problems discovered by sighted and blind users in the experiment 2 by BDB model

Number of users needed for identify more than 80% of problems in the interface	Discovery likelihood of Sighted users	Discovery likelihood of Blind users
1	15%	14%
2	28%	26%
3	39%	36%
4	48%	45%
5	56%	53%
6	62%	60%
7	68%	65%
8	73%	70%
9	77%	74%
10	**80%**	78%
11	83%	**81%**
13	86%	84%
13	88%	86%

Figure 3. Number of users needed for found more of the 80% of problems. For the ROI model, 3 sighted and blind users are needed for create a mixed panel.

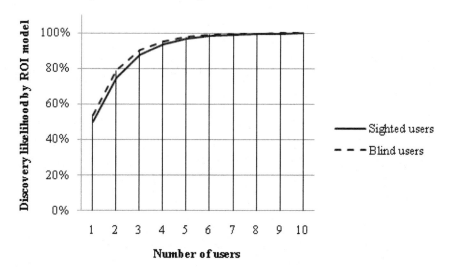

Experiment 3: DS Users' Interactions with a Website

In the experiment 3 a total of 16 problems have been found: 4 problems were identified by both not disabled users and DS users. 9 problems were identified only by not disabled users and 3 problems were identified only by DS users.

Participants:

- Control group: 6 users (3 male, 3 female, mean age = 26.7) were involved in the TA analysis of the target website.
- Experimental group: 6 users with DS (3 male, 3 female, mean age = 23.4) were in-

Table 3. Percentage of problems discovered by sighted and blind users in the experiment 2 calculated by ROI model

Number of users needed for identify more than 80% of problems in the interface	Discovery likelihood of Sighted users	Discovery likelihood of Blind users
1	50%	54%
2	75%	79%
3	**88%**	**90%**
4	94%	96%
5	97%	98%
6	98%	99%
7	99%	100%
8	100%	100%
9	100%	100%
10	100%	100%

Figure 4. Number of users needed for found more of the 80% of problems in experiment 2. For the BDB model 3 sighted users and 4 blind users are needed for create a mixed panel.

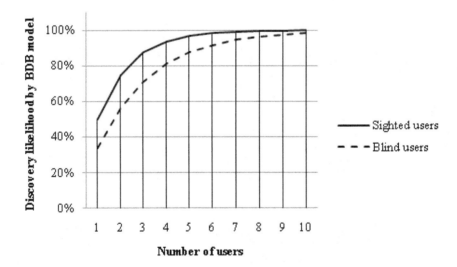

volved in the PCTA analysis of the target website.

Discovery rate results: According to the *p* value estimated by the ROI model 3 not disabled users (p =.48) and 5 DS users (p =.32) are needed to find more than the 80% of problems (see Figure 5 and Table 5).While the *p* value, estimated by the BDB model, from a side confirms the ROI model estimation of not-disabled users, from another side shows that practitioners have to add 3 more DS users—8 users for this category (p= .2)—to obtain a reliable evaluation (see Figure 6 and Table 6).

Table 4. Percentage of problems discovered by sighted and blind users in the experiment 2 calculated by BDB model

Number of users needed for identify more than 80% of problems in the interface	Discovery likelihood of Sighted users	Discovery likelihood of Blind users
1	50%	34%
2	75%	56%
3	**88%**	71%
4	94%	**81%**
5	97%	87%
6	98%	92%
7	99%	95%
8	100%	96%
9	100%	98%
10	100%	98%

Figure 5. Number of users needed for found more of the 80% of problems. For the ROI model 3 users and 5 DS users are needed for create a mixed panel.

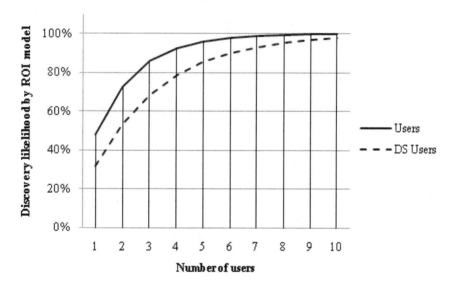

HOW TO APPLY THE BDB MODEL FOR COMPOSE A MIXED PANEL OF USERS

Our findings show that the BDB model is more accurate than the ROI in considering the abilities of the different categories of users in finding interaction problems. As showed in the experiment 1, which has been conducted on a website with many interaction problems, a great difference between the number of subjects recommended for the evaluation through the ROI model and the number of subjects estimated through the BDB model have been found—the site has been subsequently redesigned and some problems previously retrieved in other tests previously carried out (Borsci, et al., 2011) have been fixed. On the other hand, in the experiment 2, in which the tested

Table 5. Percentage of problems discovered by DS and not disabled users in the experiment 3 by ROI model

Number of users needed for identify more than 80% of problems in the interface	Discovery likelihood of users	Discovery likelihood of DS users
1	48%	32%
2	73%	54%
3	**86%**	69%
4	93%	79%
5	96%	**85%**
6	98%	90%
7	99%	93%
8	99%	95%
9	100%	97%
10	100%	98%

Figure 6. Number of users needed for found more of the 80% of problems. For the BDB model 3 users and 8 DS users are needed for create a mixed panel.

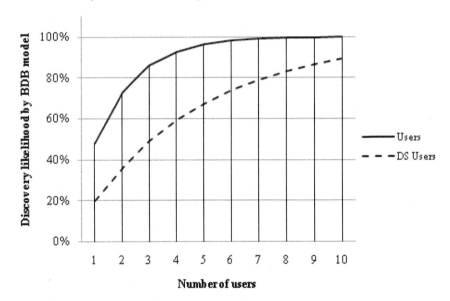

interface has been designed by following a user-centred process, the number of problems found by the two groups of users is quite low: in this case the BDB model confirmed the data obtained through the ROI model for both groups of users.

Moreover, the experiment 3, in which the users identified a great set of different problems, shows a high variance between the results obtained through the BDB model and those obtained through the

ROI model, especially for the evaluations made with the users with DS. In this case the difference between the two models seems to be due to both different approaches and strategies used by the subjects with DS towards the navigation tasks, leading them to identify a very different set of problems compared to the control group. Therefore, our results do not confirm the Nielsen's (2000) indication about testing usability with

Table 6. Percentage of problems discovered by DS and not disabled users in the experiment 3 by BDB model

Number of users needed for identify more than 80% of problems in the interface	Discovery likelihood of users	Discovery likelihood of DS users
1	48%	20%
2	73%	36%
3	**86%**	49%
4	93%	59%
5	96%	67%
6	98%	74%
7	99%	79%
8	99%	**83%**
9	100%	87%
10	100%	89%

two groups of users, i.e., that a range from 3 to 4 participants for each group can be considered as a sufficient number for a reliable evaluation. Indeed by applying the BDB model the following ranges of users for each category has to be considered by practitioners for a reliable evaluation: from 3 to 10 of not disabled participants, a range from 4 to 11 blind users, and a range from 5 to 8 DS users. Taking into account these results practitioners may start their interaction evaluations with a mixed sample composed of 5 users for each kind of group, and when users find a high number of interaction problems in the tested interfaces we recommend to add at least 5 more not disabled users, 6 blind, and 3 DS users.

CONCLUSION

In this work we have shown the application of a new tool called the BDB model, which is able to support the UCD by both endorsing the PFO approach and promoting the Design for All philosophy. The BDB model has been developed to support an interaction evaluation specialist to create a good mixed sample of disabled and not disabled users to obtain a reliable assessment of

the UX during the design process. The use of UCD process driven by a matching between users' need and the prototype's features, guarantees to the designer the possibility to obtain a final product with a great degree of UX satisfaction. In this sense, the results obtained with the BDB model clearly show that the practitioners aiming to obtain a complete evaluation of an interface have to both consider all the possible divergent navigation strategies and recruit a mixed panel of users for identifying more than the 80% of the interaction problems. Comparing our results with the indications given by the Nielsen (2000) model, at least 5 subjects for each category are needed to conduct a complete evaluation, even though practitioners have to expect a necessary increase in number for the category of blind and DS users. Practitioners are suggested to start the evaluation with a mixed sample of five users for each category. Moreover we suggest to the evaluation specialists the application of the BDB model in order to obtain an exact estimation on how many users for each category have to be added to the sample to obtain at least 80% of the interaction problems. In this way, the use of the BDB model should help practitioners to optimize the evaluation process by involving disabled users.

At the same time this model should allow both implementation and evaluation of technologies by a user-driven process.

Summarizing, the key points that make BDB better than ROI are the following:

- The BDB model computes probabilistic individual differences in problem identification.
- The BDB considers evaluated interfaces as an object *per se*, not like in an ordinal sequence, differently from the ROI, which considers the rate of the evaluators starting from the number of problems found by the first evaluator (evaluation condition).
- The BDB computes all evaluated interfaces aligning them to a start zero point independently from the first evaluator.
- The BDB model extends the representativeness of the sample resampling the population assessing all possible participants' evaluation behaviours in order to provide the number of evaluators needed for an interaction evaluation.
- The BDB provides a more accurate number of users needed for a specific interaction evaluation with and without disability.

REFERENCES

Bohman, P. R., & Anderson, S. (2005). *A conceptual framework for accessibility tools to benefit users with cognitive disabilities.* Paper presented at the International Cross-Disciplinary Workshop on Web Accessibility. Chiba, Japan.

Borsci, S., Kurosu, M., Federici, S., & Mele, M. L. (2013). *Computer systems experiences of users with and without disabilities: An evaluation guide for professionals.* London, UK: CRC Press.

Borsci, S., Londei, A., & Federici, S. (2011). The bootstrap discovery behaviour (BDB): A new outlook on usability evaluation. *Cognitive Processing, 12*(1), 23–31. doi:10.1007/s10339-010-0376-6

Caulton, D. (2001). Relaxing the homogeneity assumption in usability testing. *Behaviour & Information Technology, 20*(1), 1–7. doi:10.1080/01449290010020648

Charlton, J. I. (1998). *Nothing about us without us: Disability oppression and empowerment.* Berkeley, CA: University of California Press.

Di Giacomo, E., Didimo, W., Grilli, L., & Liotta, G. (2007). Graph visualization techniques for web clustering engines. *IEEE Transactions on Visualization and Computer Graphics, 13*(2), 294–304. doi:10.1109/TVCG.2007.40

Di Giacomo, E., Didimo, W., Grilli, L., Liotta, G., & Palladino, P. (2008). *WhatsOnWeb+: An enhanced visual search clustering engine.* Paper presented at the IEEE Pacific Visualization Symposium. Kyoto, Japan.

Efron, B. (1979). Bootstrap methods: Another look at the jackknife. *Annals of Statistics, 7*(1), 1–26. doi:10.1214/aos/1176344552

Ericsson, K. A., & Simon, H. A. (1980). Verbal reports as data. *Psychological Review, 87*(3), 215–251. doi:10.1037/0033-295X.87.3.215

Fairweather, P., & Trewin, S. (2010). Cognitive impairments and Web 2.0. *Universal Access in the Information Society, 9*(2), 137–146. doi:10.1007/s10209-009-0163-2

Federici, S., & Borsci, S. (2010). Usability evaluation: models, methods, and applications. In J. Stone & M. Blouin (Eds.), *International Encyclopedia of Rehabilitation.* Buffalo, NY: Center for International Rehabilitation Research Information and Exchange (CIRRIE). Retrieved from http://cirrie.buffalo.edu/encyclopedia/article.php?id=277&language=en.

Federici, S., Borsci, S., & Mele, M. L. (2010). Usability evaluation with screen reader users: A video presentation of the PCTA's experimental setting and rules. *Cognitive Processing, 11*(3), 285–288. doi:10.1007/s10339-010-0365-9

Federici, S., Borsci, S., Mele, M. L., & Stamerra, G. (2010). Web popularity: An illusory perception of a qualitative order in information. *Universal Access in the Information Society, 9*(4), 375–386. doi:10.1007/s10209-009-0179-7

Federici, S., Borsci, S., & Stamerra, G. (2010). Web usability evaluation with screen reader users: Implementation of the partial concurrent thinking aloud technique. *Cognitive Processing, 11*(3), 263–272. doi:10.1007/s10339-010-0358-8

Federici, S., Micangeli, A., Ruspantini, I., Borgianni, S., Corradi, F., & Pasqualotto, E. (2005). Checking an integrated model of web accessibility and usability evaluation for disabled people. *Disability and Rehabilitation, 27*(13), 781–790. doi:10.1080/09638280400014766

Feng, J., Lazar, J., Kumin, L., & Ozok, A. (2008). *Computer usage by young individuals with down syndrome: An exploratory study.* Paper presented at the 10th International ACM SIGACCESS Conference on Computers and Accessibility. Halifax, Canada.

Feng, J., Lazar, J., Kumin, L., & Ozok, A. (2010). Computer usage by children with down syndrome: Challenges and future research. *Transactions on Accessible Computing, 2*(3), 1–44. doi:10.1145/1714458.1714460

Folstein, M. F., Folstein, S. E., & McHugh, P. R. (1975). Mini-mental state: A practical method for grading the cognitive state of patients for the clinician. *Journal of Psychiatric Research, 12*(3), 189–198. doi:10.1016/0022-3956(75)90026-6

Fox, J. (2002). *An R and S-plus companion to applied regression.* Thousand Oaks, CA: SAGE.

Garrett, J. J. (2003). *The elements of user experience: User-centered design for the web.* New York, NY: New Riders Press.

Goodstein, R. L. (1963). *Boolean algebra.* Oxford, UK: Pergamon Press.

Hartson, H. R., Andre, T. S., & Williges, R. C. (2001). Criteria for evaluating usability evaluation methods. *International Journal of Human-Computer Interaction, 13*(4), 373–410. doi:10.1207/S15327590IJHC1304_03

Hertzum, M., & Jacobsen, N. E. (2003). The evaluator effect: A chilling fact about usability evaluation methods. *International Journal of Human-Computer Interaction, 15*(4), 183–204. doi:10.1207/S15327590IJHC1501_14

ISO. (1998). *ISO 9241-11: Ergonomic requirements for office work with visual display terminals.* Geneve, Switzerland: ISO.

ISO. (2010). *Ergonomics of human-system interaction – Part 210: Human-centred design for interactive systems.* Geneve, Switzerland: ISO.

Lewis, C. (2005). HCI for people with cognitive disabilities. *ACM SIGACCESS Accessibility and Computing, 83*, 12–17. doi:10.1145/1102187.1102190

Lewis, J. R. (1994). Sample sizes for usability studies: Additional considerations. *Human Factors, 36*(2), 368–378.

Lewis, J. R. (2001). Evaluation of procedures for adjusting problem-discovery rates estimated from small samples. *International Journal of Human-Computer Interaction, 13*(4), 445–479. doi:10.1207/S15327590IJHC1304_06

Lewis, J. R. (2006). Sample sizes for usability tests: Mostly math, not magic. *Interaction, 13*(6), 29–33. doi:10.1145/1167948.1167973

Luckasson, R., Borthwick-Duffy, S., Buntinx, W. H. E., Coulter, D. L., Craig, E. M., & Reeve, A. (2002). *Mental retardation: Definition, classification, and system of supports* (10th ed.). Washington, DC: AAMR.

Mele, M. L., Federici, S., Borsci, S., & Liotta, G. (2010). Beyond a visuocentric way of a visual web search clustering engine: The sonification of WhatsOnWeb. In Miesenberger, K., Klaus, J., Zagler, W., & Karshmer, A. (Eds.), *Computers Helping People with Special Needs* (*Vol. 1*, pp. 351–357). Berlin, Germany: Springer. doi:10.1007/978-3-642-14097-6_56

Nielsen, J. (1994). Heuristic evaluation. In Nielsen, J., & Mack, R. L. (Eds.), *Usability inspection methods*. New York, NY: John Wiley & Sons.

Nielsen, J. (2000). *Why you only need to test with 5 users*. Retrieved May, 20th, 2011, from http://www.useit.com/alertbox/20000319.html.

Nielsen, J., & Landauer, T. K. (1993). *A mathematical model of the finding of usability problems*. Paper presented at the Conference on Human factors in computing systems: INTERACT and CHI 1993. Amsterdam, The Netherlands.

Nielsen, J., & Mack, R. L. (Eds.). (1994). *Usability inspection methods*. New York, NY: John Wiley & Sons.

Norman, D. A. (1988). *The psychology of everyday things*. New York, NY: Basic Books.

Schalock, R. L., & Luckasson, R. (2004). American association on mental retardation's definition, classification, and system of supports and its relation to international trends and issues in the field of intellectual disabilities. *Journal of Policy and Practice in Intellectual Disabilities*, *1*(3-4), 136–146. doi:10.1111/j.1741-1130.2004.04028.x

Schmettow, M. (2008). *Heterogeneity in the usability evaluation process*. Paper presented at the 22nd British HCI Group Annual Conference on People and Computers: Culture, Creativity. Liverpool, UK.

Spool, J., & Schroeder, W. (2001). *Testing web sites: Five users is nowhere near enough*. Paper presented at the Human Factors in Computing Systems: CHI 2001. Seattle, WA.

Stephanidis, C. (2001). User interfaces for all: New perspectives into human-computer interaction. In Stephanidis, C. (Ed.), *User Interfaces for All: Concepts, Methods, and Tools* (pp. 3–17). Mahwah, NJ: Lawrence Erlbaum Associates.

Virzi, R. A. (1990). Streamlining the design process: Running fewer subjects. *Human Factors and Ergonomics Society Annual Meeting Proceedings*, *34*, 291-294.

Virzi, R. A. (1992). Refining the test phase of usability evaluation: How many subjects is enough? *Human Factors*, *34*(4), 457–468.

Wright, P. C., & Monk, A. F. (1991). A cost-effective evaluation method for use by designers. *International Journal of Man-Machine Studies*, *35*(6), 891–912. doi:10.1016/S0020-7373(05)80167-1

ADDITIONAL READING

Albert, D. M. (1999). Psychotechnology and insanity at the wheel. *Journal of the History of the Behavioral Sciences*, *35*(3), 291–305. doi:10.1002/(SICI)1520-6696(199922)35:3<291::AID-JHBS6>3.0.CO;2-1

Andronico, P., Buzzi, M., & Leporini, B. (2004). *Can I find what I'm looking for?* Paper presented at the 13th International World Wide Web Conference on Alternate Track. New York, NY.

Annett, J. (2002). Subjective rating scales in ergonomics: A reply. *Ergonomics, 45*(14), 1042–1046. doi:10.1080/00140130210166762

Annett, J. (2002). Subjective rating scales: Science or art? *Ergonomics, 45*(14), 966–987. doi:10.1080/00140130210166951

Ascott, R. (1995). The architecture of cyberception. In Toy, M. (Ed.), *Architectural Design* (pp. 38–40). London, UK: Academy Editions.

Baber, C. (2002). Subjective evaluation of usability. *Ergonomics, 45*(14), 1021–1025. doi:10.1080/00140130210166807

Brooke, J. (1996). SUS: A "quick and dirty" usability scale. In Jordan, P. W., Thomas, B., Weerdmeester, B. A., & McClelland, I. L. (Eds.), *Usability Evaluation in Industry* (pp. 189–194). London, UK: Taylor & Francis.

Bruner, J. S., & Postman, L. (1949). On the perception of incongruity: A paradigm. *Journal of Personality, 18*(2), 206–223. doi:10.1111/j.1467-6494.1949.tb01241.x

Clark, R., Williams, J., Clark, J., & Clark, C. (2003). Assessing web site usability: Construction zone. *Journal of Healthcare Information Management, 17*(2), 51–55.

De Kerckhove, D. (1995). *The skin of culture: Investigating the new electronic reality*. Toronto, CA: Somerville.

De Kerckhove, D. (2001). *The architecture of intelligence*. Berlin, Germany: Birkhäuser.

Drury, C. G. (2002). Measurement and the practising ergonomist. *Ergonomics, 45*(14), 988–990. doi:10.1080/00140130210166915

Hutchins, E. L., Hollan, J. D., & Norman, D. A. (1985). Direct manipulation interfaces. *Human-Computer Interaction, 1*(4), 311–338. doi:10.1207/s15327051hci0104_2

Jordan, P. W. (1998). *An introduction to usability*. London, UK: Taylor and Francis.

Karwowski, W. (Ed.). (2006). *International encyclopedia of ergonomics and human factors* (2nd ed.). Boca Raton, FL: CRC Press. doi:10.1201/9780849375477

Kirakowski, J. (2002). Is ergonomics empirical? *Ergonomics, 45*(14-15), 995–997. doi:10.1080/00140130210166889

Krug, S. (2000). *Don't make me think! A common sense approach to web usability*. Indianapolis, IN: New Riders.

Monk, A., Wright, P., Haber, J., & Davenport, L. (Eds.). (1993). *Improving your human computer interface: A practical technique*. New York, NY: Prentice Hall.

Nielsen, J., & Loranger, H. (2006). *Prioritizing web usability* (2nd ed.). Berkeley, CA: New Riders Press.

Nielsen, J., & Pernice, K. (2009). *Eyetracking web usability*. Berkeley, CA: New Riders.

Norman, J. (2002). Two visual systems and two theories of perception: An attempt to reconcile the constructivist and ecological approaches. *The Behavioral and Brain Sciences, 25*(1), 96–144.

Shneiderman, B. (1983). Direct manipulation: A step beyond programming languages. *Computer, 16*(8), 57–69. doi:10.1109/MC.1983.1654471

Shneiderman, B. (1987). Direct manipulation: A step beyond programming languages. In Shneiderman, B. (Ed.), *Human-Computer Interaction: A Multidisciplinary Approach* (pp. 461–467). Burlington, MA: Morgan Kaufmann. doi:10.1109/MC.1983.1654471

Stanton, N. A., & Young, M. S. (1999). *A guide to methodology in ergonomics: Design for human use*. London, UK: Taylor & Francis.

APPENDIX 1

Box 1. Bootstrap Discovery Behaviour model code for Matlab

```
function [Nsubj085,baseerr,c,gof]=BDB(errors, NBS)
  % BDB    Calculates the number of subjects for the detection of 85% of
  % problems in BDB approach by bootstrap iterations.
  %
  % [Nsubj085,baseerr,c,gof]=BDB(errors, NBS)
  %
  % errors: matrix with total amount of subjects (Nsub) rows and number of
  %         errors (Nerrors) columns.
  % NBS: number of bootstrap iterations.
  % Nsubj085: estimated number of subject to reveal the 85% of errors
  % baseerr: bias of errors considered as certainly found with no subjects.
  % c: fit object that encapsulates the result of fitting (from function
  % FIT).
  % gof: structure with fitting statistical information (from function
  % FIT).

  Nsubj=size(errors,1);
  Nerrors=size(errors,2);

  bootstrap=zeros(Nsubj,NBS);

  % Bootstrap loop
  for b=1:NBS,
      exptrial=zeros(1,Nerrors);
      ind=ceil(rand(Nsubj,1)*Nsubj);
      for k=1:Nsubj,
          exptrial=exptrial|errors(ind(k),:);
          bootstrap(k,b)=sum(exptrial');
      end
  end
  results=mean(bootstrap,2);
  stdresults=std(bootstrap,0,2);

  resultsnorm=results/Nerrors;

  % Fit of the averaged errors
  s = fitoptions('Method','NonlinearLeastSquares','Robust','LAR','Lower',[0
0 -Inf],'MaxFunEvals',2000,'MaxIter',1000,'StartPoint',[0.5 0.5 0.5]);
  f = fittype('a-(1-p)^(x+q)','options',s);
```

```
    [c,gof]=fit((1:Nsubj)',resultsnorm,f);

    plot((1:Nsubj)',resultsnorm,'x',(1:Nsubj)',c((1:Nsubj)'),'r-');

    % Find the desired parameters
    if(c.a-0.85>0)
        Nsubj085=log(c.a-0.85)/log(1-c.p) - c.q;
    else
        Nsubj085=NaN;
    end

    baseerr=Nerrors*(c.a-(1-c.p)^c.q);

    plot((1:Nsubj)',resultsnorm,'x',(1:Nsubj)',c((1:Nsubj)'),'r-');
end
```

Chapter 16
Designing "Faster" Progress Bars:
Manipulating Perceived Duration

Chris Harrison
Carnegie Mellon University, Pittsburgh, USA

Zhiquan Yeo
Carnegie Mellon University, Pittsburgh, USA

Brian Amento
AT&T Labs, USA

Scott E. Hudson
Carnegie Mellon University, Pittsburgh, USA

ABSTRACT

Human perception of time is fluid, and can be manipulated in purposeful and productive ways. In this chapter, the authors describe and evaluate how progress bar pacing behaviors and graphical design can alter users' perceptions of an operation's duration. Although progress bars are relatively simple, they provide an ideal playground in which to experiment with perceptual effects in user interface design. As a baseline in the experiments, the authors use generic, solid-color progress bars with linear pacing behaviors, prevalent in many user interfaces. In a series of direct comparison tests, they are able to rank how different progress bar designs compare to one another. Using these results, it is possible to craft perceptually-optimized progress bars that appear faster, even though their actual duration remains unchanged. Throughout, the authors include design suggestions that can contribute to an overall more responsive, pleasant, and human-centric computing experience.

DOI: 10.4018/978-1-4666-1628-8.ch016

INTRODUCTION

Progress bars, typically used to visualize the progression of an extended operation, are prevalent in current user interfaces (Myers, 1985). Users rely on progress bars to verify that an operation is proceeding successfully and to estimate its completion time. Typically, a linear function is applied such that the advancement of a progress bar is directly proportional to the amount of work that has been completed.

In desktop systems, advanced users often multitask during these periods. However, it is not uncommon for advanced users to watch an install finish or file transfer complete—especially if they are waiting on that operation. Anecdotally, novice users tend to anxiously monitor their progress bars, in hopes that some error does not occur. In non-desktop applications (e.g., ATMs, ticketing kiosks, and many mobile device platforms), novice and expert users alike have no choice but to watch progress bars frustratingly inch their way across the screen. No matter how objectively fast we make these operations, it is typically the subjective speed that mars the user experience. It has been proposed (Tognazzini, 1993) that subjective time is perhaps the most important computing factor, which, fortunately, is also the most readily manipulated.

Often overlooked in user interface design is the fact that humans perceive the passage of time in non-linear ways (Allan, 1979; Block, 1990; Hogan, 1978). With careful design and evaluation, it is possible to build perceptually optimized interfaces—ones tailored to our cognitive peculiarities. Progress bars, due to their extreme simplicity, provide an ideal playground for such experimentation. The resulting design implications can be used to craft more responsive and pleasant computing experiences, often without a computational penalty—in other words, free.

In this chapter, we leverage two perceptual effects in the aim of creating "faster" progress bars. First we explore how perceived duration can be manipulated by changing how progress bars move (e.g., pauses, accelerations)—what we call *pacing behaviors*. Secondly, we take advantage of well established visual perceptual effects and use this to inform the graphical design of progress bars. We discuss each manipulation *in situ* with their respective motivation, study, and discussion.

RELATED WORK

Myers (1985) was the first to investigate the impact of progress indicators on the user experience in graphical user interfaces. He concluded that users have a strong preference for progress indicators during long tasks, and overall, find them useful.

Conn (1995) explored the concept of time affordance. The work enumerates a series of properties an ideal progress bar would embody. This exemplar offers users an accurate and understandable method for gauging progress in interactive systems. Conn also defines another concept: the time tolerance window, which is the length of time a user is willing to wait before deciding a task is not making adequate progress. Conn goes on to describe that predictive algorithms could be applied to set user expectations for longer waits, essentially reporting progress in a non-linear manner to enhance the user experience.

Much of the work presented in this chapter borrows heavily from perceptual effects identified in other fields, but not applied to human-computer interactions. For example, duration neglect and peak-and-end effects (discussed in detail subsequently) can be seen in a variety of domains, including medicine, economics, and advertising (e.g., Redelmeier, 1996; Langer, 2005; Baumgartner, 1997). More than a decade ago, Geelhoed et al. (1995) demonstrated that similar effects are present in user interface design, by manipulating how fax transmissions were displayed over time.

Despite this early success and continued discoveries in psychophysics, there has been remarkably little interest in the broader HCI community.

Table 1. The nine progress functions

Name	Description	Rate Trend	Acceleration	Function
Linear	Progresses linearly	Constant	None	$f(x) = x$
Early Pause	Almost linear; large pause around 25%	Speeds up	Unstable near beginning	$f(x) = x+(1-\sin(x*\pi*2+\pi/2))/-8$
Late Pause	Almost linear; large pause around 75%	Slows down	Unstable near end	$f(x) = x+(1-\sin(x*\pi*2+\pi/2))/8$
Slow Wavy	Three large steps separated by pauses	Constant	Highly unstable	$f(x) = x+\sin(x*\pi*5)/20$
Fast Wavy	Increments in small, quick steps	Constant	Highly unstable	$f(x) = x+\sin(x*\pi*20)/80$
Power	Accelerates	Speeds up	Constant	$f(x) = (x+(1-x)*0.03)^2$
Inverse Power	Decelerates	Slows down	Constant	$f(x) = 1+(1-x)^{1.5} *-1$
Fast Power	Rapidly accelerates	Speeds up	Stable	$f(x) = (x+(1-x)/2)^8$
Inv. Fast Power	Rapidly decelerates	Slows down	Stable	$f(x) = 1+(1-x)^3 *-1$

This is now beginning to change as computing performance reaches the limits of Moore's law. A considerable challenge is how to make computers "faster" if processor performance plateaus. Consequently, there has been a resurgence of interest in "time design"—a discipline that looks at how temporal aspects of interactive systems can be structured and manipulated to improve the user experience (Hildebrandt, 1994; Seow, 2008).

MANIPULATING PERCEIVED DURATION THROUGH PROGRESS BAR PACING

Motivation

Fredrickson et al. (1993) suggest that duration has little effect on how pleasant an affective experience is rated (duration neglect). Instead, perception is most heavily influenced by salient features (both good and bad) during the experience and at the conclusion of the experience (peak-and-end effects). This occurs because humans do not remember experiences in a consistent and linear way, but rather recall events selectively and with various biases (Allan, 1979; Hogan, 1978). These cognitive effects can be leveraged in progress bar design.

In general, progress bars employ a linear pacing function (i.e., how a progress bar advances) where the progress of the bar is directly proportional to how much work has been completed. However, other pacing functions, coupled with humans' non-linear perception of time, allow the perceived duration of an operation to be manipulated. This section describes a study that sought to identify patterns in user perception of pacing behaviors. The results are analyzed to classify behaviors that perceptually speed up or slow down progress bars.

Study Design

We created eight non-linear functions that embodied different pacing behaviors. A linear function was included as a baseline for comparison. Table 1 and Figure 1 describe the behaviors of each pacing function. To test the human perception of these functions, an experiment interface was developed that simultaneously presented two progress bars to the user (Figure 2). The duration of each progress bar was kept at a constant 5.5 seconds to act as a control. Although this is a somewhat short duration for a progress bar, it was a necessary trade off to run the number of trials we desired and maintain user attention for the full experiment. However, as we will see in the discussion of the results from our final experiment, we believe that these types of effects can scale to at least somewhat longer durations.

Progress bars were run sequentially—when the first one finished, the second one began. Se-

Figure 1. Graphs of the nine progress functions

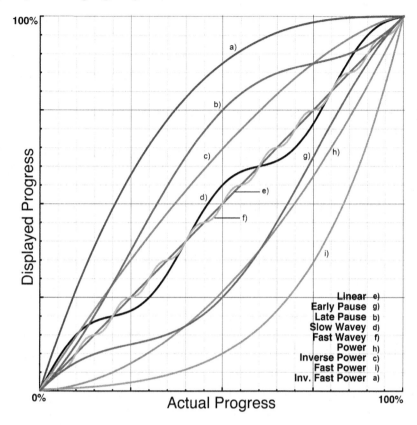

Linear	e)
Early Pause	g)
Late Pause	b)
Slow Wavey	d)
Fast Wavey	f)
Power	h)
Inverse Power	c)
Fast Power	i)
Inv. Fast Power	a)

Figure 2. Experiment interface

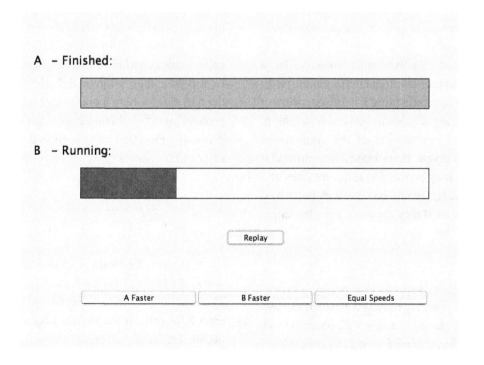

quential, rather than parallel presentation was necessary to hide the fact that the progress bars were actually the same duration. After watching the two progress bars run to completion, participants selected whether they believed the first progress bar was faster, the second progress bar was faster, or that the progress bars were equal in duration. The next trial began once an answer was provided. Participants could replay the progress bars if desired.

Comparing all distinct ordered pairs of the 9 progress functions would have required 81 trials. Initial pilot testing showed that users found the task to be fairly tedious and began to lose interest after approximately 50 sets of progress bars. To maintain participant attention and ensure a high level of response integrity, we decided to present all unique pairings of the nine progress functions (36 trials) along with the functions paired with themselves (9 trials) for a total of 45 trials per user. This kept the total task time under 15 minutes. The order of presentation was counterbalanced in two ways. First, a sequence of 45 trials was randomly selected for each pair of users. Second, within each pair of users, the order of presentation was reversed for each trial (i.e., if the first user of the pair saw linear/power, the second would see power/linear).

We recruited 22 participants from two large American computer research labs (8 female) with a mean age of approximately 37. The experiment took place in the participants' offices on a laptop. A brief verbal explanation of the comparison interface was given. Participants were told that progress bars may proceed at different rates and that they should select the one that they perceived as fastest or equal if they appeared to be the same.

Results

Participants tended to prefer (i.e., perceive as faster) whichever function they saw first. Of the 990 paired comparisons (45 trials x 22 participants), the first function was preferred 376 times (38%),

the second 262 times (26%), with no preference 352 times (36%). This finding is supported by the results of a chi-square test, discussed subsequently. This effect is controlled because the data contain equal numbers of each pair ordering.

Participants had strong preferences among the nine functions.

For every paired comparison of functions, we compute a preference score. This was calculated as ([# of trials function A was chosen as faster] − [# of trials function B was chosen as faster]) / (total number of trials of A vs. B and B vs. A). For example, in 22 comparisons of *Slow Wavy* with *Fast Wavy* (with each occurring first 11 times), 10 participants preferred *Slow Wavy*, 5 preferred *Fast Wavy*, and 7 rated the functions as equal. Consequently, the mean preference score is $(10-5)/22 = 0.23$. A positive value indicates preference for function A (in the latter example, *Slow Wavy*). Table 2 shows mean preference scores for each of the 36 function pairs. Bold values indicate statistical significance from 0 at the 0.05 level using a two-sided sign test of the null hypothesis that each function was equally likely to be preferred.

Using the mean preferences scores in Table 2, we generated a rough ordering of preferences for the nine progress functions, shown in Figure 3.

To combine information efficiently across cells, while controlling for presentation order, we fit a logistic regression model (Hosmer, 1989) to the 638 cases where a preference was given. The probability of preferring Function i to Function j given that Function i was seen first was modeled as:

$$P(i,j) = \frac{e^{\alpha+\beta_i}}{e^{\alpha+\beta_i} + e^{\beta_j}} = \frac{e^{\alpha+(\beta_i-B_j)}}{e^{\alpha+(\beta_i-\beta_j)} + 1}$$

A Hosmer-Lemeshow chi-square test (8.87 with 7 d.f.) failed to show lack of fit of the model. The parameter α, estimated to be 0.42 with standard error 0.09, reflects the tendency for participants to prefer the first function they saw. The estimated

Table 2. Preference score means for all pairs (orderings combined). Positive values indicate preference for the column label over the row label. Statistically significant results are bolded (p < .05).

	Slow Wavy	Late Pause	Inv. Fast Power	Inverse Power	Early Pause	Linear	Power	Fast Power
Fast Wavy	0.23	0.18	0.36	0.23	0.14	**0.41**	**0.45**	**0.73**
Slow Wavy		0.14	0.23	0.36	0.23	**0.36**	**0.68**	**0.77**
Late Pause			0.05	**0.45**	0.27	0.27	**0.73**	**0.59**
Inv. Fast Power				-0.14	0.00	-0.05	**0.59**	**0.50**
Inverse Power					**0.41**	-0.05	0.27	0.36
Early Pause						0.05	0.23	**0.64**
Linear							0.32	**0.59**
Power								0.00

Figure 3. A rough hierarchy of the nine progress functions. Statistically significant edges are shown with solid lines (p < .05). Dashed edges show relationships approaching significance. Mean preference scores are labeled on the edges.

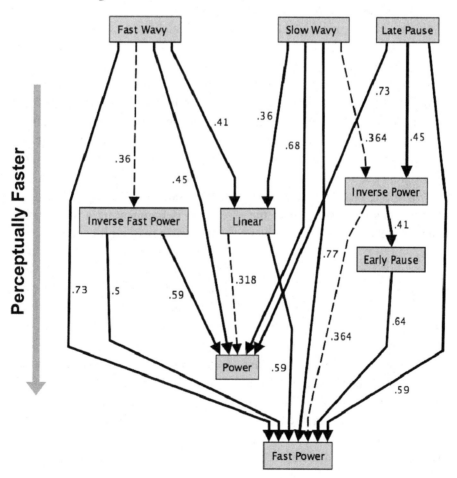

Figure 4. Number line showing relative distances from linear, which is centered at 0. Values generated from logistic regression model.

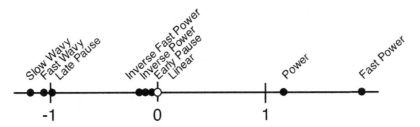

α's measure the relative preferences among the functions. Because the probabilities only depend on differences between the α's, we fixed the estimated α for linear at 0 (Figure 4). Standard errors for differences between α's ranged between 0.28 and 0.37.

The nine functions clustered cleanly into three groups (Figure 4): three that were perceived as slower than linear, four that were perceived as near linear, and two, which were perceived faster than linear. Differences between all three groups were significant but not necessarily significant within groups. The α for each function differs significantly at the 0.05 level from each function in any of the other clusters. The two functions that were perceived as faster than linear, *Power* and *Fast Power*, were both exponential functions, with the fastest progress occurring near the end of the process. *Slow Wavy, Fast Wavy,* and *Late Pause*, the only functions with pauses near the process conclusion, were all perceived as slower than linear.

Discussion

Three general findings explain the pattern of estimates, which are in line with the peak-and-end effects discussed previously. First, participants perceived progress bars with pauses as taking longer to complete (peak effect). Secondly, accelerating progress was strongly favored. The latter two effects had an exaggerated perceptual impact when located towards the end of the process

(end effect). Interestingly, the two factors appear to combine in the case of *Early Pause*, making it essentially equivalently preferred to the linear function.

Although our results could be used to enhance progress bars system-wide, there are many cases where modifying progress behavior seems inappropriate. In general, processes with known static completion conditions and stable progress are not good candidates – standard progress bars can visualize these effectively and accurately. In addition, these types of processes tend to be less affected by pauses or other negative progress behavior (sufficiently so that they are frequently accompanied by accurate time estimates). Examples of this type of process include copying a file to disk, scanning a photograph, or playing an audio file.

However, progress bars with dynamic completion conditions and roughly estimated durations (e.g., defragmenting a hard drive) can be augmented in two significant ways. First, since users seem to have a strong aversion to pauses especially towards the end of an operation, progress bars can be designed to compensate for this behavior. An intelligent progress bar can cache progress when the operation is first starting to mitigate negative progress behaviors (e.g., pauses or slow-downs) later on. Secondly, progress can be downplayed in the beginning and accelerated towards the end, providing a sense of a rapid conclusion that is highly favored by users in our experiment.

Perceptual enhancements can also be integrated into the design of multi-stage processes, such as

Table 3. The five pulsating progress bar behaviors

Behavior Name	Start Frequency (0% Progress)	End Frequency (100% Progress)
Constant	1.1 Hz	1.1 Hz
Slow Increasing	1.1 Hz	1.17 Hz
Fast Increasing	1.1 Hz	1.25 Hz
Slow Decreasing	1.1 Hz	0.95 Hz
Fast Decreasing	1.1 Hz	0.8 Hz

the installation of software. Our results suggest that negative progress behavior (e.g., stalls and inconsistent progress) at the beginning of an operation can be ameliorated by accelerated progress at the end. Hence, process stages can be arranged such that the slower or variable operations are completed first. For example, if part of an installer requires fetching updates from a remote server and network connectivity could be irregular or unreliable, it may be best to run this stage early in the install sequence. The updates themselves can always be applied later, since they run locally, with more predictable behavior.

MANIPULATING PERCEIVED DURATION THROUGH PROGRESS BAR GRAPHICAL DESIGN

In the previous section, we investigated how the pacing behaviors of progress bars could be used to manipulate perceived duration. We now turn our attention to the graphical design of progress bars, and leverage two distinct visual perceptual effects: frequency variation in rhythmic stimuli and induced motion.

Study 1: Pulsating Progress Bars

Frequency variations in rhythmic stimuli have been shown to affect peoples' perception of time (McAuley, 1995). We hypothesized that this effect could be used to reduce the perceived duration of progress bars. To test this, we designed several variations of a progress bar that used a sinusoidal visual pulsation, causing the progress bars' fill color to vary between light blue and blue.

Study Design

To investigate how pulsation can be used to manipulate perceived duration, we recruited 20 participants from an American academic institution (7 female, mean age 23) to evaluate five distinct behaviors we had created (Table 3). To identify perceptual differences, we employed the same interface as Study 1 (Figure 2); a five-second progress bar duration was used. Like in Study 1, short progress bar durations were a necessary trade-off to run a complete study.

All distinct ordered pairings of the 5 pulsation behaviors were shown to participants, for a total of 25 trials. This included testing behaviors against themselves, and both orderings of every pair, the results of which are combined to control for order effects. Presentation order was also randomized to control for time order errors (Gescheider, 1997). For functions paired against themselves, we found no significant difference in preference.

Results and Discussion

For studies in this section, we employed a two-sided sign test of the null hypothesis that each pulsation behavior was equally likely to be preferred.

287

Figure 5. Statistically significant preferences between the five pulsation behaviors. Thin lines indicate significance at p < 0.05; thick at p < 0.001. Mean preference scores are labeled on the edges.

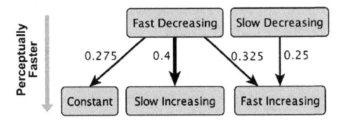

Figure 6. Progress bar used in Mac OSX

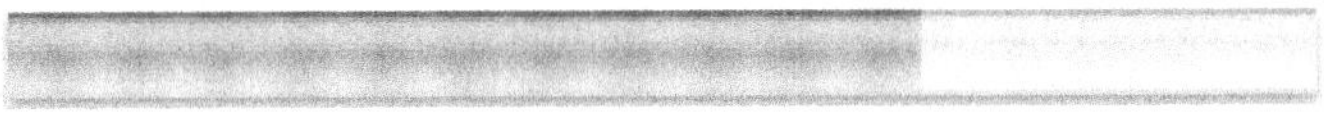

As a measure of perceptual strength, we use the same -1 to +1 preference metric as in Study 1.

There were several statistically significant differences in the preferences between the various pulsation behaviors. Figure 5 provides a partial order of these relationships, and clearly illustrates the preference towards behaviors with increasing pulsation frequencies. This result is confirmed when results are grouped by behavior type; behaviors with increasing frequency are significantly preferred over those with constant or decreasing frequencies ($p < 0.05$ and $p < 0.001$ respectively). The most preferred behavior overall was *Fast Increasing*, with a mean preference score of 0.21.

Study 2: Ribbed Progress Bars

Motivation

Ribbed progress bars have been a staple visual element of Mac OS X since its earliest releases (Figure 6). These progress bars, like others, progress from left to right, but also feature an animated ribbing which moves from right to left. The visual qualities of ribbing are well suited to take advantage of induced motion effects (Kolers, 1972; Schiffman, 1982), which state that motion

perception is not absolute, but rather relative to the surrounding visual context. Thus, ribbing moving in the opposite direction to the progress creates an illusion of increased velocity, which in turn, alters our perception of progress bar duration.

Study Design

To investigate how animated ribbing affects perception of progress bar duration, we devised seven ribbed behaviors, described in Table 4. We used the same participants as in Study 1. Figure 7 illustrates the graphical appearance of our ribbed progress bars (although not animated). Using the same study interface (Figure 2), we presented all 49 distinct ordered pairs of the seven ribbed behaviors. As before, this included testing behaviors against themselves, and both orderings of any given pair, the results of which are combined to control for order effects. Presentation order was also randomized.

Results and Discussion

Participants had strong preferences among the seven ribbed behaviors (Figure 8). When grouped by direction of ribbing, backwards-moving be-

Table 4. The seven ribbed progress bar behaviors. Negative values indicate ribbing moving to the left (opposite to the direction of progress). The progress bar moved right at 128 pixels per second.

Behavior Name	Initial Ribbing Velocity	End Ribbing Velocity
Still (no velocity)	0 mm/sec	0 mm/sec
Backwards Accel.	-7.8 mm/sec	-31.3 mm/sec
Backwards Decel.	-31.3 mm/sec	-7.8 mm/sec
Backwards Const.	-15.6 mm/sec	-15.6 mm/sec
Forwards Accel.	7.8 mm/sec	31.3 mm/sec
Forwards Decel.	31.3 mm/sec	7.8 mm/sec
Forwards Const.	15.6 mm/sec	15.6 mm/sec

Figure 7. Ribbed progress bar used in the study

haviors were significantly preferred over both still and forward ones (p < 0.001 for both), in line with our induced motion hypothesis. When grouped by change in velocity, accelerating behaviors (both forward and backwards) were significantly preferred over still ribbing (i.e., no velocity, p < 0.05), while decelerating behaviors are significantly preferred over both still and constant velocity ribbing (like that seen in Mac OSX; p < 0.05 for both).

Progress bars with backwards-moving ribbing that were either accelerating or decelerating performed the strongest. There was no significant preference between *Backwards Accelerating* and *Backwards Decelerating*. However, if the preference scores against all other behaviors are averaged, *Backwards Decelerating* has the greatest overall preference (0.34 vs. 0.29). Additionally, amongst the statistically significant relationships, *Backwards Decelerating* had both more significant and higher magnitude preferences (Figure 8).

Study 3: Pulsating and Ribbed Designs Compared

Motivation

Studies 1 and 2 identified which pulsating and ribbed behaviors were the strongest within their respective groups. However, the results offered no insight into how these visual augmentations compared against each other or generic, solid-color progress bars. Thus, a new study was devised that pitted three types of progress bars against each other: a generic, solid-color progress bar, the best-performing pulsating progress bar (*Fast Increasing*), and the best-performing ribbed progress bar (*Backwards Decelerating*).

Study Design

We recruited 10 participants from an American academic institution (5 female, mean age 19) to evaluate the relative perceived duration of the three progress bars at two different durations, 5 and 15

Figure 8. Statistically significant preferences between the seven ribbed behaviors. Line styles: dashed (p < 0.1), thin (p < 0.05), thick (p < 0.01). Mean preference scores are labeled on the edges.

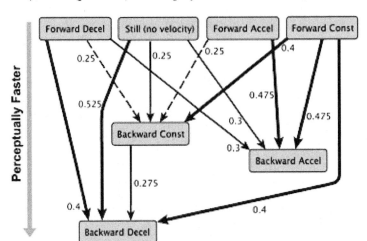

seconds. The latter time was included to explore if the perceptual effects scaled to somewhat longer intervals (both durations are well below Vierordt's threshold (Vierordt, 1868), minimizing perceptual distortion between the two conditions). Nonetheless, to control for any attenuation effects (Brown, 2008), we do not compare results across durations. Each unique ordered pair of progress bars was presented to participants twice, for a total of 18 trials. Data from repeated trials was combined, as were results from different presentation orderings of the same pair (to control for order effects). The trial order was also randomized. The study was completed for both 5- and 15-second durations (36 comparisons in total) using the same interface as the previous studies.

Results and Discussion

There was only one preference approaching significance amongst the three progress bars at the 5-second duration: the progress bar with increasing pulsation was more likely to be perceived as having a shorter duration (i.e., faster) than the generic, solid-color progress bar (p < 0.1). However, the results from the 15-second duration comparisons showed that both the ribbed and pulsating progress

bars were significantly preferred over the generic, solid-color progress bar (p < 0.05). In trials that compared ribbed with pulsating progress bars, ribbed was slightly preferred. When combining results from the 5- and 15-second duration tests, 30 trials indicated a preference for the pulsating behavior, 33 indicated a preference the animated ribbing, and 17 trials noted no preference (equal duration).

Study 4: Magnitude of Perceived Duration Manipulation

Motivation

Studies 1 through 3 indicated which visual designs led to a perception of decreased progress bar duration. However, they did not directly measure how *much* faster the progress bars "felt." In response, we conducted a final round of experimentation that was explicitly designed to gauge the magnitude of the perceptual effects we had identified.

Study Design

For our final study, we selected a progress bar that incorporated *Backwards Decelerating* ribbing, as this was slightly preferred over the pulsating behavior in Study 3. This was compared against a generic, solid color progress bar. The test interface (Figure 2), instead of simply recording participant's preferences, used the responses to warp the duration of the ribbed progress bar (the solid color progress bar had a fixed duration to act as a control). Specifically, if a user felt the ribbed progress bar was faster, its duration was extended (to slow it down). Conversely, if the user felt the ribbing was slower, the duration was reduced (to speed it up). Equal responses left the duration unchanged. The goal was to allow participants to converge to a duration where they believed the two progress bars "felt" equal—a perceptual equilibrium. For an extended discussion on *method of adjustment* experiments, please refer to (Gescheider, 1997).

As in Study 3, two progress bars durations were evaluated: 5 and 15 seconds. The latter was included as a preliminary test to see if the effects extended to longer periods (already partially demonstrated in Study 3). We piloted with longer durations, but it was clear that participants' attention suffered tremendously. We presented both orderings of each duration (solid-color first and ribbed first), yielding four distinct experimental conditions, for which duration warping was handled independently. Results from the two orderings were combined at the end of the study to control for order effects.

We recruited 16 participants from an American academic institution (6 female, mean age 22).

Participants had eight rounds to find a perceptual equilibrium for each of the four conditions. This was repeated twice (with data averaged together) for a total of 64 trials (four conditions of eight rounds each, done twice), the order of which was randomized to control for time order errors.

The time that was added or subtracted to the ribbed progress bar duration decreased linearly each round, allowing for increasing fine tuning. This delta value started at 25% of the total original duration, and then dropped by 5% each subsequent round. For the final three rounds, a fixed value of 2.5% of the original duration was used. In the first round, the "equal speeds" answer button was disabled, forcing participants to select either the generic, solid color progress bar or the ribbed progress bar as being faster. This helped to kick off the convergence. Participants could invert the relationship in as few as two rounds if they changed their mind.

Results and Discussion

Figure 9 displays the results of the duration matching trials. In both cases, the *Backwards Decelerating* ribbing was perceived to be significantly faster than a generic, solid color progress bar ($p < 0.001$). On average, a 5-second solid color progress bar felt perceptually equivalent to a 5.61-second ribbed progress bar (SE = 0.14), which is 12.2% longer in actual duration. A similar effect was seen in the case of the 15-second duration tests, where

Figure 9. Results from the perceived duration magnitude experiment

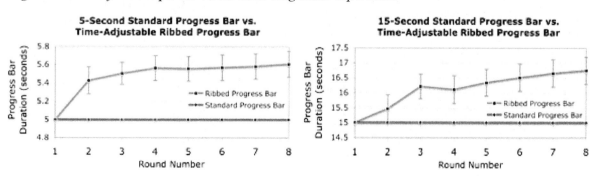

the ribbed progress bar converged to an average of 16.75 seconds (SE = 0.45), an 11.7% increase in actual time. The similarity in the magnitude of the two results suggests these effects might scale linearly to longer durations, but additional tests will be needed to confirm this.

Another interesting result is that unlike the 5-second duration results, which level off quickly (by roughly round four—see Figure 9), the 15-second results show a clearly upward trajectory, even at round eight. It is possible that the longer duration necessitates additional rounds to find a perceptual equilibrium. If this trend does exist, it would suggest an even greater perceptual performance effect is at play, and possibly that the effect magnifies as duration increases.

CONCLUSION

In this chapter, we explored how different progress bar pacing behaviors and visual design can manipulate users' perception of duration. By minimizing negative behaviors and incorporating positive behaviors, one can effectively make progress bars and their associated processes *seem* faster. In our final experiment, we took our best performing behavior, a backwards moving, and decelerating ribbed progress bar, and compared its perceived performance to that of a generic, solid color progress bar. The results show that a simple graphical design tweak could be used to make processes appear about 11% faster, when in reality, their durations remains unchanged. Importantly, this "performance boost" can be realized with little more than a software update. Finally, this work brings forward an interesting meta-question: would one rather have a computer that feels fast, but is actually slow? or a computer that is fast, but feels slow? Fortunately, it appears that we can realize the best of both worlds and have computers that are fast, and feel even faster.

ACKNOWLEDGMENT

We thank Stacey Kuznetsov and Robert Bell for their help in data collection and analysis. Additionally, this work was supported in part by grants IIS-0713509 and IIS-0840766 from the National Science Foundation. We are also grateful to Amy Ogan for help with editing.

REFERENCES

Allan, L. G. (1979). The perception of time. *Perception & Psychophysics*, *26*, 340–354. doi:10.3758/BF03204158

Baumgartner, H., Sujan, M., & Padgett, D. (1997). Patterns of affective reactions to advertisements: The integration of moment-to-moment responses into overall judgments. *JMR, Journal of Marketing Research*, *34*(2), 219–232. doi:10.2307/3151860

Block, R. (1990). *Cognitive models of psychological time*. Hillsdale, NJ: Lawrence Erlbaum Associates.

Brown, S. W. (2008). The attenuation effect in timing: Counteracting dual-task interference with time-judgment skill training. *Perception*, *37*(5), 712–724. doi:10.1068/p5698

Conn, A. P. (1995). Time affordances: The time factor in diagnostic usability heuristics. In *Proceedings of the 1995 SIGCHI Conference on Human Factors in Computing Systems,* (pp. 186-193). ACM Press.

Fredrickson, B. L., & Kahneman, D. (1993). Duration neglect in retrospective evaluations of affective episodes. *Journal of Personality and Social Psychology*, *65*, 45–55. doi:10.1037/0022-3514.65.1.45

Geelhoed, E., Toft, P., Roberts, S., & Hyland, P. (1995). To influence time perception. In *Proceedings of the Conference Companion on Human Factors in Computing Systems,* (pp. 272-273). ACM Press.

Gescheider, G. A. (1997). *Psychophysics: The fundamentals* (3rd ed.). Mahwah, NJ: Lawrence Erlbaum Associates Inc.

Hildebrandt, M., Dix, A., & Meyer, H. A. (1994). Time design. In *Proceedings of the 2004 SIGCHI Conference on Human Factors in Computing Systems, Extended Abstracts,* (pp. 1737-1738). ACM Press.

Hogan, W. H. (1978). A theoretical reconciliation of competing views of time perception. *The American Journal of Psychology, 91*(3), 417–428. doi:10.2307/1421689

Hosmer, D. W., & Lemeshow, S. (1989). *Applied logistic regression*. New York, NY: John Wiley & Sons.

Kolers, P. A. (1972). *Aspects of motion perception*. New York, NY: Pergamon Press Inc.

Langer, T., Sarin, R., & Weber, M. (2005). The retrospective evaluation of payment sequences: Duration neglect and peak-and-end effects. *Journal of Economic Behavior & Organization, 58*, 157–175. doi:10.1016/j.jebo.2004.01.001

McAuley, J. D. (1995). *On the perception of time as phase: Toward an adaptive-oscillator model of rhythm*. Ph.D. Thesis. Bloomington, IN: Indiana University.

Myers, B. A. (1985). The importance of percent-done progress indicators for computer-human interfaces. In *Proceedings of the 1985 SIGCHI Conference on Human Factors in Computing Systems,* (pp. 11-17). ACM Press.

Redelmeier, D., & Kahneman, D. (1996). Patients' memories of painful medical treatments: Real-time and retrospective evaluations of two minimally invasive procedures. *Pain, 66*, 3–8. doi:10.1016/0304-3959(96)02994-6

Schiffman, H. R. (1982). *Sensation and perception: An integrated approach* (2nd ed.). New York, NY: John Wiley & Sons.

Seow, S. C. (2008). *Designing and engineering time: The psychology of time perception in software*. Boston, MA: Pearson Education.

Tognazzini, B. (1993). Principles, techniques, and ethics of stage magic and their application to human interface design. In *Proceedings of INTERCHI, 1993*, 355–362.

Vierordt, K. V. (1868). *Der zeitsinn nach versuchen*. Tubingen, Germany: H. Laupp.

Section 5
Education and Interactive Picture Book

Chapter 17
Dynamic Generation of Adaptive Tutoring

Khulood Gaid
Royal University for Women, Bahrain

Eshaa Mohamed Alkhalifa
University of Bahrain, Bahrain

ABSTRACT

Adaptive Educational Systems are able to alter an online course as per the needs of each student. Existing technologies require significant time and effort to design and build such courses. This chapter offers a solution allowing instructors to build a practical adaptive system as they upload their lessons and tests to the online site. The system asks the instructor to associate multiple choice answers that are incorrect with error pattern names and to associate the error patterns with lessons students need to review. The result is that the adaptable system is dynamically built as the course progresses. A student views a student profile screen that is adapted to that student's level of knowledge and displays that student's misconceptions. On the other hand, an instructor can use a reports view of the system to extract common error co-occurrences and infer information about the difficulties faced by students in that course.

INTRODUCTION

Learning on the Internet has faced many challenges along the years, the most critical of which is that students are sometimes "lost in hyperspace" (Carroll, 1982). The main cause of this is that users face cognitive overload, when the learning process is interrupted by navigational concerns.

Learners are concerned with recalling the page they navigated from and the path they followed which results in low efficiency learning (Nunes & Fowell, 1996).

The main culprits for the disorientation that is faced by learners includes:

a. Learners have an incomplete conceptual model of the organization and structure of information (Elm & Wood, 1985).

DOI: 10.4018/978-1-4666-1628-8.ch017

b. Users experience a lack of closure because they do not know how much longer the lesson continues before it ends (Shneiderman, 1992).

c. Users lose track as they digress towards interesting information and forget their main goals of learning (Foss, 1989).

The problem is therefore both a design problem as well as a user problem. Designers of courseware should take these issues into account when designing educational systems to avoid the disorientation that can occur. On the other hand, users are adapting to the new world by adjusting their approach to learning.

Adaptable educational systems present one solution to this problem. Adaptive Systems are defined as systems that capable of four main tasks:

1. To manage explicitly defined learning routes adapted to each user.
2. To monitor and record the activities of students.
3. To automatically infer user trends and store them into a learner profile system.
4. To act upon available knowledge by making recommendations, or altering the course of instruction (Boticario, et al., 2006).

Brusilovsky (2004) indicated that adaptive educational systems went through three different generations. The systems that were designed during the first generation offered adaptive navigational support, adaptive presentation, direct guidance, sorting of links, hiding of links, and annotating links in different colors.

The second generation systems focused on creating adaptive web-based educational systems with a limited number of adaptive features. They also focused on producing new techniques for adaptation, as in AHA (De Bra & Calvi, 1998), which explored several approaches to link removal, while INSPIRE explored learning styles (Papanikolaou, et al., 2003). These systems also focused on development frameworks to develop adaptable learning systems.

The third generation did not register any increase in the implementation of adaptive learning system in real courses except by those who designed their own systems. Instead, educators went on to use online learning management systems as in Edu20.org and Blackboard (Blackboard Inc., 2002). These systems allow educators to upload notes offer online quizzes, and gradebooks.

Brusilovsky (2004) indicates that every single function that an LMS has, there is a matching function in adaptive systems that can do the task better. Yet, the influence of adaptive systems on education is extremely limited.

Boticario et al. (2006) indicate that building adaptive scenarios is a very complex task that covers the full life cycle of the learning process. In fact, the task is so daunting that it may dissuade many educators from following this path to build learning systems because after all that effort, the learning materials on the system may be out-of-date.

The only existing platform to develop adaptive hypermedia courses is AHA (De Bra, et al., 1998). AHA is an open source platform that can be downloaded for development of online hypertext adaptive systems. It is an extremely rich platform that allows possibilities to adapt the page content in different ways, presentation of links, with or without icons ahead of the links, to enable the same link to lead to different pages based upon the values in the user model.

However, AHA requires a full course analysis and design prior to building the adaptable course. Although the overhead required to design such systems has been significantly reduced, it is still a daunting overhead to instructors who do not know about adaptable system architecture and how it works.

This paper attempts to resolve this main critical issue by allowing educators to use an online adaptive system that generates adaptive tests. An instructor, adds lesson units, and adds multiple choice questions, then links the wrong responses of these questions to lesson units interactively.

The chapter will start by presenting user experience; first a student's experience in the system, then an instructor's experience while using the system. It will then go on to describe the architecture and how it builds the adaptive system gradually as the course progresses. The paper will later discuss an extra module that is added to give instructors more in depth knowledge of student error patterns and behavior, and then conclude with possible implications of this work.

USER EXPERIENCE IN THE DYNAMICALLY GENERATED ADAPTIVE TUTOR

Student Experience while using the System

Students have to fill in three pages of information for registration. This is necessary to create a new student profile for them so that it holds all pertinent information about them.

The Registration Step

1. Every student must provide valid username, password, email, security question and the answer.
2. The student must remember the answer to the security question because it is the only way the password can be changed.
3. After finishing this step, the student will be redirected to the log in page in order to show that the request is authentic.
4. After logging in the user will be directed to complete registration.
5. A student needs to fill the fields with valid personal data such as the first name, last name, email to communicate by, phone number and major.

6. All fields are required. If any field is not filled an error message will be given.
7. The terms and conditions agreement must be read carefully before ticking the check box for agreeing to it.
8. At this stage, a student should to specify the course he/she wants to join.
9. Provisions to include learning style preferences exist within the system for future implementation.
10. The user needs to provide the course code if he joined through a specific teacher. Otherwise this field can be left empty. Leaving it empty implies that the student is self driven to join and that this student can add courses and take tests without the supervision of a teacher. Guidance can then be provided by each teacher who has constructed an added course.
11. Then the user will be redirected to take a knowledge level test where his level can be associated. This test will save the student the effort to go through lessons he does not need to review.

Taking the Entry Test

1. The first page screen displayed contains general tips about the test.
2. When the user feels ready to take the test he/she needs to click on the begin button.
3. Question numbers are displayed as a drop down list and a student selects one to solve it and then selects another until the test is done. This approach facilitates the dynamic selection of questions for each test according to the student profile.
4. The user needs to choose only one answer per question. If more than one answer is chosen, the user will be advised to check only one answer and all radio buttons will be cleared.
5. After answering each question a user clicks the submit button.

Figure 1. A screenshot of the student profile

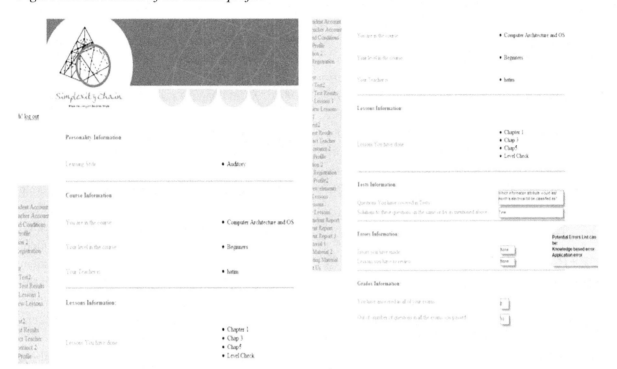

6. When the question list ends a student is redirected to the results page. Questions cannot be skipped.

7. The results page displays a list of the questions taken and under it is a list of correct answers, then a description of the mistakes that student made by using the error pattern descriptions added by an instructor. Follow that the number of questions the student answered out of the pool of questions that were chosen for him. Entry test questions do not have a maximum number of questions because they depend on what questions an instructor describes as a possible entry test question.

8. After clicking the 'DONE' button the user is redirected to the profile page.

Student Profile

A student can see the profile page containing information about a course immediately after completing the entry test for that course. If a student logs again into the system, that student has to select one of the courses in order to go to the profile page (see Figure 1).

The first part of the screen 'PERSONALITY INFORMATION' shows the student the appropriate learning style if the student has provided it.

The second part shows a student registered courses and the level for the course he joined and the supervisor for these courses.

The third part shows lessons information: Lessons already done, along with a list of questions done, correct answers to these questions, error patterns the student made while answering the questions are listed for the student to be aware of common errors and the list of recommended lessons that need to be reviewed based on the errors.

1. For example: A student may choose c, and c is a wrong answer that is associated with the description of (application error) and to the remedial lesson number 4. That student

will see this information and realize how to correct that misconception by studying that lesson.

2. From the page all updated details about the student can be found for him-her to review the progress.

Viewing a Lesson

1. In the first page the user needs to specify the course and lesson he wants to view material for. A learner can choose materials from any course that student is registered for and if many types of materials are available like (ppt. doc. Images, video, etc.) that learner can select which to learn from. An instructor that constructs the course choose the types and density of materials available for a lesson.

2. When the button go to material is clicked the user is redirected to a new page that contains a list of material available for the lesson.

3. The user need to choose from a drop down list associated with each type of material.

4. When the user chooses from the list and clicks on the view button, a conversation is opened by the browser to either save or choose a program to open the file.

5. The file can be reviewed then.

Taking a Test

1. If the user chooses to go to this page, he/she will be redirected to an initial page where a list of tips is given.

2. All tests are similar to the initial test described above except that questions will come from the domain of the concept being tested alone.

3. Taking these tests marks student progress through the lessons. Material is only marked as done if a student passes the test.

Instructor Experience while using the System

The Registration Step

1. Every teacher will need to provide a valid username, password, email, security question and the answer.

2. The teacher needs to remember the answer to the security question because it is the only way the password can be changed.

3. After finishing this step, the teacher will be redirected to the log in page in order to prove authentic.

4. The teacher will be sent an email from the administrator that contains a randomly generated code. This code is needed to identify the teacher.

5. Then after logging in the user will be redirected to the second step.

6. In this step the teacher will need to fill the fields with valid personal data such as the first name, last name, email to communicate by, phone number and profession.

7. The terms and conditions agreement must be read carefully before ticking the check box for agreeing on it.

8. If the terms are not accepted, registration will not be completed.

9. When this step is completed, the user is redirected to the third registration step.

10. In this step the teacher needs to register his class by adding the code he received by email from the site administrator who acknowledged this person as an instructor for this course.

11. This code is going to be used by students in order to register for the courses offered by the teacher.

Defining a New Attribute

(Please note that visiting this page is not compulsory; a teacher can directly go to the lessons page)

1. In this page the teacher can define classifications and general attributes that are added to the database. New course types can be added, e.g. Art, Business. New student levels can be added to the existing list (beginner, intermediate and advanced) as in levels associate with book parts, part 1, part 2, part 3. Time limits can be associated with quizzes and exams.
2. Error patterns can be added by instructors as per the needs of that particular course.
3. The teacher is allowed to define new course types, prerequisites, levels, time associations, and level types.
4. Examples of current error patterns include the following:
   ◦ Non Understanding of Place Value
   ◦ Inaccurate procedure (algorithm)
   ◦ Mechanical error
   ◦ Application error
   ◦ Knowledge based error
   ◦ Order of Operations

Defining New Courses

1. The instructor can enter a course name, choose a course type, course prerequisite, and level.
2. After finishing this step the teacher will be redirected to a page where he/she can add lessons. Additionally, objectives of the course are chosen— up to four objectives. Then, an instructor is redirected to the questions page to add questions and other details.

Defining Questions for Tests

1. The instructor will have to choose the course name from a drop down list.

2. Then the testing material question must be entered. This step is needed so the system can recognize from where can it generate questions.
3. The question must be entered in multiple choice format. More question formats will be added as this project is expanded.
4. The question level must be entered then (beginner, intermediate and advanced). The level is used to associate with question levels with student levels in the course to assess students at their own level and to inform students of their progress level in the course.
5. Then the learning objective that the question is satisfying must be determined. Objectives are defined when a new course is defined, and student profiles show what objectives the student has achieved so far.
6. The instructor needs to enter possible student choices. The correct answer will receive a "none" in the error pattern slot, while all other answers can be associated with one error pattern. If an instructor does not wish to associate an error with an error pattern the word "none" or "inapplicable" can be used to leave the choice without associating it.
7. Specify the error associated with this choice. If the choice is a correct answer then none should be chosen for error patterns.
8. If the teacher wishes to specify another question he can click on submit. Or he can choose done if he is done with adding questions.

Viewing Lessons

1. The first step that the teacher need to do here is to choose the course and lesson titles.
2. Then the teacher will be redirected to the materials page.
3. Then the teacher can choose to view the file or delete it.

Figure 2. System's architecture

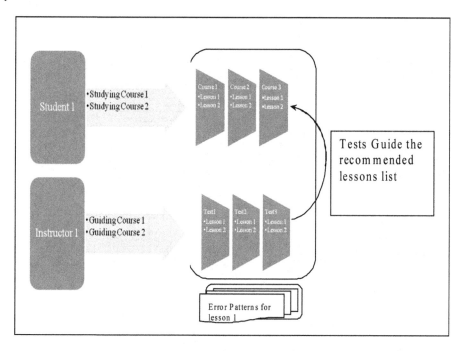

Generating Student Reports

1. The teacher needs to choose the name of the student he wants to see a report about.
2. After choosing the student the teacher will be redirected to a page where he can review the progress of the student.
3. A teacher profile that is placed so a teacher can explore details about courses he had constructed.
4. The teacher selects a course to see details about that course assuming that each instructor will teach more than one course.
5. The details he can view are the course materials, prerequisites, most common errors made by students in that course and lessons associated with that error. This will make it possible for instructors to revise lessons to increase their efficiency.

SYSTEM'S ARCHITECTURE

The system's architecture is shown in Figure 2.

This system does not require a major course design effort prior to deployment. It only requires an instructor to do what they would normally do by uploading lessons in several different formats and uploading multiple choice questions in a way that is hardly any different from existing learning management systems.

The only difference is that for every wrong answer, the teacher writes an error pattern description in normal English and then assists students in recognizing what these error patterns are. This can happen while a course is running as and when a new test is uploaded.

As students progress through the course, they will see the lessons they have to take reduce in number as they pass their tests. An increase will occur if they demonstrate an error linked to a lesson that they did not cover sufficiently well.

Figure 3. Database entity relationship diagram

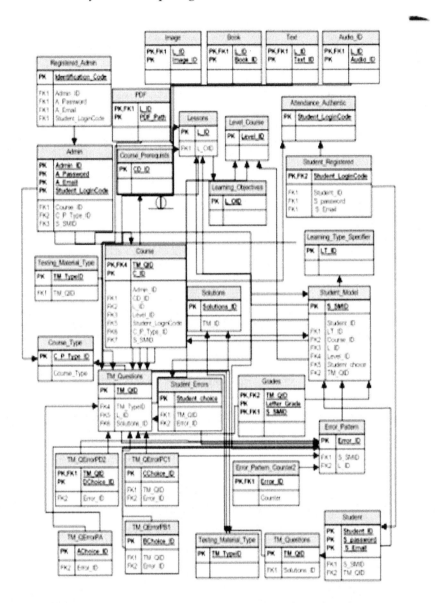

In other words, the adaptive course is deployed when the first lesson is added. The database entity relationship diagram is shown in Figure 3. It's designed to allow maximum flexibility for future expansion of the system.

FUTURE RESEARCH DIRECTIONS

Future work possibilities are many. It is possible to work on altering the presentation of multiple choice question and to allow freeform answers to be submitted. It is also possible to add learning style preferences and to link that with lesson approaches taken or offered. The current system can accommodate different types of lesson materials including PowerPoint slides, documents, images, etc. A future system can select and recommend to students which would accommodate their style of learning.

Another possibility is to expand the error mining module. In its present form, it enables instructors to know if the materials may lack a bit of information that causes most students to display the same error pattern. This would enable instructors to modify their lessons to ensure that no error patterns shows behavior beyond the statistically normal behavior that is expected of it.

CONCLUSION

The presented system has been tested on a test bed and will soon be deployed on the Internet. The goal is to make it available for use by instructors at the University and eventually to all those interested in using it in the world. The interface is guided by an adaptive engine in the background.

A central issue that may be raised by those versed in adaptable learning, is that they may say that each question in this system is an island. It is analyzed alone, and student profiles do not reflect any continuity of errors or styles.

That is true, because this system breaks up the problem of having a unified profile that generalizes student abilities into a description of how that student reacted to individual questions. That was a difficult but necessary decision, because systems as they currently stand are not able to generalize so instructors analyze courses in advance, and put that knowledge into the adaptive system. This effort became a hurdle in deployment of adaptive systems, so if it is possible to implement that small part of adaptive systems now while considering how to build an engine that would generalize for future projects, then this in itself would be an achievement.

Screens and displays as they currently exist are far from being friendly and to be honest neither is its existence as a distinct system. What educators need today is this ability added to existing learning management systems that they already use as an upgrade. If that happens, the educators will feel tempted to use it on a wide scale perhaps if only to detect misconceptions.

This work also opens a door to researchers, to think out of the box, with regards to educational tools. Algorithms or new ideas do not have to be implemented as a whole or none at all. Parts can be implemented if that is what the customers need and be effective enough to achieve their purpose.

REFERENCES

Blackboard Inc. (2002). *Blackboard course management system 5.1*. Retrieved 14 November 2010 from http://www.blackboard.com/.

Boticario, J. G. Santos, O. C., & Rosmalen, P. (2005). Technological and management issues in providing adaptive education in distance learning universities. *EADTU, 2005*. Retrieved Nov 14, 2010 from http://www.eadtu.nl/proceedings/2005/presentations/plenary/Jesus%20Boticario.pdf.

Brusilovsky, P. (2004). Adaptive educational hypermedia: From generation to generation. In *Proceedings of 4th Hellenic Conference on Information and Communication Technologies in Education*, (pp. 19-33). Athens, Greece. Retrieved 14 November 2010 from http://www2.sis.pitt.edu/~peterb/papers/PEG01.html.

De Bra, P., & Calvi, L. (1998). Towards a generic adaptive hypermedia system. In *Proceedings of the Second Workshop on Adaptive Hypertext and Hypermedia*, (pp. 5-11). Hypertext and Hypermedia.

Edu20.org. (2006). *Founded by Graham Glass*. Retrieved from http://www.edu20.org.

Nunes, J. M., & Fowell, S. P. (1996). Hypermedia as an experimental learning tool: A theoretical model. *Information Research News, 6*(4), 15-27. Retrieved 14 November 2010 from http://informationr.net/ir/2-1/paper12.html.

Papanikolaou, K. A., Grigoriadou, M., Kornilakis, H., & Magoulas, G. D. (2003). Personalizing the interaction in a web-based educational hypermedia system: The case of INSPIRE. *User Modeling and User-Adapted Interaction, 13*(3), 213–267. doi:10.1023/A:1024746731130

KEY TERMS AND DEFINITIONS

Adaptive Learning: Content that exhibits adaptive behavior that uses If..then..else rules in order to alter the choice of lessons according to a student profile.

Student Profile: A description of student standard, styles, topics mastered usually obtained through the interaction of the system with the student in a learning environment.

Intelligent Systems: Systems that exhibit a form of thinking classically associated with the description of "intelligent" where the user of the system does not necessarily know how the technology arrived at that conclusion.

Student Modeling: Techniques used to extract information about a student and to save them in what is called a student model. The techniques vary according the target information and may include natural language processing, etc.

Learning Management Systems: These systems organize the interaction between instructors and their students by allowing the exchange of information as in lesson materials, student grades, assignments, etc.

Adaptive Hypermedia: Hypermedia that can show or hide links from a web page according to information that is known about the person accessing that site.

Error Pattern: If a number of students make the same error repeatedly, then that error becomes an error pattern that can be described and documents for use in future courses.

Chapter 18
Interactive Picture Book with Story–Changeable System by Shuffling Pages

Hiroki Yamada
The University of Tokyo, Japan

Michitaka Hirose
The University of Tokyo, Japan

ABSTRACT

In this chapter, the authors introduce SequenceBook system, an interactive picture book that consists of a paper book with very thin IC (Integrated Circuit) tags embedded in each page and an RFID (Radio Frequency IDentification) antenna. This system uses a traditional paper book as an interface and realizes natural interface that keeps the affordance of traditional book and thus smoothly prompts users to experience its contents by just flipping pages in the same way as they read an ordinary book. Another important feature of the system is that users can change its storylines as they like. The system is designed like a bookbinder so that users can easily shuffle pages and make several patterns of stories.

INTRODUCTION

Since early times, picture storybook has been important tool for children and also enjoyed as entertainment by adults.

Many years later, as computers progress, people are becoming interested in making books highly computer-supported. As a result, some digital storytelling contents on computers, such as e-novels, have been created and spread into our

daily life. However, while it allows users to enjoy rich multimodal contents that traditional paper books do not have, paper books have not faded from our daily life. We think that this is because of the naturalness and familiarity as an interface of paper books.

Based on the fact that traditional paper books have been widely used until now, we aim to develop novel paper books, which users can enjoy rich multimodal contents like software on computers while keeping the affordance of a traditional book.

DOI: 10.4018/978-1-4666-1628-8.ch018

Figure 1. SequenceBook

In this chapter, we propose *SequenceBook*, which uses a traditional paper book as an interface to experience digital contents, so that it can keep the affordances of paper books while adding electronic augmentation. The aim of this study is to achieve both highly computer-supported contents and natural interface, e.g., highly efficient combination of physical and digital world. With *SequenceBook*, every person (especially who is not good at operating computers) can enjoy rich digital contents just by flipping pages (see Figure 1).

In this study, we also aim to develop an efficient and novel system to encourage creativity and activeness of users in reading. To achieve this purpose, it is very important for users to make the sequences of a story by their own hand. Therefore, *SequenceBook* was constructed like a bookbinder so that users can easily change a sequence of pages and enjoy several patterns of stories.

BACKGROUND (RELATED WORKS)

Some other media art works use a metaphor of picture book. *Moments de Jean-Jacques Rousseau* (Boissier, 2008) and *Beyond Pages* (Fujihata, 1995) are famous media art works. In addition, some researchers have been interested in visually augmented books. Augmentation of book by using Mixed Reality Technology has been also accomplished by previous works, e.g. *The Mixed Reality Book* (Grasset, et al., 2007) and *The Magic Book* (Billinghurst, et al., 2001) are representative examples. *Interactive textbook and interactive Venn diagram* (Koike, et al., 2000) attempted to project information next to the book. *Listen Reader* (Back, et al., 2001) is a system using IC tags embedded in each page like *SequenceBook*.

From a standpoint of story creation, some systems have been developed. *StoryMat* (Ryokai, et al., 1999) is a physical play mat that records voices of storytelling play and the movements of the toys.

The Lost Cosmonaut (Vogelsang, et al., 2005) is the system for narrative creation using paper as an interface. *StoryBuilder* (Antle, et al., 2003) is an online storytelling system that allows users to add to stories by others in a comic-book style.

While systems like *StoryMat* is efficient for story creation, we think that a form of traditional book has potential to prompt users to enter a world of the story rather than other forms because many stories have been recorded and read in a book form traditionally until now.

In addition, one of the biggest progress of this work is that users can change the storyline by shuffling pages; that has not been accomplished in related works using a book form.

In *the Mixed Reality Book* or *The Magic Book*, users need to put some equipments on themselves in advance, whereas, *SequenceBook* does not require any equipment on users that is not usual in reading, while some physical limitations, such as positionally-fixed book or requirement of setting up devices to a table are remaining. Its "just flip and read" interface is traditional and amiable, so it may prompt users to understand the story like they read an ordinary book.

MAIN FOCUS OF THE CHAPTER: HOW CAN ONE BOOK TELL MORE THAN ONE STORY?

Motivation

The origin of this system is our memory in childhood. We loved reading various kinds of books, especially picture books in our early years. Book was our best friend and we spent a lot of time together with wonderful books. Sometimes stories of books pleased us and sometimes made us sad. Some sad storylines and endings made us very unhappy, so we thought, "Why cannot we change the story?" Then, we came up with a good idea to change the story. That was to close the book in the middle of the story and dream our original dreamy stories.

Book is sometimes kind and sometimes not kind because book compels the reader to experience only one story. We think it is wonderful if one book has more than one story and the reader can understand the world of the book more deeply and feel familiarity with it.

Issues, Controversies, Problems

In this chapter, we focus on the topic of storytelling of picture book. As we discussed previously, one book can tell only one story. On the other hand, digital book with many stories does not have affordance and naturalness of traditional paper book.

Solutions and Recommendations

SequenceBook is a solution proposal to this issue. Readers can change the story of this picture book as they like by shuffling pages. The story of the book changes according to the order of the pages. *SequenceBook* is designed just as like a bookbinder so that readers can easily shuffle pages and make several patterns of stories. The reader also can change the storyline even in the middle of the story by shuffling the remaining pages, so they can seek their favorite storyline or ending. This interactive and augmented reality picture book consists of a paper book with very thin passive IC (Integrated Circuit) tags embedded in each page, two RFID (Radio Frequency IDentification) antennas installed under the table, and one projector set overtop. This artwork uses a traditional paper book as an interface and realizes a natural interface that keeps the affordance of ordinal book and thus smoothly prompts readers to experience its stories with movies and music by just flipping pages in the same way as they read an ordinary book.

IMPLEMENTATION

Overview of *SequenceBook* system is as follows: The user can see one book on a table in front of him. A projector is set above the table to project movie onto the pages of the book and a speaker is set under the table to play background music. The RFID (Radio Frequency IDentification) antenna is installed under the table. When the user starts to flip the pages, the RFID antenna recognizes which page the user is actually looking at. And at the same time, background music starts to play and the projector starts to project both images of characters and narrative texts (Figure 2).

Page Identification

For page identification, we selected RFID as an efficient method to identify individual pages because image processing, the most general technique for identification, is easily affected by light condition and human hands and not suitable for this case. However, IC (Integrated Circuit) tag used in previous studies is too big and thick to be naturally embedded in a page. So previous works using RFID have a problem of unnaturalness as a book.

To overcome this problem, *SequenceBook* system uses μ-chip (Hitachi, Ltd.), very small and thin (51.5mm height, 1.5mm width, 0.25mm thickness) passive IC tags for this system (Figure 3). By sandwiching them between papers (charcoal paper, 0.19mm thickness) of pages, IC tags become invisible and not touchable for users while pages keep their thinness and naturalness of ordinary papers. Therefore, users can flip pages easily like a paper book without IC tags. And they can also easily shuffle pages.

To detect embedded IC tags, the RFID antenna is installed under the table. The thickness of the table is enough thin so that it does not miss

Figure 2. Overview of SequenceBook system

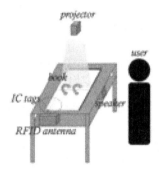

Figure 3. Embedded IC tag (μ-chip) in a page

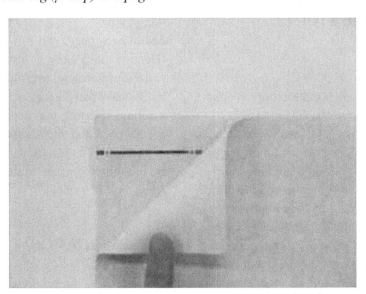

detection of tabletop IC tags. To enable the RFID antenna to work perfectly, the book with IC tags is put on designated location on the table. The RFID antenna can detect more than one tag simultaneously by its anti-collision technology. The we confirmed that the recognition rate was 99.3[%] in experiment. When users turn a page, the RFID antenna recognizes it as the change of the IC tags within its read range (about 40 [mm]). The IC tags are also embedded in book covers so that the system can also detect start and end of reading.

Page Binding and Shuffling Mechanism

To keep the IC tags within the detectable area of the RFID antenna, the book is fixed using a magnetic binder. All pages are put together using two rings with magnets and fixed to certain position of the table (Figure 4).

With the magnetic binder, users easily fix and unfix all pages to shuffle them. This is one of the most important technical innovations of *Sequence-Book*, that is, shuffling pages as users like and change the storylines. To develop this page-shuffling system, realizing manageability of pages by using very thin IC tags is essential.

While some previous works, such as *Story-Builder*, allow users to customize existing narrative

pieces (setting or characters), *SequenceBook* system allows users only recombination of pages. The reason is that story creation by simply shuffling pages does not require any electronic equipment and does not interfere with natural interaction with paper books.

Process of creating storylines by shuffling pages goes as follows: Once you take off all pages from the binder, you can see background images drown directly onto each page. Next, just shuffle pages to make different raw of sequences of a story. When you put back all pages to the binder in a different order, the RFID antenna detects rearranged IC tags and corresponding images are projected and new background music starts to play.

The number of pages should be considered for designing *SequenceBook*'s page-shuffling system. The more pages are added to the book, the more possible stories will be created. (e.g. number of pages is 2, 3, 4, 5, number of stories becomes 2, 6, 24, 120) This means too many pages make the storyline complicated and as a result, it will be impossible to arrange consistent stories in advance. Therefore, we made the book with four pages, which gives the story 24 branches. This number does not seem to be too few to create enjoyable stories.

Figure 4. Woody book covers, paper pages, and woody rings with magnets to bind pages

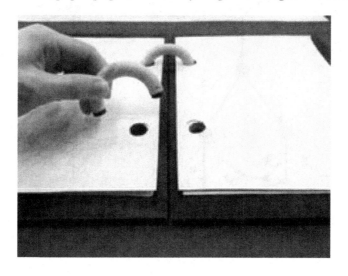

Sequence Visualization

The RFID antenna and reader send information of IC tags to the middleware (μ-chip manager, Hitachi, Ltd). The middleware reconciles data of IC tags with the hash table to translate it to page IDs (from A to D) and sends them to the software to visualize sequences (*Flash CS4, Adobe, Ltd*) after buffering for a given length of time. Then one of stories arranged in advance is called up from detected page IDs and movie of characters and narrative texts are projected onto surface of the book and background music starts to play (Figure 5).

Connection of Sequences

To shuffle pages and create their own stories easier, some kind of visual clues have to be assigned to all pages in advance. As a hint to change row of pages, the background of each scene is drawn to every page directly by palette.

To make all 24 stories attractive and motivate users to re-create stories, some ingenuities are exercised as follows: Casting is one of important factors to connect shuffled sequences smoothly.

For example, the hero is set up as a wizard to connect two different sequences by "magic," the versatile factor to connect different sequences smoothly. There are also some scene-specific characters, only appear in particular storylines to motivate users. By creating several stories, users can find some facts or characters' relationships (see Figure 6).

Figure 5. Projected images onto pages

Figure 6. Examples of storyline branches

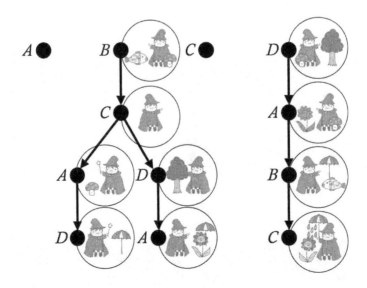

Skipping and Going Back in Reading

The system also allows users to skip pages and go back to any page. For example, if user flipped two pages (page B and C) at one time from page A, the system choices randomly one storyline from possible two patterns (A-B-C and A-C-B) and project suitable sequence of storyline arranged in advance, and the system enables users to re-create storylines at the middle of storylines. For example, after reading the storyline B-C-D-A, the user can go back to page C, and shuffle remaining two pages (page D and A) and restart reading from page D and enjoy another storyline (B-C-A-D). In this way, users can seek favorite storyline by shuffling pages again and again.

USER STUDY

We conducted a demonstration experiment of the system in *iii Exhibition 11*, the annual exhibition of technology and art in *The University of Tokyo* (Figure 7).

240 people experienced the system during the 6-day exhibition. We stayed beside the system to answer the question from users and count the number of shuffling pages for story creation. We analyzed of the result based on following two points, which characterize the system.

Naturalness of the Paper Book Interface

129 of all 240 people asked us about the mechanism of page detection. Only 5 people (about 4 percent of people interested in page detection technique) guessed that something is embedded in a page while most people had no idea or guessed that image processing is used (Figure 8). The result indicates that most people did not notice the presence of detection system inside of the thin papers, suggesting that this system keeps enough naturalness of paper even after sandwiching IC tags.

Availability of Page-Shuffling System

How many times people played with shuffling will tell how people can enjoy this system. We put the description about story change mechanism by shuffling pages, so almost all people tried to shuffle pages at least once. While some people tried

Figure 7. People playing with SequenceBook at the exhibition

Figure 8. Guess how the system detects individual pages

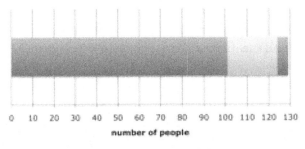

Figure 9. How many times people played with the shuffling system

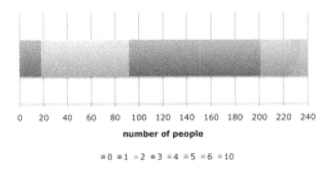

to shuffle pages only once, 225 people (about 94 percent of people) shuffled pages more than once (Figure 9). The reason why people played with this over and over are as follows: some said it is just a fun to play with, others said they tried to find the mechanism of change of storylines by shuffling pages. This result indicates that the page-shuffling system provides enjoyment to people at some level. Although further experiments are needed to validate the utility of the page-shuffling system.

ANOTHER FOCUS OF THE CHAPTER: HOW CAN ONE BOOK CHANGE ITS SCENES?

Motivation

Not only changing the stories of the picture book, but also arranging each scene seems to be inter-

esting and challenging topic for the new picture book system.

Cultural Background in Japan: "*Kototama*"

In Japan, words have been believed to have own spirits and special force since early times (Sugata, 1994). These words are called "*Kototama*" in Japanese, which means "spiritual words." So many Japanese have been taken meticulous care when they speak or write words historically. That is, words had special importance and have been esteemed in daily life. In this study, we focused attention on this cultural background and current information society in Japan. With the advancement of information technology, the more words are written or spoken in cyber space, the less people pay attention to words, the authors often feel. So we aim to develop the system for experiencing "force of words" by using augmented reality technology and reevaluate the culture of "*Kototama*" in Japan.

Solutions and Recommendations

As a solution, we propose sentence-changeable system to be embedded in *SequenceBook* system. The sentence-changeable system is AR (Augmented Reality) based system. You add (drag) and remove (withdraw) some particular words in the picture book and physically experience events in real world and feel "force of words," which is believed culturally in Japan as "*Kototama*." In this system, *SequenceBook*, you can change the world in the book not only by shuffling pages but also changing the texts.

IMPLEMANTATION

With the text-changing, "*Kototama*," system in *SequenceBook*, you can change the text by embedding the special words, "*Kototama*," into the texts of the book. The definition of "*Kototama*" here is a word which you can drawn into the book from outside space. "*Kototama*" words are projected around pages of the book as if they were "floating" outside of the world in the book. You can bring these "*Kototama*" words into the world of the book or out there by dragging the words by your fingers.

Text-Changing Mechanism: "*Kototama*" System

In *SequenceBook* system, you can change the text by embedding the special words, "*Kototama*," into the texts of the book. The definition of "*Kototama*" here is a word, which you can draw into the book from outside space. "*Kototama*" words are projected around pages of the book as if they were "floating" outside of the world of the book. You can bring these "*Kototama*" words into the

world of the book or out there by dragging the words by your fingers.

Equipment

To drag and move the "*Kototama*" words, you need a small device on his/her finger. The device is designed just like as feather (feather is called "penna" in Latin, which is the origin of "pen" in English, an instrument for vitalizing words). This feather-shaped device has an infrared LED (Light-Emitting Diode), batteries, resisters, and a switch (Figure 10). A camera with IR filter is set above the table. When the user touches the projected images on the surface of the book or the table with this feather, the switch turns on and the infrared LED lights up. The lighted infrared LED starts to be recognized by the camera with IR filter. By image processing, the device-tracking system (processing) tracks the location of the feather-shaped device.

Figure 10. Device with an infrared LED and the image of the camera with IR filter

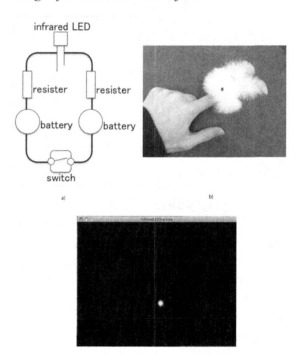

Figure 11. Dragging the "Kototama" word into the page from outside of the book

Containment and Exclusion of "*Kototama*" Words

As long as your finger with the feather-shaped device touches the surface of the table (this means the infrared LED of the device is on and the location of the device is recognized by the system), you can drag and move the "*Kototama*" words freely. If the location of the feather-shaped device matches with that of one of "*Kototama*" words projected around the book, the word starts to follow the movement of the feather-shaped device, like being dragged by your finger. You can bring the word into the page or out there by dragging them freely (Figure 11).

Record of "*Kototama*" Words in a Page

After being dragged into the book, the "*Kototama*" word is embedded into certain texts in a page. For example, the sentence "He went home." changes to "He went home in the bright sunlight." after the word "in the bright sunlight" is dragged into the page and as a result, the light overhead illuminates the book whenever that page is flipped. The "*Kototama*" words dragged into the book is

recorded on that page and corresponding event is reproduced whenever the page is flipped.

Event Reproduction Mechanism

To reproduce the event in the real world caused by "*Kototama*" words, some electronic devices are embedded in the system. All devices is connected to the microcomputer board (*Arduino Duemilanove*) and receives the signal from the system. When the page including one of "*Kototama*" words is flipped, the microcomputer board drives the corresponding device. For example, when the page including "*with breeze*" is flipped, the DC (Direct Current) fan starts to blow in under the table.

Examples of "*Kototama*" Words and Corresponding Events

Several "*Kototama*" words are prepared in advance and projected around the book. Here we introduce some examples of "*Kototama*" words (Table 1).

1. Case of "in the bright sunlight"

    In this case, if the word "in the bright sunlight" is dragged into the page, the light overhead starts to illuminate the book as if it was in the real sunlight (Figure 12).

2. Case of "with wind"

Table 1. Examples of "Kototama" words and corresponding events

"*Kototama*" word	Device	Event in the real world
"*near the river*"	speaker	sound of water
"*with wind*"	DC fan	wind blowing
"*wildly*"	vibrator	vibration
"*in the bright sunlight*"	light	illuminating

Figure 12. Dragging the word "in the bright sunlight" and change of lighting

Figure 13. Dragging the word "with wind" and blow of wind

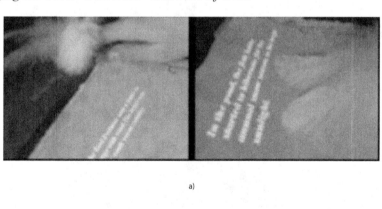

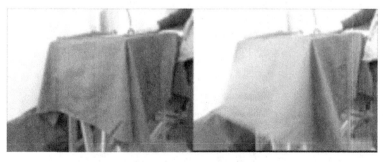

In this case, if the word "with wind" is dragged into the page, the DC fan under the table starts to blow in as if the wind is blowing in the world of the book (Figure 13).

EXHIBITIONS

We have exhibited *SequenceBook* system in three exhibitions: *"iii Exhibition"* in Japan, *"Laval Virtual 2010"* in France, and *"Ars Electronica 2010"* in Austria.

"iii Exhibition" in Japan

This exhibition was our first chance to exhibit to the public and we have executed the user study (Figure 14).

"Laval Virtual 2010" in France

This world's biggest virtual reality exhibition was hold at Laval, France in April, 2010. We have exhibited the system *SequenceBook* with *"Kototama"* function. For the exhibition, we have changed the whole stories (Figure 15).

"Ars Electronica 2010" in Austria

SequenceBook system was exhibited at Ars Electronica Center from 2010 to 2011, and to be exhibited from 2011 to 2012 at Ars Electronica Center (Linz, Austria). In this exhibition, we have removed *"Kototama"* function to let people enjoy the original and basic story-shuffling system (Figure 16).

Figure 14. The scenes of iii Exhibition

a)   b)

c)

Figure 15. The scenes of Laval Virtual 2010

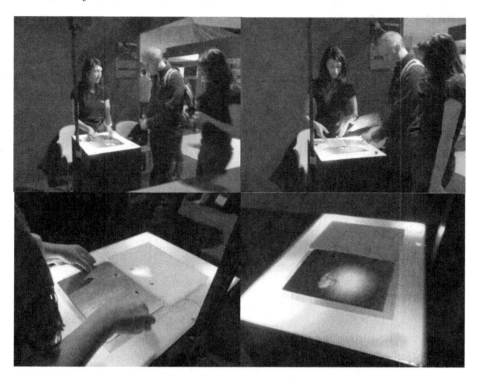

Figure 16. The scenes of Ars Electronica 2010   *Figure 17. New project*

A CURRENT PROJECT: BOOK WITHOUT PAGE-SHUFFLING SYSTEM

Now we have a project under way—development of interactive picture book without page-shuffling system. This work, "*Ephyra*," is designed by Ayako Kurihara, the artist researches new educational materials and technically supported by authors (see Figure 17).

This new picture book consists of ten pages with IC tags. The purpose of this project is to understand how the page-shuffling system affects users' interaction with book.

FUTURE RESEARCH DIRECTIONS

The *SequenceBook* will be further improved by increasing the possible number of storylines. This will be achieved by simply increasing the number of pages. However it is impossible to arrange storylines in advance with *SequenceBook* that has over 100 pages.

So an efficient algorithm to make storylines automatically will be needed. This may be challenging problem in the field of artificial intelligence.

Secondly, if users can change not only the raw of sequences, but also appearance of characters, settings or narratives, it will also improve *SequenceBook*. For example, development of image processing system to change appearance of characters at certain scenes by dragging in characters from outside of the book and dragging out them to the outside with a finger seems to be effective. This allows imagination of users to wander in any direction of the story.

CONCLUSION

The aim of this study is to add digital contents to traditional paper books. To achieve the goal, we embedded very thin IC tags in a paper of each page. From the demonstration experiments, the naturalness of the proposed page detection system has been verified. This study also proposed a page shuffling as a novel form of technique of story creation. Through the demonstration experiments, the mechanism has entertained people and showed the possibility of novel form of story creation tool.

ACKNOWLEDGMENT

We thank Hitachi Ltd. for helping development of the RFID system. And we also thank Ms. Yasuko Hayashi and Ms. Mamie Miyashita, the designer of all characters of *SequenceBook*. We deeply say a big thank you to Dr. Taro Suzuki, Dr. Chuichi Arakawa, Mr. Takashi Sagisaka, Mr. Takatsugu Kuriyama, Mr. Kenji Komoto, Ms. Emiri Hata, Mr. Hiroki Sato, and Mr. Kazuki Yanase for kind help to design *SequenceBook* system. We would like to make mention of a great work of a wonderful designer of another interactive picture book, Ms. Ayako Kurihara. We express our deepest gratitude to Dr. Akihiko Shirai, Mr. Matthieu Lépine, Mr. Takuya Sakai, Mrs. Kumiko Minobe, and Mrs. Emiko Ogawa for kind help for exhibitions.

REFERENCES

Antle, A. N. (2003). Case study: The design of CBC4Kids' StoryBuilder. In *Proceedings of Interaction Design for Children*, (pp. 59-68). ACM Press.

Back, M., Cohen, J., Gold, R., Harrison, S., & Minneman, S. (2001). Listen reader: An electronically augmented paper-based book. In *Proceedings of CHI*. ACM Press.

Billinghurst, M., Kato, H., & Poupyrev, I. (2001). The magic book – Moving seamlessly between reality and virtuality. In *Proceedings of IEEE Computer Graphics and Applications*. IEEE Press.

Grasset, R., Dünser, A., Seichter, H., & Billinghurst, M. (2007). The mixed reality book: A new multimedia reading experience. In *Proceedings of CHI 2007*. CHI.

Hitachi. (2011). *The world's smallest RFID IC μ-Chip(2.45GHz)*. Retrieved from http://www. hitachi.co.jp/Prod/mu-chip/.

Koike, H., Sato, Y., Kobayashi, Y., Tobita, H., & Kobayashi, M. (2000). Interactive textbook and interactive Venn diagram: Natural and intuitive interfaces on augmented desk system. In *Proceedings of CHI*, (pp. 121-128). ACM Press.

Ryokai, K., & Cassell, J. (1999). StoryMat: A play space with narrative memory. In *Proceedings of IUI 1999*. ACM Press.

Sugata, M. (1994). *Kototama no ama he*. Tokyo, Japan: Tachibana Inc.

Vogelsang, A., & Signer, B. (2005). The lost cosmonaut: An interactive narrative environment on basis of digitally enhanced paper. In *Proceedings of International Conference on Virtual Storytelling 2005*. ACM.

KEY TERMS AND DEFINITIONS

Page: To use two RFID antenna, the system can detect both left page and right page. By doing this, we can design page partition more freely.

RFID: We consider that RFID is the most vital technology for the next generation. In our study, we have embedded very small and thin IC tag in a page. By miniaturization technology in the future, we can develop more interesting digital toys including picture book.

Story Creation: To be exact, *SequenceBook* system itself does not create stories. We, the creators of the stories, have embedded story-changeable system in the book. However, with further research of artificial intelligence, *SequenceBook* system has the potential to become the creator of story, not only the teller of story.

Storytelling: We consider that digital storytelling tool and analog storytelling (oral, picture-card show, and so on) does not conflict. The aim of this study is to establish a mutually complementary relationship between digital storytelling and analog storytelling.

Substantiality: A lot of digital book has been spread in our daily life. However, we would like to value paper book because paper book has substantiality. Paper book really exists in our real world. We can touch it. We consider that this is most important thing for storytelling.

Visualization: To visualize the stories, we used a projector. However, this is not natural for a picture book. We are developing a visualization system without light emission for paper book with thermochromic ink and temperature control system with photothermal conversion.

World-View: One book has only one world-view. We have a plan to set more than one *SequenceBook* and let people "trade" the world-view between books.

Compilation of References

Abbott, K. R., & Sarin, S. K. (1994). Experiences with workflow management: Issues for the next generation. In *Proceedings of Conference on Computer Supported Cooperative Work,* (pp. 113-120). Chapel Hill, NC: ACM Press.

Accot, J., & Zhai, S. (1997). Beyond Fitts' law: Models for trajectory-based HCI tasks. In *Proceedings of ACM CHI Conference on Human Factors in Computing Systems,* (pp. 295–302). ACM Press.

Accot, J., & Zhai, S. (2003). Refining Fitts' law models for bivariate pointing. In *Proceedings of ACM CHI Conference on Human Factors in Computing Systems,* (pp. 193–200). ACM Press.

Achenbach, S., Moshage, W., Ropers, D., & Bachmann, K. (1998). Curved multiplanar reconstructions for the evaluation of contrast-enhanced electron-beam CT of the coronary arteries. *American Journal of Roentgenology*. Retrieved from http://www.ajronline.org/content/170/4/895.full.pdf.

Agarawala, A., & Balakrishnan, R. (2006). Keepin' it real: Pushing the desktop metaphor with physics, piles and the pen. In *Proceedings of CHI 2006: Interacting with Large Surfaces*. Montreal, Canada: ACM.

Ainsworth, S. (1999). The functions of multiple representations. *Computers & Education, 33*(2-3), 131–152. doi:10.1016/S0360-1315(99)00029-9

Ajzen, I. (1985). Action control: From cognition to behavior. In *From Intentions to Actions: A Theory of Planned Behavior* (pp. 11–39). Berlin, Germany: Springer-Verlag.

Ajzen, I., & Fishbein, M. (1980). *Understanding attitudes and predicting social behavior*. Upper Saddle River, NJ: Prentice-Hall.

Albert, W. (2002). Do web users actually look at ads? A case study of banner ads and eye-tracking technology. In *Proceedings of Usability Professional Association Conference*. Orlando, FL: Usability Professional Association.

Allan, L. G. (1979). The perception of time. *Perception & Psychophysics, 26,* 340–354. doi:10.3758/BF03204158

Allbeck, J. M., & Kress-Gazit, H. (2010). Constraints-based complex behavior in rich environments. In Allbeck, J., Badler, N., Bickmore, T., Pelachaud, C., & Safonova, A. (Eds.), *Intelligent Virtual Agents* (*Vol. 6356,* pp. 1–14). Berlin, Germany: Springer. doi:10.1007/978-3-642-15892-6_1

Allen, J. F., Kautz, H. A., Pelavin, R. N., & Tenenberg, J. D. (1991). *Reasoning about plans*. New York, NY: Morgan Kaufmann Publishers Inc.

Allport, G. W. (1937). *Personality: A psychological interpretation*. Oxford, UK: Holt.

Anderson, J. R. (1996). ACT: A simple theory of complex cognition. *The American Psychologist, 51*(4), 355–365. doi:10.1037/0003-066X.51.4.355

Anderson, J. R., Matessa, M., & Lebiere, C. (1997). ACT-R: A theory of higher level cognition and its relation to visual attention. *Human-Computer Interaction, 12*(4), 439. doi:10.1207/s15327051hci1204_5

Antle, A. N. (2003). Case study: The design of CBC4Kids' StoryBuilder. In Proceedings of Interaction Design for Children, (pp. 59-68). ACM Press.

Appert, C., Chapuis, O., & Beaudouin-Lafon, M. (2008). Evaluation of pointing performance on screen edges. In *Proceedings of Advanced Visual Interfaces*. ACM. doi:10.1145/1385569.1385590

Arroyo, E., Selker, T., & Wei, W. (2006). Usability tool for analysis of web designs using mouse tracks. In *Proceedings of the Computer-Human Interaction Extended Abstracts on Human Factors in Computing Systems*, (pp. 484-489). ACM Press.

Asch, S. E. (1951). Groups, leadership and men. In *Chapter Effects of Group Pressure upon the Modification and Distortion of Judgment*. Pittsburgh, PA: Carnegie Press.

Asch, S. E. (1955). Opinions and social pressure. *Scientific American, 193*, 31–35. doi:10.1038/scientificamerican1155-31

Back, M., Cohen, J., Gold, R., Harrison, S., & Minneman, S. (2001). Listen reader: An electronically augmented paper-based book. In Proceedings of CHI. ACM Press.

Bacon, W. F., & Egeth, H. E. (1994). Overriding stimulus-driven attentional capture. *Perception & Psychophysics, 55*, 485–496. doi:10.3758/BF03205306

Baddeley, A. D. (1992). Working memory. *Science, 255*, 556–559. doi:10.1126/science.1736359

Bade, R., Ritter, F., & Preim, B. (2005). Usability comparison of mouse-based interaction techniques for predictable 3D rotation. In *Proceedings of the 5th International Symposium on Smart Graphics: SG 2005*, (pp. 138–150). Springer.

Badr, G., & Raynal, M. (2009). Optimized interaction with word prediction list: A use case with a motor impairment. In *Proceedings of the European Conference for the Advancement of Assistive Technology in Europ (AAATE 2009)*. IOS Press.

Baldauf, D., Brugard, E., & Wittmann, M. (2009). Time perception as a workload measure in simulated car driving. *Applied Ergonomics, 40*(5), 929–935. doi:10.1016/j.apergo.2009.01.004

Ball, G., & Breese, J. (2000). Embodied conversational agents. In Cassell, J., Sullivan, J., Prevost, S., & Churchill, E. (Eds.), *Embodied Conversational Agents* (pp. 189–219). Cambridge, MA: MIT Press.

Bandura, A. (1986). *Social foundations of thought and action: A social cognitive theory*. Englewood Cliffs, NJ: Prentice-Hall.

Barclay, D., Thompson, R., & Higgins, C. (1995). The panial least squares (PLS) approach to causal modeling: Personal computer adoption and use as an illustration. *Technology Studies, 22*, 285–309.

Baron, M., & Scapin, D. (2006). *K-MAD project site*. Retrieved June 28, 2011, from http://kmade.sourceforge.net/.

Bates, J. (1994). The role of emotion in believable agents. *Communications of the ACM, 37*(7), 122–125. doi:10.1145/176789.176803

Baumgarten, F. (1933). Die charaktereigenschaften [The character traits]. *Beiträge zue Charakter-und Persönlichkeitsforschung, 1*.

Baumgartner, H., Sujan, M., & Padgett, D. (1997). Patterns of affective reactions to advertisements: The integration of moment-to-moment responses into overall judgments. *JMR, Journal of Marketing Research, 34*(2), 219–232. doi:10.2307/3151860

Baylor, A. L., & Kim, Y. (2004). Pedagogical agent design: The impact of agent realism, gender, ethnicity, and instructional role. In Lester, J. C., Vicari, R. M., & Paraguaçu, F. (Eds.), *Intelligent Tutoring Systems* (pp. 592–603). Maceio, Brazil: Springer. doi:10.1007/978-3-540-30139-4_56

Bentley, P. J. (2004). *Software seeds: The garden where perfect software grows*. Paper presented at New Scientist. London, UK.

Berti, S., Correani, F., Mori, G., Paternò, F., & Santoro, C. (2004). TERESA: A transformation-based environment for designing and development multi-device interface. In *Proceedings of the Conference on Human Factors in Computing Systems - CHI 2004*, (pp. 793-794). Vienna, Austria: ACM Press.

Billinghurst, M., Kato, H., & Poupyrev, I. (2001). The magic book – Moving seamlessly between reality and virtuality. In Proceedings of IEEE Computer Graphics and Applications. IEEE Press.

Blackboard Inc. (2002). *Blackboard course management system 5.1*. Retrieved 14 November 2010 from http://www.blackboard.com/.

Block, R. (1990). *Cognitive models of psychological time*. Hillsdale, NJ: Lawrence Erlbaum Associates.

Bodart, F., Hennebert, A., Leheureux, J., & Vanderdonckt, J. (1994). Towards a dynamic strategy for computer-aided visual placement. In *Proceedings of 2nd ACM Workshop on Advanced Visual Interfaces AVI 1994*, (pp. 78-87). New York, NY: ACM Press.

Bohman, P. R., & Anderson, S. (2005). *A conceptual framework for accessibility tools to benefit users with cognitive disabilities*. Paper presented at the International Cross-Disciplinary Workshop on Web Accessibility. Chiba, Japan.

Bohnert, F., & Zukerman, I. (2009). Non-intrusive personalisation of the museum experience. In *Proceedings of UMAP 2009*. UMAP.

Bomsdorf, B., & Szwillus, G. (1998). From task to dialogue, task-based user interface design: A CHI 98 workshop. *SIGCHI Bulletin, 30*(4).

Boroditsky, L. (1997). *Evidence for metaphoric representation: Perspective in space and time*. Paper presented at the 19th Annual Conference of the Cognitive-Science-Society. Palo Alto, CA.

Boroditsky, L., & Ramscar, M. (2002). The roles of body and mind in abstract thought. *Psychological Science, 13*(2), 185–189. doi:10.1111/1467-9280.00434

Borovik, A. V. (2009). *Mathematics under the microscope*. Washington, DC: American Mathematical Society.

Borsci, S., Kurosu, M., Federici, S., & Mele, M. L. (2013). *Computer systems experiences of users with and without disabilities: An evaluation guide for professionals*. London, UK: CRC Press.

Borsci, S., Londei, A., & Federici, S. (2011). The bootstrap discovery behaviour (BDB): A new outlook on usability evaluation. *Cognitive Processing, 12*(1), 23–31. doi:10.1007/s10339-010-0376-6

Boskamp, T., Rinck, D., Link, F., Kümmerlen, B., Stamm, G., & Mildenberger, P. (2004). New vessel analysis tool for morphometric quantification and visualization of vessels in CT and MR imaging data sets. *Radiographics, 24*(1), 287–297. doi:10.1148/rg.241035073

Boticario, J. G. Santos, O. C., & Rosmalen, P. (2005). Technological and management issues in providing adaptive education in distance learning universities. *EADTU, 2005*. Retrieved Nov 14, 2010 from http://www.eadtu.nl/proceedings/2005/presentations/plenary/Jesus%20Boticario.pdf.

Bouchet, F., & Sansonnet, J.-P. (2009). A framework for modeling the relationships between the rational and behavioral reactions of assisting conversational agents. In *Proceedings of the 7th European Workshop on Multi-Agent Systems (EUMAS 2009)*. Agia Napa, Cyprus: EUMAS.

Bouchet, F., & Sansonnet, J.-P. (2010). Classification of wordnet personality adjectives in the NEO PI-R taxonomy. In *Proceedings of the Actes du Quatrième Workshop sur les Agents Conversationnels Animés (WACA 2010)*, (pp. 83-90). Lille, France: WACA.

Boyd, S. (2006). Are you ready for social software? Retrieved January, 2011, from http://www.stoweboyd.com/post/2325281845/are-you-ready-for-social-software.

Branke, J. (2001). Dynamic graph drawing. In *Drawing Graphs: Methods and Models*. Berlin, Germany: Springer. doi:10.1007/3-540-44969-8_9

Bratman, M. E. (1990). What Is Intention? In Cohen, P. R., Morgan, J., & Pollack, M. E. (Eds.), *Intentions in Communication* (pp. 15–32). Cambridge, MA: The MIT Press.

Bratman, M. E., Israel, D. J., & Pollack, M. E. (1988). Plans and resource-bounded practical reasoning. *Computational Intelligence, 4*(4), 349–355. doi:10.1111/j.1467-8640.1988.tb00284.x

Brown, M., & Shillner, R. (1995). DeckScape: An experimental web browser. In *Proceedings of the 3rd International World Wide Web Conference*. Darmstadt, Germany: IEEE.

Brown, J. S., & Duguid, P. (2000). *The social life of information*. Boston, MA: Harvard Business School Press.

Brown, S. A., Massey, A. P., Montoya-Weiss, M. M., & Burkman, J. R. (2002). Do I really have to? User acceptance of mandated technology. *European Journal of Information Systems, 11*, 283–295. doi:10.1057/palgrave.ejis.3000438

Brown, S. W. (2008). The attenuation effect in timing: Counteracting dual-task interference with time-judgment skill training. *Perception, 37*(5), 712–724. doi:10.1068/p5698

BrowseBack. (2009). *Visual web history you can search.* Retrieved from http://www.smileonmymac.com/browse-back/.

Brusilovsky, P. (2004). Adaptive educational hypermedia: From generation to generation. In *Proceedings of 4th Hellenic Conference on Information and Communication Technologies in Education*, (pp. 19-33). Athens, Greece. Retrieved 14 November 2010 from http://www2.sis.pitt.edu/~peterb/papers/PEG01.html.

Buckley, B. C. (2000). Interactive multimedia and model-based learning in biology. *International Journal of Science Education, 22*(9), 895–935. doi:10.1080/095006900416848

Bulling, A. (2010). Toward mobile eye-based human-computer interaction. *IEEE Pervasive Computing / IEEE Computer Society and IEEE Communications Society, 9*, 8–12. doi:10.1109/MPRV.2010.86

Burgess, P. W. (2000). Real-world multitasking from a cognitive neuroscience perspective. *Control of Cognitive Processes: Attention and Performance, 18*, 465–472.

Burke, M., & Hornoff, A. J. (2001). *The effects of animated banner advertisements on a visual search task. Computer and Information Science Report.* Nantes, France: University of Nantes.

Butterworth, R., & Blandford, A. (1997). *Programmable user models: The story so far.* PUMA Working Paper WP8. Retrieved from http://www.eis.mdx.ac.uk/puma/wp8.pdf.

Caffiau, S. (2009). *Approche dirigée par les modèles pour la conception et la validation des applications interactives: Une démarche basée sur la modélisation des tâches.* Unpublished doctoral dissertation. Retrieved from http://www.lisi.ensma.fr/ftp/pub/documents/thesis/2009-thesis-caffiau.pdf.

Caffiau, S., Girard, P., Guittet, L., & Scapin, D. L. (2009). Hierarchical structure: A step for jointly designing interactive software dialog and task model. In *Human-Computer Interaction: Novel Interaction Methods and Techniques* (pp. 664–673). Berlin, Germany: Springer. doi:10.1007/978-3-642-02577-8_73

Caffiau, S., Girard, P., Scapin, D., & Guittet, L. (2007). Generating interactive applications from task models: A hard challenge. In *TAsk MOdels and DIAgrams (TAMODIA)* (pp. 267–272). Berlin, Germany: Springer. doi:10.1007/978-3-540-77222-4_22

Caffiau, S., Scapin, D., Girard, P., Baron, M., & Jambon, F. (2010). Increasing the expressive power of task analysis: Systematic comparison and empirical assessment of tool-supported task models. *Interacting with Computers, 22*(6), 569–593. doi:10.1016/j.intcom.2010.06.003

Calvary, G., Coutaz, J., Thevenin, D., Limbourg, Q., Bouillon, L., & Vanderdonckt, J. (2003). A unifying reference framework for multi-target user interfaces. *Interacting with Computers, 15*(3), 289–308. doi:10.1016/S0953-5438(03)00010-9

Card, S., Robertson, G., & York, W. (1996). The WebBook and the Web forager: An information workspace for the world-wide web. In *Proceedings of the ACM CHI 1996 Conference on Human Factors in Computing Systems.* Vancouver, Canada: ACM.

Card, S. K., English, W. K., & Burr, B. J. (1978). Evaluation of mouse, rate-controlled isometric joystick, step keys, and text keys for text selection on a CRT. *Ergonomics, 21*, 601–613. doi:10.1080/00140137808931762

Card, S. K., Moran, T. P., & Newell, A. (1983). *The psychology of human-computer interaction.* Boca Raton, FL: CRC Press.

Card, S. K., Thomas, T. P., & Newall, A. (1980). The keystroke-level model for user performance time with interactive systems. *Communications of the ACM, 23*(7), 396–410. doi:10.1145/358886.358895

Card, S. K., Thomas, T. P., & Newall, A. (1983). *The psychology of human-computer interaction.* London, UK: Lawrence Erlbaum Associates.

Card, S., Moran, T., & Newell, A. (1983). *The psychology of human-computer interaction.* Wahwah, NJ: Lawrence Erlbaum Associates.

Carlson, R. A., & Sohn, M. H. (2000). Cognitive control of multistep routines: Information processing and conscious intentions. *Control of Cognitive Processes: Attention and Performance, 18*, 443.

Carlton, E., & Shepard, R. N. (1990). Psychologically simple motions as geodesic paths: Asymmetric objects. *Journal of Mathematical Psychology, 34,* 127–188. doi:10.1016/0022-2496(90)90001-P

Casasanto, D., & Boroditsky, L. (2008). Time in the mind: Using space to think about time. *Journal of Cognition, 3*(4).

Cassell, J., Bickmore, T., Billinghurst, M., Campbell, L., Chang, K., Vilhjálmsson, H., & Yan, H. (1999). Embodiment in conversational interfaces: Rea. In *Proceedings of the SIGCHI Conference on Human Factors in Computer Systems,* (pp. 520-527). New York, NY: ACM Press.

Catledge, L., & Pitkow, J. (1995). Characterizing browsing strategies in the world-wide web. In *Proceedings of the 3rd International World Wide Web Conference.* Darmstadt, Germany: IEEE.

Cattell, R. B., Eber, H. W., & Tatsuoka, M. M. (1970). *Handbook for the sixteen personality factor questionnaire (16 PF).* Champaign, IL: Institute for Personality and Ability Testing.

Caulton, D. (2001). Relaxing the homogeneity assumption in usability testing. *Behaviour & Information Technology, 20*(1), 1–7. doi:10.1080/01449290010020648

Cellier, J. M. (1990). L'erreur human dans le travail. In Leplat, J., & De Terssac, G. (Eds.), *Les Facteurs Humains de la Fiabilite dans les Systemes Complexes. France.* Marseille.

Charlton, J. I. (1998). *Nothing about us without us: Disability oppression and empowerment.* Berkeley, CA: University of California Press.

Chater, N., & Vitanyi, P. (2003). Simplicity: A unifying principle in cognitive science? *Trends in Cognitive Sciences, 7,* 19–22. doi:10.1016/S1364-6613(02)00005-0

Chen, M., Anderson, J. R., & Sohn, M. (2001). What can a mouse cursor tell us more? Correlation of eye/mouse movements on web browsing. In *Proceedings of the Computer-Human Interactions Extended Abstracts on Human Factors in Computing Systems,* (pp. 281-282). ACM Press.

Cheverst, K., Mitchell, K., & Davies, N. (2002). The role of adaptive hypermedia in a context-aware tourist guide. *Communications of the ACM, 45*(5). doi:10.1145/506218.506244

Chi, M. T. H. (1997). Quantifying qualitative analyses of verbal data: A practical guide. *Journal of the Learning Sciences, 6*(3), 271–315. doi:10.1207/s15327809jls0603_1

Chi, M. T. H. (2005). Commonsense conceptions of emergent processes: Why some misconceptions are robust. *Journal of the Learning Sciences, 14*(2), 161–199. doi:10.1207/s15327809jls1402_1

Chi, M. T. H., Feltovich, P. J., & Glaser, R. (1981). Categorization and representation of physics problems by experts and novices. *Cognitive Science, 5*(2), 121–152. doi:10.1207/s15516709cog0502_2

Chi, M. T. H., & Roscoe, R. D. (2002). The processes and challenges of conceptual change. In Mason, M. L. A. L. (Ed.), *Reconsidering Conceptual Change: Issues in Theory and Practice* (pp. 3–27). Dordrecht, The Netherlands: Springer Netherlands. doi:10.1007/0-306-47637-1_1

Cisco. (2011). *Global internet traffic projected to quadruple by 2015.* Retrieved June 29, 2011, from http://newsroom.cisco.com/press-release-content?type=webcontent&articleId=324003.

Citrin, W., Hall, R., & Zorn, B. (1995). Programming with visual expressions. In *Proceedings of the 11ᵗʰ International IEEE Symposium on Visual Languages.* IEEE Press.

Clark, A. (1993). *Sensory qualities.* Oxford, UK: Clarendon Press.

Cockburn, A., Greenberg, S., McKenzie, B., Smith, M., & Kassten, S. (1999). WebView: A graphical aid for revisiting web pages. In *Proceedings of the 1999 Computer Human Interaction Specialist Interest Group of the Ergonomics Society of Australia (OzCHI+99).* Wagga Wagga, Australia: OzCHI.

Cockburn, A., & McKenzie, B. (2001). What do web users do? An empirical analysis of web use. *International Journal of Human-Computer Studies, 54*(6), 903–922. doi:10.1006/ijhc.2001.0459

Conn, A. P. (1995). Time affordances: The time factor in diagnostic usability heuristics. In *Proceedings of the 1995 SIGCHI Conference on Human Factors in Computing Systems,* (pp. 186-193). ACM Press.

Cooper, A., Reimann, R., & Cronin, D. (2007). *About face 3: The essentials of interaction design.* Indianapolis, IN: Wiley.

Costa, P. T., & McCrae, R. R. (1992). Normal personality assessment in clinical practice: The NEO personality inventory. *Psychological Assessment*, *4*(1), 5–13. doi:10.1037/1040-3590.4.1.5

Courage, C., & Baxter, K. (2005). *Understanding your users: A practical guide to user requirements*. New York, NY: Morgan Kaufmann Publishers.

Cover, T. M., & Thomas, J. A. (1991). *Elements of information theory*. New York, NY: John Wiley & Sons. doi:10.1002/0471200611

Crystal, A., & Ellington, B. (2004). Task analysis and human-computer interaction: approaches, techniques, and levels of analysis. In *Proceedings of the Tenth Americas Conference on Information Systems*, (pp. 1-9). New York, NY: Americas Conference.

Cutrell, E., & Guan, Z. (2007). What are you looking for? An eye-tracking study of information usage in web search. In *Proceedings of the SIGCHI Conference on Human Factors in Computing Systems*, (pp. 407-416). ACM Press.

Czerwinski, M., Horvitz, E., & Wilhite, S. (2004). A diary study of task switching and interruptions. In *Proceedings of the SIGCHI Conference on Human Factors in Computing Systems*, (pp. 175-182). ACM Press.

Das, A., & Stuerzlinger, W. (2008). Modeling learning effects in mobile texting. In *Proceedings of the 7th International Conference on MUM 2008*. ACM Press.

Dastani, M. (2008). 2APL: A practical agent programming language. *Autonomous Agents and Multi-Agent Systems*, *16*(3), 214–248. doi:10.1007/s10458-008-9036-y

Davis, F. (1986). *A technology acceptance model for empirically testing new end-user information systems: Theory and results*. Ph.D. Dissertation. Cambridge, MA: MIT Press.

Davis, F. D. (1989). Perceived usefulness, perceived ease of use, and user acceptance of information technology. *Management Information Systems Quarterly*, *13*(3), 319–340. doi:10.2307/249008

De Bra, P., & Calvi, L. (1998). Towards a generic adaptive hypermedia system. In *Proceedings of the Second Workshop on Adaptive Hypertext and Hypermedia*, (pp. 5-11). Hypertext and Hypermedia.

de Lara, J., & Vangheluwe, H. (2002). AToM3: A tool for multi-formalism and meta-modeling. In *Proceedings of the 5th International Conference on Fundamental Approaches to Software Engineering*. IEEE.

de Queiroz, J., de Oliveira, R., & Turnell, M. F. (2005). *WebQuest: A configurable web tool to prospect the user profile and user subjective satisfaction*. Paper presented at the 11th International Conference on Human-Computer Interaction. Las Vegas, NY.

Dehainsala, H., Jean, S., Dung, N. X., & Pierra, G. (2005). Ingénierie dirigée par les modèles en EXPRESS: Un exemple d'application. In *Proceedings of IDM 2005*. IDM.

Delicious. (2011). *Delicious.com*. Retrieved June 29, 2011, from www.delicious.com.

Dengler, F., Lamparter, S., Hefke, M., & Abecker, A. (2009). Collaborative process development using semantic mediawiki. *Wissensmanagement*, *145*(1), 97–107.

Denning, P. J. (2005). The locality principle. *Communications of the ACM*, *48*(7), 19–24. doi:10.1145/1070838.1070856

Depaulis, F., Jambon, F., Girard, P., & Guittet, L. (2006). Le modèle d'architecture logicielle H4: Principes, usages, outils et retours d'expérience dans les applications de conception technique. *Revue d'Interaction Homme-Machine*, *7*(1), 93–129.

Depaulis, F., Maiano, S., & Texier, G. (2002). DTS-edit: An interactive development environment for structured dialog applications. In *Proceedings of CADUI, 2002*, 75–82.

Desimone, R., & Duncan, J. (1995). Neural mechanisms of selective visual attention. *Annual Review of Neuroscience*, *18*, 193–222. doi:10.1146/annurev.ne.18.030195.001205

di Battista, G., Eades, P., Tamassia, R., & Tollis, I. G. (1998). *Graph drawing: Algorithms for the visualization of graphs*. Upper Saddle River, NJ: Prentice Hall.

Di Giacomo, E., Didimo, W., Grilli, L., Liotta, G., & Palladino, P. (2008). *WhatsOnWeb+: An enhanced visual search clustering engine*. Paper presented at the IEEE Pacific Visualization Symposium. Kyoto, Japan.

Di Giacomo, E., Didimo, W., Grilli, L., & Liotta, G. (2007). Graph visualization techniques for web clustering engines. *IEEE Transactions on Visualization and Computer Graphics, 13*(2), 294–304. doi:10.1109/TVCG.2007.40

Diaper, D., & Stanton, N. A. (Eds.). (2004). *The handbook of task analysis for human-computer interaction.* Mahwah, NJ: Lawrence Erlbaum Associates.

Dias, J., & Paiva, A. (2005). Feeling and reasoning: A computational model for emotional characters. In Bento, C., Cardoso, A., & Dias, G. (Eds.), *Progress in Artificial Intelligence* (*Vol. 3808*, pp. 127–140). Berlin, Germany: Springer. doi:10.1007/11595014_13

DiDomenico, A., & Nussbaum, M. (2008). Interactive effects of physical and mental workload on subjective workload assessment. *International Journal of Industrial Ergonomics, 38*(5), 977–983. doi:10.1016/j.ergon.2008.01.012

diSessa, A. A. (2004). Metarepresentation: Native competence and targets for instruction. *Cognition and Instruction, 22*(3), 293–331. doi:10.1207/s1532690xci2203_2

Dixon, S. R., Wickens, C. D., & McCarley, J. S. (2007). On the independence of compliance and reliance: Are automation false alarms worse than misses? *Human Factors, 49*(4), 564–572. doi:10.1518/001872007X215656

Doce, T., Dias, J., Prada, R., & Paiva, A. (2010). Creating individual agents through personality traits. In Allbeck, J., Badler, N., Bickmore, T., Pelachaud, C., & Safonova, A. (Eds.), *Intelligent Virtual Agents* (*Vol. 6356*, pp. 257–264). Berlin, Germany: Springer. doi:10.1007/978-3-642-15892-6_27

Douglas, S. A., & Mithal, A. K. (1997). *The ergonomics of computer pointing devices.* Berlin, Germany: Springer-Verlag.

Dourish, P. (2001). Process description as organisational accounting devices: The dual use of workflow technologies. In *Proceedings of Conference on Supporting Group Work (GROUP 2001),* (pp. 52–60.). New York, NY: ACM Press.

Downs, R. M., & Stea, D. (1973). Cognitive maps and spatial behavior: Process and products. In Downs, R. M., & Stea, D. (Eds.), *Image & Environment: Cognitive Mapping and Spatial Behavior* (pp. 8–26). New Brunswick, NJ: Aldine Transaction. doi:10.1002/9780470979587.ch41

Drewes, H., Luca, A. D., & Schmidt, A. (2007). Eye-gaze interaction for mobile phones. In *Proceedings of the 4th International Conference on Mobile Technology, Applications, and Systems,* (pp. 364-371). IEEE.

Droit-Volet, S. (2001). Temporal bisection in children. *Journal of Experimental Child Psychology, 80*(2), 142–159. doi:10.1006/jecp.2001.2631

Dunlop, M. D., & Crossan, A. (1999). *Dictionary based text entry method for mobile phones.* Paper presented at the Second Workshop on Human-Computer Interaction with Mobile Devices. Edinburgh, UK.

Dwyer, T., Marriott, K., & Wybrow, M. (2009). Dunnart: A constraint-based network diagram authoring tool. In *Proceedings of Graph Drawing: 16th International Symposium.* Springer.

Edu20.org. (2006). *Founded by Graham Glass.* Retrieved from http://www.edu20.org.

Efron, B. (1979). Bootstrap methods: Another look at the jackknife. *Annals of Statistics, 7*(1), 1–26. doi:10.1214/aos/1176344552

Egeth, H. E., & Yantis, S. (1997). Visual attention: Control representation and time course. *Annual Review of Psychology, 48*, 269–297. doi:10.1146/annurev.psych.48.1.269

Ehrig, K., Ermel, C., Haensgen, S., & Taentzer, G. (2005). Generation of visual editors as eclipse plug-ins. In *Proceedings of the 20th IEEE/ACM International Conference on Automated Software Engineering.* IEEE Press.

Eindhoven University of Technology. (2009). *Suite home, experimental test-bed for new features for CPN tools.* Retrieved from http://wiki.daimi.au.dk/britney/_home.wiki.

Eindhoven University of Technology. (2011). *CPN tools homepage.* Retrieved from http://wiki.daimi.au.dk/cpntools.

Ellsworth, P. C., & Scherer, K. R. (2003). Appraisal processes in emotion. In Davidson, R. J., Scherer, K. R., & Goldsmith, H. H. (Eds.), *Handbook of Affective Sciences* (pp. 572–595). New York, NY: Oxford University Press.

Erickson, T. (2008). Social systems: Designing digital systems that support social intelligence. *AI & Society, 23*(2), 147–166. doi:10.1007/s00146-007-0140-3

Ericsson, K. A., & Simon, H. A. (1980). Verbal reports as data. *Psychological Review, 87*(3), 215–251. doi:10.1037/0033-295X.87.3.215

Erol, S., Granitzer, M., Happ, S., Jantunen, S., Jennings, B., & Johannesson, P. (2009). Combining BPM and social software: Contradiction or chance? *Journal of Software Maintenance and Evolution: Research and Practice, 22*(6-7), 449–476. doi:10.1002/smr.460

Evertsz, R., Ritter, F. E., Busetta, P., & Pedrotti, M. (2008). Realistic behaviour variation in a BDI-based cognitive architecture. In *Proceedings of SimTecT 2008*. Melbourne, Australia: SimTecT.

Eysenck, H. J., & Eysenck, S. B. G. (1968). *Manual of the Eysenck personality questionnaire*. San Diego, CA: EdITS.

Eysenck, H. J. (1976). The measurement of personality. *Proceedings of the Royal Society of Medicine, 40*(2), 75–80.

Eysenck, S. B. G., Eysenck, H. J., & Barrett, P. (1985). A revised version of the psychoticism scale. *Personality and Individual Differences, 6*(1), 21–29. doi:10.1016/0191-8869(85)90026-1

Ezer, N., Fisk, A. D., & Rogers, W. A. (2008). Age-related differences in reliance behavior attributable to costs within a human-decision aid system export. *Human Factors, 50*(6), 853–863. doi:10.1518/001872008X375018

Fairweather, P., & Trewin, S. (2010). Cognitive impairments and Web 2.0. *Universal Access in the Information Society, 9*(2), 137–146. doi:10.1007/s10209-009-0163-2

Federici, S., & Borsci, S. (2010). Usability evaluation: models, methods, and applications. In J. Stone & M. Blouin (Eds.), *International Encyclopedia of Rehabilitation*. Buffalo, NY: Center for International Rehabilitation Research Information and Exchange (CIRRIE). Retrieved from http://cirrie.buffalo.edu/encyclopedia/article.php?id=277&language=en.

Federici, S., Borsci, S., & Mele, M. L. (2010). Usability evaluation with screen reader users: A video presentation of the PCTA's experimental setting and rules. *Cognitive Processing, 11*(3), 285–288. doi:10.1007/s10339-010-0365-9

Federici, S., Borsci, S., Mele, M. L., & Stamerra, G. (2010). Web popularity: An illusory perception of a qualitative order in information. *Universal Access in the Information Society, 9*(4), 375–386. doi:10.1007/s10209-009-0179-7

Federici, S., Borsci, S., & Stamerra, G. (2010). Web usability evaluation with screen reader users: Implementation of the partial concurrent thinking aloud technique. *Cognitive Processing, 11*(3), 263–272. doi:10.1007/s10339-010-0358-8

Federici, S., Micangeli, A., Ruspantini, I., Borgianni, S., Corradi, F., & Pasqualotto, E. (2005). Checking an integrated model of web accessibility and usability evaluation for disabled people. *Disability and Rehabilitation, 27*(13), 781–790. doi:10.1080/09638280400014766

Feldman, J. (1997a). Regularity-based perceptual grouping. *Computational Intelligence, 13*(4), 582–623. doi:10.1111/0824-7935.00052

Feldman, J. (1997b). The structure of perceptual categories. *Journal of Mathematical Psychology, 41*, 145–170. doi:10.1006/jmps.1997.1154

Feldman, J. (2000). Bias toward regular form in mental shape spaces. *Journal of Experimental Psychology. Human Perception and Performance, 26*, 152–165. doi:10.1037/0096-1523.26.1.152

Fellbaum, C. (1998). *WordNet: An electronic lexical database*. Cambridge, MA: MIT Press.

Feng, J., Lazar, J., Kumin, L., & Ozok, A. (2008). *Computer usage by young individuals with down syndrome: An exploratory study*. Paper presented at the 10th International ACM SIGACCESS Conference on Computers and Accessibility. Halifax, Canada.

Feng, J., Lazar, J., Kumin, L., & Ozok, A. (2010). Computer usage by children with down syndrome: Challenges and future research. *Transactions on Accessible Computing, 2*(3), 1–44. doi:10.1145/1714458.1714460

Fernandez-Duque, D., & Johnson, M. L. (2002). Cause and effect theories of attention: The role of conceptual metaphors. *Review of General Psychology, 6*(2), 153–165. doi:10.1037/1089-2680.6.2.153

Fikes, R., & Nilsson, N. (1971). STRIPS: A new approach to the application of theorem proving to problem solving. *Artificial Intelligence*. Retrieved from http://www.ai.sri.com/pubs/files/tn043r-fikes71.pdf.

Fisher, D. L., & Tan, K. C. (1989). Visual displays: The highlighting paradox. *Human Factors, 31*(1), 17–30.

Fitts, P. M. (1954). The information capacity of the human motor system in controlling amplitude of movement. *Journal of Experimental Psychology, 47*, 381–39. doi:10.1037/h0055392

Fitts, P. M., & Peterson, J. R. (1964). Information capacity of discrete motor responses. *Journal of Experimental Psychology, 67*(2), 103–112. doi:10.1037/h0045689

Flash, T., & Hogan, N. (1985). The coordination of arm movements: An experimentally confirmed mathematical model. *The Journal of Neuroscience, 5*, 1688–1703.

Fleck, M. S., & Mitroff, S. R. (2007). Rare targets are rarely missed in correctable search. *Psychological Science, 18*(11), 943–947. doi:10.1111/j.1467-9280.2007.02006.x

Folstein, M. F., Folstein, S. E., & McHugh, P. R. (1975). Mini-mental state: A practical method for grading the cognitive state of patients for the clinician. *Journal of Psychiatric Research, 12*(3), 189–198. doi:10.1016/0022-3956(75)90026-6

Foulds, R. A., Soede, M., & Van Balkom, H. (1987). Statistical disambiguation of multi-character keys applied to reduce motor requirements for augmentative and alternative communication. *Augmentative and Alternative Communication, 3*, 192–195. doi:10.1080/07434618712 331274509

Fox, J. (2002). *An R and S-plus companion to applied regression*. Thousand Oaks, CA: SAGE.

Fredrickson, B. L., & Kahneman, D. (1993). Duration neglect in retrospective evaluations of affective episodes. *Journal of Personality and Social Psychology, 65*, 45–55. doi:10.1037/0022-3514.65.1.45

Freeman, L. (2000). Visualizing social networks. *Journal of Social Structure, 1*(1).

Freer, T. W., & Ulissey, J. M. (2001). Screening mammography with computer-aided detection: Prospective study of 12,860 patients in a community breast center. *Radiology, 220*, 781–786. doi:10.1148/radiol.2203001282

Friedman, W. (1979). *The development of relational understandings of temporal and spatial terms*. Retrieved from http://www.eric.ed.gov/PDFS/ED178176.pdf.

Frijda, N. H. (2006). *The laws of emotion*. New York, NY: Psychology Press.

Frisch, M., Kleinau, S., Langner, R., & Dachselt, R. (2011). Grids & guides: Multi-touch layout and alignment tools. In *Proceedings of the 2011 Annual Conference on Human Factors in Computing Systems*. ACM Press.

Fuchs-Kittowski, F., & Köhler, A. (2005). Wiki communities in the context of work processes. In *Proceedings of the 2005 International Symposium on Wikis (WikiSym 2005)*, (pp. 33–39). New York, NY: ACM Press.

Gallistel, C. R. (1990). *The organization of learning*. Cambridge, MA: MIT Press.

Gamma, E., Helm, R., Johnson, R., & Vlissides, J. (1995). *Design patterns*. Boston, MA: Addison-Wesley.

Gärdenfors, P. (2004). *Conceptual space: The geometry of thought*. Cambridge, MA: MIT Press.

Garrett, J. J. (2003). *The elements of user experience: User-centered design for the web*. New York, NY: New Riders Press.

Geelhoed, E., Toft, P., Roberts, S., & Hyland, P. (1995). To influence time perception. In *Proceedings of the Conference Companion on Human Factors in Computing Systems*, (pp. 272-273). ACM Press.

Gentner, D. R., Grudin, J. T., Larochelle, S., Norman, D. A., & Rumelhart, D. E. (1983). A glossary of terms including classification of typing errors. In Cooper, W. E. (Ed.), *Cognitive Aspects of Skilled Typewriting* (pp. 39–43). New York, NY: Springer-Verlag. doi:10.1007/978-1-4612-5470-6_2

Gentner, D., Imai, M., & Boroditsky, L. (2002). As time goes by: Evidence for two systems in processing space-time metaphors. *Language and Cognitive Processes, 17*(5), 537–565. doi:10.1080/01690960143000317

Gerson, E. M., & Star, S. L. (1986). Analyzing the due process in the workplace. *ACM Transactions on Office Information Systems*, *4*(3), 447–465. doi:10.1145/214427.214431

Gescheider, G. A. (1997). *Psychophysics: The fundamentals* (3rd ed.). Mahwah, NJ: Lawrence Erlbaum Associates Inc.

Gillis, P. D., & Hursh, S. R. (1999). Using behavior moderators to influence CGF command entity effectiveness and performance. In *Proceedings of the Eighth Conference on Computer Generated Forces and Behavioral Representation*, (pp. 237-251). Orlando, FL: Computer Generated Forces.

Gmytrasiewicz, P. J., & Lisetti, C. L. (2002). Emotions and personality in agent design and modeling. In Meyer, J.-J. C., & Tambe, M. (Eds.), *Intelligent Agents VIII* (*Vol. 2333*, pp. 21–31). Berlin, Germany: Springer. doi:10.1007/3-540-45448-9_3

Go, K., & Carroll, J. M. (2003). The blind men and the elephant: Views of scenario-based system design. *Interaction*, *11*(6), 44–53. doi:10.1145/1029036.1029037

Goldberg, D., & Richardson, C. (1993). Touch-typing with a stylus. In *Proceedings of the INTERCHI 1993 Conference on Human Factors in Computing Systems*, (pp. 168-176). ACM Press.

Goldberg, L. R. (1981). Language and individual differences: The search for universal in personality lexicons. *Review of Personality and Social Psychology*, *2*(1), 141–165.

Goldberg, L. R. (1990). An alternative "description of personality": The big-five factor structure. *Journal of Personality and Social Psychology*, *59*, 1216–1229. doi:10.1037/0022-3514.59.6.1216

Goldberg, L. R. (1992). The development of markers for the big-five factor structure. *Psychological Assessment*, *4*(1), 26–42. doi:10.1037/1040-3590.4.1.26

González, V. M., & Mark, G. (2004). Constant, constant, multi-tasking craziness: Managing multiple working spheres. In *Proceedings of the SIGCHI Conference on Human Factors in Computing Systems*, (pp. 113-120). ACM Press.

Goodstein, R. L. (1963). *Boolean algebra*. Oxford, UK: Pergamon Press.

Graham, J. R. (2006). *MMPI-2: Assessing personality and psychopathology* (4th ed.). New York, NY: Oxford University Press.

Grasset, R., Dünser, A., Seichter, H., & Billinghurst, M. (2007). The mixed reality book: A new multimedia reading experience. In Proceedings of CHI 2007. CHI.

Gratch, J., & Marsella, S. (2004). A domain-independent framework for modeling emotion. *Cognitive Systems Research*, *5*(4), 269–306. doi:10.1016/j.cogsys.2004.02.002

Gray, W. D., John, B. E., & Atwood, M. E. (1993). Project ernestine: A validation of GOMS for prediction and explanation of real-world task performance. *Human-Computer Interaction*, *8*(3), 237–309. doi:10.1207/s15327051hci0803_3

Green, T. R. G. (1990). The cognitive dimension of viscosity: A sticky problem for HCI. In *Proceedings of the IFIP TC13 Third Interational Conference on Human-Computer Interaction (INTERACT 1990)*, (pp. 79-86). Amsterdam, The Netherlands: North-Holland Publishing Co.

Grossman, T., & Balakrishnan, R. (2005). A probabilistic approach to modeling two-dimensional pointing. *ACM Transactions on Computer-Human Interaction*, *12*(3), 435–459. doi:10.1145/1096737.1096741

Guérin, F., Laville, A., Daniellou, F., Duraffourg, J., & Kerguelen, A. (2001). *Comprendre le travail pour le transformer - La pratique de L'ergnonomie* (Ingratta, G. M., & Maffei, M., Trans.). Paris, France: Edgard Blücher Ltda.

Guerra, E., & de Lara, J. (2007). Event-driven grammars: Relating abstract and concrete levels of visual languages. In *Software and Systems Modeling, 6*(3), 317-347.

Guestrin, E. D., & Eizenman, M. (2006). General theory of remote gaze estimation using the pupil center and corneal reflections. *IEEE Transactions on Bio-Medical Engineering*, *53*(6), 1124–1133. doi:10.1109/TBME.2005.863952

Guiard, Y. (2009). The problem of consistency in the design of Fitts' law experiments: Consider either target distance and width or movement form and scale. In *Proceedings of the 27th International Conference on Human Factors in Computing Systems (CHI 2009)*, (pp. 1809-1818). ACM Press.

GVU. (1998). *10th WWW user survey*. Retrieved from http://www.cc.gatech.edu/gvu/user_surveys/survey-1998-10/.

Hart, S., & Staveland, L. (1988). Development of NASA-TLX (task load index): Results of empirical and theoretical research. In Hancock, P., & Meshkati, N. (Eds.), *Advances in Psychology: Human Mental Workload* (pp. 239–250). London, UK: Elsevier. doi:10.1016/S0166-4115(08)62386-9

Hartson, H. R., Andre, T. S., & Williges, R. C. (2001). Criteria for evaluating usability evaluation methods. *International Journal of Human-Computer Interaction, 13*(4), 373–410. doi:10.1207/S15327590IJHC1304_03

Haslam, S. A. (2004). *Psychology in organizations: The social identity approach*. Thousand Oaks, CA: SAGE Publications.

Hayes-Roth, B., Brownston, L., & van Gent, R. (1995). Multiagent collaboration in directed improvisation. In *Proceedings of the First International Conference on Multi-Agent Systems,* (pp. 148-154). San Francisco, CA: ICMAS.

Healey, C. G., Booth, K. S., & Enns, J. T. (1996). High-speed visual estimation using preattentive processing. *ACM Transactions on Human Computer Interaction, 3*(2), 107–135. doi:10.1145/230562.230563

He, P., & Kowler, E. (1989). The role of location of probability in the programming of saccades: Implications for "COG" tendencies. *Vision Research, 29*, 1165–1181. doi:10.1016/0042-6989(89)90063-1

Hertzum, M., & Jacobsen, N. E. (2003). The evaluator effect: A chilling fact about usability evaluation methods. *International Journal of Human-Computer Interaction, 15*(4), 183–204. doi:10.1207/S15327590IJHC1501_14

Hettel, T., Lawley, M., & Raymond, K. (2008). Model synchronisation: Definitions for round-trip engineering. In *Theory and Practice of Model Transformations* (pp. 31–45). Zürich, Switzerland: Springer. doi:10.1007/978-3-540-69927-9_3

Hewett, T., Baecker, R., Card, S., Carey, T., Gasen, J., & Mantei, M. (2002). *ACM SIGCHI curricula for human-computer interaction.ACM Technical Report. New York, NY.* Verplank, W.: ACM Press.

Hick, W. E. (1952). On the rate of gain of information. *The Quarterly Journal of Experimental Psychology, 4*(1), 11–26. doi:10.1080/17470215208416600

Hildebrandt, M., Dix, A., & Meyer, H. A. (1994). Time design. In *Proceedings of the 2004 SIGCHI Conference on Human Factors in Computing Systems, Extended Abstracts,* (pp. 1737-1738). ACM Press.

Hitachi. (2011). The world's smallest RFID IC μ-Chip(2.45GHz). Retrieved from http://www.hitachi.co.jp/Prod/mu-chip/.

Hix, D., & Hartson, H. R. (1993). *Developing user interfaces: Ensuring usability through product & process*. New York, NY: John Wiley & Sons, Inc.

Hoffman, J. E., & Subramaniam, B. (1995). The role of visual attention in saccadic eye movements. *Perception & Psychophysics, 57*, 787–795. doi:10.3758/BF03206794

Hoffmann, E., & Sheikh, I. (1994). Effect of target shape on movement time in a Fitts task. *Ergonomics, 37*, 1533–1548. doi:10.1080/00140139408963719

Hogan, W. H. (1978). A theoretical reconciliation of competing views of time perception. *The American Journal of Psychology, 91*(3), 417–428. doi:10.2307/1421689

Hollnagel, E. (1998). *Cognitive reliability and error analysis method (CREAM)*. London, UK: Elsevier Science.

Hong, W., Qiu, F., & Kaufman, A. (2006). A pipeline for computer aided polyp detection. *IEEE Transactions on Visualization and Computer Graphics, 12*(5), 861–868. doi:10.1109/TVCG.2006.112

Hosmer, D. W., & Lemeshow, S. (1989). *Applied logistic regression*. New York, NY: John Wiley & Sons.

Howden, N., Rönnquist, R., Hodgson, A., & Lucas, A. (2001). JACK intelligent agents-summary of an agent infrastructure. In *Proceedings of the 5th International Conference on Autonomous Agents.* Autonomous Agents.

Huber, M. J. (1999). JAM: A BDI-theoretic mobile agent architecture. In *Proceedings of the Third Annual Conference on Autonomous Agents,* (pp. 236–243). Seattle, Washington: AGENTS.

Huey, B. M., & Wickens, C. D. (1993). *Workload transition: Implications for individual and team performance.* Washington, DC: National Academy Press.

Hyman, R. (1953). Stimulus information as a determinant of reaction time. *Journal of Experimental Psychology, 45,* 188–196. doi:10.1037/h0056940

Intel. (2011). *Open source computer vision library.* Retrieved from http://www.intel.com/technology/computing/opencv/index.htm.

Interaction, H.-C. (2011). *Definition.* Retrieved from http://encyclopedia2.thefreedictionary.com/human-computer+interaction.

Iqbal, S. T., & Bailey, B. P. (2008). Effects of intelligent notification management on users and their tasks. In *Proceedings of the SIGCHI Conference on Human Factors in Computing Systems,* (pp. 93-102). ACM Press.

Iqbal, S. T., & Horvitz, E. (2007). Disruption and recovery of computing tasks: Field study, analysis, and directions. In *Proceedings of the SIGCHI Conference on Human Factors in Computing Systems,* (pp. 677-686). ACM Press.

ISO. (1998). *ISO 9241 - Ergonomic requirements for office work with visual display terminals.* Geneva, Switzerland: International Organization for Standardization.

ISO. (2010). *Ergonomics of human-system interaction – Part 210: Human-centred design for interactive systems.* Geneve, Switzerland: ISO.

Isokoski, P. (2004). Performance of menu-augmented soft keyboards. In *Proceedings of the SIGCHI Conference on Human Factors in Computing Systems (CHI 2004),* (pp. 423-430). ACM Press.

Itti, L., & Koch, C. (2000). A saliency-based search mechanism for overt and covert shifts of visual attention. *Vision Research, 40*(10-12), 1489–1506. doi:10.1016/S0042-6989(99)00163-7

Itti, L., Koch, C., & Niebur, E. (1998). A model of saliency-based fast visual attention for rapid scene analysis. *IEEE Transactions on Pattern Analysis and Machine Intelligence, 20*(11), 1254–1259. doi:10.1109/34.730558

Jacob, R. J. K. (1991). The use of eye movements in human-computer interaction techniques: What you look at is what you get. *ACM Transactions on Information Systems, 9*(2), 152–169. doi:10.1145/123078.128728

Jarman, R. F. (1979). Matching of auditory–visual and temporal–spatial information by seven- and nine-year-old children. *Child Development, 50*(2), 575–577. doi:10.2307/1129438

Jenkins, M. H. (2010). *The effects of using mental imagery as a comprehension strategy for middle school students reading science expository texts.* Retrieved from http://search.ebscohost.com/login.aspx?direct=true&db=psyh&AN=2010-99051-321&site=ehost-live.

Jensen, K. (1992). *Coloured petri nets – Basic concepts, analyses methods and practical use (Vol. 1).* Berlin, Germany: Springer.

Jhaveri, N., & Räihä, K. (2005). The advantages of a cross-session web workspace. In *Proceedings of CHI 2005 Extended Abstracts on Human Factors in Computing Systems,* (pp. 1949-1952). ACM Press.

Jiang, H., Vidal, J. M., & Huhns, M. N. (2007). EBDI: An architecture for emotional agents. In *Proceedings of the 6th International Joint Conference on Autonomous Agents and Multiagent Systems,* (pp. 11:1–11:3). Honolulu, HI: ACM Press.

Johansen, S. A., & Hansen, J. P. (2006). Do we need eye trackers to tell where people look? In *Proceedings of Computer-Human Interaction Extended Abstracts on Human Factors in Computing Systems* (pp. 923–928). ACM Press. doi:10.1145/1125451.1125630

John, E. B., & Kieras, E. D. (1996). Using GOMS for user interface design and evaluation: Which technique? *ACM Transactions on Computer-Human Interaction, 3*(4), 287–319. doi:10.1145/235833.236050

John, O. P., Naumann, L. P., & Soto, C. J. (2008). Paradigm shift to the integrative big five trait taxonomy: History, measurements, and conceptual issues. In *Handbook of Personality: Theory and Research* (3rd ed.). New York, NY: The Guilford Press.

John, O. P., Robins, R. W., & Pervin, L. A. (Eds.). (2008). *Handbook of personality: Theory and research* (3rd ed.). New York, NY: The Guilford Press.

Johnston, W. A., & Dark, V. J. (1986). Selective attention. *Annual Review of Psychology*, *37*, 43–75. doi:10.1146/annurev.ps.37.020186.000355

Jones, W., Bruce, H., & Dumais, S. (2001). Keeping found things found on the web. In *Proceedings of the Tenth International Conference on Information and Knowledge Management*, (pp. 119-126). ACM Press.

Jung, H., & Jung, H.-S. (2001). Establishment of overall workload assessment technique for various tasks and workplaces. *International Journal of Industrial Ergonomics*, *28*(6), 341–353. doi:10.1016/S0169-8141(01)00040-3

Juntumaa, M. (2010). Why consumers resist applications perceived useful? Case e-invoicing. In *Proceedings of IADIS International Conference ICT, Society and Human Beings*. IADIS.

Just, M. A., Carpenter, P. A., Keller, T. A., & Emery, L. Z. (2008). Interdependence of non-overlapping cortical systems in dual cognitive task. *NeuroImage*, *14*, 417–426. doi:10.1006/nimg.2001.0826

Kaasten, S., & Greenberg, S. (2001). Integrating back, history, and bookmarks in web browser. In *Proceedings of CHI 2001 extended Abstracts on Human Factors in Computing Systems*. Seattle, WA: ACM Press.

Kanitsar, A. (2004). *Curved planar reformation for vessel visualization*. PhD Thesis. Vienna, Austria: Vienna University of Technology.

Karahalios, K. G., & Viégas, F. B. (2006). Social visualization: Exploring text, audio, and video interaction. In *Proceedings of Extended Abstracts on Human Factors in Computing Systems (CHI 2006)*, (pp. 1667–1670). New York, NY: ACM Press.

Kavaldjian, S., Kaindl, H., Mukasa, K. S., & Falb, J. (2009). Transformations between specifications of requirements and user interfaces. In *Proceedings of MDDAUI 2009*. Sanibel Island, FL: CEUR-WS.

Kellar, M., Watters, C., & Shepherd, M. (2007). A field study characterizing Web-based information-seeking tasks. *Journal of the American Society for Information Science and Technology*, *58*(7), 999–1018. doi:10.1002/asi.20590

Kieras, D., & Meyer, D. E. (1997). An overview of the EPIC architecture for cognition and performance with application to human-computer interaction. *Human-Computer Interaction*, *12*, 391–438. doi:10.1207/s15327051hci1204_4

Kim, M. S., & Cave, K. R. (1999). Grouping effects on spatial attention in visual search. *The Journal of General Psychology*, *126*, 326–352. doi:10.1080/00221309909595370

Kirsch, L. S. (1997). Portfolios of control modes and IS project management. *Information Systems Research*, *8*(3), 215–239. doi:10.1287/isre.8.3.215

Koike, H., Sato, Y., Kobayashi, Y., Tobita, H., & Kobayashi, M. (2000). Interactive textbook and interactive Venn diagram: Natural and intuitive interfaces on augmented desk system. In Proceedings of CHI, (pp. 121-128). ACM Press.

Kolers, P. A. (1972). *Aspects of motion perception*. New York, NY: Pergamon Press Inc.

Koschmider, A., Song, M., & Reijers, H. A. (2009). Social software for modeling business processes. In *Lecture Notes in Business Information Processing* (*Vol. 17*, pp. 666–677). Berlin, Germany: Springer.

Kosslyn, S. M. (1980). *Image and mind*. Cambridge, MA: Harvard University Press.

Kosslyn, S. M. (1994). *Image and brain: The resolution of the imagery debate*. Cambridge, MA: MIT Press.

Kosslyn, S. M. (2005). Reflective thinking and mental imagery: A perspective on the development of posttraumatic stress disorder. *Development and Psychopathology*, *17*(3), 851–863. doi:10.1017/S0954579405050406

Kosslyn, S. M., Behrmann, M., & Jeannerod, M. (1995). The cognitive neuroscience of mental imagery. *Neuropsychologia*, *33*(11), 1335–1344. doi:10.1016/0028-3932(95)00067-D

Kosslyn, S. M., Murphy, G. L., Bemesderfer, M. E., & Feinstein, K. J. (1977). Category and continuum in mental comparisons. *Journal of Experimental Psychology, 106*(4), 341–375.

Kowler, E., Anderson, E., Dosher, B., & Blaser, E. (1995). The role of attention in the programming of saccades. *Vision Research, 35,* 1897–1916. doi:10.1016/0042-6989(94)00279-U

Kozma, R., Chin, E., Russell, J., & Marx, N. (2000). The roles of representations and tools in the chemistry laboratory and their implications for chemistry learning. *Journal of the Learning Sciences, 9*(2), 105–143. doi:10.1207/s15327809jls0902_1

Kozma, R., & Russell, J. (2005). Multimedia learning of chemistry. In Mayer, R. E. (Ed.), *The Cambridge Handbook of Multimedia Learning* (pp. 409–428). Cambridge, UK: Cambridge University Press.

Krech, D., Crutchfield, R., & Ballachey, E. (1962). *Individual in society: A textbook of social psychology.* New York, NY: McGraw-Hill.

Kreibig, S. (2010). Autonomic nervous system activity in emotion: A review. *Biological Psychology, 84*(3), 394–421. doi:10.1016/j.biopsycho.2010.03.010

Kristjansson, A., Wang, D., & Nakayama, K. (2002). The role of priming in conjunctive visual search. *Cognition, 85,* 37–52. doi:10.1016/S0010-0277(02)00074-4

Kroll, P., & Kruchten, P. (2003). *The rational unified process made easy: A practitioners guide to the RUP.* Boston, MA: Addison-Wesley.

Kubovy, M., & Epstein, W. (2001). Internalization: A metaphor we can live without. *The Behavioral and Brain Sciences, 24*(4), 618–625.

Laird, J. E., Newell, A., & Rosenbloom, P. S. (1987). SOAR: An architecture for general intelligence. *Artificial Intelligence, 33*(1), 1–64. doi:10.1016/0004-3702(87)90050-6

Lakoff, G. (1987). *Women, fire, and dangerous things: What categories reveal about the mind.* Chicago, IL: University of Chicago Press.

Lakoff, G., & Johnson, M. (1980). *Metaphors we live by.* Chicago, IL: University of Chicago Press.

Langer, T., Sarin, R., & Weber, M. (2005). The retrospective evaluation of payment sequences: Duration neglect and peak-and-end effects. *Journal of Economic Behavior & Organization, 58,* 157–175. doi:10.1016/j.jebo.2004.01.001

Latombe, J. C. (1991). *Robot motion planning.* Boston, MA: Kluwer.

Lee, F. J., & Taatgen, N. A. (2002). Multitasking as skill acquisition. In *Proceedings of the Twenty-Fourth Annual Conference of the Cognitive Science Society,* (pp. 572-577). Cognitive Science Society.

Leplat, J., & Cuny, X. (1977). *Introduction à la psychologie tu travail* (Domingos, H., Trans.). Lisboa, Portugal: Fundação Calouste Gulbenkian.

Lesher, G. W., & Moulton, B. J. (2000). A method for optimizing single-finger keyboards. In *Proceedings of Rehabilitation Engineering Society of North America - RESNA Annual Conference,* (pp. 91-93). RESNA.

Leuchter, S., Niessen, C., Eyferth, K., & Bierwagen, T. (1997). Modelling mental processes of experienced operators during control of a dynamic man maschine system. In *Proceedings of the 16ᵗʰ European Annual Conferece on Human Decision Making and Manual Control,* (pp. 268-276). Kassel, Germany: Universidade of Kassel.

Levine, S. H., Goodenought-Trepagnier, C., Getschow, C. O., & Minneman, S. L. (1987). Multi-character key text entry using computer disambiguation. In *Proceedings of the 10th Annual Conference of Rehabilitation Engineering,* (pp. 177-179). Washington, DC: RESNA.

Levy, J. H., Broadhurst, R. R., Ray, S., Chaney, E. L., & Pizer, S. M. (2007). Signaling local non-credibility in an automatic segmentation pipeline. In *Proceedings of the International Society for Optical Engineering Meetings on Medical Imaging,* (vol 6512). IEEE.

Lewis, C. (2005). HCI for people with cognitive disabilities. *ACM SIGACCESS Accessibility and Computing, 83,* 12–17. doi:10.1145/1102187.1102190

Lewis, J. R. (1994). Sample sizes for usability studies: Additional considerations. *Human Factors, 36*(2), 368–378.

Lewis, J. R. (2001). Evaluation of procedures for adjusting problem-discovery rates estimated from small samples. *International Journal of Human-Computer Interaction, 13*(4), 445–479. doi:10.1207/S15327590IJHC1304_06

Lewis, J. R. (2006). Sample sizes for usability tests: Mostly math, not magic. *Interaction, 13*(6), 29–33. doi:10.1145/1167948.1167973

Lewis, R. (2001). Cognitive theory, soar. In *International Encyclopedia of the Social and Behavioral Sciences*. Amsterdam, The Netherlands: Pergamon. doi:10.1016/B0-08-043076-7/01583-7

Leyton, M. (1982). *Symmetry, causality, mind*. Cambridge, MA: MIT Press.

Lim, M. Y., Dias, J., Aylett, R., & Paiva, A. (2008). Improving adaptiveness in autonomous characters. In Prendinger, H., Lester, J., & Ishizuka, M. (Eds.), *Intelligent Virtual Agents (Vol. 5208*, pp. 348–355). Berlin, Germany: Springer. doi:10.1007/978-3-540-85483-8_35

López-Aligué, F. J., Acevedo-Sotoca, I., García-Manso, A., García-Orellana, C. J., & Gallardo-Caballero, R. (2004). Microcalcifications detection in digital mammograms. In *Proceedings of the IEEE Engineering in Medicine and Biology Society*. IEEE Press.

Luckasson, R., Borthwick-Duffy, S., Buntinx, W. H. E., Coulter, D. L., Craig, E. M., & Reeve, A. (2002). *Mental retardation: Definition, classification, and system of supports* (10th ed.). Washington, DC: AAMR.

Lucquiaud, V. (2005). Proposition d'un noyau et d'une structure pour les modèles de tâches orientés utilisateurs. In Proceedings of the 17th French-Speacking Conference on Human-Computer Interaction, (pp. 83-90). Toulouse, France: HCI.

Lukander, K. (2006). A system for tracking gaze on handheld devices. *Behavior Research Methods, 38*(4), 660–666. doi:10.3758/BF03193899

Luyten, K., Clerckx, T., Coninx, K., & Vanderdonckt, J. (2003). Derivation of a dialog model from a task model by activity chain extraction. In *Proceedings of DSV-IS 2003*, (pp. 203-217). Funchal, Portugal: Springer-Verlag.

MacKay, B., & Watters, C. (2008b). Exploring multi-session web tasks. *Proceeding of the Twenty-Sixth Annual SIGCHI Conference on Human Factors in Computing Systems*, (pp. 1187-1196). ACM Press.

MacKay, B., & Watters, C. (2009). Building support for multi-session tasks. In *Proceedings of the 27th International Conference Extended Abstracts on Human Factors in Computing Systems*, (pp. 4273-4278). ACM Press.

MacKay, B., & Watters, C. (2008a). Understanding and supporting multi-session web tasks. *Proceedings of the American Society for Information Science and Technology, 45*(1), 1–13. doi:10.1002/meet.2008.1450450266

MacKenzie, I. S., & Buxton, W. A. S. (1992). Extending Fitts' law to two-dimensional tasks. In *Proceedings of ACM CHI Conference on Human Factors in Computing Systems*, (pp. 219–226). ACM Press.

MacKenzie, I. S., & Zhang, S. X. (1999). The design and evaluation of a high-performance soft keyboard. In *Proceedings of CHI 1999*, (pp. 25-31). ACM.

MacKenzie, I. S., & Soukoreff, R. W. (2002). Text entry for mobile computing: Models and methods, theory and practice. *Human-Computer Interaction, 17*(2), 147–198. doi:10.1207/S15327051HCI172&3_2

Madadhain, J., Fisher, D., Smyth, P., White, S., & Boey, Y. B. (2005). Analysis and visualization of network data using JUNG. *Journal of Statistical Software*. Retrieved from http://jung.sourceforge.net/doc/JUNG_journal.pdf.

Maes, P. (1994). Agents that reduce work and information overload. *Communications of the ACM, 37*(7), 30–40. doi:10.1145/176789.176792

Maes, P. (1995). Artificial life meets entertainment: Life-like autonomous agents. *Communications of the ACM, 38*(11), 108–114. doi:10.1145/219717.219808

Maier, S., & Minas, M. (2009). Pattern-based layout specifications for visual language editors. In *Proceedings of the 1st International Workshop on Visual Formalisms for Patterns*. ECEASST.

Maier, S., & Minas, M. (2010). Combination of different layout approaches. In *Proceedings of the 2nd International Workshop on Visual Formalisms for Patterns*. ECEASST.

Malatesta, L., Caridakis, G., Raouzaiou, A., & Karpouzis, K. (2007). Agent personality traits in virtual environments based on appraisal theory predictions. In *Proceedings of AISB 2007: Artificial and Ambient Intelligence, Language, Speech and Gesture for Expressive Characters*. Newcastle, UK: AISB.

Maljkovic, V., & Nakayama, K. (1994). Priming of pop-out: Role of features. *Memory & Cognition, 22*(6), 657–672. doi:10.3758/BF03209251

Maltz, M., & Shinar, D. (2003). New alternative methods of analyzing human behavior in cued target acquisition. *Human Factors, 45*(2), 281–295. doi:10.1518/hfes.45.2.281.27239

Mander, R., Salomon, G., & Wong, Y. Y. (1992). A pile metaphor for supporting casual organization of information. In *Proceedings of CHI 1992*. ACM Press.

Markopoulos, P., Pycock, J., Wilson, S., & Johnson, P. (1992). ADEPT - A task based design environment. In *Proceedings of the International Conference on System Sciences,* (pp. 587-596). Hawaii, HI: IEEE Computer Society Press.

Marques, J. M., & Paez, D. (1994). The "black sheep effect": Social categorization, rejection of ingroup deviates, and perception of group variability. *European Review of Social Psychology, 5*, 3768. doi:10.1080/14792779543000011

Masciocchi, C. M., Mihalas, S., Parkhurst, D., & Niebur, E. (2009). Everyone knows what is interesting: Salient locations which should be fixated. *Journal of Vision (Charlottesville, Va.), 9*(25), 1–22.

Maslow, A. H. (1968). *Toward a psychology of being* (2nd ed.). Princeton, NJ: Van Nostrand.

Masui, T. (2001). HyperSnapping. In *Proceedings of the IEEE 2001 Symposia on Human Centric Computing Languages and Environments*. IEEE Press.

Mayer, M. (2007). Web history tools and revisitation support: A survey of existing approaches and directions. *Foundations and Trends in Human-Computer Interaction, 2*(3), 173–278. doi:10.1561/1100000011

Mayer, M. (2009). *Innovation at Google: The physics of data*. Palo Alto, CA: Palo Alto Research Center.

Mayer, R. E., & Sims, V. K. (1994). For whom is a picture worth a thousand words? Extensions of a dual-coding theory of multimedia learning. *Journal of Educational Psychology, 86*(3), 389–401. doi:10.1037/0022-0663.86.3.389

McAdams, D. P. (1992). The five-factor model in personality: A critical appraisal. *Journal of Personality, 60*(2), 329–361. doi:10.1111/j.1467-6494.1992.tb00976.x

McAuley, J. D. (1995). *On the perception of time as phase: Toward an adaptive-oscillator model of rhythm*. Ph.D. Thesis. Bloomington, IN: Indiana University.

McCarthy, J. D., Sasse, M. A., & Riegelsberger, J. (2003). Can I have the menu please? An eyetracking study of design conventions. In *Proceedings of Human-Computer Interaction* (pp. 401–414). ACM Press.

McCormack, T., & Hoerl, C. (2008). Temporal decentering and the development of temporal concepts. *Language Learning, 58*(1), 89–113. doi:10.1111/j.1467-9922.2008.00464.x

McQueen, C., MacKenzie, I. S., & Zhang, S. X. (1995). An extended study of numeric entry on pen-based computers. In *Proceedings of Graphics Interface, 1995*, 215–222.

McRorie, M., Sneddon, I., Sevin, E., Bevacqua, E., & Pelachaud, C. (2009). A model of personality and emotional traits. In Ruttkay, Z., Kipp, M., Nijholt, A., & Vilhjálmsson, H. H. (Eds.), *Intelligent Virtual Agents* (*Vol. 5773*, pp. 27–33). Berlin, Germany: Springer. doi:10.1007/978-3-642-04380-2_6

Mele, M. L., Federici, S., Borsci, S., & Liotta, G. (2010). Beyond a visuocentric way of a visual web search clustering engine: The sonification of WhatsOnWeb. In Miesenberger, K., Klaus, J., Zagler, W., & Karshmer, A. (Eds.), *Computers Helping People with Special Needs* (*Vol. 1*, pp. 351–357). Berlin, Germany: Springer. doi:10.1007/978-3-642-14097-6_56

Merlin, B., & Raynal, M. (2009). *SpreadKey: Increasing software keyboard key by recycling needless ones*. Paper presented at AAATE 2009. Florence, Italia.

Meyer, D. E., Abrams, R. A., Kornblum, S., Wright, C. E., & Keith, S. J. (1998). Optimality in human motor performance: Ideal control of rapid aimed movements. *Psychological Review, 95*, 340–370. doi:10.1037/0033-295X.95.3.340

Microsoft. (2011). *User experience interaction guidelines.* Retrieved from http://msdn.microsoft.com/en-us/library/aa511258.aspx.

Milic-Frayling, N., Jones, R., Rodden, K., Smyth, G., Blackwell, A., & Sommerer, R. (2004). SmartBack: Supporting users in back navigation. In *Proceedings of WWW 2004.* New York, NY: ACM Press.

Miluzzo, E., Wang, T., & Campbell, A. T. (2010). Eye-Phone: Activating mobile phones with your eyes. In *Proceedings of the 2nd ACM SIGCOMM Workshop on Networking, Systems, and Applications on Mobile Handhelds,* (pp. 15-20). ACM Press.

Minas, M. (2006). Generating meta-model-based freehand editors. In *Proceedings of the 3rd International Workshop on Graph Based Tools.* ECEASST.

MindRetrieve. (2009). *Search your personal web.* Retrieved from http://www.mindretrieve.net/.

Mintzberg, H. (1970). Structured observation as a method to study managerial work. *Journal of Management Studies, 7*(1), 87–104. doi:10.1111/j.1467-6486.1970.tb00484.x

Mintzberg, H. (1980). *The nature of managerial work.* Englewood Cliffs, NJ: Prentice-Hall.

Miyata, Y., & Norman, D. A. (1986). Psychological issues in support of multiple activities. In *User Centered SYSTEM design* (pp. 265–284). Boca Raton, FL: CRC Press.

MOD. (2011). *The UK approach to unmanned aircraft systems.* London, UK: Ministry of Defense.

Moraglia, G. (1989). Display organization and the detection of horizontal lines segments. *Perception & Psychophysics, 45*(3), 265–272. doi:10.3758/BF03210706

Mori, G., Paternò, F., & Santoro, C. (2004). Design and development of multidevice user interfaces through multiple logical descriptions. *IEEE Transactions on Software Engineering, 30*(8), 507–520. doi:10.1109/TSE.2004.40

Morris, D., Morris, M. R., & Venolia, G. (2008). SearchBar: A search-centric web history for task resumption and information re-finding. In *Proceeding of the Twenty-Sixth Annual SIGCHI Conference on Human Factors in Computing Systems,* (pp. 1207-1216). ACM Press.

Moscovici, S. (1976). *Social influence and social change.* London, UK: Academic Press.

Mueller, D. C., Maeder, A. J., & O'Shea, P. J. (2005). Enhancing direct volume visualisation using perceptual properties. In *Proceedings of SPIE* (*Vol. 5744*, pp. 446–454). SPIE. doi:10.1117/12.594003

Muller, M. J. (2011). Catalogue of scenario-based methods and methodologies: Technical Report #99-06. *IBM Watson Research Center.* Retrieved from http://domino.watson.ibm.com/cambridge/research.nsf.

Mullet, K. E., & Sano, D. (1995). *Designing visual interfaces: Communication oriented techniques.* Mountain View, CA: SunSoft Press.

Murata, A. (1999). Extending effective target width in Fitts' law to a two-dimensional pointing task. *International Journal of Human-Computer Interaction, 11*(2), 137–152. doi:10.1207/S153275901102_4

Myers, B. A. (1985). The importance of percent-done progress indicators for computer-human interfaces. In *Proceedings of the 1985 SIGCHI Conference on Human Factors in Computing Systems,* (pp. 11-17). ACM Press.

Nagamatsu, T., Iwamoto, Y., Kamahara, J., Tanaka, N., & Yamamoto, M. (2010). Gaze estimation method based on an aspherical model of the cornea: Surface of revolution about the optical axis of the eye. In *Proceedings of the 2010 Symposium on Eye Tracking Research & Applications,* (pp. 255-258). IEEE.

Nagamatsu, T., Kamahara, J., & Tanaka, N. (2008). 3D gaze tracking with easy calibration using stereo cameras for robot and human communication. In *Proceedings of the 17th International Symposium on Robot and Human Interactive Communication (IEEE RO-MAN 2008),* (pp. 59-64). IEEE Press.

Nagel, T., & Sander, R. (2005). HyperHistory. In *Proceedings of HT 2005.* Salzburg, Austria: ACM Press.

Navalpakkam, V., & Itti, L. (2005). Modeling the influence of task on attention. *Vision Research, 45,* 205–231. doi:10.1016/j.visres.2004.07.042

Neill, J. (2008). Personality reading. *Center for Applied Psychology.* Retrieved from http://wilderdom.com/JamesNeill.htm.

Nesbat, S. B. (2003). A system for fast, full-text entry for small electronic devices. In *Proceedings of the Fifth International Conference on Multimodal Interfaces, ICMI 2003*. ACM Press.

Netto, A., Aguiar, Y., Scherer, D., & Vieira, M. D. (2009). *Context analysis during task execution: An operator model*. Paper presented at the IADIS International Conference - Interfaces and Human Computer Interaction 2009. Portugal.

Neumann, G., & Erol, S. (2009). From a social wiki to a social workflow system. In *Lecture Notes in Business Information Processing* (*Vol. 17*, pp. 698–708). Berlin, Germany: Springer. doi:10.1007/978-3-642-00328-8_70

Newell, A. (1990). *Unified theories of cognition*. Cambridge, MA: Harvard University Press.

Nguyen, P., & Chun, R. (2011). *Model driven development with interactive use cases and UML models*. Retrieved from http://www.pnguyen.tigris.org/SER4505.pdf.

Nielsen, J. (2000). *Why you only need to test with 5 users*. Retrieved May, 20th, 2011, from http://www.useit.com/alertbox/20000319.html.

Nielsen, J. (2008). *How little do users read?* Retrieved May 12, 2009 from http://www.useit.com/alertbox/percent-text-read.html.

Nielsen, J., & Landauer, T. K. (1993). *A mathematical model of the finding of usability problems*. Paper presented at the Conference on Human factors in computing systems: INTERACT and CHI 1993. Amsterdam, The Netherlands.

Nielsen, J., & Molich, R. (1990). Heuristic evaluation of user interfaces. In *Proceedings of the SIGCHI Conference on Human Factors in Computing Systems: Empowering People (CHI 1990)*, (pp. 249-256). ACM Press.

Nielsen, J., & Phillips, V. L. (1993). Estimating the relative usability of two interfaces: Heuristic, formal, and empirical methods compared. In *Proceedings of the INTERACT 1993 and CHI 1993 Conference on Human Factors in Computing Systems (CHI 1993)*, (pp. 214-221). ACM Press.

Nielsen, J. (1994). Heuristic evaluation. In Nielsen, J., & Mack, R. L. (Eds.), *Usability inspection methods*. New York, NY: John Wiley & Sons.

Nielsen, J., & Mack, R. L. (Eds.). (1994). *Usability inspection methods*. New York, NY: John Wiley & Sons.

Niessen, C., Leuchter, S., & Eyferth, K. (1998). A psychological model of air traffic control and its implementation. In F. E. Riter, & R. M. Young (Eds.), *Second European Conference on Cognitive Modelling (ECCM-98)*, (pp. 104-111). Nottingham, UK: Nottingham University Press.

Niessen, C., & Eyferth, K. (2001). A model of the air traffic controller's picture. *Safety Science, 37*(2-3), 187–202. doi:10.1016/S0925-7535(00)00048-5

Norling, E., & Ritter, F. E. (2004). Towards supporting psychologically plausible variability in agent-based human modelling. In *Proceedings of the Third International Joint Conference on Autonomous Agents and Multi-Agent Systems*. AAMAS.

Norman, D. A. (1988). *The psychology of everyday things*. New York, NY: Basic Books.

Norman, D. A. (1990). *The design of everyday things*. New York, NY: DoubleDay.

Norman, D. A. (1993). *Things that make us smart: Defending human attributes in the age of the machine*. Cambridge, MA: Perseus Books.

Norman, W. T. (1963). Toward an adequate taxonomy of personality attributes: Replicated factor structure in peer nomination personality ratings. *Journal of Abnormal and Social Psychology, 66*(6), 574–583. doi:10.1037/h0040291

Nunes, J. M., & Fowell, S. P. (1996). Hypermedia as an experimental learning tool: A theoretical model. *Information Research News, 6*(4), 15-27. Retrieved 14 November 2010 from http://informationr.net/ir/2-1/paper12.html.

Oreg, S. (2003). Resistance to change: Developing an individual differences measure. *The Journal of Applied Psychology, 88*(4), 680–693. doi:10.1037/0021-9010.88.4.680

Ortony, A. (2003). On making believable emotional agents believable. In Trappl, R., Petta, P., & Payr, S. (Eds.), *Emotions in Humans and Artifacts* (pp. 189–211). Cambridge, MA: MIT Press.

Ortony, A., Clore, G. L., & Collins, A. (1988). *The cognitive structure of emotions*. Cambridge, UK: Cambridge University Press. doi:10.1017/CBO9780511571299

Paivio, A. (1986). *Mental representations: A dual coding approach*. Oxford, UK: Oxford University Press.

Paletz, S., Bearman, C., Orasanu, J., & Holbrook, J. (2009). Socializing the human factors analysis and classification system: Incorporating social psychological phenomena into a human factors error classification system. *Human Factors*, *51*, 435–445. doi:10.1177/0018720809343588

Papanikolaou, K. A., Grigoriadou, M., Kornilakis, H., & Magoulas, G. D. (2003). Personalizing the interaction in a web-based educational hypermedia system: The case of INSPIRE. *User Modeling and User-Adapted Interaction*, *13*(3), 213–267. doi:10.1023/A:1024746731130

Parkhurst, D., Law, K., & Niebur, E. (2002). Modeling the role of salience in the allocation of overt visual attention. *Vision Research*, *42*, 107–123. doi:10.1016/S0042-6989(01)00250-4

Pashler, H. (1988). Cross-dimensional interaction and texture segregation. *Perception & Psychophysics*, *43*, 307–318. doi:10.3758/BF03208800

Pavlovych, A., & Stuerzlinger, W. (2004). Model for non-expert text entry speed on 12-button phone keypads, In *Proceedings of the SIGCHI Conference on Human Factors in Computing Systems*, (pp. 351-358). ACM Press.

Pearson, D. (2001). *New organic architecture: The breaking wave*. London, UK: Gaia.

Pelachaud, C. (2000). Some considerations about embodied agents. In *Proceedings of the Workshop on Achieving Human-Like Behavior in Interactive Animated Agents*. Barcelona, Spain: Autonomous Agents.

Petta, P., Pelachaud, C., & Cowie, R. (Eds.). (2011). *Emotion-oriented systems: The humane handbook*. Dordrecht, The Netherlands: Springer.

Piaget, J., Gruber, H. E., & Vonèche, J. (1977). *The essential Piaget*. New York, NY: Basic Books.

Poelmans, S., & Reijers, H. A. (2009). Assessing workflow management systems a quantitative analysis of a workflow evaluation model. In *Proceedings International Conference on Enterprise Information Systems (ICEIS 2009)*. ICEIS.

Poelmans, S. (1999). Workarounds and distributed viscosity in a workflow system: A case study. *SIGGROUP Bulletin*, *20*(3), 11–12.

Precedent. (2011). *Definition*. Retrieved from http://dictionary. reference.com/ browse/precedent.

Preim, B., & Oeltze, S. (2007). *Visualization in medicine and life sciences. In 3D Visualization of Vasculature: An Overview* (pp. 39–60). Berlin, Germany: Springer Verlag.

Purchase, H. C., & Samra, A. (2008). Extremes are better: Investigating mental map preservation in dynamic graphs. In *Proceedings of the 5th International Conference on Diagrammatic Representation and Inference*. Springer.

Purchase, H. C., Hoggan, E., & Goerg, C. (2007). How important is the "mental map"? An empirical investigation of a dynamic graph layout algorithm. In Kaufmann and Wagner (Eds.), *Graph Drawing: 14th International Symposium*. Springer.

Qu, H., Sun, J., & Jamjoom, H. T. (2008). SCOOP: Automated social recommendation in enterprise process management. In *Proceedings of Services Computing (SCC 2008)*, (pp. 101-108). IEEE Press.

Quintana, C., Reiser, B. J., Davis, E. A., Krajcik, J., Fretz, E., & Duncan, R. G. (2004). A scaffolding design framework for software to support science inquiry. *Journal of the Learning Sciences*, *13*(3), 337–386. doi:10.1207/s15327809jls1303_4

Rao, A. S., & Georgeff, M. P. (1995). BDI agents: From theory to practice. In *Proceedings of the 1st International Conference on Multi-Agent Systems*, (pp. 312-319). San Francisco, CA: ICMAS.

Rapp, D. N., & Kurby, C. A. (2008). The 'ins' and 'outs' of learning: Internal representations and external visualizations. In Gilbert, M. R. A. M. N. J. K. (Ed.), *Visualization: Theory and Practice in Science Education* (*Vol. 3*, pp. 29–52). Dordrecht, The Netherlands: Springer Netherlands. doi:10.1007/978-1-4020-5267-5_2

Rasmussen, J., Pejtersen, A., & Goodstein, L. (1994). *Cognitive systems engineering*. New York, NY: John Wiley & Sons, Inc.

Raynal, M., & Vigouroux, N. (2005). Genetic algorithm to generate optimized soft keyboard. In *Proceedings of CHI 2005 Extended Abstracts on Human Factors in Computing Systems (CHI 2005)*, (pp. 1729-1732). ACM Press.

Rayner, K. (1998). Eye movements in reading and information processing: 20 years of research. *Psychological Bulletin, 124*(3), 372–422. doi:10.1037/0033-2909.124.3.372

Reason, J. (1990). *Human error*. Cambridge, UK: Cambridge University Press.

Redelmeier, D., & Kahneman, D. (1996). Patients' memories of painful medical treatments: Real-time and retrospective evaluations of two minimally invasive procedures. *Pain, 66*, 3–8. doi:10.1016/0304-3959(96)02994-6

Reijers, H. A., & Poelmans, S. (2007). Re-configuring workflow management systems to facilitate a smooth flow of work. *International Journal of Cooperative Information Systems, 16*(2), 155–175. doi:10.1142/S0218843007001615

Reiss, F. (1979). *The hawthorne effect in a pilot program*. Unpublished.

Rensink, R. A. (2002). Internal vs. external information in visual perception. In *Proceedings of the 2nd International Symposium on Smart Graphics*, (pp. 63-70). IEEE.

Rice, S. (2009). Examining single and multiple-process theories of trust in automation. *The Journal of General Psychology, 136*(3), 303–319. doi:10.3200/GENP.136.3.303-322

Rizzo, P., Veloso, M., Miceli, M., & Cesta, A. (1997). Personality-driven social behaviors in believable agents. In *Proceedings of the AAAI Fall Symposium on Socially Intelligent Agents,* (pp. 109-114). AAAI.

Rogers, Y. (1994). Exploring obstacles: Integrating CSCW in evolving organisations. In *Proceedings of Conference on Computer Supported Cooperative Work (CSCW 1994)*, (pp. 67-77). New York, NY: ACM Press.

Roland, P., & Gulyas, B. (1994). Visual imagery and visual representation. *Trends in Neurosciences, 17*(7), 281–287. doi:10.1016/0166-2236(94)90057-4

Rolland, J. P., Muller, K. E., & Helvig, C. S. (1995). Visual search in medical images: A new methodology to quantify saliency. In *Proceedings of SPIE* (*Vol. 2436*, pp. 40–48). SPIE. doi:10.1117/12.206851

Rosch, E. (1975). Cognitive reference points. *Cognitive Psychology, 7*, 532–547. doi:10.1016/0010-0285(75)90021-3

Rosch, E. (1988). Principles of categorization. In Collins, A. M., & Smith, E. E. (Eds.), *Readings in Cognitive Science: A Perspective from Psychology and Artificial Intelligence* (pp. 312–322). San Mateo, CA: Morgan Kaufmann.

Rosch, E., & Mervis, C. B. (1975). Family resemblances: Studies in the internal structure of categories. *Cognitive Psychology, 7*(4), 573–605. doi:10.1016/0010-0285(75)90024-9

Rose, D. E., Mander, R., Oren, T., Ponceleon, D., Salomon, G., & Wong, Y. Y. (1993). Content awareness in a file system interface: Implementing the pile metaphor for organizing information. In *Proceedings of SIGIR 1993*. Pittsburgh, PA: ACM Press.

Rousseau, D., & Hayes-Roth, B. (1996). *Personality in synthetic agents. Technical Report No. KSL 96-21*. Palo Alto, CA: Stanford University.

Rubinstein, J. S., Meyer, D. E., & Evans, J. E. (2001). Executive control of cognitive processes in task switching. *Journal of Experimental Psychology. Human Perception and Performance, 27*(4), 763–797. doi:10.1037/0096-1523.27.4.763

Rumelhart, D. E., & McClelland, J. L. (1986). *Parallel distributed processing* (*Vol. 1-2*). Cambridge, MA: MIT Press.

Russell, S., & Norvig, P. (2009). *Artificial intelligence: A modern approach* (3rd ed.). New York, NY: Prentice Hall.

Russo Dos Santos, C., Gros, P., Abel, P., Loisel, D., Trichaud, N., & Paris, J. P. (2000). Metaphor-aware 3D navigation. In *Proceedings IEEE Symposium on Information Visualization*, (p. 155). IEEE Press.

Ryall, K., Marks, J., & Shieber, S. (1997). An interactive constraint-based system for drawing graphs. In *Proceedings of the 10th ACM Symposium on User Interface Software and Technology*. ACM Press.

Ryokai, K., & Cassell, J. (1999). StoryMat: A play space with narrative memory. In Proceedings of IUI 1999. ACM Press.

Sannella, M. (1993). Multi-way versus one-way constraints in user interfaces: Experience with the DeltaBlue algorithm. *Software, Practice & Experience, 23*(5). doi:10.1002/spe.4380230507

Sansonnet, J.-P., & Bouchet, F. (2010). Expression of behaviors in assistant agents as influences on rational execution of plans. In Allbeck, J. M., Badler, N. I., Bickmore, T. W., Pelachaud, C., & Safonova, A. (Eds.), *Intelligent Virtual Agents* (*Vol. 6356*, pp. 413–419). Philadelphia, PA: Springer. doi:10.1007/978-3-642-15892-6_45

Sardina, S. (2007). *A course on BDI architectures*. Melbourne, Australia: University of Melbourne.

Sarini, M. (2010). The activity circle: Building a bridge between workflow technology and social software. In *Proceedings of Advances in Human-Oriented and Personalized Mechanisms, Technologies and Services (CENTRIC)* (pp. 22–27). Nice, France: IEEE Press. doi:10.1109/CENTRIC.2010.18

Sarini, M., Durante, F., & Gabbiadini, A. (2010). Workflow management social systems: A new socio-psychological perspective on process management. In *Lecture Notes in Business Information Processing* (*Vol. 43*, pp. 231–242). Berlin, Germany: Springer. doi:10.1007/978-3-642-12186-9_22

Saucier, G., & Ostendorf, F. (1999). Hierarchical subcomponents of the big five personality factors: A cross-language replication. *Journal of Personality and Social Psychology, 76*(4), 613–627. doi:10.1037/0022-3514.76.4.613

Scaife, M., & Rogers, Y. (1996). External cognition: How do graphical representations work? *International Journal of Human-Computer Studies, 45*(2), 185–213. doi:10.1006/ijhc.1996.0048

Schalock, R. L., & Luckasson, R. (2004). American association on mental retardation's definition, classification, and system of supports and its relation to international trends and issues in the field of intellectual disabilities. *Journal of Policy and Practice in Intellectual Disabilities, 1*(3-4), 136–146. doi:10.1111/j.1741-1130.2004.04028.x

Scherer, D., & Vieira, M. (2008). Accounting for the human error when building the user profile. In *Proceedings of the Third IASTED International Conference Human-Computer Interaction,* (pp. 132-137). Insbruck, Austria: ACTA Press.

Scherer, D., da Costa, R., Barbosa, J., & Vieira, M. D. (2010). Taxonomy proposal for the description of accidents and incidents in electrical systems operation. In *Proceedings of the ACM SIGCHI Symposium on Engineering Interactive Computing Systems.* Berlin, Germany: ACM Press.

Scherer, D., Vieira, M., & Neto, J. (2010). Human error categorization: An extension to classical proposals applied to electrical systems operations. In P. Forbrig, F. Paternó, & A. Pejtersen (Eds.), *Proceedings of HCIS 2010, IFIP AICT,* (pp. 234-245). Brisbane, Australia: Springer.

Schiffman, H. R. (1982). *Sensation and perception: An integrated approach* (2nd ed.). New York, NY: John Wiley & Sons.

Schmettow, M. (2008). *Heterogeneity in the usability evaluation process.* Paper presented at the 22nd British HCI Group Annual Conference on People and Computers: Culture, Creativity. Liverpool, UK.

Schmidt, C., & Kastens, U. (2003). Implementation of visual languages using pattern-based specications. *Software, Practice & Experience, 33*(15). doi:10.1002/spe.560

Schmidt, K., & Bannon, L. J. (1992). Taking CSCW seriously: Supporting articulation work. *Computer Supported Cooperative Work, 1*(1–2), 7–40. doi:10.1007/BF00752449

Schmidt, K., & Simone, C. (1996). Coordination mechanisms: Towards a conceptual foundation of CSCW systems design. *Computer Supported Cooperative Work, 5*(2-3), 155–200. doi:10.1007/BF00133655

Sears, A., & Jacko, J. A. (Eds.). (2009). *Human-computer interaction: Design issues, solutions, and applications.* Boca Raton, FL: CRC Press.

Sears, A., Jacko, J. A., Chu, J., & Moro, F. (2001). The role of visual search in the design of effective soft keyboards. *Behaviour & Information Technology, 20*(3), 159–166. doi:10.1080/01449290110049790

Sellen, A. J., Murphy, R., & Shaw, K. L. (2002). How knowledge workers use the web. In *Proceedings of the SIGCHI Conference on Human Factors in Computing Systems: Changing our World, Changing Ourselves,* (pp. 227-234). ACM Press.

Sendall, S., & Küster, J. (2004). *Taming model round-trip engineering.* Paper presented in the OOPSLA Workshop on Best Practices for Model Driven Software Development. Vancouver, Canada.

Seow, S. C. (2008). *Designing and engineering time: The psychology of time perception in software.* Boston, MA: Pearson Education.

Shannon, C. (1948). A mathematical theory of communication. *Bell System Technical Journal, 27,* 379–423 & 623–656.

Shappel, S., & Wiegmann, D. (2000). *The human factors analysis and classification system - HFACS.* Oklahoma City, OK: FAA Civil Aeromedical Institute.

Shen, S.-T., Prior, S. D., & Chen, K.-M. (2009). Comparing the perspicacity, appropriateness, and preference of web browser icons. *Digital Creativity, 20*(1), 59–78. doi:10.1080/14626260902868012

Shen, S.-T., Prior, S. D., & Chen, K.-M. (2009). Testing of a novel web browser interface for the Chinese market. *Lecture Notes in Computer Science, 5623,* 413–418. doi:10.1007/978-3-642-02767-3_46

Shen, S.-T., Prior, S. D., & Chen, K.-M. (2011). Revisiting revisitation in computer interaction: Organic bookmark management. *Design Principles and Practices: An International Journal, 5*(4), 327–344.

Shen, S.-T., Prior, S. D., & Woolley, M. (2006). Towards culture-centred design. *Journal of Interacting with Computers, 18*(4), 820–852. doi:10.1016/j.intcom.2005.11.014

Shepard, R. N. (1987). Toward a universal law of generalization for psychological science. *Science, 237,* 1317–1323. doi:10.1126/science.3629243

Shepard, R. N., & Chipman, S. (1970). Second-order isomorphism of internal representations: Shapes of states. *Cognitive Psychology, 1,* 1–17. doi:10.1016/0010-0285(70)90002-2

Shepard, R. N., & Farrell, J. E. (1985). Representation of the orientations of shapes. *Acta Psychologica, 59,* 104–121. doi:10.1016/0001-6918(85)90044-7

Shih, S.-W., & Liu, J. (2004). A novel approach to 3-D gaze tracking using stereo cameras. *IEEE Transactions on Systems, Man, and Cybernetics. Part B, 34*(1), 234–245.

Silfverberg, M., MacKenzie, I. S., & Korhonen, P. (2000). Predicting text entry speed on mobile phones. In *Proceedings of the SIGCHI Conference on Human Factors in Computing Systems (CHI 2000),* (pp. 9-16). ACM Press.

Silverman, B. G., Johns, M., Cornwell, J., & O'Brien, K. (2006). Human behavior models for agents in simulators and games: Part I: Enabling science with PMFserv. *Presence (Cambridge, Mass.), 15*(2), 139–162. doi:10.1162/pres.2006.15.2.139

Simon, H. (1957). A behavioral model of rational choice. In *Models of Man, Social and Rational: Mathematical Essays on Rational Human Behavior in a Social Setting.* New York, NY: Wiley.

Sims, V. K., & Hegarty, M. (1997). Mental animation in the visuospatial sketchpad: Evidence from dual-task studies. *Memory & Cognition, 25*(3), 321–332. doi:10.3758/BF03211288

Sivik, L., & Taft, C. (1994). Color naming: A mapping in the NCS of common color terms. *Scandinavian Journal of Psychology, 35,* 144–164. doi:10.1111/j.1467-9450.1994.tb00939.x

Software Intensive Systems in the Future. (2006). *Final report//ITEA 2 symposium.* Retrieved from http://symposium.itea2.org/ symposium2006/ main/publications/ TNO_IDATE_study_ ITEA_SIS_ in_the_future_Final_Report.pdf.

Song, M., & Quintana, C. (2009). WIIS: Multimodal simulation for exploring the world beyond visual sense. In *Proceedings of the 27th International Conference Extended Abstracts on Human Factors in Computing Systems.* Boston, MA: ACM Press.

Sosnin, P. (2009). Means of question-answer interaction for collaborative development activity. *Advances in Human-Computer Interaction.* Retrieved from http://www.hindawi.com/journals/ahci/2009/619405/.

Sosnin, P. (2011). Question-answer shell for personal expert systems. In *Expert Systems for Human, Materials and Automation* (pp. 51–74). New York, NY: InTech.

Soto, C. J., & John, O. P. (2009). Ten facet scales for the big five inventory: Convergence with NEO PI-R facets, self-peer agreement, and discriminant validity. *Journal of Research in Personality, 43*(1). doi:10.1016/j.jrp.2008.10.002

Soukoreff, R. W., & MacKenzie, I. S. (1995). Theoretical upper and lower bounds on typing speeds using a stylus and soft keyboard. *Behaviour & Information Technology, 14*, 370–379. doi:10.1080/01449299508914656

Soukoreff, R. W., & MacKenzie, I. S. (2004). Towards a standard for pointing device evaluation: Perspectives on 27 years of Fitts' law research in HCI. *International Journal of Human-Computer Studies, 61*, 751–789. doi:10.1016/j.ijhcs.2004.09.001

Spink, A., Jansen, B. J., Wolfram, D., & Saracevic, T. (2002). From e-sex to e-commerce: Web search changes. *Computer, 35*(3), 107–109. doi:10.1109/2.989940

Spink, A., Park, M., Jansen, B. J., & Pedersen, J. (2006). Multitasking during Web search sessions. *Information Processing & Management, 42*(1), 264–275. doi:10.1016/j.ipm.2004.10.004

Spool, J., & Schroeder, W. (2001). *Testing web sites: Five users is nowhere near enough.* Paper presented at the Human Factors in Computing Systems: CHI 2001. Seattle, WA.

Steinberg, D., Budinsky, F., Paternostro, M., & Merks, E. (2009). *EMF: Eclipse modeling framework.* Boston, MA: Addison-Wesley.

Stephanidis, C. (2001). User interfaces for all: New perspectives into human-computer interaction. In Stephanidis, C. (Ed.), *User Interfaces for All: Concepts, Methods, and Tools* (pp. 3–17). Mahwah, NJ: Lawrence Erlbaum Associates.

Still, J. D., & Masciocchi, C. M. (2010). A saliency model predicts fixations in web interfaces. In *Proceedings of the 5th International Workshop on Model-Driven Development of Advanced User Interfaces.* Atlanta, GA: ACM Press.

Still, J. D., & Dark, V. J. (2010). Examining working memory load and congruency effects on affordances and conventions. *International Journal of Human-Computer Studies, 68*(9), 561–571. doi:10.1016/j.ijhcs.2010.03.003

Stix, A. (1996). *Creating rubrics through negotiable contracting and assessment.* Retrieved from http://www.interactiveclassroom.com/pdf/Creating_Rubrics_Through_Negotiable_Contracting_and_Assessment.pdf.

Stompernet. (2011). *Scrutinizer foveal gaze simulator.* Retrieved from http://about.stompernet.com/scrutinizer.

Suchman, L. A. (1987). *Plans and situated actions: The problem of human-machine communication.* Cambridge, UK: Cambridge University Press.

Sugata, M. (1994). *Kototama no ama he.* Tokyo, Japan: Tachibana Inc.

Suinesiaputra, A., de Koning, P. J., Zudilova-Seinstra, E. V., Reiber, J. H. C., & van der Geest, R. J. (2009). *A 3D MRA segmentation method based on tubular NURBS model.* Paper presented at the International Society for Magnetic Resonance in Medicine 2009. Honolulu, HI.

Sutherland, I. E. (1988). *Sketchpad: A man-machine graphical communication system. In 25 Years of DAC Papers on Twenty-Five Years of Electronic Design Automation.* ACM Press.

Sweller, J. (1988). Cognitive load during problem solving: Effects on learning. *Cognitive Science: A Multidisciplinary Journal, 12*(2), 257-285.

Tabard, A., Mackay, W., Roussel, N., & Letondal, C. (2007). PageLinker: Integrating contextual bookmarks within a browser. In *Proceedings of CHI 2007.* San Jose, CA: ACM Press.

Tamborello, F. P., & Byrne, M. D. (2007). Adaptive but non-optimal visual search behavior with highlighted displays. *Cognitive Systems Research, 8*(3), 182–191. doi:10.1016/j.cogsys.2007.05.003

Tarasewich, P., Pomplun, M., Fillion, S., & Broberg, D. (2005). The enhanced restricted focus viewer. *International Journal of Human-Computer Interaction, 19*(1), 35–54. doi:10.1207/s15327590ijhc1901_4

Tauscher, L., & Greenberg, S. (1997). How people revisit web pages: Empirical findings and implications for the design of history systems. *International Journal of Human-Computer Studies, 47*(1), 97–138. doi:10.1006/ijhc.1997.0125

Tenenbaum, G., & Connolly, C. (2008). Attention allocation under varied workload and effort perception in rowers. *Psychology of Sport and Exercise, 9*(5), 704–717. doi:10.1016/j.psychsport.2007.09.002

Theeuwes, J. (1992). Perceptual selectivity for color and form. *Perception & Psychophysics*, *51*, 599–606. doi:10.3758/BF03211656

Theeuwes, J. (1994). Stimulus-driven capture and attentional set: Selective search for color and visual abrupt onsets. *Journal of Experimental Psychology. Human Perception and Performance*, *20*, 799–806. doi:10.1037/0096-1523.20.4.799

Theeuwes, J. (2004). Top-down search strategies cannot override attentional capture. *Psychonomic Bulletin & Review*, *11*(1), 65–70. doi:10.3758/BF03206462

Tobii. (2011). *Tobii mobile device stand*. Retrieved from http://www.tobii.com/en/analysis-and-research/global/products/hardware-accessories/tobii-mobile-device-stand/.

Tognazzini, B. (1993). Principles, techniques, and ethics of stage magic and their application to human interface design. In *Proceedings of INTERCHI, 1993*, 355–362.

Tourniaire, F., & Pulos, S. (1985). Proportional reasoning: A review of the literature. *Educational Studies in Mathematics*, *16*(2), 181–204. doi:10.1007/BF02400937

Treisman, A. M., & Gelade, G. (1980). A feature-integration theory of attention. *Cognitive Psychology*, *12*, 97–136. doi:10.1016/0010-0285(80)90005-5

Tretter, T. R., Jones, M. G., Andre, T., Negishi, A., & Minogue, J. (2006a). Conceptual boundaries and distances: Students' and experts' concepts of the scale of scientific phenomena. *Journal of Research in Science Teaching*, *43*(3), 282–319. doi:10.1002/tea.20123

Tretter, T. R., Jones, M. G., & Minogue, J. (2006b). Accuracy of scale conceptions in science: Mental maneuverings across many orders of spatial magnitude. *Journal of Research in Science Teaching*, *43*(10), 1061–1085. doi:10.1002/tea.20155

Turnell, M. F. (2004). Accounting for human errors in a method for the conception of user interfaces. In *Proceedings of the International Mediterranean Modelling Multi-Conference - I3M 2004*, (pp. 122-130). Genova, Italy: I3M.

UCLA. (2011). *The UCLA Internet report: Surveying the digital future*. Retrieved from http://www.digitalcenter.org/pdf/InternetReportYearThree.pdf.

USC. (2009). *Center for the digital future: 2008 digital future report*. Retrieved from http://www.digitalcenter.org/pages/current_report.asp?intGlobalId=19.

Vallesi, A., Binns, M. A., & Shallice, T. (2008). An effect of spatial-temporal association of response codes: Understanding the cognitive representations of time. *Cognition*, *107*(2), 501–527. doi:10.1016/j.cognition.2007.10.011

van Schooten, B. W., van Dijk, B. M., Nijholt, A., & Reiber, J. H. (2010b). Evaluating automatic warning cues for visual search in vascular images. In *Proceeding of the 14th International Conference on Intelligent User Interfaces*, (pp. 393–396). New York, NY: ACM Press.

van Schooten, B., van Dijk, E. M. A. G., Suinesiaputra, A., & Reiber, J. H. C. (2010a). Effectiveness of visualisations for detection of errors in segmentation of blood vessels. In *Proceedings of IVAPP 2010*. IVAPP.

van Schooten, B. W., van Dijk, E. M. A. G., Zudilova-Seinstra, E. V., de Koning, P. J. H., & Reiber, J. H. C. (2009). Evaluating visualisation and navigation techniques for interpretation of MRA data. In *Proceedings of GRAPP, 2009*, 405–408.

van Schooten, B. W., van Dijk, E. M., Suinesiaputra, A., & Reiber, J. H. (2011). Interactive navigation of segmented mr angiograms using simultaneous curved planar and volume visualizations. *International Journal of Computer Assisted Radiology and Surgery*, *6*(1), 591–599. doi:10.1007/s11548-010-0534-4

Venkatesh, V., Morris, M., Davis, G., & Davis, F. (2003). User acceptance of information technology: Toward a unified view. *Management Information Systems Quarterly*, *27*(3), 425–478.

Verplanken, B., & Orbell, S. (2003). Reflections on past behavior: A self-report index of habit strength. *Journal of Applied Social Psychology*, *33*, 1313–1330. doi:10.1111/j.1559-1816.2003.tb01951.x

Vierordt, K. V. (1868). *Der zeitsinn nach versuchen*. Tubingen, Germany: H. Laupp.

Villanueva, A., & Cabeza, R. (2008). A novel gaze estimation system with one calibration point. *IEEE Transactions on Systems, Man, and Cybernetics. Part B*, *38*(4), 1123–1138.

Virzi, R. A. (1990). Streamlining the design process: Running fewer subjects. *Human Factors and Ergonomics Society Annual Meeting Proceedings, 34,* 291-294.

Virzi, R. A. (1992). Refining the test phase of usability evaluation: How many subjects is enough? *Human Factors, 34*(4), 457–468.

Vogel, E. K., Woodman, G. F., & Luck, S. J. (2001). Storage of features, conjunctions, and objects in visual working memory. *Journal of Experimental Psychology. Human Perception and Performance, 27,* 92–114. doi:10.1037/0096-1523.27.1.92

Vogelsang, A., & Signer, B. (2005). The lost cosmonaut: An interactive narrative environment on basis of digitally enhanced paper. In Proceedings of International Conference on Virtual Storytelling 2005. ACM.

Vosniadou, S., & Brewer, W. F. (1992). Mental models of the earth: A study of conceptual change in childhood. *Cognitive Psychology, 24*(4), 535–585. doi:10.1016/0010-0285(92)90018-W

Walther, D., & Koch, C. (2006). Modeling attention to salient proto-objects. *Neural Networks, 19,* 1395–1407. doi:10.1016/j.neunet.2006.10.001

Wang, Q., & Chang, H. (2010). Multitasking bar: Prototype and evaluation of introducing the task concept into a browser. In *Proceedings of CHI 2010.* Atlanta, GA: ACM Press.

Wang, Y., Gao, X., & Li, J. (2007). A feature analysis approach to mass detection in mammography based on RF-SVM. In *Proceedings of ICIP, 2007,* 9–12.

Weinger, M. B., Vredenburgh, A. G., Schumann, C. M., Macario, A., Williams, K. J., & Kalsher, M. J. (2000). Quantitative description of the workload associated with airway management procedures. *Journal of Clinical Anesthesia, 12*(4), 273–282. doi:10.1016/S0952-8180(00)00152-5

Weinreich, H., Obendorf, H., Herder, E., & Mayer, M. (2006). Off the beaten tracks: Exploring three aspects of web navigation. In *Proceedings of WWW 2006.* Edinburgh, UK: ACM Press.

Weinreich, H., Obendorf, H., Herder, E., & Mayer, M. (2008). Not quite the average: An empirical study of web use. *ACM Transactions on the Web, 2*(1), 5.1-5.31.

Weiss, G. (2000). *Multiagent systems: A modern approach to distributed artificial intelligence.* Cambridge, MA: MIT Press.

White, S. A., & Miers, D. (2008). *BPMN modeling and reference guide: Understanding and using BPMN.* New York, NY: Future Strategies Inc.

WHO. (2001). *International classification of functioning, disability and health (ICF).* Retrieved from http://www.who.int/classifications/icf/en/.

Wickens, C. D., & Andre, A. D. (1990). Proximity compatibility and information display: Effects of color, space, and objectness on information integration. *Human Factors, 32*(1), 61–77.

Wickens, C. D., & McCarley, J. S. (2008). *Applied attention theory.* Boca Raton, FL: CRC Press.

Wiebe, E., Roberts, E., & Behrend, T. (2010). An examination of two mental workload measurement approaches to understanding multimedia learning. *Computers in Human Behavior, 26*(3), 474–481. doi:10.1016/j.chb.2009.12.006

Wiese, R., Eiglsperger, M., & Kaufmann, M. (2002). yFiles: Visualization and automatic layout of graphs. In Kaufmann and Wagner (Eds.), Graph Drawing: 9th International Symposium. Springer. ENDNOTE [1] Further details about the pattern-based layout approach can be found here: http://www.unibw.de/inf2/DiaGen/Layout.

Wikipedia. (2011). *Historical origin of acre.* Retrieved from http://en.wikipedia.org/wiki/Acre#Historical_origin.

Winston, W. R. (1970). Managing the development of large software systems. In *Proceedings of IEEE Wescon,* (pp 1-9). IEEE Press.

Wittmann, M., & Paulus, M. (2007). Decision making, impulsivity and time perception. *Trends in Cognitive Sciences, 12*(1), 7–12. doi:10.1016/j.tics.2007.10.004

Wolfe, J. M. (2007). Guided search 4.0: Current progress with a model of visual search. In W. Gray (Ed.), *Integrated Models of Cognitive Systems,* (pp. 99-119). New York, NY: Oxford.

Wolfe, J. M., Butcher, S. J., Lee, C., & Hyle, M. (2003). Changing your mind: On the contributions of top-down and bottom-up guidance in visual search for feature singletons. *Journal of Experimental Psychology. Human Perception and Performance*, *29*, 483–502. doi:10.1037/0096-1523.29.2.483

Wolfe, J. M., & Horowitz, T. S. (2004). What attributes guide the deployment of visual attention and how do they do it? *Nature Reviews. Neuroscience*, *5*, 1–7. doi:10.1038/nrn1411

Wolfe, J. M., Horowitz, T. S., Kenner, N., Hyle, M., & Vasan, N. (2004). How fast can you change your mind? The speed of top-down guidance in visual search. *Vision Research*, *44*, 1411–1426. doi:10.1016/j.visres.2003.11.024

Wolff, A., & Forbrig, P. (2009). *Deriving user interfaces from task models*. Paper presented at MDDAUI 2009. Sanibel Island, FL.

Wood, D., Bruner, J. S., & Ross, G. (1976). Role of tutoring in problem-solving. *Journal of Child Psychology and Psychiatry, and Allied Disciplines*, *17*(2), 89–100. doi:10.1111/j.1469-7610.1976.tb00381.x

Wood, W., Quinn, J., & Kashy, D. (2002). Habits in everyday life: Thought, emotion, and action. *Journal of Personality and Social Psychology*, *83*(6), 1281–1297. doi:10.1037/0022-3514.83.6.1281

Woodworth, R. S. (1899). The accuracy of voluntary movement. *Psychological Review*, *3*(2), 1–4.

Wooldridge, M. J. (2000). *Reasoning about rational agents*. Cambridge, MA: MIT Press.

Wright, F. L. (1971). *The natural house*. London, UK: Pitman.

Wright, P. C., & Monk, A. F. (1991). A cost-effective evaluation method for use by designers. *International Journal of Man-Machine Studies*, *35*(6), 891–912. doi:10.1016/S0020-7373(05)80167-1

Yang, H., & Xu, X. (2010). Bias towards regular configuration in 2D pointing. In *Proceedings of ACM CHI Conference on Human Factors in Computing Systems*, (pp. 1391-1400). ACM Press.

Yeh, M., & Wickens, C. D. (2001). Display signaling in augmented reality: Effects of cue reliability and image realism on attention allocation and trust calibration. *Human Factors*, *43*(3), 355–365. doi:10.1518/001872001775898269

Zhai, S., Hunter, M., & Smith, B. A. (2000). The metropolis keyboard - An exploration of quantitative techniques for virtual keyboard design. In *Proceedings of the 13th Annual ACM Symposium on User Interface Software and Technology*, (pp. 119-128). San Diego, CA: ACM Press.

Zhai, S. (2004). Characterizing computer input with Fitts' law parameters: The information and non-information aspects of pointing. *International Journal of Human-Computer Studies*, *61*, 791–809. doi:10.1016/j.ijhcs.2004.09.006

Zhai, S., Sue, A., & Accot, J. (2002). Movement model, hits distribution and learning in virtual keyboarding. *CHI Letters*, *4*(1), 17–24.

Zhang, J., & Norman, D. (1994). The representation of relational information. In *Proceedings of the Sixteenth Annual Conference of the Cognitive Science Society*, (pp. 952-957). Cognitive Science Society.

Zhang, J. (1997). The nature of external representations in problem solving. *Cognitive Science*, *21*(2), 179–217. doi:10.1207/s15516709cog2102_3

About the Contributors

Eshaa Mohamed Alkhalifa has obtained her BSc in Computer Science of the University of Bahrain, her MS in Artificial Intelligence from the University of George Washington, and her PhD in Cognitive Science from the University of Edinburgh in Scotland. She has published a number of books, and a large number of journal and conference papers. She held the role of the Academic Vice President of the Royal University for Women until recently when she took some time off to focus on research. Her research interests include the utilization of Cognitive Science findings in increasing the efficiency of learning in general or elearning in particular.

Khulood Gaid has a Bachelor degree in Computing Science from the Royal University for Women, Bahrain. She is currently working as a System Analyst at almarwa.net. She is planning to continue research in the field of Human Computer Interaction and earn her Master's degree. Khulood had worked on many projects in the field of educational adaptive systems. Her next research projects will concentrate on the usage and implementation of cognitively informed interfaces in educational systems.

* * *

Yuska Paola Costa Aguiar was born in 1982 in Campina Grande, Paraiba, Brazil. She holds a bachelor degree in Computer Science awarded by Universidade Federal de Campina Grande (UFCG) in 2004, and a Master degree in Computer Science, also awarded by UFCG, in 2007. Since 2008, she is a doctorate student in Electrical Engineering, at UFCG, working for a double degree from the Université d'Aix Marseille III, France, where she has recently spent 18 months doing her doctorate research. She was a teacher in the Department of Mathematics and Informatics at the Universidade Estadual da Paraiba (UEPB) between 2008 and 2009. Currently, she is a member of the Human-Machine Interface Group (GIHM), working at the Laboratory of Human-Machine Interface (LIHM). Her research focus include usability evaluation and the study of human behavior, user interface design, software development processes, and software testing.

Brian Amento is a Principal Technical Staff Member at AT&T Labs – Research for 14 years, working in the Human Computer Interface Research group. Brian received his PhD in Computer Science from Virginia Polytechnic Institute and State University. His research interests include novel interaction techniques, mining implicit social data and enabling ubiquitous collaboration. He has served as an Adjunct Faculty member at New York University and a Research Professor at the New Jersey Institute of Technology. His current research work includes collaborative music listening, vibration-based networking, and large multi-touch surface interfaces.

Simone Borsci, PhD, is Research Fellow for the Match and Match Plus Project at the Brunel University. He obtained a PhD (2010) in Cognitive Psychology at the Sapienza University of Rome. He is a member of Interuniversity Center for Research on Cognitive Processing in Natural and Artificial Systems (ECONA) and CognitiveLab of University of Perugia (www.cognitivelab.it). He collected 20 international and national publications on psychotechnologies, web accessibility and usability, and user experience evaluation.

François Bouchet received a Master's degree in Engineering from ESIEA and in Computer Science from University Paris-Sud 11 in 2005 and 2006, respectively, and a PhD in Computer Science from University Paris-Sud 11 in 2010. During those years, his research interests gradually evolved from corpus analysis and Natural Language Processing of requests made to assistant conversational agents, to the design of architectures for believable cognitive agents with personality and emotions. He is now a postdoctoral fellow at McGill University, in Pr. Roger Azevedo's team, working on emotionally-aware agent-based intelligent tutoring systems.

Sybille Caffiau is Assistant Professor at the University Joseph Fourier at Grenoble (France) and performs its research at the LIG (computer science lab of Grenoble). Her research is at the intersection of ergonomics, model-driven engineering, and human computer interaction. She works on user-centered design of interactive applications. Her work is based on the use of models in an iterative approach for which the design is validated by the user activity that is expressed from specifications, evaluations, and feedback in the form of task models. She is author of several papers on national and international conferences and journals.

Huiyou Chang Ph.D. in Computer Science, experienced researcher on Human Computer Interaction, Workflow Management Coalition, Computer Integrated Manufacturing System, Computer Integrated Technology and Application, Artificial Optimization and Intelligent Algorithm, and Complex Problem Modeling and Algorithm. Professor of School of Software, Sun Yat-Sen University, teaching courses on Embedded Software and Systems, Software Engineering, Operating Systems, and Software Engineering Training. In recent years, he presided over more than 20 scientific and technological projects over the national, provincial, and municipal levels. He has published papers in dozens of international and domestic core academic journals, and has had more than thirty papers accepted by SCI, EI index . His research interests are in workflow management coalition, computer integrated manufacturing systems, and artificial optimization and intelligent algorithms.

Stefano Federici, PhD, is currently Associate Professor of General Psychology at the University of Perugia and Visiting Professor of Psychotechnologies for Integration and Adaptation at the Sapienza University of Rome, Faculty of Psychology. He is member of: the editorial board of *Disability and Rehabilitation: Assistive Technology International Journal* and *Cognitive Processing: International Quarterly of Cognitive Science*; and the Scientific Committee of the the International Conference on Space Cognition (ICSC). He is the coordinator of research team of CognitiveLab at University of Perugia (www.cognitivelab.it). He has collected more than 120 international and national publications on cognitive psychology, psychotechnology, disability, and usability.

Patrick Girard is Professor in Computer Science at the University of Poitiers. His research laboratory is situated in the French Engineering School of Mechanics and Aerotechnics, on the Futuroscope Scientific Area. He is the head of the Human Computer Interaction group, which works on Validation and Verification of Interactive Systems. He is mainly concerned with formal modelization and model-driven approaches for interactive system design. He has been the supervisor of ten PHD students, and is involved in several workgroups in model-based approaches. He has been for four years the president of the French Association for Human Computer Interaction.

Chris Harrison is a Ph.D. student in the Human-Computer Interaction Institute at Carnegie Mellon University. His research interests primarily focus on novel input methods and interaction technologies—especially those that enable people to interact with "small devices in big ways." Chris has worked on several projects in the area of social computing and input methods at IBM Research, AT&T Labs, and most recently, Microsoft Research and Disney Research. Since 2009, Chris has been the Editor-in-Chief of *XRDS*, ACM's flagship magazine for its student members.

Michitaka Hirose was born in Kanagawa, Japan, in 1954. He received the B.S. degree in Engineering from The University of Tokyo, in 1977, and Ph.D. degree, in 1982, respectively. He currently is a Professor of The University of Tokyo. His research interests include virtual reality, augmented reality, and their applications.

Scott Hudson is a Professor in the Human-Computer Interaction Institute within the School of Computer Science at Carnegie Mellon University, where he was until recently the founding director of the HCII PhD program. He received his Ph.D. in Computer Science from the University of Colorado in 1986, and has previously held faculty positions at the University of Arizona and the Georgia Institute of Technology. Elected to the CHI Academy in 2006, he has published extensively on technology-oriented HCI topics. He has regularly served on program committees for the ACM SIGCHI Conference on Human Factors in Computing Systems and ACM Symposium on User Interface Software and Technology (UIST), and served as the papers co-chair for the SIGCHI 2009 and 2010 conferences.

Huiyang Liu is a graduate student in School of Information Science and Technology, Sun Yat-Sen University, interested in Human Computer Interaction, User Experience, and utilizing browser history on collaboration and navigation. He has several years experience in the design and development of software, and is interested in software project management and Web 2.0 programming.

Alessandro Londei, PhD, graduated in Physics in 1991, doctorate in Electronic Engineering in 1996 at the SapienzaUniversity of Rome. His main area of interests are neural networks theory, artificial intelligence algorithms, nonlinear dynamics, and functional magnetic resonance analysis. At present, he works as a scientific consultant at the Sapienza University in several European Projects.

Sonja Maier studied Computer Science at the Technical University Munich, Germany, where she focused on Mathematics. Furthermore, she holds a Master's degree in Computer Science from the Georgia Institute of Technology, USA. At the Georgia Institute of Technology, she mainly focused on Human Computer Interaction. Currently, she is a Ph.D. student at the Computer Science Department of the Universität der Bundeswehr München, Germany. She is working in the fields of Meta-Modeling, and Visual Domain-Specific Language Engineering, and is mainly interested in tool creation and tool integration for visual domain-specific languages. In her Ph.D., she focuses on layout support for visual language editors. Her research is heavily influenced by her background in mathematics, human computer interaction, and software engineering.

Christopher M. Masciocchi is a Lecturer in the Department of Psychology at Frostburg State University. Christopher received his Master's and Ph.D. in Psychology from Iowa State University, where he primarily studied the effects of semantics on visual attention. His research showed that semantically relevant information affects visual attention in many of the same ways as salient information, namely that it attracts additional attentional resources. He is also interested in visual and semantic effects on attention in natural and artificial scenes, and is currently involved in projects on investigating attention in websites, and critical thinking and decision making.

Maria Laura Mele, PhD, Cognitive Psychology at the ECONA of the Sapienza University of Rome. Her research topics are User eXperience, accessibility, usability, user centered design, assistive technologies, and eye-tracking methodology. She is a member of CognitiveLab research team of University of Perugia (www.cognitivelab.it).

Bruno Merlin is a Computer Sciences Professor at the Federal University of Pará (UFPa, Belém-Brazil), member of the ICEN (Exact and Natural sCience Institute). PhD in Human-Computer Interaction at University of Toulouse III (2011, Toulouse-France). Master in Human-Computer Interaction at the ENAC (2003, French Civil Aviation Engineering School, Toulouse-France). Actual researches in design and evaluation of assistive tools to improve text input in mobile contexts and to assist motor impairment, and in pointing task instrumentation. Designer of the HMI toolkit IntNovate (http://www.intnovate.org/) providing predefined behaviors and widgets to map data with advanced graphical representations and advanced interactions. 2004-2009, Researches and HMI design for air traffic control: providing new paradigms to improve the air traffic control and smoothing the transition between former and new tools in order to improve the new paradigm acceptability (concept of interfaces multi-layer).

Mark Minas holds Diploma and Doctoral degrees in Computer Science from the Friedrich-Alexander-University Erlangen-Nuremberg, Germany. He is a full professor of Computer Science at the Computer Science Department of the Universität der Bundeswehr München, Germany. He is working in the fields of graph grammars, meta-modeling, and visual domain-specific language engineering. He focuses on tool creation and tool integration for visual domain-specific languages. The tool set comprises editors that are tailored to particular visual domain-specific languages and transformation tools that transform models expressed in one domain-specific language into a different language for further processing. Mark Minas has published many papers in particular on automatically creating visual editors from language specifications based on graph grammars or meta-models.

Takashi Nagamatsu received the B.E. and M.E. degrees in Electrical Engineering from Kyoto University, Japan, in 1994 and 1996, respectively. In 1996, he joined Mitsubishi Heavy Industries Ltd. In 1999, he joined Kyoto University as a Research Associate. In 2000, he moved to Kobe University of Mercantile Marine and is presently an Assistant Professor at Kobe University. He received the Ph.D. degree in Energy Science from Kyoto University, Japan, in 2004. He is involved in research on human-computer interaction, and so on.

Ademar Virgolino da Silva Netto is a doctorate student at Federal University of Campina Grande (UFCG), in Brazil. He received his Electrical Engineer degree from UFCG, in 2008, and his Master degree in Electrical Engineering from UFCG in 2010. He is a lecturer at the Information System Department at the private institution FACISA-CESED, since 2011. He is one of the shareholders of the company INTERFACEIS Technology and Automation Consultancy. He is a member of the Human Machine Interface Group (GIHM—Research Groups at CNPq—Brazil). His research interests include human-computer interaction, product usability evaluation, and industrial operator training.

Anton Nijholt received his MSc in Mathematics and Computer Science (1974) from Delft University of Technology and his PhD in Computer Science from the Vrije Universiteit Amsterdam. He has held positions at various universities in Canada, Belgium, and the Netherlands. Since 1989, he has been a Full Professor of Computer Science at the University of Twente (Enschede, The Netherlands). He is now member of the Human Media Interaction research group at the Department of Computer Science of the University of Twente. Nijholt is author of numerous journal papers and book chapters. He has edited books and special issues of journals on parsing theory, artificial intelligence, interactive entertainment, and brain-computer interfaces. His current interests include multimodal interaction, affective computing, entertainment computing, and brain-computer interfacing.

Domenico Polimeno is a MSc student at Faculty of Psychology of the Sapienza University of Rome. He obtained a BA in Experimental Psychology at the Sapienza University of Rome. After six years in the IT industries as a Programmer and Web Developer, he is now a consultant in the field of User Experience and Applied Psychology. His fields of interest are HCI, usability engineering, accessibility, general psychology, cognitive ergonomic. He is a member of CognitiveLab research team of University of Perugia (www.cognitivelab.it).

Stephen Prior gained a BEng Mechanical Engineering degree, in 1987, and a PhD in Rehabilitation Robotics from Middlesex University, London, in 1993. He is a Chartered Mechanical Engineer, Corporate Member of the IMechE, and Fellow of the Higher Education Academy. His research interests are in the areas of Mechatronics, Autonomous Unmanned Systems, Robotics, and Design Education. He was the project leader for the MoD Grand Challenge i-Spy team in 2008 and is currently leading a team in the DARPA UAV Forge competition 2011. He is the Director of the Autonomous Systems Lab at Middlesex University which designs, develops and manufactures nano unmanned aerial systems for the military and security forces in collaboration with BCB International Ltd., http://www.eis.mdx.ac.uk/research/robotics/.

Mathieu Raynal is an Assistant Professor and teaches Computer Science at University of Toulouse, since 2006. He is a member of the ELIPSE team in the IRIT lab. His research in Human Computer Interaction focuses on model, design, and evaluation of new text input systems and pointing devices for contexts in which these interactions are difficult (disability or mobility) or new interaction spaces such as

3D virtual environments. His current research projects include the study of soft keyboards augmented by character and word predictions systems, and he is particularly interested in modeling user performance in pointing and text input tasks.

Johan H. C. Reiber received his M.Sc. EE-degree from the Delft University of Technology in 1971 and his M.Sc and Ph.D. from Stanford University, USA, in 1975 and 1976, respectively. In 1977, he founded the Division of Image Processing (LKEB) at the Thoraxcenter, Erasmus University in Rotterdam, and continued these activities at the Department of Radiology, Leiden University Medical Center (LUMC) in the Netherlands, since 1990. Since 1995, he has been Professor of Medical Image Processing at the LUMC. In 2000, he became a member of the Royal Netherlands Academy of Arts and Sciences (KNAW). He is (co)-author of more than 660 scientific papers, and co-author/editor of 15 books. He is editor-in-chief of the International Journal of Cardiovascular Imaging. In 2004, he became an IEEE Fellow for his contributions to medical image analysis and its applications. Other fellowships include those of the European Society of Cardiology (FESC, 1988) and the American College of Cardiology (FACC, 2010). His research interests include (knowledge guided) image processing and its clinical applications.

Jean-Paul Sansonnet received a PhD degree in Computer Science in 1977 and a full Doctorate of State in 1982 from the University of Toulouse, France, for his research on early Lisp-Machines. Then he joined the Alcatel Research Centre in Paris for six years where he developed new architectures for Artificial Intelligence Applications. In 1988, he became CNRS Research Director at the CNRS-LRI Laboratory in Paris and worked on massively Distributed Artificial Intelligence architectures and languages. Since 2000, he is Senior Research Director at CNRS-LIMSI in Paris, where he heads the Interaction research group. His current research is related to Conversational Agents, which is dedicated to the study of communicative interaction, with strong semantic and linguistic components, between human and/or software agents in mediated information systems.

Marcello Sarini was born in Milan (Italy) in 1968. He received a Degree in Computer Science from the University of Milano, in 1997, and a PhD in Computer Science from the University of Torino in 2003. Since 2003, he has been with the University of Milano-Bicocca, Italy, where he is an Assistant Professor in Computer Science. His research interests focus on the analysis and design of technologies to support collaboration, communication, coordination, and knowledge sharing among human practitioners in complex work settings such as hospitals and biological laboratories. In particular, he is involved in a research agenda to exploit a human-centered approach, on the one hand, to investigate the relevant factors for the acceptance of collaboration technology by end users; and on the other hand, to design social visualization mechanisms to facilitate the acceptance of such technology.

Hiroshi Sato received his BE in Information Science from Kwansei Gakuin University in 2010. He is currently a master course student in Graduate School of Science and Technology, Kwansei Gakuin University. He is interested in gaze interaction, and so on.

Daniel Scherer was born in 1977 in Novo Hamburgo, Rio Grande do Sul, Brazil. Since 2010, he has been lecturing on Human-Computer Interface Project in the Computer Department at the State University of Paraiba. There he is the course director of the teaching degree in Computer Sciences. He is a research fellow in the Human Machine Interface Group (GIHM) at Federal University of Campina Grande. He has a BS in Computer Science from the Centro Universitário Feevale and a MSc. in Computer Sciences. He also holds a Doctorate in Electrical Engineering from the Federal University of Campina Grande. His research focuses on human-computer interaction, human error studies. Currently he leads the Research Group on Computer Education at the State University of Paraiba.

Siu-Tsen Shen has studied widely, gaining her Masters degree in Industrial Design Research from the Design Academy of Eindhoven, and her PhD in Design from Goldsmiths College, University of London. She is currently an Associate Professor in Multimedia Design at the National Formosa University, Taiwan. Her research interests lie in the areas of HCI, User-Centred Design, Cross-Cultural Research, User Interface Design, and Design Team Formation using Personality Type. She has taught on a number of different programmes including Introduction to Multimedia Design, Creative Thinking and Design Methods, Cognitive Psychology, and Emerging Technology.

Minyoung Song is currently a Ph.D. candidate in Learning Technologies at the School of Education in the University of Michigan. Prior to studying Learning Technologies, she studied Human-Computer Interaction at the School of Information of the University of Michigan, where she earned the degree of Masters in Science in Information. She holds B.A. in Education and Computer Science from Ewha Women's University in Seoul, Korea. Her main research topic is renovating and designing educational technologies by incorporating multimodal interfaces. Her other research interest includes augmented reality, information visualization, and psychometrics.

Peter Sosnin was born in Ulyanovsk in the USSR in 1945. He graduated from the Ulyanovsk Polytechnic Institute (1968). His employment experience included the Ulianovsk Polytechnic Institute and Ulyanovsk State Technical University. Sosnin defended full doctor degree in Moscow Aviation Institute (1994). His research interests focus on Artificial Intelligence Applications. He is the author and co-author of about 300 publications (including 9 monographs). He has been the scientific adviser of over 50 M.Sc. theses, as well as 19 Ph.D. dissertations and 2 Doctors dissertations. Professor Sosnin is a member of European Association of Artificial Intelligence, a chair of the Ulyanovsk affiliate of the Russian Artificial Intelligence Association, an active member of 3 dissertation boards. He is a Member of IEEE, Computer Society, and ACM.

Jeremiah D. Still is an Assistant Professor in the Department of Psychology at Missouri Western State University. He is director and developer of the first Human Factors graduate program in Missouri. Their Masters of Applied Science curriculum combines MBA and HCI coursework. Jeremiah received his Ph.D. from Iowa State University in Human-Computer Interaction. His research is driven by a desire to help designers make products better. He focuses on understanding human-centered design from a cognitive viewpoint: how a user will perceive, process, and respond to a product's design. Jeremiah's recent projects draw from cognitive theories to improve product design theories and methodologies. For further information please visit: JeremiahStill.info.

Avan Suinesiaputra finished his undergraduate study in Computer Science (Institut Teknologi Bandung, Indonesia), graduate study in Computational Science (University of Amsterdam, the Netherlands) with Cum Laude, and doctoral study in Medical Imaging (University of Leiden, the Netherlands). His thesis focused on a computer-aided diagnosis method for cardiac MRI by using statistical shape analysis. He worked as a post-doc researcher at Leiden University Medical Center, the Netherlands, in a project to develop a semi-automated segmentation method for carotid arteries from MRA images. He recently joined the University of Auckland, New Zealand, as a fellow researcher to work on the Cardiac Atlas Project. His main research interests include model-based image analysis, statistical shape analysis of medical data and probabilistic methods for computer-aided diagnosis.

Betsy van Dijk took a MSc degree in Mathematics at the Radboud University Nijmegen and a PhD in Computer Science and Educational Technology at the University of Twente in Enschede, The Netherlands. She worked as a researcher and teacher at Nijmegen University and Arnhem University of Applied Sciences. At this moment, she is an Assistant Professor at the University of Twente in the Human Media Interaction Research Group of the Department of Computer Science. She works in the area of human-computer interaction where she focuses on user experience design and evaluation, multimodal interaction, human-robot/virtual agent interaction, and interaction in smart environments. She is involved in several national and international research projects.

Boris van Schooten earned his MSc degree in Computer Science at the University of Twente, Netherlands, in 1997. He worked as a PhD student at the same university and obtained his PhD degree in 2003 with a thesis titled "Development and Specification of Virtual Environments." In the period of 2004 to 2010, he worked as a postdoc researcher on multimodal question answering dialogue systems and visualization of and interaction with 3D medical images. Right now he works as a Software Engineer for Roessingh Research and Development developing innovative telehabilitation software. His research interests include novel input and output devices, visualizations, human-computer interaction, and software engineering.

Maria de Fatima Queiroz Vieira is an academic with experience in industrial automation. She is currently Associate Professor in the Department of Electrical Engineering at the Federal University of Campina Grande (UFCG), Brazil. She holds first degrees in Physics and Electronic Engineering, an MSc degree in Electronic Engineering (UFCG) and a PhD in Electrical and Electronic Engineering (UK). Her recent research focuses on ergonomic aspects of human-machine interfaces in automated industrial systems and on human error studies. Her work has been applied to the Electricity Supply Industry. She works in collaboration with research groups in France, at the Department of Industrial Engineering, University of Marseille, and with the group of Cognitive Ergonomics, University of Provence. She is also an Honorary Senior Research Fellow in CeSIP at the University of Strathclyde, UK. Since 1986, she has led the Human Interface Laboratory at UFCG and the Human Interface Research Group.

Qing Wang, Ph.D. in Computer Science and Member of SIGCHI, experienced researcher on Human Computer Interaction, User Experience, Collaborative Software, and Interoperability of Enterprise Software and Application, and especially interested in utilizing browser history on collaboration. Assistant Professor of School of Software, Sun Yat-Sen University, teaching courses on Web Programming, Software Engineering, Software Analysis and Design, and Software Engineering Training. Over ten years' experience in the design and development of software. Proficient in JEE and Web 2.0. Seasoned in software project management, especially in Agile and XP software processes and best practices.

Hiroki Yamada was born in Kanagawa, Japan, in 1984. He received the B.Sc. and M.Sc. degrees from Osaka University in 2007 and 2009, respectively. He is currently a Ph.D. candidate at Research Center for Advanced Science and Technology, The University of Tokyo. He is with Cyber Interface Lab (Hirose-Tanikawa Laboratory), which studies virtual reality, human interface, and multimodal interfaces since 2009. His research interests include product design, information visualization, tangible user interface, and media arts. He established and works as a researcher at Tokyo Interaction Center, a nonprofit operation which promotes collaborations between designers, researchers, engineers, and artists since 2010.

Michiya Yamamoto received his BE in Electrical Engineering from Kyoto University, in 1997, ME and doctoral degrees in Energy Science from Kyoto University, in 1999 and 2002, respectively. Since 2002, he is working as an Assistant Professor at Okayama Prefectural University. In 2009, he moved to Kwansei Gakuin University as an Associate Professor. His research interests are embodied interaction and communication support, and so on.

Huahai Yang is a Cognitive Psychologist and Computer Scientist with a specialization in human-computer interaction; he is currently a Research Staff Member in the Computer Science Department of IBM Research – Almaden, San Jose, California. He has a B.S. in Psychology from East China Normal University and a M.S. in Engineering Psychology from Institute of Psychology, Chinese Academy of Sciences. He earned his Ph.D. in Information from School of Information, University of Michigan – Ann Arbor. He is interested in theoretical and cognitive issues in human-computer interaction, with an emphasis on the combination of formal and empirical approaches. He is also keen on designing and developing advanced user interface systems for managing complex information.

Zhiquan "ZQ" Yeo is an experienced Software Developer and User Experience Practitioner. He is also experienced in Human-Computer Interaction research and has published several papers at the Association for Computing Machinery's CHI conference. Zhiquan has a variety of research interests, including interaction methods, novel sensor systems, as well as visual and emotive interfaces. He has worked at Disney Research Pittsburgh, where he worked on sensing systems for interaction. Zhiquan has also founded, and worked for, several startup companies, where he worked on web development and iOS applications. He is currently a User Experience Analyst at Bloomberg LP, where he works with a team of user experience professionals to develop software. Zhiquan obtained his B.Sc. in Computer Science and Masters in Human-Computer Interaction from Carnegie Mellon University in 2009 and 2010, respectively.

Index